WHERE "HIAWATHA" HAD ITS BEGINNING. JOHNSTON-SCHOOLCRAFT HOME AT SAULT STE. MARIE, MICHIGAN, BUILT ABOUT 1815.

Schoolcraft >⟶ Longfellow >⟶ Hiawatha

By
CHASE S. OSBORN and STELLANOVA OSBORN

THE JAQUES CATTELL PRESS
LANCASTER, PENNSYLVANIA
1942

THE SCIENCE PRESS PRINTING COMPANY
LANCASTER, PENNSYLVANIA

This Book Is Dedicated to

THE GREAT LAKES REGION OF NORTH AMERICA

Which Is Without Equal

Also to

ITS STURDY PIONEERS BOTH WHITE AND RED

Who Inspired Schoolcraft and Longfellow

CONTENTS

LIST OF ILLUSTRATIONS

PROLEGOMENA

THE publication of this book was suggested by the profound Dr. William Cole Jones, chief editorial writer of the *Atlanta Journal,* Atlanta, Georgia. His generous comment is included.

Behind it all lies an interesting human drama.

In the fall of 1855, a small book containing *The Song of Hiawatha* was given to the public. A few weeks after its appearance, the statement was made by a writer in a Washington, D. C., newspaper that Longfellow had taken "the entire form, spirit, and many of the most striking incidents" from the Finnish *Kalevala.* For a while critics amused themselves with preferring charges of plagiarism against this latest production of the poet. Spurred on by hunger for publicity, Poe once had led such an attack viciously. Longfellow and his friends had no great trouble in refuting the disagreeable assertions. In his notes to the poem, Longfellow gave full credit to Henry Rowe Schoolcraft's writings as the source of practically all of his material. When Schoolcraft's *The Myth of Hiawatha* appeared in 1856 the slanders were effectually scotched.

In 1899 Nathan Haskell Dole published a learned discussion of the relation of *Hiawatha* to the *Kalevala,* in which Longfellow was completely vindicated; but no one has ever adequately presented the important part played by Henry Rowe Schoolcraft in the creation of the great American epic.

Also, the rare contribution of the Ojibway Indians of the Lake Superior country is forgotten, even in Michigan, while the figment of literary piracy from the Finns persists.

Recently a writer in *John O'London's Weekly* revived the old story of plagiarism by Longfellow, and for the sake of sensation took Poe's side. Malcolm Wallace Bingay, editorial director of the *Detroit Free Press,* reprinted the attack of the English writer in his own personal column. He ended it by calling Longfellow a son-of-a-gun, which was not only vulgar but plainly suggested a worse phrase. Special emphasis was given to the false statement that *Hiawatha* was stolen from the Finnish epic, the *Kalevala,* about which Mr. Bingay's lack of knowledge was apparent.

In order to present the subject once again in its true light, for the present generation, Mr. Osborn replied to Mr. Bingay. This irritated the latter and so wounded his vanity that he became angry. It surprised and pained Mr. Osborn to have his warm personal friend assume that attitude.

To indicate how little reason there was for any resentment on the part of Mr. Bingay, it appeared, in the same connection, that Miss Stellanova Osborn, Mr. Osborn's daughter, had never heard of the *Kalevala,* although she is a summa cum laude graduate of the Literary College of the University of Michigan, and a Phi Beta Kappa, with a master of arts degree and credit toward a doctorate in English literature. Another scholar, in the person of William Kline Kelsey, able Commentator of the *Detroit News,* confessed he had never heard of the *Kalevala.* These instances show how completely unnecessary it was for Mr. Bingay to feel hurt.

The incident brings out several interesting points that bear on modern schooling.

Malcolm Bingay's education began in the sand lots, where Mr. Osborn's also started. Mr. Bingay took a course in personal study and followed it so persistently that he became one of the intellectuals of America.

Mr. Osborn had certain other training. He traveled into every country in the world, to all the islands of the seas, and within seven degrees of the North Pole and eleven degrees of the South Pole. This gave him an opportunity for as much intellectual development as he had capacity for, including incidental knowledge of such world-literature as the *Kalevala.*

The foregoing contrast in methods of education indicates that two distinguished graduates of a great University have not apparently covered much more ground than Mr. Bingay and Mr. Osborn.

Henry Ford is one of the best educated men in America

in his specialty.   He told Mr. Osborn that he did not go to
school beyond the third grade.   His is another instance of
education outside of school.

Aristotle did not go to school.   Socrates did not.   Moses
was not a collegian.   Lao-Tse never went to a university.
Neither did Confucius.   Endless illustrations could be given.
It appears conclusive that anyone who wishes to acquire learning can do so by a constant endeavor to satisfy a great and
wholesome curiosity.

Nothing said herein is intended to disparage or discredit
academic courses.   How necessary they are is problematical.
The matter in question, however, does emphasize that college
training is still insular.

On the other hand, while formal education does not yet
cover the world as it may some time do, neither does it teach
the facts of local history as well as might be profitable.   For
example, the background of the State of Michigan is scarcely
known even to native Michiganians.   Without some intimate
appreciation of the significant and colorful facts of local history, lore, and literary traditions, there can be no deep roots for
the attachments of affectionate pride, patriotic enthusiasm,
and confident, constructive citizenship.

There is a clear suggestion to educators here.

The unwarranted attack on Longfellow in the *Detroit
Free Press* has revealed, startlingly, that Henry Rowe Schoolcraft, without whose work *Hiawatha* could never have been
written, whose twenty years in Michigan made him outstanding in the history of that State and gave him a unique place
in the development of the nation, is practically unknown today.
Yet, if comparison between two figures as majestic as Schoolcraft and Longfellow were not invidious, the statement could
be made and would be, that Schoolcraft was the major of the
two.   In the eastern end of the Upper Peninsula of Michigan
Schoolcraft's name is slightly familiar and a few have a dim
idea of his activities, but generally speaking his life and contributions have been allowed to sink into oblivion.   It is time
that this facet of our State and national tradition should begin

to be part of the common heritage. This book is an effort
toward that end.

Malcolm Wallace Bingay's columns about Longfellow and
the Hiawatha epic will—like all of his writings—have been of
great value to Michigan and America if they result in wider
popular appreciation of Henry Rowe Schoolcraft, and of the
Lake Superior region as the Hiawatha country.

LONGFELLOW'S BIRTHDAY

An Editorial from the Evening News, Sault Ste. Marie, Michigan, February 27, 1940

Today the *Evening News* celebrates the birth date of the great
poet Henry Wadsworth Longfellow with a special edition. The
forthright tribute by Chase S. Osborn was inspired by the strange
error made by the *Detroit Free Press* and its Editorial Director as
well as its Business Director in a recent issue.

We all owe a great debt to Longfellow whose *Hiawatha* has
given to the school children of the world more widespread information concerning the Sault country than all the publicity that since
has been issued. It is a text book in schools not only in the United
States but of many other countries of the world.

The idea of *Hiawatha* was given Longfellow by Henry Rowe
Schoolcraft, the first and highest American Indian authority of the
world. Schoolcraft's residence at Sault Ste. Marie made possible
the foundation of the great poem and we honor him for his scholarly
assistance.

The United States government has put out a special Longfellow
stamp in commemoration of the poet's 133rd anniversary. Millions pay tribute to the great American and his *Hiawatha,* including a prediction of Bayard Taylor that *"The Song of Hiawatha* will
live after the Indian race has vanished from our continent."

Long shall we of the Hiawatha country revere Longfellow and
his friend, Schoolcraft.

ASSOCIATED PRESS CARRIES NEWS OF THE FORGOTTEN FACT THAT THE MATERIAL FOR "HIAWATHA" CAME OUT OF MICHIGAN

POULAN, GEORGIA, February 27, 1940 (AP).—Chase S. Osborn, beloved former Governor of Michigan, paid tribute today to the genius of Henry Wadsworth Longfellow on the occasion of the 133rd anniversary of the poet's birth—and broke a friendly, literary lance with Malcolm Bingay of the *Detroit Free Press*.

Writing from his winter home, Possum Poke in Possum Lane, Osborn cited one of Bingay's recent columns in which the Detroit newspaperman discussed the origins of Longfellow's *Hiawatha* and its resemblance to the Finnish folk epic, *The Kalevala*.

Bingay had written:

In 1835 Elias Lonnrot, the Finnish poet, gathered as many of these ancient rune songs as possible and put them into a book and in 1849 enlarged it into the present *Kalevala*. Longfellow ran across the German translation and helped himself to the mustard.

The son of a gun.

To this Osborn took objection.

The similarity in verse form of the *Kalevala* and *Hiawatha*, however great, is no warrant for any such malign charges as are made against Longfellow. All poets could be branded plagiarists if the use of similar rhythms and number of measures and arrangement of lines in stanzas, constituted literary theft. Every sonneteer except the first would be a thief. All except the first who ever wrote blank verse would be literary outcasts. This of course is utter nonsense. Verse forms do not belong to any one person any more than the multiplication table, the alphabet, or the air and sunlight.

Osborn said Longfellow made no secret of his admiration for the *Kalevala* or for the work that Henry Rowe Schoolcraft did in gathering together the Indian legends of Upper Michigan.

The entire matter of *Hiawatha* is particularly interesting to Michigan folk because it is a beautiful story taken from the traditions of the Chippewas, who were especially a Lake Superior tribe of Indians. . . .

The vibrant and colorful background of early North America, through Longfellow, has won a first place in world literature. No poet has ever shown more originality or creative genius than he did when he seized upon the beautiful folklore of the Indians of our Great Lakes country and formed it into new and intimately appropriate verse.

In recognition of Michigan's debt to Longfellow, the Sault Ste. Marie *News*, which is published by Osborn's son, George, today issued a special edition in honor of the poet.

"There never was a more legitimate creation in the world than that of *Hiawatha*," wrote the elder Osborn, "nor was there ever a nobler song-writer on earth in any language than Henry Wadsworth Longfellow."

THE ATLANTA JOURNAL APPLAUDS

An Editorial, "In Defense of Hiawatha," by Dr. William Cole Jones, March 31, 1940

(According to *Who's Who in America*, William Cole Jones, associate editor of the *Atlanta Journal*, was born at Macon, Georgia, December 13, 1881. He holds the degrees of Bachelor of Arts and Master of Arts, and the honorary degree of Doctor of Laws, from Mercer University, and for a time was instructor in English and elementary Greek in that institution. He is a member of Phi Beta Kappa and of the Atlanta Historical Society; and trustee of the Decatur, Georgia, Public Library. On the *Atlanta Journal* he has served as reporter and chief editorial writer, as well as in his present capacity. In addition to his contributions to that newspaper, he has published numerous distinguished essays and notable verse.)

It was an ill-starred hour for the genial and gifted Malcolm Bingay when he wrote in his "Good Morning" column in the *Detroit Free Press* that Longfellow's *Hiawatha* was stolen from the Finnish national epic, *Kalevala*. The accusation fell under the piercing eye of that versatile genius and part-time Georgian, former Governor Chase Osborn of Michigan. If there be any land or sea or subject which the "Governor" has not explored, we doubt that it will be found on the maps or in the encyclopedias. And if there be one province of literature, history and geography with which he is more familiar than with others, it must be the Hiawatha Country around Sault Ste. Marie, whither he turns every summer from his winter home at "Possum Poke in Possum Lane," Worth County, Georgia.

When he saw what the noted editor and columnist and his own warm friend had done, he could scarcely believe his eyes. But there it was, in cold print: the charge, first made 85 years ago and recently exhumed by a British scribe in *John O'London's Weekly*, that Longfellow's classic on the American Indian had been plagiarized from the epic of the Finns. More in sorrow than in anger, but with the might of Ulysses' bow and the mortal sureness of its arrow's aim, Chase Osborn's pen replied. The product appears in the Longfellow anniversary edition of the Sault Ste. Marie *Evening News*, which itself is an altogether admirable piece of journalism. The Governor's article, running 18 columns or more, ought to be republished in book form and preserved in the nation's libraries as the definitive utterance on the *Hiawatha* controversy. It treats the subject from alpha to omega, views it with telescopic range and with microscopic particularity, turns it upside down, inside out, and leaves it as utterly disposed of as was the body of Hector when Achilles had dragged it seven times behind his chariot wheels around the walls of Troy.

The mere fact that the verse form of Longfellow's poem is similar to that of the *Kalevala* prompts Governor Osborn to observe, "All poets could be branded plagiarists if the use of similar rhythms and number of measures and arrangement of lines in stanzas, constituted literary theft. Every sonneteer except the first would be a 'thief.' This, of course, is utter nonsense. Verse forms do not belong to one person any more than the multiplication table, the alphabet, or the air and sunlight." In its essence the *Song of Hiawatha* is as native to America as are the Indian lore and legends it embodies. Governor Osborn has done a timely and characteristic service, and in the spirit of him who cried "My foot is on my native heath, and my name is MacGregor."

OTHER ACKNOWLEDGMENTS

FOR assistance in the gathering of material for this book, we are indebted to a number of efficient institutions and many gracious individuals.

Especially we wish to thank Miss Alice B. Clapp, Librarian at Sault Ste. Marie, Michigan, and Miss Margaret I. Smith, Superintendent of the Reading Room of the General Library of the University of Michigan, for their cooperation.

Dr. William Warner Bishop, Librarian of the University of Michigan, and Dr. Randolph Greenfield Adams, Director of the William L. Clements Library of the same institution, have generously provided reprints, photostat copies, books on inter-library loan, and bibliographical data, as well as much valuable information. Henry D. Brown has extended to us every resource of the Michigan Historical Collections of the University of Michigan.

Dr. Milo Milton Quaife, distinguished secretary-editor of the Burton Historical Collection of the Detroit Public Library, has not only replied to inquiries with ample letters based on extended special research but has volunteered facts that led to interesting discoveries. We are also indebted to the Detroit Public Library for books on inter-library loan, the good offices of Miss Helen Ellis, and an unusually fine piece of research by Mrs. Bernice Sprenger, in addition to the interested helpfulness of Miss Gracie B. Krum and Mrs. Elleine H. Stones, former and present Chief of the Burton Historical Collection.

Dr. George N. Fuller, Secretary-Editor of the Michigan Historical Commission, Lansing, Michigan, has made available all the resources at his command. At the Michigan State Library, Lansing, Michigan, Gail Curtis, Harriet Ann Nelson, and Marjorie Hazard have extended courtesies for State Librarian Loleta D. Fyan.

The Library of Congress, Washington, D. C., is one of

the great institutions in the world.   It is a representative of America at its best.   The efficiency and the graciousness of this organization are on the highest level ever attained by humans at any period, anywhere.   We wish to mention with particular appreciation the kindnesses of Secretary Louise G. Caton; Robert C. Gooch, Chief of the Book Service; Chief Bibliographer Florence S. Hellman, and Anne L. Baden, Acting Chief Bibliographer; H. S. Parsons, Chief of the Periodical Division; and Dr. St. George L. Sioussat, Chief of the Division of Manuscripts; and the personally interested as well as professionally expert work of Vincent L. Eaton of the Manuscript Division, in the preparation of a Schoolcraft bibliography. This special acknowledgment to members of the staff of the Congressional Library includes also James B. Childs, Chief of the Division of Documents; Luther H. Evans, Chief Assistant Librarian; Frederick R. Goff, Acting Chief of the Rare Book Collection; Leicester B. Holland, Chief of the Division of Fine Arts; D. W. McClellan, of the Photoduplication Service; and David C. Mearns, Reference Librarian.

For their assistance we express our gratefulness to Secretary C. G. Abbot, of the Smithsonian Institution; Dr. Leila F. Clark, Acting Librarian; Librarian William L. Corbin; H. W. Dorsey, Administrative Assistant to the Secretary; Associate Director J. E. Graf; and Dr. M. W. Stirling, Chief of the Bureau of American Ethnology.

The courtesy of the War Department, through W. U. Carter of the Adjutant General's Office, and of the Bureau of the Census, through Chief Statistician T. F. Murphy, has supplied valuable details.   In the Office of Indian Affairs, Department of the Interior, Librarian Anita S. Tilden has been splendidly cooperative; and the National Archives have yielded many useful facts through the unstinted interest of P. M. Hamer, Chief of the Division of Reference.

The form of *The Song of Hiawatha* presented is the only one authorized by the author, or his heirs, for school use, and is published with the assent of Houghton Mifflin Company, the only authorized publisher of the works of Longfellow.

We are also happy to remember the assistance given us by Elsie Andrews, Librarian, Michigan State Normal College, Ypsilanti; Harry C. Beattie, Richmond, Virginia; B. A. Black, for Francis J. Scott, Superintendent, Consolidated Chippewa Agency, Cass Lake, Minnesota; Maud D. Brooks, City Historian, Olean, New York; Emma A. Bull, Charleston, South Carolina; Geneva Campbell, Sault Ste. Marie, Michigan; Ella Ruth Kennon Carter, Poulan, Georgia; Lena Smith Chandler, Ruth Joan Chandler, John Paul Chandler, of Sault Ste. Marie; Dr. Richard Clyde Ford, Michigan State Normal College; Beulah Glover, Walterboro, South Carolina; Arthur B. Gregg, Altamont, New York; Edward and Georgia Hastings, Charlotte, Michigan; W. M. Heinline, Superintendent of the Congressional Cemetery, Washington, D. C.; Dr. William Herbert Hobbs, Professor Emeritus of Geology, University of Michigan; John W. Howard, Savannah, Georgia; Edward A. Hoyt, Librarian-Curator, Vermont Historical Society; Henry Schoolcraft Hulbert, Detroit, Michigan; Mrs. J. A. Johnston, Assistant Secretary, Virginia Historical Society, Richmond, Virginia; William Kline Kelsey, The Commentator, *Detroit News*, Detroit, Michigan; Dr. Vernon Kinietz, University Museums, University of Michigan; Reverend Father Joseph Ling, Mackinac Island, Michigan; Anna L. Lynch, Sault Ste. Marie, Michigan; the Honorable T. R. L. MacInnes, Secretary, Indian Affairs Branch, Department of Mines and Resources, Ottawa, Canada; Mabel L. Martin, Historian, Vernon, New York; the New York Public Library, through Paul North Rice and Robert W. Hill; Grace Lee Nute, Curator of Manuscripts, Minnesota Historical Society, Saint Paul, Minnesota; George Augustus Osborn, Publisher, *Evening News*, Sault Ste. Marie, Michigan; Wyman Parker, Librarian, Middlebury College, Middlebury, Vermont; Elizabeth T. Platt, Librarian, American Geographical Society, New York City; Dr. Arthur Pound, State Historian, and Director of Archives and History of the University of New York, Albany, New York; S. Gilbert Prentiss, Librarian, Elmira, N. Y.; *Richmond* (Virginia) *Times Dispatch;* Mabel Runnette, Librarian, Beaufort, South Carolina; Dr. A. S. Salley, Secretary, Historical Commission of South Carolina; Milford L. Smith, *The Spectator,* Hamilton, Canada; Shirley Wheeler Smith, Vice-President and Secretary, University of Michigan; United States Office of Education—Educational Radio Script Exchange; Freda F. Waldon, Librarian, Public Library, Hamilton, Canada; A. J. Wall, Jr., the New-York Historical Society; Dr. John Wargelin, Former President, Suomi College, Hancock, Michigan; Irene B. Warming, Reference Assistant, Minnesota Historical Society, Saint Paul, Minnesota; Mrs. Joan B. Williman, Charleston, South Carolina; Janet Lewis Winters, Los Altos, California; Mary Gilliam (Mrs. Coleman) Wortham, Richmond, Virginia; H. Heyward Burnet, Waycross, Georgia; Emma P. Burnet, East Orange, New Jersey; Mrs. Georgia H. Dove, Baltimore, Maryland; William J. Fox, Librarian, Academy of Natural Sciences of Philadelphia; Viola B. Hardage, Poulan, Georgia; Reference Librarian Maud Jeffrey, Ohio State University Library; New York State Library—Edna L. Jacobsen and June Lambert; C. A. Paquin, Michigan State Department of Conservation; Director Frank E. Robbins, University of Michigan Press; Reference Librarian Harold Russell, University of Minnesota Library; Alma Stone Skaggs of the University of North Carolina Library; Nella Rutledge Burnet Stoddart, Hershey, Pennsylvania; Robert James Usher, Librarian, Tulane University; J. B. Waddill, Waycross, Georgia; and Dr. M. L. Williams, Department of English, University of Michigan.

This book is better than it would have been in many ways because of the suggestions of Dr. Milo Milton Quaife, who has graciously read it in proof.

PART ONE

I. HIAWATHA AND THE KALEVALA

A Letter by Chase S. Osborn

Published in the Evening News, Sault Ste. Marie, Michigan, Special Longfellow-School-craft-Ojibway Edition, February 27, 1940, in Reply to

An Essay by Malcolm W. Bingay

Published in the Detroit Free Press, Detroit, Michigan, January 27, 1940

Henry Wadsworth Longfellow is not a thief.

The *Detroit Free Press* says he is.   It is not true.

Longfellow is America's greatest poet and a custodian of American literary honor and genius.

On January 27, 1940, in the *Detroit Free Press,* occurred one of those strange errors that are almost inexplicable.   The guilty person—and there is guilt, without malice—is Dr. Malcolm Wallace Bingay.   I know Dr. Bingay as Dearest Bing—a brilliant newspaperman, almost a journalist (whatever that may mean), and not only Editorial Director of the *Detroit Free Press* but also one of the Business Directors of that great institution.   These are high positions that carry with them prestige, influence, reputation, and great responsibility!

All this ponderous preface is because of the fact that he has been betrayed into traducing one of America's most beloved literary luminaries.

Dr. Bingay read an article in *John O'London's Weekly,* by George Goodwin, a contemporary English writer, directly accusing Henry Wadsworth Longfellow of being a poetical thief.

The man who wrote for the English publication did not know what he was considering or stating, but simply wished

1

to sensationalize untruth.   He may not have known it was a
falsehood.   Criticism of him and condemnation cannot be too
severe.

But that the great American Bingay—a writer of experience in both this country and England—should fall into the
flimsy trap, is as amazing as it is mysterious!   The brilliant
controversialist Bingay told the story as the English writer
gave it, and endorsed it fully!   More than that, in his traduc-
tion of the nationally beloved American poet, Dr. Bingay used
the worst language, in referring to Longfellow, that I have ever
known him to indulge in.   In the last sentence of his attack,
he calls Longfellow a "son-of-a-gun," which, even though
euphemistic, may easily be thought of in its disrespectful impli-
cations as something even more vulgar.

Longfellow is charged with plagiarizing the *Kalevala* in
his famous *Hiawatha*.

It appears that two great American writers have just discovered the *Kalevala*.   The first one that I noticed who did
so was Dr. William Kline Kelsey, erudite Commentator of the
Detroit News and one of the keenest analysts of any subject
he treats who writes in any land.   Bill Kelsey is as honest
intellectually as he is morally.   That is what most of us are
not.   We permit things to fool us.   Dr. Kelsey admitted
frankly he might not have known of the *Kalevala* if it had not
been for the war of the Union of Socialist Soviet Republics
upon Finland.   That is not so strange, because the *Kalevala*
has never had a tremendous popular vogue.

Dr. Bingay repeated the cheap English charge, with
enough power to help blacken the name of the great Longfellow if it could be done.

Goodwin accuses Longfellow, and Bingay abets him, of
stealing his brilliant Indian epic folktale of *Hiawatha* from the
Finnish *Kalevala*.   There isn't a scintilla of truth in the statement, and yet Dr. Bingay swallowed it.

The English Goodwin based his statement on the similarity of the meter in the two poems.   An old edition of the
Encyclopaedia Britannica printed over thirty years ago might

be considered particeps criminis. This edition, fathered by the masters and scholars of the University of Cambridge, says, misleadingly: "The poem (*Kalevala*) is written in eight-syllabled trochaic verse and an idea of its style may be obtained from Longfellow's Hiawatha, which is a pretty true imitation of the Finnish epic." The usually meticulous Britannica, by this obscure statement of the fact of similarity in style of versification, made possible an interpretation that the American epic was an imitation of the Finnish. More recent editions of the English Encyclopaedia corrected this ambiguity by adding another sentence, which definitely narrows the parallel to that of metrical form.

The fact that Longfellow used, in *Hiawatha*, the same style of versification as, or one similar to that of the *Kalevala*, has nothing to do with the case, any more than the use of blank verse by Milton has to do with the originality of *Paradise Lost*.

There has always been jealousy between English and American writers of songs, as well as of other things. It is true we have no Shakespeare. We have no medieval history, and our national life has not been long. Otherwise our American writers have been quite the equal, if not the superior, of any who have been upon the stage of the English language. I do not claim to be an authority on such things, but I have the blood of Fitz-Greene Halleck in my veins and I have stories and traditions of the many things that were said by the English of his classical *Marco Bozzaris*. Also I have Revolutionary blood. Despite these facts I feel I can be entirely fair to the English. I like Kit Marlowe, the brilliant, who died too young, likely because of a tavern brawl. Also I bow to Shakespeare. (He is almost as much of a myth as Homer.) Dr. Owens of Detroit tried to prove for years with his Baconian cipher that Bacon wrote the Shakespearian plays. I never took any stock in his claim at all, though it is possible he could be correct. I do not think in terms of destruction and detraction of the great Elizabethan dramas because they were tales taken boldly wherever they were found, and poured in timeworn blank verse molds. The sonnets of Shakespeare and

Elizabeth Barrett Browning are not the less noble and original because their form is similar to that of Dante's sonnets.

The famous line in Milton's *Paradise Lost,* which is generally quoted as the keynote of Satan's character—

"Better to reign in hell than serve in heaven—"
was apparently taken bodily from a mystery play, *Lucifer.* Milton's character of Satan is characterized by eminent British literary authorities as a perfect amalgam of this Lucifer and of Marlowe's Faustus. Such recognized and common practice constitutes no crime.

The poetic form of the *Kalevala* itself may not have been original with the Finns. It is even possible that one of those unknown Homers who set Greek legends into singing phrases might have wandered into the far north. Who can tell? Runic characters are even thought to be of Greek and Roman origin. They may date to the first recession of the latest ice age that is known about. They may even have been the first connected tangible intelligent laryngal, labial, and lingual, and pharyngeal sounds.

The similarity in verse form of the *Kalevala* and *Hiawatha,* however great, is no warrant for any such malign charges as are made against Longfellow. All poets could be branded plagiarists if the use of similar rhythms, and number of measures, and arrangement of lines in stanzas, constituted literary theft. Every sonneteer except the first would be a thief. All except the first who ever wrote blank verse would be literary outcasts. This of course is utter nonsense. Verse forms do not belong to one person any more than the multiplication table, the alphabet, or the air and sunlight.

The whole matter hinges on the question as to whether Longfellow's tale of Hiawatha is the same as that of the *Kalevala.* The story is as different as anything can possibly be. Dr. Bingay echoes the English literary vandal by citing as "a deadly parallel," the departure of Vainamoinen in a boat for Heaven, and the sailing away of Hiawatha in a canoe for the Happy Hunting Grounds. The *Kalevala* had no proprietary right in such an imaginative presentation of the passing of a hero from the earth. The Arthurian romances, for instance, have King Arthur sail mysteriously away in a boat that never returned. Final transportation alive is a world myth. A poet's reputation cannot be guillotined on such inconsequential evidence.

It is one of the most remarkable and praiseworthy things about Longfellow that, although he was so thoroughly steeped in European culture, he always remained an American. I went to all the countries of Europe, not many years after Longfellow traveled there. I visited more of them, but my object was the study of iron-bearing rocks, which took me to all the nooks and corners of the earth. While doing this work, whenever there was time I gave attention to the people—their language, literature, art, and modes of life. What I was after especially, I got in a satisfactory way, but in literature, art and language I obtained only a smattering of what Longfellow absorbed thoroughly. It is an apexial tribute to the great poet that he always returned to America a better American, instead of being won away to some foreign country, as so many English and American writers have been.

The *Kalevala* is worth knowing, not only in relation to this discussion but for its own values.

Until the nineteenth century it existed only in fragments in the memories and on the lips of peasants. A collection of a few of these scattered songs was published first in 1822 by Dr. Zacharius Topelius. They did not speak of them as folklore in that sense but as songs may be folklore. It was not until 1835 that anything like a complete and systematic collection was given to the world, by Dr. Elias Lonnrot. In fact, the Finnish language had never been used in literature until that time. So it is all quite new.

For years Dr. Lonnrot wandered from place to place in the most remote districts, living with the peasantry and taking down from their lips all that they knew of their popular myths and songs. Some of the most valuable material was gathered in the governments of Archangel and Olonetz.

After unwearying diligence, Lonnrot was successful in collecting 12,000 lines. These he arranged as methodically as he could into thirty-two cantos, which he published as he heard them sung or chanted. Continuing his researches, in 1849 Dr. Lonnrot published a new edition of 22,793 lines in fifty cantos. A still more complete version was published by A. V. Forsman in 1887. The word rune really means signs or symbols that finally constituted a crude alphabet.

The importance of this indigenous epic, the *Kalevala,* was at once recognized in Europe and finally in America. Translations were made into Swedish, German and French. There are several translations in English, the fullest being that of J. M. Crawford in 1888. The best foreign editions are those of Castrén, in Swedish, in 1844; Leouzon le Duc in French, in 1845 and 1868; and Schiefner, in German, in 1852.

The *Kalevala* is named for the three sons of Kalewa or Kaleva, whose adventures are wound about a plot for securing in marriage the hand of the daughter of Louhi, a hero of a land of the cold north. In the main it is a lengthy recital of a struggle to recover, from this land of the cold north, a magic mill which grinds out meal, salt and gold, and gives prosperity to whoever possesses it. It begins with a poetical theory of the origin of the world and ends with what is understood to be an allegorical account of the conquest of Paganism by Christianity. It is utterly unlike *Hiawatha.*

To call *Hiawatha* a spurious folksong, of which the *Kalevala* is the original, is simply grotesque and worse than that.

The lawless attempt to blacken the reputation of Longfellow makes me sad. The story of *Hiawatha* is almost completely a Michigan epic of the Ojibway Indians. It is our own local, loved and priceless heritage.

Michigan has so many grandeurs. Lake Superior is one of the wonders of the world. All our marvelous Lake area and splendors we cannot adequately comprehend. Our colorful State history, picturesque background and surroundings, real and imaginative folklore, and literary traditions are practically unknown to us. It is time to be aroused understandingly and to evaluate them vibrantly. To be misled into fouling our own nest, without cause, is sorrowful and to be repented and remedied. Dr. Bingay is as noble and big a soul as ever lived. No one will be more deeply regretful than he for anything that he has done to soil the garments of Longfellow who holds so high a place in the affection and respect and gratitude and reverence of Michigan and the world.

The worst feature of Dr. Bingay's deplorable claim is that it is not news. The question is eighty-five years old and was settled long ago. It is an ancient slander, that never should have been repeated by an American newspaper or anybody.

A few weeks after the appearance of *Hiawatha,* the charge was made by a writer in a Washington newspaper that the poet had borrowed "the entire form, spirit, and many of the most striking incidents" of the *Kalevala.*

The origin of the onslaught was an English literary jealousy of Longfellow. The immediate demand for *Hiawatha* was unprecedented both in England and the United States. On either side of the water there was no poet living at that time, nor since, who made even a distant approach to Longfellow's popularity. The lesser writers disliked this. The real ones loved him.

Longfellow felt keenly the unreasonableness of the attack upon his honesty in the charge that he had borrowed meter and incidents both from the *Kalevala.*

He made no secret of the suggestion of the meter—he had used an acknowledged form, which was not exclusively Finnish. His diary under date of June 5, 1854, says: "I am reading with great delight the Finnish epic, *Kalevala.* It is charming." Later, on June 22, 1854, he wrote illuminatingly: "I have at length hit upon a plan for a poem on the American Indians, which seems to me the right one, and the only. It is to weave together their beautiful traditions into a whole. I have hit upon a measure, too, which I think the right and only one for such a theme." Then on June 25, 1854, he chronicled: "I could not help this evening making a beginning of Manabozho or whatever the poem is to be called. His adventures will form the theme, at all events."

About the calumny in the Washington newspaper, Longfellow said, in a letter, in 1855:

This is truly one of the greatest literary outrages I ever heard of. But I think it is done mainly to show the alleged learning of the writer. . . . He will stand finally in the position of a man who makes public assertions which he cannot substantiate. You see what the charge of imitation amounts to, by the extracts given. As to my having "taken many of the most striking incidents of the Finnish Epic and transferred them to the American Indians"—it is absurd. I can give chapter and verse for these Indian legends. Their chief value is that they *are Indian* legends. I know the *Kalevala* quite well; and that some of its legends resemble the Indian stories preserved by Schoolcraft is very true. But the idea of making me responsible for that is too ludicrous.

When the friend who later translated *Hiawatha* into German, wrote to Longfellow, mentioning their reading the *Kalevala* together thirteen years before, and said, "The characteristic feature, which shows that you have fetched the meter from the Finns, is the parallelism adopted so skilfully and so gracefully in *Hiawatha,*—" Mr. Longfellow noted in his diary, "He does not seem to be aware that the parallelism, or repetition is as much the characteristic of Indian as of Finnish song."

What Longfellow meant by this is plain in the following passage from Schoolcraft:

In 1759 a Chippewa girl, named Paig-wain-e-oshe-e, or White Eagle, met at the Lake of Two Mountains a young Algonquin belonging to the French mission. They fell in love; and she is said to have composed the following song, the first stanza of which in the original runs thus:

<blockquote>
Ia indenaindum,
Ia indenaindum,
Ma Kow we yah,
Nin denaindum we,
O dishquadumee.
</blockquote>

Schoolcraft translated this verse as follows: "Ah me! When I think of him, when I think of him—my sweetheart, my Algonquin." Longfellow's graceful molding of the thought into perfect rhythmic form is:

When I think of my beloved,
Ah me! think of my beloved,
When my heart is thinking of him,
O my sweetheart, my Algonquin!

The use of repetition by Indian singers is their own, and Longfellow adapted it admirably in the epic he wrote for them. The work he did in the creation of *Hiawatha* was as legitimate as that of any poet in the history of literature.

Nathan Haskell Dole in 1899, in his edition of *The Song of Hiawatha,* gave most careful consideration to its relation to the *Kalevala,* devoting a number of pages to passages where resemblances might be considered. He says that the translator of the *Kalevala* into English was influenced in his phraseology by the language of *Hiawatha.* However consciously or unconsciously Longfellow may have carried the Suomi epic in his mind while he was writing *Hiawatha,* the form did not belong to the Finns. Longfellow merely worked as Virgil did, when, knowing Homer, he wrote his Aeneid.

In regard to the meter of *Hiawatha* nothing further need be said, except to quote what a sound critic observed in this connection a hundred years ago: "The author who first makes popular a peculiar style or measure must expect to be charged with plagiarism by the ignoramus who makes the wonderful discovery that such style or measure did not originate with the writer through whose agency it became known to him."

Undoubtedly it is also a temptation in literary criticism to make a display of knowledge by gravely discovering to the public, as evidence of stealing or at least borrowing, some chance similitude in subject. In his diary, July 31, 1857, Longfellow records and comments:

My friend the Abbé Rouquette, in Louisiana, sends me Émile Montégut's review of *Hiawatha,* from the *Revue des Deux Mondes;* very friendly, and carefully written. Only he thinks the legend of "Mondamin" taken from Burns's *John Barleycorn.* This is rather too bad, after I had stated that my legends were real Indian legends. He seems to imagine that I invented them.

In view of Schoolcraft's "Mon-daw-min" and other tales, printed later in this book, all such affectations of erudition are reduced to sources of amusement.

Longfellow was attracted to his theme, not by the *Kalevala*, but by a great contemporary American—another statured figure in Michigan history—Henry Rowe Schoolcraft. Both Longfellow and Schoolcraft are in their works so much a part of Sault Ste. Marie, Michigan, and the Lake Superior country, that the whole subject has burnished interest for this region as well as world-wide significance.

The source of the material for *Hiawatha* is plainly stated by Longfellow in his notes to the poem, as follows:

This Indian Edda—if I may so call it—is founded on a tradition, prevalent among the North American Indians, of a personage of miraculous birth, who was sent among them to clear their rivers, forests, and fishing-grounds, and to teach them the arts of peace. He was known among different tribes by the several names of Michabou, Chiabo, Manabozo, Tarenyawagon, and Hiawatha. Mr. Schoolcraft gives an account of him in his *Algic Researches*, Volume 1, page 134; and in his *History, Condition, and Prospects of the Indian Tribes of the United States*, Part III, page 314, may be found the Iroquois form of the tradition, derived from the verbal narrations of an Onondaga chief.

Into this old tradition I have woven other curious Indian legends, drawn chiefly from the various and valuable writings of Mr. Schoolcraft, to whom the literary world is greatly indebted for his indefatigable zeal in rescuing from oblivion so much of the legendary lore of the Indians.

The scene of the poem is among the Ojibways on the southern shore of Lake Superior.

The general purpose to make use of Indian legends had been in the poet's mind some time before 1854. Prose tales about them had a place in his early plans. He had seen a few Algonquins in Maine and had read Heckewelder while he was in college. A few years afterwards he entertained the Ojibway chief Kah-ge-ga-gahbowh from Le Saut country in his home.

Tales told him by a former student upon his return from the West finally focused this interest. The poet found Schoolcraft's *Algic Researches,* published in 1839. About this collection of Indian tales and legends, mythologic and allegoric, an eminent critic said:

The legends preserved in this and other writings of Schoolcraft showed the Indians to have possessed unwritten literature of vast value in both poetic and dramatic sense. There was much delicacy in the conception of these tales of the spirits of earth and air, with a genuine quaintness showing an affinity with the fairy stories of the northern races of Europe.

In fact the Ojibways are thought by some ethnic scholars to be boreal.

Longfellow said, "I pored over Mr. Schoolcraft's writings nearly three years, before I resolved to appropriate something of them to my own use."

It was from Schoolcraft that Longfellow learned stories of Manabozho and the Windigo and other fascinating things. There was also an actual Iroquois chieftain of legendary ability, named Hiawatha. Consequently the poem embraces facts and fancies of the Six Nations of the Iroquois that Hiawatha is credited with forming. It was more convenient for Longfellow to follow the Ojibways, than any other group, because Schoolcraft knew so much about them, and because they were still active, and their old chiefs living and in power. Longfellow studied the Indians of Michigan, and spent months ripening into years in getting the folk tales and myths of the Ojibways. He rescued and vivified the ancient imaginative lore of our own region.

Schoolcraft not only told Longfellow most of the Hiawatha legends but put him in touch with Chief Mendoskong on the American side at the Sault, who lived up to my own time and whom I knew. Some of the material that Longfellow got was from the lips of this splendid Indian, who lived and ruled the Chippewas in the region of Sault Ste. Marie. For a long time he made his own home on Jim Island in the St. Marys River. The island now is charted as Gem Island. I talked with Mendoskong about Longfellow and learned of his work.

Longfellow, through Schoolcraft, was introduced also to

Shingwauk (whose name in English means Tall Pine) and others, near the Canadian Sault.   At Sault Ste. Marie, Ontario, there is a home for Indians called Shingwauk, which does good work now, and has been doing so for more than half a century.

In my own time, the daughters of Henry Wadsworth Longfellow came to Michigan, before the death of their father, to check on some of his understandings of the fundamentals of *Hiawatha.*   I talked to them on several occasions.   When I saw them at Garden River, near the Sault, they were being guided by the most intellectual Chippewa Indian on the reservation.   His name was Kabiosa.   At times he was a chief and always friendly and interesting to the whites.   As a young man he had helped their father, working under Shingwauk. The half-breeds called Kabiosa "Kaboose," and he was so known by most whites rather than as Kabiosa, his true name. Kabiosa told me about helping Longfellow as a boy.

Longfellow began *Manabozho,* as he at first called *Hiawatha,* June 25, 1854.   The next day he wrote in his diary:

"Look over Schoolcraft's great book on the Indians; three huge quartos, ill-digested, and without any index.   I wrote a few lines of the poem."

September 19, he recorded: "Working away with Tanner [of the Sault], Heckewelder, and sundry books about the Indians"; and September 28, "Worked at the disentanglement of Indian legends."

"Having composed nearly five hundred verses," Longfellow told a friend afterwards, "I suddenly changed my mind, and abandoned what I had written.   Then I began again, and continued writing to the end."

It was not until some time after the publication of the poem that I looked upon it as of much value, and only when I was assured of its appreciation on the part of my critical readers did I begin to realize how much I stood indebted to Mr. Schoolcraft.   I was anxious to tell him that I was his largest debtor, and I did so at the earliest opportunity.

It should never be forgotten that it was Henry Rowe Schoolcraft—so long a resident at Sault Ste. Marie, Michigan

—who first called attention to this department of our national literature. Without his poetical interest in the subject, much of the material he has preserved would probably have been lost and *Hiawatha* would never have been written.

Schoolcraft's respect and admiration for Longfellow is expressed in the letter of dedication in his *The Myth of Hiawatha, and Other Oral Legends, Mythologic and Allegoric, of the North American Indians,* published in 1856, which reads as follows:

To Professor Henry Wadsworth Longfellow.

Sir,—Permit me to dedicate to you this volume of Indian myths and legends, derived from the story-telling circle of the native wigwams. That they indicate the possession, by the vesperic tribes, of mental resources of a very characteristic kind,—furnishing, in fact, a new point from which to judge the race and to excite intellectual sympathies,—you have most felicitously shown in your poem of *Hiawatha*. Not only so, but you have demonstrated, by this pleasing series of pictures of Indian life, sentiment, and invention, that the theme of the native lore reveals one of the true sources of our literary independence. Greece and Rome, England and Italy, have so long furnished, if they have not exhausted, the field of poetic culture, that it is at least refreshing to find, both in theme and meter, something new.

Very truly yours,

HENRY R. SCHOOLCRAFT

This entire matter of *Hiawatha* is particularly interesting to Michigan folk because it is a beautiful story taken from the traditions of the Chippewas, who were especially a Lake Superior tribe of Indians. Some hundreds and even thousands of Chippewas still live in Michigan. Just across the international border within a few miles of our boundaries, are still several Chippewa reservations. Within my memory there have been grouped Chippewa Indians in many portions of the Upper Peninsula and in the northern part of the Lower Peninsula. I have been an adopted member of the tribe for many years, although I have no Indian blood in my veins. The great Schoolcraft is the highest ethnic authority, living or dead, on Ojibway Indians. He married one.

By far the best dictionary of the Ojibway language was made in Michigan by Father Baraga, for whom the town and county of Baraga are named.

From still another standpoint both *Hiawatha* and the *Kalevala* are of unusual interest in this region. The latter poem revolves around one of the most important foreign elements in the citizenry of Michigan.

Dr. Bingay in his criticism of Longfellow confesses that he knew nothing about the Finns until the Russo-Finn war broke out. That is surprising, because he is one of the best-informed men I have ever met. He should have known and could have known and it is marvelous that he did not know that there are about one hundred thousand Finns in Michigan. Nearly three-quarters of them are in the Upper Peninsula. There are also many in Northern Wisconsin and others in Northern Minnesota. The number of foreign-born Finns in Michigan is almost equal to the number of foreign-born Italians in the state. Some regions have no such proportion of Finns, because races are attracted in their migrations to similar latitudes. One does not find many people of southern countries in the north, and north country people may not thrive in the south.

One of the best Finnish educational institutions in the world is in Michigan. It is Suomi, located in the copper district of the Upper Peninsula. Just a few months ago I met a woman physician in the fine hospital at Thomasville, Georgia, who had been educated at Suomi College. The name Suomi is another term for the Finns, and also for their language. Also at Hancock there is a Finnish Lutheran book concern and a Suomi publishing company.

In addition to this Suomic distinction in the Upper Peninsula, there was in the Twelfth District one of the most brilliant congressmen, a Finn, who was ever elected from any part of Michigan. He was and is the Honorable Oscar Larsen, who at the present time is a practicing attorney at Duluth, Minnesota. I know him well and count him as a great friend. He proved that by making a nominating speech for me at one of the Michigan state conventions.

One of the best books ever written by a Michigan author is a Finn and Indian story, *Joe Pete*. The scene is Sugar Island. It is by my neighbor and friend, of whom I am proud, Miss Florence McClinchey, now a teacher at Central Michigan College of Education at Mt. Pleasant.

I have lived for years with Finns as neighbors in the more undeveloped regions of Michigan. There are 2,000 of them in Chippewa county, three-quarters of them American-born. Nearly three hundred are on Sugar Island, where I owned twelve miles of shore line until I gave it to the University of Michigan. I found these Finlanders most agreeable and always dependable when sane.

There is a class among the Finns, as in all nationalities, who drink to excess. This tends to increase the percentage of insanity among them.

At one time I employed Sugar Island Finns to build a log lodge for me. They did the best work I have ever seen performed by any hewers with axes. They asked me if I would not permit them to build a Finnish stove. These I had seen when I was in their country where I have been several times. I at once consented. So they built a stove of ordinary brick, lined with firebrick, which had the flues so indirectly arranged that, although the draft was good, you could build a fire in it and practically bank it, and it would last for three days and nights. That cabin and stove now belong to the University of Michigan.

The Finns are a resourceful people. I know them in their home country and in Michigan and I like them. They supply our Duck Island camp with eggs and milk and good butter and are thrifty, industrious citizens and good neighbors. A young Finnish girl had the mail route on Sugar Island for some time. She gained some notice throughout the country by finding in a snowdrift the body of an Indian who had perished in a blinding storm through which she traveled safely.

There are five Finnish churches in Chippewa county:

Evangelical Lutheran and Apostolic Lutheran at Rudyard; Finnish Lutheran at Dafter; Finnish Pentecostal at Brimley; and St. John's Finnish church at Sault Ste. Marie.

Michigan has three Finnish newspapers: *Amerikan Suometar*, at Hancock; *Opas,* at Calumet; and *Walvoja,* at Calumet. Other Suomi newspapers published in the United States are *Lannen Suometar*, at Astoria, Oregon; *Minnesotan Uutiset,* New York Mills, Minnesota; *Paivalehti,* Duluth, Minnesota; *New Yorkin Uutiset,* Brooklyn, N. Y.; the socialist paper *Raivaaja*, Fitchburg, Massachusetts; and two communist papers, *Eteenpain,* New York, N. Y., and *Tyomies,* Superior, Wisconsin.

It is not surprising to me that the Finns fight the Russians as they do, because I have been familiar with their clan rows in Michigan for fifty years and more. When they go on a bender and start a fight, the knives fly, and do deadly execution. In no instance have I known of one making a complaint against another. They were all private fights. When their spree would be over they would go into a Finnish bath and recover.

This primitive and rude Finnish bath is as interesting as can be. Those on Sugar Island, Michigan, are the same as those in parts of Finland similarly developed. They build a log cabin without an opening of any kind in it—no ventilation whatever except a door. Into this they put a tank either of masonry or metal. The receptacle is filled with water. To heat it and make a great volume of steam they put rocks in a fire until they are red-hot, then carry them into the bath house and submerge them in the water. In the resulting steam they luxuriate until everything scales off that they hope to get rid of.

The Finns are good, square fighters. However, without minifying their valor, it is necessary to take into consideration, in their present exhibition against the Russians, that an invading army must have a greatly preponderating force in order to conquer. Genghiz and Kublai Khan and Alexander the Great understood this. It is a realization of this fact, and the knowledge that none of them has the necessary numbers, that keep

England, France and Germany in the present war from attempting to invade each other's territory. Napoleon learned this truth, to his unending sorrow, at Moscow. The Russians apparently have forgotten the lesson taught by Napoleon's disastrous campaign, or else they have never comprehended its significance. The better the organization of the country invaded, the larger must be the proportion of the invading army. The fact that the Finns have been able to withstand the Russian onslaught is less amazing, when this is comprehended, but not the less admirable.

Inasmuch as I am a Dane myself, my interest in the Scandinavian corner of the earth has always been unusually keen and concentrated. I feel a kinship with it somewhere in my blood and bones. My name in Danish is Esbjerne, which soon came to be Osborn, spelled variously, after two jarls named Esbjerne who landed in England in the eighth century to assist in a war of conquest. Someone promptly killed one of the brothers. The other survived. He is my ancestor.

When I was traveling in this fascinating portion of the world, I attended lectures at the University of Upsala and also the University of Helsingfors. Some things I got there I could not have procured any other place. It was particularly enjoyable to visit Throndhjem. The old cathedral there is a most perfect example of ancient Scandinavian architecture.

In order to know the Finnish people in their own country, I went to Finland fifty years ago: First to Helsingfors, which now may be Helsinki, and from there to the Abo Islands. Then I visited Uleaborg. After that I made a trip into the remotest parts of Finland and onward for three hundred miles in Arctic Lapland. My impressions of the trip are still vivid.

Everything reminded me of the Upper Peninsula of Michigan, northern Wisconsin, and northern Minnesota. Of course I went farther north than the American regions mentioned.

The interesting settlements at Tornea and Gellivare were among the points I visited. My first sight of the midnight sun was from the Dundret. Then I went into the Norwegian sea to visit the Ofoten Islands Maelstrom and on to Dunderland farther north.   It was fascinating to proceed from Narvik to Tromsoe and Hammerfest and cover that region.

While in that part of the world, I paid studied visits to Kirunavaara and Luosavaara, all within the Arctic zone. That is where the Krupps of Essen later got so much iron ore for use in the World War. I was particularly interested in the iron-bearing rocks of the region.   In addition, however, I studied the peoples: their culture, their business methods, agriculture, industries, and everything else pertaining to their activities.   I tried to get Carnegie and Rockefeller interested in the Kirunavaara and Luosavaara vast iron ore ranges. There was a little too much titanium in the ore, and our metal-lurgists had not learned how to mix it with other ores and use it successfully as the Germans did.

The greatest physical feat I performed, perhaps, was to learn to ride in a Lapland sledge called by some of them a suka. It looks exactly like a Hoosier hog-trough made of a log four or five feet long, scooped out so you can put your hips and body in it and lean back against a support.   It is drawn by a rein-deer or reindeers with reindeer thongs fastened to reindeer-bone hames, stretched between the forelegs and hindlegs, and attached to the suka.   It is as hard to balance, for one who has not ridden in it before, as a bicycle is for a novice.   In a day or so, after being spilled a half hundred or more times, I learned to keep the thing right side up and enjoyed it.   Snow and ice often was from thirty to sixty feet deep and perhaps more.

It was interesting to find that the Lapps bury their dead during certain seasons.   Often they transport them long dis-tances for this purpose.   In July or August of each year, when the thals (valleys) thaw, the Lapps bring them down from the highlands and inter them.

The rule of the Lapps by women enmeshed me.   They are the chiefs in every way and officially in control by common consent.

I am writing something of the Lapps because the *Kalevala* contains some of their folk tales and songs.   They have no country of their own, but live along the mountainous north coast of Scandinavia and Finland. When Lonnrot was collecting his folk songs of the Finns he naturally got some from the Lapps. The *Kalevala* has also Eskimo, Russian, and Scandinavian lore. Even some Icelandic influence may be detected.

Mr. Bingay says that the Finns are the best educated people in Europe. How is he going to prove this? Some of them are certainly scholarly, and the percentage of literacy is high enough. If I were to guess at the most learned people in Europe, I would claim the distinction for the Germans. And I might be just as wrong as Mr. Bingay, because there are so many to be found on the intellectual planes, from the commonest to the highest, in Great Britain, France, Italy, Switzerland, and even in Russia—in fact, all the old European civilizations.

As to the antiquity of their culture, it is interesting to note that there was no literary composition in the Finnish language prior to 1835. Before that time, the literature of Finland was written in Swedish.

The Finns as a group, under this name, first appear in history about the beginning of the eighth century. Provoked by frequent raids, Sweden conquered Finland in 1157, and held it until Russia took it in 1716. For centuries Finland was the cockpit of the struggle between Sweden and Russia. Its present independence of both countries began in 1919. Mr. Bingay speaks of the government of Finland as a modern republic. It is well organized and efficient, but I would call it a republican autocracy.

Domination by the Swedes was unfavorable to the development of anything like a Finnish literature. The poets of Finland preferred to write in Swedish in order to secure a wider audience.

The earliest writer in the Finnish vernacular was Michael Agricola. About the middle of the sixteenth century he published an A B C book, and a number of religious and educational works, also a version of the New Testament in Finnish, and some books of the Old Testament. This was only a few decades before Catholic missionaries in America were translating the Bible into Chippewa and other Indian tongues. The myths of Finland may not be as old as those of the Ojibways.

It was not until after the *Kalevala* was published in 1835 that the Finnish language was used for literary composition. Their culture in this respect, therefore, is of recent development. They have indeed made admirable progress in view of their difficulties and late start.

When I went to Yasnaya Polyana to see Tolstoi I found the most delightful and simple and impressive man I have ever met in my life. He reminded me of Jesus Christ. Tolstoi had just given away his fortune and had not been any too wise about it. He was living the life of a kindly, heart-loving Russian moujik.

It was from Tolstoi that I got the idea that some of the tales of the *Kalevala* were as much Russian as they are Finnish. The fact is, the Finns and Russians are quite nearly related in some ethnic respects. That may be why the Finns are as much inclined toward Communism as are the Russians. In my own county of Chippewa in Michigan, on Sugar Island, may be seen in a Finnish graveyard at least one permanent monument with the hammer and sickle of the Russian Union of Socialist Soviet Republics carved on it in bold relief.

Tolstoi was the father of the idea of communism in Russia so far as it represents the application of the principles of the brotherhood of man. Landless men and manless land, he considered an indictment of the heart and intellect of mankind. As illustrations, he cited the situation in Australia, where an area of three million square miles was at that time occupied by three million people; and in Canada where five million inhabitants were spread over a country larger than the United States. He thought it was a sad injustice that a few individuals should leech all the money, and a few nations be porcine with the earth's surface. It was his hope, he said, that Russia might some day approximate conditions in the United States, where the government was founded on the idea of brotherhood and practical communal principles; but he feared it might take a long period of time before his country could develop to our stage of human justice.

Russia has departed in many ways from the visions that Tolstoi had for it, not only in its present war on Finland, but in its government, which, under Stalin, is as autocratic as that of Napoleon or Hitler or Mussolini.

I am reminded of Tolstoi, not only in connection with the Russo-Finnish war, but in relation to the art of Henry Wadsworth Longfellow. Tolstoi believed that appreciation by the masses is a fundamental quality of greatest art. It is only reasonable to believe that many of the verses and lines of Longfellow which are now an integral part of the common speech of the American people, may, in a thousand years, constitute a classic remnant of our present-day literature similar to the legacy Greece gave the world.

I repeat that it does not matter where Longfellow got the idea of his verse form for *Hiawatha*. He was the first to use it in the English language. Longfellow enriched the ars poetica of English by introducing into it a primitive singing rhythm hitherto unfamiliar to moderns.

The vibrant and colorful background of early North America, through Longfellow, has won a first place in world literature. No poet has ever shown more originality or creative genius than he did when he seized upon the beautiful folklore of the Indians of our Great Lakes country and formed it into new and intimately appropriate verse.

The first purpose of all the foregoing is to do justice to Henry Wadsworth Longfellow. I am happy at the same time in trying to say some kindly and just things of the Finns.

Longfellow is a great American. His fame is Immortal. He is enshrined in the sacred memory of the American people and the literary world. He needs no defense, but those who would traduce him do need to be corrected.

My affection for Dr. Malcolm Wallace Bingay is undimmed. I am sorry for him, as I think I would be for myself if I was entangled by such a snare. His article in full follows.

Dr. Bingay's revival of the worn-out charge would not be entitled to so much attention except that it puts Longfellow in a bad light in the eyes of a younger generation who do not know that all of this was settled a century ago. The libel is especially unfortunate because of the great circulation of the *Free Press* and Dr. Bingay's own prominence and prestige which make the thing serious as well as ridiculous. A great reason for concern is not so much the attack on Longfellow as it is on the American literary school of which he still remains the chief.

———◆———

GOOD MORNING
By Malcolm W. Bingay
The Detroit Free Press, January 27, 1940

HIAWATHA STOLEN?

Funny thing about this little country of Finland. Here we have been going along all these years without paying the slightest attention to the Finns either here or abroad. Finns to us were just so many folks who chopped down trees in the lumber camps or did railroad work or rubbed in bath houses. Not that we had anything against them, you understand; it was just that they did not register with us. When we thought of them at all we thought of reindeer and Eskimos.

Their names were hard to pronounce and, anyway, they just didn't belong to our social set. You see, there are only about four million of them over there and not many of them in the United States.

* * *

In a vague way we did know, of course, that there was a great Finnish composer and a great Finnish architect but it never occurred to us that they must have had a background of an ancient culture to have risen to such eminence. Oh, yes, they did have a fellow named Nurmi who could run all day and all night.

Then came the Communist threat to crush this little country. And we didn't get so excited about even that. No more, in fact, than when Stalin grabbed portions of Poland and other small Baltic countries. Just one of those things, happening all the time, we said. But when the Finns startled the world by kicking the daylight out of Stalin's troops and putting up a fight not equalled in history since the tragically glorious days of Thermopylae we began to sit up and take notice.

"Hardy men of the North," we said, "great fighters because they are a primitive people."

*   *   *

Wrong again! Now we learn that they are not only a deeply religious people with a culture far older even than that of the English and French, but that they are among the best educated of all the nationals in Europe. In the brief time of their freedom from Russia they have established a democracy that is almost unique in its efficiency. And now comes the worst blow of all to our pride.

*   *   *

All these years we of the United States have been listening to or reciting snatches of Longfellow's *Hiawatha*. We have looked upon it as the great Homeric classic of our Indian folklore. And now we are informed that Mr. Longfellow stole the whole thing, almost bodily from the national epic of Finland—a saga of a people that is so old it is lost in the dim gray dusks of antiquity.

Just to think of our good old New England poet baldly plagiarizing a song that may be as old as the tales of Homer! The Finnish national epic, because of the peculiarities of their language is little known outside the homeland. It is called *Kalevala* (pronounced something like kah-lev-a-lah). Those who know both the Longfellow effort and the original say the American poet's effort is a very poor imitation.

*   *   *

Of course, the charge that Longfellow helped himself to what he liked is not new. Edgar Allan Poe published an article in 1846 bitterly accusing the good gray poet of being a plagiarist and in it he pulled many a deadly parallel.

Poe, f'rinstance, took a Scottish poem by William Motherwell, published in 1827, and showed how Longfellow rewrote it as his own in 1843.   Here is the way Poe lined them up:

Motherwell	*Longfellow*
Hie upon Hielands	High on the Highlands
And far upon Tay	And deep in the day
Bonnie George Campbell	The good George Campbell
Rode out on a day.	Rode free and away.
Saddled and booted	All saddled and bridled
And gallant rode he.	Gay garments he wore.
Hame cam his gude horse,	Home came his good steed
But never cam he.	But he never more!

But Poe, nor no one else until now, accused the old man of helping himself to a national folk song.   A German translation of *Kalevala* was published in 1852.   Three years later Longfellow gave to the world his *Hiawatha* as something peculiarly American.   And we have been thinking all these years that the peculiar meter was proof of Longfellow's genius in catching the lilting, musical speech of the American Indian. Shucks!

*   *   *

Poe is long gone.   This new exposure of Longfellow is made by George Goodwin, writing in *John O'London's Weekly*. Here is another deadly parallel:

Hiawatha

On the shore stood Hiawatha,
Turned and waved his hands at parting;
On the clear and luminous water
Launched his birch canoe for sailing,
From the pebbles of the margin
Shoved it forth into the water;
Whispered to it, "Westward! westward!"

Kalevala

Then the aged Vainamoinen
Went upon his journey singing,

Sailing in his boat of copper,
In his vessel made of copper,
Sailed away to loftier regions,
To the land beneath the heavens.

Ironically enough the original folksong is hardly known outside of its native land while the spurious one, with the scene supposed to be Michigan, is world famous.

* * *

The saga of the *Kalevala* was handed down from generation to generation, century after century, even as were the tales of Homer. These rune singers traveled about the country as part of a lifetime profession.

In 1835 Elias Lonnrot, the Finnish poet, gathered as many of these ancient rune songs as possible and put them into a book and in 1849 enlarged it into the present *Kalevala*. Longfellow ran across the German translation and helped himself to the mustard.

The son of a gun!

———◆———

HENRY WADSWORTH LONGFELLOW

Hiawatha was a bold venture on the part of Longfellow. The result was a triumph, and the passage of long years has only intensified the admiration of the world for his masterpiece. It has been translated into many languages, has outlived innumerable travesties, and is the national epic of the Indian race—"the one tribute that the whites have rendered to offset all the abuses which the race have imposed on their predecessors."

The whole country could afford the pleasure and profit and justice of reading the life of Longfellow. The standard biography is that written by the poet's brother, the Reverend Samuel Longfellow. H. E. Scudder, relying upon this biography, has issued impressive material about the great American.

There has not been much improvement upon the edition of Longfellow's works in 1886. This edition is published in eleven volumes. Two are given to prose, six to verse, and three to the translation of Dante. The extent of Longfellow's works ought to be more popularly appreciated.

Henry Wadsworth Longfellow was not only the greatest poet, but one of the best students and scholars that America has produced.

He was born in the house that may still stand at the corner of Fore and Hancock Streets, Portland, Maine, February 27, 1807. His first schooling was at Portland Academy. He entered Bowdoin College when he was fourteen and graduated there at eighteen, at which time he received an invitation to teach modern languages in his Alma Mater, with leave of absence for travel and study in Europe.

He sailed for France when he was nineteen, and spent the rest of the year in that country. Early in 1827 he went to Spain for eight months. A year followed in Italy. After six months spent in Germany he returned to America in 1829, having been three years abroad. In September of that year he entered upon his duties at Bowdoin as professor of modern languages.

His study and his writing during his residence at Bowdoin College made him feel restricted in opportunity. Unexpectedly he was asked by Harvard to succeed George Ticknor as Smith Professor of Modern Languages in Harvard University. This offer he accepted. They told him if he wished he could spend a year or a year and a half more in Europe for the purpose of perfecting himself, especially in German.

He studied in England, Norway, Sweden, Denmark and Holland before going to Germany. He wintered at Heidelberg, devoting himself to close study. Later he was in the Tyrol and spent the succeeding summer in Switzerland. He returned to America in the fall of 1836, and went to work at Harvard in earnest. Longfellow had become an advanced scholar in the culture of the times.

These major attainments did not satisfy him. He continued to advance along the lines of intellectual development. It was not all an expansion of his brain. His heart grew, and his soul, and he became a humanist of deepest convictions.

HENRY WADSWORTH LONGFELLOW.

No demonstration of woe and sorrow failed to affect him. His poetic temperament was marching through his entire being to a great future. He said his whole soul burned ardently for improvement.

Longfellow's first poems were written when he was eighteen. They did not satisfy him, of course. Onward he went in his musical literary career. At Harvard he became notable as an interpreter of foreign literature both as a teacher and writer. Indeed one of his first books was his translation of *Coplas de Manrique,* which he termed the most beautiful moral poem in Spanish.

There is so much of monumental scholarship in Longfellow's career that it is impossible to assail him or criticize him successfully, except in so far as he was a man of the earth, and he was more than that in the sense that he was accorded Heavenly inspiration and guidance. This developed within him a controlling religious nature. It made him honest and noble and considerate.

Before Longfellow died he developed to such a degree that he was recognized as the leading litterateur of the world in English. It is utterly ridiculous to accuse him of anything unfair let alone that which would approach literary theft or plagiarism in any form.

His *Hiawatha* is as original as anything written in the world in any language because it is a story of American Indian myths done in a most appropriate poetic style.

This came to him in a degree from the *Kalevala* but that poem had nothing whatsoever to do with the poem of *Hiawatha* or the myths it develops. The *Kalevala* may well indeed have suggested the poetic measure, but that is no more than to have had something come to him from the beautiful wind music of an aeolian harp. The meter of the *Kalevala* did not belong to the author or authors of that epic. It had been used before. It was no man's property, any more than the musical scale belongs to any one composer.

Longfellow himself gives generous credit for the legends

and material of *Hiawatha* to Schoolcraft's great *Algic Researches*.

The poet began writing *Hiawatha* June 25, 1854. It was finished March 29, 1855. Thus it was a work of nearly a year. It was first published November 10, 1855. One of his critics writes that he is doubtful if the poet wrote any of his works with more enjoyment of the task or a keener sense of the *originality* of his venture, and, by consequence, with more perplexity when he thought of his readers. He tried the poem on his friends more frequently than had been customary with him, and with varying results. His own mind, as he neared the test of publication, wavered a little in its moods. In his diary he wrote:

"I am growing idiotic about this song and no longer know whether it is good or bad." Again he stated he was "in great doubt about a canto of *Hiawatha*—whether to retain or suppress it," and continued, "It is odd how confused one's mind becomes about such matters from long looking at the same subject."

The moment it was published Hiawatha became a contagion of popularity.

There never was a more legitimate creation in the world than that of *Hiawatha,* nor was there ever a nobler song-writer on earth in any language than Henry Wadsworth Longfellow.

MALCOLM W. BINGAY'S REPLY

Published in the Detroit Free Press,
February 28, 1940

MAH FRIEND!

When Chase S. Osborn wrote me that he was going to criticize me sharply for a mistake I had made I was amusingly puzzled as to which mistake he was going to denounce. I have made so many! He said he hoped that what he was going to say would not affect our friendship. I wrote to say what he pleased.

"I cannot believe that you are going to criticize me," I said, "because of the long years you have proclaimed your friendship for me.   A true friend, Chase, tells *you* your faults, not others."

*   *   *

Well, he not only slammed me for thirty-five pages but gave copies of it to the Associated Press to spread to the whole world—and ordered a special edition of his newspaper, the Sault *News,* to give his remarks special attention.   There's a pal!

All because I confessed I had never heard of the Finnish poem, the *Kalevala,* nor the charges that Longfellow had plagiarized it in writing his American Indian epic, *Hiawatha.*

*   *   *

If I had Mr. Osborn's omniscience and a friend of mine made a mistake of this nature, I think I would write him and say: "You pulled a boner on that one.   I hope nobody else has noticed it."

Nobody else did notice my mistake—if it was one—except Mr. Osborn.   But in his eagerness to show his vast erudition he proclaims my error (again, if it was one) to the universe. Now everybody is in a position to suspect that the Old Architect is not infallible after all.   Darn it!

*   *   *

Since receiving a copy of his thirty-five-page epistle proclaiming the greatness of Longfellow—and incidentally not forgetting himself—I've been doing some reading.

Says Mr. Osborn, "Nor was there ever a nobler songwriter on earth in any language than Henry Wadsworth Longfellow."   All right.   I turn the whole quarrel over to Edgar Allan Poe, a far greater poet if not a nobler song-writer.

Mr. Poe was a contemporary of Mr. Longfellow and the old professor was Mr. Poe's pet bete noire.   Poe charged that Mr. Longfellow not only helped himself to the works of foreign authors but that he had also borrowed from Poe's own works. In his review on Longfellow's "play" he wrote:

Throughout "The Spanish Student," as well as throughout other compositions of its author, there runs a very obvious vein of

imitation.   We are perpetually reminded of something we have seen
before, some old acquaintance in manner or matter; and even where
the similarity cannot be said to amount to plagiarism, it is still
injurious to the poet in the good opinion of him who reads.

*   *   *

Poe wrote a lengthy essay entitled "Mr. Longfellow and
Other Plagiarists."   Longfellow was at the zenith of his powers
then and had ample opportunity to refute, if possible, the
charges made against him.   This was, of course, long before
Hiawatha was written.

*   *   *

Poe repeatedly called attention to this imitative art of
Longfellow, collating, for example, that poet's "The Death of
the Old Year" with Tennyson's much better and original effort,
"Midnight Mass for the Dying Year."

This imitation is too palpable to be mistaken . . . and belongs
to the most barbarous class of literary piracy, that class in which,
while the words of the wronged author are avoided, his most intan-
gible and, therefore, least defensible and least reclaimable property
is appropriated. . . . Tennyson is robbed. . . . What is not taken from
Tennyson is made up mosaically, from the death scene of Cordelia
in Lear.

*   *   *

As to the strange parallel between the Scottish verse
(quoted yesterday) and written by William Motherwell, Poe
dwells at length, reprinting, side by side, all three verses, showing how Longfellow helped himself line for line, with very few
changes in the original text.

Longfellow defended himself against this charge by saying
he translated it from the German of O. L. B. Wolff and that
Wolff must have copied it from the Scottish poet.   Poe wrote
in answer to this:

I am willing to believe almost anything than so gross a plagiarism as this seems to be; but there are difficulties which should be
cleared up.   In the first place, how happens it that, in the trans-
mission from the German into English, not only the versification

should have been rigidly preserved, but the rhymes and alliterations?

Again, how are we to imagine Mr. Longfellow, with his known intimate acquaintance with Motherwell's "Minstrelsy," did not at once recognize so remarkable a poem when he met it in Wolff?

I have now before me a large volume of songs, ballads, etc., collected by Wolff; but there is no such poem.

He says there were other collections, perhaps, from the German Wolff—"But in such a case it must have been plainly acknowledged as a translation, with its origin designated. How, then, could Mr. Longfellow have translated it as original with Wolff? These are mysteries yet to be solved."

* * *

All this, of course, is aside from the issue and is only printed here because it is interesting to note that in the profundity of my ignorance I am not alone—that is to say, there's Mr. Poe.

Funny thing, this starting over again—by accident—a now ninety-eight-year-old controversy. With the world on fire and civilization in chaos we must get into a lather about what Mr. Longfellow said in 1842!

No, Chase, our friendship remains unaffected as far as I'm concerned. Your onslaught afforded me some pleasant hours of reading.

END OF THE LONGFELLOW WAR
The Last Word on the Plagiarism Libel,
by Chase S. Osborn and Stellanova Osborn

Dr. Malcolm Wallace Bingay quoted statements of Edgar Allan Poe as authoritative evidence that Henry Wadsworth Longfellow stole his ballad, "The Good George Campbell," from the ballad "Bonnie George Campbell" published in Motherwell's *Minstrelsy.*

Longfellow denied the charge, as soon as it had been made, in a letter to *Graham's Magazine* in which his poem had appeared, and showed that his poem was what it purported to be, a translation from the German.

The George Campbell ballad has an interesting history. There are at least four versions of it in print. In addition to the poem in Motherwell, and its German translation by O. L. B. Wolf, and Longfellow's re-translation from Wolf's poem into English from the German, there is another fragment of the same old Scotch ballad called "Hame Never Came He." We are concerned here, however, with only the first three.

The first two lines of the Motherwell version, the German translation, and Longfellow's re-translation of the German, furnish unmistakable proof of Longfellow's statement, if his words needed support against the words of Poe.

BONNIE GEORGE CAMPBELL
(Motherwell)
Hie upon Hielands
And low upon Tay,

DER GUTE GEORGE CAMPBELL
(Wolf)
Hoch auf dem Hochland,
Und tief an dem Tag,

THE GOOD GEORGE CAMPBELL
(Longfellow)
High on the Highlands
And deep in the day,

The fact that Longfellow's second line reproduced the German error *Tag* (*day*), instead of using the name of the River *Tay* as in the Motherwell poem, is complete proof that the German poem was Longfellow's source.

A review of the circumstances leading up to and closing what has been called in criticism "the Longfellow war," leads to the inevitable conclusion that Poe is the last man in the world to be quoted as an authority.

Poe's attack upon Longfellow was based on a natural antagonism of ideas and ideals. It was made acrid by Poe's jealousy of Longfellow's popularity and success as compared with his own uphill struggle for recognition. Poe's mind was diseased, and unbalanced. He killed himself by his excesses.

Drunkenness and dope-addiction made him irresponsible. His egotism also was irrational.

Poe's need for money led him to many questionable actions. At one time he put new titles on clippings of his old book reviews and resold them. One of the outstanding incidents of his career was his acceptance of an engagement in Boston to give a poem, and then, when he was unable to write one for the occasion, palming off a juvenile composition. This disappointed his audience and resulted in severe criticism of his action when it was discovered what he had done. In defense of himself, Poe concocted a story in which there was at least one outright lie. He circulated, and so far as he could, practically accredited, falsehoods concerning himself. He approved reports of his wildness in youth, and took no pains to explain questionable incidents of his career, because as his star began to ascend he believed the notoriety was all to his advantage. He was willing to besmirch his own reputation for temporary financial gain.

Poe and an associate publisher made advertising capital out of the notoriety surrounding Poe's attack on Longfellow.

Poe had launched his charge of plagiarism in the *Mirror*, a New York publication, at a time when he had achieved sudden recognition because of his poem, *The Raven*. The onslaught was one of the features of the part he was then playing, of the fearless critic. When his connection with the *Mirror* ended, its editor stated his entire dissent from all the disparagement of Longfellow that had been published in that paper.

The one-sided war was carried on by Poe in the *Broadway Journal*. His associate on this publication was Charles F. Briggs, who said of Poe, at the beginning, that he was a "monomaniac on the subject of plagiarism." While Briggs believed that the Longfellow war would end as it began, in smoke, he was not averse to it because in the meantime it would be the source of great publicity for the paper. Some time later, though still delighted by the advertising value of Poe's charges, Briggs repeated that he did not like his "fol-de-rol about plagiarism," and said that Poe had a high admiration for Longfellow which he would admit before he was done. At the end of four months' association with him, Briggs made plans to get rid of Poe, because he no longer had any sympathy with him, and had become completely undeceived of his first impressions of Poe's independence and learning in his criticisms, because they were so verbal and so purely selfish.

Poe has been described by an intimate associate as a characterless character—a person utterly deficient of high motive who could not conceive of anybody's doing anything except for his own personal advantage. Although he never dared to publish such opinions, or was unable to obtain a publisher for them, he revealed in conversations that he had no reverence for Homer, Shakespeare, or Milton; that he considered *Orion* the greatest poem in the language; and that he thought the Bible was all rigmarole.

This is the man to whose irresponsible statements Dr. Malcolm Wallace Bingay consigned the reputation of Henry Wadsworth Longfellow.

On the other side we have Longfellow's categorical denial, and documentary proof.

Dr. Bingay is already sorry like the gentleman he is. He is not the first good man fooled by poor, miserable Edgar Allan Poe.

A FINNISH-MICHIGANIAN SCHOLAR'S STATEMENT
CONCERNING THE KALEVALA AND HIAWATHA
Published in the Daily Mining Gazette,
Houghton, Michigan, March 23, 1940

Dr. John Wargelin, the erudite President of Suomi College at Hancock, Michigan, and noted litterateur, has given even more proof of the legitimacy of Longfellow's *Hiawatha*. He traces a phase of the matter far beyond conjecture and anchors it in the Psalms. His illustrations are invulnerable.

Dr. Wargelin is one of the best Finnish and English scholars. He has studied both the *Kalevala* and *Hiawatha* in the original. His research and logic have finality.

In addition to his work as president and manager of Suomi College and Theological Seminary, Dr. Wargelin is notary of the Consistory and president of the Board of Education of Suomi Synod; and is prominent in Finnish Lutheran religious work in three States. In 1927 and 1928 he was a member of the board of directors of the Finnish National Temperance Association.

He was born in Finland, September 26, 1881, the son of Isaac and Elizabeth Uitto Wargelin. From 1896 to 1906, he attended Suomi College (where he was graduated with an A.B. degree) and Suomi Seminary. He was ordained in 1906. After studying for several summers at the University of Michigan and the University of Chicago, he was granted the Master of Arts degree in Education at the University of Michigan in 1923. Wittenberg College conferred an honorary D.D. degree upon him in 1925. He is a member of Phi Delta Kappa, and of the Order of the White Rose in Finland.

President Wargelin is the author of *The Americanization of the Finns* and *Kristillinen Hyvantekevaisyys,* as well as of numerous articles on educational and religious topics, and he has edited several volumes. His leadership in civic, educational, and church activities has been widely recognized in Finland, as well as North America.

His contribution to the discussion of the *Kalevala* and *Hiawatha* is as follows:

Now that Finland has peace again—a forced peace—we are ready to give attention to other matters pertaining to Finland, besides war. To the fame of Finland's prowess in athletics, music, and architecture can now be added the heroism of her soldiers, a fact established long ago, for example, by the Finnish "Hakkapelitans" in the Thirty Years' War, but the deeds of small nations rarely come to the focus of the world in general. The fate of Finland in her recent heroic struggle may be compared to that of Belgium during the World War. May the admiration of the world be expressed again, as it was in the case of Belgium, in aiding Finland in her work of reconstruction after the war.   Our purpose, however, was not to discuss these matters, but rather to point to a discussion of the theme appearing at the head of this article.

In the *Detroit Free Press* of January 27, 1940, Dr. Malcolm W. Bingay charges that Henry Wadsworth Longfellow plagiarized the Finnish epic, *Kalevala,* in writing his *Hiawatha.* He writes: "Mr. Longfellow stole the whole thing, almost bodily, from the national epic of Finland—a saga of a people that is so old it is lost in the dim gray dusks of antiquity."

This charge was ably answered by one of the most scholarly and illustrious citizens of Michigan, former Governor Chase S. Osborn, in a lengthy three-page review of the whole subject, appearing in the Sault *Evening News* on February 27, 1940.   Besides writing a commendable essay on Longfellow, Mr. Osborn relates in an interesting way his travels in Norway and Finland, some fifty years ago, when he had an opportunity to study these peoples, their culture and life in general.   He also visited Count Leo Tolstoi in Russia, of whom he gives a very pleasant description.   But back to the *Hiawatha-Kalevala* controversy.

Mr. Osborn writes: "His (Longfellow's) *Hiawatha* is as original as anything written in the world in any language because it is a story of American Indian myths done in a most appropriate poetic style.   This came to him in a degree from the *Kalevala,* but that poem had nothing whatsoever to do with the poem of *Hiawatha* or the myths it develops.   The *Kalevala* may well indeed have suggested the poetic measure, but that is no more than to have had something come to him from the beautiful wind music of an aeolian harp."   Of the Finnish *Kalevala* Mr. Osborn says that it is worth knowing, not only in relation to this discussion but for its own worth.

Having studied both the *Kalevala* and the *Hiawatha* in the originals, the writer wishes to add his personal comment here.   Although there are certain similarities in the two epics, *e.g.,* both of them use the trochaic meter and parallelism of thought, and the *Kalevala* may have inspired Longfellow in

other particulars, it has never occurred to the writer to accuse
Longfellow of plagiarism. Longfellow had a perfect right to
use the simple monotonous trochaic meter in his work for it so
well suited the description of the primitive, nature-loving life
of the Indians. Its use need not end with the *Kalevala*, although Longfellow became acquainted with its modern use
first in the *Kalevala*.

And as to the parallelism, it is an ancient poetic form
found in some of the oldest literature of the world, for example
in the Hebrew Psalms. We add here examples of a few parallelisms:

> Thou shalt break them with a rod of iron;
> Thou shalt dash them in pieces like a potter's vessel.
>
> (Psalms 2:9)
>
> Let the people praise Thee, O God;
> Let all the people praise Thee.   (Psalms 67:5)
>
> They gave me also gall for my meat;
> And in my thirst they gave me vinegar to drink.
>
> (Psalms 69:21)

Longfellow, whose one-hundred-thirty-third birthday anniversary occurred on February 27, 1940, was the first poet to
use the *Hiawatha* meter in the English language, and has thus
enriched, as Mr. Osborn says, the ars poetica of English.

"There never was a more legitimate creation in the world
than that of *Hiawatha,* nor was there ever a nobler song-writer
on earth in any language than Henry Wadsworth Longfellow."

With a humble sense of our judgment concerning these
matters, we agree with Mr. Osborn that the honored and beloved name of our foremost American poet should not be
besmirched with a charge of plagiarism. This charge has been
fully met and answered satisfactorily long before this, and no
echo of it should be resounded again.

Hiawatha should be of special interest to the people of the
Upper Peninsula of Michigan for it was here the legends were
gathered and the center of the story moves here.

LONGFELLOW FOUND THE METER OF HIAWATHA
BY FOLLOWING AN AMERICAN TRAIL

The controversy over the actual source of the verse form of *Hiawatha* was satisfactorily ended, among those who study such matters and know what they are talking about, by the statements of F. Freiligrath, the German translator of the poem, in articles published in the *London Athenaeum*, December, 1855, and in *Blackwood's Magazine* for February, 1856.

Another informed critic had previously pointed out that rhymeless trochaic verses are common in Old Russian, Bohemian, Serbian, and Spanish; had declared that Longfellow's non-alliterative verse was unlike the old national meter of Finland; and suggested that the American poem might derive its measure from the Swedish translation of the *Kalevala* by Castrén or the German translation by Schiefner. Freiligrath, agreeing that *Hiawatha* is not in the old national meter of Finland, demonstrated its similarity to a modified form of that meter used in von Schröter's German translation of the *Kalevala*.

Although at first Freiligrath had cited the parallelisms of *Hiawatha* as evidence of its debt to the *Kalevala,* he admitted afterwards, on page x of the foreword to his *Der Sang von Hiawatha,* that parallelism was characteristic also of American Indian expression. Longfellow, in asserting this fact to his German friend and others, might have quoted conclusively the American Indian authority, Schoolcraft:

Most of the attempts to record poetic sentiments in the race have encountered difficulties, from the employment of some forms of the Grecian metres; or, still less adapted to it, English laws of rhyme. They have neither. It is far better suited, as the expression of strong poetic feeling, to the freedom of the Hebrew measure; the repetitious style of which reminds one of both the Indian sepulchral or burial chant, and eulogy. There is indeed in the flow of their oratory, as well as songs, a strong tendency to the figure of parallelism.

This statement on page 328 of part 3 of *Historical and Statistical Information Respecting the . . . Indian Tribes,* conspicuously headed "Poetic Development of the Indian Mind," was inescapably part of the Schoolcraft material that Longfellow had discovered and studied.

The critical pronouncement of Freiligrath as to the source of the *Hiawatha* meter stood unchallenged down almost to the present time.   In the last decade, however, it was importantly illuminated by Wilbur Lang Schramm of the University of Iowa, to whom should be accorded wider appreciation than is generally given scholarship in American literature.

When Longfellow read von Schröter's *Finnische Runen* with Freiligrath in 1842, he did what any master craftsman would do—he took the pattern of it for possible future use, to be stored in his memory with hundreds of other verse forms. When the time for *Hiawatha* came, he selected this particular meter as the most appropriate mold into which to pour the molten substance of his poetic thought.   How thoroughly American were the factors that influenced Longfellow to choose this measure, Dr. Schramm shows convincingly in the *Philological Quarterly,* October, 1932.   Furthermore, he proves that the form is far more American than has hitherto been recognized.

To begin with, Dr. Schramm reminds that upwards of a dozen Indian verse romances had been published in the United States before *Hiawatha.* Analyzing eleven of them, he discloses a well-grounded tradition, of which Longfellow must have been conscious when he began his famous poem.   Ten of these earlier romances show a predominance of tetrameter lines.   Any American poet in the 1850's, following the fashion of sixty years of Indian verse romances, says Dr. Schramm, would have chosen a lyric meter, probably tetrameter, and, quite possibly, trochaic tetrameter.   So that Longfellow's selection was quite close to the American tradition.

Still more than this: Longfellow was not only constrained to write in tetrameter by an American tradition as old as 1790. Schoolcraft, both in practice and in theory, specifically told him to write in trochees.

Henry Rowe Schoolcraft's Indian romance, *Alhalla,* published in 1843, which is one of the eleven considered by Dr. Schramm, is in trochaic tetrameter, and in the preface to that poem there is the following explicit information:

The measure [tetrameter] is thought to be not ill adapted to the Indian mode of enunciation. Nothing is more characteristic of their harangues and public speeches, than the vehement, yet broken and continued strain of utterance, which would be subject to the charge of monotony, were it not varied by an extraordinary compass in the stress of voice, broken by the repetition of high and low accent, and often terminated with an exclamatory vigor, which is sometimes startling. It is not the less in accordance with these traits that nearly EVERY INITIAL SYLLABLE OF THE MEASURE CHOSEN, IS UNDER ACCENT. This at least may be affirmed, that it imparts a movement to the narrative, which, at the same time that it obviates languor, favors that repetitious rhythm, or pseudo-parallelism, which so strongly marks their highly compound lexicography.

Dr. Schramm, in his distinguished contribution to American literary criticism, disclaims any attempt to prove that Longfellow found his meter elsewhere than in one of the *Kalevala* translations. He does, however, assert that the great American was guided to his choice of the *Finnische Runen* line by well-marked blazes made by pioneer poets of America. Above all of these looms Henry Rowe Schoolcraft. Intimately acquainted with the Ojibways and their language, intensely interested in the technical problems of versification, Schoolcraft pointed out to the poetic genius Longfellow exactly what his meter ought to accomplish, and declared that a trochaic tetrameter would come perhaps nearest that achievement.

II. THE HIAWATHA COUNTRY

THE Hiawatha country is one of the most interesting, beautiful and wholesome regions on earth. It may be defined as the woods and waters, many of them still in a state of nature, where the Ojibway Indians lived and trapped, fished and fought. Although this tribe sometimes got over the heights of land into the drainage area of other of the Great Lakes, the Hiawatha territory may be roughly described as the basin whose waters flow into Lake Superior. It seems an established fact that some of the Chippewas have resided north of this Lake from time immemorial.

> By the shores of Gitche Gumee,
> By the shining Big-Sea-Water,
> Stood the wigwam of Nokomis,
> Daughter of the Moon, Nokomis.
> Dark behind it rose the forest,
> Rose the black and gloomy pine-trees,
> Rose the firs with cones upon them;
> Bright before it beat the water,
> Beat the clear and sunny water,
> Beat the shining Big-Sea-Water.
>   There the wrinkled old Nokomis
> Nursed the little Hiawatha.

The grandeurs of the Lake Superior region are unsurpassable. Its shores are majestic in their contours and their colorings. Its water is as emerald and as pure as earth water can be. The sunshine is golden and the air is fragrant with balsam and other evergreens. It is the center of the greatest snow precipitation east of the Mississippi. Quite commonly it is transformed by the glorious phenomenon of the Northern Lights. The winds that blow from the Northwest, even today are never breathed by man until they get to where the Indians lived and where the whites now have taken their place.

The picturesque islands and waters of the blue Mediterranean gave rise to the Homeric tales of gods and men. The noble rock and sea scapes of Scandinavia inspired epic imaginings of Thor and Odin.   Such stories of men who strove with gods, to whom they were mysteriously akin, appear to be the effect of beautiful earth scenes upon the religious instinct of primitive men.   It was quite natural that the Lake Superior country, with its appeal and its austerity, should turn the minds of the Ojibways, as it does the thoughts of men today, toward interpretations of the Deity and man's relation to Him, in terms of beauty and of human needs.

What the Grecian peninsula and archipelago was to Homer, and what the Scandinavian region was to Northern mythology, the Lake Superior country has been to *Hiawatha*, the world-famous epic of the aboriginals of North America. An actual Indian leader named Hiawatha is known to have lived in New York State and to have become the nucleus of some traditions, but the bulk of the supernatural and other legends that have been combined to create the character of Hiawatha as we know it, were born in and of the sublimity of the Lake Superior country, where Henry Rowe Schoolcraft found them, and preserved them, and made them available to Longfellow.

Carver wrote that "The entrance into Lake Superior affords one of the most pleasing prospects in the world."

Schoolcraft's description of the gigantic basin is vivid:

Few portions of America can vie in scenic attractions with this interior sea.   Its size alone gives it all the elements of grandeur; but these have been heightened by the mountain masses which nature has piled along its shores.   In some places, these masses consist of vast walls, of coarse gray, or drab-colored sandstone, placed horizontally, until they have attained many hundred feet in height above the water.   The action of such an immense liquid area, forced against these crumbling walls by tempests, has caused wide and deep arches to be worn into the solid structure, at their base, into which the billows roll, with a noise resembling low-pealing thunder.   By this means, large areas of the impending mass are at length undermined and precipitated into the lake, leaving the split and rent parts, from which they have separated, standing like huge misshapen turrets and battlements.   Such is the varied coast, called the Pictured Rocks.

At other points of the coast, volcanic forces have operated, lifting up these level strata into positions nearly vertical, and leaving them to stand, like the leaves of a vast open book. At the same time, the volcanic rocks sent up from below, have risen in high mountains, with ancient gaping craters. Such is the condition of the disturbed stratification at the Porcupine Mountains.

The basin and bed of this lake act like a vast geological mortar, in which the masses of broken and fallen stones are whirled about and ground down, till all the softer ones, such as the sandstones, are brought into the state of pure yellow sand. This sand is driven ashore by the waves, where it is shoved up in long wreaths, and dried by the sun. The winds now take it up, and spread it inland, or pile it immediately along the coast, where it presents itself in mountain masses. Such are the great sand dunes of the Grande Sables.

There are yet other theatres of action for this sublime mass of inland waters, where the lake has manifested, perhaps, still more strongly, its abrasive powers. The whole force of its waters, under the impulse of a northwest tempest, is directed against prominent portions of the shore, which consist of black and hard volcanic rocks. Solid as these are, the waves have found an entrance in veins of spar, or minerals of softer texture, and have thus been led on their devastating course inland, tearing up large fields of amygdaloid, or other rock; or, left portions of them standing in rugged knobs, or promontories. Such are the east and west coasts of the great peninsula of Keweena, which have recently become the theatre of mining operations.

When the visitor to these remote and boundless waters comes to see this wide and varied scene of complicated geological disturbances and scenic magnificence, he is absorbed in wonder and astonishment. The eye, once introduced to this panorama of waters, is never done looking and admiring. Scene after scene, cliff after cliff, island after island, and vista after vista are presented. One day's scenes of the traveller are but the prelude to another; and when weeks, and even months, have been spent in picturesque rambles along its shores, he has only to ascend some of its streams, and go inland a few miles, to find falls, and cascades, and cataracts of the most beautiful or magnificent character. Go where he will, there is something to attract him. Beneath his feet are pebbles of agates; the water is of the most crystalline purity. The sky is filled, at sunset with the most gorgeous piles of clouds. The air itself is of the purest and most inspiring kind. To visit such a scene is to draw health from its purest sources, and while the eye revels in intellectual delights, the soul is filled with the liveliest symbols of God, and the most striking evidences of his creative power.

There are lifetimes of rare experience in the accounts of this country by Schoolcraft, Carver, and Alexander Henry and his nephew.

If Lake Superior were not so tremendous it would be seen more easily by the popular eye, and be the greatest modern Mecca of summer travel, even more so than Niagara Falls, for which it supplies fully half the water. The greatest of the Great Lakes is a major wonder of the world.

No one has finished seeing the earth with satisfaction until he has circled Lake Superior both by land and water. At one time one of the authors of this book went around this inland ocean on foot. At another time he paddled and sailed a canoe completely around its shores.

The north shore has promontories, like Point Noble, that once seen are remembered forever. They remind one of the Croatian shores of the Adriatic, except that Lake Superior water is fresh and sweet and potable. Also the North Superior shore is somewhat like the southern shores of Alaska. Between its archipelago of wooded islands and the mainland are deep channels and many safe harbors, which make an ideal cruising ground. A first sight of the islands off Port Arthur is breath-taking and transporting.

All the islands of Lake Superior have a nobility of their own. Isle Royale is one of the gems of creation. When one approaches it by way of Houghton, after a long trip across windswept open water that reaches to the sky on all horizons, the first warm land breeze from Isle Royale, laden with the fragrance of evergreens, comes like a breath from the Isles of Spice, and the first sight of the island is like a landfall to an ocean voyager. Michipicoten is attractive not only because of its scenic beauty but because it gives promise of valuable minerals. Pie Island has a lovely setting. So has Parisian. Caribou Island is a wild spot that Alexander Henry found overrun with caribou. It was called the Isle of the Golden Sands because its shores are a lovely gamboge. There is no

gold in the sands there, although it is found in the rocks elsewhere on Lake Superior. Henry went ashore and got thirteen
caribou for his larder in one day. Finally the animals were
exterminated. In recent years they have been successfully
reintroduced.

On the south shore, the Huron Mountains and the Porcupine Mountains limned against the sky are never to be forgotten. Remnants of an ancient range, they are thought-provok-
ing as well as spirit-stirring. The highest peak in Michigan,
which is 2,023 feet above sea level, is in the Porcupines.

In a general way, the south shore of Lake Superior may
be likened to the North Atlantic coast. Steep cliffs and
rocky promontories contrast with long stretches of sand
beaches and deep bays. Harbors are infrequent. There is
none from Whitefish Bay to Munising. Beginning east of
Marquette are high, perpendicular sandstone cliffs, characterized by variegated colorings and by the fantastic carvings made
in them by winds and waves. There are arches and caves into
which large craft can enter, and forms that the imagination
pleasurably construes into castles and battlements. From the
beginning of the history of this region, the group known as the
Pictured Rocks has been a source of enjoyment and wonder-
ment. They were originally the most famous of our natural
phenomena and are still without a counterpart in coastal
scenery. Geologically, these sandstone cliffs are interesting as
remnants of the beach of the prehistoric Nipissing Great Lakes.
This chain of three great lakes, including what we now know
as Lakes Superior, Michigan and Huron, was as much deeper
than the present Lakes as these cliffs indicate. This was
immediately after the continental icecap had ceased to interfere with these giant bodies of water, and for the time being
they emptied by way of Lake Nipissing and the Mattawa River
into the ocean which at that period reached a line west of what
is now the city of Ottawa, Ontario.

As might be expected, the remarkable Pictured Rocks had
a place in the traditions of the Ojibway Indians. The mis-

chief-maker Pau-Puk-Keewis, finally driven here by Hiawatha, met his end in one of the many awe-inspiring caverns.

Every rock tells its own story of the vast changes that have taken place in ages past, and that are continuously in progress under our unseeing eyes. The basalt flows on the north shore, and other volcanic rocks, prove this to have been an eruptive zone at one time. The story of the aeons is also to be read where the many waterfalls of the Upper Peninsula of Michigan reveal the chapters recorded in the eloquent rocks. There are many beautiful falls in this part of the Lake Superior country. Among them are Munising, Miner's, Tannery, Laughing Whitefish, Wagner, Au Train, Sable ;and, best known of all, the Tahquamenon, in some respects the largest falls west of Niagara. It was the Tahquamenon River that Hiawatha cleared for navigation, with the help of the very strong man, Kwasind, and in this stream that Kwasind later was lured to his destruction.

Among other interesting phenomena on the south Lake Superior shore are the dunes of perpetual ice between Grand Marais and Munising. At Au Sable banks the snows and ice of centuries have piled up and the winds have driven the sand over them until there are repeated layers of congelations. The Indians used these banks as refrigerators. White men do the same now. All that is necessary to keep fish or game, is to dig a hole in the sand two or three feet or until one reaches frozen conditions. The Chippewa tale of the origin of the dunes is told in the Hiawatha epic.

"Two of the most sublime natural objects in the United States," says Schoolcraft,

the Grand Sable and the pictured rocks are to be found upon this coast. The former is an immense hill of sand, extending for some miles along the lake, of great elevation and precipitous ascent. The latter is an unbroken wall of rocks, rising perpendicularly from the lake to the height of 300 feet, assuming every grotesque and fanciful appearance, and presenting to the eye of the passenger a spectacle as tremendous as the imagination can conceive, or as reason itself can well sustain.

We almost held our breath in passing the coast; and when, at

THE PICTURED ROCKS OF LAKE SUPERIOR—CHAPEL ROCK. SHOWING NIPISSING
AND MODERN SHORES.

night, we compared our observations around the camp-fire, there was no one who could recall such a scene of simple novelty and grandeur in any other part of the world; and all agreed that, if a storm should have arisen while we were passing, inevitable destruction must have been our lot.

The Doric Rock and the offerings made to it by the Chippewas are described by Peter Esprit Radisson, an explorer as well as a trader with the Indians, from 1652 to 1684.

Some two hundred streams are tributary to Lake Superior, on the surface. There appears also to be evidence of subterranean inlets. This is easily possible, because the streams of water on the surface of the earth are but a visible cross-section of the streams that flow at varying depths below the ground. Moreover, as far as data can be obtained, the visible discharge of water from Lake Superior is much greater than any visible inflow. The greatest depth of Lake Superior is eight hundred feet below the surface of the Atlantic Ocean. This eight hundred feet conjecturally almost without a doubt is the receptacle of much underground water. This may be the only way to account for the fact that the level of Lake Superior has not varied much more than an average of ten inches a year since records have been kept.

One of the interesting things about Lake Superior is the slight variation in its temperature throughout the year. Although lying north of latitude 46 North, the temperature of the water is reported to vary less than nine degrees in winter and summer, with almost no difference whatsoever at a depth of a hundred feet. This gives rise to the statement that Lake Superior never gives up its dead. Ordinarily it is too cold to permit fermentation of the bodies of those who drown in it, unless they happen to be cast into shallow bays, and there are not many of those. The case of Hiawatha's friend, Chibiabos the sweet-singer, appears to have been one of the exceptional instances. The low temperature of the water in Lake Superior, and its invariability throughout the year, has suggested that its subterranean inlets flow from the north and could be thought of as underground rivers from Arctic regions.

This greatest body of fresh water in the world, suspended as it were some six hundred feet above the level of the sea, is four hundred fifty miles long and one hundred sixty-seven miles wide. It has an area of thirty-two thousand square miles and a maximum depth of fourteen hundred feet. Gitche Gumee it is indeed! A comparison with two other vast fresh water lakes is illuminating.

Lake Victoria Nyanza, the source of the Nile, in Africa, has an area commonly given as twenty-seven thousand square miles but actually it has a larger surface. Its greatest recorded depth is two hundred seventy feet, although the soundings may not be complete or accurate.

Although Victoria Nyanza is three thousand eight hundred feet above sea level, it is within the tropics and the temperature of its water often runs above seventy degrees. Its water teems with living infusoria and holds in suspense various forms of life that are not much more than colloidal. It is claimed that there are living diatoms in it. When I examined the water of that lake I did not have the microscopic equipment that would permit classifications of the water burden.

The other rival of Lake Superior in size and volume is Lake Baikal in Siberia, which is three hundred ninety-seven miles long and forty-five miles wide on the average and has an area of thirteen thousand two hundred square miles. I have visited Baikal several times and each time have tried to get accurate data as to its depth. This I have been unable to do, although I have especially consulted the Trans-Baikal and Circum-Baikal railway reports. It is commonly said to have an average depth exceeding two thousand feet, or six hundred more than Lake Superior at its maximum. A sounding of four thousand seven hundred twenty-five feet ranks Baikal as the deepest lake in the world. Even so it remains a fact that in volume of fresh water Superior is the largest lake on earth.

Gold and silver and precious stones are superficially considered wealth, but water to drink is much more precious. It would make Lake Superior a major wonder of creation merely to be nature's greatest reservoir of deep, pure water in the world. Health is wealth. Not only are the waters of the region pleasantly potable. The air is the clearest and most vitalizing on earth, for it is as invigorating as that of the Alps without the danger and discomfort attendant on high altitude. Before the white men came, with pork and whisky poisoning, there were no such things as syphilis, cancer, and tuberculosis known among the Indians. There is not a dangerously noxious thing. Mosquitoes do not spread malaria. Black flies are disagreeable but they never kill. These exist only at certain seasons. The mosquito works mostly at night and the black fly in the daytime. The Indians were immune to both. White explorers are also. The region is internationally famous as a refuge from hay fever. Most of the ailments that man is heir to are alleviated in the Hiawatha country. Especially tired man is born anew.

If one had nothing else to do for a lifetime but explore Lake Superior and its environs, he could not finish. There are those who have been traveling and studying it for more than half a hundred years who feel that they have not much more than begun. One need not be driven by curiosity alone but can be sure of the possibility of economic results that are highly worth while. Those who discovered the mineral zones of Lake Superior made fortunes. Many more have been wrung from the ranges since, and these are still a source of vast riches. In the heart of the Hiawatha country, adjacent to the shores of Lake Superior, are some of the greatest mineral deposits in the world.

Native copper deposits first made Lake Superior a lure for explorers. There is evidence on Isle Royale and other places that early Norsemen may have discovered and worked this metal. The Indians realized its usefulness. At first they worked it to produce forms resembling those of their stone implements. Copper proved too soft to supersede stone as a material for the manufacture of implements, but copper celts, hatchets, awls, knives, drills, spearheads, and other simple tools have been found. Occasional specimens are grooved for hafting. The color and other properties of copper led to its use also for personal ornaments. By the time the white men arrived, this mineral had spread over the greater part of the country. It is considered likely that most if not all of the objects of sheet-copper with repoussé designs that have been found in Indian mounds and graves from Illinois to Florida had their source in the Lake Superior country. Sites of copper mines are marked by extensive pittings in exposing the copper-bearing rocks and breaking them up to release the masses of native copper by means of heavy boulders from the Lake shore. Thousands of these rude hammers are found about the pits.

In 1820, Henry Rowe Schoolcraft, as geologist with Governor Lewis Cass's expedition, traversed the south shore of Lake Superior. Among the material he took back East with him was a large specimen of native copper. It is interesting to know that this finally reached the hands of Secretary of War John Calhoun, who led in developing the first appreciable gold discovery in the American States, at Dahlonega, Georgia, and established the first mint there. John Calhoun cut up the specimen of native copper from Michigan and presented pieces of it to foreign ministers at Washington and other gentlemen from abroad, in order to advertise the resources of the country.

Henry Rowe Schoolcraft's journal of this 1820 expedition is more than a scientific notebook. For the general reader, it is a real adventure. So is the narrative of his expedition in 1832; or the summary narrative of both, published in 1855.

Gold was found in some quantity in the Upper Peninsula and mines were wrought. Marble and granite, and verdi antique that equals the Italian, are there; also gypsum, slate, sandstone, dolomite, and highest grade limestone for carbide and sugar and for steel manufacture. But more productive of wealth than everything else put together were and are the iron deposits. Great ranges of iron ore tributary to Lake Superior are real but seem fabulous. The Mesaba range has produced tremendous tonnage. The Marquette range has been rich and still is. The Menominee and Gogebic and Vermilion, with their ramifications, are apparently endless. The country has been only half explored.

On Isle Royale there are precious stones. Thomsonites do not class as a true gem but are near enough to pass the pseudo stage. Chlorastrolites are true gems. The name means green star stone. On the north shore are amethysts that are clear purple and others bluish violet. These tintings, so delicate and appealing, are supposed to be due to the presence of manganese. Wherever there are rocks around the Lake, agates may be found on the shores.

For the Indians, the lure of the Lake Superior country lay in the elemental necessities of living that could be won from its woods and waters.

Cedar logs for the walls of their homes, and cedar and black ash bark for coverings, were plentiful. There was birch bark for canoes, spruce roots to sew them with, spruce gum for caulking. Out of the swamps they dug tamarack knees perhaps a century old which made perfect ribs for water vehicles. The birch-bark canoe of the Indian has never been superseded by lighter or cleverer craft. The Hudson's Bay Company had single birch-bark canoes that would carry tons of cargo. Some of these are still to be seen, as exhibits, in the Hiawatha country.

When the white man came he found everywhere white pine without a knot, yielding perfect drafting boards. These are rare now. As late as this year there was cut one log from one tree that was sixteen feet long and ten feet in diameter and yielded over a thousand feet board measure. The spruce swamps have provided many things, including measureless quantities of the best pulpwood. Balsam, and the poplar of the Hiawatha country that is called popple, have been another great source of raw material for paper mills. Where the tamaracks grow with their delicate greens in the springtime, men sought that wood for car timbers and other purposes. Intermingled with these softer woods were millions of acres of the finest mahogany birch, beech, basswood, ash, and elm, sugar or hardwood maple in solid stands, and birdseye trees. These caused the establishment of many woodworking plants and the largest wood charcoal furnaces in the world.   Maple sugar was one of the preservable foods of the Indians.   The possibilities of the maple syrup and maple sugar industry in the north country have not yet been realized.

Characteristic of the Hiawatha country are the tall, tortured, twisted hemlock trees.   Along the winding Tahquamenon, especially in late fall when gnarliness of trunk and limb is most apparent, they are impressive in their picturesqueness. The Indian expressed his evaluation of the tree in a short story. After the Great Spirit made the beautiful pine tree, with its long straight trunk and fine wood, the Bad Spirit saw it.   It made him jealous.   So the Bad Spirit tried to make a pine tree himself.   The hemlock was what he made instead.   It is crooked and trouble-causing and not good for much.

Great changes have occurred since the Ojibway Indians had this country to themselves, and even since Schoolcraft lived among them and made records of their doings and traditions.   Today certain sections of this land have proven to be highly fertile.   Potatoes and beans, clover and timothy, and all vegetables and root crops grow riantly.   Dairy products of high grade are plentiful.   Chippewa County lamb is the finest in the world.   But for the Indians the question of food was always a serious consideration.

Although the early explorers found the Garden River Valley and similar locations famous for Indian corn, that was a late development in Indian life.   The Lake Superior Ojibways were not naturally agricultural.   They depended on wild rice and berries, on maple syrup and the maple sugar that they stored in makaks made of birch bark, and on the game that they could take from forest and stream.   At best their living was precarious.

Deer are probably more plentiful today than they were in the pre-white-man era.   Now they are completely protected from hunters most of the year and partially all of the year. Their deadly enemies, the timber wolves, have been practically exterminated.   The area of the cover in which they roam is much less than in former days, so that the deer are concentrated. When the little Hiawatha waited on the deer runway and got his buck, it was really more of an exploit than it is for many modern hunters. And when as a young man he laid his kill at the feet of Minnehaha, in indication of his intent to ask her hand in marriage, that was an act of prime significance. Deer and moose and bear and beaver and muskrat and squirrel and varying hare, such as are still in the forests of the Upper Peninsula of Michigan, were not always to be found when the Indians needed them most. Hiawatha, with all his supernatural powers, was unable to prevent the death of Minnehaha from fever following famine, which was an all too common cause of death, especially after the fur-trade made its effects felt on wild life.

According to Perrot, the Chippewas were using both guns and bows and arrows in 1718. They were also adept in the use of snares to take large game. He stated that a band of Chippewas made an extraordinary catch of more than twenty-four hundred moose in the winter of 1670–1671 on Manitoulin Island, using only snares.

Schoolcraft records the statement of an Indian from Fond du Lac on Lake Superior that his band numbered two hundred twenty, of whom fifty-four were hunters; and that these fifty-four hunters had killed, during the season of 1828, nine hundred ninety-four bears.

Charlevoix, in 1721, wrote:

When we discovered this vast continent it was full of wild beasts. A handful of Frenchmen has made them almost entirely disappear in less than an age, and there are some the species of which is entirely destroyed. They killed the elks and moose-deer merely for the pleasure of killing them, and to show their dexterity.

"This senseless slaughter of our wild game has continued even to this day," said Charles S. Wheeler, as late as 1902, writing about all of Michigan,

until the bison or buffalo, elk, moose, caribou, panther, and wolverine are extinct in the State. The early mammals numbered about fifty species. They were the bison or buffalo, the caribou, elk, moose, common deer, panther, lynx, wild-cat, gray wolf, fisher, sable or pine marten, red fox, gray fox, ermine or white weasel, mink, badger, skunk, otter, wolverine, black bear, raccoon, four bats, two moles, two shrews, flying squirrel, red squirrel, black and gray squirrel, fox squirrel, two chipmunks, striped gopher, woodchuck, beaver, five kinds of mice, muskrat, common rabbit, white hare, porcupine and opossum. Three hundred and thirty-six kinds of birds have been reported as residents or migrants. Dr. Miles records 43 reptiles, including turtles, snakes, frogs, toads, and lizards; also 161 land and fresh-water mollusks. The number of fishes, insects, and lower orders of animal life are unknown.

However, Iagoo, the great boaster, did not get all the wild animals of the Hiawatha country. In 1941, hunters crossing the Straits of Mackinac took home 11,000 deer, which lately are increasing in number. There are still many moose and bear. The most valuable fur in the region is the silver gray fox, then the black fox, the cross fox, and the red fox. In bulk, beaver is the most valuable of all. There are plenty of skunks, and enough lynxes which are the nearest to a panther in this part of the earth. Also there are bobcats and porcupines and innumerable small creatures, including flying squirrels.

Fish were the Indians' mainstay. They are still plentiful in the Hiawatha country. In all the tributaries of Lake Superior are found the gamiest and finest brook trout in the world. The trout streams that emerge from the dark forests on the north shore are clear and turbulent and plunge suddenly down the steep watershed into the crystal depths of the lake. Those on the Michigan shore are of a deep wine color, dyed by the roots of hemlock, and the speckled trout in them take on darker shades of brown and orange and red, in contrast with the silver and pink of those in the lake. In Lake Superior are lake trout weighing over a hundred pounds, in instances. There are muskellunge, which are fine food at any size, and sturgeon. Whitefish have been taken weighing more than thirty pounds to the fish.

An interesting volume might be written about the whitefish of Lake Superior.

Baron La Hontan, who came in 1688, said,

You can scarcely believe what vast shoals of whitefish are seen about the middle of the channel, between the continent and the Isle of Missilimakinac. This sort of whitefish, in my opinion, is the only one from all these lakes that can really be called good. Above all, it has one singular property; namely, that all sorts of sauces spoil it, so that it is always eaten either broiled or boiled, without any manner of seasoning.

Father Marquette established his mission at Point St. Ignace in 1671 because here the whitefish, his source of food, was found in great abundance. This territory was referred to by the Indians as Pe-kwa-de-nong, meaning "the place of the fishes."

In 1688–89 Father Claude Dablon visited Sault Ste. Marie and left this note:

At the foot of these rapids, and even among these boiling waters, extensive fishing is carried on, from early spring until winter, of a kind of fish usually found only in Lake Superior and the Lake of the Hurons. . . . It is very white and very excellent. In truth it furnishes food almost by itself to the greater part of all these peoples.

Mrs. Jameson, an Englishwoman who visited Sault Ste. Marie in 1837, wrote about the whitefish:

Here, at the foot of the rapids, the celebrated whitefish of the lakes is caught in its highest perfection. The people down below (that is, in the neighborhood of Lake Ontario and Lake Erie) who boast of the excellence of the whitefish, really know nothing of the matter. There is no more comparison between the whitefish of the lower lakes and the whitefish of St. Marys, than between plaice and turbot, or between a clam and a Sandwich oyster. I ought to be a judge, who have eaten them fresh out of the river four times a day, and I declare to you that I never tasted anything of the fish kind half so exquisite. If the Roman Apicius had lived in these latter days, he would certainly have made a voyage up Lake Huron to breakfast on the whitefish of St. Marys River. Really it is the most luxurious delicacy that swims the waters. It is said by Alexander Henry that people never tire of them. Mr. McMurray, missionary at the Canadian Sault, tells me that he has eaten them every day of his life for seven years.

Dablon gives an interesting account of the Ojibway method of taking whitefish in the earliest times:

Dexterity and strength are needed for this kind of fishing; for one must stand upright in a bark canoe, and there, among the whirlpools, with muscles tense, thrust deep into the water a rod, at the end of which is fastened a net made in the form of a pocket, into which the fish are made to enter. One must look for them as they glide between the rocks, pursue them when they are seen; and, when they have been made to enter the net, raise them with a sudden strong pull into the canoe. This is repeated over and over again, six or seven large fish being taken each time, until a load of them is obtained.

Not all persons are fitted for this fishing; and sometimes those are found who, by the exertions they are forced to make, overturn the canoe, for want of possessing sufficient skill and experience.

Dr. Vernon Kinietz, of the University of Michigan Museums, comments:

The Chippewa, including the Missisauga and the Nipissing, appear to have been the only ones whose men were sufficiently skillful to practice this fishing in the swiftest water where the yield was greatest. The Chippewa caught more whitefish than they could eat and carried the surplus to Mackinac, where they sold it at a high price to both French and Indians. Another part of the heavy autumn catch was dried on frames over a fire to preserve it for winter use.

"I used to admire the fishermen on the Arno," wrote Mrs. Jameson,

and those on the Laguna, and above all the Neapolitan fishermen, hauling in their nets, or diving like ducks, but I never saw anything like these Indians. The manner in which they keep their position upon a footing of a few inches, is to me as incomprehensible as the beauty of their forms and attitudes, swayed by every movement and turn of their dancing, fragile barks, is admirable.

Those who taste the famous Lake Superior whitefish, one of the greatest delicacies any waters produce, should know that it is one of the history-making products of North America. Indeed it deserves recognition together with the codfish that lured Europeans to the Newfoundland banks and the gold that brought about the Spanish conquest of Mexico.

In the earliest days, Mukwa, the bear, when he was hungry, walked to the shore and scooped out a luscious whitefish with his paw. Then came the Ojibways, who complimented, cajoled, and exhorted "Addik-kum-maig" to come and be caught, promising that the utmost respect would be shown their bones. The Indians thought it necessary to propitiate the spirit of the whitefish, lest they forsake them. Addik-kum-maig, or deer of the waters, they named it, because it compared with the deer in importance as a means of subsistence.

Its never-failing abundance from spring to winter at the foot of the rapids of the St. Marys River caused the gathering there of the largest Indian village in North America. Dablon says it furnished food, almost by itself, to the greater part of all these people. French and British trappers, fur traders, and soldiers congregated at this point and fought for dominion over it. It was one of the greatest fur-trading centers on the continent. Expeditions were outfitted here for distant parts of the country. "Poisson blanc," the Frenchman called the choice catch that fed the village. "Whitefish," said the advance guard of British conquerors. Thus the whitefish was the reason for the beginning and the growth of the oldest French town in the United States—Sault Ste. Marie, Michigan.

When the fur trade diminished, the catching and shipping of whitefish became a major industry of Michigan. A traveler in the State in 1870 said, "A fleet of two hundred fishing boats are engaged in and about the Straits (of Mackinac). Each boat will average one barrel of fish a day during the fishing season."

At the time this book is written, well on toward the middle of the twentieth century, with the fishing industry still the sole support of many thousands in Michigan, the whitefish remains the most desired of all catches and has been recently selected as the outstandingly representative food of the State.

The economics of geography are interesting in their effect upon the wars and migrations of nations. Also they play a part in the background of other human dramas. The concentration of Ojibways at Sault Ste. Marie and LaPointe set the scene for Schoolcraft, and through him for the great poem of Hiawatha.

The frontier settlement of Sault Ste. Marie, which Schoolcraft saw for the first time in 1820, decided for him what his lifework was to be and gave him his Indian bride.   It was here that the eminent American ethnologist gained his detailed and intimate knowledge of the life and legends of the Ojibways.

Then Henry Wadsworth Longfellow created *Hiawatha,* a diadem of literature, from the jewels that Henry Rowe Schoolcraft discovered on the shores of Lake Superior.

III. HIAWATHA'S PEOPLE

Their Origin, Wars and Migrations

THE largest settlement of the Ojibways, and, in fact, the most numerous primitive Indian village in the United States, was their ancient capital at the outlet of Lake Superior, on the Saint Marys River at the foot of the Rapids,—what is now known as Sault Ste. Marie. The crane was its totem.

Their legend that tells of its establishment is almost as interesting as the historic explanation. Schoolcraft preserved this under the title of "Mash-kwa-sha-kwong" in *Oneóta*, as George Johnston wrote it for him, which is practically as follows:

Mash-kwa-sha-kwong was a first rate hunter, and he loved the chase exceedingly and pursued it with unceasing vigilance. One day, on his return home, arriving at his lodge, he was informed by his two sons, who were but small then, that they were very lonesome, because their mother was in the habit of daily leaving them alone, and this occurred so soon as he started upon his daily chase. This circumstance was not unknown to Mash-kwa-sha-kwong, but he seemed fully aware of it. He took his boys in his arms and kissed them and told them that their mother behaved improperly and was acting the part of a wicked and faithless woman. But Mash-kwa-sha-kwong behaved towards his wife as if ignorant of her vile course. One morning, rising very early, he told his sons to take courage and that they must not be lonesome; he also strictly enjoined them not to be absent themselves or quit their lodge; after this injunction was given to the boys he made preparations, and, starting much earlier than usual, he traveled but a short distance from his lodge, when he halted and secreted himself. After waiting a short time he saw his wife coming out of the lodge, and immediately after a man made his appearance and meeting Mash-kwa-sha-kwong's wife, they greeted one another. His suspicions were now confirmed and when he saw them in the act of carrying on an illegal intercourse, his anger arose; he went up to them and killed them with one blow. He then dragged them both to his lodge, and tying them together, he dug a hole beneath the fireplace in his lodge and buried them. He then told his sons that it was necessary that he should go away, as he would surely be killed if he remained, and their safety would depend upon their ability to keep the matter a secret. He gave his elder son a small bird (Kichig-e-chig-aw-na-she) to roast for his small brother over the ashes and embers where their mother was buried; he also provided a small leather bag, and then told his sons the necessity of his immediate flight to heaven, or to the skies; and that it would be expedient for them to fly and journey southward, and thus prepared their minds for the separation about to take place. "By and bye," said Mash-kwa-sha-kwong to his sons,"persons will come to you and inquire for me and your mother; you will say to them that I am gone hunting, and your little brother in the mean-time will continually point to the fireplace; this will lead the persons to whom I allude to make inquiries of the cause of this pointing, and you will tell them that you have a little bird roasting for your brother; this will cause them to desist from further inquiry at the time. As soon as they are gone, escape! While you are journeying, agreeable to my instructions, I will look from on high upon you; I will lead and conduct you and you shall hear my voice from day to day." Mash-kwa-sha-kwong at this time gave his sons an awl, a beaver's tooth, and a hone, also a dry coal, and directed them to place a small piece of the coal on the ground every evening, so soon as they should encamp, from which fire would be produced and given to them; he told his elder son to place his brother in the leather bag and in that manner carry him upon his back; he then bade them farewell.

The two boys being thus left alone in the lodge, and while in the act of roasting the little bird provided for them, a man came in, and then another and another, until they numbered ten in all. The younger boy would from time to time point at the fire, and the men inquired to know the reason. The elder boy said that he was roasting a bird for his brother, and, digging the ashes, produced it. They inquired where their father and mother were; the boy answered them, saying that their father was absent hunting, and that their mother had gone to chop and collect wood. Upon this information the men rose and searched around the outskirts of the lodge, endeavoring to find traces of the man and his wife, but they were not successful, and returned to the lodge. Before this, however, and during the absence of the ten men, Mash-kwa-sha-kwong's elder son placed his little brother in the leather bag (Ouskemood), and ran away southward.

One of the ten men observed that the smaller boy had repeatedly pointed to the fireplace, and that they might find out something by digging; they set to work and found the woman and the man tied together. On this discovery their wrath was kindled; they brandished their weapons, pronouncing imprecations upon Mash-kwa-sha-kwong, who was, of course, suspected of having committed the deed.

The ten men renewed their search in order to avenge themselves upon the perpetrator of this dark deed; but Mash-kwa-sha-kwong in order to avoid instant death, had sought a large hollow tree, and entering at the bottom or root part, passed through and reached the top of it, from whence he took his flight upwards to the sky. His pursuers finally traced him, and followed him as far as the tree, and into the sky, with loud and unceasing imprecations of revenge and their determination to kill him. The spirit of the mother alone followed her children. About mid-day, the boys heard as they ran, a noise in the heavens like the rolling of distant thunder. The boys continued the journey south, when the noise ceased. Towards night they encamped; they put a small piece of the coal on the ground, then a log of firewood was dropped down from the skies to them, from whence a good blazing fire was kindled. This was done daily, and when the fire was lighted, a raccoon would fall from on high upon the fire, and in this manner the boys were fed; and this overruling care they experienced daily. In the evenings at their camping place, and sometimes during the day, the Red Head's voice was heard speaking to his children, and encouraging them to use their utmost exertions to fly from the pursuit of their mother. To aid them in escaping they were told to throw away their awl, and immediately there grew a strong and almost impassable hedge of thorn bushes behind them, in their path, which the pursuing mother could scarcely penetrate, and thus impeding her progress, tearing away her whole body and leaving nothing but the head. So they escaped the first day.

The next day they resumed their march and could distinctly hear the noise of combat in the sky, as if it were a roaring thunder; they also heard the noise of their mother behind them, desiring her elder son to stop and wait for her, saying that she wished to give the breast to his brother; then again Mash-kwa-sha-kwong's voice encouraging his sons to fly for their lives and saying that if their mother overtook them she would surely kill them.

In the evening of the second day the boys prepared to encamp and the noise of combat on high ceased; on placing a small piece of the coal on the ground a log and some firewood was let down as on the preceding night, and the fire was kindled, and then the raccoon placed on it for their food. This was fulfilling the promise made by their father, that they would be provided for during their flight. The beaver's tooth was here thrown away, and this is the cause why the northern country now abounds with beaver; and also the innumerable little lakes and marshes, and consequently the rugged and tedious traveling now experienced.

On the third day the boys resumed their flight and threw away their hone, and it became a high, rocky, mountainous ridge, the same now seen on the north shore of these straits (St. Marys) which was a great obstacle in the way of the woman of the Head, for this was now her name, because that part alone remained of her whole frame, and with it she was incessantly uttering determinations to kill her elder son; the boys finally reached the fishing place known as the eddy of

Wah-zah-zhawing at the rapids of Bawating (Sault Ste. Marie) situated on the north shore of the river. Here Mash-kwa-sha-kwong told his sons that he himself had been overtaken in his flight by his pursuers and killed; and he appeared to them in the shape of a red-headed woodpecker, or a *mama*. This is a bird that is seldom or never attacked by birds of prey, for no vestiges of his remains are ever seen or found by the Indian hunter. "Now, my sons," said the red-headed woodpecker, "I have brought you to this river; you will now see your grand-father and he will convey you across to the opposite side." Then the boys looked to the southern shore of the river, and they saw in the middle of the rapid an Oshuggay standing on a rock. To the Oshuggay the boys spoke, and accosted him as their grandfather, requesting him to carry them across the river Bawating. The Oshuggay, stretching his long neck over the river to the place where the boys stood, told them to get upon his head and neck, and again stretching to the southern shore, he landed the boys in safety upon a prairie; the crane was seen walking in state up and down the prairie.

The persevering mother soon arrived at Wah-zah-hawing, and immediately requested the Oshuggay to cross her over; stating that she was in pursuit of her children and that she wished to overtake them, but the Oshuggay seemed well aware of her character and objected to conveying her across, giving her to understand that she was a lewd and bad woman; he continued giving her a long moral lecture upon the course she had pursued and the bad results to mankind in consequence, such as quarrels, murders, deaths, and hence widowhood.

The Woman of the Head persisted in her request to be conveyed across. Objections and entreaties followed. She talked as if she were still a woman whose favors were to be sought, and he as if he were above such favors. After this dialogue the Oshuggay said that he would convey her across on the condition that she would adhere strictly to his injunctions; he told her not to touch the bare part of his head, but to get upon the hollow or crooked part of his neck; to this she agreed and got on. The Oshuggay then withdrew his long neck to about half way across, when, feeling that she had forgotten her pledge, he dashed her head upon the rocks, and the small fish that were so abundant instantly fed upon the brain and fragments of the skull and became large white fish. "A fish," said the Oshuggay, "that from this time forth shall be abundant and remain in these rapids to feed the Indians and their issue from generation to generation."

After this transaction of the Oshuggay's landing the boys safely across, and dashing the woman's head upon the rocks, he spake to the crane, and mutually consulting one another in relation to Mash-kwa-sha-kwong's sons, they agreed to invite two women from the eastward of the tribe of the Wassissig, and the two lads took them for wives. The Oshuggay plucked one of his largest wing feathers and gave it to the elder boy, and the crane likewise did the same, giving his feather to the younger; they were told to consider the feathers as their sons after this; one feather appeared like an Oshuggay and the other like a young crane. By and by they appeared like human beings to the lads. Thus the alliance was formed with the Wassissig, and the circumstances of the Oshuggay and crane interesting themselves in behalf of the boys, and the gift to them of their feathers and the result is the origin of the Indian Totem.

Here Mash-kwa-sha-kwong's sons were told that they would be considered as chieftains, and that this office would be hereditary and continue in their generations. After this they multiplied exceedingly and became strong and powerful.

Population increased so rapidly at Bawating that it was necessary to form new villages, some settling on the Garden River, some upon the Pakaysaugauegan River, and others upon the Island of St. Joseph's and upon the Menashkong bay and Mashkotay Saugie river. . . . The Oshuggays and the Cranes quarreled, and this quarrel commenced on a trivial point. It appears that the Cranes took a pole, without leave, from the Oshuggays and they broke the pole; this circumstance led to a separation. The Oshuggays emigrated south, and are now known as the Shawnees.

Among other dim ideas of their origin is a suggestion that they originally dwelt in a country destitute of snows; also the belief that they migrated from the east to the west. A version of the latter is that, many strings of lives before, they were led by a kindly spirit to migrate from the shores of the great salt sea to the more pleasant land of the sweet-water seas. This spirit manifested itself in the form of a beautiful seashell rising from the water in the direction of the setting sun.

The earliest traditions of the Ojibways were of their troubles with the Iroquois. Together with other tribes of the Algonquian stock to which they belong, the Chippewas originally seem to have crossed the St. Lawrence and dispersed themselves along the shores of Lake Ontario, and Lake Huron and its islands. Then the Iroquois, who had obtained guns and other steel-age implements from the Dutch colonists on the Atlantic seaboard and were boldly over-running all the western lake country, endeavored to possess themselves of the hunting grounds of the Chippewas. A bitter and lasting feud resulted.

The tribes of the Algonquian linguistic stock, which includes the majority of Canadian Indians from the Atlantic seaboard to the Rocky Mountains, were no less brave than the Iroquois. However, they were patrilineal and not so well developed in political sense and cohesiveness. Certainly they were less aggressive in warfare, at least not unitedly so. The Iroquois League completely destroyed a number of other Indian nations who lived in large, palisaded towns. The Algonquians, who were more scattered, generally withstood them longer. They had a strategy all their own. When attacked they disappeared into the deeper forest, much as Marion's men in the South sought the jungles and hiddenmost parts of swamps when they were fleeing for their lives.

Less than twenty miles above Sault Ste. Marie, Iroquois Point projects into the narrow foot of Lake Superior known as Whitefish Bay. The Indian name of this cape means The Place of Iroquois Bones. Here, according to tradition, a wild and terrific engagement occurred, in which the Ojibway tribe inflicted a disastrous defeat upon the Iroquois.

The Six Nation Indians or Iroquois, after a victorious onslaught on the Ojibways, encamped, a thousand strong, upon this Point, where, thinking themselves secure, they made a war-feast to torture and devour their prisoners. Their orgies rose to heights of wild delirium such as only Indians can create. The Chippewas, beholding the humiliation and sufferings of their brothers from the opposite shore, were roused to sudden fury. Collecting their warriors, only three hundred in all, they crossed the channel, and at break of day fell upon the Iroquois, then sleeping after their horrible excesses. Tradition says that they massacred all the Iroquois—men, women, and children—except two, and stuck their heads on stakes which they embedded in the ground at intervals for some miles along the point. The bodies were left to bleach on the shore. Bones and skulls were found there long after the fight had faded into old men's memories. The Ojibways, so runs the tale, lost but one warrior, who was stabbed with a crude awl by an old woman who was sitting at the entrance of her wigwam stitching moccasins. The two Iroquois that were not killed were mutilated and sent to their home country to show their people and tell them what the Chippewas would do if they were attacked again.

The battle at Iroquois Point was not a minor local skirmish. It was a turning point in Ojibway history—the greatest single achievement of the tribe. In point of emphasis, it was to them what Waterloo was to the nations who on that battle-field stopped the encroachments of Napoleon; and what Vienna was to a Europe struggling against a flood of invaders from the East. The Battle of the Bloody Marshes on St. Simons Island, Georgia, has profound significance to the English because it marked the end of the advance of Spanish dominion in North America. Just so the place of Iroquois Bones near Sault Ste. Marie looms large in the lore of the Ojibways, because there they stemmed the tide of Iroquois invasion, and set a boundary to that League's conquest in the west. The details and the importance of this battle, however, exist only in the traditions of the tribe. Historically, the encounter was unrecorded and without great significance. What the Chippewas did not know is that the western raids of the Iroquois were halted, not because of this overthrow, but because the Carignan-Saliere Regiment invaded their homeland and dictated terms of peace, in 1666.

In their retreat westward, the Ojibway tribe were joined by two other tribes, the Ottawas and the Potawatamis, who also were Algonquian. With these they formed a loose union known as The Three Fires, or the Lake Confederacy. Presumably the three crossed the St. Marys River, then separated at Mackinac, the Ottawas and Potawatamis going southward in Michigan while the Ojibways spread to the west along both shores of Lake Superior. On the north the Chippewas are so closely connected with the Crees and Maskegons that the three can be distinguished only by those intimately acquainted with their dialects and customs. The triumph of the Ojibways at Iroquois Point established them in their new country.

It is likely that the Ojibways had not occupied the Lake Superior region for many generations before the white man recorded them there, in the Jesuit Relation, 1640. It is possible that Nicollet found them in 1634. When first known, they were confined to a comparatively narrow, heavily-wooded area close along the shore, hemmed in by the hostile Sioux and Foxes in the more open country on the west and south.

The Jesuit fathers Jogues and Raymbault visited the Sault in 1641 at the request of some Chippewas who had seen the results of their work on Lake Huron. In 1668 Fathers Marquette and Dablon established a mission at the Falls of St. Mary, built the first house, erected the first church, cleared and planted the first land, and founded the first permanent white settlement in what is now the State of Michigan. Of the two thousand Indians they found there, practically all were Algonquian.

The Chippewa tribe of the Algonquian linguistic stock should not be confused with the Chipewyan tribe of Athabascan stock settled around Lake Athabasca in Canada. They are different peoples. The Chippewas, as they are most frequently called popularly, still are both Canadian and American Indians. They called themselves "Anishinabeg," which means "spontaneous men." The French spoke of them as Saulteurs, which means people of the falls. Ojibois is another name given them by the French. The English called them Ojibways, Ojibwas, or, in the corrupted form, Chippewas. The names Chippewa and Ojibway are from a word meaning "to roast till puckered" or "drawn up." It has been suggested that this refers to a peculiar seam in their moccasins, but other explanations also are given.

The University of Michigan Press has just published a thorough study, by Dr. Vernon Kinietz, of early books and of the archives of Ottawa, Montreal, Quebec, Chicago, Detroit, Ann Arbor, and Washington, D. C., relating to the Indians of the Great Lakes region during the initial period of their contact with the white man, from 1615 to 1760. Interrupted quotations from this valuable work are incorporated in the pages following.

The Chippewa resident in Michigan were not very numerous at the time of first contact. The small groups in the Lower Peninsula and on the St. Marys River in the Upper Peninsula appear to have been the advance guard of a general southern and western movement.

From the earliest mention of them in 1640 throughout the next one hundred and twenty years the customary designation was some form of *saut* (old spelling, *sault*, "fall" or "rapid"), in reference to the rapids in the St. Marys River, the only early settled abode of the tribe. Examples of these names are: nation or people of the saut, sault, or salt; sauteurs, saulteurs, saulteux, or sauteux. If other names were given, they were usually in addition to or qualified by one of the foregoing. Examples of these are: Baouichitigouian, Pauoitugoueieuhak, Pawating, Panoestigonce, Outchibouec, Pahou-itingwach Irini, Outhipoue, Paouitikoungraentaouak, and Achipoes. The French name of Sauteurs was given very naturally, as the Huron appellation was Eskiaeronnon—"people of the *Skia,e*" ("falls"). Most of the foregoing native names were applied to the tribe prior to 1670 and all before 1700. There is some significance in this, for in 1670 Dablon reported that the principal and native inhabitants at the mission of Sainte Marie du Sault were those who called themselves Pahouitingwach Irini, and whom the French called Saulteurs. These numbered only one hundred and fifty souls, but united themselves with three other tribes which numbered more than five hundred and fifty persons. . . . The inference is that the original small group at the Sault was lost in the southern movement of a large and probably cognate group of Chippewa and that at least part of the newcomers carried the name Ojibwa, which later became corrupted to Chippewa. The name Sauteur remained to the newcomers about the Sault and stayed with them when they went elsewhere.

The Sauteurs were settled along the St. Marys River during the seasons of abundant fishing and wintered farther west on the Upper Peninsula of Michigan, where part of the tribe were resident the year around. The St. Marys River is the earliest situation known for the Chippewa; they were there from 1640 to about 1650, when fear of the Iroquois drove them from the Sault. They returned sometime between 1662 and 1667. From the latter date to the close of the contact period their occupancy of the Sault region was continuous.

The increase in their number resulted in settlements at Chaquamegon, before 1695, Keweenaw, before 1710, and other places along the southern shore of Lake Superior. In 1703 some Chippewa and Missisauga formed a village near Detroit. There were villages of Chippewa along the Saginaw in 1723. Others were with Ottawa at Mackinac in 1729, and when the major part of the latter removed to L'Arbre Croche in 1740 the Chippewa expanded even more in that neighborhood. In 1737 the River aux Sables began to be mentioned as the location of some Chippewa. A Chippewa village was reported on La Grosse Ile (Bois Blanc Island) in 1747. Another village on the Beaver Islands was reported in 1751. In 1757 the Chippewa were settled at or in the vicinity of the following places south of Lake Superior: Sault Sainte Marie, Mackinac, Beaver Islands, Chaquamegon, Keweenaw, Carp River, River aux Sables, Saginaw, Detroit, and the following unidentified villages, Coasekimagen and Cabibonke.

The first record that gives any clue to the number of the Saulteurs stated that there were two hundred men from the Nation of the Sault, and the same number of Missisauga and Nipissing, joining a war party against the Iroquois in 1653. There is no evidence of the size of the village or villages from which they were drawn.

Apparently, the Saulteurs met with some disasters, for in 1670, according to Dablon, they numbered only one hundred and fifty souls. After they made a cession of rights in their native country to some other bands and united with them, their total was seven hundred.

This group which was originally given the name Saulteurs by the French appears to have been either the advance guard of the incoming Chippewa or a small cognate band which was absorbed by the Chippewa. The Chippewa before their arrival south of Lake Superior seem to have had no agriculture and were primarily hunters and nomads. Most of the bands were small, constantly moving, and seldom in contact with French establishments. None of the French statements of their numbers are satisfactory. A few of them estimated the Chippewa, including the Amikwa and Missisauga, as being as many as sixteen hundred persons.

About the beginning of the eighteenth century, after the Chippewas had been given firearms by the traders, they aggressively pushed their way westward. They were alternately at peace and at war with the Sioux and in almost constant conflict with the Foxes. First they drove out the Foxes from northern Wisconsin, and the Sioux from the headwaters of the Mississippi. Then they continued their victorious trail until they occupied the upper Red River country and established their westernmost band in the Turtle Mountains on the boundary between North Dakota and Manitoba.

While the main division of the tribe was thus extending its possessions in the West, others overran the peninsula between Lake Huron and Lake Erie which had long been claimed by the Iroquois through conquest. The Iroquois were forced to withdraw, and the whole region was occupied by the Chippewa bands, most of whom are now known as Missisauga, although they still call themselves Ojibway.

In the latter half of the eighteenth century and till the close of the War of 1812, they had, with the other tribes of the Northwest, kept up warfare with the border settlements. Throughout the Colonial wars they were uniformly friendly in their relations with the French. They joined Pontiac. Then in the War of Independence, and its closing engagements in 1812–1814, they were with the English and Tecumseh. Since the treaty of 1815, the Ojibways have been generally at peace with the whites; and since 1825, when the government made a treaty for adjustment of intertribal disputed boundaries in the Northwest, they have been reconciled with the Sioux, their hereditary enemies. Unofficially, however, on a private and isolated scale, the Sioux-Chippewa warfare continued at least to the close of the Civil War.

THEIR CHARACTERISTICS

The long and successful contest of the Chippewas with the Sioux and Foxes exhibited their bravery and determination. Schoolcraft describes their attitude of mind:

It seems to be the object of the Indian, before he sets out on a war expedition, to divest himself of every other passion but that of warlike glory. Every thing like the love of life and its pleasures, is dismissed from his thoughts. He prepares himself for death. He fasts,—he recites the warlike exploits of his forefathers in the war-dance,—he supplicates the Great Spirit, to make his heart strong, and to give him success in his enterprise. By this course of preparation, he purifies his mind from all thoughts of sensual enjoyments, and he appears to feel assured of victory, in proportion as he conquers his desires for worldly pleasure, and his lingering attachments to home. In this way he works up his courage to the highest point, he adopts the maxims of severe virtue, which his new character requires; and he puts on a severity of manners and a seriousness of deportment, which is not relaxed until he returns successful. Then feasting succeeds to fasting, and gayety for a season usurps the place of stoical reserve, and inflexible gravity. It is remarkable with what singleness of purpose, wariness, and expedition, an Indian thus disciplined will move; and it should no longer excite surprise, that with inferior numbers they have uniformly committed such havoc upon our frontiers, and so often prevailed in their desperate attacks.

William W. Warren, of St. Paul, Minnesota, highly-educated half-breed of the tribe, who is not disposed to accept any statement that tends to disparage the character of his people, affirmed that, according to tradition, the division of the tribe residing at LaPointe practised cannibalism. Father Belcourt states that, although the Chippewas of Canada treated the vanquished with most horrible barbarity and at these times ate human flesh, they looked upon cannibalism, except under such conditions, with horror. Alexander Henry records an instance of it at Mackinac Island. According to Schoolcraft, tales of cannibalism current among the northern voyageurs were due to the fact that the latter were generally more intent on raising the fears or wonder of their auditors than scrupulous about the truth. He said that the habit among northern Indians of feasting on human flesh was confined to times of great excitement, usually in war. It was the custom of the Pillager band to allow a warrior who scalped an enemy to wear on his head two eagle feathers, and the act of capturing a wounded prisoner on the battlefield earned the distinction of wearing five.

Schoolcraft says:

The Indians do not regard the approach of death with horror. Deists in religion, they look upon it as a change of state, which is mainly for the better. It is regarded as the close of a series of wanderings and hardships, which must sooner or later cease, which it is desirable should not take place until old age, but which, happen when it may, if it puts a period to their worldly enjoyments, also puts a period to their miseries. Most of them look to an existence in a future state, and expect to lead a happier life in another sphere. And they are not without the idea of rewards and punishments. But what this happiness is to be, where it is to be enjoyed, and what is to be the nature of the rewards and punishments, does not appear to be definitely fixed in the minds of any. If a man dies, it is said, he has gone to the happy land before us—he has outrun us in the race, but we shall soon follow.

They handle their dead without apparent emotion. After the body has been dressed in the best clothing possessed by the deceased, or the most costly and valuable that can be furnished by the relatives or friends, a funeral address is pronounced over it. This pious office is generally performed by some relative, or aged person of sense and discretion, who is versed in their ancient customs and traditions. The deceased is addressed as if still living, and capable of hearing and understanding what is said.

"You have reached," says the orator, "the place of sleep before us; but we shall soon lie down with you. You are going to another country, which we trust you will find pleasant; but in your journey thither, you will have to be very cautious how you travel, for your path is beset with dangers. There is one place in particular, where you must be extremely cautious. You have a dark stream to cross, which is wide and deep, and the water runs rapidly. There is but a single tree lying across it, and you will be compelled to cross over it, without the help of a staff.

"My Brother,—If your actions have been pleasing to the Great Spirit in this world, if you have been a good man in your tribe, you will get safely over; but if not, you will surely fall into the stream.

"We shall not allow you to leave us without an attendant, and a part of the provisions you have left in your lodge. At such a time (naming it) and such a place (naming it), I killed one of our enemies, and took his scalp. He is my slave. He will henceforward be yours. You will meet him on your way, and must bid him follow you. He will cut wood and make fire for you at night; he will hunt, and provide food for you on the way, and render you every assistance, which is necessary for the comfort of your perilous journey.

"We also lay by you, your gun and tomahawk, for your slave to use; and your small kettle, in which he will boil your corn. This wooden dish contains some provisions for you to eat at the commencement of your journey. We also kill your dog, who will follow you."

When a Chippewa died it was customary to place the body in a grave facing west, often in a sitting posture, or to scoop a shallow cavity in the earth and deposit the body therein on its back or side, covering it with earth so as to form a small mound, over which boards, poles, or birch bark were placed. According to McKenney, the Chippewas of Fond du Lac on Lake Superior practised scaffold burial, the corpse being inclosed in a box. They imagined that the shade, after the death of the body, followed a wide-beaten path leading toward the west, finally arriving in a country abounding in everything the Indian desires. It is a general belief among the northern Chippewas that the spirit often returns to visit the grave, so long as the body is not reduced to dust. Mourning for a lost relative continued for a year, unless shortened by the meda or by certain exploits in war.

Their creation myth is that common among the northern Algonquians. Like most other tribes they believe that a mysterious power dwells in all objects, animate and inanimate. Such objects are manitos, which are ever wakeful and quick to hear everything in the summer, but in winter, after snow falls, are in a torpid state. The Chippewas regard dreams as revelations, and some object which appears therein is often chosen as a tutelary deity.

"The master of the spirits of the lakes and the god of waters, whom Pachot called Bichi Bichy, was the Michapoux of Raudot and other writers," says Dr. Kinietz. "It was he who crushed in the beaver dam at Sault Ste. Marie, leaving it a rapids. Raudot said that from what the Indians said of this god he must have been as tall as Gargantua, and the tales they told of him were very much the same as those told about that fabulous giant."

The Medewiwin, or grand medicine society, was formerly a powerful organization of the Chippewas, which controlled the movements of the tribe and was a formidable obstacle to the introduction of Christianity. Living mostly in small groups they were not readily approached by the missionaries. Although long friendly with the whites they appear to have been highly resistant to Christian teachings and slow to adopt European articles and ways. The group that settled near Detroit furnished an instance of this aloofness: a number of Chippewas, part of whom were designated as Missisauga, were attracted to Cadillac's settlement, but, unlike the other tribes that made their villages in the shadow of the fort, they established theirs on one of the islands at the northern end of Lake St. Clair.

The Chippewas were hospitable, proud, redoubtable to their enemies, improvident, and uneconomical, according to La Potherie. Raudot termed them great thieves. Sabrevois said they were very industrious. There is abundant evidence that polygamy was common.

Like most Algonquian tribes, they were not much given to farming. They are a timber people. Some of them living south of Lake Superior in 1670–1699 cultivated maize, although they subsisted chiefly on fish, game, wild rice, other wild seed, wild fruits, and sugar. The possession of wild-rice fields was one of the chief causes of their wars with the Dakota, Fox and other nations. The sugar extracted from the maple they stored in birch-bark boxes or makaks. They made no pottery, but they were skillful mat-weavers and made the best snowshoes and the most perfect light birch-bark canoes. They were expert in the use of birch-bark canoes, and in their early history depended largely on fish for food. Lacking salt to cure the whitefish they hung them up on sticks with the heads down, thus keeping them all winter.

Their wigwams were made with strips of birch bark or grass mats. The framework consisted of poles, planted in the ground in a circle, with the tops bent together and tied. In covering them, a smoke-hole was left at the top. The strips of birch bark were twenty feet or more long and about three feet wide, made of small pieces sewn together. They rolled up into small bundles and were easily packed in a canoe or carried.

The beautiful birch bark also gave them paper on which to scratch their simple pictograph records.

The Chippewas were superior in every ethnic way, if undeveloped and unlettered people can be called that. Really they were not uneducated and illiterate, in a sense, because their language is meaningful and eloquent. A remarkable Otchiptwe dictionary that is now rare but is still to be had was compiled by Father Baraga. The good priest also wrote a grammar to complement his lexicon.

"The language of the Chippewas," wrote Mrs. Jameson,

however figurative and significant, is not copious. In their speeches and songs they are emphatic and impressive by the continual repetition of the same phrase or idea; and the simple eloquence of this seems to affect them like the perpetual recurrence of a few simple notes in music, by which I have been myself wound up to painful excitement or melted to tears.

The story-tellers were estimated according to their eloquence and powers of invention, and were always welcome, sure of the best place in the lodge, and the choicest mess of food wherever they went. Some individuals, not story-tellers by profession, possessed and exercised these gifts of memory and invention. Mrs. Henry Rowe Schoolcraft mentioned an Indian living at Sault Ste. Marie, who in this manner amused and instructed his family almost every night before they went to rest. Her own mother also was celebrated for her stock of traditional lore, and her poetical and inventive faculties, which she inherited from her father, Waub-ojeeg, who was the greatest poet and story-teller as well as the greatest warrior of his tribe. Henry Rowe Schoolcraft is an important source of information for their lore and everything concerning them.

THEIR ORGANIZATION

Authors differ as to the names and number of the Chippewa gentes, which range all the way from eleven to twenty-three. Lewis Henry Morgan names the following twenty-three gentes: Myeengun (Wolf), Makwa (Bear), Ahmik (Beaver), Mesheka (Mud Turtle), Mikonoh (Snapping Turtle), Meskwadare (Little Turtle), Ahdik (Reindeer), Chueskweskewa (Snipe), Ojeejek (Crane), Kakake (Pigeon Hawk) [= Kagagi, Raven], Omegeeze (Bald Eagle), Mong (Loon), Ahahweh (Duck), [= Waʰwaʰ, Swan], Zheshebe (Duck), Kenabig (Snake), Wazhugh (Muskrat), Wabezhaze (Marten), Mooshkaoooze (Heron), Ahwahsissa (Bullhead), Namabin (Carp), [Catfish], Name (Sturgeon), Kenozhe (Pike) [= Kinega, Pickerel]. Tanner gives also the Pepegewizzains (Sparrow-hawk), Mussundummo (Water Snake), and the forked tree as totems among the Ottawas and Chippewas. Warren gives twenty-one gentes, of which the following are not included among those named by Morgan: Manumaig (Catfish), Nebaunaubay (Merman), Besheu (Lynx), Mous (Moose), Nekah (Goose), Udekumaig (Whitefish), Gyaushk (Gull). Some of them, Warren says, have but few members and are not known to the tribe at large.

As the Chippewas were scattered over a region extending one thousand miles from east to west, they had a large number of villages, bands, and local divisions. Some of the bands bore the name of the village, lake, or river near which they resided, but these were grouped under larger divisions or subtribes which occupied certain fixed limits and were distinguished by marked differences. According to Warren there were ten of these principal divisions: Kechegummewininewug, on the southern shore of Lake Superior; Betonukeengainubejig, in

A TYPE OF HIAWATHA. SHINGABAWOSSIN, THE IMAGE STONE. LEADING CHIEF
ON THE AMERICAN SIDE AT THE SAULT IN SCHOOLCRAFT'S TIME.

northern Wisconsin; Munominikasheenhug, on the headwaters of St. Croix River in Wisconsin and Minnesota; Wahsuahgune-wininiewug, at the head of the Wisconsin River in northern Wisconsin; Ottawa Lake Men, on Lac Courte Oreilles, Wisconsin; Kechesebewininewug, on the upper Mississippi in Minnesota; Mukmeduawininewug, or Pillagers, on Leech Lake, Minnesota; Sugwaundugahwininewug, north of Lake Superior; Kojejewininewug, on Rainy Lake and River about the northern boundary of Minnesota; and Omushkasug, on the northwestern side of Lake Superior at the Canadian border.

Besides these general divisions the following collective or local names are recognized as belonging to various settlements, bands, or divisions of the tribe: Angwassag, Big Rock, Little Forks, Menitegow, Blackbird, Menoquet's Village, Ketche-waundaugenink, Kawkawling, Kishkawbawee, Saginaw, Thunder Bay, Nagonabe, Ommunise, Shabwasing, Beaver Islands, Nabobish, Cheboygan, Otusson, Reaum's Village, and Wapisiwisibiwininiwak, in lower Michigan; Red Cedar Lake, Sukaauguning, Knife Lake, Kechepukwaiwah, Long Lake, Chetac Lake, Turtle Portage, Rice Lake, Yellow Lake, Trout Lake, Pawating, Ontonagon, Wauswagiming, Lac Courte Oreilles, Shaugwaumikong, Burnt Woods, Gatagetegauning, Bay du Noc, Wequadong, Mekadewagamitigweyawininiwak, Michilimackinac, St. Francis Xavier, and Wiaquahheche-gumeeng, in Wisconsin and upper Michigan; Grand Portage, Pokegama, Fond du Lac, Red Cliff, Crow Wing River, Gull Lake, Onepowesepewenenewak, Miskwagamiwisagaigan, Wabasemowenenewak (?), Wanamakewajenenik, Mikinak-wadshiwininiwak, Misisagaikaniwininiwak, Gasakaskuatchim-mekak, Oschekkamegawenenewak, Winnebegoshishiwinini-wak, Gamiskwakokawininiwak, Gawababiganikak, Anibimi-nanisibiwininiwak, Kahmetahwungaguma, and Rabbit Lake, in Minnesota and the Dakotas; Oueschekgagamioulimy, Walpole Island, Obidgewong, Michipicoten, Doki's Band, Bago-ache, Epinette (1744), Ouasouarini, Mishtawayawininiwak, Nopeming, and Nameuilni, in Ontario; Portage de Prairie,

Mattawan, and Pic River in Manitoba; and Nibowisibiwinini-wak in Saskatchewan.

The Chippewas Today

After 1855 the Ojibway people ceased to exist as a treaty-making entity. With the exception of a small band of Swan Creek and Black River Chippewas, who sold their lands in southern Michigan in 1836 and are now with the Munsee in Franklin County, Kansas, the American members of the tribe are all residing on reservations or other land within their original territory in Michigan, Wisconsin, Minnesota, and North Dakota.

It is difficult even to approximate their number. An estimate by the British after taking possession of Canada set this at twenty-five thousand. In the twentieth century they are believed to have increased to more than thirty thousand. A few thousand in Michigan are so intermingled with Ottawas that an accurate count is not possible. They are about equally divided between Canada and the United States.

In the Dominion, under the Robinson Treaty of 1850, they hold twelve reserves in the Port Arthur district, nine in the vicinity of Sault Ste. Marie, and thirteen around Georgian Bay and the northern part of Lake Huron. The Garden River Reservation near Sault Ste. Marie, Ontario, and West Bay on Manitoulin Island in that Province, are characteristic Canadian Ojibway settlements.

In the United States, the Consolidated Chippewa Agency at Cass Lake, Minnesota, in April, 1940, had 13,610 enrolled. This is exclusive of many not enrolled with any reservation and a number transient among the Indians of Canada. The reservations under the Cass Lake jurisdiction are at White Earth, Mille Lacs, Greater Leech Lake, Fond du Lac, Nett Lake, and Grand Portage. A typical group of unenrolled Ojibways are the three hundred on Sugar Island near the American Sault.

The Chippewas have made good progress as such is measured. There has been much admixture of French and English with the tribe in various regions, so that a full-blooded Ojibway is no longer common. Like all other elements of the melting pot, they are gradually being fused into the composite American.

Under modern conditions, and with the help of various emergency agencies of the government, the range of individual initiative is asserting itself. Their homes range from old log cabins and flimsy frame structures to modern dwellings. Their craftsmanship asserts itself in the manufacture of seaworthy boats for customers, instead of canoes for fishing; in log cabins, cedar furniture, hooked rugs, beadwork and handmade snowshoes for summer visitors.

Preservation of the ancient arts and crafts of the Michigan Indians, something that has been slipping away from the younger generation, is a movement that has been undertaken with satisfactory results under the Supervision of the Bureau of Indian Affairs, State Conservation Department, Works Progress Administration and National Youth Administration. The work of the Indians in the Great Lakes region has never been as widely publicized and commercialized as some Indian handicrafts in other sections of the country, but these people have long been producing many useful and attractive articles.

Results of the wages paid out of federal emergency funds are seen in the fact that the blueberry plains, and the patches on the Algoma rocks, are being left almost uninvaded except by thrifty whites. Hitherto, during berry season they were temporary Indian tenting grounds.

At the Consolidated Chippewa Agency in Minnesota they are building modern homes; young men and women are becoming skilled in trade and professional fields; and agricultural, social and cultural activities are being carried on at a remarkable pace. They have a monthly mimeographed bulletin with clever illustrations and cartoons, articles on scarlet fever, fire fighting, opportunities in forestry, the Indian division of the Civilian Conservation Corps, 4-H clubs, nursery schools, and drunken driving, with such contemporary language as cheerio, and gone with the wind.

Wild rice has been from earliest times a staple of the diet of the tribe. Also it was esteemed by the traders, who purchased it by the fawn-skin or the half-fawn-skin. Schoolcraft records that a failure of this crop, as in 1830, caused much suffering among both traders and Indians. In 1900 ten thousand Chippewas in the United States were using it. Originally it was a chief cause of feuds and warfare. Now the government provides for its harvesting with licenses and camp sites; and cooperative equipment for its threshing, cleaning, and marketing.

With the aid of agricultural extension work, including credit, the Chippewas are enlarging their livestock and agricultural enterprises, improving their methods, and developing their own resources to a larger degree. Productive loans are now in force not only for farming, but for cooperative stores, fishing enterprises, operation of summer resorts, and other commercial undertakings.

In the last seven years much has been done. The Allotment Act of 1887 had resulted in trimming the 139,000,000 total acres of Indian holdings in the United States that year to 47,000,000 acres in 1933. On the reservations everything was being done to destroy normal Indian life. The Indian Reorganization Act of 1934 altered this trend. It forbade alienation of Indian lands, granted the tribes the right to organize local governments with written constitutions, and gave those governments definite powers which the Indian Bureau and Department of the Interior were bound to respect. Now, in addition to these reservation councils giving them self-government in various functions, there are nationwide Indian Service Conferences, in which their representatives meet with those of the Washington and Reservation offices, to discuss social rehabilitation, law and order, juvenile delinquency, home and community life, and educational advancement. Recently a medal was conferred on an Indian as the leader of Indian progress in the United States. A definite advance has been achieved toward making the Indian more conscious of his responsibilities as a member of his community, and the aim is to increase the incentive and training to earn a living, and offer opportunities to earn it.

Eighty-five years ago Indian Commissioner Manypenny pleaded for authority from Congress to compile the laws referring directly or indirectly to Indian affairs. Schoolcraft was one of those who supported him, for the purpose of securing a general repeal of confusing, conflicting, outworn laws. This significant compilation of forty-six volumes has now been completed.

While so much is being done, under something of the old paternalistic system on the reservations, and in government projects, those who are not enrolled are advancing in their own way.

On Sugar Island, Chippewa County, Michigan, there is Ne-on-gib-gay-gah-wah-nib, who is honest, dependable, and loyal, a gentleman instinctively and an ingenious craftsman, who prefers to be called Charles Andrew except by his best friends. He has been a chauffeur in Chicago, is in charge at Duck Island, has wintered in South Georgia, and once tried in vain to converse in Indian with a Seminole on the Tamiami Trail in Florida. His brother, Waba-binaysi (Graybird) or Joe Andrew, who is as creditable in every way, is caretaker of the University of Michigan Preserve.

Mus-ko-mini-doantz or Redbug, who can be found either at Payment, Michigan, or the Garden River Reservation in Canada, and may easily be the greatest bear hunter and sturgeon fisherman in the world as well as a famous guide, goes popularly by the name of Joe Corbiere. We call him Wah-zhushk, Muskrat, for short. When he shows visitors the Indian mission church, he sings hymns for them, in Chippewa and in Latin, accompanying himself on the organ, which he has learned to play by ear. Or he will imitate a bird call, with a pleasantly musical intonation, and tell you that the bird is saying

> Bwan tchiman!
> Tchigibig!
> Tchigibig!

which means

> Sioux canoe!
> Near the shore!
> Near the shore!

Thus, after more than a hundred years, the echoes of the old feud still linger.

The first full-blooded Indian to serve as commander of an American Legion Post is A. A. Bonno of Sault Ste. Marie, Michigan. M. L. Burns, Coordinator of Indian Affairs in the Great Lakes Area, is an Ojibway Indian. Francis Mee, a young Chippewa from Minnesota, now sails the seas as Commander of the destroyer U. S. S. *Ellet*. He is a graduate of the United States Naval Academy at Annapolis. A full-blooded Ojibway woman of Sault Ste. Marie, Michigan, who, not so long ago, wore feathers in her hair and always sat on the floor instead of on a chair, had a great-granddaughter who graduated at Vassar and became head of a graduate reading room in the great library of the University of Michigan,—the late brilliant and able Miss Henriette Scranton.

Descendants of the original tribesmen are today ornamenting and contributing to every phase of responsible contemporary society. The Chippewas may be increasing in number so far as census figures show. Also they are merging with the general population of North America.

SHORT BIBLIOGRAPHY OF THE CHIPPEWAS

Based on circular issued by the United States Office of Indian Affairs

Baraga, Frederic. A dictionary of the Otchipwe language, explained in English. Cincinnati, O., 1853. 662 p.

Beltrami, J. C. A pilgrimage in Europe and America, leading to the discovery of the sources of the Mississippi and Bloody river. 2 v. London, England, Hunt & Clarke, 1828.

Blair, Emma H., ed. The Indian tribes of the upper Mississippi valley and region of the Great Lakes, as described by Nicolas Perrot, French commandant in the northwest; Bacqueville de la Potherie, French royal commander to Canada; Morrell Marston, American army officer; and Thos. Forsyth, United States Indian agent at Fort Armstrong. Cleveland, O., Arthur H. Clark Co. 2 v.

Bond, J. Wesley. Minnesota and its resources. Chicago, Keene & Lee; Philadelphia, Chas. DeSilver; 1856.

Carver, Jonathan. Travels through the interior parts of North America in the years 1766, 1767, and 1768. London, 1781. New York, Harper & Bros., 1838.

Chittenden, Hiram M., and Richardson, Alfred T. Life, letters and travels of Father Pierre-Jean de Smet, S.J., 1801–1873 (edited). New York, N. Y., Francis P. Harper, 1905. 4 v. 1624 p. ill.

Copway, George. The life, history, and travels of Kah-ge-ga-gah-bowh (George Copway), written by himself. Philadelphia, J. Harmstead, 1847.

Copway, George. Indian life and Indian history. Boston, Albert Colby & Co., 1860.

Coues, Elliott, ed. Forty years a fur trader on the upper Missouri: the personal narrative of Charles Larpenteur, 1833–1872. New York, N. Y., Francis P. Harper, 1898. 2 v., ill., maps.

Densmore, Frances. Chippewa music. Washington, D. C., Bureau of American Ethnology, Bulletins 45 and 53.

Donaldson, Thomas. The George Catlin Indian gallery in the United States National Museum. (From Smithsonian report for 1885). Washington, 1887.

Folwell, William W. A history of Minnesota. St. Paul, Minnesota Historical Society, 4 v., 1921, 1922, 1924, 1926.

Heard, Isaac V. D. History of the Sioux war and massacres of 1862 and 1863. New York, N. Y., Harper & Bros., 1865.

Hoffman, W. J. The mide'wiwin or "grand medicine society" of the Ojibwa. (7th annual report, bureau of American ethnology). Washington, D. C., 1891.

Hulbert, Thomas. Hymns in the Chippewa or Ottawa language, to which is appended a short summary of Christian doctrine. 1846.

James, Edwin, ed. A narrative of the captivity and adventures of John Tanner (United States interpreter at the Sault de Ste. Marie), during thirty years' residence among the Indians in the interior of North America. New York, N. Y., 1830.

Jenks, Albert E. The wild rice gatherers of the upper lakes; a study in American primitive economics. (19th annual report, bureau of American ethnology). Washington, D. C., 1900.

Jones, P. History of the Ojebway Indians, 1861.

Jones, William. Ojibwa texts. American ethnological society. Publications, v. 7, pt. 2.

Kappler, Charles J. Indian affairs, laws and treaties. Washington, D. C., Government Printing Office. 4 v.

Kenton, Edna, ed. The Jesuit relations and allied documents; travels and explorations of the Jesuit missionaries in North America (1610–1791). New York, N. Y., Albert and Charles Boni, 1925.

Kinietz, W. Vernon. The Indians of the western Great Lakes 1615–1760. Ann Arbor, Michigan, University of Michigan Press, 1940.

Laidlaw, G. E. Certain Ojibwa myths. Toronto, Canada, Archaeological report, 1914, 1915, 1916.

Longfellow, Alice M. A visit to Hiawatha's people. (In: Longfellow, Henry W., The song of Hiawatha, Boston, 1883, p. v–xii and 193).

Morse, Jedidiah. A report to the Secretary of War of the United States, on Indian affairs, comprising a narrative of a tour performed in the year 1820. New Haven, Conn., S. Converse, 1822.

Murray, Charles A. Travels in North America during the years 1834–36. London, England, 1839.

Neill, Edward D. History of the Ojibways, and their connection with the fur traders. (Minnesota historical society. Collections, v. 5).

Parkman, Francis, Jr. History of the conspiracy of Pontiac. Boston, Mass., Little, Brown & Co., 1851.

Petitot. Dictionary. Paris, 1876. 455 p.

Pike, Zebulon M. Exploratory travels through the western territories of North America, performed in the years 1805, 1806, 1807. London, England, 1811.

Royce, Charles C. Indian land cessions in the United States. (18th annual report, bureau of American ethnology, pt. 2). Washington, D. C., 1899.

Schoolcraft, Henry R. Narrative journal of travels . . . in the year 1820; Personal memoirs; Narrative of an expedition . . . to Itasca Lake; Summary narrative of an exploratory expedition; History, condition and prospects of the Indian tribes of the United States; and other works. See Schoolcraft Bibliography later in this book.

Smith, William R., comp. The history of Wisconsin. Madison, Wis., 1854. 3 v.

Thwaites, Reuben Gold, ed. Early western travels, 1748–1846. Cleveland, Arthur H. Clark Co., 1904.

Verwyst, C. Missionary labors of Father Marquette, Menard and Allouez in the Lake Superior region. Chicago, 1886.

Verwyst, C. Chippewa exercises, being a practical introduction into the study of the Chippewa language. Harbor Springs, Mich., Holy Childhood School Print, 1901.

Warren, W. W.   History of the Ojibways.   Minnesota historical society.   Collections, v. 5, 1885.

Will, George F., and Hyde, George E.   Corn among the Indians
of the upper Missouri.   St. Louis, Mo., Wm. Harvey Miner Co.,
1917.   (Little Histories of the North American Indians, no. 5).

Yarrow, H. C.   A further contribution to the study of the mor-
tuary customs of the North American Indians.   (1st annual report,
bureau of American ethnology).   Washington, D. C., 1881.

Annual reports, War Department (to 1849).
Annual reports, Bureau of Indian Affairs.
Annual reports and bulletins, Bureau of American Ethnology.
Publications of the Michigan, Wisconsin, Minnesota, and
Kansas Historical Societies.

IV. THE GENEALOGY OF HIAWATHA

"In the realm of poetry," said Justice Joseph Hall Steere, "Hiawatha becomes one of Michigan's honored citizens."

More than that, he is the best known personality that the State has yet produced; for, in many languages, the story of the Indian leader is familiar around the world.

Hiawatha, the epic personification of Ojibway hope and imagination, was a native of Michigan, born and cradled in a log house, part of which may still be seen, on the shore of the noblest of all earth's rivers, the St. Marys, at Sault Ste. Marie. Many years later Longfellow adopted him and moulded his maturity. Schoolcraft discovered his first breathing and fostered his infancy and childhood. His origin, as a literary figure, leads back through the marriage of Schoolcraft into the family of Waub-ojeeg.

In the following personal story of Jane Johnston Schoolcraft's mother, intimate traditions of the Ojibway tribe and the origin of Hiawatha are intertwined. It is an adaptation of Mrs. Jameson's account, which is sympathetic and has authority. She repeated what she heard in 1837 by the fireplace where the Hiawatha epic drew its initial breath of life.

When the Chippewas first penetrated to the Lake Superior region, they came in contact with the Outagamis or Foxes. These Indians being descended from the same stock, received the Chippewas as brothers, and at first ceded to them a part of their boundless hunting-grounds. The Outagamis, moreover, were friends and allies of the Sioux, so these three nations continued for some time friends, and intermarriages and family alliances took place.

Soon, however, the increasing power of the Chippewas excited the jealousy and apprehension of the other two tribes. The Outagamis committed inroads on the Chippewa hunting-grounds, and when the Chippewas sent an embassy to complain of the injury and desired the Outagamis to restrain their

OZHAW-GUSCODAY-WAYQUAY, THE POCAHONTAS OF THE OJIBWAYS, DAUGHTER
OF WAUB-OJEEG, WIFE OF JOHN JOHNSTON, MOTHER OF JANE JOHNSTON
SCHOOLCRAFT.

young men within the stipulated bounds, the latter returned an insulting answer. The result was that the war-hatchet was raised, and the Sioux and the Outagamis united against the Chippewas. This was soon after 1700. From that time for over a hundred years there was no peace between the Chippewas and Sioux.

Before the declaration of war, a young Chippewa girl had been married to a Sioux chief of great distinction, and had borne him two sons. When hostilities commenced the Sioux chief retired to his own tribe, and his wife remained with her relations, according to Indian custom. The two children, belonging to both tribes, were hardly safe with either; but as the father was best able to protect them, it was at last decided that they should accompany him. The Sioux chief and his boys departed to join his warriors. His Chippewa wife and her relations accompanied them till they were in safety; then the young wife returned home weeping and inconsolable for the loss of her husband and children.

Some years afterwards she consented to become the wife of the great chief at Chequamegon. Her son by this second marriage was Mamongazide or Mongazida, the Loon's Foot, a chief of great celebrity, who led a strong party of his nation in the Canadian wars between the French and English, fighting on the side of the French. He was present at the battle of Quebec, when Wolfe was killed, and according to the Indian tradition, the Marquis Montcalm died in Mongazida's arms.

After the war was over, Mongazida "shook hands" with the English. He was at the grand assemblage of chiefs, convened by Sir William Johnson at Niagara, and from him received a rich gorget and broad belt of wampum, as pledges of peace and alliance with the English. These relics were preserved in the family with great veneration. They were inherited first by his second son, Waub-ojeeg, and afterwards by a younger one, but were lost and never recovered when the latter and all his family were overtaken by famine and starved to death, on a winter hunt near the River Brule.

Waub-ojeeg, the White Fisher, who was the grandfather

of Mrs. Henry Rowe Schoolcraft, was not only the grandson
of the great chief at Chequamegon and son of the famous
Mongazida, but an outstanding leader in his own right. Once
when he was eight years old, when his father Mongazida went
out on his fall hunts, on the grounds near the Sioux territory,
taking all his relatives with him, upwards of twenty in number, they were attacked by the Sioux at early dawn, in the
usual manner. The first volley had gone through the lodges.
Before the second could be fired, Mongazida rushed out, and,
proclaiming his own name with a loud voice, demanded if
Wabash, his mother's son by her first marriage to the Sioux
chief, was among the assailants. There was a pause, and then
a tall figure in his war-dress, with a profusion of feathers in his
head, stepped forward and gave his hand to his half-brother.
They all repaired to the lodge in peace together. But at the
moment the Sioux chief stooped to enter, the boy Waub-ojeeg,
who had planted himself at the entrance to defend it, struck
him a blow on the forehead with his small war-club. Wabash,
enchanted, took him up in his arms and prophesied that he
would become a great war-chief, and an implacable enemy of
the Sioux. Subsequently the prophecy was accomplished, and
Waub-ojeeg commanded his nation in all the war-parties
against the Sioux and Outagamis. He was generally victorious, and so entirely defeated the Outagamis that they never
afterwards ventured to oppose him, but retired down the Wisconsin River, where they settled.

Waub-ojeeg was something more and better than merely
a successful warrior. He was remarkable also for his eloquence,
and composed a number of war songs, which were sung through
the Chippewa villages. Some of these his daughter, Mrs.
Schoolcraft's mother, could repeat. He was no less skillful in
hunting than in war. His hunting-grounds extended to the
river Brule, at Fond du Lac; and he killed anyone who dared
to intrude on his district. The skins he took annually were
worth three hundred fifty dollars, a sum amply sufficient to
make him rich in clothing, arms, powder, vermilion, and
trinkets.

Like Tecumseh, Waub-ojeeg would not marry early lest it should turn his attention from war, but at the age of thirty he married a widow, by whom he had two sons. Afterward, becoming tired of this elderly helpmate, he took a young wife, a beautiful girl of fourteen, by whom he had six children. Of these, the mother of Mrs. Schoolcraft was the eldest. She described her father as affectionate and domestic, and said there was always plenty of bear's meat and deer's flesh in the lodge.

He had a splendid wigwam, sixty feet in length, which he was fond of ornamenting. In the center there was a strong post, which rose several feet above the roof, and on the top there was the carved figure of an owl which veered with the wind. This owl was the insignia of his power and of his presence. When absent on his long winter hunts the lodge was shut up and the owl taken down.

A chief seat of the Ojibways was upon a promontory at the farthest end of Lake Superior, near what is now Ashland, Wisconsin. The French called this La Pointe du St. Esprit or La-Pointe. The Indians knew it as Che-goi-me-gon, Chagou amigon, Shaga waumikong. It appeared by one name or the other on most early maps. Schoolcraft translates Shaugwame-gin as low lands. By some the word is thought to mean needle, as the sandy point projected in this shape. Chequamegon was noted for its fish. Its totem was the addik or reindeer. The Indians lived on the shore of the Lake only during the summer. As soon as they harvested their crops of corn and squashes they returned to their hunting grounds.

On account of the number of Indians found at Chequamegon, the traders made it a center. A mission was located there in 1665 but was abandoned in 1671 on account of attacks from the Sioux. Father Marquette in 1670 wrote about the community's barbarous customs and crimes. It was there he first heard, from a slave bought from the Illinois Indians, about the Mississippi River and formed the idea of discovering it. The French, in 1692, reestablished a trading post at this place, which became an important Chippewa settlement.

Here at Chequamegon was the grand national council fire. Governor Lewis Cass, in 1820, said that the care of the sacred fire was committed to male and female guardians. Its extinction foretold, if it did not occasion, some dread national calamity. This may have been taught to frighten the Indians into guarding precious flame. If it went out, they had no easy way to rekindle it.

Chequamegon also was the residence of the presiding chief of the tribe. The Ojibways had many brave warriors. They were among the first in historic times to defeat the Iroquois.

Noted among these war leaders was Waub-ojeeg. Tall and commanding in person, with full, black, piercing eyes, eloquent in his native language, he was a recognized war-chief at twenty-two and equally popular as a civil ruler. He died in 1793 of tuberculosis before the age of fifty and was buried at LaPointe. A sketch of the life of Waub-ojeeg is given in *Oneóta;* also the following famous war song, as preserved by his son-in-law, John Johnston. It was uttered after his victory at the falls of the St. Croix over the Sioux and Outagamis, which raised the name of the White Fisher to the zenith of his renown among his people.

> On that day when our heroes lay low—lay low,
> > On that day when our heroes lay low,
> I fought by their side, and thought ere I died,
> > Just vengeance to take on the foe,
> > Just vengeance to take on the foe.
>
> On that day, when our chieftains lay dead—lay dead,
> > On that day when our chieftains lay dead,
> I fought hand to hand, at the head of my band,
> > And here, on my breast, have I bled,
> > And here, on my breast, have I bled.
>
> Our chiefs shall return no more—no more,
> > Our chiefs shall return no more,
> Nor their brothers of war, who can show scar for scar,
> > Like women their fates shall deplore—deplore,
> > Like women their fate shall deplore.
>
> Five winters in hunting we'll spend—we'll spend,
> > Five winters in hunting we'll spend,

Till our youth, grown to men, we'll to war lead again,
And our days, like our fathers, we'll end,
And our days, like our fathers, we'll end.

The skill of Waub-ojeeg as a hunter and trapper, brought him into friendly communication with a fur-trader named John Johnston, in the year 1791. This young man, of good Irish family, came out to Canada with such strong letters of recommendation to Lord Dorchester, that he was invited to reside in the government house till a vacancy occurred in his favor in one of the official departments. Meantime, being of an active and adventurous turn, he joined a party of traders going up the lakes, merely as an excursion. The result was that he became so enamoured of the fur-traders' wild life as to adopt it in earnest. On one of his expeditions, when encamped at Chequamegon and trafficking with Waub-ojeeg, he saw the eldest daughter of the chief, and ended by asking his Indian friend to give him the beautiful Ozhaw-guscoday-wayquay.

"White man!" said the chief with dignity, "Your customs are not our customs! You white men desire our women. You marry them, and when they cease to please your eye, you say they are not your wives, and you forsake them. Return, young friend, with your load of skins, to Monreal; and if, there, the women of the palefaces do not put my child out of your mind, return hither in the spring and we will talk further. She is young, and can wait."

The young Irishman, ardently in love, and impatient and impetuous after the manner of his countrymen, tried arguments, entreaties, presents, in vain. He was obliged to submit. He went down to Montreal, and the following spring returned and claimed his bride. The chief, after making him swear that he would take her as his wife, according to the law of the white man, till death, gave him his daughter, with a long speech of advice to both.

Mrs. Johnston described how, previous to her marriage, she had fasted according to the universal Indian custom, for a guardian spirit. To perform this ceremony she went away to the summit of an eminence, built herself a little lodge of cedar boughs, painted herself black, and began her fast in solitude. She dreamed continually of a white man, who approached her with a cup in his hand saying, "Poor thing! Why are you punishing yourself? Why do you fast? Here is food for you!" He was always accompanied by a dog, which looked up in her face as though he knew her.

Also she dreamed of being on a high hill, which was surrounded by water and from which she beheld many canoes, full of Indians, coming to her and paying her homage.

After this she felt as if she were carried up into the heavens. Looking down upon the earth, she perceived it was on fire, and said to herself, "All my relations will be burned!" But a voice answered and said, "No, they will not be destroyed, they will be saved;" and she knew it was a spirit because the voice was not human. She fasted for ten days, during which time her grandmother brought her at intervals some water.

When satisfied that she had obtained a guardian spirit in the white stranger who haunted her dreams, she returned to her father's lodge, carrying green cedar boughs, which she threw on the ground, stepping on them as she went. When she entered the lodge, she threw some more down upon her usual place, next her mother, and took her seat. During the ten succeeding days she was not permitted to eat any meat, nor anything but a little corn boiled with a bitter herb. Then for ten days more she ate meat smoked in a particular manner, after which she partook of the usual food of her family.

Notwithstanding that her future husband and greatness had been so clearly prefigured in this dream, the pretty Ozhawguscoday-wayquay, having always regarded a white man with awe and as a being of quite another species, perhaps the more so in consequence of her dream, seems to have felt nothing throughout the whole negotiation for her hand but reluctance, terror, and aversion. On being carried with the usual ceremonies to her husband's lodge, she fled into a dark corner, rolled herself up in her blanket, and would not be comforted nor even looked upon. It is to the honor of Johnston that he took no cruel advantage of their mutual position, but treated her with the utmost tenderness and respect, and sought by every gentle means to overcome her fear and gain her affection, during the ten days she remained in his lodge. After a lapse of over forty years this was related tenderly and gratefully by his bride.

On the tenth day, however, she ran away from him in a paroxysm of terror, and after fasting in the woods for four days reached her grandfather's wigwam.

Meantime, her father, Waub-ojeeg, who was far off in his hunting camp, dreamed that his daughter had not conducted herself, according to his advice, with proper wifelike docility. He returned in haste two days' journey to see after her; and, finding all things according to his dream, gave her a good beating with a stick and threatened to cut off her ears. Then he took her back to her husband, with a propitiatory present of furs and Indian corn, and many apologies and exculpations of his own honor.

Johnston, who settled at the Sault in 1793, took her there as a bride, where she lived most happily with him until his death in 1828.

Many of the Indians that dwelt at Sault Ste. Marie, like those at LaPointe, left their village twice a year. In June, after planting their corn, they dispersed along the shores of Lake Huron, where they gathered bark for canoes and wigwams, picked blueberries, and speared sturgeon. When the time came for grain to ripen they returned home and remained at the Sault through the autumn to enjoy the whitefish, before they left on their winter expeditions to the shores of the lake to kill beaver and moose until the spring and corn-planting time. But at the Sault there were also many of the tribe who stayed the year around. On both sides of the river they put up their permanent tepees. They almost depopulated the adjacent country of game but their source of fish was never depleted. When the whitefish migrated to spawn they took them in great quantities and preserved them by drying and smoking. These were hoarded. They used game until they were forced to eat their fish as a reserve. This was done almost up to the present time.

Sault Ste. Marie was not only their ancient capital, first fixed settlement, and largest center, but also the first permanent settlement of white men in the State of Michigan, and an important outfitting point for trade on both sides of Lake Superior, and the Upper Mississippi.

Thither came Ozhaw-guscoday-wayquay as the wife of the patriarch of the village. The home built for her in 1794 was considered pretentious, as befitting the establishment of her husband. It was constructed of small logs squared on the outside, the crevices plastered with mortar. The house fronted on the north, toward the river, on which side it had a comfortable porch. On the south side was a massive chimney for the ample fireplace of the main room, which was about twenty-five by twenty. The sleeping rooms were on the west, and in the loft which was lighted by dormer windows.

Growing to young womanhood as the daughter of the ruling chief at Chequamegon, spending most of her life at Sault Ste. Marie as wife of its leading citizen, Ozhaw-guscoday-wayquay was a commanding figure in the two great Ojibway centers. This full-blooded Indian woman united in her background the most highly-developed characteristics of her people and manifested it in her own remarkable capacities.

John Johnston was the first English settler in Sault Ste. Marie, Michigan. His education, and intercourse with polished society up to his thirtieth year, gave him many striking advantages over the inhabitants of that remote region—indeed fitted him to shine anywhere. His grandfather, a civil engineer, had planned and executed the waterworks at Belfast. One aunt, on his mother's side, was the wife of the Bishop of Dromore; one of his cousins was the attorney general for Ireland. He had made a number of trips to Great Britain and Ireland, Montreal, Toronto, and New York.

Schoolcraft likened the marriage of Ozhaw-guscoday-wayquay and John Johnston to that of Pocahontas and Rolfe. Although her descendants have not been to the North Country what those of Pocahontas are in Virginia, Ozhaw-guscoday-wayquay herself was indeed the Pocahontas of the Chippewas, and in her own personality shows more striking qualities than the Indian maiden of the Eastern coast. She saved the Cass expedition of 1820 from the attack of a superior force of Indians, not by betraying her own people but by reasoning with them. If Ozhaw-guscoday-wayquay's name had been as short and rememberable as Pocahontas her fame might have been wider. Not only did she play the part of a wise woman chieftain in the critical flag incident of General Cass. It was her family traditions, her memory and talents, her home and her children, that gave to Henry Rowe Schoolcraft the legends and sympathetic understanding that culminated in the classic *Hiawatha*.

A measured and eloquent tribute to her character is that of Colonel Thomas L. McKenney of the Indian Department at Washington, who, as a joint commissioner with Governor Cass in negotiating the treaty of Fond du Lac in 1826, visited the Johnston home.

Mrs. Johnston is genuine Chippewa, without the smallest admixture of white blood. She is tall and large, but uncommonly active and cheerful. She dresses nearly in the costume of her nation—a petticoat of blue cloth, a short gown of calico, with leggins worked with beads, and moccasins. Her hair is black. She plaits and fastens it up behind with a comb. Her eyes are black and expressive, and pretty well marked, according to phrenologists, with the development of language. She has fine teeth; indeed her face, taken altogether (with her high cheek-bones, compressed forehead and jutting brows) denotes a vigorous intellect and great firmness of character, and needs only to be seen to satisfy even a tyro in physiognomy like myself that she required only the advantages of education and society to place her on a level with the most distinguished of her sex. As it is she is a prodigy. As a wife she is devoted to her husband, as a mother tender and affectionate, as a friend faithful. She manages her domestic concerns in a way that might afford lessons to the better instructed. They are rarely exceeded anywhere, whilst she vies with her generous husband in his hospitality to strangers. She understands but will not speak English. As to influence, there is no chief in the Chippewa nation who exercises it, when it is necessary for her to do so, with equal success.

This has been often tested, but especially at the treaty of cession

at this place in 1820.   Governor Cass, the commissioner, was made
fully sensible of her power then; for when every evidence was given
that the then pending negotiations would issue not only in resistance
on the part of the Indians to the propositions of the commissioner,
but in a serious rupture, she, at this critical moment, sent for some
of the principal chiefs, directing that they should, to avoid the observation of the great body of Indians, make a circuit and meet her in
an avenue at the back of her residence, and there, by her luminous
exposition of their own weakness and the power of the United States,
and by assurances of the friendly disposition of the government
towards them and of their own mistaken views of the entire object
of the commissioner, produced a change which resulted on that same
evening in the conclusion of the treaty.

I have heard Governor Cass say that he felt himself under the
greatest obligations to Mrs. Johnston for her co-operation at that
critical moment; and that the United States is debtor to her, not
only on account of that act, but on many others.   She has never
been known in a single instance to counsel her people contrary to her
conceptions of what was best for them, and never in opposition to
the views of the government.

The United States refused to confirm the claims of her
husband to a tract of land in Sault Ste. Marie, on which the
Johnston residence and other buildings had been built, but it
was not unmindful of the services rendered by Mrs. Johnston.
In the treaty of Fond du Lac of Lake Superior, concluded
August 5, 1826, a section of land was given to her, and a like
acreage to each of her children, and each of her grandchildren.
Part of this was selected from the highlands of Sugar Island, a
few miles below the Sault.

Ozhaw-guscoday-wayquay, Woman of the Green Glade,
who was baptized Susan at the time of her Christian marriage
to John Johnston in 1823, was the mother of eight children,
four girls and four boys, all born at the Sault.   Several were
prominent actors in the history-making events of their time.

Lewis Saurin, born in 1793, served on board the Queen
Charlotte when she was captured by one of the United States
gunboats under Commodore Perry on Lake Erie in 1813.   He
died at Malden, Upper Canada, in 1825, an officer in the British
Indian Department.

George, born in 1796, served in the British Army and was in the engagement at Mackinac Island, August 4, 1814. Later he worked for the United States government as interpreter, and as Indian carpenter at the mission of Grand Traverse Bay. With Lewis he had acquired the common branches of an English education and the French language at Montreal. He was a great reader and gave valuable assistance to Schoolcraft, who said of him, after the elder Johnston was dead, that he was "the only man in the Johnston family who shows any interest in matters of literature and research." He died at the Sault January 6, 1861. Three of George's sons—James, Sam, and Benjamin—were killed in the Civil War.

The unhappy William, who was born in 1811, had some education at Cornwall, Ontario, and Chambly, Quebec, was an Indian interpreter at various times for the United States government, and, for a short time, keeper of the Indian dormitory at Mackinac. Schoolcraft preserved a series of his letters about the fur trade. William died at Mackinac in 1866.

The youngest child, John McDougall, who was born in 1816 and died at the Sault February 14, 1895, was schooled briefly in New York State. He was Indian interpreter for his brother-in-law for two years; two years Indian farmer at Grand Traverse Bay; interpreter for the 1838 delegation of Ottawas and Ojibways from Saginaw to look over lands west of the Mississippi, then for one agent or another, and for the last Chippewa treaty in 1855. Subsequently he was paymaster as long as the government gave tribal annuities to the Ojibways, till sometime in the seventies.

Anna Maria, or Omiskabu-goquay, Woman of the Red Leaf, the youngest daughter, was born in 1814, and became the wife of James L. Schoolcraft. After his untimely death she married the Reverend O. Taylor and moved to Pontiac, Michigan, where she died in 1856.

Charlotte, Woman of the Wild Rose, Ogebu-noquay, who was born in 1806, grew to be a woman of elegance and beauty. When the Reverend Abel Bingham first went to the Sault in 1828 as Baptist missionary to both whites and Indians, Charlotte sat by his side in the Sabbath afternoon services and interpreted his sermon into the musical phrases of her mother's language.   In 1833 she became the wife of a clergyman named William McMurray, who was then a missionary of the Anglican Church at the Canadian Sault but afterwards became Archdeacon of Niagara.   Charlotte died in Ontario in 1878.

Eliza, a woman of beauty and accomplishments, more Indian in her appearance and in refusing to speak English,— although, with Charlotte, she had been sent to a private school at Sandwich, Ontario,—never married.   She was born in 1802 and lived till 1888.   Her Ojibway name, Wahbunnung-oquay means Woman of the Morning Star.

The distinguished story of Jane, the eldest daughter,— Obahbahm-wawa-geezhagoquay, Woman of the Sound the Stars Make Rushing Through the Sky,—who became the wife of Henry Rowe Schoolcraft in 1823, is told at length later in this volume.

Commissioner McKenney, continuing his description of the Johnston family in his letter to his wife in 1827, said:

When I look upon this group of interesting children, and reflect that their mother is a native of our wilds, I wish for the sake of the Indians, that every representative of the people and all who might have influence to bring about a complete system for the preservation and improvement, of at least the rising generation, could see them too.

Following the death of her husband in 1828, Ozhaw-guscoday-wayquay turned her attention to the manufacture of maple sugar on her lands and each year marketed several tons.

In the fall she would go with her people in canoes to the entrance of Lake Superior to fish in the bays and creeks for a fortnight, and return with a load of fish cured for the winter's consumption.   In her youth she had hunted, and was accounted the surest eye and fleetest foot among the women of her tribe.   Her talents, energy, activity and strength of mind, and her skill in all the domestic vocations of the Indian women, have maintained comfort and plenty within her dwelling in spite of the losses sustained by her husband, while her descent from the blood of their ancient chiefs renders her an object of great veneration among the Indians around, who in all their miseries, maladies and difficulties, applied to her for aid or for counsel. . . . She inherited the poetical talent of her father Waub-ojeeg.

Colonel McKenney then quoted a fable which was written down from her recitation and translated by her daughter. He commented further:

During the first quarter of the last century, the Johnston family's old homestead, with its spacious sitting room, large, open fire place and highly polished beams and woodwork, was to the traveler, the resident of the Saut, and the army officer from Fort Brady, a place of the most pleasurable resort, taking the place of the opera house in the cities. During the long winter evenings while Kabbebonicca (the northwest storm spirit) was breathing his icy breath of the severest blasts, "with no earth beneath and no sky above," the visitors who would be seated with the family and who always found this home a welcome retreat, would frequently observe a sudden commotion, and find, from the countenances of the family, that agreeable news had arrived. "Old ——————— has come!" There is general joy.

An old Indian enters, enfeebled by years and no longer able to join warriors and hunters now, perhaps, absent on some dangerous enterprise. He possesses a memory retentive of the traditions of the tribe, and probably an imagination quick at invention or embellishment. He loves to repeat his tales, and all dearly love to listen. The old man, seated and surrounded by an attentive circle, begins his tale, and as the interest rises, and the narrative requires it, he now changes his tone to imitate different speakers, varies his countenance and attitude or moves across the room to personate the character he describes. Thus the Indians hand down their traditions of different kinds from generation to generation.

The best of Ojibway imagination and spirit and art and tradition was thus conveyed to the minds and hearts of the white race by Ozhaw-guscoday-wayquay and her children, and through her daughter Jane in greater part.

Longfellow in 1855 created a sensation in the literary circles of the world with his North American Indian *Song of Hiawatha,* written at Boston. But it was in the flickering firelight and vesperian shadows of a log house on the St. Marys River, at Sault Ste. Marie, Michigan, that Hiawatha was actually born; and it was Henry Rowe Schoolcraft, in *Algic Researches* published in 1839, who told of his discovery there.

The original John Johnston log house, built in 1794, the second year after his marriage, was destroyed during the War of 1812. It was replaced about 1815 by the main portion of the building shown in the frontispiece of this volume. Later owners covered the logs with clapboarding.

The wooden mantel and frame of the fireplace of this cradling place of Hiawatha were in the pioneer museum at Lansing, Michigan. Remains of its chimney may still be seen at Sault Ste. Marie. The part of the house still standing on the Great Lakes Towing Company property fronting Water Street was built in time for the marriage of Jane Johnston to Henry Rowe Schoolcraft in 1823, and was their first home.

PART TWO

THE MANABOZHO–HIAWATHA LEGENDS

As Gathered and Preserved by

HENRY ROWE SCHOOLCRAFT

And as Transmuted by

HENRY WADSWORTH LONGFELLOW

in

THE SONG OF HIAWATHA

"I pored over Mr. Schoolcraft's writings nearly three years."—Longfellow.

"In bringing these curious traditions to light, valuable as an historical index to the character of the tribes, as well as for their invention, Mr. Schoolcraft ought ever to merit and receive the grateful remembrance of the reading portion of the public. He it was who first called attention to this department of our national literature, and without his poetical interest in the subject, very much of the material which he has preserved would probably have been lost, and,—we speak from knowledge,—the poem of *Hiawatha* would never have been written."—George Lowell Austin.

THE extent and character of the contribution of Schoolcraft as shown in the succeeding pages is amazing. Longfellow obtained not only the Ojibway but the Iroquois legendary matter from him. In addition to the long passages quoted, there is an imponderable wealth of detail—of characteristics, manners, family life, picture-writing, canoe-making, tribal names, Ojibway expressions—that Longfellow used to spin the thread from which he wove the actual fabric of his poem. Even in his happy choice of meter Longfellow followed Schoolcraft's specific advice.

Equally overwhelming, in this juxtaposition of the work of these two men, is the manifestation of the creative genius of Henry Wadsworth Longfellow. No mountainous credit given to Schoolcraft can overshadow Longfellow's achievement.

Hiawatha appears all the more clearly a masterpiece of selection, organization, and imaginative development.   Longfellow separated the preponderating goodness of Manabozho from his inconsistent mischievousness.   He gave to the maze of stories a beginning and an end, and a direction.   In Hiawatha's wooing there is a striking exhibition of his originative powers.

Most of the Schoolcraft material is taken from *Algic Researches,* volumes one and two; *Oneóta;* and the first three volumes of *Historical and Statistical Information Respecting the History, Condition and Prospects of the Indian Tribes of the United States.*   In the references the last-named work is indicated by the initials *H. & S. I.*

This reprinting of the unadorned versions of the Indian tales, as collected by Schoolcraft, must also add to the renown of the Ojibway tribe today.   For several seasons a dramatization of *Hiawatha* was presented by a band of seventy-five of them at Point Kensington near Sault Ste. Marie.   It ought to be revived as an annual memorial.

INTRODUCTION

Should you ask me, whence these stories,
Whence these legends and traditions,
With the odors of the forest,
With the dew and damp of meadows,
With the curling smoke of wigwams,
With the rushing of great rivers,
With their frequent repetitions,
And their wild reverberations,
As of thunder in the mountains?
    I should answer, I should tell you,
"From the forests and the prairies,
From the great lakes of the Northland,
From the land of the Ojibways,
From the land of the Dacotahs,
From the mountains, moors, and fen-lands
Where the heron, the Shuh-shuh-gah,
Feeds among the reeds and rushes.
I repeat them as I heard them
From the lips of Nawadaha,
The musician, the sweet singer."

Should you ask where Nawadaha
Found these songs so wild and wayward,
Found these legends and traditions,
I should answer, I should tell you,
"In the bird's-nests of the forest,
In the lodges of the beaver,
In the hoof-prints of the bison,
In the eyry of the eagle!
    "All the wild-fowl sang them to him,
In the moorlands and the fen-lands,
In the melancholy marshes;
Chetowaik, the plover, sang them,
Mahng, the loon, the wild goose, Wawa,
The blue heron, the Shuh-shuh-gah,
And the grouse, the Mushkodasa!"
    If still further you should ask me,
Saying, "Who was Nawadaha?
Tell us of this Nawadaha,"
I should answer your inquiries
Straightway in such words as follow.
    "In the Vale of Tawasentha,*
In the green and silent valley,
By the pleasant water-courses,
Dwelt the singer Nawadaha.
Round about the Indian village
Spread the meadows and the cornfields,
And beyond them stood the forest,
Stood the groves of singing pine-trees,
Green in Summer, white in Winter,
Ever sighing, ever singing.
    "And the pleasant water-courses,
You could trace them through the valley,
By the rushing in the Spring-time,
By the alders in the Summer,
By the white fog in the Autumn,
By the black line in the Winter;
And beside them dwelt the singer,
In the vale of Tawasentha,
In the green and silent valley.
    "There he sang of Hiawatha,
Sang the Song of Hiawatha,

* Henry Rowe Schoolcraft was born in the valley of the Tawasentha, now called Normanskill, in Albany County, New York.

Sang his wondrous birth and being,
How he prayed and how he fasted,
How he lived, and toiled, and suffered,
That the tribes of men might prosper,
That he might advance his people!"
   Ye who love the haunts of Nature,
Love the sunshine of the meadow,
Love the shadow of the forest,
Love the wind among the branches,
And the rain-shower and the snow-storm,
And the rushing of great rivers
Through their palisades of pine-trees,
And the thunder in the mountains,
Whose innumerable echoes
Flap like eagles in their eyries;—
Listen to these wild traditions,
To this Song of Hiawatha!
   Ye who love a nation's legends,
Love the ballads of a people,
That like voices from afar off
Call to us to pause and listen,
Speak in tones so plain and childlike,
Scarcely can the ear distinguish
Whether they are sung or spoken;—
Listen to this Indian Legend,
To this Song of Hiawatha!
   Ye whose hearts are fresh and simple,
Who have faith in God and Nature,
Who believe that in all ages
Every human heart is human,
That in even savage bosoms
There are longings, yearnings, strivings
For the good they comprehend not,
That the feeble hands and helpless,
Groping blindly in the darkness,
Touch God's right hand in that darkness
And are lifted up and strengthened;—
Listen to this simple story,
To this song of Hiawatha!
   Ye who sometimes, in your rambles
Through the green lanes of the country,
Where the tangled barberry-bushes
Hang their tufts of crimson berries

THE VALE OF TAWASENTHA. VALLEY OF THE NORMANSKILL, ALBANY COUNTY,
NEW YORK, WHERE SCHOOLCRAFT WAS BORN.

Over stone walls gray with mosses,
Pause by some neglected graveyard,
For a while to muse, and ponder
On a half-effaced inscription,
Written with little skill of song-craft,
Homely phrases, but each letter
Full of hope and yet of heart-break,
Full of all the tender pathos
Of the Here and the Hereafter;—
Stay and read this rude inscription,
Read this song of Hiawatha!

I

THE PEACE-PIPE

. . . SUDDENLY there arose a great alarm at the invasion of a ferocious band of warriors from the north of the Great Lakes. As they advanced, an indiscriminate slaughter was made of men, women, and children. Destruction threatened to be alike the fate of those who boldly resisted, or quietly submitted. The public alarm was extreme. Hiawatha advised them not to waste their efforts in a desultory manner, but to call a general council of all the tribes that could be gathered together from the east to the west; and he appointed the meeting to take place on an eminence on the banks of Onondaga lake.

Accordingly all the chief men assembled at this spot. The occasion brought together vast multitudes of men, women, and children; for there was an expectation of some great deliverance. Three days had already elapsed, and there began to be a general anxiety lest Hiawatha should not arrive. Messengers were despatched for him to Tioto, who found him in a pensive mood, to whom he communicated his strong presentiments that evil betided his attendance. These were overruled by the strong representations of the messengers, and he again put his wonderful vessel in its element, and set out for the council, taking his only daughter with him. She timidly took her seat in the stern, with a light paddle, to give direction to the vessel; for the strength of the current of the Seneca river was sufficient to give velocity to the motion till arriving at

So-hah-hi, the Onondaga outlet. At this point the powerful exertions of the aged chief were required, till they entered on the bright bosom of the Onondaga.

The grand council, that was to avert the threatened danger, was quickly in sight, and sent up its shouts of welcome, as the venerated man approached, and landed in front of the assemblage. An ascent led up the banks of the lake to the place occupied by the council. As he walked up this, a loud sound was heard in the air above, as if caused by some rushing current of wind. Instantly the eyes of all were directed upward to the sky, where a spot of matter was discovered descending rapidly, and every instant enlarging in its size and velocity. Terror and alarm were the first impulses, for it appeared to be descending into their midst, and they scattered in confusion.

Hiawatha, as soon as he had gained the eminence, stood still, and caused his daughter to do the same; deeming it cowardly to fly, and impossible, if it were attempted, to divert the designs of the Great Spirit. The descending object had now assumed a more definite aspect, and as it came down, revealed the shape of a gigantic white bird, with wide extended and pointed wings, which came down, swifter and swifter, with a mighty swoop, and crushed the girl to the earth. Not a muscle was moved in the face of Hiawatha. His daughter lay dead before him, but the great and mysterious white bird was also destroyed by the shock. Such had been the violence of the concussion, that it had completely buried its beak and head in the ground. But the most wonderful sight was the carcass of the prostrated bird, which was covered with beautiful plumes of snow-white shining feathers. Each warrior stepped up, and decorated himself with a plume. And it hence became a custom to assume this kind of feathers on the war-path. Succeeding generations substituted the plumes of the white heron, which led this bird to be greatly esteemed.

But yet a greater wonder ensued. On removing the carcass of the bird, not a human trace could be discovered of the daughter. She had completely vanished. At this the father was greatly afflicted in spirits, and disconsolate. But he roused himself, as from a lethargy, and walked to the head of the council with a dignified air, covered with his simple robe of wolf-skins; taking his seat with the chief warriors and counsellors, and listening with attentive gravity to the plans of the different speakers. One day was given to these discussions; on the next day, he arose and said:

My friends and brothers; you are members of many tribes, and have come from a great distance. We have met to promote the common interest, and our mutual safety. How shall it be accomplished? To oppose these northern hordes in tribes singly, while we are at variance often with each other, is impossible. By uniting in a common band of brotherhood, we may hope to succeed. Let this be done, and we shall drive the enemy from our land. Listen to me by tribes.

You (the Mohawks), who are sitting under the shadow of the Great Tree, whose roots sink deep in the earth, and whose branches spread wide around, shall be the first nation, because you are warlike and mighty.

You (the Oneidas), who recline your bodies against the Everlasting Stone, that cannot be moved, shall be the second nation, because you always give wise counsel.

You (the Onondagas), who have your habitation at the foot of the Great Hills, and are overshadowed by their crags, shall be the third nation, because you are all greatly gifted in speech.

You (the Senecas), whose dwelling is in the Dark Forest, and whose home is everywhere, shall be the fourth nation, because of your superior cunning in hunting.

And you (the Cayugas), the people who live in the Open Country, and possess much wisdom, shall be the fifth nation, because you understand better the art of raising corn and beans, and making houses.

Unite, you five nations, and have one common interest, and no foe shall disturb and subdue you. You, the people who are as the feeble bushes, and you, who are a fishing people, may place yourselves under our protection, and we will defend you.

And you of the south and of the west may do the same, and we will protect you.   We earnestly desire the alliance and friendship of you all.

Brothers, if we unite in this great bond, the Great Spirit will smile upon us, and we shall be free, prosperous, and happy. But if we remain as we are, we shall be subject to his frown. We shall be enslaved, ruined, perhaps annihilated.   We may perish under the war-storm, and our names be no longer remembered by good men, nor be repeated in the dance and song.

Brothers, these are the words of Hiawatha.   I have said it. I am done.

The next day the plan of union was again considered, and adopted by the council. . . . *H. & S. I.*, pt. 3, p. 315–17.   Also see *Notes on the Iroquois* (1847), p. 272–83, 476–78.

> On the Mountains of the Prairie,
> On the great Red Pipe-stone Quarry,
> Gitche Manito, the mighty,
> He the Master of Life, descending,
> On the red crags of the quarry
> Stood erect, and called the nations,
> Called the tribes of men together.
>   From his footprints flowed a river,
> Leaped into the light of morning,
> O'er the precipice plunging downward
> Gleamed like Ishkoodah, the comet.
> And the Spirit, stooping earthward,
> With his finger on the meadow
> Traced a winding pathway for it,
> Saying to it, "Run in this way!"
>   From the red stone of the quarry
> With his hand he broke a fragment,
> Moulded it into a pipe-head,
> Shaped and fashioned it with figures;
> From the margin of the river
> Took a long reed for a pipe-stem,
> With its dark green leaves upon it;
> Filled the pipe with bark of willow,
> With the bark of the red willow;
> Breathed upon the neighboring forest,
> Made its great boughs chafe together,

Till in flame they burst and kindled;
And erect upon the mountains,
Gitche Manito, the mighty,
Smoked the calumet, the Peace-Pipe,
As a signal to the nations.

And the smoke rose slowly, slowly,
Through the tranquil air of morning,
First a single line of darkness,
Then a denser, bluer vapor,
Then a snow-white cloud unfolding,
Like the tree-tops of the forest,
Ever rising, rising, rising,
Till it touched the top of heaven,
Till it broke against the heaven,
And rolled outward all around it.

From the Vale of Tawasentha,
From the Valley of Wyoming,
From the groves of Tuscaloosa,
From the far-off Rocky Mountains,
From the Northern lakes and rivers,
All the tribes beheld the signal,
Saw the distant smoke ascending,
The Pukwana of the Peace-Pipe.

And the Prophets of the nations
Said: "Behold it, the Pukwana!
By this signal from afar off,
Bending like a wand of willow,
Waving like a hand that beckons,
Gitche Manito, the mighty,
Calls the tribes of men together,
Calls the warriors to his council!"

Down the rivers, o'er the prairies,
Came the warriors of the nations,
Came the Delawares and Mohawks,
Came the Choctaws and Camanches,
Came the Shoshonies and Blackfeet,
Came the Pawnees and Omahas,
Came the Mandans and Dacotahs,
Came the Hurons and Ojibways,
All the warriors drawn together
By the signal of the Peace-Pipe,
To the Mountains of the Prairie,
To the great Red Pipe-stone Quarry.

And they stood there on the meadow,
With their weapons and their war-gear,
Painted like the leaves of Autumn,
Painted like the sky of morning,
Wildly glaring at each other;
In their faces stern defiance,
In their hearts the feuds of ages,
The hereditary hatred,
The ancestral thirst of vengeance.
    Gitche Manito, the mighty,
The creator of the nations,
Looked upon them with compassion,
With paternal love and pity;
Looked upon their wrath and wrangling
But as quarrels among children,
But as feuds and fights of children!
    Over them he stretched his right hand
To subdue their stubborn natures,
To allay their thirst and fever,
By the shadow of his right hand;
Spake to them with voice majestic
As the sound of far-off waters
Falling into deep abysses,
Warning, chiding, spake in this wise:—
    "O my children! my poor children!
Listen to the words of wisdom,
Listen to the words of warning,
From the lips of the Great Spirit,
From the Master of Life, who made you.
    "I have given you lands to hunt in,
I have given you streams to fish in,
I have given you bear and bison,
I have given you roe and reindeer,
I have given you brant and beaver,
Filled the marshes full of wild-fowl,
Filled the rivers full of fishes;
Why then are you not contented?
Why then will you hunt each other?
    "I am weary of your quarrels,
Weary of your wars and bloodshed,
Weary of your prayers for vengeance,
Of your wranglings and dissensions;
All your strength is in your union,

All your danger is in discord;
Therefore be at peace henceforward,
And as brothers live together.

. . . About this time a person in the shape of a human being came down from the sky; his clothing was exceedingly pure and white; he was seated as it were in a nest with a very fine cord attached to it, by which this mysterious person was let down, and the cord or string reached heaven. He addressed the Indians in a very humane, mild, and compassionate tone, saying that they were very poor and needy, but telling them that they were perpetually asleep, and this was caused by the Mache Monedo who was in the midst of them and leading them to death and ruin.

This mysterious personage informed them also that above, where he came from, there was no night, that the inhabitants never slept, that it was perpetually day and they required no sleep; that Kezha Monedo was their light. He then invited four of the Indians to ascend up with him, promising that they would be brought back in safety; that an opportunity would thereby present itself to view the beauty of the sky, or heavens. But the Indians doubted and feared lest the cord should break, because it appeared to them so small. They did not believe it possible it could bear their weight. With this objection they excused themselves. They were, however, again assured that the cord was sufficiently strong, and that Kezha Monedo had the power to make it so. Yet the Indians doubted and feared, and did not accompany the messenger sent down to them. After this refusal the mysterious person produced a small bow and arrows with which he shot at the Indians in different parts of their bodies; the result was the killing of multitudes of small white worms, which he showed to them, telling them that they were the Mache Monedo which caused them to sleep, and prevented their awakening from their death-like state.

This divine messenger then gave to the Indians laws and rules whereby they should be guided; first, to love and fear Kezha Monedo, and next, that they must love one another, and be charitable and hospitable; and finally that they must not covet their neighbors' property, but acquire it by labor and honest industry. . . . From "Mash-kwa-sha-kwong," in *Oneóta,* p. 144.

Tarenyawago taught the Six Nations arts and knowledge. He had a canoe which would move without paddles. It was only necessary to will it, to compel it to go. With this he ascended the streams and lakes. He taught the people to raise corn and beans, removed obstructions from their water-courses, and made their fishing-grounds clear. He helped them to get the mastery over the great monsters which overran the country, and thus prepared the forests for their hunters. His wisdom was as great as his power. The people listened to him with admiration, and followed his advice gladly. There was nothing in which he did not excel good hunters, brave warriors, and eloquent orators.

He gave them wise instructions for observing the laws and maxims of the Great Spirit. Having done these things, he laid aside the high powers of his public mission, and resolved to set them an example of how they should live. . . . From "Hiawatha, or, The Origin of the Onondaga Council-Fire," in *H. & S. I.,* pt. 3, 314-15.

"I will send a Prophet to you,
A Deliverer of the nations,
Who shall guide you and shall teach you,
Who shall toil and suffer with you.
If you listen to his counsels,
You will multiply and prosper;
If his warnings pass unheeded,
You will fade away and perish!
"Bathe now in the stream before you,
Wash the war-paint from your faces,
Wash the blood-stains from your fingers,
Bury your war-clubs and your weapons,
Break the red stone from this quarry,
Mould and make it into Peace-Pipes,
Take the reeds that grow beside you,
Deck them with your brightest feathers,
Smoke the calumet together,
And as brothers live henceforward!"

Then upon the ground the warriors
Threw their cloaks and shirts of deer-skin,
Threw their weapons and their war-gear,
Leaped into the rushing river,
Washed the war-paint from their faces.
Clear above them flowed the water,
Clear and limpid from the footprints
Of the Master of Life descending;
Dark below them flowed the water,
Soiled and stained with streaks of crimson,
As if blood were mingled with it!
　　From the river came the warriors,
Clean and washed from all their war-paint;
On the banks their clubs they buried,
Buried all their warlike weapons.
Gitche Manito, the mighty,
The Great Spirit, the creator,
Smiled upon his helpless children!
　　And in silence all the warriors
Broke the red stone of the quarry,
Smoothed and formed it into Peace-Pipes,
Broke the long reeds by the river,
Decked them with their brightest feathers,
And departed each one homeward,
While the Master of Life, ascending,
Through the opening of cloud-curtains,
Through the doorways of the heaven,
Vanished from before their faces,
In the smoke that rolled around him,
The Pukwana of the Peace-Pipe!

II

THE FOUR WINDS

MUDJEKEWIS and nine brothers conquered the Mammoth
Bear, and obtained the Sacred Belt of Wampum, the great
object of previous warlike enterprise, and the great means of
happiness to men. The chief honour of this achievement was
awarded to Mudjekewis, the youngest of the ten, who received
the government of the West Winds. He is therefore called
Kabeyun, the father of the winds. To his son, Wabun, he
gave the East; to Shawondasee, the south, and to Kabibonokka,

the North.   Manabozho, being an illegitimate son, was left unprovided.   When he grew up, and obtained the secret of his birth, he went to war against his father, Kabeyun, and having brought the latter to terms, he received the government of the Northwest Winds, ruling jointly with his brother Kabibonokka the tempests from that quarter of the heavens. . . . From "Shawondasee," in *Algic Researches,* v. 2, p. 214.

They continued to see the remains of former warriors, who had been to the place where *they* were now going, some of whom had retreated as far back as the place where they first saw the bones, beyond which no one had ever escaped.   At last they came to a piece of rising ground, from which they plainly distinguished, sleeping on a distant mountain, a mammoth bear.

The distance between them was very great, but the size of the animal caused him plainly to be seen.   "There," said the leader, "it is he to whom I am leading you; here our troubles only will commence, for he is a Mishemokwa* and a Manito. It is he who has that we prize so dearly (i.e., *wampum*), to obtain which, the warriors whose bones we saw sacrificed their lives.   You must not be fearful.   Be manly.   We shall find him asleep."   They advanced boldly till they came near, when they stopped to view him more closely.   He was asleep.   Then the leader went forward and touched the belt around the animal's neck.   "This," he said, "is what we must get.   It contains the wampum."   They then requested the eldest to try and slip the belt over the bear's head, who appeared to be fast asleep, as he was not in the least disturbed by the attempt to obtain the belt.   All their efforts were in vain, till it came to the one next the youngest.   He tried, and the belt moved nearly over the monster's head, but he could get it no farther. Then the youngest one and leader made his attempt, and succeeded.   Placing it on the back of the oldest, he said, "Now we must run," and off they started.   When one became fatigued with its weight, another would relieve him.   Thus they ran till they had passed the bones of all former warriors, and

* A she-bear—also a male having the ferocity of a she-bear.

were some distance beyond, when, looking back, they saw the monster slowly rising. He stood some time before he missed his wampum. Soon they heard his tremendous howl, like distant thunder, slowly filling all the sky; and then they heard him speak and say, "Who can it be that has dared to steal my wampum? Earth is not so large but that I can find them." And he descended from the hill in pursuit. As if convulsed, the earth shook with every jump he made. Very soon he approached the party. They however kept the belt, exchanging it from one to another, and encouraging each other. But he gained on them fast. . . . Striking him with one of the clubs, it broke in pieces. The bear stumbled. Renewing the attempt with the other war-club, that also was broken, but the bear fell senseless. Each blow the old man gave him sounded like a clap of thunder, and the howls of the bear ran along till they filled the heavens.

The young men had now run some distance, when they looked back. They could see that the bear was recovering from the blows. First he moved his paws, and soon they saw him rise on his feet. . . .

Mudjikewis struck him a tremendous blow on the head, and gave the saw-saw-quan. The bear's limbs doubled under him, and he fell stunned by the blow. . . .

Mudjikewis, stepping up, gave a yell and struck him a blow upon the head. This he repeated till it seemed like a mass of brains.—From "Iamo, or, The Undying Head, an Ottowa Tale," in *Algic Researches*, v. 1, p. 102–4, 106–7, 108, 111–12.

> "Honor be to Mudjekeewis!"
> Cried the warriors, cried the old men,
> When he came in triumph homeward
> With the sacred Belt of Wampum,
> From the regions of the North-Wind,
> From the kingdom of Wabasso,
> From the land of the White Rabbit.
>   He had stolen the Belt of Wampum
> From the neck of Mishe-Mokwa,
> From the Great Bear of the mountains,

From the terror of the nations,
As he lay asleep and cumbrous
On the summit of the mountains,
Like a rock with mosses on it,
Spotted brown and gray with mosses.
    Silently he stole upon him,
Till the red nails of the monster
Almost touched him, almost scared him,
Till the hot breath of his nostrils
Warmed the hands of Mudjekeewis,
As he drew the Belt of Wampum
Over the round ears, that heard not,
Over the small eyes, that saw not,
Over the long nose and nostrils,
The black muffle of the nostrils,
Out of which the heavy breathing
Warmed the hands of Mudjekeewis.
    Then he swung aloft his war-club,
Shouted loud and long his war-cry,
Smote the mighty Mishe-Mokwa
In the middle of the forehead,
Right between the eyes he smote him.
    With the heavy blow bewildered,
Rose the Great Bear of the mountains;
But his knees beneath him trembled,
And he whimpered like a woman,
As he reeled and staggered forward,
As he sat upon his haunches;
And the mighty Mudjekeewis,
Standing fearlessly before him,
Taunted him in loud derision,
Spake disdainfully in this wise:—
    "Hark you, Bear! you are a coward,
And no Brave, as you pretended;
Else you would not cry and whimper
Like a miserable woman!
Bear! you know our tribes are hostile,
Long have been at war together;
Now you find that we are strongest,
You go sneaking in the forest,
You go hiding in the mountains!
Had you conquered me in battle
Not a groan would I have uttered;

But you, Bear! sit here and whimper,
And disgrace your tribe by crying,
Like a wretched Shaugodaya,
Like a cowardly old woman!"
  Then again he raised his war-club,
Smote again the Mishe-Mokwa
In the middle of his forehead,
Broke his skull, as ice is broken
When one goes to fish in Winter.
Thus was slain the Mishe-Mokwa,
He the Great Bear of the mountains,
He the terror of the nations.
  "Honor be to Mudjekeewis!"
With a shout exclaimed the people,
"Honor be to Mudjekeewis!
Henceforth he shall be the West-Wind,
And hereafter and forever
Shall he hold supreme dominion
Over all the winds of heaven.
Call him no more Mudjekeewis,
Call him Kabeyun, the West-Wind!"
  Thus was Mudjekeewis chosen
Father of the Winds of Heaven.
For himself he kept the West-Wind,
Gave the others to his children;
Unto Wabun gave the East-Wind,
Gave the South to Shawondasee,
And the North-Wind, wild and cruel,
To the fierce Kabibonokka.
  Young and beautiful was Wabun;
He it was who brought the morning,
He it was whose silver arrows
Chased the dark o'er hill and valley;
He it was whose cheeks were painted
With the brightest streaks of crimson,
And whose voice awoke the village,
Called the deer, and called the hunter.
  Lonely in the sky was Wabun;
Though the birds sang gayly to him,
Though the wild-flowers of the meadow
Filled the air with odors for him,
Though the forests and the rivers
Sang and shouted at his coming,

Still his heart was sad within him,
For he was alone in heaven.

   But one morning, gazing earthward,
While the village still was sleeping,
And the fog lay on the river,
Like a ghost, that goes at sunrise,
He beheld a maiden walking
All alone upon a meadow,
Gathering water-flags and rushes
By a river in the meadow.

   Every morning, gazing earthward,
Still the first thing he beheld there
Was her blue eyes looking at him,
Two blue lakes among the rushes.
And he loved the lonely maiden,
Who thus waited for his coming;
For they both were solitary,
She on earth and he in heaven.

   And he wooed her with caresses,
Wooed her with his smile of sunshine,
With his flattering words he wooed her,
With his sighing and his singing,
Gentlest whispers in the branches,
Softest music, sweetest odors,
Till he drew her to his bosom,
Folded in his robes of crimson,
Till into a star he changed her,
Trembling still upon his bosom;
And forever in the heavens
They are seen together walking,
Wabun and the Wabun-Annung,
Wabun and the Star of Morning.

   But the fierce Kabibonokka
Had his dwelling among icebergs,
In the everlasting snow-drifts,
In the kingdom of Wabasso,
In the land of the White Rabbit.
He it was whose hand in Autumn
Painted all the trees with scarlet,
Stained the leaves with red and yellow.
He it was who sent the snow-flakes,
Sifting, hissing through the forest,
Froze the ponds, the lakes, the rivers,

Drove the loon and sea-gull southward,
Drove the cormorant and curlew
To their nests of sedge and sea-tang
In the realms of Shawondasee.

There was once a Shingebiss (the name of a kind of duck) living alone in a solitary lodge, on the shores of the deep bay of a lake, in the coldest winter weather. The ice had formed on the water, and he had but four logs of wood to keep his fire. Each of these, would, however, burn a month, and as there were but four cold winter months, they were sufficient to carry him through till spring.

Shingebiss was hardy and fearless, and cared for no one. He would go out during the coldest day, and seek for places where flags and rushes grew through the ice, and plucking them up with his bill, would dive through the openings, in quest of fish. In this way he found plenty of food, while others were starving, and he went home daily to his lodge, dragging strings of fish after him, on the ice.

Kabebonicca observed him, and felt a little piqued at his perseverance and good luck in defiance of the severest blasts of wind he could send from the northwest. "Why! this is a wonderful man," said he; "he does not mind the cold, and appears as happy and contented, as if it were the month of June. I will try, whether he cannot be mastered." He poured forth ten-fold colder blasts, and drifts of snow, so that it was next to impossible to live in the open air. Still the fire of Shingebiss did not go out: he wore but a single strip of leather around his body, and he was seen, in the worst weather, searching the shores for rushes, and carrying home fish.

"I shall go and visit him," said Kabebonicca, one day, as he saw Shingebiss dragging along a quantity of fish. And accordingly, that very night, he went to the door of his lodge. Meantime Shingebiss had cooked his fish, and finished his meal, and was lying, partly on his side, before the fire singing his songs. After Kabebonicca had come to the door, and stood listening there, he sang as follows:

Ka	Neej	Ka	Neej
Be	In	Be	In
Bon	In	Bon	In
Oc	Ee.	Oc	Ee.
Ca	We-ya!	Ca	We-ya!

The number of words, in this song, are few and simple, but they are made up from compounds which carry the whole of their original meanings, and are rather suggestive of the ideas floating in the mind, than actual expressions of those ideas. Literally he sings:

Spirit of the North West—you are but my fellow man.

By being broken into syllables, to correspond with a simple chant, and by the power of intonation and repetition, with a chorus, these words are expanded into melodious utterance, if we may be allowed the term, and may be thus rendered:

Windy god, I know your plan,
You are but my fellow man,
Blow you may your coldest breeze,
Shingebiss you cannot freeze,
Sweep the strongest wind you can,
Shingebiss is still your man,
Heigh! for life——and ho! for bliss,
Who so free as Shingebiss?

The hunter knew that Kabebonicca was at his door, for he felt his cold and strong breath; but he kept on singing his songs, and affected utter indifference. At length Kabebonicca entered, and took his seat on the opposite side of the lodge. But Shingebiss did not regard, or notice him. He got up, as if nobody were present, and taking his poker, pushed the log, which made his fire burn brighter, repeating as he sat down again:

You are but my fellow man.

Very soon the tears began to flow down Kabebonicca's cheeks, which increased so fast, that, presently, he said to himself, "I cannot stand this—I must go out." He did so, and left Shingebiss to his songs; but resolved to freeze up all the flag orifices, and make the ice thick, so that he could not get any more fish. Still Shingebiss, by dint of great diligence, found means to pull up new roots, and dive under for fish. At last Kabebonicca was compelled to give up the contest. "He must be aided by some Monedo," said he, "I can neither freeze him, nor starve him, he is a very singular being—I will let him alone."—"Shingebiss, From the Odjibwa-Algonquin," in *Oneóta,* p. 11–12; also in *H. & S. I.,* pt. 3, 324–26.

> Once the fierce Kabibonokka
> Issued from his lodge of snow-drifts,
> From his home among the icebergs,
> And his hair, with snow besprinkled,
> Streamed behind him like a river,
> Like a black and wintry river,
> As he howled and hurried southward,
> Over frozen lakes and moorlands.
> There among the reeds and rushes
> Found he Shingebis, the diver,
> Trailing strings of fish behind him,
> O'er the frozen fens and moorlands,
> Lingering still among the moorlands,
> Though his tribe had long departed
> To the land of Shawondasee.
> Cried the fierce Kabibonokka,
> "Who is this that dares to brave me?
> Dares to stay in my dominions,
> When the Wawa has departed,
> When the wild-goose has gone southward,
> And the heron, the Shuh-shuh-gah,
> Long ago departed southward?
> I will go into his wigwam,
> I will put his smouldering fire out!"
> And at night Kabibonokka
> To the lodge came wild and wailing,
> Heaped the snow in drifts about it,
> Shouted down into the smoke-flue,
> Shook the lodge-poles in his fury,
> Flapped the curtain of the door-way.
> Shingebis, the diver, feared not,
> Shingebis, the diver, cared not;
> Four great logs had he for fire-wood,
> One for each moon of the winter,
> And for food the fishes served him.
> By his blazing fire he sat there,

Warm and merry, eating, laughing,
Singing, "O Kabibonokka,
You are but my fellow-mortal!"
    Then Kabibonokka entered,
And though Shingebis, the diver,
Felt his presence by the coldness,
Felt his icy breath upon him,
Still he did not cease his singing,
Still he did not leave his laughing,
Only turned the log a little,
Only made the fire burn brighter,
Made the sparks fly up the smoke-flue.
    From Kabibonokka's forehead,
From his snow-besprinkled tresses,
Drops of sweat fell fast and heavy,
Making dints upon the ashes,
As along the eaves of lodges,
As from drooping boughs of hemlock,
Drips the melting snow in spring-time,
Making hollows in the snow-drifts.
    Till at last he rose defeated,
Could not bear the heat and laughter,
Could not bear the merry singing,
But rushed headlong through the door-way,
Stamped upon the crusted snow-drifts,
Stamped upon the lakes and rivers,
Made the snow upon them harder,
Made the ice upon them thicker,
Challenged Shingebis, the diver,
To come forth and wrestle with him,
To come forth and wrestle naked
On the frozen fens and moorlands.
    Forth went Shingebis, the diver,
Wrestled all night with the North-Wind,
Wrestled naked on the moorlands
With the fierce Kabibonokka,
Till his panting breath grew fainter,
Till his frozen grasp grew feebler,
Till he reeled and staggered backward
And retreated, baffled, beaten,
To the kingdom of Wabasso,
To the land of the White Rabbit,
Hearing still the gusty laughter,

Hearing Shingebis, the diver,
Singing, "O Kabibonokka,
You are but my fellow-mortal!"

. . . Shawondasee is represented as an affluent, plethoric old man, who has grown unwieldy from repletion, and seldom moves. He keeps his eyes steadfastly fixed on the north. When he sighs, in autumn, we have those balmy southern airs, which communicate warmth and delight over the northern hemisphere, and make the Indian Summer.

One day, while gazing toward the north, he beheld a beautiful young woman of slender and majestic form, standing on the plains. She appeared in the same place for several days, but what most attracted his admiration, was her bright and flowing locks of yellow hair. Ever dilatory, however, he contented himself with gazing. At length he saw, or fancied he saw, her head enveloped in a pure white mass like snow. This excited his jealousy toward his brother Kabibonokka, and he threw out a succession of short and rapid sighs—when lo! the air was filled with light filaments of a silvery hue, but the object of his affections had for ever vanished. In reality, the southern airs had blown off the fine-winged seed-vessels of the prairie dandelion. . . . From "Shawondasee," in *Algic Researches,* v. 2, p. 214-15.

Shawondasee, fat and lazy,
Had his dwelling far to southward,
In the drowsy, dreamy sunshine,
In the never-ending Summer.
He it was who sent the wood-birds,
Sent the robin, the Opechee,
Sent the bluebird, the Owaissa,
Sent the Shawshaw, sent the swallow,
Sent the wild-goose, Wawa, northward,
Sent the melons and tobacco,
And the grapes in purple clusters.
From his pipe the smoke ascending
Filled the sky with haze and vapor,
Filled the air with dreamy softness,
Gave a twinkle to the water,
Touched the rugged hills with smoothness,
Brought the tender Indian Summer

To the melancholy North-land,
In the dreary Moon of Snow-shoes.
    Listless, careless Shawondasee!
In his life he had one shadow,
In his heart one sorrow had he.
Once, as he was gazing northward,
Far away upon a prairie
He beheld a maiden standing,
Saw a tall and slender maiden
All alone upon a prairie;
Brightest green were all her garments,
And her hair was like the sunshine.
    Day by day he gazed upon her,
Day by day he sighed with passion,
Day by day his heart within him
Grew more hot with love and longing
For the maid with yellow tresses.
But he was too fat and lazy
To bestir himself and woo her;
Yes, too indolent and easy
To pursue her and persuade her.
So he only gazed upon her,
Only sat and sighed with passion
For the maiden of the prairie.
    Till one morning, looking northward,
He beheld her yellow tresses
Changed and covered o'er with whiteness
Covered as with whitest snow-flakes.
"Ah! my brother from the North-land,
From the kingdom of Wabasso,
From the land of the White Rabbit!
You have stolen the maiden from me,
You have laid your hand upon her,
You have wooed and won my maiden,
With your stories of the North-land!"
    Thus the wretched Shawondasee
Breathed into the air his sorrow;
And the South-Wind o'er the prairie
Wandered warm with sighs of passion,
With the sighs of Shawondasee,
Till the air seemed full of snow-flakes,
Full of thistle-down the prairie,
And the maid with hair like sunshine

Vanished from his sight forever;
Never more did Shawondasee
See the maid with yellow tresses!
    Poor, deluded Shawondasee!
'T was no woman that you gazed at,
'T was no maiden that you sighed for,
'T was the prairie dandelion
That through all the dreamy Summer
You had gazed at with such longing,
You had sighed for with such passion,
And had puffed away forever,
Blown into the air with sighing.
Ah! deluded Shawondasee!
    Thus the Four Winds were divided;
Thus the sons of Mudjekeewis
Had their stations in the heavens,
At the corners of the heavens;
For himself the West-Wind only
Kept the mighty Mudjekeewis.

III

HIAWATHA'S CHILDHOOD

. . . HE [Manabozho] is not presented here as an historical personage, or in any other light than as the native narrators themselves depict him, when they have assembled a group of listeners in the lodge, and begin the story of Manabozho. His birth and parentage are obscure. Story says his grandmother was the daughter of the moon. Having been married but a short time, her rival attracted her to a grapevine swing on the banks of a lake, and by one bold exertion pitched her into its centre, from which she fell through to the earth. Having a daughter, the fruit of her lunar marriage, she was very careful in instructing her, from early infancy, to beware of the west wind, and never, in stooping, to expose herself to its influence. In some unguarded moment this precaution was neglected. In an instant, the gale, invading her robes, scattered them upon its wings, and accomplishing its Tarquinic purpose, at the same moment annihilated her. At the scene of this catastrophe her mother found a foetus-like mass, which she carefully and tenderly nursed till it assumed the beautiful and striking lineaments of the infant Manabozho . . . —From "Manabozho; or, The Great Incarnation of the North, an Algic Legend," in *Algic Researches*, v. 1, p. 135–36.

> Downward through the evening twilight,
> In the days that are forgotten,
> In the unremembered ages,
> From the full moon fell Nokomis,
> Fell the beautiful Nokomis,
> She a wife but not a mother.
>   She was sporting with her women,
> Swinging in a swing of grape-vines,
> When her rival, the rejected,
> Full of jealousy and hatred,
> Cut the leafy swing asunder,
> Cut in twain the twisted grape-vines,
> And Nokomis fell affrighted
> Downward through the evening twilight,
> On the Muskoday, the meadow,
> On the prairie full of blossoms.
> "See! a star falls!" said the people,
> "From the sky a star is falling!"
>   There among the ferns and mosses,
> There among the prairie lilies,
> On the Muskoday, the meadow,
> In the moonlight and the starlight,
> Fair Nokomis bore a daughter.
> And she called her name Wenonah,
> As the first-born of her daughters.
> And the daughter of Nokomis
> Grew up like the prairie lilies,
> Grew a tall and slender maiden,
> With the beauty of the moonlight,
> With the beauty of the starlight.
>   And Nokomis warned her often,
> Saying oft, and oft repeating,
> "Oh, beware of Mudjekeewis,
> Of the West-Wind, Mudjekeewis;
> Listen not to what he tells you,
> Lie not down upon the meadow,
> Stoop not down among the lilies,
> Lest the West-Wind come and harm you."

But she heeded not the warning,
Heeded not those words of wisdom.
And the West-Wind came at evening,
Walking lightly o'er the prairie,
Whispering to the leaves and blossoms,
Bending low the flowers and grasses,
Found the beautiful Wenonah,
Lying there among the lilies,
Wooed her with his words of sweetness,
Wooed her with his soft caresses,
Till she bore a son in sorrow,
Bore a son of love and sorrow.

Thus was born my Hiawatha,
Thus was born the child of wonder;
But the daughter of Nokomis,
Hiawatha's gentle mother,
In her anguish died deserted
By the West-Wind, false and faithless,
By the heartless Mudjekeewis.

For her daughter, long and loudly
Wailed and wept the sad Nokomis;
"Oh that I were dead!" she murmured,
"Oh that I were dead, as thou art!
No more work, and no more weeping,
Wahonowin! Wahonowin!"

. . . Very little is told of his early boyhood. We take him up in the following legend at a period of advanced youth, when we find him living with his grandmother. And at this time he possessed, although he had not yet *exercised,* all the anomalous and contradictory powers of body and mind, of manship and divinity, which he afterward evinced. . . . He often conversed with animals, fowls, reptiles, and fishes. He deemed himself related to them, and invariably addressed them by the term "my brother"; and one of his greatest resources, when hard pressed, was to change himself into their shapes. . . .

. . . Manabozho was living with his grandmother near the edge of a wide prairie. On this prairie he first saw animals and birds of every kind. He there also saw exhibitions of divine power in the sweeping tempests, in the thunder and lightning, and the various shades of light and darkness, which form a never-ending scene of observation. Every new sight he beheld in the heavens was a subject of remark; every new animal or bird an object of deep interest; and every sound uttered by the animal creation a new lesson, which he was expected to learn. He often trembled at what he heard and saw. To this scene his grandmother sent him at an early age to watch. The first sound he heard was that of the owl, at which he was greatly terrified, and, quickly descending the tree he had climbed, he ran with alarm to the lodge. "Noko! Noko!"* he cried, "I have heard a monedo." She laughed at his fears, and asked him what kind of a noise it made. He answered, "It makes a noise like this: Ko-ko-ko-ho." She told him that he was young and foolish; that what he had heard was only a bird, deriving its name from the noise it made.

He went back and continued his watch. . . . From "Manabozho," in *Algic Researches,* v. 1, p. 136–38.

The tickenagun, or Indian cradle, . . . consists of three pieces. . . . These are tied together with deer's sinews or pegged. The whole structure is very light, and is carved with a knife by the men, out of the linden or maple tree. Moss constitutes the bed of the infant. . . .

> Who is this?
> Who is this?
> Giving light (meaning the light of the eye)
> On the top of my lodge.
>
> It is I—the little owl
>   Coming,
> It is I—the little owl
>   Coming,
> Down! Down!

. . . The e-we-yea of the Indian woman is entirely analogous to the lul la by of our language, and will be seen to be exceedingly pretty in itself.—From "Nursery and Cradle Songs of the Forest," in *Oneóta,* p. 212–14.

* An abbreviated term for "my grandmother," derived from no-komiss.

By the shores of Gitche Gumee,
By the shining Big-Sea-Water,
Stood the wigwam of Nokomis,
Daughter of the Moon, Nokomis.
Dark behind it rose the forest,
Rose the black and gloomy pine-trees,
Rose the firs with cones upon them;
Bright before it beat the water,
Beat the clear and sunny water,
Beat the shining Big-Sea-Water.
 There the wrinkled old Nokomis
Nursed the little Hiawatha,
Rocked him in his linden cradle,
Bedded soft in moss and rushes,
Safely bound with reindeer sinews;
Stilled his fretful wail by saying,
"Hush! the Naked Bear will hear thee!"
Lulled him into slumber, singing,
"Ewa-yea! my little owlet!
Who is this, that lights the wigwam?
With his great eyes lights the wigwam?
Ewa-yea! my little owlet!"
 Many things Nokomis taught him
Of the stars that shine in heaven;
Showed him Ishkoodah, the comet,
Ishkoodah, with fiery tresses;
Showed the Death-Dance of the spirits,
Warriors with their plumes and war-clubs,
Flaring far away to northward
In the frosty nights of Winter;
Showed the broad white road in heaven,
Pathway of the ghosts, the shadows,
Running straight across the heavens,
Crowded with the ghosts, the shadows.

In the hot summer evenings, the children of the Chippewa Algonquins, along the shores of the upper lakes, and in the northern latitudes, frequently assemble before their parents' lodges, and amuse themselves by little chants of various kinds, with shouts and wild dancing. Attracted by such shouts of merriment and gambols, I walked out one evening, to a green lawn skirting the edge of the St. Mary's river, with the fall in full view, to get hold of the meaning of some of these chants. The air and the plain were literally sparkling with the phosphorescent light of the fire-fly.   By dint of attention, repeated on one or two occasions, the following succession of words was caught.   They were addressed to this insect:

> Wau wau tay see!
> Wau wau tay see!
> E mow e shin
> Tshe bwau ne baun-e wee!
> Be eghaun—be eghaun—ewee!
> Wa wau tay see!
> Wa wau tay see!
> Was sa koon ain je gun
> Was sa koon ain je gun.

Literal translation: Flitting-white-fire-insect!   Waving-white-fire-bug! give me light before I go to bed! give me light before I go to sleep.   Come little dancing-white-fire-bug! Come little flitting-white-fire-beast!   Light me with your bright white-flame-instrument—your little candle.

Metre there was none, at least, of a regular character: they were the wild improvisations of children in a merry mood. . . .

> Fire-fly, fire-fly! bright little thing,
> Light me to bed, and my song I will sing.
> Give me your light, as you fly o'er my head,
> That I may merrily go to my bed.
> Give me your light o'er the grass as you creep,
> That I may joyfully go to my sleep.
> Come little fire-fly—come little beast—
> Come! and I'll make you to-morrow a feast.
> Come little candle that flies as I sing,
> Bright little fairy-bug—night's little king;
> Come, and I'll dance as you guide me along,
> Come, and I'll pay you, my bug, with a song.
> —"Chant to the Fire-Fly," in *Oneóta*, p. 61.

> At the door on summer evenings
> Sat the little Hiawatha;
> Heard the whispering of the pine-trees,
> Heard the lapping of the waters,
> Sounds of music, words of wonder;

"Minne-wawa!" said the pine-trees.
"Mudway-aushka!" said the water.
    Saw the fire-fly, Wah-wah-taysee,
Flitting through the dusk of evening,
With the twinkle of its candle
Lighting up the brakes and bushes,
And he sang the song of children,
Sang the song Nokomis taught him:
"Wah-wah-taysee, little fire-fly,
Little, flitting, white-fire insect,
Little, dancing, white-fire creature,
Light me with your little candle,
Ere upon my bed I lay me,
Ere in sleep I close my eyelids!"
    Saw the moon rise from the water
Rippling, rounding from the water,
Saw the flecks and shadows on it,
Whispered, "What is that, Nokomis?"
And the good Nokomis answered:
"Once a warrior, very angry,
Seized his grandmother, and threw her
Up into the sky at midnight;
Right against the moon he threw her;
'T is her body that you see there."
    Saw the rainbow in the heaven,
In the eastern sky, the rainbow,
Whispered, "What is that, Nokomis?"
And the good Nokomis answered:
"'T is the heaven of flowers you see there;
All the wild-flowers of the forest,
All the lilies of the prairie,
When on earth they fade and perish,
Blossom in that heaven above us."
    When he heard the owls at midnight,
Hooting, laughing in the forest,
"What is that?" he cried in terror,
"What is that," he said, "Nokomis?"
And the good Nokomis answered:
"That is but the owl and owlet,
Talking in their native language,
Talking, scolding at each other."
    Then the little Hiawatha
Learned of every bird its language,

Learned their names and all their secrets,
How they built their nests in Summer,
Where they hid themselves in Winter,
Talked with them whene'er he met them,
Called them "Hiawatha's Chickens."
  Of all beasts he learned the language,
Learned their names and all their secrets,
How the beavers built their lodges,
Where the squirrels hid their acorns,
How the reindeer ran so swiftly,
Why the rabbit was so timid,
Talked with them whene'er he met them,
Called them "Hiawatha's Brothers."
  Then Iagoo, the great boaster,
He the marvellous story-teller,
He the traveller and the talker,
He the friend of old Nokomis,
Made a bow for Hiawatha;
From a branch of ash he made it,
From an oak-bough made the arrows,
Tipped with flint, and winged with feathers,
And the cord he made of deer-skin.
  Then he said to Hiawatha:
"Go, my son, into the forest,
Where the red deer herd together,
Kill for us a famous roebuck,
Kill for us a deer with antlers!"
  Forth into the forest straightway
All alone walked Hiawatha
Proudly, with his bow and arrows;
And the birds sang round him, o'er him,
"Do not shoot us, Hiawatha!"
Sang the robin, the Opechee,
Sang the bluebird, the Owaissa,
"Do not shoot us, Hiawatha!"
  Up the oak-tree, close beside him,
Sprang the squirrel, Adjidaumo,
In and out among the branches,
Coughed and chattered from the oak-tree,
Laughed, and said between his laughing,
"Do not shoot me, Hiawatha!"
  And the rabbit from his pathway
Leaped aside, and at a distance

Sat erect upon his haunches,
Half in fear and half in frolic,
Saying to the little hunter,
"Do not shoot me, Hiawatha!"
   But he heeded not, nor heard them,
For his thoughts were with the red deer;
On their tracks his eyes were fastened,
Leading downward to the river,
To the ford across the river,
And as one in slumber walked he.
   Hidden in the alder-bushes,
There he waited till the deer came,
Till he saw two antlers lifted,
Saw two eyes look from the thicket,
Saw two nostrils point to windward,
And a deer came down the pathway,
Flecked with leafy light and shadow.
And his heart within him fluttered,
Trembled like the leaves above him,
Like the birch-leaf palpitated,
As the deer came down the pathway.
   Then, upon one knee uprising,
Hiawatha aimed an arrow;
Scarce a twig moved with his motion,
Scarce a leaf was stirred or rustled,
But the wary roebuck started,
Stamped with all his hoofs together,
Listened with one foot uplifted,
Leaped as if to meet the arrow;
Ah! the singing, fatal arrow;
Like a wasp it buzzed and stung him!
   Dead he lay there in the forest,
By the ford across the river;
Beat his timid heart no longer,
But the heart of Hiawatha
Throbbed and shouted and exulted,
As he bore the red deer homeward,
And Iagoo and Nokomis
Hailed his coming with applauses.
   From the red deer's hide Nokomis
Made a cloak for Hiawatha,
From the red deer's flesh Nokomis
Made a banquet in his honor.

All the village came and feasted,
All the guests praised Hiawatha,
Called him Strong-Heart, Soan-ge-taha!
Called him Loon-Heart, Mahn-go-taysee!

IV

HIAWATHA AND MUDJEKEEWIS

. . . THE timidity and rawness of the boy quickly gave way in the courageous developments of the man. He soon evinced the sagacity, cunning, perseverance, and heroic courage which constitute the admiration of the Indians. And he relied largely upon these in the gratification of an ambitious, vainglorious, and mischief-loving disposition. In wisdom and energy he was superior to any one who had ever lived before. Yet he was simple when circumstances required it, and was ever the object of tricks and ridicule in others. He could transform himself into any animal he pleased, being man or manito, as circumstances rendered necessary. . . . From "Manabozho," in *Algic Researches*, v. 1, 136–37.

. . . He thought to himself, "It is singular that I am so simple, and my grandmother so wise, and that I have neither father nor mother. I have never heard a word about them. I must ask and find out." He went home and sat down silent and dejected. At length his grandmother asked him, "Manabozho, what is the matter with you?" He answered, "I wish you would tell me whether I have any parents living, and who my relatives are." Knowing that he was of a wicked and revengeful disposition, she dreaded telling him the story of his parentage, but he insisted on her compliance. "Yes," she said, "you have a father and three brothers living. Your mother is dead. She was taken without the consent of her parents by your father the West. Your brothers are the North, East, and South, and, being older than yourself, your father has given them great power with the winds, according to their names. You are the youngest of his children. I have nourished you from your infancy, for your mother died in giving you birth, owing to the ill treatment of your father. I have no relations besides you this side of the planet in which I was born, and from which I was precipitated by female jealousy. Your mother was my only child, and you are my only hope."

He appeared to be rejoiced to hear that his father was living, for he had already thought in his heart to try and kill him. He told his grandmother he should set out in the morning to visit him. She said it was a long distance to the place where Ningabiun* lived. But that had no effect to stop him, for he had now attained manhood, possessed a giant's height, and was endowed by nature with a giant's strength and power. . . . *Ibid.*, p. 139–40.

> Out of childhood into manhood
> Now had grown my Hiawatha,
> Skilled in all the craft of hunters,
> Learned in all the lore of old men,
> In all youthful sports and pastimes,
> In all manly arts and labors.
>   Swift of foot was Hiawatha;
> He could shoot an arrow from him,
> And run forward with such fleetness
> That the arrow fell behind him!
> Strong of arm was Hiawatha;
> He could shoot ten arrows upward,
> Shoot them with such strength and swiftness
> That the tenth had left the bow-string
> Ere the first to earth had fallen!
> He had mittens, Minjekahwun,
> Magic mittens made of deer-skin;
> When upon his hands he wore them,
> He could smite the rocks asunder,
> He could grind them into powder.
> He had moccasins enchanted,
> Magic moccasins of deer-skin;
> When he bound them round his ankles,
> When upon his feet he tied them,
> . At each stride a mile he measured!
>   Much he questioned old Nokomis
> Of his father Mudjekeewis;

* This is a term for the west wind. It is a derivative from Ka-bian-oong, the proper appellation for the occident.

Learned from her the fatal secret
Of the beauty of his mother,
Of the falsehood of his father;
And his heart was hot within him,
Like a living coal his heart was.
    Then he said to old Nokomis,
"I will go to Mudjekeewis,
See how fares it with my father,
At the doorways of the West-Wind,
At the portals of the Sunset!"
    From his lodge went Hiawatha,
Dressed for travel, armed for hunting,
Dressed in deer-skin shirt and leggings,
Richly wrought with quills and wampum;
On his head his eagle-feathers,
Round his waist his belt of wampum,
In his hand his bow of ash-wood,
Strung with sinews of the reindeer;
In his quiver oaken arrows,
Tipped with jasper, winged with feathers;
With his mittens, Minjekahwun,
With his moccasins enchanted.
    Warning said the old Nokomis,
"Go not forth, O Hiawatha!
To the kingdom of the West-Wind,
To the realms of Mudjekeewis,
Lest he harm you with his magic,
Lest he kill you with his cunning!"

. . . He set out and soon reached the place, for every step
he took covered a large surface of ground. The meeting took
place on a high mountain in the West. His father was very
happy to see him. He also appeared pleased. They spent
some days in talking with each other. One evening Manabozho
asked his father what he was most afraid of on earth. He
replied, "Nothing." "But is there not something you dread
here? tell me." At last his father said, yielding, "Yes, there is
a black stone found in such a place. It is the only thing earthly
I am afraid of; for if it should hit me or any part of my body,
it would injure me very much." He said this as a secret, and
in return asked his son the same question. Knowing each
other's power, although the son's was limited, the father feared

him on account of his great strength. Manabozho answered, "Nothing!" intending to avoid the question, or to refer to some harmless object as the one of which he was afraid. He was asked again and again, and answered "Nothing!" But the West said, "There must be something you are afraid of." "Well! I will tell you," says Manabozho, "what it is." But, before he would pronounce the word, he affected great dread. "Ie-ee—Ie-ee—it is—it is," said he, "yeo! yeo! I cannot name it, I am seized with a dread." The West told him to banish his fears. He commenced again, in a strain of mock sensitiveness repeating the same words; at last he cried out, "It is the root of the apukwa [bulrush]." He appeared to be exhausted by the effort of pronouncing the word, in all this skilfully acting a studied part.

Some time after he observed, "I will get some of the black rock." The West said, "Far be it from you; do not do so, my son." He still persisted. "Well," said the father, "I will also get the apukwa root." Manabozho immediately cried out, "Kago! kago!" [Do not—do not!] affecting, as before, to be in great dread of it, but really wishing, by this course, to urge on the West to procure it, that he might draw him into combat. He went out and got a large piece of the black rock, and brought it home. The West also took care to bring the dreaded root.

In the course of conversation he asked his father whether he had been the cause of his mother's death. The answer was "Yes!" He then took up the rock and struck him. Blow led to blow, and here commenced an obstinate and furious combat, which continued several days. Fragments of the rock, broken off under Manabozho's blows, can be seen in various places to this day. The root did not prove as mortal a weapon as his well-acted fears had led his father to expect, although he suffered severely from the blows. This battle commenced on the mountains. The West was forced to give ground. Manabozho drove him across rivers, and over mountains and lakes, and at last he came to the brink of this world.

"Hold!" cried he, "my son, you know my power, and that it is impossible to kill me. Desist, and I will also portion you

out with as much power as your brothers.   The four quarters
of the globe are already occupied; but you can go and do a
great deal of good to the people of this earth, which is infested
with large serpents, beasts, and monsters, who make great
havoc among the inhabitants.   Go and do good.   You have
the power now to do so, and your fame with the beings of this
earth will last forever.   When you have finished your work, I
will have a place provided for you.   You will then go and sit
with your brother Kabibboonocca in the north."

Manabozho was pacified.   He returned to his lodge, where
he was confined by the wounds he had received.   But from his
grandmother's skill in medicines he was soon recovered. . . .
From "Manabozho," in *Algic Researches,* v. 1, 140–43.

> But the fearless Hiawatha
> Heeded not her woman's warning;
> Forth he strode into the forest,
> At each stride a mile he measured;
> Lurid seemed the sky above him,
> Lurid seemed the earth beneath him,
> Hot and close the air around him,
> Filled with smoke and fiery vapors,
> As of burning woods and prairies.
> For his heart was hot within him,
> Like a living coal his heart was.
> So he journeyed westward, westward,
> Left the fleetest deer behind him,
> Left the antelope and bison;
> Crossed the rushing Esconaba,*
> Crossed the mighty Mississippi,
> Passed the Mountains of the Prairie,
> Passed the land of Crows and Foxes,
> Passed the dwellings of the Blackfeet,
> Came unto the Rocky Mountains,
> To the kingdom of the West-Wind,
> Where upon the gusty summits
> Sat the ancient Mudjekeewis,
> Ruler of the winds of heaven.
> Filled with awe was Hiawatha

* A river of the Upper Peninsula of Michigan, emptying into the Little
Bay de Noc.   Now spelled Escanaba.

At the aspect of his father.
On the air about him wildly
Tossed and streamed his cloudy tresses,
Gleamed like drifting snow his tresses,
Glared like Ishkoodah, the comet,
Like the star with fiery tresses.

Filled with joy was Mudjekeewis
When he looked on Hiawatha,
Saw his youth rise up before him
In the face of Hiawatha,
Saw the beauty of Wenonah
From the grave rise up before him.

"Welcome!" said he, "Hiawatha,
To the kingdom of the West-Wind!
Long have I been waiting for you!
Youth is lovely, age is lonely,
Youth is fiery, age is frosty;
You bring back the days departed,
You bring back my youth of passion,
And the beautiful Wenonah!"

Many days they talked together,
Questioned, listened, waited, answered;
Much the mighty Mudjekeewis
Boasted of his ancient prowess,
Of his perilous adventures,
His indomitable courage,
His invulnerable body.

Patiently sat Hiawatha,
Listening to his father's boasting;
With a smile he sat and listened,
Uttered neither threat nor menace;
Neither word nor look betrayed him,
But his heart was hot within him,
Like a living coal his heart was.

Then he said, "O Mudjekeewis,
Is there nothing that can harm you?
Nothing that you are afraid of?"
And the mighty Mudjekeewis,
Grand and gracious in his boasting,
Answered, saying, "There is nothing,
Nothing but the black rock yonder,
Nothing but the fatal Wawbeek!"

And he looked at Hiawatha

With a wise look and benignant,
With a countenance paternal,
Looked with pride upon the beauty
Of his tall and graceful figure,
Saying, "O my Hiawatha!
Is there anything can harm you?
Anything you are afraid of?"
    But the wary Hiawatha
Paused awhile, as if uncertain,
Held his peace, as if resolving,
And then answered, "There is nothing,
Nothing but the bulrush yonder,
Nothing but the great Apukwa!"
    And as Mudjekeewis, rising,
Stretched his hand to pluck the bulrush,
Hiawatha cried in terror,
Cried in well-dissembled terror,
"Kago! kago! do not touch it!"
"Ah, kaween!" said Mudjekeewis,
"No indeed, I will not touch it!"
    Then they talked of other matters:
First of Hiawatha's brothers,
First of Wabun, of the East-Wind,
Of the South-Wind, Shawondasee,
Of the North, Kabibonokka;
Then of Hiawatha's mother,
Of the beautiful Wenonah,
Of her birth upon the meadow,
Of her death, as old Nokomis
Had remembered and related.
    And he cried, "O Mudjekeewis,
It was you who killed Wenonah,
Took her young life and her beauty,
Broke the Lily of the Prairie,
Trampled it beneath your footsteps;
You confess it! you confess it!"
And the mighty Mudjekeewis
Tossed upon the wind his tresses,
Bowed his hoary head in anguish,
With a silent nod assented.
    Then up started Hiawatha,
And with threatening look and gesture
Laid his hand upon the black rock,
On the fatal Wawbeek laid it,

With his mittens, Minjekahwun,
Rent the jutting crag asunder,
Smote and crushed it into fragments,
Hurled them madly at his father,
The remorseful Mudjekeewis,
For his heart was hot within him,
Like a living coal his heart was.

But the ruler of the West-Wind
Blew the fragments backward from him,
With the breathing of his nostrils,
With the tempest of his anger,
Blew them back at his assailant;
Seized the bulrush, the Apukwa,
Dragged it with its roots and fibres
From the margin of the meadow,
From its ooze, the giant bulrush;
Long and loud laughed Hiawatha!

Then began the deadly conflict,
Hand to hand among the mountains;
From his eyry screamed the eagle,
The Keneu, the great war-eagle,
Sat upon the crags around them,
Wheeling flapped his wings above them.

Like a tall tree in the tempest
Bent and lashed the giant bulrush;
And in masses huge and heavy
Crashing fell the fatal Wawbeek;
Till the earth shook with the tumult
And confusion of the battle,
And the air was full of shoutings,
And the thunder of the mountains,
Starting, answered, "Baim-wawa!"

Back retreated Mudjekeewis,
Rushing westward o'er the mountains,
Stumbling westward down the mountains,
Three whole days retreated fighting,
Still pursued by Hiawatha
To the doorways of the West-Wind,
To the portals of the Sunset,
To the earth's remotest border,
Where into the empty spaces
Sinks the sun, as a flamingo
Drops into her nest at nightfall,
In the melancholy marshes.

"Hold!" at length cried Mudjekeewis,
"Hold, my son, my Hiawatha!
'T is impossible to kill me,
For you cannot kill the immortal.
I have put you to this trial,
But to know and prove your courage;
Now receive the prize of valor!

"Go back to your home and people,
Live among them, toil among them,
Cleanse the earth from all that harms it,
Clear the fishing-grounds and rivers,
Slay all monsters and magicians,
All the Wendigoes, the giants,
All the serpents, the Kenabeeks,
As I slew the Mishe-Mokwa,
Slew the Great Bear of the mountains.

"And at last when Death draws near you,
When the awful eyes of Pauguk
Glare upon you in the darkness,
I will share my kingdom with you,
Ruler shall you be thenceforward
Of the Northwest-Wind, Keewaydin,
Of the home-wind, the Keewaydin."

Thus was fought that famous battle
In the dreadful days of Shah-shah,
In the days long since departed,
In the kingdom of the West-Wind.
Still the hunter sees its traces
Scattered far o'er hill and valley;
Sees the giant bulrush growing
By the ponds and water-courses,
Sees the masses of the Wawbeek
Lying still in every valley.

Homeward now went Hiawatha;
Pleasant was the landscape round him,
Pleasant was the air above him,
For the bitterness of anger
Had departed wholly from him,
From his brain the thought of vengeance,
From his heart the burning fever.

. . . He continued making bows and arrows without number, but he had no heads for his arrows. At last Noko told him that an old man who lived at some distance could make them.

He sent her to get some. She soon returned with her conaus or wrapper full. Still he told her he had not enough, and sent her again. She returned with as much more. He thought to himself, "I must find out the way of making these heads." Cunning and curiosity prompted him to make the discovery. But he deemed it necessary to deceive his grandmother in so doing. "Noko," said he, "while I take my drum and rattle, and sing my war songs, go and try to get me some *larger* heads for my arrows, for those you brought me are all of the same size. Go and see whether the old man cannot make some a little larger." He followed her as she went, keeping at a distance, and saw the old artificer at work, and so discovered his process. He also beheld the old man's daughter, and perceived that she was very beautiful. He felt his breast beat with a new emotion, but said nothing. He took care to get home before his grandmother, and commenced singing as if he had never left his lodge. When the old woman came near, she heard his drum and rattle, without any suspicion that he had followed her. She delivered him the arrow-heads. . . . From "Manabozho," in *Algic Researches,* v. 1, 147–48.

> Only once his pace he slackened,
> Only once he paused or halted,
> Paused to purchase heads of arrows
> Of the ancient Arrow-maker,
> In the land of the Dacotahs,
> Where the Falls of Minnehaha
> Flash and gleam among the oak-trees,
> Laugh and leap into the valley.
> There the ancient Arrow-maker
> Made his arrow-heads of sandstone,
> Arrow-heads of chalcedony,
> Arrow-heads of flint and jasper,
> Smoothed and sharpened at the edges,
> Hard and polished, keen and costly.
> With him dwelt his dark-eyed daughter,
> Wayward as the Minnehaha,
> With her moods of shade and sunshine,
> Eyes that smiled and frowned alternate,
> Feet as rapid as the river,
> Tresses flowing like the water,

And as musical a laughter;
And he named her from the river,
From the water-fall he named her,
Minnehaha, Laughing Water.

Was it then for heads of arrows,
Arrow-heads of chalcedony,
Arrow-heads of flint and jasper,
That my Hiawatha halted
In the land of the Dacotahs?

Was it not to see the maiden,
See the face of Laughing Water
Peeping from behind the curtain,
Hear the rustling of her garments
From behind the waving curtain,
As one sees the Minnehaha
Gleaming, glancing through the branches,
As one hears the Laughing Water
From behind its screen of branches?

Who shall say what thoughts and visions
Fill the fiery brains of young men?
Who shall say what dreams of beauty
Filled the heart of Hiawatha?
All he told to old Nokomis,
When he reached the lodge at sunset,
Was the meeting with his father,
Was his fight with Mudjekeewis;
Not a word he said of arrows,
Not a word of Laughing Water!

V

HIAWATHA'S FASTING

. . . ONE evening the old woman said, "My son, you ought to
fast before you go to war, as your brothers frequently do, to
find out whether you will be successful or not." He said he
had no objection, and immediately commenced a fast for several days. He would retire every day from the lodge so far as
to be out of reach of his grandmother's voice. . . . From
"Manabozho," in *Algic Researches,* v. 1, 148–50.

In times past, a poor Indian was living with his wife and
children in a beautiful part of the country. He was not only

poor, but inexpert in procuring food for his family, and his children were all too young to give him assistance. Although poor,
he was a man of a kind and contented disposition. He was always thankful to the Great Spirit for everything he received.
The same disposition was inherited by his eldest son, who had
now arrived at the proper age to undertake the ceremony of
the Ke-ig-uish-im-o-win, or fast, to see what kind of a spirit
would be his guide and guardian through life. Wunzh, for this
was his name, had been an obedient boy from his infancy, and
was of a pensive, thoughtful, and mild disposition, so that he
was beloved by the whole family. As soon as the first indications of spring appeared, they built him the customary little
lodge, at a retired spot some distance from their own, where he
would not be disturbed during this solemn rite. In the mean
time he prepared himself, and immediately went into it and
commenced his fast. The first few days he amused himself in
the mornings by walking in the woods and over the mountains,
examining the early plants and flowers, and in this way prepared himself to enjoy his sleep, and, at the same time, stored
his mind with pleasant ideas for his dreams. While he rambled
through the woods, he felt a strong desire to know how the
plants, herbs, and berries grew, without any aid from man, and
why it was that some species were good to eat, and others possessed medicinal or poisonous juices. He recalled these
thoughts to mind after he became too languid to walk about,
and had confined himself strictly to the lodge; he wished he
could dream of something that would prove a benefit to his
father and family, and to all others. "True!" he thought, "the
Great Spirit made all things, and it is to him that we owe our
lives. But could he not make it easier for us to get our food,
than by hunting animals and taking fish? I must try to find
out this in my visions."

On the third day he became weak and faint, and kept his
bed. He fancied, while thus lying, that he saw a handsome
young man coming down from the sky and advancing towards
him. He was richly and gayly dressed, having on a great

many garments of green and yellow colours, but differing in their deeper or lighter shades. He had a plume of waving feathers on his head, and all his motions were graceful.

"I am sent to you, my friend," said the celestial visiter, "by that Great Spirit who made all things in the sky and on the earth. He has seen and knows your motives in fasting. He sees that it is from a kind and benevolent wish to do good to your people, and to procure a benefit for them, and that you do not seek for strength in war or the praise of warriors. I am sent to instruct you, and show you how you can do your kindred good." He then told the young man to arise, and prepare to wrestle with him, as it was only by this means that he could hope to succeed in his wishes. Wunzh knew he was weak from fasting, but he felt his courage rising in his heart, and immediately got up, determined to die rather than fail. He commenced the trial, and, after a protracted effort, was almost exhausted, when the beautiful stranger said, "My friend, it is enough for once; I will come again to try you;" and, smiling on him, he ascended in the air in the same direction from which he came. The next day the celestial visiter reappeared at the same hour and renewed the trial. Wunzh felt that his strength was even less than the day before, but the courage of his mind seemed to increase in proportion as his body became weaker. Seeing this, the stranger again spoke to him in the same words he used before, adding, "To-morrow will be your last trial. Be strong, my friend, for this is the only way you can overcome me, and obtain the boon you seek." On the third day he again appeared at the same time and renewed the struggle. The poor youth was very faint in body, but grew stronger in mind at every contest, and was determined to prevail or perish in the attempt. He exerted his utmost powers, and after the contest had been continued the usual time, the stranger ceased his efforts and declared himself conquered. For the first time he entered the lodge, and sitting down beside the youth, he began to deliver his instructions to him, telling him in what manner he should proceed to take advantage of his victory.

"You have won your desires of the Great Spirit," said the

stranger. "You have wrestled manfully. To-morrow will be the seventh day of your fasting. Your father will give you food to strengthen you, and as it is the last day of trial, you will prevail. I know this, and now tell you what you must do to benefit your family and your tribe. To-morrow," he repeated, "I shall meet you and wrestle with you for the last time; and, as soon as you have prevailed against me, you will strip off my garments and throw me down, clean the earth of roots and weeds, make it soft, and bury me in the spot. When you have done this, leave my body in the earth, and do not disturb it, but come occasionally to visit the place, to see whether I have come to life, and be careful never to let the grass or weeds grow on my grave. Once a month cover me with fresh earth. If you follow my instructions, you will accomplish your object of doing good to your fellow-creatures by teaching them the knowledge I now teach you." He then shook him by the hand and disappeared.

In the morning the youth's father came with some slight refreshments, saying, "My son, you have fasted long enough. If the Great Spirit will favour you, he will do it now. It is seven days since you have tasted food, and you must not sacrifice your life. The Master of Life does not require that." "My father," replied the youth, "wait till the sun goes down. I have a particular reason for extending my fast to that hour." "Very well," said the old man, "I shall wait till the hour arrives, and you feel inclined to eat."

At the usual hour of the day the sky-visiter returned, and the trial of strength was renewed. Although the youth had not availed himself of his father's offer of food, he felt that new strength had been given to him, and that exertion had renewed his strength and fortified his courage. He grasped his angelic antagonist with supernatural strength, threw him down, took from him his beautiful garments and plume, and finding him dead, immediately buried him on the spot, taking all the precautions he had been told of, and being very confident, at the same time, that his friend would again come to life. He then returned to his father's lodge, and partook sparingly of the meal that had been prepared for him.   But he never for a moment forgot the grave of his friend.   He carefully visited it throughout the spring, and weeded out the grass, and kept the ground in a soft and pliant state.   Very soon he saw the tops of the green plumes coming through the ground; and the more careful he was to obey his instructions in keeping the ground in order, the faster they grew.   He was, however, careful to conceal the exploit from his father.   Days and weeks had passed in this way.   The summer was now drawing towards a close, when one day, after a long absence in hunting, Wunzh invited his father to follow him to the quiet and lonesome spot of his former fast.   The lodge had been removed, and the weeds kept from growing on the circle where it stood, but in its place stood a tall and graceful plant, with bright-coloured silken hair, surmounted with nodding plumes and stately leaves, and golden clusters on each side.   "It is my friend," shouted the lad; "it is the friend of all mankind.   It is *Mondawmin*.   We need no longer rely on hunting alone; for, as long as this gift is cherished and taken care of, the ground itself will give us a living."   He then pulled an ear.   "See, my father," said he, "this is what I fasted for.   The Great Spirit has listened to my voice, and sent us something new, and henceforth our people will not alone depend upon the chase or upon the waters."

He then communicated to his father the instructions given him by the stranger.   He told him that the broad husks must be torn away, as he had pulled off the garments in his wrestling; and having done this, directed him how the ear must be held before the fire till the outer skin became brown, while all the milk was retained in the grain.   The whole family then united in a feast on the newly-grown ears, expressing gratitude to the Merciful Spirit who gave it.   So corn came into the world, and has ever since been preserved.—"Mon-daw-min; or, The Origin of Indian Corn, An Odjibwa Tale," in *Algic Researches,* v. 1, p. 122–28.   Revised as "Mondamin, or the Origin of the Zea Maize," in *H. & S. I.,* pt. 2, p. 230–32.   The incident also occurs in "The Magician of Lake Huron; an Ottowa Tale . . . ," in *Oneóta,* p. 483–84.

You shall hear how Hiawatha
Prayed and fasted in the forest,
Not for greater skill in hunting,
Not for greater craft in fishing,
Not for triumphs in the battle,
And renown among the warriors,
But for profit of the people,
For advantage of the nations.
    First he built a lodge for fasting,
Built a wigwam in the forest,
By the shining Big-Sea-Water,
In the blithe and pleasant Spring-time,
In the Moon of Leaves he built it,
And, with dreams and visions many,
Seven whole days and nights he fasted.
    On the first day of his fasting
Through the leafy woods he wandered;
Saw the deer start from the thicket,
Saw the rabbit in his burrow,
Heard the pheasant, Bena, drumming,
Heard the squirrel, Adjidaumo,
Rattling in his hoard of acorns,
Saw the pigeon, the Omeme,
Building nests among the pine-trees,
And in flocks the wild goose, Wawa,
Flying to the fen-lands northward,
Whirring, wailing far above him.
"Master of Life!" he cried, desponding,
"Must our lives depend on these things?"
    On the next day of his fasting
By the river's brink he wandered,
Through the Muskoday, the meadow,
Saw the wild rice, Mahnomonee,
Saw the blueberry, Meenahga,
And the strawberry, Odahmin,
And the gooseberry, Shahbomin,
And the grape-vine, the Bemahgut,
Trailing o'er the alder-branches,
Filling all the air with fragrance!
"Master of Life!" he cried, desponding,
"Must our lives depend on these things?"
    On the third day of his fasting
By the lake he sat and pondered,
By the still, transparent water;

Saw the sturgeon, Nahma, leaping,
Scattering drops like beads of wampum,
Saw the yellow perch, the Sahwa,
Like a sunbeam in the water,
Saw the pike, the Maskenozha,
And the herring, Okahahwis,
And the Shawgashee, the craw-fish!
"Master of Life!" he cried, desponding,
"Must our lives depend on these things?"
　　On the fourth day of his fasting
In his lodge he lay exhausted;
From his couch of leaves and branches
Gazing with half-open eyelids,
Full of shadowy dreams and visions,
On the dizzy, swimming landscape,
On the gleaming of the water,
On the splendor of the sunset.
　　And he saw a youth approaching,
Dressed in garments green and yellow,
Coming through the purple twilight,
Through the splendor of the sunset;
Plumes of green bent o'er his forehead,
And his hair was soft and golden.
　　Standing at the open doorway,
Long he looked at Hiawatha,
Looked with pity and compassion
On his wasted form and features,
And, in accents like the sighing
Of the South-Wind in the tree-tops,
Said he, "O my Hiawatha!
All your prayers are heard in heaven,
For you pray not like the others;
Not for greater skill in hunting,
Not for greater craft in fishing,
Not for triumph in the battle,
Nor renown among the warriors,
But for profit of the people,
For advantage of the nations.
　　"From the Master of Life descending,
I, the friend of man, Mondamin,
Come to warn you and instruct you,
How by struggle and by labor
You shall gain what you have prayed for.

Rise up from your bed of branches,
Rise, O youth, and wrestle with me!"
    Faint with famine, Hiawatha
Started from his bed of branches,
From the twilight of his wigwam
Forth into the flush of sunset
Came, and wrestled with Mondamin;
At his touch he felt new courage
Throbbing in his brain and bosom,
Felt new life and hope and vigor
Run through every nerve and fibre.
    So they wrestled there together
In the glory of the sunset,
And the more they strove and struggled,
Stronger still grew Hiawatha;
Till the darkness fell around them,
And the heron, the Shuh-shuh-gah,
From her nest among the pine-trees,
Gave a cry of lamentation,
Gave a scream of pain and famine.
    "'T is enough!" then said Mondamin,
Smiling upon Hiawatha,
"But to-morrow, when the sun sets,
I will come again to try you."
And he vanished, and was seen not;
Whether sinking as the rain sinks,
Whether rising as the mists rise,
Hiawatha saw not, knew not,
Only saw that he had vanished,
Leaving him alone and fainting,
With the misty lake below him,
And the reeling stars above him.
    On the morrow and the next day,
When the sun through heaven descending
Like a red and burning cinder
From the hearth of the Great Spirit,
Fell into the western waters,
Came Mondamin for the trial,
For the strife with Hiawatha;
Came as silent as the dew comes,
From the empty air appearing,
Into empty air returning,
Taking shape when earth it touches

But invisible to all men
In its coming and its going.
   Thrice they wrestled there together
In the glory of the sunset,
Till the darkness fell around them,
Till the heron, the Shuh-shuh-gah,
From her nest among the pine-trees,
Uttered her loud cry of famine,
And Mondamin paused to listen.
   Tall and beautiful he stood there
In his garments green and yellow;
To and fro his plumes above him
Waved and nodded with his breathing,
And the sweat of the encounter
Stood like drops of dew upon him.
   And he cried, "O Hiawatha!
Bravely have you wrestled with me,
Thrice have wrestled stoutly with me,
And the Master of Life, who sees us,
He will give to you the triumph!"
   Then he smiled and said: "To-morrow
Is the last day of your conflict,
Is the last day of your fasting.
You will conquer and o'ercome me;
Make a bed for me to lie in,
Where the rain may fall upon me,
Where the sun may come and warm me;
Strip these garments, green and yellow,
Strip this nodding plumage from me,
Lay me in the earth and make it
Soft and loose and light above me.
   "Let no hand disturb my slumber,
Let no weed nor worm molest me,
Let not Kahgahgee, the raven,
Come to haunt me and molest me,
Only come yourself to watch me,
Till I wake, and start, and quicken,
Till I leap into the sunshine."
   And thus saying, he departed;
Peacefully slept Hiawatha,
But he heard the Wawonaissa,
Heard the whippoorwill complaining,
Perched upon his lonely wigwam;
Heard the rushing Sebowisha,

Heard the rivulet rippling near him,
Talking to the darksome forest;
Heard the sighing of the branches,
As they lifted and subsided
At the passing of the night-wind,
Heard them, as one hears in slumber
Far-off murmurs, dreamy whispers:
Peacefully slept Hiawatha.

On the morrow came Nokomis,
On the seventh day of his fasting,
Came with food for Hiawatha,
Came imploring and bewailing,
Lest his hunger should o'ercome him,
Lest his fasting should be fatal.

But he tasted not, and touched not,
Only said to her, "Nokomis,
Wait until the sun is setting,
Till the darkness falls around us,
Till the heron, the Shuh-shuh-gah,
Crying from the desolate marshes,
Tells us that the day is ended."

Homeward weeping went Nokomis,
Sorrowing for her Hiawatha,
Fearing lest his strength should fail him,
Lest his fasting should be fatal.
He meanwhile sat weary waiting
For the coming of Mondamin,
Till the shadows, pointing eastward,
Lengthened over field and forest,
Till the sun dropped from the heaven,
Floating on the waters westward,
As a red leaf in the Autumn
Falls and floats upon the water,
Falls and sinks into its bosom.

And behold! the young Mondamin,
With his soft and shining tresses,
With his garments green and yellow,
With his long and glossy plumage,
Stood and beckoned at the doorway.
And as one in slumber walking,
Pale and haggard, but undaunted,
From the wigwam Hiawatha
Came and wrestled with Mondamin.

Round about him spun the landscape,

Sky and forest reeled together,
And his strong heart leaped within him
As the sturgeon leaps and struggles
In a net to break its meshes.
Like a ring of fire around him
Blazed and flared the red horizon,
And a hundred suns seemed looking
At the combat of the wrestlers.
   Suddenly upon the greensward
All alone stood Hiawatha,
Panting with his wild exertion,
Palpitating with the struggle;
And before him, breathless, lifeless,
Lay the youth, with hair dishevelled,
Plumage torn, and garments tattered,
Dead he lay there in the sunset.
   And victorious Hiawatha
Made the grave as he commanded,
Stripped the garments from Mondamin,
Stripped his tattered plumage from him,
Laid him in the earth, and made it
Soft and loose and light above him;
And the heron, the Shuh-shuh-gah,
From the melancholy moorlands,
Gave a cry of lamentation,
Gave a cry of pain and anguish!
   Homeward then went Hiawatha
To the lodge of old Nokomis,
And the seven days of his fasting
Were accomplished and completed.
But the place was not forgotten
Where he wrestled with Mondamin;
Nor forgotten nor neglected
Was the grave where lay Mondamin,
Sleeping in the rain and sunshine,
Where his scattered plumes and garments
Faded in the rain and sunshine.
   Day by day did Hiawatha
Go to wait and watch beside it;
Kept the dark mould soft above it,
Kept it clean from weeds and insects,
Drove away, with scoffs and shoutings,
Kahgahgee, the king of ravens.
   Till at length a small green feather

From the earth shot slowly upward,
Then another and another,
And before the Summer ended
Stood the maize in all its beauty,
With its shining robes about it,
And its long, soft, yellow tresses;
And in rapture Hiawatha
Cried aloud, "It is Mondamin!
Yes, the friend of man, Mondamin!"
    Then he called to old Nokomis
And Iagoo, the great boaster,
Showed them where the maize was growing,
Told them of his wondrous vision,
Of his wrestling and his triumph,
Of this new gift to the nations,
Which should be their food forever.
    And still later, when the Autumn
Changed the long, green leaves to yellow,
And the soft and juicy kernels
Grew like wampum hard and yellow,
Then the ripened ears he gathered,
Stripped the withered husks from off them,
As he once had stripped the wrestler,
Gave the first Feast of Mondamin,
And made known unto the people
This new gift of the Great Spirit.

VI

Hiawatha's Friends

At a certain time, a great Manito came on earth, and took a wife of men.   She had four sons at a birth, and died in ushering them into the world.   The first was Manabozho, who is the friend of the human race.   The second Chibiabos, who has the care of the dead, and presides over the country of souls. . . .

Manabozho . . . and his brother Chibiabos lived retired, and were very intimate, planning things for the good of men, and were of superior and surpassing powers of mind and body. . . . From "Allegorical Traditions of the Origin of Men . . . ," in *H. & S. I.*, pt. 1, p. 317.

Two good friends had Hiawatha,
Singled out from all the others,

Bound to him in closest union,
And to whom he gave the right hand
Of his heart, in joy and sorrow;
Chibiabos, the musician,
And the very strong man, Kwasind.

Straight between them ran the pathway,
Never grew the grass upon it;
Singing birds, that utter falsehoods,
Story-tellers, mischief-makers,
Found no eager ear to listen,
Could not breed ill-will between them,
For they kept each other's counsel,
Spake with naked hearts together,
Pondering much and much contriving
How the tribes of men might prosper.

Most beloved by Hiawatha
Was the gentle Chibiabos,
He the best of all musicians,
He the sweetest of all singers.
Beautiful and childlike was he,
Brave as man is, soft as woman,
Pliant as a wand of willow,
Stately as a deer with antlers.

When he sang, the village listened;
All the warriors gathered round him,
All the women came to hear him;
Now he stirred their souls to passion,
Now he melted them to pity.

From the hollow reeds he fashioned
Flutes so musical and mellow,
That the brook, the Sebowisha,
Ceased to murmur in the woodland,
That the wood-birds ceased from singing,
And the squirrel, Adjidaumo,
Ceased his chatter in the oak-tree,
And the rabbit, the Wabasso,
Sat upright to look and listen.

Yes, the brook, the Sebowisha,
Pausing, said, "O Chibiabos,
Teach my waves to flow in music,
Softly as your words in singing!"

Yes, the bluebird, the Owaissa,
Envious, said, "O Chibiabos,
Teach me tones as wild and wayward,

Teach me songs as full of frenzy!"
   Yes, the robin, the Opechee,
Joyous, said, "O Chibiabos,
Teach me tones as sweet and tender,
Teach me songs as full of gladness!"
   And the whippoorwill, Wawonaissa,
Sobbing, said, "O Chibiabos,
Teach me tones as melancholy,
Teach me songs as full of sadness!"
   All the many sounds of nature
Borrowed sweetness from his singing;
All the hearts of men were softened
By the pathos of his music;
For he sang of peace and freedom,
Sang of beauty, love, and longing;
Sang of death, and life undying
In the Islands of the Blessed,
In the kingdom of Ponemah,
In the land of the Hereafter.
   Very dear to Hiawatha
Was the gentle Chibiabos,
He the best of all musicians,
He the sweetest of all singers;
For his gentleness he loved him,
And the magic of his singing.

Manabozho traverses the whole earth. He is the friend
of man. He killed the ancient monsters whose bones we now
see under the earth; and cleared the streams and forests of
many obstructions which the Bad Spirit had put there, to fit
them for our residence.—From "Allegorical Traditions of the
Origin of Men," in *H. & S. I.*, pt. 1, p. 319.

Pauwating* was a village where the young men amused
themselves very much in ancient times, in sports and ball-
playing.

One day as they were engaged in their sports, one of the
strongest and most active, at the moment he was about to
succeed in a trial of lifting, slipped and fell upon his back.
"Ha! ha! ha!" cried the lookers on, "you will never rival

* Place of shallow cataract, named Sault de Ste. Marie on the arrival
of the French. This is the *local* form of the word. The substantive proper
terminates in *eeg*.

Kwasind." He was deeply mortified, and when the sport was over, these words came to his mind. He could not recollect any man of this name. He thought he would ask the old man, the story-teller of the village, the next time he came to the lodge. The opportunity soon occurred.

"My grandfather," said he, "who was Kwasind? I am very anxious to know what he could do."

Kwasind, the old man replied, was a listless idle boy. He would not play when the other boys played, and his parents could never get him to do any kind of labour. He was always making excuses. His parents took notice, however, that he fasted for days together, but they could not learn what spirit he supplicated, or had chosen as the guardian spirit to attend him through life. He was so inattentive to his parents' requests, that he, at last, became a subject of reproach.

"Ah," said his mother to him one day, "is there any young man of your age, in all the village, who does so little for his parents? You neither hunt nor fish. You take no interest in any thing, whether labour or amusement, which engages the attention of your equals in years. I have often set my nets* in the coldest days of winter, without any assistance from you. And I have taken them up again, while you remained inactive at the lodge fire. Are you not ashamed of such idleness? Go, I bid you, and wring out that net, which I have just taken from the water."

Kwasind saw that there was a determination to make him obey. He did not therefore make any excuses, but went out and took up the net. He carefully folded it, doubled and re-doubled it, forming it into a roll, and then with an easy twist of his hands wrung it short off, with as much ease as if every twine had been a thin brittle fibre. Here, they at once saw, the secret of his reluctance. He possessed supernatural strength.

After this, the young men were playing one day on the plain, where there was lying one of those large, heavy, black

---

* Nets are set in winter, in high northern latitudes, through orifices cut in the ice.

pieces of rock, which Manabozho is said to have cast at his father. Kwasind took it up with much ease, and threw it into the river. After this, he accompanied his father on a hunting excursion into a remote forest. They came to a place where the wind had thrown a great many trees into a narrow pass. "We must go the other way," said the old man, "it is impossible to get the burdens through this place." He sat down to rest himself, took out his smoking apparatus, and gave a short time to reflection. When he had finished, Kwasind had lifted away the largest pine trees, and pulled them out of the path.

Sailing one day in his canoe, Kwasind saw a large furred animal, which he immediately recognized to be the king of beavers. He plunged into the water in pursuit of it. His companions were in the greatest astonishment and alarm, supposing he would perish. He often dove down and remained a long time under water, pursuing the animal from island to island; and at last returned with the kingly prize. After this, his fame spread far and wide, and no hunter would presume to compete with him. . . . From "Kwasind, or The Fearfully Strong Man," in *Algic Researches,* v. 2, p. 160–63.

> Dear, too, unto Hiawatha
> Was the very strong man, Kwasind,
> He the strongest of all mortals,
> He the mightiest among many;
> For his very strength he loved him,
> For his strength allied to goodness.
> Idle in his youth was Kwasind,
> Very listless, dull, and dreamy,
> Never played with other children,
> Never fished and never hunted,
> Not like other children was he;
> But they saw that much he fasted,
> Much his Manito entreated,
> Much besought his Guardian Spirit.
> "Lazy Kwasind!" said his mother,
> "In my work you never help me!
> In the Summer you are roaming
> Idly in the fields and forests;
> In the Winter you are cowering

O'er the firebrands in the wigwam!
In the coldest days of Winter
I must break the ice for fishing;
With my nets you never help me!
At the door my nets are hanging,
Dripping, freezing with the water;
Go and wring them, Yenadizze!
Go and dry them in the sunshine!"

Slowly, from the ashes, Kwasind
Rose, but made no angry answer;
From the lodge went forth in silence,
Took the nets, that hung together,
Dripping, freezing at the doorway;
Like a wisp of straw he wrung them,
Like a wisp of straw he broke them,
Could not wring them without breaking,
Such the strength was in his fingers.

"Lazy Kwasind!" said his father,
"In the hunt you never help me;
Every bow you touch is broken,
Snapped asunder every arrow;
Yet come with me to the forest,
You shall bring the hunting homeward."

Down a narrow pass they wandered,
Where a brooklet led them onward,
Where the trail of deer and bison
Marked the soft mud on the margin,
Till they found all further passage
Shut against them, barred securely
By the trunks of trees uprooted,
Lying lengthwise, lying crosswise,
And forbidding further passage.

"We must go back," said the old man,
"O'er these logs we cannot clamber;
Not a woodchuck could get through them,
Not a squirrel clamber o'er them!"
And straightway his pipe he lighted,
And sat down to smoke and ponder.
But before his pipe was finished,
Lo! the path was cleared before him:
All the trunks had Kwasind lifted,
To the right hand, to the left hand,
Shot the pine-trees swift as arrows,
Hurled the cedars light as lances.

"Lazy Kwasind!" said the young men,
As they sported in the meadow;
"Why stand idly looking at us,
Leaning on the rock behind you?
Come and wrestle with the others,
Let us pitch the quoit together!"
    Lazy Kwasind made no answer,
To their challenge made no answer,
Only rose, and, slowly turning,
Seized the huge rock in his fingers,
Tore it from its deep foundation,
Poised it in the air a moment,
Pitched it sheer into the river,
Sheer into the swift Pauwating,
Where it still is seen in Summer.
    Once as down that foaming river,
Down the rapids of Pauwating,
Kwasind sailed with his companions,
In the stream he saw a beaver,
Saw Ahmeek, the King of Beavers,
Struggling with the rushing currents,
Rising, sinking in the water.
    Without speaking, without pausing,
Kwasind leaped into the river,
Plunged beneath the bubbling surface,
Through the whirlpools chased the beaver,
Followed him among the islands,
Stayed so long beneath the water,
That his terrified companions
Cried, "Alas! good-by to Kwasind!
We shall never more see Kwasind!"
But he reappeared triumphant,
And upon his shining shoulders
Brought the beaver, dead and dripping,
Brought the King of all the Beavers.
    And these two, as I have told you,
Were the friends of Hiawatha,
Chibiabos, the musician,
And the very strong man, Kwasind.
Long they lived in peace together,
Spake with naked hearts together,
Pondering much and much contriving
How the tribes of men might prosper.

VII

Hiawatha's Sailing

. . . The latter [Mishosha] possessed a magic canoe which would rush forward through the water on the utterance of a charm, with a speed that would outstrip the wind. Hundreds of miles were performed in as many minutes. . . . From "Mythology, Superstitions, and Religion of the Algonquins," in *Oneóta,* p. 460.

. . . When Hiawatha assumed the duties of an individual, at Tioto, he carefully drew out from the water his beautiful talismanic canoe, which had served for horses and chariot, in his initial excursions through the Iroquois territories, and it was carefully secured on land, and never used except in his journeys to attend the general councils. . . . From "Hiawatha . . . ," in *H. & S. I.,* pt. 3, p. 315.

"Give me of your bark, O Birch-Tree!
Of your yellow bark, O Birch-Tree!
Growing by the rushing river,
Tall and stately in the valley!
I a light canoe will build me,
Build a swift Cheemaun for sailing,
That shall float upon the river,
Like a yellow leaf in Autumn,
Like a yellow water-lily!
  "Lay aside your cloak, O Birch-Tree!
Lay aside your white-skin wrapper,
For the Summer-time is coming,
And the sun is warm in heaven,
And you need no white-skin wrapper!"
  Thus aloud cried Hiawatha
In the solitary forest,
By the rushing Taquamenaw,*
When the birds were singing gayly,
In the Moon of Leaves were singing,
And the sun, from sleep awaking,
Started up and said, "Behold me!
Gheezis, the great Sun, behold me!"

*A river of Chippewa and Luce counties, Upper Peninsula of Michigan.

And the tree with all its branches
Rustled in the breeze of morning,
Saying, with a sigh of patience,
"Take my cloak, O Hiawatha!"
    With his knife the tree he girdled;
Just beneath its lowest branches,
Just above the roots, he cut it,
Till the sap came oozing outward;
Down the trunk, from top to bottom,
Sheer he cleft the bark asunder,
With a wooden wedge he raised it,
Stripped it from the trunk unbroken.
    "Give me of your boughs, O Cedar!
Of your strong and pliant branches,
My canoe to make more steady,
Make more strong and firm beneath me!"
    Through the summit of the Cedar
Went a sound, a cry of horror,
Went a murmur of resistance;
But it whispered, bending downward,
"Take my boughs, O Hiawatha!"
    Down he hewed the boughs of cedar,
Shaped them straightway to a framework,
Like two bows he formed and shaped them,
Like two bended bows together.
    "Give me of your roots, O Tamarack!
Of your fibrous roots, O Larch-Tree!
My canoe to bind together,
So to bind the ends together
That the water may not enter,
That the river may not wet me!"
    And the Larch, with all its fibres,
Shivered in the air of morning,
Touched his forehead with its tassels,
Said, with one long sigh of sorrow,
"Take them all, O Hiawatha!"
    From the earth he tore the fibres,
Tore the tough roots of the Larch-Tree,
Closely sewed the bark together,
Bound it closely to the framework.
    "Give me of your balm, O Fir-Tree!
Of your balsam and your resin,
So to close the seams together

That the water may not enter,
That the river may not wet me!"
    And the Fir-Tree, tall and sombre,
Sobbed through all its robes of darkness,
Rattled like a shore with pebbles,
Answered wailing, answered weeping,
"Take my balm, O Hiawatha!"
    And he took the tears of balsam,
Took the resin of the Fir-Tree,
Smeared therewith each seam and fissure,
Made each crevice safe from water.
    "Give me of your quills, O Hedgehog!
All your quills, O Kagh, the Hedgehog!
I will make a necklace of them,
Make a girdle for my beauty,
And two stars to deck her bosom!"
    From a hollow tree the Hedgehog
With his sleepy eyes looked at him,
Shot his shining quills, like arrows,
Saying, with a drowsy murmur,
Through the tangle of his whiskers,
"Take my quills, O Hiawatha!"
    From the ground the quills he gathered,
All the little shining arrows,
Stained them red and blue and yellow,
With the juice of roots and berries;
Into his canoe he wrought them,
Round its waist a shining girdle,
Round its bows a gleaming necklace,
On its breast two stars resplendent.
    Thus the Birch Canoe was builded
In the valley, by the river,
In the bosom of the forest;
And the forest's life was in it,
All its mystery and its magic,
All the lightness of the birch-tree,
All the toughness of the cedar,
All the larch's supple sinews;
And it floated on the river,
Like a yellow leaf in Autumn,
Like a yellow water-lily.
    Paddles none had Hiawatha,
Paddles none he had or needed,

TAHQUAMENON FALLS.   IN THE UPPER PENINSULA OF MICHIGAN.

For his thoughts as paddles served him,
And his wishes served to guide him;
Swift or slow at will he glided,
Veered to right or left at pleasure.
   Then he called aloud to Kwasind,
To his friend, the strong man, Kwasind,
Saying, "Help me clear this river
Of its sunken logs and sand-bars."
   Straight into the river Kwasind
Plunged as if he were an otter,
Dived as if he were a beaver,
Stood up to his waist in water,
To his arm-pits in the river,
Swam and shouted in the river,
Tugged at sunken logs and branches,
With his hands he scooped the sand-bars,
With his feet the ooze and tangle.
   And thus sailed my Hiawatha
Down the rushing Taquamenaw,
Sailed through all its bends and windings,
Sailed through all its deeps and shallows,
While his friend, the strong man, Kwasind,
Swam the deeps, the shallows waded.
   Up and down the river went they,
In and out among its islands,
Cleared its bed of root and sand-bar,
Dragged the dead trees from its channel,
Made its passage safe and certain,
Made a pathway for the people,
From its springs among the mountains,
To the waters of Pauwating,
To the bay of Taquamenaw.

VIII

Hiawatha's Fishing

. . . "WHEN he [Nokomis' grandfather] was alive," she [No-
komis] continued, "I was never without oil to put on my head,
but now my hair is fast falling off for the want of it." "Well!"
said he, "Noko, get cedar bark and make me a line, whilst I
make a canoe." When all was ready, he went out to the middle

of the lake to fish. He put his line down, saying, "Me-she-nah-ma-gwai (the name of the kingfish), take hold of my bait." He kept repeating this for some time. At last the king of the fishes said, "Manabozho troubles me. Here, Trout, take hold of his line." The trout did so. He then commenced drawing up his line, which was very heavy, so that his canoe stood nearly perpendicular; but he kept crying out, "Wha-ee-he! wha-ee-he!" till he could see the trout. As soon as he saw him, he spoke to him. "Why did you take hold of my hook? Esa! esa! [Shame! shame!] you ugly fish." The trout, being thus rebuked, let go.

Manabozho put his line again in the water, saying, "King of fishes, take hold of my line." But the king of the fishes told a monstrous sunfish to take hold of it; for Manabozho was tiring him with his incessant calls. He again drew up his line with difficulty, saying as before, "Wha-ee-he! wha-ee-he!" while his canoe was turning in swift circles. When he saw the sunfish, he cried, "Esa! esa! you odious fish! why did you dirty my hook by taking it in your mouth? Let go, I say, let go." The sunfish did so, and told the king of fishes what Manabozho said. Just at that moment the bait came near the king, and hearing Manabozho continually crying out, "Me-she-nah-ma-gwai, take hold of my hook," at last he did so, and allowed himself to be drawn up to the surface, which he had no sooner reached than, at one mouthful, he took Manabozho and his canoe down. When he came to himself, he found that he was in the fish's belly, and also his canoe. He now turned his thoughts to the way of making his escape. Looking in his canoe, he saw his war-club, with which he immediately struck the heart of the fish. He then felt a sudden motion, as if he were moving with great velocity. The fish observed to the others, "I am sick at stomach for having swallowed this dirty fellow Manabozho." Just at this moment he received another more severe blow on the heart. Manabozho thought, "If I am thrown up in the middle of the lake, I shall be drowned; so I must prevent it." He drew his canoe and placed it across the fish's throat, and just as he had finished the fish commenced vomiting, but to no effect. In this he was aided by a squirrel, who had accompanied him unperceived until that moment. This animal had taken an active part in helping him to place his canoe across the fish's throat. For this act he named him, saying, "For the future, boys shall always call you Ajidaumo."*

He then renewed his attack upon the fish's heart, and succeeded, by repeated blows, in killing him, which he first knew by the loss of motion, and by the sound of the beating of the body against the shore. He waited a day longer to see what would happen. He heard birds scratching on the body, and all at once the rays of light broke in. He could see the heads of gulls, who were looking in by the opening they had made. "Oh!" cried Manabozho, "my younger brothers, make the opening larger, so that I can get out." They told each other that their brother Manabozho was inside of the fish. They immediately set about enlarging the orifice, and in a short time liberated him. After he got out he said to the gulls, "For the future you shall be called Kayoshk† for your kindness to me."

The spot where the fish happened to be driven ashore was near his lodge. He went up and told his grandmother to go and prepare as much oil as she wanted. . . . From "Manabozho," in *Algic Researches*, v. 1, 144–46. Another version of this fish story occurs in "The Little Monedo, or Boy-Man," in *H. & S. I.*, pt. 3, p. 320, and *Oneóta*, p. 262–63.

> Forth upon the Gitche Gumee,
> On the shining Big-Sea-Water,
> With his fishing-line of cedar,
> Of the twisted bark of cedar,
> Forth to catch the sturgeon Nahma,
> Mishe-Nahma, King of Fishes,
> In his birch canoe exulting
> All alone went Hiawatha.
>   Through the clear, transparent water
> He could see the fishes swimming
> Far down in the depths below him;
> See the yellow perch, the Sahwa,

* Animal tail, or bottom upward.

† A free translation of this expression might be rendered, noble scratchers, or grabbers.

Like a sunbeam in the water,
See the Shawgashee, the craw-fish,
Like a spider on the bottom,
On the white and sandy bottom.
  At the stern sat Hiawatha,
With his fishing-line of cedar;
In his plumes the breeze of morning
Played as in the hemlock branches;
On the bows, with tail erected,
Sat the squirrel, Adjidaumo;
In his fur the breeze of morning
Played as in the prairie grasses.
  On the white sand of the bottom
Lay the monster Mishe-Nahma,
Lay the sturgeon, King of Fishes;
Through his gills he breathed the water,
With his fins he fanned and winnowed,
With his tail he swept the sand-floor.
  There he lay in all his armor;
On each side a shield to guard him,
Plates of bone upon his forehead,
Down his sides and back and shoulders
Plates of bone with spine projecting!
Painted was he with his war-paints,
Stripes of yellow, red, and azure,
Spots of brown and spots of sable;
And he lay there on the bottom,
Fanning with his fins of purple,
As above him Hiawatha
In his birch canoe came sailing,
With his fishing-line of cedar.
  "Take my bait!" cried Hiawatha,
Down into the depths beneath him,
"Take my bait, O Sturgeon, Nahma!
Come up from below the water,
Let us see which is the stronger!"
And he dropped his line of cedar
Through the clear, transparent water,
Waited vainly for an answer,
Long sat waiting for an answer,
And repeating loud and louder,
"Take my bait, O King of Fishes!"
  Quiet lay the sturgeon, Nahma,
Fanning slowly in the water,

Looking up at Hiawatha,
Listening to his call and clamor,
His unnecessary tumult,
Till he wearied of the shouting;
And he said to the Kenozha,
To the pike, the Maskenozha,
"Take the bait of this rude fellow,
Break the line of Hiawatha!"
  In his fingers Hiawatha
Felt the loose line jerk and tighten;
As he drew it in, it tugged so,
That the birch canoe stood endwise,
Like a birch log in the water,
With the squirrel, Adjidaumo,
Perched and frisking on the summit.
  Full of scorn was Hiawatha
When he saw the fish rise upward,
Saw the pike, the Maskenozha,
Coming nearer, nearer to him,
And he shouted through the water,
"Esa! esa! shame upon you!
You are but the pike, Kenozha,
You are not the fish I wanted,
You are not the King of Fishes!"
  Reeling downward to the bottom
Sank the pike in great confusion,
And the mighty sturgeon, Nahma,
Said to Ugudwash, the sun-fish,
To the bream, with scales of crimson,
"Take the bait of this great boaster,
Break the line of Hiawatha!"
  Slowly upward, wavering, gleaming,
Rose the Ugudwash, the sun-fish,
Seized the line of Hiawatha,
Swung with all his weight upon it,
Made a whirlpool in the water,
Whirled the birch canoe in circles,
Round and round in gurgling eddies,
Till the circles in the water
Reached the far-off sandy beaches,
Till the water-flags and rushes
Nodded on the distant margins.
  But when Hiawatha saw him
Slowly rising through the water,

Lifting up his disk refulgent,
Loud he shouted in derision,
"Esa! esa! shame upon you!
You are Ugudwash, the sun-fish,
You are not the fish I wanted,
You are not the King of Fishes!"
  Slowly downward, wavering, gleaming,
Sank the Ugudwash, the sun-fish,
And again the sturgeon, Nahma,
Heard the shout of Hiawatha,
Heard his challenge of defiance,
The unnecessary tumult,
Ringing far across the water.
  From the white sand of the bottom
Up he rose with angry gesture,
Quivering in each nerve and fibre,
Clashing all his plates of armor,
Gleaming bright with all his war-paint;
In his wrath he darted upward,
Flashing leaped into the sunshine,
Opened his great jaws, and swallowed
Both canoe and Hiawatha.
  Down into that darksome cavern
Plunged the headlong Hiawatha,
As a log on some black river
Shoots and plunges down the rapids,
Found himself in utter darkness,
Groped about in helpless wonder,
Till he felt a great heart beating,
Throbbing in that utter darkness.
  And he smote it in his anger,
With his fist, the heart of Nahma,
Felt the mighty King of Fishes
Shudder through each nerve and fibre,
Heard the water gurgle round him
As he leaped and staggered through it,
Sick at heart, and faint and weary.
  Crosswise then did Hiawatha
Drag his birch-canoe for safety,
Lest from out the jaws of Nahma,
In the turmoil and confusion,
Forth he might be hurled and perish.
And the squirrel, Adjidaumo,
Frisked and chattered very gayly,

Toiled and tugged with Hiawatha
Till the labor was completed.
   Then said Hiawatha to him,
"O my little friend, the squirrel,
Bravely have you toiled to help me;
Take the thanks of Hiawatha,
And the name which now he gives you;
For hereafter and forever
Boys shall call you Adjidaumo,
Tail-in-air the boys shall call you!"
   And again the sturgeon, Nahma,
Gasped and quivered in the water,
Then was still, and drifted landward
Till he grated on the pebbles,
Till the listening Hiawatha
Heard him grate upon the margin,
Felt him strand upon the pebbles,
Knew that Nahma, King of Fishes,
Lay there dead upon the margin.
   Then he heard a clang and flapping,
As of many wings assembling,
Heard a screaming and confusion,
As of birds of prey contending,
Saw a gleam of light above him,
Shining through the ribs of Nahma,
Saw the glittering eyes of sea-gulls,
Of Kayoshk, the sea-gulls, peering,
Gazing at him through the opening,
Heard them saying to each other,
" 'T is our brother, Hiawatha!"
   And he shouted from below them,
Cried exulting from the caverns:
"O ye sea-gulls! O my brothers!
I have slain the sturgeon, Nahma;
Make the rifts a little larger,
With your claws the openings widen,
Set me free from this dark prison,
And henceforward and forever
Men shall speak of your achievements,
Calling you Kayoshk, the sea-gulls,
Yes, Kayoshk, the Noble Scratchers!"
   And the wild and clamorous sea-gulls
Toiled with beak and claws together,
Made the rifts and openings wider

In the mighty ribs of Nahma,
And from peril and from prison,
From the body of the sturgeon,
From the peril of the water,
They released my Hiawatha.

He was standing near his wigwam,
On the margin of the water,
And he called to old Nokomis,
Called and beckoned to Nokomis,
Pointed to the sturgeon, Nahma,
Lying lifeless on the pebbles,
With the sea-gulls feeding on him.

"I have slain the Mishe-Nahma,
Slain the King of Fishes!" said he;
"Look! the sea-gulls feed upon him,
Yes, my friends Kayoshk, the sea-gulls;
Drive them not away, Nokomis,
They have saved me from great peril
In the body of the sturgeon,
Wait until their meal is ended,
Till their craws are full with feasting,
Till they homeward fly, at sunset,
To their nests among the marshes;
Then bring all your pots and kettles,
And make oil for us in Winter."

And she waited till the sun set,
Till the pallid moon, the Night-sun,
Rose above the tranquil water,
Till Kayoshk, the sated sea-gulls,
From their banquet rose with clamor,
And across the fiery sunset
Winged their way to far-off islands,
To their nests among the rushes.

To his sleep went Hiawatha,
And Nokomis to her labor,
Toiling patient in the moonlight,
Till the sun and moon changed places,
Till the sky was red with sunrise,
And Kayoshk, the hungry sea-gulls,
Came back from the reedy islands,
Clamorous for their morning banquet.

Three whole days and nights alternate
Old Nokomis and the sea-gulls
Stripped the oily flesh of Nahma,

Till the waves washed through the rib-bones,
Till the sea-gulls came no longer,
And upon the sands lay nothing
But the skeleton of Nahma.

IX

HIAWATHA AND THE PEARL-FEATHER

. . . SHE [Nokomis] told him that his grandfather, who had come to the earth in search of her, had been killed by Megissogwon [the wampum or pearl feather], who lived on the opposite side of the great lake. . . . From "Manabozho," in *Algic Researches,* v. 1, p. 143.

. . . All besides [what Nokomis wanted of the oil of the great fish], he informed her, he should keep for himself.

Some time after this, he commenced making preparations for a war excursion against the Pearl Feather, the Manito who lived on the opposite side of the great lake, who had killed his grandfather. The abode of this spirit was defended, first, by fiery serpents, who hissed fire so that no one could pass them; and, in the second place, by a large mass of gummy matter lying on the water, so soft and adhesive, that whoever attempted to pass, or whatever came in contact with it, was sure to stick there. . . . *Ibid.,* p. 146–47.

After having finished his term of fasting and sung his war-song—from which the Indians of the present day derive the custom—he embarked in his canoe, fully prepared for war. In addition to the usual implements, he had a plentiful supply of oil. He travelled rapidly night and day, for he had only to will or speak, and the canoe went. At length he arrived in sight of the fiery serpents. He stopped to view them. He saw they were some distance apart, and that the flame only which issued from them reached across the pass. He commenced talking as a friend to them; but they answered, "We know you, Manabozho, you cannot pass." He then thought of some expedient to deceive them, and hit upon this. He pushed his canoe as near as possible. All at once he cried out, with a loud and terrified voice, "What is that behind you?" The serpents instantly turned their heads, when, at a single word, he passed them. "Well!" said he, placidly, after he had got by, "how do you like my exploit?" He then took up his bow and arrows, and with deliberate aim shot them, which was easily done, for the serpents were stationary, and could not move beyond a certain spot. They were of enormous length and of a bright colour.

Having overcome the sentinel serpents, he went on in his canoe till he came to a soft gummy portion of the lake, called Pigiu-wagumee, or Pitchwater. He took the oil and rubbed it on his canoe, and then pushed into it. The oil softened the surface and enabled him to slip through it with ease, although it required frequent rubbing, and a constant reapplication of the oil. Just as his oil failed, he extricated himself from this impediment, and was the first person who ever succeeded in overcoming it.

He now came in view of land, on which he debarked in safety, and could see the lodge of the Shining Manito, situated on a hill. He commenced preparing for the fight, putting his arrows and clubs in order, and just at the dawn of day began his attack, yelling and shouting, and crying with triple voices, "Surround him! surround him! run up! run up!" making it appear that he had many followers. He advanced crying out, "It was you that killed my grandfather," and with this shot his arrows. The combat continued all day. Manabozho's arrows had no effect, for his antagonist was clothed with pure wampum. He was now reduced to three arrows, and it was only by extraordinary agility that he could escape the blows which the Manito kept making at him. At that moment a large woodpecker (the ma-ma) flew past, and lit on a tree. "Manabozho," he cried, "your adversary has a vulnerable point; shoot at the lock of hair on the crown of his head." He shot his first arrow so as only to draw blood from that part. The Manito made one or two unsteady steps, but recovered himself. He began to parley, but, in the act, received a second arrow, which brought him to his knees. But he again recovered. In so doing, however, he exposed his head, and gave his adversary a chance to fire his third arrow, which penetrated deep, and brought him a lifeless corpse to the ground. Manabozho uttered his saw-saw-quan, and taking his scalp as a trophy, he called the woodpecker to come and receive a reward for his information. He took the blood of the Manito and rubbed it on the woodpecker's* head, the feathers of which are red to this day.

After this victory he returned home, singing songs of triumph and beating his drum. When his grandmother heard him, she came to the shore and welcomed him with songs and dancing. . . . *Ibid.,* v. 1, p. 151–54.

> On the shores of Gitche Gumee,
> Of the shining Big-Sea-Water,
> Stood Nokomis, the old woman,
> Pointing with her finger westward,
> O'er the water pointing westward,
> To the purple clouds of sunset.
>   Fiercely the red sun descending
> Burned his way along the heavens,
> Set the sky on fire behind him,
> As war-parties, when retreating,
> Burn the prairies on their war-trail;
> And the moon, the Night-sun, eastward,
> Suddenly starting from his ambush,
> Followed fast those bloody footprints,
> Followed in that fiery war-trail,
> With its glare upon his features.
>   And Nokomis, the old woman,
> Pointing with her finger westward,
> Spake these words to Hiawatha:
> "Yonder dwells the great Pearl-Feather,
> Megissogwon, the Magician,
> Manito of Wealth and Wampum,
> Guarded by his fiery serpents,
> Guarded by the black pitch-water.
> You can see his fiery serpents,
> The Kenabeek, the great serpents,
> Coiling, playing in the water;

* The tuft feathers of the red-headed woodpecker are used to ornament the stems of the Indian pipe, and are symbolical of valour.

You can see the black pitch-water
Stretching far away beyond them,
To the purple clouds of sunset!
   "He it was who slew my father,
By his wicked wiles and cunning,
When he from the moon descended,
When he came on earth to seek me.
He, the mightiest of Magicians,
Sends the fever from the marshes,
Sends the pestilential vapors,
Sends the poisonous exhalations,
Sends the white fog from the fen-lands,
Sends disease and death among us!
   "Take your bow, O Hiawatha,
Take your arrows, jasper-headed,
Take your war-club, Puggawaugun,
And your mittens, Minjekahwun,
And your birch canoe for sailing,
And the oil of Mishe-Nahma,
So to smear its sides, that swiftly
You may pass the black pitch-water;
Slay this merciless magician,
Save the people from the fever
That he breathes across the fen-lands,
And avenge my father's murder!"
   Straightway then my Hiawatha
Armed himself with all his war-gear,
Launched his birch canoe for sailing;
With his palm its sides he patted,
Said with glee, "Cheemaun, my darling,
O my Birch-canoe! leap forward,
Where you see the fiery serpents,
Where you see the black pitch-water!"
   Forward leaped Cheemaun exulting,
And the noble Hiawatha
Sang his war-song wild and woful,
And above him the war-eagle,
The Keneu, the great war-eagle,
Master of all fowls with feathers,
Screamed and hurtled through the heavens.
   Soon he reached the fiery serpents,
The Kenabeek, the great serpents,
Lying huge upon the water,
Sparkling, rippling in the water,

Lying coiled across the passage,
With their blazing crests uplifted,
Breathing fiery fogs and vapors,
So that none could pass beyond them.
　But the fearless Hiawatha
Cried aloud, and spake in this wise:
"Let me pass my way, Kenabeek,
Let me go upon my journey!"
And they answered, hissing fiercely,
With their fiery breath made answer:
"Back, go back! O Shaugodaya!
Back to old Nokomis, Faint-heart!"
　Then the angry Hiawatha
Raised his mighty bow of ash-tree,
Seized his arrows, jasper-headed,
Shot them fast among the serpents;
Every twanging of the bow-string
Was a war-cry and a death-cry,
Every whizzing of an arrow
Was a death-song of Kenabeek.
　Weltering in the bloody water,
Dead lay all the fiery serpents,
And among them Hiawatha
Harmless sailed, and cried exulting:
"Onward, O Cheemaun, my darling!
Onward to the black pitch-water!"
　Then he took the oil of Nahma,
And the bows and sides anointed,
Smeared them well with oil, that swiftly
He might pass the black pitch-water.
　All night long he sailed upon it,
Sailed upon that sluggish water,
Covered with its mould of ages,
Black with rotting water-rushes,
Rank with flags and leaves of lilies,
Stagnant, lifeless, dreary, dismal,
Lighted by the shimmering moonlight,
And by will-o'-the-wisps illumined,
Fires by ghosts of dead men kindled,
In their weary night-encampments.
　All the air was white with moonlight,
All the water black with shadow,
And around him the Suggema,
The mosquito, sang his war-song,

And the fire-flies, Wah-wah-taysee,
Waved their torches to mislead him;
And the bull-frog, the Dahinda,
Thrust his head into the moonlight,
Fixed his yellow eyes upon him,
Sobbed and sank beneath the surface;
And anon a thousand whistles,
Answered over all the fen-lands,
And the heron, the Shuh-shuh-gah,
Far off on the reedy margin,
Heralded the hero's coming.

Westward thus fared Hiawatha,
Toward the realm of Megissogwon,
Toward the land of the Pearl-Feather,
Till the level moon stared at him,
In his face stared pale and haggard,
Till the sun was hot behind him,
Till it burned upon his shoulders,
And before him on the upland
He could see the Shining Wigwam
Of the Manito of Wampum,
Of the mightiest of Magicians.

Then once more Cheemaun he patted,
To his birch-canoe said, "Onward!"
And it stirred in all its fibres,
And with one great bound of triumph
Leaped across the water-lilies,
Leaped through tangled flags and rushes,
And upon the beach beyond them
Dry-shod landed Hiawatha.

Straight he took his bow of ash-tree,
On the sand one end he rested,
With his knee he pressed the middle,
Stretched the faithful bow-string tighter,
Took an arrow, jasper-headed,
Shot it at the Shining Wigwam,
Sent it singing as a herald,
As a bearer of his message,
Of his challenge loud and lofty:
"Come forth from your lodge, Pearl-Feather!
Hiawatha waits your coming!"

Straightway from the Shining Wigwam
Came the mighty Megissogwon,
Tall of stature, broad of shoulder,

Dark and terrible in aspect,
Clad from head to foot in wampum,
Armed with all his warlike weapons,
Painted like the sky of morning,
Streaked with crimson, blue and yellow,
Crested with great eagle-feathers,
Streaming upward, streaming outward.
  "Well I know you, Hiawatha!"
Cried he in a voice of thunder,
In a tone of loud derision.
"Hasten back, O Shaugodaya!
Hasten back among the women,
Back to old Nokomis, Faint-heart!
I will slay you as you stand there,
As of old I slew her father!"
  But my Hiawatha answered,
Nothing daunted, fearing nothing:
"Big words do not smite like war-clubs,
Boastful breath is not a bow-string,
Taunts are not so sharp as arrows,
Deeds are better things than words are,
Actions mightier than boastings!"
  Then began the greatest battle
That the sun had ever looked on,
That the war-birds ever witnessed.
All a Summer's day it lasted,
From the sunrise to the sunset;
For the shafts of Hiawatha
Harmless hit the shirt of wampum,
Harmless fell the blows he dealt it
With his mittens, Minjekahwun,
Harmless fell the heavy war-club;
It could dash the rocks asunder,
But it could not break the meshes
Of that magic shirt of wampum.
  Till at sunset Hiawatha,
Leaning on his bow of ash-tree,
Wounded, weary, and desponding,
With his mighty war-club broken,
With his mittens torn and tattered,
And three useless arrows only,
Paused to rest beneath a pine-tree,
From whose branches trailed the mosses,
And whose trunk was coated over

With the Dead-man's Moccasin-leather,
With the fungus white and yellow.
   Suddenly from the boughs above him
Sang the Mama, the woodpecker:
"Aim your arrows, Hiawatha,
At the head of Megissogwon,
Strike the tuft of hair upon it,
At their roots the long black tresses;
There alone can he be wounded!"
   Winged with feathers, tipped with jasper,
Swift flew Hiawatha's arrow,
Just as Megissogwon, stooping,
Raised a heavy stone to throw it.
Full upon the crown it struck him,
At the roots of his long tresses,
And he reeled and staggered forward,
Plunging like a wounded bison,
Yes, like Pezhekee, the bison,
When the snow is on the prairie.
   Swifter flew the second arrow,
In the pathway of the other,
Piercing deeper than the other,
Wounded sorer than the other;
And the knees of Megissogwon
Shook like windy reeds beneath him,
Bent and trembled like the rushes.
   But the third and latest arrow
Swiftest flew, and wounded sorest,
And the mighty Megissogwon
Saw the fiery eyes of Pauguk,
Saw the eyes of Death glare at him,
Heard his voice call in the darkness;
At the feet of Hiawatha
Lifeless lay the great Pearl-Feather,
Lay the mightiest of Magicians.
   Then the grateful Hiawatha
Called the Mama, the woodpecker,
From his perch among the branches
Of the melancholy pine-tree,
And, in honor of his service,
Stained with blood the tuft of feathers
On the little head of Mama;
Even to this day he wears it,

Wears the tuft of crimson feathers,
As a symbol of his service.
   Then he stripped the shirt of wampum
From the back of Megissogwon,
As a trophy of the battle,
As a signal of his conquest.
On the shore he left the body,
Half on land and half in water,
In the sand his feet were buried,
And his face was in the water.
And above him, wheeled and clamored
The Keneu, the great war-eagle,
Sailing round in narrower circles,
Hovering nearer, nearer, nearer.
   From the wigwam Hiawatha
Bore the wealth of Megissogwon,
All his wealth of skins and wampum,
Furs of bison and of beaver,
Furs of sable and of ermine,
Wampum belts and strings and pouches,
Quivers wrought with beads of wampum,
Filled with arrows, silver-headed.
   Homeward then he sailed exulting,
Homeward through the black pitch-water,
Homeward through the weltering serpents,
With the trophies of the battle,
With a shout and song of triumph.
   On the shore stood old Nokomis,
On the shore stood Chibiabos,
And the very strong man, Kwasind,
Waiting for the hero's coming,
Listening to his song of triumph.
And the people of the village
Welcomed him with songs and dances,
Made a joyous feast, and shouted:
"Honor be to Hiawatha!
He has slain the great Pearl-Feather,
Slain the mightiest of Magicians,
Him who sent the fiery fever,
Sent the white fog from the fen-lands,
Sent disease and death among us!"
   Ever dear to Hiawatha
Was the memory of Mama!
And in token of his friendship,

As a mark of his remembrance,
He adorned and decked his pipe-stem
With the crimson tuft of feathers,
With the blood-red crest of Mama.
But the wealth of Megissogwon,
All the trophies of the battle,
He divided with his people,
Shared it equally among them.

X

HIAWATHA'S WOOING

HAVING accomplished the victory over the reptiles, Mana-bozho returned to his former place of dwelling, and married the arrow-maker's daughter.—From "Manabozho," in *Algic Researches,* v. 1, p. 171.

For this purpose [to set an example of how his people should live], he selected a beautiful spot on the southern shore of one of the lesser and minuter lakes, which is called Tioto (Cross lake) by the natives, to this day. Here he erected his lodge, planted his field of corn, kept by him his magic canoe, and selected a wife.   In relinquishing his former position, as a subordinate power to the Great Spirit, he also dropped his name [Tarenyawago], and, according to his present situation, took that of Hiawatha, meaning a person of very great wisdom, which the people spontaneously bestowed on him.

He now lived in a degree of respect scarcely inferior to that which he before possessed.   His words and counsels were im-plicitly obeyed.   The people flocked to him from all quarters, for advice and instruction.   Such persons as had been promi-nent in following his precepts, he favored, and they became eminent on the war-path and in the council-room. . . .

He had elected to become a member of the Onondaga tribe, and chose the residence of this people, in the shady recesses of their fruitful valley, as the central point of their government.

After the termination of his higher mission from above, years passed away in prosperity, and the Onondagas assumed an elevated rank, for their wisdom and learning, among the

other tribes, and there was not one of these which did not yield
its assent to their high privilege of lighting the general council-
fire.—From "Hiawatha," in *H. & S. I.,* v. 3, p. 315.

"As unto the bow the cord is,
So unto the man is woman,
Though she bends him, she obeys him,
Though she draws him, yet she follows,
Useless each without the other!"
    Thus the youthful Hiawatha
Said within himself and pondered,
Much perplexed by various feelings,
Listless, longing, hoping, fearing,
Dreaming still of Minnehaha,
Of the lovely Laughing Water,
In the land of the Dacotahs.
    "Wed a maiden of your people,"
Warning said the old Nokomis;
"Go not eastward, go not westward,
For a stranger, whom we know not!
Like a fire upon the hearth-stone
Is a neighbor's homely daughter,
Like the starlight or the moonlight
Is the handsomest of strangers!"
    Thus dissuading spake Nokomis,
And my Hiawatha answered
Only this: "Dear old Nokomis,
Very pleasant is the firelight,
But I like the starlight better,
Better do I like the moonlight!"
    Gravely then said old Nokomis:
"Bring not here an idle maiden,
Bring not here a useless woman,
Hands unskilful, feet unwilling;
Bring a wife with nimble fingers,
Heart and hand that move together,
Feet that run on willing errands!"
    Smiling answered Hiawatha:
"In the land of the Dacotahs
Lives the Arrow-maker's daughter,
Minnehaha, Laughing Water,
Handsomest of all the women.
I will bring her to your wigwam,
She shall run upon your errands,

Be your starlight, moonlight, firelight,
Be the sunlight of my people!"
    Still dissuading said Nokomis:
"Bring not to my lodge a stranger
From the land of the Dacotahs!
Very fierce are the Dacotahs,
Often is there war between us,
There are feuds yet unforgotten,
Wounds that ache and still may open!"
    Laughing answered Hiawatha:
"For that reason, if no other,
Would I wed the fair Dacotah,
That our tribes might be united,
That old feuds might be forgotten,
And old wounds be healed forever!"
    Thus departed Hiawatha
To the land of the Dacotahs,
To the land of handsome women;
Striding over moor and meadow,
Through interminable forests,
Through uninterrupted silence.
    With his moccasins of magic,
At each stride a mile he measured;
Yet the way seemed long before him,
And his heart outran his footsteps;
And he journeyed without resting,
Till he heard the cataract's laughter,
Heard the Falls of Minnehaha
Calling to him through the silence.
"Pleasant is the sound!" he murmured,
"Pleasant is the voice that calls me!"
    On the outskirts of the forest,
'Twixt the shadow and the sunshine,
Herds of fallow deer were feeding,
But they saw not Hiawatha;
To his bow he whispered, "Fail not!"
To his arrow whispered, "Swerve not!"
Sent it singing on its errand,
To the red heart of the roebuck;
Threw the deer across his shoulder,
And sped forward without pausing.
    At the doorway of his wigwam
Sat the ancient Arrow-maker,
In the land of the Dacotahs,

Making arrow-heads of jasper,
Arrow-heads of chalcedony.
At his side, in all her beauty,
Sat the lovely Minnehaha,
Sat his daughter, Laughing Water,
Plaiting mats of flags and rushes;
Of the past the old man's thoughts were,
And the maiden's of the future.

   He was thinking, as he sat there,
Of the days when with such arrows
He had struck the deer and bison,
On the Muskoday, the meadow;
Shot the wild goose, flying southward,
On the wing, the clamorous Wawa;
Thinking of the great war-parties,
How they came to buy his arrows,
Could not fight without his arrows.
Ah, no more such noble warriors
Could be found on earth as they were!
Now the men were all like women,
Only used their tongues for weapons!

   She was thinking of a hunter,
From another tribe and country,
Young and tall and very handsome,
Who one morning, in the Spring-time,
Came to buy her father's arrows,
Sat and rested in the wigwam,
Lingered long about the doorway,
Looking back as he departed.
She had heard her father praise him,
Praise his courage and his wisdom;
Would he come again for arrows
To the Falls of Minnehaha?
On the mat her hands lay idle,
And her eyes were very dreamy.

   Through their thoughts they heard a footstep,
Heard a rustling in the branches,
And with glowing cheek and forehead,
With the deer upon his shoulders,
Suddenly from out the woodlands
Hiawatha stood before them.

   Straight the ancient Arrow-maker
Looked up gravely from his labor,
Laid aside the unfinished arrow,

Bade him enter at the doorway,
Saying, as he rose to meet him,
"Hiawatha, you are welcome!"
    At the feet of Laughing Water
Hiawatha laid his burden,
Threw the red deer from his shoulders;
And the maiden looked up at him,
Looked up from her mat of rushes,
Said with gentle look and accent,
"You are welcome, Hiawatha!"
    Very spacious was the wigwam,
Made of deer-skin dressed and whitened,
With the Gods of the Dacotahs
Drawn and painted on its curtains,
And so tall the doorway, hardly
Hiawatha stooped to enter,
Hardly touched his eagle-feathers
As he entered at the doorway.
    Then uprose the Laughing Water,
From the ground fair Minnehaha,
Laid aside her mat unfinished,
Brought forth food and set before them,
Water brought them from the brooklet,
Gave them food in earthen vessels,
Gave them drink in bowls of bass-wood,
Listened while the guest was speaking,
Listened while her father answered,
But not once her lips she opened,
Not a single word she uttered.
    Yes, as in a dream she listened
To the words of Hiawatha,
As he talked of old Nokomis,
Who had nursed him in his childhood,
As he told of his companions,
Chibiabos, the musician,
And the very strong man, Kwasind,
And of happiness and plenty
In the land of the Ojibways,
In the pleasant land and peaceful.
    "After many years of warfare,
Many years of strife and bloodshed,
There is peace between the Ojibways
And the tribe of the Dacotahs."
Thus continued Hiawatha,

And then added, speaking slowly,
"That this peace may last forever,
And our hands be clasped more closely,
And our hearts be more united,
Give me as my wife this maiden,
Minnehaha, Laughing Water,
Loveliest of Dacotah women!"
    And the ancient Arrow-maker
Paused a moment ere he answered,
Smoked a little while in silence,
Looked at Hiawatha proudly,
Fondly looked at Laughing Water,
And made answer very gravely:
"Yes, if Minnehaha wishes;
Let your heart speak, Minnehaha!"
    And the lovely Laughing Water
Seemed more lovely, as she stood there,
Neither willing nor reluctant,
As she went to Hiawatha,
Softly took the seat beside him,
While she said, and blushed to say it,
"I will follow you, my husband!"
    This was Hiawatha's wooing!
Thus it was he won the daughter
Of the ancient Arrow-maker,
In the land of the Dacotahs!
    From the wigwam he departed,
Leading with him Laughing Water;
Hand in hand they went together,
Through the woodland and the meadow,
Left the old man standing lonely
At the doorway of his wigwam,
Heard the Falls of Minnehaha
Calling to them from the distance,
Crying to them from afar off,
"Fare thee well, O Minnehaha!"
    And the ancient Arrow-maker
Turned again unto his labor,
Sat down by his sunny doorway,
Murmuring to himself, and saying:
"Thus it is our daughters leave us,
Those we love, and those who love us!
Just when they have learned to help us,
When we are old and lean upon them,

Comes a youth with flaunting feathers,
With his flute of reeds, a stranger
Wanders piping through the village,
Beckons to the fairest maiden,
And she follows where he leads her,
Leaving all things for the stranger!"
      Pleasant was the journey homeward,
Through interminable forests,
Over meadow, over mountain,
Over river, hill, and hollow.
Short it seemed to Hiawatha,
Though they journeyed very slowly,
Though his pace he checked and slackened
To the steps of Laughing Water.
      Over wide and rushing rivers
In his arms he bore the maiden;
Light he thought her as a feather,
As the plume upon his head-gear;
Cleared the tangled pathway for her,
Bent aside the swaying branches,
Made at night a lodge of branches,
And a bed with boughs of hemlock,
And a fire before the doorway
With the dry cones of the pine-tree.
      All the travelling winds went with them,
O'er the meadow, through the forest;
All the stars of night looked at them,
Watched with sleepless eyes their slumber;
From his ambush in the oak-tree
Peeped the squirrel, Adjidaumo,
Watched with eager eyes the lovers;
And the rabbit, the Wabasso,
Scampered from the path before them,
Peering, peeping from his burrow,
Sat erect upon his haunches,
Watched with curious eyes the lovers.
      Pleasant was the journey homeward!
All the birds sang loud and sweetly
Songs of happiness and heart's-ease;
Sang the bluebird, the Owaissa,
"Happy are you, Hiawatha,
Having such a wife to love you!"
Sang the robin, the Opechee,

"Happy are you, Laughing Water,
Having such a noble husband!"
From the sky the sun benignant
Looked upon them through the branches,
Saying to them, "O my children,
Love is sunshine, hate is shadow,
Life is checkered shade and sunshine,
Rule by love, O Hiawatha!"
From the sky the moon looked at them,
Filled the lodge with mystic splendors,
Whispered to them, "O my children,
Day is restless, night is quiet,
Man imperious, woman feeble;
Half is mine, although I follow;
Rule by patience, Laughing Water!"
Thus it was they journeyed homeward;
Thus it was that Hiawatha
To the lodge of old Nokomis
Brought the moonlight, starlight, firelight,
Brought the sunshine of his people,
Minnehaha, Laughing Water,
Handsomest of all the women
In the land of the Dacotahs,
In the land of handsome women.

XI

Hiawatha's Wedding-Feast

For Schoolcraft's account of Pau-Puk-Keewis, see XVI
and XVII.

You shall hear how Pau-Puk-Keewis,
How the handsome Yenadizze
Danced at Hiawatha's wedding;
How the gentle Chibiabos,
He the sweetest of musicians,
Sang his songs of love and longing;
How Iagoo, the great boaster,
He the marvellous story-teller,
Told his tales of strange adventure,
That the feast might be more joyous,
That the time might pass more gayly,
And the guests be more contented.
Sumptuous was the feast Nokomis

Made at Hiawatha's wedding;
All the bowls were made of bass-wood,
White and polished very smoothly,
All the spoons of horn of bison,
Black and polished very smoothly.

She had sent through all the village
Messengers with wands of willow,
As a sign of invitation,
As a token of the feasting;
And the wedding guests assembled,
Clad in all their richest raiment,
Robes of fur and belts of wampum,
Splendid with their paint and plumage,
Beautiful with beads and tassels.

First they ate the sturgeon, Nahma,
And the pike, the Maskenozha,
Caught and cooked by old Nokomis;
Then on pemican they feasted,
Pemican and buffalo marrow,
Haunch of deer and hump of bison,
Yellow cakes of the Mondamin,
And the wild rice of the river.

But the gracious Hiawatha,
And the lovely Laughing Water,
And the careful old Nokomis,
Tasted not the food before them,
Only waited on the others,
Only served their guests in silence.

And when all the guests had finished,
Old Nokomis, brisk and busy,
From an ample pouch of otter,
Filled the red stone pipes for smoking
With tobacco from the South-land,
Mixed with bark of the red willow,
And with herbs and leaves of fragrance.

Then she said, "O Pau-Puk-Keewis,
Dance for us your merry dances,
Dance the Beggar's Dance to please us,
That the feast may be more joyous,
That the time may pass more gayly,
And our guests be more contented!"

Then the handsome Pau-Puk-Keewis,
He the idle Yenadizze,
He the merry mischief-maker,

Whom the people called the Storm-Fool,
Rose among the guests assembled.
   Skilled was he in sports and pastimes,
In the merry dance of snow-shoes,
In the play of quoits and ball-play;
Skilled was he in games of hazard,
In all games of skill and hazard,
Pugasaing, the Bowl and Counters,
Kuntassoo, the Game of Plum-stones.
Though the warriors called him Faint-Heart,
Called him coward, Shaugodaya,
Idler, gambler, Yenadizze,
Little heeded he their jesting,
Little cared he for their insults,
For the women and the maidens
Loved the handsome Pau-Puk-Keewis.
   He was dressed in shirt of doe-skin,
White and soft, and fringed with ermine,
All inwrought with beads of wampum;
He was dressed in deer-skin leggings,
Fringed with hedgehog quills and ermine,
And in moccasins of buck-skin,
Thick with quills and beads embroidered.
On his head were plumes of swan's down,
On his heels were tails of foxes,
In one hand a fan of feathers,
And a pipe was in the other.
   Barred with streaks of red and yellow,
Streaks of blue and bright vermilion,
Shone the face of Pau-Puk-Keewis.
From his forehead fell his tresses,
Smooth, and parted like a woman's,
Shining bright with oil, and plaited,
Hung with braids of scented grasses,
As among the guests assembled,
To the sound of flutes and singing,
To the sound of drums and voices,
Rose the handsome Pau-Puk-Keewis,
And began his mystic dances.
   First he danced a solemn measure,
Very slow in step and gesture,
In and out among the pine-trees,
Through the shadows and the sunshine,
Treading softly like a panther.

Then more swiftly and still swifter,
Whirling, spinning round in circles,
Leaping o'er the guests assembled,
Eddying round and round the wigwam,
Till the leaves went whirling with him,
Till the dust and wind together
Swept in eddies round about him.
　　Then along the sandy margin
Of the lake, the Big-Sea-Water,
On he sped with frenzied gestures,
Stamped upon the sand, and tossed it
Wildly in the air around him;
Till the wind became a whirlwind,
Till the sand was blown and sifted
Like great snowdrifts o'er the landscape,
Heaping all the shores with Sand Dunes,
Sand Hills of the Nagow Wudjoo!
　　Thus the merry Pau-Puk-Keewis
Danced his Beggar's Dance to please them,
And, returning, sat down laughing
There among the guests assembled,
Sat and fanned himself serenely
With his fan of turkey-feathers.
　　Then they said to Chibiabos,
To the friend of Hiawatha,
To the sweetest of all singers,
To the best of all musicians,
"Sing to us, O Chibiabos!
Songs of love and songs of longing,
That the feast may be more joyous,
That the time may pass more gayly,
And our guests be more contented!"

I once had (alas! *had*) a correspondent, whose letters, for a few brief years, dated from "La Pointe, Wisconsin Territory, Lake Superior." . . . The accompanying song seems to be a mixture of the Ottawa and Ojibway, (or Chippewa,) . . . [At the end of the Indian version,—which begins with the exclamation *Onaiweh!*—the following literal translation is given:]

Awake! flower of the forest—beautiful bird of the prairie.
Awake! awake! thou with the eyes of the fawn.

When you look at me I am happy; like the flowers when
  they feel the dew.

The breath of thy mouth is sweet as the fragrance of the
  flowers in the morning;—sweet as their fragrance at
  evening in the moon of the fading leaf.*

Does not the blood of my veins spring towards thee, like
  the bubbling springs to the sun—in the moon of the
  brightest nights?†

My heart sings to thee when thou art near; like the dancing
  branches to the wind, in the moon of strawberries.‡

When thou art not pleased, my beloved, my heart is
  darkened like the shining river when shadows fall from
  the clouds above.

Thy smiles cause my troubled heart to be brightened, as
  the sun makes to look like gold the ripple which the
  cold wind has created.

Myself! behold me!—blood of my beating heart.

The earth smiles—the waters smile—the heavens smile,
  but I—I lose the way of smiling when thou art not
  near—Awake, awake! my beloved.

—From "Indian Serenade," in *Littell's Living Age,* v. 25, April,
1850, p. 45.   (See footnote to this item in the Bibliography.)

   And the gentle Chibiabos
  Sang in accents sweet and tender,
  Sang in tones of deep emotion,
  Songs of love and songs of longing;
  Looking still at Hiawatha,
  Looking at fair Laughing Water,
  Sang he softly, sang in this wise:
   "Onaway! Awake, beloved!
  Thou the wild-flower of the forest!
  Thou the wild-bird of the prairie!
  Thou with eyes so soft and fawn-like!
   "If thou only lookest at me,
  I am happy, I am happy,
  As the lilies of the prairie,
  When they feel the dew upon them!
   "Sweet thy breath is as the fragrance
  Of the wild-flowers in the morning,

* October.
† April.
‡ June.

As their fragrance is at evening,
In the Moon when leaves are falling.
    "Does not all the blood within me
Leap to meet thee, leap to meet thee,
As the springs to meet the sunshine,
In the Moon when nights are brightest?
    "Onaway! my heart sings to thee,
Sings with joy when thou art near me,
As the sighing, singing branches
In the pleasant Moon of Strawberries!
    "When thou art not pleased, beloved,
Then my heart is sad and darkened,
As the shining river darkens
When the clouds drop shadows on it!
    "When thou smilest, my beloved,
Then my troubled heart is brightened,
As in sunshine gleam the ripples
That the cold wind makes in rivers.
    "Smiles the earth, and smile the waters,
Smile the cloudless skies above us,
But I lose the way of smiling
When thou art no longer near me!
    "I myself, myself! behold me!
Blood of my beating heart, behold me!
O awake, awake, beloved!
Onaway! awake, beloved!"
    Thus the gentle Chibiabos
Sang his song of love and longing;
And Iagoo, the great boaster,
He the marvellous story-teller,
He the friend of old Nokomis,
Jealous of the sweet musician,
Jealous of the applause they gave him,
Saw in all the eyes around him,
Saw in all their looks and gestures,
That the wedding guests assembled
Longed to hear his pleasant stories,
His immeasurable falsehoods.

Iagoo is the name of a personage noted in Indian lore for
having given extravagant narrations of whatever he had seen,
heard, or accomplished. It seems that he always saw extraordinary things, made extraordinary journeys, and performed

extraordinary feats. He could not look out of his lodge and see things as other men did. If he described a bird, it had a most singular variety of brilliant plumage. The animals he met with were all of the monstrous kind; they had eyes like orbs of fire, and claws like hooks of steel, and could step over the top of an Indian lodge. He told of a serpent he had seen, which had hair on its neck like a mane, and feet resembling a quadruped; and if one were to take his own account of his exploits and observations, it would be difficult to decide whether his strength, his activity, or his wisdom should be most admired.

Iagoo did not appear to have been endowed with the ordinary faculties of other men. His eyes appeared to be magnifiers, and the tympanum of his ears so constructed that what appeared to common observers to be but the sound of a zephyr, to him had a far closer resemblance to the noise of thunder. His imagination appeared to be of so exuberant a character, that he scarcely required more than a drop of water to construct an ocean, or a grain of sand to form an earth. And he had so happy an exemption from both the restraints of judgment and moral accountability, that he never found the slightest difficulty in accommodating his facts to the most enlarged credulity. Nor was his ample thirst for the marvellous ever quenched by attempts to reconcile statements the most strange, unaccountable, and preposterous.

Such was Iagoo, the Indian story-teller, whose name is associated with all that is extravagant and marvellous, and has long been established in the hunter's vocabulary as a perfect synonym for liar, and is bandied about as a familiar proverb. If a hunter or warrior, in telling his exploits, undertakes to embellish them; to overrate his merits, or in any other way to excite the incredulity of his hearers, he is liable to be rebuked with the remark, "So here we have Iagoo come again." And he seems to hold the relative rank in oral narration which our written literature awards to Baron Munchausen, Jack Falstaff, and Captain Lemuel Gulliver.

Notwithstanding all this, there are but a few scraps of his

actual stories to be found. He first attracted notice by giving an account of a water lily, a single leaf of which, he averred, was sufficient to make a petticoat and upper garments for his wife and daughter. One evening he was sitting in his lodge, on the banks of a river, and hearing the quacking of ducks on the stream, he fired through the lodge door at a venture. He killed a swan that happened to be flying by, and twenty brace of ducks in the stream. But this did not check the force of his shot; they passed on, and struck the heads of two loons, at the moment they were coming up from beneath the water, and even went beyond and killed a most extraordinary large fish called Moshkeenozha [muscalunge]. On another occasion he had killed a deer, and after skinning it, was carrying the carcass on his shoulders, when he spied some stately elks on the plain before him. He immediately gave them chase, and had run, over hill and dale, a distance of half a day's travel, before he recollected that he had the deer's carcass on his shoulders.

One day, as he was passing over a tract of *mushkeeg,* or bog-land, he saw musquitoes of such enormous size, that he staked his reputation on the fact that a single wing of one of the insects was sufficient for a sail to his canoe, and the proboscis as big as his wife's shovel. But he was favoured with a still more extraordinary sight, in a gigantic ant, which passed him, as he was watching a beaver's lodge, dragging the entire carcass of a hare.

At another time, for he was ever seeing or doing something wonderful, he got out of smoking weed, and in going into the woods in search of some, he discovered a bunch of the red willow, or maple bush, of such a luxuriant growth, that he was industriously occupied half a day in walking round it.—"Iagoo, from the Mythology of the Chippewas," in *Algic Researches,* v. 2, 229–32.

> Very boastful was Iagoo;
> Never heard he an adventure
> But himself had met a greater;
> Never any deed of daring
> But himself had done a bolder;

Never any marvellous story
But himself could tell a stranger.
Would you listen to his boasting,
Would you only give him credence,
No one ever shot an arrow
Half so far and high as he had;
Ever caught so many fishes,
Ever killed so many reindeer,
Ever trapped so many beaver!
None could run so fast as he could,
None could dive so deep as he could,
None could swim so far as he could;
None had made so many journeys,
None had seen so many wonders,
As this wonderful Iagoo,
As this marvellous story-teller!
Thus his name became a by-word
And a jest among the people;
And whene'er a boastful hunter
Praised his own address too highly,
Or a warrior, home returning,
Talked too much of his achievements,
All his hearers cried, "Iagoo!
Here's Iagoo come among us!"
He it was who carved the cradle
Of the little Hiawatha,
Carved its framework out of linden,
Bound it strong with reindeer sinews;
He it was who taught him later
How to make his bows and arrows,
How to make the bows of ash-tree,
And the arrows of the oak-tree.
So among the guests assembled
At my Hiawatha's wedding
Sat Iagoo, old and ugly,
Sat the marvellous story-teller.
And they said, "O good Iagoo,
Tell us now a tale of wonder,
Tell us of some strange adventure,
That the feast may be more joyous,
That the time may pass more gayly,
And our guests be more contented!"
And Iagoo answered straightway,

"You shall hear a tale of wonder,
You shall hear the strange adventures
Of Osseo, the Magician,
From the Evening Star descended."

XII

The Son of the Evening Star

. . . . The swan was still there. He shot the first arrow with
great precision, and came very near to it. The second came
still closer; as he took the last arrow, he felt his arm firmer, and
drawing it up with vigour, saw it pass through the neck of the
swan a little above the breast.   Still it did not prevent the bird
from flying off, which it did, however, at first slowly, flapping
its wings and rising gradually into the air, and then flying off
toward the sinking of the sun. . . . From "The Red Swan," in
Algic Researches, v. 2, p. 12.

Can it be the sun descending
O'er the level plain of water?
Or the Red Swan floating, flying,
Wounded by the magic arrow,
Staining all the waves with crimson,
With the crimson of its life-blood,
Filling all the air with splendor,
With the splendor of its plumage?
　Yes; it is the sun descending,
Sinking down into the water;
All the sky is stained with purple,
All the water flushed with crimson!
No; it is the Red Swan floating,
Diving down beneath the water;
To the sky its wings are lifted,
With its blood the waves are reddened!
　Over it the Star of Evening
Melts and trembles through the purple,
Hangs suspended in the twilight.
No; it is a bead of wampum
On the robes of the Great Spirit,
As he passes through the twilight,
Walks in silence through the heavens.
　This with joy beheld Iagoo
And he said in haste: "Behold it!

See the sacred Star of Evening!
You shall hear a tale of wonder,
Hear the story of Osseo!
Son of the Evening Star, Osseo!

There once lived an Indian in the north, who had ten daughters, all of whom grew up to womanhood. They were noted for their beauty, but especially Oweenee, the youngest, who was very independent in her way of thinking. She was a great admirer of romantic places, and paid very little attention to the numerous young men who came to her father's lodge for the purpose of seeing her. Her elder sisters were all solicited in marriage from their parents, and one after another, went off to dwell in the lodges of their husbands, or mothers-in-law, but she would listen to no proposals of the kind. At last she married an old man called Osseo, who was scarcely able to walk, and was too poor to have things like others. They jeered and laughed at her, on all sides, but she seemed to be quite happy, and said to them, "It is my choice, and you will see in the end, who has acted the wisest." Soon after, the sisters and their husbands and their parents were all invited to a feast, and as they walked along the path, they could not help pitying their young and handsome sister, who had such an unsuitable mate. Osseo often stopped and gazed upwards, but they could perceive nothing in the direction he looked, unless it was the faint glimmering of the evening star. They heard him muttering to himself as they went along, and one of the elder sisters caught the words, "Sho-wain-ne-me-shin nosa."* "Poor old man," said she, "he is talking to his father, what a pity it is, that he would not fall and break his neck, that our sister might have a handsome young husband." Presently they passed a large hollow log, lying with one end toward the path. The moment Osseo, who was of the turtle totem, came to it, he stopped short, uttered a loud and peculiar yell, and then dashing into one end of the log, he came out at the other, a most beautiful young man, and springing back to the road, he led off the party with

* Pity me, my father.

steps as light as the reindeer.*   But on turning round to look for his wife, behold, she had been changed into an old, decrepit woman, who was bent almost double, and walked with a cane. The husband, however, treated her very kindly, as she had done him during the time of his enchantment, and constantly addressed her by the term of ne-ne-moosh-a, or my sweetheart.

When they came to the hunter's lodge with whom they were to feast, they found the feast ready prepared, and as soon as their entertainer had finished his harangue (in which he told them his feasting was in honour of the Evening, or Woman's Star) they began to partake of the portion dealt out, according to age and character, to each one.   The food was very delicious, and they were all happy but Osseo, who looked at his wife and then gazed upward, as if he was looking into the substance of the sky.   Sounds were soon heard, as if from far-off voices in the air, and they became plainer and plainer, till he could clearly distinguish some of the words.

"My son—my son," said the voice, "I have seen your afflictions and pity your wants.   I come to call you away from a scene that is stained with blood and tears.   The earth is full of sorrows.   Giants and sorcerers, the enemies of mankind, walk abroad in it, and are scattered throughout its length. Every night they are lifting their voices to the Power of Evil, and every day they make themselves busy in casting evil in the hunter's path.   You have long been their victim, but shall be their victim no more.   The spell you were under is broken. Your evil genius is overcome.   I have cast him down by my superior strength, and it is this strength I now exert for your happiness.   Ascend, my son—ascend into the skies, and partake of the feast I have prepared for you in the stars, and bring with you those you love.

"The food set before you is enchanted and blessed.   Fear not to partake of it.   It is endowed with magic power to give immortality to mortals, and to change men to spirits.   Your bowls and kettles shall be no longer wood and earth.   The one shall become silver, and the other wampum.   They shall shine

* Caribou, once common in North America, north of latitude 46°.

like fire, and glisten like the most beautiful scarlet. Every female shall also change her state and looks, and no longer be doomed to laborious tasks. She shall put on the beauty of the starlight, and become a shining bird of the air, clothed with shining feathers. She shall dance and not work—she shall sing and not cry."

"My beams," continued the voice, "shine faintly on your lodge, but they have a power to transform it into the lightness of the skies, and decorate it with the colours of the clouds. Come, Osseo, my son, and dwell no longer on earth. Think strongly on my words, and look steadfastly at my beams. My power is now at its height. Doubt not—delay not. It is the voice of the Spirit of the stars that calls you away to happiness and celestial rest."

The words were intelligible to Osseo, but his companions thought them some far-off sounds of music, or birds singing in the woods. Very soon the lodge began to shake and tremble, and they felt it rising into the air. It was too late to run out, for they were already as high as the tops of the trees. Osseo looked around him as the lodge passed through the topmost boughs, and behold! their wooden dishes were changed into shells of a scarlet colour, the poles of the lodge to glittering wires of silver, and the bark that covered them into the gorgeous wings of insects. A moment more, and his brothers and sisters, and their parents and friends, were transformed into birds of various plumage. Some were jays, some partridges and pigeons, and others gay singing birds, who hopped about displaying their glittering feathers, and singing their songs. But Oweenee still kept her earthly garb, and exhibited all the indications of extreme age. He again cast his eyes in the direction of the clouds, and uttered that peculiar yell, which had given him the victory at the hollow log. In a moment the youth and beauty of his wife returned; her dingy garments assumed the shining appearance of green silk, and her cane was changed into a silver feather. The lodge again shook and trembled, for they were now passing through the uppermost clouds, and they immediately after found themselves in the Evening Star, the residence of Osseo's father.

"My son," said the old man, "hang that cage of birds, which you have brought along in your hand, at the door, and I will inform you why you and your wife have been sent for." Osseo obeyed the directions, and then took his seat in the lodge. "Pity was shown to you," resumed the king of the star, "on account of the contempt of your wife's sister, who laughed at her ill fortune, and ridiculed you while you were under the power of that wicked spirit, whom you overcame at the log. That spirit lives in the next lodge, being a small star you see on the left of mine, and he has always felt envious of my family, because we had greater power than he had, and especially on account of our having had the care committed to us of the female world. He failed in several attempts to destroy your brothers-in-law and sisters-in-law, but succeeded at last in transforming yourself and your wife into decrepit old persons. You must be careful and not let the light of his beams fall on you, while you are here, for therein is the power of his enchantment; a ray of light is the bow and arrows he uses."

Osseo lived happy and contented in the parental lodge, and in due time his wife presented him with a son, who grew up rapidly, and was the image of his father. He was very quick and ready in learning every thing that was done in his grandfather's dominions, but he wished also to learn the art of hunting, for he had heard that this was a favourite pursuit below. To gratify him his father made him a bow and arrows, and he then let the birds out of the cage that he might practise in shooting. He soon became expert, and the very first day brought down a bird, but when he went to pick it up, to his amazement, it was a beautiful young woman with the arrow sticking in her breast. It was one of his younger *aunts*. The moment her blood fell upon the surface of that pure and spotless planet, the charm was dissolved. The boy immediately found himself sinking, but was partly upheld, by something like wings, till he passed through the lower clouds, and he then suddenly dropped upon a high, romantic island in a large lake.

He was pleased on looking up, to see all his aunts and uncles following him in the form of birds, and he soon discovered the silver lodge, with his father and mother, descending with its waving barks looking like so many insects' gilded wings. It rested on the highest cliffs of the island, and here they fixed their residence. They all resumed their natural *shapes,* but were diminished to the *size* of fairies, and as a mark of homage to the King of the Evening Star, they never failed, on every pleasant evening, during the summer season, to join hands, and dance upon the top of the rocks. These rocks were quickly observed by the Indians to be covered, in moonlight evenings, with a larger sort of Puk Wudj Ininees, or little men, and were called Mish-in-e-mok-in-ok-ong, or turtle spirits, and the island is named from them to this day.* Their shining lodge can be seen in the summer evenings when the moon shines strongly on the pinnacles of the rocks, and the fishermen, who go near those high cliffs at night, have even heard the voices of the happy little dancers.—"Osseo, or The Son of the Evening Star," in *Algic Researches,* v. 2, p. 152–59.

> "Once, in days no more remembered,
> Ages nearer the beginning,
> When the heavens were closer to us,
> And the Gods were more familiar,
> In the North-land lived a hunter,
> With ten young and comely daughters,
> Tall and lithe as wands of willow;
> Only Oweenee, the youngest,
> She the wilful and the wayward,
> She the silent, dreamy maiden,
> Was the fairest of the sisters.
> "All these women married warriors,
> Married brave and haughty husbands;
> Only Oweenee, the youngest,
> Laughed and flouted all her lovers,
> All her young and handsome suitors,
> And then married old Osseo,

* Michilimackinac, the term alluded to, is the original French orthography of Mish en i mok in ong, the *local* form (sing. and plu.) of Turtle Spirits.

Old Osseo, poor and ugly,
Broken with age and weak with coughing,
Always coughing like a squirrel.
    "Ah, but beautiful within him
Was the spirit of Osseo,
From the Evening Star descended,
Star of Evening, Star of Woman,
Star of tenderness and passion!
All its fire was in his bosom,
All its beauty in his spirit,
All its mystery in his being,
All its splendor in his language!
    "And her lovers, the rejected,
Handsome men with belts of wampum,
Handsome men with paint and feathers,
Pointed at her in derision,
Followed her with jest and laughter.
But she said: 'I care not for you,
Care not for your belts of wampum,
Care not for your paint and feathers,
Care not for your jest and laughter;
I am happy with Osseo!'
    "Once to some great feast invited,
Through the damp and dusk of evening
Walked together the ten sisters,
Walked together with their husbands;
Slowly followed old Osseo,
With fair Oweenee beside him;
All the others chatted gayly,
These two only walked in silence.
    "At the western sky Osseo
Gazed intent, as if imploring,
Often stopped and gazed imploring
At the trembling Star of Evening,
At the tender Star of Woman;
And they heard him murmur softly,
'Ah, showain nemeshin, Nosa!
Pity, pity me, my father!'
    " 'Listen!' said the elder sister,
'He is praying to his father!
What a pity that the old man
Does not stumble in the pathway,
Does not break his neck by falling!'

And they laughed till all the forest
Rang with their unseemly laughter.
    "On their pathway through the woodlands
Lay an oak, by storms uprooted,
Lay the great trunk of an oak-tree,
Buried half in leaves and mosses,
Mouldering, crumbling, huge and hollow.
And Osseo, when he saw it,
Gave a shout, a cry of anguish,
Leaped into its yawning cavern,
At one end went in an old man,
Wasted, wrinkled, old, and ugly;
From the other came a young man,
Tall and straight and strong and handsome.
    "Thus Osseo was transfigured,
Thus restored to youth and beauty;
But, alas for good Osseo,
And for Oweenee, the faithful!
Strangely, too, was she transfigured.
Changed into a weak old woman,
With a staff she tottered onward,
Wasted, wrinkled, old, and ugly!
And the sisters and their husbands
Laughed until the echoing forest
Rang with their unseemly laughter.
    "But Osseo turned not from her,
Walked with slower step beside her,
Took her hand, as brown and withered
As an oak-leaf is in Winter,
Called her sweetheart, Nenemoosha,
Soothed her with soft words of kindness,
Till they reached the lodge of feasting,
Till they sat down in the wigwam,
Sacred to the Star of Evening,
To the tender Star of Woman.
    "Wrapt in visions, lost in dreaming,
At the banquet sat Osseo;
All were merry, all were happy,
All were joyous but Osseo.
Neither food nor drink he tasted,
Neither did he speak nor listen,
But as one bewildered sat he,
Looking dreamily and sadly,

First at Oweenee, then upward
At the gleaming sky above them.
  "Then a voice was heard, a whisper,
Coming from the starry distance,
Coming from the empty vastness,
Low, and musical, and tender;
And the voice said: 'O Osseo!
O my son, my best beloved!
Broken are the spells that bound you,
All the charms of the magicians,
All the magic powers of evil;
Come to me; ascend, Osseo!
  " 'Taste the food that stands before you:
It is blessed and enchanted,
It has magic virtues in it,
It will change you to a spirit.
All your bowls and all your kettles
Shall be wood and clay no longer;
But the bowls be changed to wampum,
And the kettles shall be silver;
They shall shine like shells of scarlet,
Like the fire shall gleam and glimmer.
  " 'And the women shall no longer
Bear the dreary doom of labor,
But be changed to birds, and glisten
With the beauty of the starlight,
Painted with the dusky splendors
Of the skies and clouds of evening!'
  "What Osseo heard as whispers,
What as words he comprehended,
Was but music to the others,
Music as of birds afar off,
Of the whippoorwill afar off,
Of the lonely Wawonaissa
Singing in the darksome forest.
  "Then the lodge began to tremble,
Straight began to shake and tremble,
And they felt it rising, rising,
Slowly through the air ascending,
From the darkness of the tree-tops
Forth into the dewy starlight,
Till it passed the topmost branches;
And behold! the wooden dishes
All were changed to shells of scarlet!

And behold! the earthen kettles
All were changed to bowls of silver!
And the roof-poles of the wigwam
Were as glittering rods of silver,
And the roof of bark upon them
As the shining shards of beetles.
    "Then Osseo gazed around him,
And he saw the nine fair sisters,
All the sisters and their husbands,
Changed to birds of various plumage.
Some were jays and some were magpies,
Others thrushes, others blackbirds;
And they hopped, and sang, and twittered,
Perked and fluttered all their feathers,
Strutted in their shining plumage,
And their tails like fans unfolded.
    "Only Oweenee, the youngest,
Was not changed, but sat in silence,
Wasted, wrinkled, old, and ugly,
Looking sadly at the others;
Till Osseo, gazing upward,
Gave another cry of anguish,
Such a cry as he had uttered
By the oak-tree in the forest.
    "Then returned her youth and beauty,
And her soiled and tattered garments
Were transformed to robes of ermine,
And her staff became a feather,
Yes, a shining silver feather!
    "And again the wigwam trembled,
Swayed and rushed through airy currents,
Through transparent cloud and vapor,
And amid celestial splendors
On the Evening Star alighted,
As a snow-flake falls on snow-flake,
As a leaf drops on a river,
As the thistle-down on water.
    "Forth with cheerful words of welcome
Came the father of Osseo,
He with radiant locks of silver,
He with eyes serene and tender.
And he said: 'My son, Osseo,
Hang the cage of birds you bring there,
Hang the cage with rods of silver,

And the birds with glistening feathers,
At the doorway of my wigwam.'
　"At the door he hung the bird-cage,
And they entered in and gladly
Listened to Osseo's father,
Ruler of the Star of Evening,
As he said: 'O my Osseo!
I have had compassion on you,
Given you back your youth and beauty,
Into birds of various plumage
Changed your sisters and their husbands;
Changed them thus because they mocked you;
In the figure of the old man,
In that aspect sad and wrinkled,
Could not see your heart of passion,
Could not see your youth immortal;
Only Oweenee, the faithful,
Saw your naked heart and loved you.
　" 'In the lodge that glimmers yonder,
In the little star that twinkles
Through the vapors, on the left hand,
Lives the envious Evil Spirit,
The Wabeno, the magician,
Who transformed you to an old man.
Take heed lest his beams fall on you,
For the rays he darts around him
Are the power of his enchantment,
Are the arrows that he uses.'
　"Many years, in peace and quiet,
On the peaceful Star of Evening
Dwelt Osseo with his father;
Many years, in song and flutter,
At the doorway of the wigwam,
Hung the cage with rods of silver,
And fair Oweenee, the faithful,
Bore a son unto Osseo,
With the beauty of his mother,
With the courage of his father.
　"And the boy grew up and prospered,
And Osseo, to delight him,
Made him little bows and arrows,
Opened the great cage of silver,
And let loose his aunts and uncles,

All those birds with glossy feathers,
For his little son to shoot at.
  "Round and round they wheeled and darted,
Filled the Evening Star with music,
With their songs of joy and freedom;
Filled the Evening Star with splendor,
With the fluttering of their plumage;
Till the boy, the little hunter,
Bent his bow and shot an arrow,
Shot a swift and fatal arrow,
And a bird, with shining feathers,
At his feet fell wounded sorely.
  "But, O wondrous transformation!
'T was no bird he saw before him!
'T was a beautiful young woman,
With the arrow in her bosom!
  "When her blood fell on the planet,
On the sacred Star of Evening,
Broken was the spell of magic,
Powerless was the strange enchantment,
And the youth, the fearless bowman,
Suddenly felt himself descending,
Held by unseen hands, but sinking
Downward through the empty spaces,
Downward through the clouds and vapors,
Till he rested on an island,
On an island, green and grassy,
Yonder in the Big-Sea-Water.
  "After him he saw descending
All the birds with shining feathers,
Fluttering, falling, wafted downward,
Like the painted leaves of Autumn;
And the lodge with poles of silver,
With its roof like wings of beetles,
Like the shining shards of beetles,
By the winds of heaven uplifted,
Slowly sank upon the island,
Bringing back the good Osseo,
Bringing Oweenee, the faithful.
  "Then the birds, again transfigured,
Reassumed the shape of mortals,
Took their shape, but not their stature;
They remained as Little People,

Like the pygmies, the Puk-Wudjies,
And on pleasant nights of Summer,
When the Evening Star was shining,
Hand in hand they danced together
On the island's craggy headlands,
On the sand-beach low and level.
"Still their glittering lodge is seen there,
On the tranquil Summer evenings,
And upon the shore the fisher
Sometimes hears their happy voices,
Sees them dancing in the starlight!"
When the story was completed,
When the wondrous tale was ended,
Looking round upon his listeners,
Solemnly Iagoo added:
"There are great men, I have known such,
Whom their people understand not,
Whom they even make a jest of,
Scoff and jeer at in derision.
From the story of Osseo
Let us learn the fate of jesters!"
All the wedding guests delighted
Listened to the marvellous story,
Listened laughing and applauding,
And they whispered to each other:
"Does he mean himself, I wonder?
And are we the aunts and uncles?"
Then again sang Chibiabos,
Sang a song of love and longing,
In those accents sweet and tender,
In those tones of pensive sadness,
Sang a maiden's lamentation
For her lover, her Algonquin.

The following song, taken from the oral traditions of the north, is connected with a historical incident, of note, in the Indian wars of Canada. In 1759, great exertions were made by the French Indian department, under Gen. Montcalm, to bring a body of Indians into the valley of the lower St. Lawrence, and invitations, for this purpose reached the utmost shores of Lake Superior. In one of the canoes from that quarter, which was left on their way down, at the lake of Two Mountains, near the mouth of the Utawas, while the warriors proceeded farther, was a Chippewa girl called Paig-wain-e-osh-e, or the White Eagle, driven by the wind. While the party awaited there, the result of events at Quebec, she formed an attachment for a young Algonquin belonging to the French mission of the Two Mountains. This attachment was mutual, and gave origin to the song, of which the original words, with a literal prose translation, are subjoined:

I

Ia indenaindum
Ia indenaindum
Ma kow we yah
Nin denaindum we.

Ah me! when I think of him—when I think of him—my sweetheart, my Algonquin.

II

Pah bo je aun
Ne be nau be koning
Wabi megwissun
Nene mooshain we
    Odishquagumee.

As I embarked to return, he put the white wampum around my neck—a pledge of truth, my sweetheart, my Algonquin.

III

Keguh wejewin
Ain dah nuk ke yun
Ningee egobun
Nene mooshain we
    Odishquagumee.

I shall go with you, he said, to your native country—I shall go with you, my sweetheart—my Algonquin.

IV

Nia! nin de nah dush
Wassahwud gushuh
Aindahnuk ke yaun
Ke yau ninemooshai wee
    Odishquagumee.

Alas! I replied—my native country is far, far away—my sweetheart; my Algonquin.

V

Kai aubik oween
Ain aube aunin
Ke we naubee
Ne ne mooshai we
      Odishquagumee.

When I looked back again—where we parted, he was still looking after me, my sweetheart; my Algonquin.

VI

Apee nay we ne bow
Unishe bun
Aungwash agushing
Ne ne mooshai we
      Odishquagumee.

He was still standing on a fallen tree—that had fallen into the water, my sweetheart; my Algonquin.

VII

Nia! indenaindum
Nia! indenaindum
Ma kow we yuh
Nin de nain dum we
      Odishquagumee.

Alas! when I think of him—when I think of him—It is when I think of him; my Algonquin.—"Odjibwa Song," in *Oneóta,* p. 15–16.

> "When I think of my beloved,
> Ah me! think of my beloved,
> When my heart is thinking of him,
> O my sweetheart, my Algonquin!
>   "Ah me! when I parted from him,
> Round my neck he hung the wampum,
> As a pledge, the snow-white wampum,
> O my sweetheart, my Algonquin!
>   "I will go with you, he whispered,
> Ah me! to your native country;

Let me go with you, he whispered,
O my sweetheart, my Algonquin!
"Far away, away, I answered,
Very far away, I answered,
Ah me! is my native country,
O my sweetheart, my Algonquin!
"When I looked back to behold him,
Where we parted, to behold him,
After me he still was gazing,
O my sweetheart, my Algonquin!
"By the tree he still was standing,
By the fallen tree was standing,
That had dropped into the water,
O my sweetheart, my Algonquin!
"When I think of my beloved,
Ah me! think of my beloved,
When my heart is thinking of him,
O my sweetheart, my Algonquin!"
Such was Hiawatha's Wedding,
Such the dance of Pau-Puk-Keewis,
Such the story of Iagoo,
Such the songs of Chibiabos;
Thus the wedding banquet ended,
And the wedding guests departed,
Leaving Hiawatha happy
With the night and Minnehaha.

XIII

Blessing the Corn-Fields

It is well known that corn-planting and corn-gathering, at least among all the still *uncolonized* tribes, are left entirely to the females and children, and a few superannuated old men. It is not generally known, perhaps, that this labor is not compulsory, and that it is assumed by the females as a just equivalent, in their view, for the onerous and continuous labor of the other sex in providing meats, and skins for clothing, by the chase, and in defending their villages against their enemies and keeping intruders off their territories. A good Indian housewife deems this a part of her prerogative, and prides herself to have a store of corn to exercise her hospitality, or duly honor her husband's hospitality, in the entertainment of the lodge guests. . . .

A singular proof of this belief, in both sexes, of the mysterious influence of the steps of a woman on the vegetable and insect creation, is found in an ancient custom which was related to me respecting corn-planting. It was the practice of the hunter's wife, when the field of corn had been planted, to choose the first dark or over-clouded evening, to perform a secret circuit, *sans habillement,* around the field. For this purpose she slipped out of the lodge in the evening, unobserved, to some obscure nook, where she completely disrobed. Then taking her *matchecota,* or principal garment, in one hand, she dragged it around the field. This was thought to ensure a prolific crop, and to prevent the assaults of insects and worms upon the grain. It was supposed they could not creep over the charmed line.—From "Corn-Planting, and Its Incidents," in *Oneóta,* p. 82, 83.

Sing, O Song of Hiawatha,
Of the happy days that followed,
In the land of the Ojibways,
In the pleasant land and peaceful!
Sing the mysteries of Mondamin,
Sing the Blessing of the Corn-fields!
  Buried was the bloody hatchet,
Buried was the dreadful war-club,
Buried were all warlike weapons,
And the war-cry was forgotten.
There was peace among the nations;
Unmolested roved the hunters,
Built the birch canoe for sailing,
Caught the fish in lake and river,
Shot the deer and trapped the beaver;
Unmolested worked the women,
Made their sugar from the maple,
Gathered wild rice in the meadows,
Dressed the skins of deer and beaver.
  All around the happy village
Stood the maize-fields, green and shining,
Waved the green plumes of Mondamin,
Waved his soft and sunny tresses,
Filling all the land with plenty.

'T was the women who in Spring-time
Planted the broad fields and fruitful,
Buried in the earth Mondamin;
'T was the women who in Autumn
Stripped the yellow husks of harvest,
Stripped the garments from Mondamin,
Even as Hiawatha taught them.

Once, when all the maize was planted,
Hiawatha, wise and thoughtful,
Spake and said to Minnehaha,
To his wife, the Laughing Water:
"You shall bless to-night the corn-fields,
Draw a magic circle round them,
To protect them from destruction,
Blast of mildew, blight of insect,
Wagemin, the thief of corn-fields,
Paimosaid, who steals the maize-ear!

"In the night, when all is silence,
In the night, when all is darkness,
When the Spirit of Sleep, Nepahwin,
Shuts the doors of all the wigwams,
So that not an ear can hear you,
So that not an eye can see you,
Rise up from your bed in silence,
Lay aside your garments wholly,
Walk around the fields you planted,
Round the borders of the corn-fields,
Covered by your tresses only,
Robed with darkness as a garment.

"Thus the fields shall be more fruitful,
And the passing of your footsteps
Draw a magic circle round them,
So that neither blight nor mildew,
Neither burrowing worm nor insect,
Shall pass o'er the magic circle;
Not the dragon-fly, Kwo-ne-she,
Nor the spider, Subbekashe,
Nor the grasshopper, Pah-puk-keena,
Nor the mighty caterpillar,
Way-muk-kwana, with the bear-skin,
King of all the caterpillars!"

On the tree-tops near the corn-fields
Sat the hungry crows and ravens,
Kahgahgee, the King of Ravens,

With his band of black marauders,
And they laughed at Hiawatha,
Till the tree-tops shook with laughter,
With their melancholy laughter
At the words of Hiawatha.
"Hear him!" said they; "hear the Wise Man,
Hear the plots of Hiawatha!"
    When the noiseless night descended
Broad and dark o'er field and forest,
When the mournful Wawonaissa
Sorrowing sang among the hemlocks,
And the Spirit of Sleep, Nepahwin,
Shut the doors of all the wigwams,
From her bed rose Laughing Water,
Laid aside her garments wholly,
And with darkness clothed and guarded,
Unashamed and unaffrighted,
Walked securely round the corn-fields,
Drew the sacred, magic circle
Of her footprints round the corn-fields.
    No one but the Midnight only
Saw her beauty in the darkness,
No one but the Wawonaissa
Heard the panting of her bosom;
Guskewau, the darkness, wrapped her
Closely in his sacred mantle,
So that none might see her beauty,
So that none might boast, "I saw her!"
    On the morrow, as the day dawned,
Kahgahgee, the King of Ravens,
Gathered all his black marauders,
Crows and blackbirds, jays and ravens,
Clamorous on the dusky tree-tops,
And descended, fast and fearless,
On the fields of Hiawatha,
On the grave of the Mondamin.
    "We will drag Mondamin," said they,
"From the grave where he is buried,
Spite of all the magic circles
Laughing Water draws around it,
Spite of all the sacred footprints
Minnehaha stamps upon it!"
    But the wary Hiawatha,
Ever thoughtful, careful, watchful,

Had o'erheard the scornful laughter
When they mocked him from the tree-tops.
"Kaw!" he said, "my friends the ravens!
Kahgahgee, my King of Ravens!
I will teach you all a lesson
That shall not be soon forgotten!"

Manabozho was the author of arts and improvements. He taught men how to make agákwuts (axes), lances, and arrow-points, and all implements of bone and stone, and also how to make snares, and traps, and nets, to take animals, and birds, and fishes.—From "Allegorical Traditions of the Origin of Men," in *H. & S. I.*, pt. 1, p. 317.

He had risen before the daybreak,
He had spread o'er all the corn-fields
Snares to catch the black marauders,
And was lying now in ambush
In the neighboring grove of pine-trees,
Waiting for the crows and blackbirds,
Waiting for the jays and ravens.
Soon they came with caw and clamor,
Rush of wings and cry of voices,
To their work of devastation,
Settling down upon the corn-fields,
Delving deep with beak and talon,
For the body of Mondamin.
And with all their craft and cunning,
All their skill in wiles of warfare,
They perceived no danger near them,
Till their claws became entangled,
Till they found themselves imprisoned
In the snares of Hiawatha.
From his place of ambush came he,
Striding terrible among them,
And so awful was his aspect
That the bravest quailed with terror.
Without mercy he destroyed them
Right and left, by tens and twenties,
And their wretched, lifeless bodies
Hung aloft on poles for scarecrows
Round the consecrated corn-fields,
As a signal of his vengeance,
As a warning to marauders.

Only Kahgahgee, the leader,
Kahgahgee, the King of Ravens,
He alone was spared among them
As a hostage for his people.
With his prisoner-string he bound him,
Led him captive to his wigwam,
Tied him fast with cords of elm-bark
To the ridge-pole of his wigwam.
  "Kahgahgee, my raven!" said he,
"You the leader of the robbers,
You the plotter of this mischief,
The contriver of this outrage,
I will keep you, I will hold you,
As a hostage for your people,
As a pledge of good behavior!"
  And he left him, grim and sulky,
Sitting in the morning sunshine
On the summit of the wigwam,
Croaking fiercely his displeasure,
Flapping his great sable pinions,
Vainly struggling for his freedom,
Vainly calling on his people!
  Summer passed, and Shawondasee
Breathed his sighs o'er all the landscape,
From the South-land sent his ardors,
Wafted kisses warm and tender;
And the maize-field grew and ripened,
Till it stood in all the splendor
Of its garments green and yellow,
Of its tassels and its plumage,
And the maize-ears full and shining
Gleamed from bursting sheaths of verdure.
  Then Nokomis, the old woman,
Spake, and said to Minnehaha:
" 'T is the Moon when leaves are falling;
All the wild-rice has been gathered,
And the maize is ripe and ready;
Let us gather in the harvest,
Let us wrestle with Mondamin,
Strip him of his plumes and tassels,
Of his garments green and yellow!"

But if corn-planting be done in a lively and satisfied, and
not a slavish spirit, corn-gathering and husking is a season of

decided thankfulness and merriment. At these gatherings, the chiefs and old men are mere spectators, although they are pleased spectators, the young only sharing in the sport. Who has not seen, the sedate ogema in such a vicinage, smoking a dignified pipe with senatorial ease. On the other hand, turning to the group of nature's red daughters and their young cohorts, it may be safely affirmed that laughter and garrulity constitute no part of the characteristics of civilization. . . .

If one of the young female huskers finds a red ear of corn, it is typical of a brave admirer, and is regarded as a fitting present to some young warrior. But if the ear be crooked, and tapering to a point, no matter what colour, the whole circle is set in a roar, and *wa ge min* is the word shouted aloud. It is the symbol of a thief in the cornfield. It is considered as the image of an old man stooping as he enters the lot. . . .

The term wagemin, which unfolds all these ideas, and reveals, as by a talisman, all this information, is derived in part, from the tri-literal form Waweau, that which is bent or crooked. . . . This term is taken as the basis of the cereal chorus or corn song, as sung by the northern Algonquin tribes. It is coupled with the phrase Paimosaid. . . . Its literal meaning is, he who walks, or the walker; but the ideas conveyed by it, are, he who walks at night to pilfer corn. . . . The chorus is entirely composed of these two terms, variously repeated, and may be set down as follows:

> Wagemin,
> Wagemin,
> Paimosaid.
> Wagemin,
> Wagemin,
> Paimosaid.

When this chant has been sung, there is a pause, during which some one who is expert in these things, and has a turn for the comic or ironic, utters a short speech, in the manner of a recitative, in which a peculiar intonation is given, and generally interrogates the supposed pilferer, as if he were present to answer questions, or accusations. There can be no pretence, that this recitative part of the song is always the same, at different times and places, or even that the same person should not vary his phraseology. On the contrary, it is often an object to vary it. It is a perfect improvisation, and it may be supposed that the native composer is always actuated by a desire to please, as much as possible by novelty. The whole object indeed is, to keep up the existing merriment, and excite fun and laughter.

Cereal chorus:

> Wagemin! wagemin!
> Thief in the blade,
> Blight of the cornfield
> Paimosaid.

—From "Corn Planting and Its Incidents," in *Oneóta*, p. 83, 254–55.

> And the merry Laughing Water
> Went rejoicing from the wigwam,
> With Nokomis, old and wrinkled,
> And they called the women round them,
> Called the young men and the maidens,
> To the harvest of the corn-fields,
> To the husking of the maize-ear.
> On the border of the forest,
> Underneath the fragrant pine-trees,
> Sat the old men and the warriors
> Smoking in the pleasant shadow.
> In uninterrupted silence
> Looked they at the gamesome labor
> Of the young men and the women;
> Listened to their noisy talking,
> To their laughter and their singing,
> Heard them chattering like the magpies,
> Heard them laughing like the blue-jays,
> Heard them singing like the robins.
> And whene'er some lucky maiden
> Found a red ear in the husking,
> Found a maize-ear red as blood is,
> "Nushka!" cried they all together,
> "Nushka! you shall have a sweetheart,
> You shall have a handsome husband!"

"Ugh!" the old men all responded,
From their seats beneath the pine-trees.
    And whene'er a youth or maiden
Found a crooked ear in husking,
Found a maize-ear in the husking
Blighted, mildewed, or misshapen,
Then they laughed and sang together,
Crept and limped about the corn-fields,
Mimicked in their gait and gestures
Some old man, bent almost double,
Singing singly or together:
"Wagemin, the thief of corn-fields!
Paimosaid, who steals the maize-ear!"
    Till the corn-fields rang with laughter,
Till from Hiawatha's wigwam
Kahgahgee, the King of Ravens,
Screamed and quivered in his anger,
And from all the neighboring tree-tops
Cawed and croaked the black marauders.
"Ugh!" the old men all responded,
From their seats beneath the pine-trees!

XIV

PICTURE-WRITING

In those days said Hiawatha,
"Lo! how all things fade and perish!
From the memory of the old men
Pass away the great traditions,
The achievements of the warriors,
The adventures of the hunters,
All the wisdom of the Medas,
All the craft of the Wabenos,
All the marvellous dreams and visions
Of the Jossakeeds, the Prophets!
    "Great men die and are forgotten,
Wise men speak; their words of wisdom
Perish in the ears that hear them,
Do not reach the generations
That, as yet unborn, are waiting
In the great, mysterious darkness
Of the speechless days that shall be!
    "On the grave-posts of our fathers

Are no signs, no figures painted;
Who are in those graves we know not,
Only know they are our fathers.
Of what kith they are and kindred,
From what old, ancestral Totem,
Be it Eagle, Bear or Beaver,
They descended, this we know not,
Only know they are our fathers.
    "Face to face we speak together,
But we cannot speak when absent,
Cannot send our voices from us
To the friends that dwell afar off;
Cannot send a secret message,
But the bearer learns our secret,
May pervert it, may betray it,
May reveal it unto others."
    Thus said Hiawatha, walking
In the solitary forest,
Pondering, musing in the forest,
On the welfare of his people.
    From his pouch he took his colors,
Took his paints of different colors,
On the smooth bark of a birch-tree
Painted many shapes and figures,
Wonderful and mystic figures,
And each figure had a meaning,
Each some word or thought suggested.

["Indian Pictography," in *H. & S. I.*, part 1, occupies pages 333 to 430 and includes many plates of illustrations. The study given this material by Longfellow, and the extent to which he utilized it, can only be suggested here. The details used in his description of the symbols for the Love-Song are on pages 403–4.]

Gitche Manito the Mighty,
He, the Master of Life, was painted
As an egg, with points projecting
To the four winds of the heavens.
Everywhere is the Great Spirit,
Was the meaning of this symbol.
    Mitche Manito the Mighty,
He the dreadful Spirit of Evil,

As a serpent was depicted,
As Kenabeek, the great serpent.
Very crafty, very cunning,
Is the creeping Spirit of Evil,
Was the meaning of this symbol.
　Life and Death he drew as circles,
Life was white, but Death was darkened;
Sun and moon and stars he painted,
Man and beast, and fish and reptile,
Forests, mountains, lakes, and rivers.
　For the earth he drew a straight line,
For the sky a bow above it;
White the space between for day-time,
Filled with little stars for night-time;
On the left a point for sunrise,
On the right a point for sunset,
On the top a point for noontide,
And for rain and cloudy weather
Waving lines descending from it.
　Footprints pointing towards a wigwam
Were a sign of invitation,
Were a sign of guests assembling;
Bloody hands with palms uplifted
Were a symbol of destruction,
Were a hostile sign and symbol.
　All these things did Hiawatha
Show unto his wondering people,
And interpreted their meaning,
And he said: "Behold, your grave-posts
Have no mark, no sign, nor symbol.
Go and paint them all with figures;
Each one with its household symbol,
With its own ancestral Totem;
So that those who follow after
May distinguish them and know them."
　And they painted on the grave-posts,
On the graves yet unforgotten,
Each his own ancestral Totem,
Each the symbol of his household;
Figures of the Bear and Reindeer,
Of the Turtle, Crane, and Beaver,
Each inverted as a token
That the owner was departed,

That the chief who bore the symbol
Lay beneath in dust and ashes.
    And the Jossakeeds, the Prophets,
The Wabenos, the Magicians,
And the Medicine-men, the Medas,
Painted upon bark and deer-skin
Figures for the songs they chanted,
For each song a separate symbol,
Figures mystical and awful,
Figures strange and brightly colored;
And each figure had its meaning,
Each some magic song suggested.
    The Great Spirit, the Creator,
Flashing light through all the heaven;
The Great Serpent, the Kenabeek,
With his bloody crest erected,
Creeping, looking into heaven;
In the sky the sun, that glistens,
And the moon eclipsed and dying;
Owl and eagle, crane and hen-hawk,
And the cormorant, bird of magic;
Headless men, that walk the heavens,
Bodies lying pierced with arrows,
Bloody hands of death uplifted,
Flags on graves, and great war-captains
Grasping both the earth and heaven!
    Such as these the shapes they painted
On the birch-bark and the deer-skin;
Songs of war and songs of hunting,
Songs of medicine and of magic,
All were written in these figures,
For each figure had its meaning,
Each its separate song recorded.
    Nor forgotten was the Love-Song,
The most subtle of all medicines,
The most potent spell of magic,
Dangerous more than war or hunting!
Thus the Love-Song was recorded,
Symbol and interpretation.
    First a human figure standing,
Painted in the brightest scarlet;
'T is the lover, the musician,
And the meaning is, "My painting
Makes me powerful over others."

Then the figure seated, singing,
Playing on a drum of magic,
And the interpretation, "Listen!
'T is my voice you hear, my singing!"
    Then the same red figure seated
In the shelter of a wigwam,
And the meaning of the symbol,
"I will come and sit beside you
In the mystery of my passion!"
    Then two figures, man and woman,
Standing hand in hand together
With their hands so clasped together
That they seem in one united,
And the words thus represented
Are, "I see your heart within you,
And your cheeks are red with blushes!"
    Next the maiden on an island,
In the centre of an island;
And the song this shape suggested
Was, "Though you were at a distance,
Were upon some far-off island,
Such the spell I cast upon you,
Such the magic power of passion,
I could straightway draw you to me!"
    Then the figure of the maiden
Sleeping, and the lover near her,
Whispering to her in her slumbers,
Saying, "Though you were far from me
In the land of Sleep and Silence,
Still the voice of love would reach you!"
    And the last of all the figures
Was a heart within a circle,
Drawn within a magic circle;
And the image had this meaning:
"Naked lies your heart before me,
To your naked heart I whisper!"
    Thus it was that Hiawatha,
In his wisdom, taught the people
All the mysteries of painting,
All the art of Picture-Writing,
On the smooth bark of the birch-tree,
On the white skin of the reindeer,
On the grave-posts of the village.

XV

HIAWATHA'S LAMENTATION

. . . NEXT day the old wolf addressed him thus: "My brother, I am going to separate from you, but I will leave behind me one of the young wolves to be your hunter." He then departed. In the act Manabozho was disenchanted, and again resumed his mortal shape. He was sorrowful and dejected, but soon resumed his wonted air of cheerfulness. The young wolf who was left with him was a good hunter, and never failed to keep the lodge well supplied with meat. One day he addressed him as follows: "My grandson, I had a dream last night, and it does not portend good. It is of the large lake which lies in *that* direction (pointing). You must be careful never to cross it, even if the ice should appear good. If you should come to it at night weary or hungry, you must make the circuit of it." Spring commenced, and the snow was melting fast before the rays of the sun, when one evening the wolf came to this lake, weary with the day's chase. He disliked to go so far to make the circuit of it. "Hwooh!" he exclaimed, "there can be no great harm in trying the ice as it appears to be sound. Nesho* is over cautious on this point." But he had not got half way across when the ice gave way and he fell in, and was immediately seized by the serpents, who knew it was Manabozho's grandson, and were thirsting for revenge upon him. Manabozho sat pensively in his lodge.

Night came on, but no son returned. The second and third night passed, but he did not appear. He became very desolate and sorrowful. "Ah!" said he, "he must have disobeyed me, and has lost his life in that lake I told him of. Well!" said he at last, "I must mourn for him." So he took coal and blackened his face. But he was much perplexed as to the right mode. "I wonder," said he, "how I must do it? I will cry 'Oh! my grandson! Oh! my grandson!'" He burst out a laughing. "No! no! that won't do. I will try so—'Oh! my heart! Oh! my heart! ha! ha! ha!' That won't do either. I

---

* Abbreviated from Neshomiss, my grandfather.

will cry 'Oh my grandson obiquadj!' "* This satisfied him, and he remained in his lodge and fasted, till his days of mourning were over. "Now," said he, "I will go in search of him." He set out and travelled some time. At last he came to a great lake. He then raised the same cries of lamentation for his grandson which had pleased him. He sat down near a small brook that emptied itself into the lake, and repeated his cries. Soon a bird called Ke-ske-mun-i-see† came near to him. The bird inquired, "What are you doing here?" "Nothing," he replied; "but can you tell me whether any one lives in this lake, and what brings you here yourself?" "Yes!" responded the bird; "the Prince of Serpents lives here, and I am watching to see whether the obiquadj of Manabozho's grandson will not drift ashore, for he was killed by the serpents last spring. . . . From "Manabozho," in *Algic Researches*, v. 1, 162–64.

The Manitos who live in the air, the earth, and the water, became jealous of their great power, and conspired against them. Manabozho had warned his brother against their machinations, and cautioned him not to separate himself from his side; but one day Chibiabos ventured alone on one of the Great Lakes. It was winter, and the whole surface was covered with ice. As soon as he had reached the centre the malicious Manitos broke the ice, and plunged him to the bottom, where they hid his body.

Manabozho wailed along the shores. He waged a war against all the Manitos, and precipitated numbers of them to the deepest abyss. He called on the dead body of his brother. He put the whole country in dread by his lamentations. He then besmeared his face with black, and sat down six years to lament, uttering the name of Chibiabos. The Manitos consulted what to do to appease his melancholy and his wrath. The oldest and wisest of them, who had had no hand in the death of Chibiabos, offered to undertake the task of reconcili-

---

* That part of the intestines of a fish, which, by its expansion from air in the first stage of decomposition, causes the body to rise and float. The expression here means float.

† The Alcedo or kingfisher.

ation. They built a sacred lodge close to that of Manabozho, and prepared a sumptuous feast. They procured the most delicious tobacco, and filled a pipe. They then assembled in order, one behind the other, and each carrying under his arm a sack formed of the skin of some favorite animal, as a beaver, an otter, or a lynx, and filled with precious and curious medicines, culled from all plants. These they exhibited, and invited him to the feast with pleasing words and ceremonies. He immediately raised his head, uncovered it, and washed off his mourning colors and besmearments, and then followed them. When they had reached the lodge, they offered him a cup of liquor prepared from the choicest medicines, as, at once, a propitiation, and an initiative rite. He drank it at a single draught. He found his melancholy departed, and felt the most inspiring effects. They then commenced their dances and songs, united with various ceremonies. Some shook their bags at him as a token of skill. Some exhibited the skins of birds filled with smaller birds, which, by some art, would hop out of the throat of the bag. Others showed curious tricks with their drums. All danced, all sang, all acted with the utmost gravity, and earnestness of gestures; but with exactness of time, motion, and voice. Manabozho was cured; he ate, danced, sung, and smoked the sacred pipe. In this manner the mysteries of the Grand Medicine Dance were introduced.

The before recreant Manitos now all united their powers, to bring Chibiabos to life. They did so, and brought him to life, but it was forbidden him to enter the lodge. They gave him, through a chink, a burning coal, and told him to go and preside over the country of souls, and reign over the land of the dead. They bid him with the coal to kindle a fire for his aunts and uncles, a term by which is meant all men who should die thereafter, and make them happy, and let it be an everlasting fire.

Manabozho went to the Great Spirit after these things. He then descended to the earth, and confirmed the mysteries of the medicine-dance, and supplied all whom he initiated with medicines for the cure of all diseases. It is to him that we owe the growth of all the medical roots, and antidotes to every disease and poison. He commits the growth of these to Misukumigakwa, or the mother of the earth, to whom he makes offerings.—From "Allegorical Traditions of the Origin of Men," in *H. & S. I.*, pt. 1, p. 317–19.

. . . He [the divine messenger] then instituted the grand medicine or metay-we-win dance; this ceremony was to be observed annually, and with due solemnity, and the Indians, said Nabinoi, experienced much good from it; but unfortunately, the foolish young men were cheated by Mache Monedo, who caused them to adopt the Wabano dance and its ceremonies. This latter is decidedly an institution of the sagemaus, or evil spirits, and this was finally introduced into the metay-we-wining (i.e., medicine dance) and thereby corrupted it.
—From "Mash-kwa-sha-kwong," in *Oneóta*, p. 144–45.

In those days the Evil Spirits,
All the Manitos of mischief,
Fearing Hiawatha's wisdom,
And his love for Chibiabos,
Jealous of their faithful friendship,
And their noble words and actions,
Made at length a league against them,
To molest them and destroy them.
  Hiawatha, wise and wary,
Often said to Chibiabos,
"O my brother! do not leave me,
Lest the Evil Spirits harm you!"
Chibiabos, young and heedless,
Laughing shook his coal-black tresses,
Answered ever sweet and childlike,
"Do not fear for me, O brother!
Harm and evil come not near me!"
  Once when Peboan, the Winter,
Roofed with ice the Big-Sea-Water,
When the snow-flakes, whirling downward,
Hissed among the withered oak-leaves,
Changed the pine-trees into wigwams,
Covered all the earth with silence,—
Armed with arrows, shod with snow-shoes,
Heeding not his brother's warning,

Fearing not the Evil Spirits,
Forth to hunt the deer with antlers
All alone went Chibiabos.
    Right across the Big-Sea-Water
Sprang with speed the deer before him.
With the wind and snow he followed,
O'er the treacherous ice he followed,
Wild with all the fierce commotion
And the rapture of the hunting.
    But beneath, the Evil Spirits
Lay in ambush, waiting for him,
Broke the treacherous ice beneath him,
Dragged him downward to the bottom,
Buried in the sand his body.
Unktahee, the god of water,
He the god of the Dacotahs,
Drowned him in the deep abysses
Of the lake of Gitche Gumee.
    From the headlands Hiawatha
Sent forth such a wail of anguish,
Such a fearful lamentation,
That the bison paused to listen,
And the wolves howled from the prairies,
And the thunder in the distance
Starting answered "Baim-wawa!"
    Then his face with black he painted,
With his robe his head he covered,
In his wigwam sat lamenting,
Seven long weeks he sat lamenting,
Uttering still this moan of sorrow:—
    "He is dead, the sweet musician!
He the sweetest of all singers!
He has gone from us forever,
He has moved a little nearer
To the Master of all music,
To the Master of all singing!
O my brother, Chibiabos!"
    And the melancholy fir-trees
Waved their dark green fans above him,
Waved their purple cones above him,
Sighing with him to console him,
Mingling with his lamentation
Their complaining, their lamenting.
    Came the Spring, and all the forest

Looked in vain for Chibiabos;
Sighed the rivulet, Sebowisha,
Sighed the rushes in the meadow.
    From the tree-tops sang the bluebird,
Sang the bluebird, the Owaissa,
"Chibiabos! Chibiabos!
He is dead, the sweet musician!"
    From the wigwam sang the robin,
Sang the robin, the Opechee,
"Chibiabos! Chibiabos!
He is dead, the sweetest singer!"
    And at night through all the forest
Went the whippoorwill complaining,
Wailing went the Wawonaissa,
"Chibiabos! Chibiabos!
He is dead, the sweet musician!
He the sweetest of all singers!"

. . . The mysteries of the Meda . . . according to Pottawatomie tradition, were introduced by the Manitos to revive Manabozho out of his gloom, on account of the death of Chebiábos.—From "Rites and Symbolic Notations of the Songs of the Wabeno," in *H. & S. I.*, pt. 1, p. 366. The description of this and kindred ceremonials occupies pages 358–401. A comparison of this account with that in *Hiawatha* affords a good example of Longfellow's powers of selection and organization. His adaptations of such details as "I blow my brother strong," on page 363, and of the cabalistic chorus on page 370, are typical.

    Then the medicine-men, the Medas,
The magicians, the Wabenos,
And the Jossakeeds, the Prophets,
Came to visit Hiawatha;
Built a Sacred Lodge beside him,
To appease him, to console him,
Walked in silent, grave procession,
Bearing each a pouch of healing,
Skin of beaver, lynx, or otter,
Filled with magic roots and simples,
Filled with very potent medicines.
    When he heard their steps approaching,
Hiawatha ceased lamenting,

Called no more on Chibiabos;
Naught he questioned, naught he answered,
But his mournful head uncovered,
From his face the mourning colors
Washed he slowly and in silence,
Slowly and in silence followed
Onward to the Sacred Wigwam.

There a magic drink they gave him,
Made of Nahma-wusk, the spearmint,
And Wabeno-wusk, the yarrow,
Roots of power, and herbs of healing;
Beat their drums, and shook their rattles;
Chanted singly and in chorus,
Mystic songs, like these, they chanted.

"I myself, myself! behold me!
'T is the great Gray Eagle talking;
Come, ye white crows, come and hear him!
The loud-speaking thunder helps me;
All the unseen spirits help me;
I can hear their voices calling,
All around the sky I hear them!
I can blow you strong, my brother,
I can heal you, Hiawatha!"

"Hi-au-ha!" replied the chorus,
"Way-ha-way!" the mystic chorus.

"Friends of mine are all the serpents!
Hear me shake my skin of hen-hawk!
Mahng, the white loon, I can kill him;
I can shoot your heart and kill it!
I can blow you strong, my brother,
I can heal you, Hiawatha!"

"Hi-au-ha!" replied the chorus,
"Way-ha-way!" the mystic chorus.

"I myself, myself! the prophet!
When I speak the wigwam trembles,
Shakes the Sacred Lodge with terror,
Hands unseen begin to shake it!
When I walk, the sky I tread on
Bends and makes a noise beneath me!
I can blow you strong, my brother!
Rise and speak, O Hiawatha!"

"Hi-au-ha!" replied the chorus,
"Way-ha-way!" the mystic chorus.

Then they shook their medicine-pouches

O'er the head of Hiawatha,
Danced their medicine-dance around him;
And upstarting wild and haggard,
Like a man from dreams awakened,
He was healed of all his madness.
As the clouds are swept from heaven,
Straightway from his brain departed
All his moody melancholy;
As the ice is swept from rivers,
Straightway from his heart departed
All his sorrow and affliction.
    Then they summoned Chibiabos
From his grave beneath the waters,
From the sands of Gitche Gumee
Summoned Hiawatha's brother.
And so mighty was the magic
Of that cry and invocation,
That he heard it as he lay there
Underneath the Big-Sea-Water;
From the sand he rose and listened,
Heard the music and the singing,
Came, obedient to the summons,
To the doorway of the wigwam,
But to enter they forbade him.
    Through a chink a coal they gave him,
Through the door a burning fire-brand;
Ruler in the Land of Spirits,
Ruler o'er the dead, they made him,
Telling him a fire to kindle
For all those that died thereafter,
Camp-fires for their night encampments
On their solitary journey
To the kingdom of Ponemah,
To the land of the Hereafter.
    From the village of his childhood,
From the homes of those who knew him,
Passing silent through the forest,
Like a smoke-wreath wafted sideways,
Slowly vanished Chibiabos!

All things retained their natural colors and shapes. The woods and leaves, and streams and lakes, were only more bright and comely than he had ever witnessed. Animals bounded across his path with a freedom and confidence which seemed to tell him, there was no blood shed there. Birds of beautiful plumage inhabited the groves, and sported in the waters. There was but one thing in which he saw a very unusual effect. He noticed that his passage was not stopped by trees or other objects. He appeared to walk directly through them: they were, in fact, but the images or shadows of material forms. He became sensible that he was in the land of souls.

When he had travelled half a day's journey, through a country which was continually becoming more attractive, he came to the banks of a broad lake, in the centre of which was a large and beautiful island. He found a canoe of white shining stone, tied to the shore.—From "The Island of the Blessed; or the Hunter's Dream," in *H. & S. I.*, pt. 1, p. 322. Also printed as "The White Stone Canoe," in *Oneóta*, p. 6.

> Where he passed, the branches moved not,
> Where he trod, the grasses bent not,
> And the fallen leaves of last year
> Made no sound beneath his footsteps.
>   Four whole days he journeyed onward
> Down the pathway of the dead men;
> On the dead man's strawberry feasted,
> Crossed the melancholy river,
> On the swinging log he crossed it,—
> Came unto the Lake of Silver,
> In the Stone Canoe was carried
> To the Islands of the Blessed,
> To the land of ghosts and shadows.
>   On that journey, moving slowly,
> Many weary spirits saw he,
> Panting under heavy burdens,
> Laden with war-clubs, bows and arrows,
> Robes of fur, and pots and kettles,
> And with food that friends had given
> For that solitary journey.
>   "Ay! why do the living," said they,
> "Lay such heavy burdens on us!
> Better were it to go naked,
> Better were it to go fasting,
> Than to bear such heavy burdens
> On our long and weary journey!"
>   Forth then issued Hiawatha,

Wandered eastward, wandered westward,
Teaching men the use of simples
And the antidotes for poisons,
And the cure of all diseases.
Thus was first made known to mortals
All the mystery of Medamin,
All the sacred art of healing.

XVI

PAU-PUK-KEEWIS

A MAN of large stature, and great activity of mind and body, found himself standing alone on a prairie. He thought to himself, "How came I here? Are there no beings on this earth but myself? I must travel and see. I must walk till I find the abodes of men." So soon as his mind was made up, he set out, he knew not where, in search of habitations. No obstacles could divert him from his purpose. Neither prairies, rivers, woods, nor storms had the effect to daunt his courage or turn him back. After travelling a long time he came to a wood, in which he saw decayed stumps of trees, as if they had been cut in ancient times, but no other traces of men. Pursuing his journey, he found more recent marks of the same kind; and after this, he came to fresh traces of human beings; first their footsteps, and then the wood they had cut, lying in heaps. Continuing on, he emerged towards dusk from the forest, and beheld at a distance a large village of high lodges, standing on rising ground. He said to himself, "I will arrive there on a run." Off he started with all his speed; on coming to the first large lodge, he jumped over it. Those within saw something pass over the opening, and then heard a thump on the ground.

"What is that?" they all said.

One came out to see, and invited him in. He found himself in company with an old chief and several men, who were seated in the lodge. Meat was set before him, after which the chief asked him where he was going and what his name was. He answered, that he was in search of adventures, and his name was Paup-Puk-Keewiss. A stare followed.

"Paup-Puk-Keewiss!"* said one to another, and a general titter went round.—From "Paup-Puk-Keewiss," in *Algic Researches,* v. 1, 200–201.

You shall hear how Pau-Puk-Keewis,
He, the handsome Yenadizze,
Whom the people called the Storm Fool,
Vexed the village with disturbance;
You shall hear of all his mischief,
And his flight from Hiawatha,
And his wondrous transmigrations,
And the end of his adventures.
  On the shores of Gitche Gumee,
On the dunes of Nagow Wudjoo,
By the shining Big-Sea-Water
Stood the lodge of Pau-Puk-Keewis.
It was he who in his frenzy
Whirled these drifting sands together,
On the dunes of Nagow Wudjoo,
When, among the guests assembled,
He so merrily and madly
Danced at Hiawatha's wedding,
Danced the Beggar's Dance to please them.
  Now, in search of new adventures,
From his lodge went Pau-Puk-Keewis,
Came with speed into the village,
Found the young men all assembled
In the lodge of old Iagoo,
Listening to his monstrous stories,
To his wonderful adventures.

Ojeeg told the Otter to make the first attempt to try and make a hole in the sky. He consented with a grin. He made a leap, but fell down the hill stunned by the force of his fall; and the snow being moist, and falling on his back, he slid with velocity down the side of the mountain. When he found himself at the bottom, he thought to himself, it is the last time I make such another jump, so I will make the best of my way

* This word appears to be derived from the same root as Paup-puk-ke-nay, a grasshopper, the inflection iss making it personal. The Indian idea is that of harum scarum. He is regarded as a foil to Manabozho, with whom he is frequently brought in contact in aboriginal story craft.

home. Then it was the turn of the Beaver, who made the attempt, but fell down senseless; then of the Lynx and Badger, who had no better success.

"Now," says the Fisher to the Wolverine, "try your skill; your ancestors were celebrated for their activity, hardihood, and perseverance, and I depend on you for success. Now make the attempt." He did so, but also without success. He leaped the second time, but now they could see that the sky was giving way to their repeated attempts. Mustering strength, he made the third leap, and went in. The Fisher nimbly followed him.—From "Ojeeg Annung; or, The Summer-Maker," in *Algic Researches*, v. 1, p. 62–63.

> He was telling them the story
> Of Ojeeg, the Summer-Maker,
> How he made a hole in heaven,
> How he climbed up into heaven,
> And let out the summer-weather,
> The perpetual, pleasant Summer;
> How the Otter first essayed it;
> How the Beaver, Lynx, and Badger
> Tried in turn the great achievement,
> From the summit of the mountain
> Smote their fists against the heavens,
> Smote against the sky their foreheads,
> Cracked the sky, but could not break it;
> How the Wolverine, uprising,
> Made him ready for the encounter,
> Bent his knees down, like a squirrel,
> Drew his arms back, like a cricket.
> "Once he leaped," said old Iagoo,
> "Once he leaped, and lo! above him
> Bent the sky, as ice in rivers
> When the waters rise beneath it;
> Twice he leaped, and lo! above him
> Cracked the sky, as ice in rivers
> When the freshet is at highest!
> Thrice he leaped, and lo! above him
> Broke the shattered sky asunder,
> And he disappeared within it,
> And Ojeeg, the Fisher Weasel,
> With a bound went in behind him!"

"Hark you!" shouted Pau-Puk-Keewis
As he entered at the doorway;
"I am tired of all this talking,
Tired of old Iagoo's stories,
Tired of Hiawatha's wisdom.
Here is something to amuse you,
Better than this endless talking."

This is the principal game of hazard among the northern tribes. It is played with thirteen pieces, hustled in a vessel called onágun, which is a kind of wooden bowl. They are represented, and named, as follows.

The pieces marked No. 1, in this cut, of which there are two, are called Ininewug, or men. They are made tapering, or wedge-shaped in thickness, so as to make it possible, in throwing them, that they may stand on their base. Number 2, is called Gitshee Kenabik, or the Great Serpent. It consists of two pieces, one of which is fin-tailed, or a water-serpent, the other truncated, and is probably designed as terrestrial. They are formed wedge-shaped, so as to be capable of standing on their bases lengthwise. Each has four dots. Number 3 is called Pugamágun, or the war club. It has six marks on the handle, on the *red side*, and four radiating from the orifice of the club end; and four marks on the handle of the *white side;* and six radiating marks from the orifice on the club-end, making ten on each side. Number 4 is called Keego, which is the generic name for a fish. The four circular pieces of brass, slightly concave, with a flat surface on the apex, are called Ozawábiks. The three bird-shaped pieces, Sheshebwug, or ducks.

All but the circular pieces are made out of a fine kind of bone. One side of the piece is white, of the natural colour of the bones, and polished, the other red. The brass pieces have the convex side bright, the concave black. They are all shaken together, and thrown out of the onágun, as dice. The term pugasaing denotes this act of throwing. It is the participial form of the verb.

The following rules govern the game:

1. When the pieces are turned on the red side, and one of

the Ininewugs stands upright on the bright side of one of the brass pieces, it counts 158.

2. When all the pieces turn red side up, and the Gitshee Kenabik with the tail stands on the bright side of the brass piece, it counts 138.

3. When all turn up red, it counts 58 whether the brass pieces be bright or black side up.

4. When the Gitshee Kenabik and his associate, and the two Ininewugs turn up white side, and the other pieces red, it counts 58, irrespective of the concave or convex position of the brass pieces.

5. When all the pieces turn up white, it counts 38, whether the Ozawábiks be bright or black.

6. When the Gitshee Kenabik and his associate turn up red, and the other white, it counts 38, the brass pieces immaterial.

7. When one of the Ininewugs stands up, it counts 50, without regard to the position of all the rest.

8. When either of the Gitshee Kenabiks stands upright, it counts 40, irrespective of the position of the others.

9. When all the pieces turn up white, excepting one, and the Ozawábiks dark, it counts 20.

10. When all turn up red, except one, and the brass pieces bright, it counts 15.

11. When the whole of the pieces turn up white, but one, with the Ozawábiks bright, it counts 10.

12. When a brass piece turns up dark, the two Gitshee Kenabiks and the two men red, and the remaining pieces white, it counts 8.

13. When the brass piece turns up bright, the two Gitshee Kenabiks and one of the men red, and all the rest white, it is 6.

14. When the Gitshee Kenabik in chief, and one of the men turn up red, the Ozawábiks, bright, and all the others white, it is 4.

15. When both the Kenabiks, and both men, and the three ducks, turn up red, the brass piece black, and either the Keego, or a duck white, it is 5.

16. When all the pieces turn up red, but one of the Inine-wugs, and the brass piece black, it counts 2.

The limit of the game is stipulated. The parties throw up for the play.

This game is very fascinating to some portions of the Indians. They stake at it their ornaments, weapons, clothing, canoes, horses, everything in fact they possess; and have been known, it is said, to set up their wives and children, and even to forfeit their own liberty. Of such desperate stakes, I have seen no examples, nor do I think the game itself in common use. It is rather confined to certain persons, who hold the relative rank of gamblers in Indian society—men who are not noted as hunters or warriors, or steady providers for their families. Among these are persons who bear the term of Ienadizze-wug, that is, wanderers about the country, braggadocios, or fops. It can hardly be classed with the popular games of amusement, by which skill and dexterity are acquired. I have generally found the chiefs and graver men of the tribes, who encouraged the young men to play ball, and are sure to be present at the customary sports, to witness, and sanction, and applaud them, speak lightly and disparagingly of this game of hazard. Yet it cannot be denied that some of the chiefs, distinguished in war and the chase, at the west, can be referred to, as lending their example to its fascinating power.

An analysis of this game, to show its arithmetical principles and powers, might be gone into; but it is no part of the present design to take up such considerations here, far less to pursue the comparison and extension of customs of this kind among the modern western tribes. It may be sufficient to say, from the foregoing rules, that there seems to be no unit in the throw, and that the count proceeds by decimals, for all numbers over 8. Doubtless these rules are but a part of the whole series known to experienced players. They comprise, however, all that have been revealed to me.

Gambling is not peculiar to our race,
The Indian gambles with as fixed a face.

—"Pugasaing; or, The Game of the Bowl," in *Oneóta,* p. 85–87; also in *H. & S. I.,* pt. 2, p. 72–74; with illustrations.

Then from out his pouch of wolf-skin
Forth he drew, with solemn manner,
All the game of Bowl and Counters,
Pugasaing, with thirteen pieces.
White on one side were they painted,
And vermilion on the other;
Two Kenabeeks or great serpents,
Two Ininewug or wedge-men,
One great war-club, Pugamaugun,
And one slender fish, the Keego,
Four round pieces, Ozawabeeks,
And three Sheshebwug or ducklings.
All were made of bone and painted,
All except the Ozawabeeks;
These were brass, on one side burnished,
And were black upon the other.
In a wooden bowl he placed them,
Shook and jostled them together,
Threw them on the ground before him,
Thus exclaiming and explaining:
"Red side up are all the pieces,
And one great Kenabeek standing
On the bright side of a brass piece,
On a burnished Ozawabeek;
Thirteen tens and eight are counted."
Then again he shook the pieces,
Shook and jostled them together,
Threw them on the ground before him,
Still exclaiming and explaining:
"White are both the great Kenabeeks,
White the Ininewug, the wedge-men,
Red are all the other pieces;
Five tens and an eight are counted."
Thus he taught the game of hazard,
Thus displayed it and explained it,
Running through its various chances,
Various changes, various meanings:
Twenty curious eyes stared at him,
Full of eagerness stared at him.
"Many games," said old Iagoo,

"Many games of skill and hazard
Have I seen in different nations,
Have I played in different countries.
He who plays with old Iagoo
Must have very nimble fingers;
Though you think yourself so skilful
I can beat you, Pau-Puk-Keewis,
I can even give you lessons
In your game of Bowl and Counters!"
    So they sat and played together,
All the old men and the young men,
Played for dresses, weapons, wampum,
Played till midnight, played till morning,
Played until the Yenadizze,
Till the cunning Pau-Puk-Keewis,
Of their treasures had despoiled them,
Of the best of all their dresses,
Shirts of deer-skin, robes of ermine,
Belts of wampum, crests of feathers,
Warlike weapons, pipes and pouches.
Twenty eyes glared wildly at him,
Like the eyes of wolves glared at him.

He was not easy in his new position; the village was too small to give him full scope for his powers, and after a short stay he made up his mind to go farther, taking with him a young man who had formed a strong attachment for him, and might serve him as his mesh-in-au-wa.—"Paup-Puk-Keewiss," in *Algic Researches,* v. 1, p. 201.

    Said the lucky Pau-Puk-Keewis:
"In my wigwam I am lonely,
In my wanderings and adventures
I have need of a companion,
Fain would have a Meshinauwa,
An attendant and pipe-bearer.
I will venture all these winnings,
All these garments heaped about me,
All this wampum, all these feathers,
On a single throw will venture
All against the young man yonder!"
'T was a youth of sixteen summers,
'T was a nephew of Iagoo;
Face-in-a-Mist, the people called him.

As the fire burns in a pipe-head
Dusky red beneath the ashes,
So beneath his shaggy eyebrows
Glowed the eyes of old Iagoo.
"Ugh!" he answered very fiercely;
"Ugh!" they answered all and each one.
   Seized the wooden bowl the old man,
Closely in his bony fingers
Clutched the fatal bowl, Onagon,
Shook it fiercely and with fury,
Made the pieces ring together
As he threw them down before him.
   Red were both the great Kenabeeks,
Red the Ininewug, the wedge-men,
Red the Sheshebwug, the ducklings,
Black the four brass Ozawabeeks,
White alone the fish, the Keego;
Only five the pieces counted!
   Then the smiling Pau-Puk-Keewis
Shook the bowl and threw the pieces;
Lightly in the air he tossed them,
And they fell about him scattered;
Dark and bright the Ozawabeeks,
Red and white the other pieces,
And upright among the others
One Ininewug was standing,
Even as crafty Pau-Puk-Keewis
Stood alone among the players,
Saying, "Five tens! mine the game is!"
   Twenty eyes glared at him fiercely,
Like the eyes of wolves glared at him,
As he turned and left the wigwam,
Followed by his Meshinauwa,
By the nephew of Iagoo,
By the tall and graceful stripling,
Bearing in his arms the winnings,
Shirts of deer-skin, robes of ermine,
Belts of wampum, pipes and weapons.
   "Carry them," said Pau-Puk-Keewis,
Pointing with his fan of feathers,
"To my wigwam far to eastward,
On the dunes of Nagow Wudjoo!"
   Hot and red with smoke and gambling
Were the eyes of Pau-Puk-Keewis

As he came forth to the freshness
Of the pleasant Summer morning.
All the birds were singing gayly,
All the streamlets flowing swiftly,
And the heart of Pau-Puk-Keewis
Sang with pleasure as the birds sing,
Beat with triumph like the streamlets,
As he wandered through the village,
In the early gray of morning,
With his fan of turkey-feathers,
With his plumes and tufts of swan's down,
Till he reached the farthest wigwam,
Reached the lodge of Hiawatha.

After wandering a long time, he came to the lodge of
Manabozho, who was absent. He thought he would play him
a trick, and so turned everything in the lodge upside down, and
killed his chickens. Now Manabozho calls all the fowls of the
air his chickens; and among the number was a raven, the mean-
est of birds, which Paup-Puk-Keewiss killed and hung up by
the neck to insult him. He then went on till he came to a very
high point of rocks running out into the lake, from the top of
which he could see the country back as far as the eye could
reach. While sitting there, Manabozho's mountain chickens
flew round and past him in great numbers. So, out of spite,
he shot them in great numbers, for his arrows were sure and
the birds very plenty, and he amused himself by throwing the
birds down the rocky precipice. At length a wary bird cried
out, "Paup-Puk-Keewiss is killing us. Go and tell our father."
Away flew a delegation of them, and Manabozho soon made his
appearance on the plain below.—*Ibid.*, p. 216.

Silent was it and deserted;
No one met him at the doorway,
No one came to bid him welcome;
But the birds were singing round it,
In and out and round the doorway,
Hopping, singing, fluttering, feeding,
And aloft upon the ridge-pole
Kahgahgee, the King of Ravens,
Sat with fiery eyes, and, screaming,
Flapped his wings at Pau-Puk-Keewis.

"All are gone! the lodge is empty!"
Thus it was spake Pau-Puk-Keewis,
In his heart resolving mischief;—
"Gone is wary Hiawatha,
Gone the silly Laughing Water,
Gone Nokomis, the old woman,
And the lodge is left unguarded!"

By the neck he seized the raven,
Whirled it round him like a rattle,
Like a medicine-pouch he shook it,
Strangled Kahgahgee, the raven,
From the ridge-pole of the wigwam
Left its lifeless body hanging,
As an insult to its master,
As a taunt to Hiawatha.

With a stealthy step he entered,
Round the lodge in wild disorder
Threw the household things about him,
Piled together in confusion
Bowls of wood and earthen kettles,
Robes of buffalo and beaver,
Skins of otter, lynx, and ermine,
As an insult to Nokomis,
As a taunt to Minnehaha.

Then departed Pau-Puk-Keewis,
Whistling, singing through the forest,
Whistling gayly to the squirrels,
Who from hollow boughs above him
Dropped their acorn-shells upon him,
Singing gayly to the wood-birds,
Who from out the leafy darkness
Answered with a song as merry.

Then he climbed the rocky headlands
Looking o'er the Gitche Gumee,
Perched himself upon their summit,
Waiting full of mirth and mischief
The return of Hiawatha.

Stretched upon his back he lay there;
Far below him plashed the waters,
Plashed and washed the dreamy waters;
Far above him swam the heavens,
Swam the dizzy, dreamy heavens;
Round him hovered, fluttered, rustled,
Hiawatha's mountain chickens,

Flock-wise swept and wheeled about him,
Almost brushed him with their pinions.
    And he killed them as he lay there,
Slaughtered them by tens and twenties,
Threw their bodies down the headland,
Threw them on the beach below him,
Till at length Kayoshk, the sea-gull,
Perched upon a crag above them,
Shouted: "It is Pau-Puk-Keewis!
He is slaying us by hundreds!
Send a message to our brother,
Tidings send to Hiawatha!"

XVII

The Hunting of Pau-Puk-Keewis

PAUP-PUK-KEEWISS made his escape on the opposite side.
Manabozho cried out from the mountain, "The earth is not so
large but I can get up to you." Off Paup-Puk-Keewiss ran, and
Manabozho after him. He ran over hills and prairies with all
his speed, but still saw his pursuer hard after him.—From
"Paup-Puk-Keewiss," in *Algic Researches*, v. 1, p. 216–17.

Full of wrath was Hiawatha
When he came into the village,
Found the people in confusion,
Heard of all the misdemeanors,
All the malice and the mischief,
Of the cunning Pau-Puk-Keewis.
    Hard his breath came through his nostrils,
Through his teeth he buzzed and muttered
Words of anger and resentment,
Hot and humming like a hornet.
"I will slay this Pau-Puk-Keewis,
Slay this mischief-maker!" said he.
"Not so long and wide the world is,
Not so rude and rough the way is,
That my wrath shall not attain him,
That my vengeance shall not reach him!"
    Then in swift pursuit departed
Hiawatha and the hunters
On the trail of Pau-Puk-Keewis,

Through the forest, where he passed it,
To the headlands where he rested;
But they found not Pau-Puk-Keewis,
Only in the trampled grasses,
In the whortleberry-bushes,
Found the couch where he had rested,
Found the impress of his body.
    From the lowlands far beneath them,
From the Muskoday, the meadow,
Pau-Puk-Keewis, turning backward,
Made a gesture of defiance,
Made a gesture of derision;
And aloud cried Hiawatha,
From the summit of the mountains:
"Not so long and wide the world is,
Not so rude and rough the way is,
But my wrath shall overtake you,
And my vengeance shall attain you!"

After walking a while he came to a lake, which flooded the trees on its banks; he found it was only a lake made by beavers. He took his station on the elevated dam, where the stream escaped, to see whether any of the beavers would show themselves. He soon saw the head of one peeping out of the water to see who disturbed them.

"My friend," said Paup-Puk-Keewiss, "could you not turn me into a beaver like yourself?" for he thought, if he could become a beaver, he would see and know how these animals lived.

"I do not know," replied the beaver; "I will go and ask the others."

Soon all the beavers showed their heads above the water, and looked to see if he was armed; but he had left his bow and arrows in a hollow tree at a short distance. When they were satisfied, they all came near.

"Can you not, with all your united power," said he, "turn me into a beaver? I wish to live among you."

"Yes," answered their chief; "lay down"; and he soon found himself changed into one of them.

"You must make me large," said he; "larger than any of you."

"Yes, yes!" said they. "By-and-by, when we get into the lodge, it shall be done."

In they all dove into the lake; and, in passing large heaps of limbs and logs at the bottom, he asked the use of them; they answered, "It is for our winter's provisions." When they all got into the lodge, their number was about one hundred. The lodge was large and warm.

"Now we will make you large," said they. "Will that do?" exerting their power.

"Yes," he answered, for he found he was ten times the size of the largest.

"You need not go out," said they. "We will bring your food into the lodge, and you will be our chief."

"Very well," Paup-Puk-Keewiss answered. He thought, "I will stay here and grow fat at their expense." But, soon after, one ran into the lodge out of breath, saying, "We are visited by Indians." All huddled together in great fear. The water began to lower, for the hunters had broken down the dam, and they soon heard them on the roof of the lodge, breaking it up. Out jumped all the beavers into the water, and so escaped. Paup-Puk-Keewiss tried to follow them; but, alas! they had made him so large that he could not creep out of the hole. He tried to call them back, but to no effect; he worried himself so much in trying to escape, that he looked like a bladder. He could not turn himself back into a man, although he heard and understood all the hunters said. One of them put his head in at the top of the lodge.

"Ty-au!" cried he; "Tut Ty-au! Me-shau-mik—king of the beavers is in." They all got at him, and knocked his scull till it was as soft as his brains. He thought, as well as ever he did, although he was a beaver. Seven or eight of them then placed his body on poles and carried him home. As they went, he reflected in this manner: "What will become of me? my ghost or shadow will not die after they get me to their lodges." Invitations were immediately sent out for a grand feast. The women took him out into the snow to skin him; but, as soon as his flesh got cold, his Jee-bi went off.—*Ibid.*, p. 206–209.

Over rock and over river,
Thorough bush, and brake, and forest,
Ran the cunning Pau-Puk-Keewis;
Like an antelope he bounded,
Till he came unto a streamlet
In the middle of the forest,
To a streamlet still and tranquil,
That had overflowed its margin,
To a dam made by the beavers,
To a pond of quiet water,
Where knee-deep the trees were standing,
Where the water-lilies floated,
Where the rushes waved and whispered.

On the dam stood Pau-Puk-Keewis,
On the dam of trunks and branches,
Through whose chinks the water spouted,
O'er whose summit flowed the streamlet.
From the bottom rose the beaver,
Looked with two great eyes of wonder,
Eyes that seemed to ask a question,
At the stranger, Pau-Puk-Keewis.

On the dam stood Pau-Puk-Keewis,
O'er his ankles flowed the streamlet,
Flowed the bright and silvery water,
And he spake unto the beaver,
With a smile he spake in this wise:
"O my friend Ahmeek, the beaver,
Cool and pleasant is the water;
Let me dive into the water,
Let me rest there in your lodges;
Change me, too, into a beaver!"

Cautiously replied the beaver,
With reserve he thus made answer:
"Let me first consult the others,
Let me ask the other beavers."
Down he sank into the water,
Heavily sank he, as a stone sinks,
Down among the leaves and branches,
Brown and matted at the bottom.

On the dam stood Pau-Puk-Keewis,
O'er his ankles flowed the streamlet,
Spouted through the chinks below him,
Dashed upon the stones beneath him,
Spread serene and calm before him,

And the sunshine and the shadows
Fell in flecks and gleams upon him,
Fell in little shining patches,
Through the waving, rustling branches.
      From the bottom rose the beavers,
Silently above the surface
Rose one head and then another,
Till the pond seemed full of beavers,
Full of black and shining faces.
      To the beavers Pau-Puk-Keewis
Spake entreating, said in this wise:
"Very pleasant is your dwelling,
O my friends! and safe from danger;
Can you not with all your cunning,
All your wisdom and contrivance,
Change me, too, into a beaver?"
      "Yes!" replied Ahmeek, the beaver,
He the King of all the beavers,
"Let yourself slide down among us,
Down into the tranquil water."
      Down into the pond among them
Silently sank Pau-Puk-Keewis;
Black became his shirt of deer-skin,
Black his moccasins and leggins,
In a broad black tail behind him
Spread his fox-tails and his fringes;
He was changed into a beaver.
      "Make me large," said Pau-Puk-Keewis,
"Make me large and make me larger,
Larger than the other beavers."
"Yes," the beaver chief responded,
"When our lodge below you enter,
In our wigwam we will make you
Ten times larger than the others."
      Thus into the clear brown water
Silently sank Pau-Puk-Keewis;
Found the bottom covered over
With the trunks of trees and branches,
Hoards of food against the winter,
Piles and heaps against the famine,
Found the lodge with arching doorway,
Leading into spacious chambers.
      Here they made him large and larger,
Made him largest of the beavers,

Ten times larger than the others.
"You shall be our ruler," said they;
"Chief and king of all the beavers."
    But not long had Pau-Puk-Keewis
Sat in state among the beavers,
When there came a voice of warning
From the watchman at his station
In the water-flags and lilies,
Saying, "Here is Hiawatha!
Hiawatha with his hunters!"
    Then they heard a cry above them,
Heard a shouting and a tramping,
Heard a crashing and a rushing,
And the water round and o'er them
Sank and sucked away in eddies,
And they knew their dam was broken.
    On the lodge's roof the hunters
Leaped, and broke it all asunder;
Streamed the sunshine through the crevice,
Sprang the beavers through the doorway,
Hid themselves in deeper water,
In the channel of the streamlet;
But the mighty Pau-Puk-Keewis
Could not pass beneath the doorway;
He was puffed with pride and feeding,
He was swollen like a bladder.
    Through the roof looked Hiawatha,
Cried aloud, "O Pau-Puk-Keewis!
Vain are all your craft and cunning,
Vain your manifold disguises!
Well I know you, Pau-Puk-Keewis!"
With their clubs they beat and bruised him,
Beat to death poor Pau-Puk-Keewis,
Pounded him as maize is pounded,
Till his skull was crushed to pieces.
    Six tall hunters, lithe and limber,
Bore him home on poles and branches,
Bore the body of the beaver;
But the ghost, the Jeebi in him,
Thought and felt as Pau-Puk-Keewis,
Still lived on as Pau-Puk-Keewis.
    And it fluttered, strove, and struggled,
Waving hither, waving thither,
As the curtains of a wigwam

Struggle with their thongs of deer-skin,
When the wintry wind is blowing;
Till it drew itself together,
Till it rose up from the body,
Till it took the form and features
Of the cunning Pau-Puk-Keewis
Vanishing into the forest.
　But the wary Hiawatha
Saw the figure ere it vanished,
Saw the form of Pau-Puk-Keewis
Glide into the soft blue shadow
Of the pine-trees of the forest;
Toward the squares of white beyond it,
Toward an opening in the forest,
Like a wind it rushed and panted,
Bending all the boughs before it,
And behind it, as the rain comes,
Came the steps of Hiawatha.

. . . on coming to a large lake with a sandy beach, he saw a large flock of brant, and, speaking to them, asked them to turn him into a brant.

"Yes," they replied.

"But I want to be very large," he said.

"Very well," they answered; and he soon found himself a large brant, all the others standing gazing in astonishment at his large size.

"You must fly as leader," they said.

"No," answered Paup-Puk-Keewiss, "I will fly behind."

"Very well," they said. "One thing more we have to say to you. You must be careful, in flying, not to look down, for something may happen to you."

"Well! it is so," said he; and soon the flock rose up into the air, for they were bound north. They flew very fast, he behind. One day, while going with a strong wind, and as swift as their wings could flap, while passing over a large village, the Indians raised a great shout on seeing them, particularly on Paup-Puk-Keewiss's account, for his wings were broader than two large aupukwa [mats]. They made such a noise, that he forgot what had been told him, about looking down. They were now

going as swift as arrows; and, as soon as he brought his neck
in and stretched it down to look at the shouters, his tail was
caught by the wind, and over and over he was blown. He tried
to right himself, but without success. Down, down he went,
making more turns than he wished for, from a height of several
miles. The first thing he knew was, that he was jammed into
a large hollow tree. To get back or forward was out of the
question, and there he remained till his brant life was ended by
starvation. His Jee-bi again left the carcass, and he once more
found himself in the shape of a human being.—*Ibid.*, p. 210–12.

> To a lake with many islands
> Came the breathless Pau-Puk-Keewis
> Where among the water-lilies
> Pishnekuh, the brant, were sailing;
> Through the tufts of rushes floating,
> Steering through the reedy islands.
> Now their broad black beaks they lifted,
> Now they plunged beneath the water,
> Now they darkened in the shadow,
> Now they brightened in the sunshine.
> "Pishnekuh!" cried Pau-Puk-Keewis,
> "Pishnekuh! my brothers!" said he,
> "Change me to a brant with plumage,
> With a shining neck and feathers,
> Make me large, and make me larger,
> Ten times larger than the others."
> Straightway to a brant they changed him,
> With two huge and dusky pinions,
> With a bosom smooth and rounded,
> With a bill like two great paddles,
> Made him larger than the others,
> Ten times larger than the largest,
> Just as, shouting from the forest,
> On the shore stood Hiawatha.
> Up they rose with cry and clamor,
> With a whirr and beat of pinions,
> Rose up from the reedy islands,
> From the water-flags and lilies.
> And they said to Pau-Puk-Keewis:
> "In your flying, look not downward,
> Take good heed, and look not downward,

Lest some strange mischance should happen,
Lest some great mishap befall you!"
　　Fast and far they fled to northward,
Fast and far through mist and sunshine,
Fed among the moors and fen-lands,
Slept among the reeds and rushes.
　　On the morrow as they journeyed,
Buoyed and lifted by the South-wind,
Wafted onward by the South-wind,
Blowing fresh and strong behind them,
Rose a sound of human voices,
Rose a clamor from beneath them,
From the lodges of a village,
From the people miles beneath them.
　　For the people of the village
Saw the flock of brant with wonder,
Saw the wings of Pau-Puk-Keewis
Flapping far up in the ether,
Broader than two doorway curtains.
　　Pau-Puk-Keewis heard the shouting,
Knew the voice of Hiawatha,
Knew the outcry of Iagoo,
And, forgetful of the warning,
Drew his neck in, and looked downward,
And the wind that blew behind him
Caught his mighty fan of feathers,
Sent him wheeling, whirling downward!
　　All in vain did Pau-Puk-Keewis
Struggle to regain his balance!
Whirling round and round and downward,
He beheld in turn the village
And in turn the flock above him,
Saw the village coming nearer,
And the flock receding farther,
Heard the voices growing louder,
Heard the shouting and the laughter;
Saw no more the flock above him,
Only saw the earth beneath him;
Dead out of the empty heaven,
Dead among the shouting people,
With a heavy sound and sullen,
Fell the brant with broken pinions.
　　But his soul, his ghost, his shadow,
Still survived as Pau-Puk-Keewis,

Took again the form and features
Of the handsome Yenadizze,
And again went rushing onward,
Followed fast by Hiawatha,
Crying: "Not so wide the world is,
Not so long and rough the way is,
But my wrath shall overtake you,
But my vengeance shall attain you!"

He then pushed on in the pursuit of Paup-Puk-Keewiss, and had got so near as to put out his arm to seize him; but Paup-Puk-Keewiss dodged him, and immediately raised such a dust and commotion by whirlwinds as made the trees break, and the sand and leaves dance in the air. Again and again Manabozho's hand was put out to catch him; but he dodged him at every turn, and kept up such a tumult of dust, that in the thickest of it, he dashed into a hollow tree which had been blown down, and changed himself into a snake, and crept out at the roots. Well that he did; for at the moment he had got out, Manabozho, who is Ogee-bau-ge-mon (a species of lightning), struck it with his power, and it was in fragments. Paup-Puk-Keewiss was again in human shape; again Manabozho pressed him hard. At a distance he saw a very high bluff of rock jutting out into the lake, and ran for the foot of the precipice, which was abrupt and elevated. As he came near, the local manito of the rock opened his door and told him to come in. The door was no sooner closed than Manabozho knocked.

"Open it!" he cried, with a loud voice.

The manito was afraid of him, but he said to his guest,

"Since I have sheltered you, I would sooner die with you than open the door."

"Open it!" Manabozho again cried.

The manito kept silent. Manabozho, however, made no attempt to open it by force. He waited a few moments. "Very well," he said; "I give you only till night to live." The manito trembled, for he knew he would be shut up under the earth.

Night came. The clouds hung low and black, and every moment the forked lightning would flash from them. The black clouds advanced slowly, and threw their dark shadows afar, and behind there was heard the rumbling noise of the coming thunder. As they came near to the precipice, the thunders broke, the lightning flashed, the ground shook, and the solid rocks split, tottered, and fell. And under their ruins were crushed the mortal bodies of Paup-Puk-Keewiss and the manito.

It was only then that Paup-Puk-Keewiss found he was really dead. He had been killed in different animal shapes; but now his body, in human shape, was crushed. Manabozho came and took their Jee-bi-ug or spirits.

"You," said he to Paup-Puk-Keewiss, "shall not be again permitted to live on the earth. I will give you the shape of the war-eagle, and you will be the chief of all fowls, and your duty shall be to watch over their destinies."—*Ibid.*, p. 218–20.

> And so near he came, so near him,
> That his hand was stretched to seize him,
> His right hand to seize and hold him,
> When the cunning Pau-Puk-Keewis
> Whirled and spun about in circles,
> Fanned the air into a whirlwind,
> Danced the dust and leaves about him,
> And amid the whirling eddies
> Sprang into a hollow oak-tree,
> Changed himself into a serpent,
> Gliding out through root and rubbish.
> With his right hand Hiawatha
> Smote amain the hollow oak-tree,
> Rent it into shreds and splinters,
> Left it lying there in fragments.
> But in vain; for Pau-Puk-Keewis,
> Once again in human figure,
> Full in sight ran on before him,
> Sped away in gust and whirlwind,
> On the shores of Gitche Gumee,
> Westward by the Big-Sea-Water,
> Came unto the rocky headlands,
> To the Pictured Rocks of sandstone,
> Looking over lake and landscape.
> And the Old Man of the Mountain,
> He the Manito of Mountains,
> Opened wide his rocky doorways,

CAVERN IN THE PICTURED ROCKS OF LAKE SUPERIOR.   FROM AN ENGRAVING
BY EASTMAN FROM A SKETCH BY SCHOOLCRAFT.

Opened wide his deep abysses,
Giving Pau-Puk-Keewis shelter
In his caverns dark and dreary,
Bidding Pau-Puk-Keewis welcome
To his gloomy lodge of sandstone.
  There without stood Hiawatha,
Found the doorways closed against him,
With his mittens, Minjekahwun,
Smote great caverns in the sandstone,
Cried aloud in tones of thunder,
"Open! I am Hiawatha!"
But the Old Man of the Mountain
Opened not, and made no answer
From the silent crags of sandstone,
From the gloomy rock abysses.
  Then he raised his hands to heaven,
Called imploring on the tempest,
Called Waywassimo, the lightning,
And the thunder, Annemeekee;
And they came with night and darkness,
Sweeping down the Big-Sea-Water
From the distant Thunder Mountains;
And the trembling Pau-Puk-Keewis
Heard the footsteps of the thunder,
Saw the red eyes of the lightning,
Was afraid, and crouched and trembled.
  Then Waywassimo, the lightning,
Smote the doorways of the caverns,
With his war-club smote the doorways,
Smote the jutting crags of sandstone,
And the thunder, Annemeekee,
Shouted down into the caverns,
Saying, "Where is Pau-Puk-Keewis!"
And the crags fell, and beneath them
Dead among the rocky ruins
Lay the cunning Pau-Puk-Keewis,
Lay the handsome Yenadizze,
Slain in his own human figure.
  Ended were his wild adventures,
Ended were his tricks and gambols,
Ended all his craft and cunning,
Ended all his mischief-making,
All his gambling and his dancing,
All his wooing of the maidens.

Then the noble Hiawatha
Took his soul, his ghost, his shadow,
Spake and said: "O Pau-Puk-Keewis!
Never more in human figure
Shall you search for new adventures;
Never more with jest and laughter
Dance the dust and leaves in whirlwinds,
But above there in the heavens
You shall soar and sail in circles;
I will change you to an eagle,
To Keneu, the great war-eagle,
Chief of all the fowls with feathers,
Chief of Hiawatha's chickens."

In these storms, when each inmate of the lodge has his conaus, or wrapper, tightly drawn around him, and all are cowering around the cabin fire, should some sudden puff of wind drive a volume of light snow into the lodge, it would scarcely happen, but that some one of the group would cry out "Ah, Pauppukeewiss is now gathering his harvest," an expression which has the effect to put them all into good humour.

Pauppukeewiss was a crazy brain, who played many queer tricks, but took care, nevertheless, to supply his family and children with food. But, in this, he was not always successful. Many winters have passed since he was overtaken, at this very season of the year, with great want, and he, with his whole family, was on the point of starvation. Every resource seemed to have failed. The snow was so deep, and the storm continued so long, that he could not even find a partridge or a hare. And his usual resource of fish had entirely failed. His lodge stood in a point of woods, not far back from the shores of the Gitchiguma, or great water, where the autumnal storms had piled up the ice into high pinnacles, resembling castles.

"I will go," said he to his family one morning, "to these castles, and solicit the pity of the spirits, who inhabit them, for I know that they are the residence of some of the spirits of Kabiboonoka." He did so, and found that his petition was not disregarded. They told him to fill his mushkemoots, or sacks, with the ice and snow, and pass on toward his lodge, without looking back, until he came to a certain hill. He must then drop his sacks, and leave them till morning, when he would find them filled with fish.

They cautioned him, that he must by no means look back, although he would hear a great many voices crying out to him, in abusive terms, for these voices were nothing but the wind playing through the branches of the trees. He faithfully obeyed the injunction, although he found it hard to avoid turning round, to see who was calling out to him. And when he visited his sacks in the morning, he found them filled with fish. —From "La Poudre, or The Storm-Fool," in *Algic Researches,* v. 2, p. 123–25.

> And the name of Pau-Puk-Keewis
> Lingers still among the people,
> Lingers still among the singers,
> And among the story-tellers;
> And in Winter, when the snow-flakes
> Whirl in eddies round the lodges,
> When the wind in gusty tumult
> O'er the smoke-flue pipes and whistles,
> "There," they cry, "comes Pau-Puk-Keewis;
> He is dancing through the village,
> He is gathering in his harvest!"

XVIII

THE DEATH OF KWASIND

SLEEP is personified by the Algic race, under the name of Weeng.* But the power of the Indian Morpheus is executed in a peculiar manner, and by a novel agency. Weeng seldom acts directly in inducing sleep, but he exercises dominion over hosts of gnome-like beings, who are everywhere present, and are constantly on the alert. These beings are invisible to common eyes. Each one is armed with a tiny puggamaugon, or club, and when he observes a person sitting or reclining under circumstances favourable to sleep, he nimbly climbs upon his forehead and inflicts a blow. The first blow only creates drowsiness, the second makes the person lethargic, so that he

---

* This word has the g sounded hard, as if it were followed by a half sound of k—a common sound for g final in the Odjibwa.

occasionally closes his eyelids, the third produces sound sleep. It is the constant duty of these little emissaries to put every one to sleep whom they encounter—men, women, and children. And they are found secreted around the bed, or on small protuberances of the bark of the Indian lodges. They hide themselves in the Gushkeepitaugun, or smoking pouch of the hunter, and when he sits down to light his pipe in the woods, are ready to fly out and exert their sleep-compelling power. If they succeed, the game is suffered to pass, and the hunter obliged to return to his lodge without a reward.

In general, however, they are represented to possess friendly dispositions, seeking constantly to restore vigour and elasticity to the exhausted body. But being without judgment, their power is sometimes exerted at the hazard of reputation, or even life. Sleep may be induced in a person carelessly floating in his canoe, above a fall; or in a war party, on the borders of an enemy's country; or in a female, without the protection of the lodge circle. Although their peculiar season of action is in the night, they are also alert during the day.

While the forms of these gnomes are believed to be those of ininees, little or fairy men, the figure of Weeng himself is unknown, and it is not certain that he has ever been seen. Most of what is known on this subject, is derived from Iagoo, who related, that going out one day with his dogs to hunt, he passed through a wide range of thicket, where he lost his dogs. He became much alarmed, for they were faithful animals, and he was greatly attached to them. He called out, and made every exertion to recover them in vain. At length he came to a spot where he found them asleep, having incautiously run near the residence of Weeng. After great exertions he aroused them, but not without having felt the power of somnolency himself. As he cast up his eyes from the place where the dogs were lying, he saw the Spirit of Sleep sitting upon a branch of a tree. He was in the shape of a giant insect, or monetoas, with many wings from his back, which made a low deep murmuring sound, like distant falling water. But Iagoo himself, being a very great liar and braggart, but little credit was given to his narration.

Weeng is not only the dispenser of sleep, but it seems, he is also the author of dulness, which renders the word susceptible of an ironical use. If an orator fails, he is said to be struck by Weeng. If a warrior lingers, he has ventured too near the sleepy god. If children begin to nod or yawn, the Indian mother looks up smilingly, and says, "they have been struck by Weeng," and puts them to bed.—"Weeng, From the Mythology of the Chippewas," in *Algic Researches*, v. 2, p. 226–28.

. . . He performed so many feats of strength and skill, that he excited the envy of the Puck-wudj In-in-ee-sug, or fairies, who conspired against his life. "For," said they, "if this man is suffered to go on, in his career of strength and exploits, we shall presently have no work to perform. Our agency in the affairs of men must cease. He will undermine our power, and drive us, at last, into the water, where we must all perish, or be devoured by the wicked Neebanawbaig.*

The strength of Kwasind was all concentrated in the crown of his head. This was, at the same time, the only vulnerable part of his body; and there was but one species of weapon which could be successfully employed in making any impression upon it. The fairies carefully hunted through the woods to find this weapon. It was the burr or seed vessel of the white pine. They gathered a quantity of this article, and waylaid Kwasind at a point on the river, where the red rocks jut into the water, forming rude castles—a point which he was accustomed to pass in his canoe. They waited a long time, making merry upon these rocks, for it was a highly romantic spot. At last the wished-for object appeared, Kwasind came floating calmly down the stream, on the afternoon of a summer's day, languid with the heat of the weather, and almost asleep. When his canoe came directly beneath the cliff, the tallest and stoutest fairy began the attack. Others followed his example. It was a long time before they could hit the vulner-

* A kind of water spirits.

able part, but success at length crowned their efforts, and Kwasind sunk, never to rise more.

Ever since this victory, the Puck Wudj Ininee have made that point of rock a favourite resort. The hunters often hear them laugh, and see their little plumes shake as they pass this scene on light summer evenings.—From "Kwasind, or The Fearfully Strong Man," in *Algic Researches*, v. 2, 163–64.

> Far and wide among the nations
> Spread the name and fame of Kwasind;
> No man dared to strive with Kwasind,
> No man could compete with Kwasind.
> But the mischievous Puk-Wudjies,
> They the envious Little People,
> They the fairies and the pygmies,
> Plotted and conspired against him.
> "If this hateful Kwasind," said they,
> "If this great, outrageous fellow
> Goes on thus a little longer,
> Tearing everything he touches,
> Rending everything to pieces,
> Filling all the world with wonder,
> What becomes of the Puk-Wudjies?
> Who will care for the Puk-Wudjies?
> He will tread us down like mushrooms,
> Drive us all into the water,
> Give our bodies to be eaten
> By the wicked Nee-ba-naw-baigs,
> By the Spirits of the water!"
> So the angry Little People
> All conspired against the Strong Man,
> All conspired to murder Kwasind,
> Yes, to rid the world of Kwasind,
> The audacious, overbearing,
> Heartless, haughty, dangerous Kwasind!
> Now this wondrous strength of Kwasind
> In his crown alone was seated;
> In his crown too was his weakness;
> There alone could he be wounded,
> Nowhere else could weapon pierce him,
> Nowhere else could weapon harm him.
> Even there the only weapon

That could wound him, that could slay him
Was the seed-cone of the pine-tree,
Was the blue cone of the fir-tree.
This was Kwasind's fatal secret,
Known to no man among mortals;
But the cunning Little People,
The Puk-Wudjies, knew the secret,
Knew the only way to kill him.

So they gathered cones together,
Gathered seed-cones of the pine-tree,
Gathered blue cones of the fir-tree,
In the woods by Taquamenaw,
Brought them to the river's margin,
Heaped them in great piles together,
Where the red rocks from the margin
Jutting overhang the river.
There they lay in wait for Kwasind,
The malicious Little People.

'T was an afternoon in Summer;
Very hot and still the air was,
Very smooth the gliding river,
Motionless the sleeping shadows;
Insects glistened in the sunshine,
Insects skated on the water,
Filled the drowsy air with buzzing,
With a far-resounding war-cry.

Down the river came the Strong Man,
In his birch canoe came Kwasind,
Floating slowly down the current
Of the sluggish Taquamenaw,
Very languid with the weather,
Very sleepy with the silence.

From the overhanging branches,
From the tassels of the birch-trees,
Soft the Spirit of Sleep descended;
By his airy hosts surrounded,
His invisible attendants,
Came the Spirit of Sleep, Nepahwin;
Like the burnished Dush-kwo-ne-she,
Like a dragon-fly, he hovered
O'er the drowsy head of Kwasind.

To his ear there came a murmur
As of waves upon a sea-shore,

As of far-off tumbling waters,
As of winds among the pine-trees;
And he felt upon his forehead
Blows of little airy war-clubs,
Wielded by the slumbrous legions
Of the Spirit of Sleep, Nepahwin,
As of some one breathing on him.

At the first blow of their war-clubs,
Fell a drowsiness on Kwasind;
At the second blow they smote him,
Motionless his paddle rested;
At the third, before his vision
Reeled the landscape into darkness,
Very sound asleep was Kwasind.

So he floated down the river,
Like a blind man seated upright,
Floated down the Taquamenaw,
Underneath the trembling birch-trees,
Underneath the wooded headlands,
Underneath the war encampment
Of the pygmies, the Puk-Wudjies.

There they stood, all armed and waiting,
Hurled the pine-cones down upon him,
Struck him on his brawny shoulders,
On his crown defenceless struck him.
"Death to Kwasind!" was the sudden
War-cry of the Little People.

And he sideways swayed and tumbled,
Sideways fell into the river,
Plunged beneath the sluggish water
Headlong, as an otter plunges;
And the birch canoe, abandoned,
Drifted empty down the river,
Bottom upward swerved and drifted:
Nothing more was seen of Kwasind.

But the memory of the Strong Man
Lingered long among the people,
And whenever through the forest
Raged and roared the wintry tempest,
And the branches, tossed and troubled,
Creaked and groaned and split asunder,
"Kwasind!" cried they; "that is Kwasind!
He is gathering in his fire-wood!"

XIX

The Ghosts

THERE lived a hunter in the north who had a wife and one child. His lodge stood far off in the forest, several days' journey from any other. He spent his days in hunting, and his evenings in relating to his wife the incidents that had befallen him. As game was very abundant he found no difficulty in killing as much as they wanted. Just in all his acts, he lived a peaceful and happy life.

One evening during the winter season, it chanced that he remained out later than usual, and his wife began to feel uneasy, for fear some accident had befallen him. It was already dark. She listened attentively and at last heard the sound of approaching footsteps. Not doubting it was her husband, she went to the door and beheld two strange females. She bade them enter, and invited them to remain.

She observed that they were total strangers in the country. There was something so peculiar in their looks, air, and manner, that she was uneasy in their company. They would not come near the fire; they sat in a remote part of the lodge, were shy and taciturn, and drew their garments about them in such a manner as nearly to hide their faces. So far as she could judge, they were pale, hollow-eyed, and long-visaged, very thin and emaciated. There was but little light in the lodge, as the fire was low, and served by its fitful flashes, rather to increase than dispel their fears. "Merciful spirit!" cried a voice from the opposite part of the lodge, "there are two corpses clothed with garments." The hunter's wife turned around, but seeing nobody, she concluded the sounds were but gusts of wind. She trembled, and was ready to sink to the earth.

Her husband at this moment entered and dispelled her fears. He threw down the carcass of a large fat deer. "Behold what a fine and fat animal," cried the mysterious females, and they immediately ran and pulled off pieces of the whitest fat,*

* The fat of animals is esteemed by the N. A. Indians among the choicest parts.

which they ate with greediness. The hunter and his wife looked on with astonishment, but remained silent. They supposed their guests might have been famished. Next day, however, the same unusual conduct was repeated. The strange females tore off the fat and devoured it with eagerness. The third day the hunter thought he would anticipate their wants by tying up a portion of the fattest pieces for them, which he placed on the top of his load. They accepted it, but still appeared dissatisfied, and went to the wife's portion and tore off more. The man and his wife felt surprised at such rude and unaccountable conduct, but they remained silent, for they respected their guests, and had observed that they had been attended with marked good luck during the residence of these mysterious visitors.

In other respects the deportment of the females was strictly unexceptionable. They were modest, distant, and silent. They never uttered a word during the day. At night they would occupy themselves in procuring wood, which they carried to the lodge, and then returning the implements exactly to the places in which they had found them, resume their places without speaking. They were never known to stay out until daylight. They never laughed or jested.

The winter had nearly passed away, without anything uncommon happening, when, one evening the hunter staid out very late. The moment he entered and laid down his day's hunt as usual before his wife, the two females began to tear off the fat, in so unceremonious a way, that her anger was excited. She constrained herself, however, in a measure, but did not conceal her feelings, although she said but little. The guests observed the excited state of her mind, and became unusually reserved and uneasy. The good hunter saw the change, and carefully inquired into the cause, but his wife denied having used any hard words. They retired to their couches, and he tried to compose himself to sleep, but could not, for the sobs and sighs of the two females were incessant. He arose on his couch and addressed them as follows:

"Tell me," said he, "what is it that gives you pain of mind, and causes you to utter those sighs. Has my wife given you offence, or trespassed on the rights of hospitality?"

They replied in the negative. "We have been treated by you with kindness and affection. It is not for any slight we have received, that we weep. Our mission is not to you only. We come from the land of the dead to test mankind, and to try the sincerity of the living. Often we have heard the bereaved by death say that if the dead could be restored, they would devote their lives to make them happy. We have been moved by the bitter lamentations which have reached the place of the dead, and have come to make proof of the sincerity of those who have lost friends. Three moons were allotted us by the Master of life to make the trial. More than half the time had been successfully past, when the angry feelings of your wife indicated the irksomeness you felt at our presence, and has made us resolve on our departure."

They continued to talk to the hunter and his wife, gave them instructions as to a future life, and pronounced a blessing upon them.

"There is one point," they added, "of which we wish to speak. You have thought our conduct very strange in rudely possessing ourselves of the choicest parts of your hunt. *That* was the point of trial selected to put you to. It is the wife's peculiar privilege. For another to usurp it, we knew to be the severest trial of her, and consequently of your temper and feelings. We know your manners and customs, but we came to prove you, not by a compliance with them, but a violation of them. Pardon us. We are the agents of him who sent us. Peace to your dwelling, adieu!"

When they ceased total darkness filled the lodge. No object could be seen. The inmates heard the door open and shut, but they never saw more of the two Jeebi-ug.

The hunter found the success which they had promised. He became celebrated in the chase, and never wanted for any thing. He had many children, all of whom grew up to manhood, and health, peace, and long life were the rewards of his hospitality.—"The Two Jeebi-ug, or A Trial of Feeling, From the Odjibwa," in *Algic Researches,* v. 2, p. 61–66; also a version, "The Two Ghosts, or Hospitality Rewarded," in *Travels in the Central Portions of the Mississippi Valley,* p. 412–20.

Never stoops the soaring vulture
On his quarry in the desert,
On the sick or wounded bison,
But another vulture, watching
From his high aerial look-out,
Sees the downward plunge, and follows;
And a third pursues the second,
Coming from the invisible ether,
First a speck, and then a vulture,
Till the air is dark with pinions.
   So disasters come not singly;
But as if they watched and waited,
Scanning one another's motions,
When the first descends, the others
Follow, follow, gathering flock-wise
Round their victim, sick and wounded,
First a shadow, then a sorrow,
Till the air is dark with anguish.
   Now, o'er all the dreary Northland,
Mighty Peboan, the Winter,
Breathing on the lakes and rivers,
Into stone had changed their waters.
From his hair he shook the snow-flakes,
Till the plains were strewn with whiteness,
One uninterrupted level,
As if, stooping, the Creator
With his hand had smoothed them over.
   Through the forest, wide and wailing,
Roamed the hunter on his snow-shoes;
In the village worked the women,
Pounded maize, or dressed the deer-skin;
And the young men played together
On the ice the noisy ball-play,
On the plain the dance of snow-shoes.
   One dark evening, after sundown,
In her wigwam Laughing Water
Sat with old Nokomis, waiting
For the steps of Hiawatha
Homeward from the hunt returning.
   On their faces gleamed the fire-light,

Painting them with streaks of crimson,
In the eyes of old Nokomis
Glimmered like the watery moonlight,
In the eyes of Laughing Water
Glistened like the sun in water;
And behind them crouched their shadows
In the corners of the wigwam,
And the smoke in wreaths above them
Climbed and crowded through the smoke-flue.
    Then the curtain of the doorway
From without was slowly lifted;
Brighter glowed the fire a moment,
And a moment swerved the smoke-wreath,
As two women entered softly,
Passed the doorway uninvited,
Without word of salutation,
Without sign of recognition,
Sat down in the farthest corner,
Crouching low among the shadows.
    From their aspect and their garments,
Strangers seemed they in the village;
Very pale and haggard were they,
As they sat there sad and silent,
Trembling, cowering with the shadows.
    Was it the wind above the smoke-flue,
Muttering down into the wigwam?
Was it the owl, the Koko-koho,
Hooting from the dismal forest?
Sure a voice said in the silence:
"These are corpses clad in garments,
These are ghosts that come to haunt you,
From the kingdom of Ponemah,
From the land of the Hereafter!"
    Homeward now came Hiawatha
From his hunting in the forest,
With the snow upon his tresses,
And the red deer on his shoulders.
At the feet of Laughing Water
Down he threw his lifeless burden;
Nobler, handsomer she thought him,
Than when first he came to woo her,
First threw down the deer before her,
As a token of his wishes,
As a promise of the future.

Then he turned and saw the strangers,
Cowering, crouching with the shadows;
Said within himself, "Who are they?
What strange guests has Minnehaha?"
But he questioned not the strangers,
Only spake to bid them welcome
To his lodge, his food, his fireside.

When the evening meal was ready,
And the deer had been divided,
Both the pallid guests, the strangers,
Springing from among the shadows,
Seized upon the choicest portions,
Seized the white fat of the roebuck,
Set apart for Laughing Water,
For the wife of Hiawatha;
Without asking, without thanking,
Eagerly devoured the morsels,
Flitted back among the shadows
In the corner of the wigwam.

Not a word spake Hiawatha,
Not a motion made Nokomis,
Not a gesture Laughing Water;
Not a change came o'er their features;
Only Minnehaha softly
Whispered, saying, "They are famished;
Let them do what best delights them;
Let them eat, for they are famished."

Many a daylight dawned and darkened,
Many a night shook off the daylight
As the pine shakes off the snow-flakes
From the midnight of its branches;
Day by day the guests unmoving
Sat there silent in the wigwam;
But by night, in storm or starlight,
Forth they went into the forest,
Bringing fire-wood to the wigwam,
Bringing pine-cones for the burning,
Always sad and always silent.

And whenever Hiawatha
Came from fishing or from hunting,
When the evening meal was ready,
And the food had been divided,
Gliding from their darksome corner,
Came the pallid guests, the strangers,

Seized upon the choicest portions
Set aside for Laughing Water,
And without rebuke or question
Flitted back among the shadows.
    Never once had Hiawatha
By a word or look reproved them;
Never once had old Nokomis
Made a gesture of impatience;
Never once had Laughing Water
Shown resentment at the outrage.
All had they endured in silence,
That the rights of guest and stranger,
That the virtue of free-giving,
By a look might not be lessened,
By a word might not be broken.
    Once at midnight Hiawatha,
Ever wakeful, ever watchful,
In the wigwam, dimly lighted
By the brands that still were burning,
By the glimmering, flickering fire-light,
Heard a sighing, oft repeated,
Heard a sobbing as of sorrow.
    From his couch rose Hiawatha,
From his shaggy hides of bison,
Pushed aside the deer-skin curtain,
Saw the pallid guests, the shadows,
Sitting upright on their couches,
Weeping in the silent midnight.
    And he said: "O guests! why is it
That your hearts are so afflicted,
That you sob so in the midnight?
Has perchance the old Nokomis,
Has my wife, my Minnehaha,
Wronged or grieved you by unkindness,
Failed in hospitable duties?"
    Then the shadows ceased from weeping,
Ceased from sobbing and lamenting,
And they said, with gentle voices:
"We are ghosts of the departed,
Souls of those who once were with you.
From the realms of Chibiabos
Hither have we come to try you,
Hither have we come to warn you.
    "Cries of grief and lamentation

Reach us in the Blessed Islands:
Cries of anguish from the living,
Calling back their friends departed,
Sadden us with useless sorrow.
Therefore have we come to try you;
No one knows us, no one heeds us.
We are but a burden to you,
And we see that the departed
Have no place among the living.
  "Think of this, O Hiawatha!
Speak of it to all the people,
That henceforward and forever
They no more with lamentations
Sadden the souls of the departed
In the Islands of the Blessed.

Git-Chee-Gau-Zinee, after a few days' illness, suddenly expired in the presence of his friends, by whom he was beloved and lamented. He had been an expert hunter, and left, among other things, a fine gun, which he had requested might be buried with his body. There were some who thought his death a suspension and not an extinction of the animal functions, and that he would again be restored. His widow was among the number, and she carefully watched the body for the space of four days. She thought that by laying her hand upon his breast she could discover remaining indications of vitality. Twenty-four hours had elapsed, and nearly every vestige of hope had departed, when the man came to life. He gave the following narration to his friends:

"After death, my Jeebi travelled in the broad road of the dead toward the happy land, which is the Indian paradise. I passed on many days without meeting with any thing of an extraordinary nature. Plains of large extent, and luxuriant herbage, began to pass before my eyes. I saw many beautiful groves, and heard the songs of innumerable birds. At length I began to suffer for the want of food. I reached the summit of an elevation. My eyes caught the glimpse of the city of the dead. But it appeared to be distant, and the intervening space, partly veiled in silvery mists, was spangled with glittering lakes and streams. At this spot I came in sight of numerous herds of stately deer, moose, and other animals, which walked near my path, and appeared to have lost their natural timidity. But having no gun I was unable to kill them. I thought of the request I had made to my friends, to put my gun in my grave, and resolved to go back and seek for it.

"I found I had the free use of my limbs and faculties, and I had no sooner made this resolution, than I turned back. But I now beheld an immense number of men, women, and children, travelling toward the city of the dead, every one of whom I had to face in going back. I saw, in this throng, persons of every age, from the little infant—the sweet and lovely Penaisee,* to the feeble gray-headed man, stooping with the weight of years. All whom I met, however, were heavily laden with implements, guns, pipes, kettles, meats, and other articles. One man stopped me and complained of the great burdens he had to carry. He offered me his gun, which I however refused, having made up my mind to procure my own. Another offered me a kettle. I saw women who were carrying their basket work and painted paddles, and little boys, with their ornamented war clubs and bows and arrows—the presents of their friends.

"After encountering this throng for two days and nights, I came to the place where I had died. But I could see nothing but a great fire, the flames of which rose up before me, and spread around me. Whichever way I turned to avoid them, the flames still barred my advance. I was in the utmost perplexity, and knew not what to do. At length I determined to make a desperate leap, thinking my friends were on the other side, and in this effort, I awoke from my trance." Here the chief paused, and after a few moments concluded his story with the following admonitory remarks:

"My chiefs and friends," said he, "I will tell you of one practice, in which our forefathers have been wrong. They have been accustomed to deposit too many things with the dead. These implements are burthensome to them. It requires a longer time for them to reach the peace of repose, and almost every one I have conversed with, complained bitterly to me of

* The term of endearment for a young son.

the evil. It would be wiser to put such things only, in the grave, as the deceased was particularly attached to, or made a formal request to have deposited with him. If he has been successful in the chase, and has abundance of things in his lodge, it would be better that they should remain for his family, or for division among his friends and relatives."—From "Git-Chee-Gau-Zinee, or The Trance," in *Algic Researches,* v. 2, p. 128–31.

"Do not lay such heavy burdens
In the graves of those you bury,
Not such weight of furs and wampum,
Not such weight of pots and kettles,
For the spirits faint beneath them.
Only give them food to carry,
Only give them fire to light them.
    "Four days is the spirit's journey
To the land of ghosts and shadows,
Four its lonely night encampments;
Four times must their fires be lighted.
Therefore, when the dead are buried,
Let a fire, as night approaches,
Four times on the grave be kindled,
That the soul upon its journey
May not lack the cheerful fire-light,
May not grope about in darkness.
    "Farewell, noble Hiawatha!
We have put you to the trial,
To the proof have put your patience,
By the insult of our presence,
By the outrage of our actions.
We have found you great and noble.
Fail not in the greater trial,
Faint not in the harder struggle."
    When they ceased, a sudden darkness
Fell and filled the silent wigwam.
Hiawatha heard a rustle
As of garments trailing by him,
Heard the curtain of the doorway
Lifted by a hand he saw not,
Felt the cold breath of the night air,
For a moment saw the starlight;
But he saw the ghosts no longer,

Saw no more the wandering spirits
From the kingdom of Ponemah,
From the land of the Hereafter.

XX

THE FAMINE

AFTER Manabozho had killed the Prince of Serpents, he was living in a state of great want, completely deserted by his powers, as a deity, and not able to procure the ordinary means of subsistence. He was at this time living with his wife and children, in a remote part of the country, where he could get no game. He was miserably poor. It was winter, and he had not the common Indian comforts.—From "The Moose and Woodpecker," in *Algic Researches,* v. 2, p. 217.

O the long and dreary Winter!
O the cold and cruel Winter!
Ever thicker, thicker, thicker
Froze the ice on lake and river,
Ever deeper, deeper, deeper,
Fell the snow o'er all the landscape,
Fell the covering snow, and drifted
Through the forest, round the village.
  Hardly from his buried wigwam
Could the hunter force a passage;
With his mittens and his snow-shoes
Vainly walked he through the forest,
Sought for bird or beast and found none,
Saw no track of deer or rabbit,
In the snow beheld no footprints,
In the ghastly, gleaming forest
Fell, and could not rise from weakness,
Perished there from cold and hunger.
  O the famine and the fever!
O the wasting of the famine!
O the blasting of the fever!
O the wailing of the children!
O the anguish of the women!
  All the earth was sick and famished;
Hungry was the air around them,
Hungry was the sky above them,

And the hungry stars in heaven
Like the eyes of wolves glared at them!
    Into Hiawatha's wigwam
Came two other guests as silent
As the ghosts were, and as gloomy,
Waited not to be invited,
Did not parley at the doorway,
Sat there without word of welcome
In the seat of Laughing Water;
Looked with haggard eyes and hollow
At the face of Laughing Water.
    And the foremost said: "Behold me!
I am Famine, Bukadawin!"
And the other said: "Behold me!
I am Fever, Ahkosewin!"
    And the lovely Minnehaha
Shuddered as they looked upon her,
Shuddered at the words they uttered,
Lay down on her bed in silence,
Hid her face, but made no answer;
Lay there trembling, freezing, burning
At the looks they cast upon her,
At the fearful words they uttered.
    Forth into the empty forest
Rushed the maddened Hiawatha;
In his heart was deadly sorrow,
In his face a stony firmness;
On his brow the sweat of anguish
Started, but it froze and fell not.
    Wrapped in furs and armed for hunting,
With his mighty bow of ash-tree,
With his quiver full of arrows,
With his mittens, Minjekahwun,
Into the vast and vacant forest
On his snow-shoes strode he forward.
    "Gitche Manito, the Mighty!"
Cried he with his face uplifted
In that bitter hour of anguish,
"Give your children food, O father!
Give us food, or we must perish!
Give me food for Minnehaha,
For my dying Minnehaha!"
    Through the far-resounding forest,

Through the forest vast and vacant
Rang that cry of desolation,
But there came no other answer
Than the echo of his crying,
Than the echo of the woodlands,
"Minnehaha! Minnehaha!"
  All day long roved Hiawatha
In that melancholy forest,
Through the shadow of whose thickets,
In the pleasant days of Summer,
Of that ne'er forgotten Summer,
He had brought his young wife homeward
From the land of the Dacotahs;
When the birds sang in the thickets,
And the streamlets laughed and glistened,
And the air was full of fragrance,
And the lovely Laughing Water
Said with voice that did not tremble,
"I will follow you, my husband!"
  In the wigwam with Nokomis,
With those gloomy guests that watched her,
With the Famine and the Fever,
She was lying, the Beloved,
She the dying Minnehaha.
  "Hark!" she said; "I hear a rushing,
Hear a roaring and a rushing,
Hear the Falls of Minnehaha
Calling to me from a distance!"
"No, my child!" said old Nokomis,
"'T is the night-wind in the pine-trees!"
  "Look!" she said; "I see my father
Standing lonely at his doorway,
Beckoning to me from his wigwam
In the land of the Dacotahs!"
"No, my child!" said old Nokomis,
"'T is the smoke, that waves and beckons!"

Pauguk, according to this authority, is the personification
of death. He is represented as existing without flesh or blood.
He is a hunter, and besides his bow and arrows, is armed with
a puggamagon, or war club. But he hunts only men, women,
and children. He is an object of dread and horror. To see him
is a sure indication of death. Some accounts represent his

bones as covered by a thin transparent skin, and his eye sockets
as filled with balls of fire.

Pauguk never speaks. Unlike the Jeebi or ghost, his limbs
never assume the rotundity of life, neither is he to be con-
founded in form with the numerous class of minor Manitoes, or
spirits. He does not possess the power of metamorphosis. Un-
varied in repulsiveness, he is ever an object of fear; and often,
according to Indian story, has the warrior, flushed with the
ardour of battle, rushing forward to seize the prize of victory,
clasped the cold and bony hand of Pauguk.—From "Pauguk,"
in *Algic Researches,* v. 2, p. 240–41.

> "Ah!" said she, "the eyes of Pauguk
> Glare upon me in the darkness,
> I can feel his icy fingers
> Clasping mine amid the darkness!
> Hiawatha! Hiawatha!"
> And the desolate Hiawatha,
> Far away amid the forest,
> Miles away among the mountains,
> Heard that sudden cry of anguish,
> Heard the voice of Minnehaha
> Calling to him in the darkness,
> "Hiawatha! Hiawatha!"
> Over snow-fields waste and pathless,
> Under snow-encumbered branches,
> Homeward hurried Hiawatha,
> Empty-handed, heavy-hearted,
> Heard Nokomis moaning, wailing:
> "Wahonowin! Wahonowin!
> Would that I had perished for you,
> Would that I were dead as you are!
> Wahonowin! Wahonowin!"
> And he rushed into the wigwam,
> Saw the old Nokomis slowly
> Rocking to and fro and moaning,
> Saw his lovely Minnehaha
> Lying dead and cold before him,
> And his bursting heart within him
> Uttered such a cry of anguish,
> That the forest moaned and shuddered,

That the very stars in heaven
Shook and trembled with his anguish.
　　Then he sat down, still and speechless,
On the bed of Minnehaha,
At the feet of Laughing Water,
At those willing feet, that never
More would lightly run to meet him,
Never more would lightly follow.
　　With both hands his face he covered.
Seven long days and nights he sat there,
As if in a swoon he sat there,
Speechless, motionless, unconscious
Of the daylight or the darkness.
　　Then they buried Minnehaha;
In the snow a grave they made her,
In the forest deep and darksome,
Underneath the moaning hemlocks;
Clothed her in her richest garments,
Wrapped her in her robes of ermine,
Covered her with snow, like ermine;
Thus they buried Minnehaha.
　　And at night a fire was lighted,
On her grave four times was kindled,
For her soul upon its journey
To the Islands of the Blessed.
From his doorway Hiawatha
Saw it burning in the forest,
Lighting up the gloomy hemlocks;
From his sleepless bed uprising,
From the bed of Minnehaha,
Stood and watched it at the doorway,
That it might not be extinguished,
Might not leave her in the darkness.
　　"Farewell!" said he, "Minnehaha!
Farewell, O my Laughing Water!
All my heart is buried with you,
All my thoughts go onward with you!
Come not back again to labor,
Come not back again to suffer,
Where the Famine and the Fever
Wear the heart and waste the body.
Soon my task will be completed,
Soon your footsteps I shall follow

To the Islands of the Blessed,
To the Kingdom of Ponemah,
To the Land of the Hereafter!"

XXI

THE WHITE MAN'S FOOT

An old man was sitting alone in his lodge, by the side of a frozen stream. It was the close of winter, and his fire was almost out. He appeared very old and very desolate. His locks were white with age, and he trembled in every joint. Day after day passed in solitude, and he heard nothing but the sounds of the tempest, sweeping before it the new-fallen snow.

One day, as his fire was just dying, a handsome young man approached and entered his dwelling. His cheeks were red with the blood of youth, his eyes sparkled with animation, and a smile played upon his lips. He walked with a light and quick step. His forehead was bound with a wreath of sweet grass, in place of a warrior's frontlet, and he carried a bunch of flowers in his hand.

"Ah, my son," said the old man, "I am happy to see you. Come in. Come, tell me of your adventures, and what strange lands you have been to see. Let us pass the night together. I will tell you of my prowess and exploits, and what I can perform. You shall do the same, and we will amuse ourselves."

He then drew from his sack a curiously-wrought antique pipe, and having filled it with tobacco, rendered mild by an admixture of certain leaves, handed it to his guest. When this ceremony was concluded they began to speak.

"I blow my breath," said the old man, "and the streams stand still. The water becomes stiff and hard as clear stone."

"I breathe," said the young man, "and flowers spring up all over the plains."

"I shake my locks," retorted the old man, "and snow covers the land. The leaves fall from the trees at my command, and my breath blows them away. The birds get up from the water, and fly to a distant land. The animals hide themselves from my breath, and the very ground becomes as hard as flint."

"I shake my ringlets," rejoined the young man, "and warm showers of soft rain fall upon the earth. The plants lift up their heads out of the earth, like the eyes of children glistening with delight. My voice recalls the birds. The warmth of my breath unlocks the streams. Music fills the groves wherever I walk, and all nature rejoices."

At length the sun began to rise. A gentle warmth came over the place. The tongue of the old man became silent. The robin and bluebird began to sing on the top of the lodge. The stream began to murmur by the door, and the fragrance of growing herbs and flowers came softly on the vernal breeze.

Daylight fully revealed to the young man the character of his entertainer. When he looked upon him, he had the icy visage of Peboan.* Streams began to flow from his eyes. As the sun increased, he grew less and less in stature, and anon had melted completely away. Nothing remained on the place of his lodge fire but the miskodeed,† a small white flower, with a pink border, which is one of the earliest species of Northern plants.—"Peboan and Seegwun, An Allegory of the Seasons," in *Algic Researches,* v. 1, p. 84–86.

> In his lodge beside a river,
> Close beside a frozen river,
> Sat an old man, sad and lonely.
> White his hair was as a snow-drift;
> Dull and low his fire was burning,
> And the old man shook and trembled,
> Folded in his Waubewyon,
> In his tattered white-skin-wrapper,
> Hearing nothing but the tempest
> As it roared along the forest,
> Seeing nothing but the snow-storm,
> As it whirled and hissed and drifted.
>   All the coals were white with ashes,
> And the fire was slowly dying,

* Winter.
† The *Claytonia virginica.*

As a young man, walking lightly,
At the open doorway entered.
Red with blood of youth his cheeks were,
Soft his eyes, as stars in Spring-time,
Bound his forehead was with grasses,
Bound and plumed with scented grasses;
On his lips a smile of beauty,
Filling all the lodge with sunshine,
In his hand a bunch of blossoms
Filling all the lodge with sweetness.

    "Ah, my son!" exclaimed the old man,
"Happy are my eyes to see you.
Sit here on the mat beside me,
Sit here by the dying embers,
Let us pass the night together.
Tell me of your strange adventures,
Of the lands where you have travelled;
I will tell you of my prowess,
Of my many deeds of wonder."

    From his pouch he drew his peace-pipe,
Very old and strangely fashioned;
Made of red stone was the pipe-head,
And the stem a reed with feathers;
Filled the pipe with bark of willow,
Placed a burning coal upon it,
Gave it to his guest, the stranger,
And began to speak in this wise:
"When I blow my breath about me,
When I breathe upon the landscape,
Motionless are all the rivers,
Hard as stone becomes the water!"

    And the young man answered, smiling:
"When I blow my breath about me,
When I breathe upon the landscape,
Flowers spring up o'er all the meadows,
Singing, onward rush the rivers!"

    "When I shake my hoary tresses,"
Said the old man, darkly frowning,
"All the land with snow is covered;
All the leaves from all the branches
Fall and fade and die and wither,
For I breathe, and lo! they are not.
From the waters and the marshes

Rise the wild goose and the heron,
Fly away to distant regions,
For I speak, and lo! they are not.
And where'er my footsteps wander,
All the wild beasts of the forest
Hide themselves in holes and caverns,
And the earth becomes as flintstone!"

"When I shake my flowing ringlets,"
Said the young man, softly laughing,
"Showers of rain fall warm and welcome,
Plants lift up their heads rejoicing,
Back unto their lakes and marshes
Come the wild goose and the heron,
Homeward shoots the arrowy swallow,
Sing the bluebird and the robin,
And where'er my footsteps wander,
All the meadows wave with blossoms,
All the woodlands ring with music,
All the trees are dark with foliage!"

While they spake, the night departed;
From the distant realms of Wabun,
From his shining lodge of silver,
Like a warrior robed and painted,
Came the sun, and said, "Behold me!
Gheezis, the great sun, behold me!"

Then the old man's tongue was speechless
And the air grew warm and pleasant,
And upon the wigwam sweetly
Sang the bluebird and the robin,
And the stream began to murmur,
And a scent of growing grasses
Through the lodge was gently wafted.

And Segwun, the youthful stranger,
More distinctly in the daylight
Saw the icy face before him;
It was Peboan, the Winter!

From his eyes the tears were flowing,
As from melting lakes the streamlets,
And his body shrunk and dwindled
As the shouting sun ascended,
Till into the air it faded,
Till into the ground it vanished,
And the young man saw before him,

On the hearth-stone of the wigwam,
Where the fire had smoked and smouldered,
Saw the earliest flower of Spring-time,
Saw the Beauty of the Spring-time,
Saw the Miskodeed in blossom.
   Thus it was that in the North-land
After that unheard-of coldness,
That intolerable Winter,
Came the Spring with all its splendor,
All its birds and all its blossoms,
All its flowers and leaves and grasses.
   Sailing on the wind to northward,
Flying in great flocks, like arrows,
Like huge arrows shot through heaven,
Passed the swan, the Mahnahbezee,
Speaking almost as a man speaks;
And in long lines waving, bending
Like a bow-string snapped asunder,
Came the white goose, Waw-be-wawa;
And in pairs, or singly flying,
Mahng the loon, with clangorous pinions,
The blue heron, the Shuh-shuh-gah,
And the grouse, the Mushkodasa.
   In the thickets and the meadows
Piped the bluebird, the Owaissa,
On the summit of the lodges
Sang the robin, the Opechee,
In the covert of the pine-trees
Cooed the pigeon, the Omemee,
And the sorrowing Hiawatha,
Speechless in his infinite sorrow,
Heard their voices calling to him,
Went forth from his gloomy doorway,
Stood and gazed into the heaven,
Gazed upon the earth and waters.
   From his wanderings far to eastward,
From the regions of the morning,
From the shining land of Wabun,
Homeward now returned Iagoo,
The great traveller, the great boaster,
Full of new and strange adventures,
Marvels many and many wonders.
   And the people of the village

Listened to him as he told them
Of his marvellous adventures,
Laughing answered him in this wise:
"Ugh! it is indeed Iagoo!
No one else beholds such wonders!"

He had seen, he said, a water
Bigger than the Big-Sea-Water,
Broader than the Gitche Gumee,
Bitter so that none could drink it!
At each other looked the warriors,
Looked the women at each other,
Smiled, and said, "It cannot be so!
Kaw!" they said, "it cannot be so!"

O'er it, said he, o'er this water
Came a great canoe with pinions,
A canoe with wings came flying,
Bigger than a grove of pine-trees,
Taller than the tallest tree-tops!
And the old men and the women
Looked and tittered at each other;
"Kaw!" they said, "we don't believe it!"

From its mouth, he said, to greet him,
Came Waywassimo, the lightning,
Came the thunder, Annemeekee!
And the warriors and the women
Laughed aloud at poor Iagoo;
"Kaw!" they said, "what tales you tell us!"

In it, said he, came a people,
In the great canoe with pinions
Came, he said, a hundred warriors;
Painted white were all their faces,
And with hair their chins were covered!
And the warriors and the women
Laughed and shouted in derision,
Like the ravens on the tree-tops,
Like the crows upon the hemlocks.
"Kaw!" they said, "what lies you tell us!
Do not think that we believe them!"

Only Hiawatha laughed not,
But he gravely spake and answered
To their jeering and their jesting:
"True is all Iagoo tells us;
I have seen it in a vision,

Seen the great canoe with pinions,
Seen the people with white faces,
Seen the coming of this bearded
People of the wooden vessel
From the regions of the morning,
From the shining land of Wabun.
   "Gitche Manito the Mighty,
The Great Spirit, the Creator,
Sends them hither on his errand,
Sends them to us with his message.
Wheresoe'er they move, before them
Swarms the stinging fly, the Ahmo,
Swarms the bee, the honey-maker;
Wheresoe'er they tread, beneath them
Springs a flower unknown among us,
Springs the White-man's Foot in blossom.
   "Let us welcome, then, the strangers,
Hail them as our friends and brothers,
And the heart's right hand of friendship
Give them when they come to see us.
Gitche Manito, the Mighty,
Said this to me in my vision.
   "I beheld, too, in that vision
All the secrets of the future,
Of the distant days that shall be.
I beheld the westward marches
Of the unknown, crowded nations.
All the land was full of people,
Restless, struggling, toiling, striving,
Speaking many tongues, yet feeling
But one heart-beat in their bosoms.
In the woodlands rang their axes,
Smoked their towns in all the valleys,
Over all the lakes and rivers
Rushed their great canoes of thunder.
   "Then a darker, drearier vision
Passed before me, vague and cloud-like:
I beheld our nation scattered,
All forgetful of my counsels,
Weakened, warring with each other;
Saw the remnants of our people
Sweeping westward, wild and woful,
Like the cloud-rack of a tempest,
Like the withered leaves of Autumn!"

XXII

HIAWATHA'S DEPARTURE

THE period of his labours and adventures having expired, he withdrew to dwell with his brother in the North, where he is understood to direct those storms which proceed from points west of the pole. He is regarded as the spirit of the northwest tempests, but receives no worship from the present race of Indians. It is believed by them that he is again to appear, and to exercise an important power in the final disposition of the human race.—From "Manabozho," in *Algic Researches*, v. 1, p. 172–73.

Manabozho, it is believed, yet lives on an immense flake of ice in the Arctic Ocean. We fear the white race will some day discover his retreat, and drive him off. Then the end of the world is at hand, for as soon as he puts his foot on the earth again, it will take fire, and every living creature perish in the flames.—From "Allegorical Traditions of the Origin of Men," in *H. & S. I.*, pt. 1, p. 319.

Conceiving this [the decision of the Five Nations to unite] to be the accomplishment of his mission to the Iroquois, the tutelar patron of this rising confederacy addressed them in a speech elaborate with wise counsels, and then announced his withdrawal to the skies. At its conclusion, he went down to the shore, and assumed his seat in his mystical vessel. Sweet music was heard in the air at the same moment, and as its cadence floated in the ears of the wondering multitude, it rose in the air, higher and higher, till it vanished from the sight, and disappeared in the celestial regions inhabited only by Owayneo and his hosts.—From "Hiawatha," in *H. & S. I.*, pt. 3, p. 317.

> By the shore of Gitche Gumee,
> By the shining Big-Sea-Water,
> At the doorway of his wigwam,
> In the pleasant summer morning,
> Hiawatha stood and waited.
> All the air was full of freshness,
> All the earth was bright and joyous,
> And before him, through the sunshine,

Westward toward the neighboring forest
Passed in golden swarms the Ahmo,
Passed the bees, the honey-makers,
Burning, singing in the sunshine.

Bright above him shone the heavens,
Level spread the lake before him;
From its bosom leaped the sturgeon,
Sparkling, flashing in the sunshine;
On its margin the great forest
Stood reflected in the water,
Every tree-top had its shadow,
Motionless beneath the water.

From the brow of Hiawatha
Gone was every trace of sorrow,
As the fog from off the water,
As the mist from off the meadow.
With a smile of joy and triumph,
With a look of exultation,
As of one who in a vision
Sees what is to be, but is not,
Stood and waited Hiawatha.

Toward the sun his hands were lifted,
Both the palms spread out against it,
And between the parted fingers
Fell the sunshine on his features,
Flecked with light his naked shoulders,
As it falls and flecks an oak-tree
Through the rifted leaves and branches.

O'er the water floating, flying,
Something in the hazy distance,
Something in the mists of morning,
Loomed and lifted from the water,
Now seemed floating, now seemed flying,
Coming nearer, nearer, nearer.

Was it Shingebis the diver?
Or the pelican, the Shada?
Or the heron, the Shuh-shuh-gah?
Or the white goose, Waw-be-wawa,
With the water dripping, flashing
From its glossy neck and feathers?

It was neither goose nor diver,
Neither pelican nor heron,
O'er the water floating, flying,
Through the shining mist of morning,

But a birch canoe with paddles,
Rising, sinking on the water,
Dripping, flashing in the sunshine;
And within it came a people
From the distant land of Wabun,
From the farthest realms of morning
Came the Black-Robe chief, the Prophet,
He the Priest of Prayer, the Pale-face,
With his guides and his companions.
　　And the noble Hiawatha,
With his hands aloft extended,*
Held aloft in sign of welcome,
Waited, full of exultation,
Till the birch canoe with paddles
Grated on the shining pebbles,
Stranded on the sandy margin,
Till the Black-Robe chief, the Pale-face,
With the cross upon his bosom,
Landed on the sandy margin.
　　Then the joyous Hiawatha
Cried aloud and spake in this wise:
"Beautiful is the sun, O strangers,
When you come so far to see us!
All our town in peace awaits you;
All our doors stand open for you;
You shall enter all our wigwams,
For the heart's right hand we give you.
　　"Never bloomed the earth so gayly,
Never shone the sun so brightly,
As to-day they shine and blossom
When you come so far to see us!
Never was our lake so tranquil,
Nor so free from rocks and sand-bars;
For your birch canoe in passing
Has removed both rock and sand-bar.
　　"Never before had our tobacco
Such a sweet and pleasant flavor,
Never the broad leaves of our corn-fields
Were so beautiful to look on,
As they seem to us this morning,
When you come so far to see us!"

* In this manner and with such words was Father Marquette received
by the Illinois.

And the Black-Robe chief made answer,
Stammered in his speech a little,
Speaking words yet unfamiliar:
"Peace be with you, Hiawatha,
Peace be with you and your people,
Peace of prayer, and peace of pardon,
Peace of Christ, and joy of Mary!"
Then the generous Hiawatha
Led the strangers to his wigwam,
Seated them on skins of bison,
Seated them on skins of ermine,
And the careful old Nokomis
Brought them food in bowls of bass-wood,
Water brought in birchen dippers,
And the calumet, the peace-pipe,
Filled and lighted for their smoking.
All the old men of the village,
All the warriors of the nation,
All the Jossakeeds, the prophets,
The magicians, the Wabenos,
And the medicine-men, the Medas,
Came to bid the strangers welcome;
"It is well," they said, "O brothers,
That you come so far to see us!"
In a circle round the doorway,
With their pipes they sat in silence,
Waiting to behold the strangers,
Waiting to receive their message;
Till the Black-Robe chief, the Pale-face,
From the wigwam came to greet them,
Stammering in his speech a little,
Speaking words yet unfamiliar;
"It is well," they said, "O brother,
That you come so far to see us!"
Then the Black-Robe chief, the prophet,
Told his message to the people,
Told the purport of his mission,
Told them of the Virgin Mary,
And her blessed Son, the Saviour,
How in distant lands and ages
He had lived on earth as we do;
How he fasted, prayed, and labored;
How the Jews, the tribe accursed,
Mocked him, scourged him, crucified him;

How he rose from where they laid him,
Walked again with his disciples,
And ascended into heaven.
    And the chiefs made answer, saying:
"We have listened to your message,
We have heard your words of wisdom,
We will think on what you tell us.
It is well for us, O brothers,
That you come so far to see us!"
    Then they rose up and departed
Each one homeward to his wigwam,
To the young men and the women
Told the story of the strangers
Whom the Master of Life had sent them
From the shining land of Wabun.
    Heavy with the heat and silence
Grew the afternoon of Summer,
With a drowsy sound the forest
Whispered round the sultry wigwam,
With a sound of sleep the water
Rippled on the beach below it;
From the corn-fields shrill and ceaseless
Sang the grasshopper, Pah-puk-keena;
And the guests of Hiawatha,
Weary with the heat of Summer,
Slumbered in the sultry wigwam.
    Slowly o'er the simmering landscape
Fell the evening's dusk and coolness,
And the long and level sunbeams
Shot their spears into the forest,
Breaking through its shields of shadow,
Rushed into each secret ambush,
Searched each thicket, dingle, hollow;
Still the guests of Hiawatha
Slumbered in the silent wigwam.
    From his place rose Hiawatha,
Bade farewell to old Nokomis,
Spake in whispers, spake in this wise,
Did not wake the guests, that slumbered;
    "I am going, O Nokomis,
On a long and distant journey,
To the portals of the Sunset,
To the regions of the home-wind,
Of the Northwest-Wind, Keewaydin.

But these guests I leave behind me,
In your watch and ward I leave them.
See that never harm comes near them,
See that never fear molests them,
Never danger nor suspicion,
Never want of food or shelter,
In the lodge of Hiawatha!"
　　Forth into the village went he,
Bade farewell to all the warriors,
Bade farewell to all the young men,
Spake persuading, spake in this wise:
　　"I am going, O my people,
On a long and distant journey;
Many moons and many winters
Will have come, and will have vanished,
Ere I come again to see you.
But my guests I leave behind me;
Listen to their words of wisdom,
Listen to the truth they tell you,
For the Master of Life has sent them
From the land of light and morning!"
　　On the shore stood Hiawatha,
Turned and waved his hand at parting;
On the clear and luminous water
Launched his birch canoe for sailing,
From the pebbles of the margin
Shoved it forth into the water;
Whispered to it, "Westward! westward!"
And with speed it darted forward.
　　And the evening sun descending
Set the clouds on fire with redness,
Burned the broad sky, like a prairie,
Left upon the level water
One long track and trail of splendor,
Down whose stream, as down a river,
Westward, westward Hiawatha
Sailed into the fiery sunset,
Sailed into the purple vapors,
Sailed into the dusk of evening.
　　And the people from the margin
Watched him floating, rising, sinking,
Till the birch canoe seemed lifted
High into that sea of splendor,
Till it sank into the vapors

Like the new moon slowly, slowly
Sinking in the purple distance.
   And they said, "Farewell forever!"
Said, "Farewell, O Hiawatha!"
And the forests, dark and lonely,
Moved through all their depths of darkness,
Sighed, "Farewell, O Hiawatha!"
And the waves upon the margin
Rising, rippling on the pebbles,
Sobbed, "Farewell, O Hiawatha!"
And the heron, the Shuh-shuh-gah,
From her haunts among the fen-lands,
Screamed, "Farewell, O Hiawatha!"
   Thus departed Hiawatha,
Hiawatha the Beloved,
In the glory of the sunset,
In the purple mists of evening,
To the regions of the home-wind,
Of the Northwest-Wind, Keewaydin,
To the Islands of the Blessed,
To the Kingdom of Ponemah,
To the Land of the Hereafter!

PART THREE

HENRY ROWE SCHOOLCRAFT

A BIOGRAPHY

His Ancestry

At St. Louis, Missouri, in 1818, Henry Rowe Schoolcraft said: "By extending our military posts to the Yellowstone, and the Falls of St. Anthony, the fur trade of the northwest regions, and the Upper Missouri, which is now engrossed by the British traders, and carried on through the Lakes and Montreal, will in a few years, be turned into its natural channels, the Mississippi and the Missouri. St. Louis will then become the great depot of this trade, as Montreal is now, and by the supplies it will furnish, and the furs and peltries it will receive in return, will add yearly to its wealth and increase. This measure will also be attended with the most important benefits to the frontier settlements, who will thereby be protected from savage invasions and wars, and be enabled to extend themselves into countries which would otherwise remain a wilderness for at least half a century longer."

This is more than mere economic vision. It shows statesmanship, not of the European school but of the hard-experienced, tradition-taught, frontier-facing American. Border conflict between English, French, Spanish, Indians, and Americans was in the blood of Henry Rowe Schoolcraft and of three generations back of him.

The family history that follows is taken from the sketch of the life of Henry Rowe Schoolcraft that precedes his *Memoirs*. If not actually written by him, or by his second wife, this must at least have had his editorial sanction. Whatever historical inconsistencies such traditions present, they have value as a part of the psychological background of the individual who believed them, in addition to what facts they may preserve.

To begin with, his great-grandfather, James Calcraft, was

294

present in the operations connected with the building by the English of Forts Anne and Edward on the North River, and Fort William Henry on Lake George. He had embarked at Liverpool, England, in the reign of George II—that is, after 1727—in a detachment of veteran troops intended to act against the French in Canada. Before that he had served in the armies of the Duke of Marlborough, during the reign of Queen Anne, with high reputation for bravery and loyalty. He had been present in Marlborough's celebrated triumphs on the continent, in one of which engagements Calcraft lost an eye from the premature explosion of the priming of a cannon. He was a descendant of a family that went to England with William the Conqueror and settled, under grants from the crown, in Nottinghamshire and Lincolnshire. Three separate branches of the family received the honor of knighthood for their military services. The name appears also as Colcroft and Colcraft.

At the conclusion of his campaigns with the English army against New France, James Calcraft made his home in Eastern New York, which continued to be the residence of the family for more than a century.

James Calcraft was a man of education as well as military distinction. At first he devoted himself to the business of a land surveyor, in which capacity he was employed by Colonel Adam Vroman to resurvey the boundaries of his tract of land in the frontier settlement of Schoharie, New York. At the latter place, he married Anna, the only child of Christian Camerer, one of the Palatines—a body of determined Saxons who had emigrated from the Upper Rhine in 1712, under the assurance or expectation of a patent from Queen Anne. By this marriage he had eight children: James, Christian, John, Margaret, Elizabeth, Lawrence, William, and Helen.

For many years, during his old age, he conducted a large school in this settlement. It was the first English school in that frontier part of the country. This appears to be the only tenable reason that has been assigned for the change of the family name from Calcraft or Colcraft to Schoolcraft. When far advanced in life he went to live with his son William, on the New York grants on Otter Creek, south of Lake Champlain— now included in Vermont.   There he died at the great age of one hundred and two.

After the death of James Calcraft, when the troubles of the American Revolution began, William, his youngest son, moved into Lower Canada.   The other children all remained in this section of New York, except one.   Christian, when the jangling land disputes and conflicts of titles arose in Schoharie, followed Conrad Wiser, Esq. (a near relative), to the banks of the Susquehanna.   He appears eventually to have pushed his way to Buchanan River, one of the sources of the Monongahela, in Lewis County, Virginia.   Some of his descendants became deeply involved in the Indian wars which the Shawnees kept up on the frontiers of Virginia.   In this struggle they took an active part, and were visited with the severest retribution by the marauding Indians.   Between 1770 and 1779, not less than fifteen of this family, men, women, and children, were killed or taken prisoners, and carried into captivity.

Of the other children of the original progenitor, James, the eldest son, died a bachelor.   Lawrence was the ancestor of the persons of this name in Schoharie County.   Elizabeth and Helen married, in that County, in the families of Rose and Haines, and Margaret, the eldest daughter, married Colonel Green Brush, at the house of General Bradstreet, Albany.   Her daughter, Miss Frances Brush, cousin of Schoolcraft's father, married the celebrated Colonel Ethan Allen, six years after his return from the Tower of London.

John Schoolcraft, third son of James and grandfather of Henry Rowe Schoolcraft, settled in Watervliet, in the valley of the Normanskill—or, as the Indians called it, Tawasentha— Albany County, New York.   He served in a winter's campaign against Oswego, in 1757, and took part also in the successful siege of Fort Niagara, under Brigadier General Prideaux and Sir William Johnson, in the summer of 1759.   His wife was Anna Barbara Boss.   They had three children: Anne, Lawrence, and John.   He died at the age of sixty-four, leaving a local reputation for great intrepidity, unusual muscular power, and unyielding decision of character.

Henry Rowe Schoolcraft's father, Lawrence, the eldest son of John, had entered his seventeenth year when the American Revolution began. He was in the first revolutionary procession that marched through the settlement, with martial music and the Committee of Safety at its head, to canvass the region and determine who was Whig and who was Tory. At once he enlisted among the defenders of his country, as a private, in the Third Regiment of Albany County.

He was present, in 1776, when the Declaration of Independence was read to the troops drawn up in hollow square at Ticonderoga. He marched with one of the forces sent to relieve the remnant of Montgomery's ill-fated expedition against Quebec, and continued to be an indomitable actor in various positions, civil and military, in the great drama of the Revolution during its entire continuance.

In 1777, the darkest and most hopeless period of the contest, he led a reinforcement from Albany to Fort Schuyler, up the Mohawk Valley, then alive with hostile Indians and Tories, and escaped them all. He was in this fort, under Colonel Gansevoort, during its close, nineteen-day siege by Colonel St. Leger and his Indian allies.

The whole embodied militia of the Mohawk Valley marched to its relief, under the bold and patriotic General Herkimer. They were met by the Mohawks, Onondagas, and Senecas, and British loyalists, lying in ambush on the banks of the Oriskany, eight miles from the fort. A dreadful battle ensued. It was one of the most bitterly contested engagements of the Revolution. This battle made orphans of half the inhabitants of the Mohawk Valley. It was a desperate struggle between neighbors, who were ranged on opposite sides as Whig and Tory, and it was an American triumph, Herkimer remaining master of the field.

During the hottest of the battle, Colonel Willett stepped on to the esplanade of the fort, where the troops were paraded, and requested all who were willing to fight for liberty and join a party for the relief of Herkimer, to step forward one pace. Lawrence Schoolcraft was the first to advance. Two hundred and fifty men followed him. An immediate sally was made. They carried the camp of Sir John Johnson; took all his baggage, military-chest, and papers; drove him through the Mohawk River; and then turned upon the howling Mohawks and swept and fired their camp. The results of this battle were brilliant. The booty was immense. The lines of the besiegers, which had been thinned by the forces sent to Oriskany, were carried.

The most dangerous enemy to the cause of American freedom was not to be found in the field, but among neighbors who were lurking at midnight around the scenes of home. The districts of Albany and Schoharie were infested by Tories, and young Lawrence Schoolcraft was ever on the qui vive to ferret out these elusive and deadly effective instruments of the enemy. On one occasion he detected a Tory who had returned from Canada with a lieutenant's commission in his pocket. He immediately clapped spurs to his horse, and reported him to Governor George Clinton, Chairman of the Committee of Safety at Albany. Within three days the lieutenant was seized, tried, condemned, and hanged.

About the close of the Revolutionary War, Lawrence Schoolcraft married Miss Margaret Ann Barbara Rowe, a native of Fishkill, Dutchess County, New York. It is highly probable that he was connected with the glassworks on the Hungerkill, in what was then Watervliet township, from its early days under the De Neufvilles and learned his trade under them. It is certain he was in the neighborhood as early as 1788, and became superintendent of the plant in 1802. The records of the Dutch Reformed Church of the Helderberg show him as one of its deacons and elders, at various times; his place in the "West Men's Seats," and where Margaret Rou, his wife, sat in the "South West Weomans' Block." The baptisms of their various children are recorded. They had thirteen. He assisted in calling the first regular pastor of this congregation, and in building the structure that replaced the log prayer house. In October, 1808, he left Hamilton to take the management of a new glass factory then under construction in Vernon, Oneida County, New York. His contributions to glassmaking history are discussed in succeeding pages of this book, together with those of his son, Henry Rowe Schoolcraft.

Lawrence Schoolcraft had come out of the Revolutionary War with an adjutant's commission and a high reputation for bravery. When the War of 1812 appeared inevitable, General Gansevoort, his old commanding officer at Fort Schuyler, placed him in command of the first regiment of uniformed volunteers who were mustered into service for that conflict.

He had served his country eagerly and with credit in its wars, and between times advanced the new nation's industrial interests with distinction. Also he shouldered a good share of community responsibilities. Among the local offices he held were those of excise commissioner and justice of the peace. His skill and activity and character, consistently shown through many years, won for him the consideration and respect of his townsmen. It was said of Lawrence Schoolcraft that he was never governed by expediency but by right, and that in all his expressions of opinion he was original and fearless of consequences. His monument, on the banks of the Skenando, bears the inscription: "A patriot, a Christian, and an honest man." He died at Vernon, Oneida County, New York, June 7, 1840.

BIRTH, YOUTH, AND SCHOOLING

Should you ask me, whence these stories?
Whence these legends and traditions,
With the odors of the forest,
With the dew and damp of meadows. . . .
I should answer, I should tell you, . . .
I repeat them as I heard them
From the lips of Nawadaha,
The musician, the sweet singer. . . .

If still further you should ask me,
Saying, "Who was Nawadaha?
Tell us of this Nawadaha,"
I should answer your inquiries
Straightway in such words as follow.

"In the vale of Tawasentha,
In the green and silent valley,
By the pleasant water-courses,
Dwelt the singer Nawadaha. . . ."

HENRY WADSWORTH LONGFELLOW, in his notes to *Hiawatha,* in his diary, and in his recorded conversations, has given Henry Rowe Schoolcraft unmeasured credit as his collaborator. Schoolcraft was born

"In the vale of Tawasentha,
In the green and silent valley,
By the pleasant water-courses."

Longfellow, who pored over Schoolcraft's works some three years, absorbing material, surely did not use the name Tawasentha accidentally. It is further recognition of the poet's nobility of heart and mastery of his craft to interpret his introductory lines as another, fragrant tribute to the man who made *Hiawatha* possible.

The most prominent feature of Albany County, New York, is the Helderberg, a spur of the Catskill Mountains. This highest range divides the County into two general levels of unequal width, characterized as being above or below that elevation. The plateau section, which extends northwest-wardly from the Hudson to the valley of the Mohawk, is sixteen miles from river to river, by about half the distance in breadth, with an area of a hundred and twenty square miles. Known as the great Pine Plains, because they were originally covered with a magnificent forest of *Pinus resinosa,* in time this sandy stretch became well-nigh denuded. The winds insinuated into the sides of its hills, creating a species of dunes. Across this plateau plain lay the ancient path of the Iroquois in their journeys from the West.

The deepest cutting into the geological column of Albany County is that of the Tawasentha. Originating, in its western fork, on the Helderberg, it empties into the Hudson River. At points in Guilderland township its perpendicular facades of slate are from eighty to a hundred twenty feet high. The musical Iroquois name for this stream, which means "place of the dead," refers to an ancient Indian burying ground on a curious natural mound near its mouth. Schoolcraft did much to perpetuate this beautiful name and its associations, although, since the days of Jan Bradt de Norman, an early Dutch settler who built a mill on its banks, it has been known as the Normanskill.

The Hungerkill, one of the tributaries of the Tawasentha, is formed by the confluence of several gorges in the Pine Plains, each contributing its spring-sourced waters. Though small in volume, this stream is of unsurpassed purity and unfailing supply and flows with a force sufficient to sink its channel through the deep clay stratum. The site of the now decayed manufacturing village of Hamilton is on the Hungerkill a mile from where it joins the Tawasentha.

Here Henry Rowe Schoolcraft was born "March 28, 1793, in the Manor of Rensselaerswyck, Albany County, in the State of New York."

All the details in the foregoing paragraph are indicated in the sermon delivered at his funeral by one of his close friends in Washington. Albany County, New York, and the same date, are given in the biographical introduction to his *Memoirs,* which Schoolcraft edited. At other places in that sketch the statements are made that Schoolcraft was a native of New York State; and that he was born during the second presidential term of Washington—which began March 4, 1793. In *Iosco* Schoolcraft writes of the Vale of Norma as "my native land." On March 28, 1834, he noted in his *Memoirs* that the day was his forty-first birthday. The baptismal records of the Reformed Church of the Hellebergh at New Salem, New York, in volume one, on page eighteen, contain the following entry: [parents] Lourens Scoelcraft, Margariet Rou; [child] Hendrik; [time of birth] Maart 28; [witnesses, sponsors] Hendrik Apple, Eva Wagenaar." The date of the christening ceremony was May 16, 1793.

This accumulation of evidence places beyond any idle questioning the time and place of his birth.

The general background of Schoolcraft's ancestry and

youth is given in an interesting book, *Old Hellebergh*. This tells in documented detail something of the happenings of two hundred and fifty years in the valley of the Normanskill, immediately west of the city of Albany, New York. The activities of peace, and the tides of war that swept back and forth with surge of action and ebb of suffering, in that crescent-shaped bit of New York State between Albany and Schenectady, are informatively sketched.

The story of the birthplace of Henry Rowe Schoolcraft is there: In the days when it was known only as the West Manor of Rensselaerswyck; through the period marked by the Dowesburgh Glass Works on the Hungerkill, which was given up by the famous glassmaking De Neufvilles about the time Henry was born; how a company of Albany capitalists planted there the glass-manufacturing town of Hamilton, when he was three years old.

> Can pleased memory, pass the hill top by,
> Where once caloric vapours pierced the sky,
> High pent in walls,—where art's alchemic power,
> Transmuted well the product of the hour
> Giving o'er all the circle of the plain,
> Bread to the poor, and to the wealthy gain.

Afterwards the community was called Hamiltonville for a while. Much later it became, what it is today, the village of Guilderland.

The township of Guilderland received its name much earlier, in 1803, when Schoolcraft was a boy of ten. When the first town meeting of Guilderland was held, that year, the gathering was in the tavern owned by Hendrik Apple, who had been sponsor for Henry Schoolcraft at his baptism, in the church opposite. Hendrik Apple was a compatriot in arms of Lawrence Schoolcraft. He is the man for whom Henry Schoolcraft was named. Of course the second name, Rowe, was Henry's mother's. The crossroads where the Dutch Reformed Church and Apple's tavern stood was known as Apple's Corners—now Osborn's Corners, near Guilderland Center.

A State historical marker points out Colonel Lawrence

BOYHOOD HOME OF SCHOOLCRAFT. AT GUILDERLAND, NEW YORK.

Schoolcraft's house—where Henry Rowe Schoolcraft was born—which is still standing in Guilderland village on Willow Street. This street was part of what was known as the old Schoharie Road, built about 1750 to connect that Palatine settlement with Albany. The Schoolcraft dwelling was the first two-story house erected in the community. Schoolcraft refers to it, with some truth as well as poetic license, as a manse, or mansion, in his *Helderbergia*. In *Iosco* he tells of the funeral of his older favorite brother from this place. The story of the large coffin and the difficulty of getting it down the narrow stairs is still current in Guilderland. The burying ground that Schoolcraft mentions in the same poem is still marked by a few prostrate stones a short distance up the street.

Among the glimpses of his boyhood afforded in *Iosco* are the following:

And thou, my Norma! stream of waters bright,
Flung sparkling from thy bold cerulean heighth,
Oft on thy banks my early footsteps roved,
And clung to solitudes that fancy loved;
There first I leapt the cool and grassy brim,
And learned the health preserving art to swim,
And oft of garments half disrobed, or rolled,
Walked up thy summer bed of slate and gold;
Less bent, as elder youth, on finny prey,
Than, laughter-smit, to scare the fish away.

High o'er the brow of yond bold sandy heighth,
I, with my chum, oft clambered with delight,
And gathered fruits or pennyroyal sweet,
Careless of time, or only time to cheat;
Or flushed with play-day vigor, leapt we grand,
The high denuded bank of yellow sand;
Or culled the pebbles from the crystal brook,
Each grove a volume, and each stream a book;
Or climbed the wild fruit in the distant glen,
And laughed at all the meaner cares of men.

Angling ne'er fired my mind; but gun and horn
With animation rife, employed my morn,
And oft my noon and eve, and many a mile,
Hope drew me on, and flattered with a smile,

Still whispering other woods, and glades more wide,
Would grant the spoils that nearer spots denied:
And well doth memory picture one and all,
The woods and shores that saw the squirrel fall,
Or bramble copse, half forest and half heath,
In which the proud beau pheasant fell in death.

. . . who can now, the blooming treasures name,
Thence gathered gaily when vacation came,—
And wood-ward bent, the frolic village school,
Threw by each occult, dry, scholastic rule,
And with high mettle scampered to the wood,
Let friends and grandames counsel all they could.

Schoolcraft also has preserved some of the flavor of the days of his youth in an excellent narrative, "The Rabid Wolf." Following are a few pictorial paragraphs from that sketch:

It was at other times tried to trap them [the wolves], and to bait them in sundry ways. I recollect that we all had implicit faith in the village schoolmaster, one Cleanthus, who knew some Latin, and a little of almost everything; and among other arts which he cherished, and dealt out in a way to excite wonder for his skill, he knew how to make the wolves follow his tracks, by smearing his shoes with aesofoedita, or some other substance, and then ensconcing himself at night in a log pen, where he might bid defiance to the best of them, and shoot at them besides. But I never could learn that there were any of these pestiferous animals killed, either by the schoolmaster and his party, or any other party, except it was the luckless poor animal I am about to write of. . . .

A beautiful and clear stream of sparkling cold water, called the Hungerkill, after gathering its crystal tributaries from the deep gorges of the plains, ran through the village, and afforded one or two seats for mills, and after winding and doubling on its track a mile or two, rendered its pellucid stores into the Norman's Kill. . . . No stream in the country was more famous for the abundance of its fine brook trout, and the neighboring plains served to shelter the timid hare, and the fine species of northern partridge, which is there always called a pheasant.

The village was supported by its manufacturing interests, and was quite populous. It had a number of long streets, some of which reached across the stream, and over a spacious mill pond, and others swept at right angles along the course of the great Cherry Valley Turnpike. In its streets were to be heard, in addition to the English, nearly all the dialects of the German between the Rhine and the Danube; the Low Dutch as spoken by the common country people on the manor of Rensselaerswyck, the Erse and Gaelic, as not unfrequently used by the large proportion of its Irish and Scotch, and what seemed quite as striking to one brought up in seclusion from it, the genuine Yankee, as discoursed by the increasing class of factory wood choppers, teamsters, schoolmasters, men out at the elbows, and travelling wits. The latter were indeed but a sorry representation of New England, as we have since found it. . . .

If one would take every thing as it was given, there had been more acts of bravery, conduct, and firm decision of character and foresight, displayed in encountering these wild vixens of the plains and valleys by night, than would, if united, have been sufficient to repel the inroads of Burgoyne, St. Leger, or Sir John Johnson, with Brant and all his hosts of Tories and Indians, during the American revolution.

I chanced one night to have left the city of Albany, in company with one of these heroic spirits. We occupied my father's chaise, an old-fashioned piece of gentility now out of vogue, drawn by a prime horse, one which he always rode on parades. It was late before we got out of the precincts of the city, and up the hill, and night overtook us away in the pine woods, at Billy McKown's, a noted public-house seated half way between the city and Hamilton, where it was customary in those days to halt; for besides that he was much respected, and one of the most sensible and influential men in the town, it was not thought right, whatever the traveler might require, that a horse should be driven eight miles without drawing breath, and having a pail of water. As I was but young, and less of a charioteer than my valiant companion, he held the whip and reins thus far; but after the wolf stories that poured in upon us at McKown's that evening, he would hold them no longer. Every man, he thought, was responsible to himself. He did not wish to be wolf's meat that night, so he hired a fleet horse from our host, and a whip and spurs, and set off with the speed of a Jehu, leaving me to make my way, in the heavy chaise, through the sandy plains, as best I could.

In truth we had just reached the most sombre part of the plain, where the trees were more thick, the sand deep and heavy, and not a house but one, within the four miles. To render it worse, this was the chief locality of wolf insolence, where he had even ventured to attack men. It was on this route too, that the schoolmaster had used his medical arts, which made it better known through the country as the supposed centre of their power. Nothing harmed me, however; the horse was fine, and I reached home not only uneaten, but unthreatened by a wolf's jaw.

His tale of the wild chase of the mad wolf indicates that for once, at least, young Henry Schoolcraft was out most of that night. This was a radical departure from his custom. Usually he was at home, not with the crowd.

From his earliest years Henry Rowe Schoolcraft was a natural scholar. Even as a small boy he combined curiosity, initiative, and intelligence with the accuracy, industry, and persistence of character. He showed marked bents in directions that are usually incompatible—for the arts of painting and poetry and for many of the sciences.

The valley of the Normanskill and the mountains of the Hellebergh attracted him not only for their natural beauty and their associations with play and animals and war and Indians, but for their rocks, specimens of which he carried home and studied.

His room at home, while he was a boy, offered more educational atmosphere than most schoolrooms of the period. It afforded a small library of good books, a cabinet of mineral specimens, and an exhibit of drawings—all the result of his own taste and efforts. At a time and in a place where even schoolbooks were so difficult to get that hand-written copies were in use, he had several editions of English classics that were purchased at a private sale in Albany.

At an early age he wrote verse, both lyrical and historical, and essays along the lines of geology, history and ethnology. Some of these, published locally, attracted considerable attention. Lieutenant-Governor Jeremiah Van Rensselaer, a director of the glassworks, observed the activities of the boy and gave him some encouragement. Steps taken by him to place young Schoolcraft with a master to study painting did not lead to anything, presumably because the painting of buildings was involved in the apprenticeship.

After finishing his primary studies he prepared himself, under a special instructor, to enter Union College at Schenectady. He did not attend that institution. A career in glass-manufacturing prevented. Several years later, while he was at Salisbury, Vermont, superintending glassworks there, he resumed his studies by himself and also, ex academia, under a professor of Middlebury College. Schoolcraft wrote of himself, in *Oneóta:*

I had, from early youth, cultivated a taste for mineralogy, long indeed it may be said, before I knew that mineralogy was a science; and, as opportunities increased, had been led by my inquiries (which I followed with ardor but with very slight helps) to add to this some knowledge of elementary chemistry and experimental philosophy, and to supply myself, from Boston and New York, with books, apparatus, and tests. I do not know that there were any public lectures on mineralogy, etc., at this time, say from 1810 to 1816; certainly there were none within my reach. I gleaned from the best sources I could, and believe that the late Professor Frederick Hall was the only person to whom I was indebted even for occasional instructions in these departments. He was a man strongly devoted to some of the natural sciences, particularly mineralogy; and was erudite in the old authors on the subject, whom he liked to quote; and I may say that I continued to enjoy his confidence and friendship to the time of his death, which happened in 1843.

At the same time, at Salisbury, he read French with instructors, took some work in natural philosophy and medicine, and taught himself Hebrew and German by means of grammars and dictionaries.

The following letter, from L. L. Van Kleeck to Dr. R. W. Griswold, dated June 4, 1851, bears witness to his achievements and reputation as a boy:

I revert with great pleasure to the scenes of my residence, in the part of Albany County which was also the residence of Henry R. Schoolcraft. I went to reside at the village of Hamilton, in the town of Guilderland, in 1803. Colonel Lawrence Schoolcraft, the father of Henry, had then the direction of the large manufactories of glass, for which that place was long noted. The standing of young Henry, I remember, at his school, for scholarship, was then very noted, and his reputation in the village most prominent. He was spoken of as a lad of great promise, and a very learned boy at twelve. Mr. Robert Buchanan, a Scotchman, and a man of learning, took much pride in his advances, and finally came to his father and told him that he had taught him all he knew. In Latin, I think he was taught by Cleanthus Felt. He was at this age very arduous and assiduous in the pursuit of knowledge. He discovered great mechanical ingenuity. He drew and painted in water colors. . . . At an early age he manifested a taste for mineralogy and natural science, which was then (I speak of about 1808) almost unknown in the country. He was generally to be found at home, at his studies, when other boys of his age were attending horseraces, cock-fights, and other vicious amusements for which the village was famous.

On Schoolcraft's return from the Northwest in 1820, Governor De Witt Clinton of New York gave him the use of his private library while the preparation of his journal for the press was in progress, and offered suggestions in the way of reading that were of lasting benefit.

After 1822, on the frontier at the Sault, he made constant use of the Johnston and Fort Brady book collections. Later, the spacious rooms of Elmwood were lined with cabinets of specimens and books like a museum-library. Whenever he was not engaged with Indian affairs or research, or on expeditions, or writing, he read voraciously. He carried forward the education of Jane Johnston Schoolcraft, instructed his children, studied Hebrew.

From youth to maturity, the assiduity of Schoolcraft, his love of method, the great value he attached to time, and his indomitable perseverance in whatever study or research he undertook, were invaluable assets. His life is a clear illustration of how far such qualities will carry the mind in spite of early disadvantages.

EARLY AMERICAN GLASS MANUFACTURER

THERE were harder lessons ahead. Right on the heels of the high promise and expectations of his childhood, came seven years of industry and ambition that ended in complete financial disaster.

The site of the one-time flourishing Hamilton glass factory of which Lawrence Schoolcraft was superintendent is only a stone's throw off the main road through the village of Guilderland of today. A State historical marker ten miles west of the city docks of Albany, New York, indicates the point nearest it on Route 20. The big glass works went the way of so many in its period. No trace remains except fragments of its products which antiquarians dig up or plows unearth. But the operation of this plant for more than a quarter of a century started Lawrence and Henry Rowe Schoolcraft on a career which won them prominence in glass-making history in America.

The details of Henry Rowe Schoolcraft's involvement in the ruin of once-flourishing industrial enterprises have been known for only a short time and then by few except unusual students of antique glass. Not long ago the discovery was made, in Michigan, of two collections of papers that preserved many facts about the background of his early years. Scholars in more than one field are indebted to Mr. Harry Hall White of Detroit for the careful studies and interpretations he has published in the magazine *Antiques*. The DeNeufville papers, belonging to Forest H. Sweet of Battle Creek, Michigan, have afforded definite knowledge of the Dowesburgh Glass Company on the Hungerkill. New information concerning the glassmaking activities of the Schoolcrafts in that valley and elsewhere in New York, as well as in Vermont and New Hampshire, were brought to light by Mr. White from unpublished Schoolcraft correspondence, 1809 to 1824, which he consulted in copies of Smithsonian manuscripts in the Burton Historical Collection of the Detroit Public Library.

One must take friendly issue with Mr. White, however, in his statement that Henry Rowe Schoolcraft was "obviously miscast in the role of glass factory manager." Schoolcraft made his mark nationally and internationally in many fields. He was eminently versatile as well as able. There was a marked economic bent in all his interests. He was a practical operator and had ambitions in that direction, as his activities in the lead mine region of Missouri show. In that Territory he studied methods of mining, smelting and pumping; gathered statistics; considered transportation possibilities and tenure of leases; and recommended appointment of a Federal superintendent, which position he desired himself. His scholarly studies did not interfere with his glass factory management, but aided it. A widening knowledge of mineralogy and chemistry was applied by him at once to glassmaking problems. Even after his long series of misfortunes in connection with the glass industry, he was still so much enmeshed with it that he undertook the writing of a practical treatise on the subject. During all his early explorations in the West the possibilities of glassmaking seem to have been constantly in his mind. There can be no doubt either of his ability, or his enthusiasm.

Schoolcraft's series of failures in glass factories is no proof he was miscast in his part as a glass manufacturer. If the mere fact of financial misfortune meant that, then practically all of the early American glass producers were miscast. The London Company ventures in Virginia, and the Massachusetts undertakings at Salem and Germantown, as well as the exceptionally well-financed and manned operations of Amelung at Frederick, Maryland, are representative of the long series of abortive efforts at glassmaking in the United States. Even Henry William Stiegel, who is credited with having produced the most beautiful glass ever blown in America, ended with complete financial failure. The plain fact is that the trouble lay with the glass-making business in this country in that day,—not with individuals; and that Henry Rowe Schoolcraft, with all his love of art and science, his energy and applied interest, and excellent commercial judgment, went down with the wreck of practically the entire industry as then conducted east of the Alleghenies. In many ways it is fortunate that Schoolcraft's abilities were blocked in that direction, to break over into wider channels of usefulness.

A sketch of the development of American glassmaking is necessary background for an understanding of the first decade of Schoolcraft's maturity. The industry from the beginning encountered almost insurmountable difficulties in the United States. Its problems in the new country were different from those in other lands.

Early American furnaces were handicapped by a scarcity of operatives. Glassmaking and glass-blowing are crafts that require complex traditional knowledge and a variety of technical skills. They require long and disciplined training. American artisans did not enjoy the assistance and patronage of guilds and trades societies as European workers did. The simple apprentice system proved ineffectual. Foreign nations, appreciating the value of glass-workers, passed laws preventing their emigration. Those who came to America were smuggled from their home countries. They were inclined to be arrogant and unwilling to impart their knowledge to others. There was tense competition among glassworks for the men who were available. The nomadic tendencies of these craftsmen hampered the industry; also their addiction to drink. The health-destroying conditions of this work limited their usefulness to six or nine months a year. Many of the operatives were lost because farming proved more attractive.

The earthenware vats required for melting, until about 1863, presented another serious problem. The making of these involved three ripening periods extending over a period of two years, and a vat lasted on the average less than two months. The special clay necessary to resist intense and prolonged heat and the chemical action of the glass matrix had to be imported from England until early in the nineteenth century when suitable clay was discovered in Delaware and Missouri.

Poor silica bed ingredients as well as poor pot-clay, the constant recurrence of fires, and an apathetic attitude on the part of the public toward the struggling industry, were other factors that doomed nearly every venture almost before it started. The greater number of glassmen were financial failures until the advent of the machine age. Not till 1818 was the secret of red-lead-making fathomed. The glass pressing machine was invented in 1827.

The apparently unlimited supply of wood for fuel, which had caused glass from Jamestown to be the first industrial export from America, soon began to give out. This aggravated the already complex situation. Wood for glass factory furnaces was gradually supplanted by coal, after the discovery of that mineral near Pittsburgh in 1797. That marks the beginning of the great glassmaking development west of the Appalachians.

Added to these difficulties peculiar to the industry, were the local and national troubles of the fifty years succeeding the American Revolution—sporadic wars, political agitations, land-bubbles, panics, high transportation rates, long credits and poor collections. Then came the War of 1812. The increasing demands of a growing population encouraged glass manufacturers. When the war shut off the supply of foreign-made glass, the industry enjoyed a brief boom period in America. Quickly it collapsed. The close of hostilities permitted importation of great accumulated stocks of foreign glassware that was sold at low prices to begin with and at auction rates for remainders. The War of 1812 in coming and going wrecked many fortunes. It is illuminating to consider that while Schoolcraft's glassmaking enterprises were failing in the Eastern States, the war was also sweeping away the lifetime accumulations, and cutting short the lives as well, of two men in far-removed places and occupations who were destined to be his fathers-in-law: John Johnston, merchant outfitter for the fur-trade at Sault Ste. Marie, Michigan Territory; and James Howard, wealthy cotton plantation owner in South Carolina. Theirs were the individual tragedies of war.

The glassworks on the Hungerkill, in Albany County, New York, with which Schoolcraft was first associated, was in operation in all about thirty years. The Dutch De Neufvilles, father and son, had opened the Dowesburgh glass house, as it then was called, in 1785, hoping to retrieve through it the hereditary fortune they had sacrificed in Holland. They built their glass plant in the wilderness because of the availability of sand, plenty of wood for fuel, the water power from the Hungerkill, and the potash which was manufactured locally. By 1788, however, they were petitioning for State aid. In 1789 they were granted a State loan. By 1793 they had quit. The elder De Neufville died in 1796, leaving his widow destitute.

The year Henry Rowe Schoolcraft was born, 1793, under new management the glasshouse was again asking State aid. This they obtained. Nevertheless, twice during 1795 it was reorganized. The Legislature then, in 1796, gave encouragement by exempting the company and their workmen from all taxation for five years and a permanent manufacturing town was built under the name of Hamilton. The firm became the Hamilton Manufacturing Society. Then followed a period of successful operation.

It was during this time of prosperity that Lawrence Schoolcraft became superintendent of the works, in 1802. No mention of his earlier connection with the plant has been found, but his presence in the locality in 1788 is proven by the original Dutch records of the Reformed Church at Watervliet. The probability of his having served his apprenticeship under the De Neufvilles is further strengthened by his later manifest ability as a glassmaker and engineer in glass factory construction. It was at the Hamilton glassworks he taught his son, Henry Rowe Schoolcraft, the art of glassmaking, in which both father and son were destined to become national figures. The sketch of the life of the latter, introducing his *Memoirs,* has the following to say of Lawrence Schoolcraft:

His disciplinary knowledge and tact in the government of men, united to amenity of manners, led to his selection in 1802, by the Honorable Jeremiah Van Rensselaer as director of his extensive glass works at Hamilton, near Albany, which he conducted with high reputation so many years. The importance of this manufacture to the new settlements at that early day was deeply felt, and his ability and skill in the management of these works were widely known and appreciated.

. . . His celebrity in the manufacture of glass led capitalists in Western New York to offer him large inducements to remove there, where he first introduced this manufacture during the settlement of that new and attractive part of the State, in which a mania for manufactories was then rife. In this new field the sphere of his activity and skill were much enlarged.

The correspondence of Schoolcraft and his father indicates that the latter left Hamilton because of some disagreement. This was in October, 1808, when he undertook the management of a glasshouse to be erected in Vernon, Oneida County, New York. The new plant was later known as the Sherman Works of the Oneida Glass Factory Company. Lawrence

Schoolcraft's influence was widespread as a consultant, throughout the East, especially at Utica, New York, and Salisbury, Vermont, as well as at Keene, New Hampshire, where for a time he was closely associated with his son.

Henry Rowe Schoolcraft had learned the art and business of glassmaking at Hamilton, under his father. At the age of fifteen he had already achieved sufficient responsibility to be entrusted with the task of going to Philadelphia to purchase a shipload of English clay. About a year after his father went to Vernon, he followed, in the late fall of 1809.

Toward the end of the first decade of the nineteenth century, there was a boom in glassmaking in western New York. The technical ability of the Schoolcraft family was in demand. In his *Memoirs* Henry Rowe Schoolcraft says:

Early in the spring of 1810, I accompanied Mr. Alexander Bryan Johnson of Utica, a gentleman of wealth, intelligence, and enterprise, to the area of the Genesee country, for the purpose of superintending a manufactory for a company incorporated by the State Legislature. After visiting Sodus Bay, on Lake Ontario, it was finally resolved to locate this company's works near Geneva, on the banks of Seneca Lake.

Among the Schoolcraft papers in the Smithsonian collection is an agreement between him and the Ontario Glass Works, at Geneva, Ontario County, New York, dated February 4, 1810, providing that he should receive one share of stock in return for every workman he secured.

"During my residence here," Schoolcraft says, writing of Geneva,

the War of 1812 broke out; the events of which fell with severity on this frontier, particularly on the lines included between the Niagara and Lake Champlain, where contending armies and navies operated. While these scenes of alarm and turmoil were enacting, and our trade with Great Britain was cut off, an intense interest arose for manufactures of first necessity, needed by the country, particularly for that indispensable article of new settlements, window glass. In directing the foreign artisans employed in the making of this product of skill, my father, Colonel Lawrence Schoolcraft, had, from an early period after the American Revolution, acquired celebrity, by the general superintendency of the noted works of this kind near Albany, and afterwards in Oneida County. Under his auspices, I directed the erection of similar works in Western New York and in the States of Vermont and New Hampshire.

His correspondence indicates plainly that Henry Schoolcraft was not happy long at Geneva. Things did not go smoothly between him and his associates. The preparations for war had a disturbing effect. In his letters to his sister he shows an unsettled state of mind.

Sometime prior to March 31, 1813, he left Geneva, New York, and went to Salisbury, Vermont. There is a possibility that in the meantime he may have spent a short term at Cheshire. Mr. White suggests this on the basis of a sentence in Appleton's American Encyclopedia of 1879. However, this may refer only to Schoolcraft's glassmaking later at Keene, in the County of Cheshire, New Hampshire.

By May, 1813, he had indicated to his father that things at Salisbury were not to his liking. The War of 1812–1814 was at the root of his unrest. He wrote of the possibility of a military commission, and at another time intimated a desire to find a place in the glass factories at Vernon, where his father lived. Peter Schoolcraft, Henry's brother, his senior by three years, who also was at Salisbury, had made up his mind to leave. Henry, however, obedient to his father's urging, decided to remain. The contract that he signed with the president and director of the Vermont Glass Factory, August 30, 1813, is printed in full in Mr. White's articles which, indeed, are a concatenation of direct quotations from the Smithsonian Schoolcraft papers.

In this memorandum, Schoolcraft agreed to superintend the Vermont Glass Factory "now erected on the northern bank of Lake Dunmore in Salisbury . . . for five years to commence on the 15th day of July, 1813, . . . provided the discharge of those duties is not rendered impracticable by want of materials to carry on the works." The considerations were a salary of $1000, office and stationery, eight acres of land, $40 a year for house rent; and $100 reward, sixty days from the commence-

ment of blowing, for his voluntary attention to the building of
the above-mentioned glass factory.

This contract does not parallel the following statement
made by Schoolcraft in his *Memoirs:* "While in Vermont I
received a salary of eighteen hundred dollars per annum. . . .
In conversation with President Davis of Middlebury College
I learned that this was the highest salary paid in the State, he
himself receiving eleven hundred, and the Governor of the
State but eight hundred." But the agreement does not pre-
clude the possibility of other arrangements, involving possibly
stock or partial interest in the plant. There was some basis for
Schoolcraft's statement one can be sure, from the consistent
character of the man. The contract is interesting, but it carries
no guarantee that, with it, the facts of the situation are complete.

Further light on Schoolcraft's activities at Salisbury, Vermont, is given in two articles in the *American Collector* of
August and September, 1937. Dates and other facts about
Schoolcraft in this are not to be accepted without careful questioning. This may be true about most accounts of Schoolcraft,
in which original errors have been copied and multiplied to an
unusual degree. The following is interesting:

On October 27, 1813, an advertisement in the *Vermont Mirror,*
published at Middlebury, over the signature of Henry R. Schoolcraft, superintendent, offered in the name of the president and directors of the Vermont Glass Factory one hundred dollars reward "to
any person who shall discover, within the state of Vermont a bed of
such clay found equal to the manufacture of crucibles for melting
pots."

He is definite regarding the type of clay required, stating that
it must be similar to that found in the neighborhood of Philadelphia
and in sufficient quantities to assure the glassworks an adequate
supply. He makes it entirely clear also that no reward will be paid
until samples have been thoroughly tested. Then he gives full details of places where such clay is usually found and other information
helpful to those who might be interested.

The reward evidently had the desired effect, for in an article
about the glasshouse at Lake Dunmore which appeared December,

1813, in *The Literary and Philosophical Repertory,* of Middlebury, Vermont, Schoolcraft is quoted as follows:

"Sand is found on the shores of the lake. Wood stands in exhaustless abundance in the immediate vicinity of the factory. Firestone, an article hitherto brought, at great expense, from Connecticut, has been discovered within ten miles of the works. And the enormous charges heretofore incurred in the transporting of clay from Philadelphia, for the manufacture of pots for melting glass, is about to be avoided by the discovery that the Monkton, Vermont, porcelain earth will answer a good purpose. From the unusual success that has attended these works since their commencement, the many advantages which they hold and the variety of the materials with which the place abounds for the making of all kinds of glass, we are led to believe they will become one of the first establishments in the Union."

The article in the *Repertory* stated that glass was first blown at the Lake Dunmore glasshouse in September, 1813, that "it is now on sale in the Middlebury stores and is beginning to circulate through a large section of the country."

The Ormsbee-Allen article in the *American Collector* goes on to say, about what they term the earliest and most interesting attempt at glassmaking in Vermont:

In the Chemistry Department of Middlebury College is preserved a group of pieces which tradition, handed down within the faculty, attributes to the workmen of the Vermont Glass Company. Jarius Kennan [No; it was Frederick Hall] was professor of chemistry and mineralogy and it was under him that Schoolcraft studied before he left for the West. Could anything have given the latter greater pleasure than to provide his professor with needed, if crude, pieces of chemical apparatus especially blown at either East Middlebury or Lake Dunmore under Schoolcraft's supervision?

The outlook for the Vermont Glass Company was so rosy that within three years the organization had a second glass factory in operation in the neighboring village of East Middlebury where bottles were blown. But the company was too ambitious. Overextended, it could not weather the financial stringency that came with the Treaty of Ghent. First the bottle factory was lost by foreclosure; then the glasshouse on the shore of Lake Dunmore had to discontinue. In 1816 the East Middlebury property was lost. On August 30, 1817, the company suspended all operations.

But many months before that Henry Rowe Schoolcraft had gone. His correspondence indicates that, whatever his salary at Salisbury, he had difficulty collecting it. Other conditions had never been to his liking. An offer of an interest in a flint glass plant to be erected at Keene, New Hampshire, lured him to leave the Vermont Glass Company. The amount due him for salary at Salisbury he left for collection in the hands of an attorney. This was $1,062.17.

It is worth noting here that the Hamilton Glassworks, where he had learned the business, which had had an output of five hundred thousand feet of window glass in 1813, by 1815 had permanently suspended operations.

Early in 1815 Schoolcraft went to Keene, New Hampshire, where he became the operating manager and possibly the manager of the Marlboro Street Works. The contract with his first partner, Timothy Twitchell, for the erection of a plant at Keene to manufacture flint glass and other wares, dated in pencil July 25, 1815, specified that their salaries,—$1000 for Schoolcraft as general superintendent and a less amount for Twitchell as business manager—began February 1, 1815. They were to share equally in expenses of building and operation and profits. The same year their plant began making glass. Henry Rowe Schoolcraft had successfully launched a prominent glass manufactory, for himself. To operate it with equal satisfaction was another problem. Of this he wrote, years later, under Personal Reminiscences, in *Oneóta*:

The year 1814 constituted a crisis, not only in our political history, but also in our commercial, manufacturing, and industrial interests. The treaty of Ghent [proclaimed February 18, 1815], which put a period to the war with England, was a blessing to many individuals and classes in America; but, in its consequences, it had no small share of the effects of a curse upon that class of citizens who were engaged in certain branches of manufactures. It was a peculiarity of the crisis, that these persons had been stimulated by double motives, to invest their capital and skill in the perfecting and establishment of the manufactories referred to, by the actual wants of the country and the high prices of the foreign articles. No pains and no cost had been spared, by many of them, to supply this demand; and it was another result of the times, that no sooner had they got well established, and were in the high road of prosperity than the peace came and plunged them headlong from the pinnacle of success. This blow fell heavier upon some branches than others. It was most fatal to those manufacturers who had undertaken to produce fabrics of the highest order, or which belong to an advanced state of the manufacturing prosperity of a nation. Be this as it may, however, it fell with crushing force upon that branch in which I was engaged. As soon as the American ports were opened to these fabrics, the foreign makers who could undersell us, poured in cargo on cargo; and when the first demands had been met, these cargoes were ordered to be sold at auction; the prices immediately fell to the lowest point, and the men who had staked in one enterprise their zeal, skill and money, were ruined at a blow.

Schoolcraft had signed an agreement with a new partner, Nathaniel Sprague, March 20, 1816. He kept on fighting. Among his letters is one, addressed to his new concern, from a Boston shipping firm. It is dated July 19, 1816: "We cannot at present recommend your sending any glassware here, as our market is completely over-stocked with all kinds of glass and crockery ware, which makes it very low and dull sale." Insufficient tariff protection permitted the sale of foreign glassware below American costs.

A few months more and Schoolcraft was writing letters to various glassworks in an attempt to find employment. While waiting, he planned and wrote a work on vitreology. By early December, 1817, he was back at his father's home in Vernon, New York, soliciting subscriptions in advance for this proposed book.

An inventory of his assets, conservatively estimated, April 5, 1817, valued them at $3856.50. Six months later, September 27, this amount had shrunk to $683.64. In the spring of 1818, when he left the family sleigh at Olean, New York, and started down river into the great West, he had less than a hundred dollars.

Little is known of what he actually produced as a glass-maker. At Salisbury, Vermont, July 7, 1814, in his twenty-first year, he had been made a Mason by initiation in the Union

Masonic Lodge. A Masonic flask, bearing his initials, has survived, as one of a series particularly dear to the collector. It is
described as unusually fine—bold, heavy and dignified—and is
attributed to his Keene, New Hampshire, period. Two important pieces of an early type—a ribbed sunburst flask and a
Masonic flask—also are assigned tentatively to him, either at
Geneva or Salisbury.

This was the end of seven years! And he was twenty-five
years old! All he had for his hard work was the bitterness of
failure; and sixty dollars.

Yet it was far from all. He possessed what he had studied
with his heart as well as his mind at Hamilton and Salisbury:
English literature and Hebrew and French and painting and
chemistry and medicine and natural history—and mineralogy.
Above all, he had the burgeoning hope of youth and an inner
exultation at the vast promise of the Great West! Also, though
he did not know it then, as he turned his face toward new
things, he had won for himself a place in American glassmaking
history.

Prospective Lead Mine Superintendent

THE WAR of 1812 was an unsettling influence in many
ways. One of its after-effects in the United States was a great
fever of migration westward. Henry Rowe Schoolcraft finally
was seized by this, as he bears witness, in *Oneóta:*

If this contest had brought no golden showers on American
manufacturers (as I could honestly testify in my own case), it had
opened to emigration and enterprise the great area west of the Alleghenies. The armies sent out to battle with Indian, and other foes,
on the banks of the Wabash, the Illinois, the Detroit, the Raisin and
the Miami of the Lakes, had opened to observation attractive scenes
for settlement; and the sword was no sooner cast aside, than emigrants seized hold of the axe and the plough. This result was worth
the cost of the whole contest, honor and glory included. The total
prostration of the moneyed system of the country, the effects of city-
lot and other land speculations, while the system was at its full flow,
and the backward seasons of 1816 and 1817, attended with late and
early frosts which extensively destroyed the corn crop in the Atlantic
States, all lent their aid in turning attention towards the west and

south-west. . . . It appeared to me that information, geographical and other, of such a wide and varied region, whose boundaries were but ill-defined, must be interesting at such a period; and I was not without the hope that the means of my future advancement would be found in connexion with the share I might take in the exploration of it. With such views I resolved to go west. . . .

Means constitute the first object of solicitude in all such undertakings. The ebbing tide of manufacturing prosperity to which I have referred, had left me very poor. From the fragments of former acquisitions, for which, however, I was exclusively indebted to my own industry, I raised a small sum of money—much smaller I think than most men would be willing to start with, who had resolved to go so far. I had, in truth, but sixty dollars in the world; but I possessed a very good wardrobe, and some other personal means such as it may be supposed will adhere to a man who has lived in abundance for many years. I put up a miniature collection of mineralogical specimens, to serve as a standard of comparison in the west, a few implements for analysis, some books which I thought it would be difficult to meet with in that region, and some drawing materials. I had connected these things in some way with my future success. In other respects, I had the means, as above hinted, of making a respectable appearance. Thus prepared, I bade adieu to my father and mother, and also to three sisters and a brother, all younger than myself, and set forward. The winter of [1817–] 1818 had opened before I reached my brother's house at Geneva, in western New York. . . .

My brother drove me, in his own sleigh, as far as Angelica. By the time we reached that place, being no traveller and much fatigued with the intricacies and roughness of the road, he was fain to give over his undertaking, and I parted from him, sending back the sleigh from Olean, to take him home.

Schoolcraft reached Olean, New York, on the source of the Allegheny River, early in 1818, while the snow was yet on the ground, several weeks before the opening of that stream. He was surprised to see the great number of persons, from various quarters, who had pressed to this point, awaiting the opening of navigation.

I mingled in this crowd, and, while listening to the anticipations indulged in, it seemed to me that the war had not, in reality, been fought for free trade and sailors' rights where it commenced, but to gain a knowledge of the world beyond the Alleghenies.

Many came with their household stuff, which was to be embarked in arks and flat boats. The children of Israel could scarcely have presented a more motley array of men and women, with their kneading troughs on their backs, and their little ones, than were there assembled, on their way to the new land of promise.

To judge by the tone of general conversation, they meant, in their generation, to plough the Mississippi Valley from its head to its foot. There was not an idea short of it. What a world of golden dreams was there!

With Schoolcraft's varied training and versatility, and the unlimited opportunity of the new country, the Westward trail had, indeed, numerous possibilities for him. Two general interests had prominence in his mind. One was his own urge for scientific investigation. Another was the belief that an account of the natural history of the West would find a ready market. Yet, predominating over these indefinite ideas, he had a fixed aim and a set goal. His geographical objective appears to have been the Missouri lead mines, and his prime purpose to find a means to earn a livelihood. Without a doubt the emphasis in his interest in 1818 was still that of the industrialist.

This was natural. He was born and reared in a manufacturing center, of which his father and his family were the focus. He had been an apprentice in glassmaking, then a superintendent, and finally an entrepreneur in his own right. By nature he was no idle dreamer, but had a strong sense of personal responsibility.

When he left New York State he knew where he was going and went there without delay. The first book he wrote, at once and rapidly, was his *A View of the Lead Mines of Missouri.* It was not till after his visit to Missouri in 1821, that he stressed the more scientific aspects of its geology and these were not published until 1825.

At least as late as 1823, his hope of being appointed superintendent of the lead mines of Missouri remained alive. According to the biographical sketch prefacing his *Memoirs,* he was still awaiting action at Washington in regard to this, when he was appointed Indian Agent on the northwestern frontier.

The noticeable amount of space in *A View of the Lead Mines of Missouri* that is given to practical discussion of the relation of lead and its by-products to glassmaking is another indication that when Schoolcraft went West in 1818 he was still predominantly the practical works manager, despite his brilliance in scientific directions and his zeal as a writer. It was not to be expected that he could shake off at once, even after all the misfortunes he had suffered from it, his attachment to the industry that had been the sustaining activity of his family all his life and for years before his birth. Glassmaking was in his blood. In his brief treatise on the lead mines he writes about glass at every opportunity. For instance, from pages 80 to 85 there is a discussion of the possibilities in Missouri for materials for window glass and glass bottles with something about manufacturing methods, chiefly in connection with basalt. At another point he considers in detail the suitability of the slag, at all the mines where ash furnaces had been erected, to be blown into junk bottles, and, with a different admixture, into green bottles. Sublimate of lead he thought ought to be converted into pig lead or used as a possible flux in the manufacture of flint glass. The plastic white clay at Gray Mine, Missouri, served to recall a similar deposit at Zanesville, Ohio, and provoked the statement that it might prove valuable in the manufacture of pottery—particularly glasshouse pots, which require a clay of the utmost purity and infusibility. Then follow three pages on this subject. He reverts to his glassmaking background in examining beads found on Big River in Missouri as well as those noted earlier at Hamburg, New York. There are two pages on the use of manganese or "glass soap" in making enamels and artificial gems, and on the art of melting. Again, for eight pages following 141, he introduces recipes for synthetic gems, flint glass, and other vitreous products. A discussion of glass-sands, pages 186–188, occurs in conjunction with a mention of siliceous ingredient for flint glass.

The overtures of the Austin family in an endeavor to attract him to their vast undertaking in Spanish Texas, did not turn him from his idea of exploring the interior of Missouri and Arkansas. This expedition in 1818–1819, although incidentally it permitted investigation of other phases of the Ozark country and, also incidentally, led to the publication later of a journal of exploration, was unquestionably directed to a point twenty miles above the junction of Findley Creek and the James River branch of the White River, because of known important lead deposits there. Notwithstanding the fact that he lost his way, reaching Arkansas on another fork of the White River, and regardless of dangers, discouragements and many disagreeable conditions, he would not be deflected from his destination on the James River. When he reached it, he built a temporary cabin, remained some days investigating the lead deposits, then at once turned back. This seems ample proof that the lead mines were his goal. The journal of this Missouri exploration was not published until some time after his lead-mine treatise. The story of his route from Olean to Potosi seems not to have appeared until 1844, in *Oneóta*. The fact that another edition of *A View of the Lead Mines of Missouri* was issued in 1853 as only an appendix to *Scenes and Adventures in the Semi-Alpine Region of the Ozark Mountains of Missouri and Arkansas* serves to emphasize his mining engineering interest in 1819.

The plant at Keene, New Hampshire, in which Schoolcraft had been interested last, was a flint glassworks. The composition of flint glass is chiefly distinguished from that of other types by the introduction of a high percentage of lead, which is largely employed both as a flux and as a permanent material of the ware. Up to 1818, in spite of earnest investigations, American glassmakers had been unable to produce crystal glass or lead flint that could be cut in the English manner, because none of the manufacturers had yet solved the secret of compounding red-lead or litharge. The future of the industry, in fact, hinged considerably on the success of these experiments. All this clearly explains the origin of Schoolcraft's interest in the lead mines of Missouri, and his concentration on them.

It is equally easy to understand how, after he had thoroughly investigated the Missouri mining situation, his preoccupation shifted from glassmaking to lead-mining, from that of the manufacturer to the mining engineer.

In the preface to *A View of the Lead Mines of Missouri*, dated New York, November 25, 1819, Schoolcraft states

We are still in want of a detailed account of the mines of Missouri, the extent and quality of the ore, the character of the accompanying minerals, the methods of mining, the nature of the contiguous country, its character, value, population, and resources, its advantages for water-mills and manufactories, the facilities it affords by its streams for internal navigation, with other facts necessary in estimating the collective value and importance of those mines.

Then he adds, "A want of information is also felt in regard to the physical history of the western country, particularly its minerals, fossils, geology, antiquities, &c." This nicely indicates the relative importance of the two parts into which this book is divided by him, logically.

The second part, described in the subsidiary title as "Observations on the Mineralogy, Geology, Geography, &c. of the Western Country," is a miscellany of facts, gathered together into 144 pages, of which the following summary may be useful: geographical outline of Missouri Territory; catalogue of the minerals and fossils of the Western Country; journal of a voyage up the Mississippi River from the mouth of the Ohio to St. Louis, with some account of that city; and a topographical account of the White River in Arkansas Territory. A final chapter of various writings relates to the Hot Springs of Arkansas; steamboat and other traffic on the Mississippi; precious stones of Missouri; reprints of items about manganese in Kentucky, beads unearthed in Hamburg, New York, and supposed dwarf skeletons on a farm near St. Louis, Missouri; an antique silver cup taken from a mound at Marietta, Ohio; and a note on the lead mines of Millersburg, Kentucky.

Part I, consisting of 150 pages, the actual body of the book, is a well-knit, comprehensive contribution to the mining engineering and economic geology of its time. As such it played an important part in the development of Missouri and in Schoolcraft's own career.

Pittsburgh, the great manufacturing city of the West, Schoolcraft had regarded as "the alpha" in his route to the Mississippi Valley. He visited its various workshops and foundries, including the large glassworks of Bakewell and of O'Hara, and collected accurate data of the cost of raw materials, the places where they were obtained, the expense of manufacture, and the price of the finished product. "I had thus a body of facts which enabled me . . . to give my friends in the east suitable data and to compare the advantages of manufacturing here with those possessed by the eastern and middle states." He mentioned briefly the rich coal and iron mines which had caused the phenomenal growth of Pittsburgh and were the promise for its future, and took time to explore the geology of the Monongahela Valley as far as Williamsport.

His notes on three weeks spent in Cincinnati feature an experimental structure there in which it was proposed to realize a practical mechanical power from the rarefaction of the atmosphere; the fact that he was called on, in an advisory capacity, to remove defects in the processes of manufacture at the Cincinnati white lead works; and the effects of the depression on that community.

At Louisville, Kentucky, where he stopped several weeks, he wrote notices for one of the papers about manganese on Sandy River, lead at Millersburg, and other items of western natural history. The fact that these were copied by eastern newspapers confirmed his theory that there was a general desire in the Atlantic States for information about the West.

Levi Pettibone, formerly of Vernon, New York, lived at St. Louis. Schoolcraft visited him a few days, saw the scientific sights of the place, then buried himself for almost a full year in the lead-mining district.

Henry Rowe Schoolcraft was the first mineralogist to visit the region. His purpose to investigate and publicize gave him immediate standing. At Potosi, center of activities, Mr. Stephen F. Austin invited him to take rooms at the old Austin mansion, provided a room for his mineralogical collections, and rode out with him to examine several mines.

I found rising of forty principal mines scattered over a district of some twenty miles, running parallel to, and about thirty miles west of, the banks of the Mississippi. I spent about three months in these examinations, and as auxiliary means thereto, built a chemical furnace, for assays, in Mr. Austin's old smelting-house.

In the month of October, he resolved to push his investigations west beyond the line of settlement, and to extend them into the Ozark Mountains. This journey southwestward began at Potosi, Missouri, November 6, 1818. After reaching certain lead deposits on the James River branch of the White River in Missouri, by a circuitous route, he retraced his way along the James and White Rivers, and then traveled some distance farther down the latter stream till it crossed the postroad leading from the capital of Arkansas Territory to St. Louis. Over this road he reached Potosi, February 4, 1819.

Schoolcraft had personally visited every mine or digging of consequence in the Missouri country, and had traced the geological relations between Missouri and Arkansas. At once he sat down to draw up a description of the mine region and its various mineral resources. His preparation of the manuscript of *A View of the Lead Mines of Missouri* consumed February and March, 1819.

Although shorn of every personal mention, this work is a unique contribution to his biography, for it reveals Henry Rowe Schoolcraft in a way that nothing else that he has written has done. The compact essay is really a concentrate of his practical ability and comprehensive vision, which in other fields are only indirectly and sporadically evidenced.

He had acquired an unusual knowledge of mineralogy at a time when that branch had scarcely emerged from the vague science of natural history. His exploratory zeal was only equaled by his initiative, his energy, and an intelligent purposefulness that could not be turned aside by obstacles. The estimates made by him of the minerals and the ores that he saw were based on his own personal examination and even his own assays. He knew enough of chemistry to make analyses. Combining his geology and his knowledge of machinery, he saw the wastage of the methods of mining then followed and the great advantages that would attend mechanical improvements. He was able to suggest the benefits of pumps and other steam engines. In his drawings of the lead furnaces, he was minutely correct. These were from actual measurements done under his own eye, and corrected by an operative builder of approved skill. The furnaces, he found, were inefficient both in material and construction. He was ahead of his times in his vision of the possibilities of by-products, not only with regard to those of the mines, but of those obtainable in manufacture through chemical processing.

Statistics formed the basis of his report. His estimates were conservative. He reached a figure for the probable production of a year, from incomplete data, in two different ways. Although this was for a year when the mines were in a manifest state of decline, were wrought wholly by individuals, in competition with foreign mines and without any systematic organization of the domestic mining interest, he adopted it as the average annual production for the fifteen years during which the territory had been in the possession of the United States, and showed that the return of more than three million dollars in that time was one-fifth of the purchase price of all of Louisiana! The mines in Missouri Territory were reserved to the Government but worked by individuals under three-year leases. In order to encourage capital he advocated outright sale of properties or increasing the period of leasage to fifteen years. His own unfortunate experience of the effect of a low tariff on infant industry in a new country taught him to propose an increase from 1% to $2\frac{1}{2}\%$ in the tariff on pig and bar lead. The necessity for further exploration was stressed. Existing facilities for transportation were noted in detail— even to the number, names, character, capacity, rates, and value and kinds of freight, of steamboats then operating on the Mississippi.

He saw the region as a whole; its streams, soil, climate, settlements, and future combination of mining, agriculture, and industry. The treatise began with a historical sketch of the mines from 1712, when Anthony Crozat obtained a grant from Louis XIV of France, and ended with a summary of the uses of lead and an outline of the needs of the region in 1819. Because of lack of supervision much mining was carried on by farmer-miners without the lease supposedly required by law. Suppression of this illegal practice, and encouragement of more efficient methods by responsible concerns, would produce great increases in output and profit not only for the mining interests and Missouri Territory but for the nation. The problem of managing the lead mines in the Territory, as part of the public domain, belonged properly, as he saw it, to the Federal Government. An appointment of a United States superintendent of mines for the region was recommended.

Schoolcraft's report is concise, comprehensive, convincing. Logically enough, he saw himself as a proper person for the proposed superintendency. A fortuitous meeting at Herculaneum with the government expedition to the Yellowstone, under Major Long, and a discussion with members of that party, drew his attention to the interest of the Secretary of War in practical matters of this kind. With characteristic incisiveness, he determined to present the matter personally to Secretary Calhoun in Washington. A few days later he was on his way down the Mississippi en route to New York City via New Orleans.

In the few weeks that elapsed between August 3 and November 25, 1819, when his *A View of the Lead Mines of Missouri* came off the press, he had not only supervised its publication, in New York, but found time and means swiftly to make a place for himself in scientific circles in America.

As soon as his book was announced, he took copies of it and went to Washington. He contacted President Monroe, Secretary of War Calhoun and Secretary of the Treasury Crawford, and was favorably received. The President made memoranda of Schoolcraft's recommendations. John C. Calhoun had a definite personal interest in mining. Some ten years later he became the owner of the famous Calhoun gold mine in North Georgia, shortly after its discovery. Mr. Calhoun stated that the jurisdiction of the lead mines was not in his department, and that some Congressional action would be necessary; but, as Schoolcraft writes,

he had received a memoir from General Cass, Governor of Michigan, proposing to explore the sources of the Mississippi, through the Lakes, and suggesting that a naturalist, conversant with mineralogy, should accompany him, to inquire into the supposed value of the Lake Superior copper mines. He tendered me the place, and stated the compensation. The latter was small, but the situation appeared to me to be one which was not to be overlooked. I accepted it. It seemed to be the bottom step in a ladder which I ought to climb. . . . In the mean time, while I accepted this place, the subject of the management and superintendence of the western mines appeared to be fully appreciated by Mr. Calhoun and Mr. Crawford, the latter of whom requested a written statement on the subject; and it was held for further consideration.

Schoolcraft's effort eventually resulted in action by the Government on the matter of the lead mines. President Monroe presented it to the consideration of Congress in the fall. A superintendent was subsequently appointed. Meantime, in 1822, while the lead-mine situation was still under advisement at Washington, Henry Rowe Schoolcraft was appointed by President Monroe as Agent for Indian Affairs on the northwestern frontier. However unusual his ability as an industrialist, he was destined for another, wider field of activity.

MINERALOGIST AND GEOLOGIST

HENRY ROWE SCHOOLCRAFT had gone West in 1818 as an amateur of natural history, hoping to find a market for the record of his observations, expecting to find a useful place for himself in the new country. On his return, late the next year, he had the high anticipation of an appointment as Federal Superintendent of Mines of Missouri Territory. Then, suddenly, within a few months, he emerged as a scientific figure in America, with a place on the technical staff of a Government expedition to the Northwest.

His transition from industrial management to science was effected with finality without his realization of what was happening. In fact, for four years after his connection with the Cass Expedition he clung to the hope of being superintendent of mines in the Ozarks. His life work, however, was not to be in that direction.

What happened to Schoolcraft in the last months of 1819 was unusual but easily explainable. When he arrived in New York in August with the manuscript of his *A View of the Lead Mines of Missouri,* he was completely an unknown. When he reached Washington, D. C., with the finished book, in November of that year, a considerable reputation as a mineralogist had preceded him. There was nothing miraculous about this. It was not the result of the work of even a year or two but the fruit of uncounted hours from boyhood.

Rocks had been his toys. At first the heavy drift stratum of Albany County, as seen in the bed of Normanskill, and its deep cuttings in the slate and other rocks, were his field of mineralogical inquiries. Afterwards, while living in Vermont, he revised and systematized the study under an instructor. His remarks in the *Literary and Philosophical Repertory* on the evolvement of hydrogen gas from the strata of Western New York, under the name of Burning Springs, evinced his early aptitude. For years the clays and sands of the East helped him earn his livelihood. His heart was in the subject.

At the beginning of his Mississippi Valley venture, when the ice in the Allegheny at Olean delayed his start down river, he made use of it to cross on foot and examine evidence of the coal formation on the other side. At the end of that long journey, when held in quarantine because of an epidemic of yellow fever, he spent the time happily in mineralogical and geological exploration of Staten Island. His success in life, reduced to its prime terms, shows hard, persistent work as the predominating factor.

He displayed another element of genius in his recognition and deft seizure of opportunity. Natural science at the time was in its infancy in the United States. Schoolcraft nevertheless sensed that the general public, now keenly curious about the whole Mississippi Valley, would welcome scientific facts about it. He had tested his idea while in Louisville, Kentucky, by writing a few items for the newspapers and watching Eastern publications to see if his contributions were noticed. Results confirmed his previous convictions. The possibilities of mineral wealth in new regions had more than once in history aroused popular imagination.

How well Schoolcraft had judged his times he makes clear in telling what happened on his return to New York:

I had now completed, by land and water, a circuit of the Union, having traveled some six thousand miles. My arrival was opportune. No traveler of modern times had thrown himself upon the success of his scientific observations, and I was hailed, by the scientific public, as the first one who had ever brought a collection of the mineral productions of the Mississippi Valley. My collection, which was large and splendid, was the means of introducing me to men of science at New York and elsewhere. Dr. Samuel L. Mitchill and Dr. D. Hosack, who were then in the zenith of their fame, cordially received me. The natural sciences were then chiefly in the hands of physicians, and there was scarcely a man of note in these departments of inquiry who was not soon numbered among my acquaintances. Dr. John Torrey was then a young man, who had just published his first botanical work. Dr. A. W. Ives warmly interested himself in my behalf, and I had literary friends on every side. Among these Governor DeWitt Clinton was prominent.

His practical treatise on the lead mines was dedicated to a contemporary scientist—member of the Antiquarian Society of Massachusetts and of the Literary and Philosophical and of the Historical Society of New York. Schoolcraft had not only carried East a choice selection from his mineralogical gleanings but enough duplicates to enrich the cabinets of others. A letter by him on the resources of the West was published by the Corresponding Association of Internal Improvements. The Lyceum of Natural History of New York and the New-York Historical Society, each admitted him to membership. In short, he created a considerable sensation and gave a strong impulse to the study of mineralogy and geology.

In addition to the impressiveness of his long trip on his own initiative; the publication of the letter by him about the mines; his own book under his arm, containing evidence of comprehensive knowledge and a sound proposal about the region; and the favorable reception accorded him in scholarly circles, Schoolcraft had another means of effective approach to the administration at Washington.

Fortune had collaborated again with his unusual qualities in making at least one friend at court for him in the person of the Honorable Jesse B. Thomas, Senator from Illinois. The incident had occurred on his way down the Ohio. In the little fleet with which his ark traveled from Pittsburgh to Cincinnati, there was a flatboat owned by Senator Thomas. This barge, loaded with a valuable cargo of farm machinery, was somehow crowded into a slanting position between the larger craft. It began to leak above the caulked seams, filled rapidly, and was about to sink. They cut it loose and were leaving it to its fate. Those held up by the mishap were sitting on the shore, idling away the time of the delay. Schoolcraft decided, however, that two men bailing with all their might could empty the water faster than it poured in and lighten the craft until it could rise again above the line of leakage. A companion agreed to help him. When the point was proven, others volunteered. He organized shifts. The ark with its costly cargo was saved and enabled to proceed. Senator Thomas naturally responded with respect for the young man's ability, as well as gratitude and friendship, which stood Schoolcraft in good stead when he arrived in Washington.

Another factor in the circumstances that proved the turning point in his career was, again, a further instance of his rare vision. At the same time as General Lewis Cass, Governor of the Territory of Michigan, he saw the need of mineralogical exploration of the upper Great Lakes and Mississippi region. Perhaps he expressed it even sooner. He knew about the famous Ontonagon copper boulder and the specimens of native copper that made the western Lake Superior region glamorous. Even backwoods hunters and traders in Missouri told wild tales of it. His poem, *Transallegania,* published soon after returning from the Ozarks, has an interesting reference to the

Michigan copper country. His investigations of the Missouri
lead mines made him eager to extend his observations to the
deposits of that mineral on the Upper Mississippi, and also into
the copper-bearing regions of that latitude. Acting promptly
on this urge, before he left Missouri Territory he wrote to Senator Thomas, suggesting the desirability of federal investigation
of these northern possibilities. The same idea was put forward
in his letter of October 5, 1819, to the New York Corresponding
Association. There was not much of the fortuitous, therefore,
in the selection of Henry Rowe Schoolcraft by Secretary of War
Calhoun, when Governor Cass made his proposal for an expedition from Detroit to the sources of the Mississippi and asked
for an assistant acquainted with zoology, botany, and mineralogy.

Schoolcraft accepted the offer of this place although it
paid only one dollar and a half a day for the time actually put
in. It was a step on his way. Abraham Lincoln is supposed to
have said, "I will study and prepare myself and some day my
chance will come." Henry Rowe Schoolcraft wished to be useful. He studied; worked; and did not wait for a great opportunity, but took what came.

After two months in Washington he returned to New York
City for a month before setting out, by stage, on March 5, 1820,
for the West. From Buffalo he visited Niagara Falls, by horse
and buggy, May 1. Taking passage, then, on the steamer
Walk-in-the-Water, he reached Detroit May 8. Sixteen days
later the memorable Cass Expedition of 1820 was on its way.

As in the case of his explorations in Missouri, Schoolcraft's
emphasized concern was mining possibilities. Yet he examined,
as carefully as opportunity permitted, practically all the
American shores of the three upper Great Lakes, the banks of
the Upper Mississippi to within one hundred fifty miles of its
as yet undiscovered source, and the connecting river routes.
He obtained special permission from Governor Cass to visit
the lead mines at Dubuque. "Among the objects secured," he
wrote, "were fine specimens of the various forms of native
copper and its ores, together with crystallized sulphurets of

ROUTE OF THE EXPEDITION OF 1820. NOTE THAT UPPER LINE MARKS INTERNATIONAL BOUNDARY

lead, zinc, and iron; native muriate of soda, graphite, sulphate of lime, and strontian; and the attractive forms which the species of the quartz family assume, in the shore debris of the lakes, under the names of agate, carnelian, etc."

Information about the "reported" Lake Superior copper mines was the outstanding geological objective. The expedition spent four days exploring this region. Schoolcraft's detailed report to Secretary of War Calhoun, made in November, 1820, is an interesting document. Published in advance by the *American Journal of Science,* and by order of the Senate of the United States, it is the earliest scientific account of the mineral affluence of the Lake Superior basin. Although Schoolcraft did not locate the copper deposits, he noted the first appearance of the ore as at Keweenaw Point, and dwelt in some detail on the occurrence of frequent masses of drift copper, several of them extraordinary, for two hundred miles along the South Superior shore. The copper mines located among the hills of the Ontonagon he characterized as "so-called."

He described the finding of the large block of native copper on the shore of the Ontonagon River, gave a picture of it, and offered some remarks on its probable origin. Definitely, he said, it was not in place. Even in its then reduced size, he characterized it as one of the largest and most remarkable bodies of native copper on the globe. More than twenty years later, when the famous boulder was exhibited in Detroit, Schoolcraft reappraised it as by far the largest known and described specimen. Earlier rumors of a larger piece in South America had proved unfounded. Even in 1843 its weight was only estimated. There were no scales in Detroit capable of weighing it.*

* Merwin W. Youngs, able editor of the *Daily Mining Gazette,* at Houghton, Michigan, says: The Ontonagon boulder is far from being the largest mass of native copper ever found. However, it has a certain fascination because it was the earliest of the large masses and incidents in its history are of interest. A dislodged boulder or "float," almost spherical in shape, it weighed 3,750 pounds. After several unsuccessful efforts to take it from the Ontonagon River, it was finally moved by James K. Paull, who managed to get it to the mouth of the stream. There a Major Cunning-

Various early accounts of the search for the copper mines were quoted by Schoolcraft, and the report was included of a recent analysis, at the University of Leyden, of one specimen that proved to be native copper in a state of uncommon purity.

In short, while he found no body of the metal sufficiently extensive to mine profitably, he unqualifiedly confirmed the expectation that a more intimate knowledge of the country would result in the discovery of valuable ores of copper, in the working of which "occasional masses and veins of the native metal may materially enhance the advantage of mining."

Two years later, in his general report to the Secretary of War on the geology and mineralogy of the Lake Superior country, he impressively reiterated his belief that the region was destined to be the future theater of extensive mining operations; and called particular attention to the need of a mineralogical survey of the lead formation at Dubuque, Iowa. His reply to the inquiry of the Senate of the United States concerning the value and extent of the mineral lands on Lake Superior, October 1, 1822, further stresses the possibility that expecta-

---

ham of the United States Army endeavored to confiscate it, but Paull defied him and eventually sold it to a man named Eldred. Eldred resold it to the government at a nice profit and for many years the boulder was lodged outside the door of the War Department in Washington. It now is in the Smithsonian Institution.

Many big copper masses have been found in the same district. The largest ever discovered was in the old Minnesota mine in Ontonagon County. It weighed 520 *tons*, before it was cut up in small pieces and sold. Many masses weighing 50 or 60 tons have been found in the Quincy mine, which has been in operation for over ninety years and is still working. Many more were yielded by the old Cliff and Central mines in Keweenaw County.

Of course there have been numerous mass copper deposits in the district, the one in Ahmeek being particularly impressive. This was a mass fissure vein running at right angles to the regular lode formation. It was something like 1,200 feet long and 600 feet wide, and varied in thickness, narrowing in places to a few inches.

Mounted on a base on the campus of the Michigan College of Mining and Technology at Houghton, Michigan, is a mass of "float" copper larger than the Ontonagon boulder. It weighs about 3,900 pounds. This was ploughed up in a field in the South range district.

tions would be justified by stating that the mines would prove not only fertile but unparalleled in extent. Their location, he showed, presented no hindrance to their profitable operation. The purchase of the mines from the Indians would be beneficial to the tribes rather than otherwise. In short, the mines could be wrought with eminent advantage to the republic.

These reports, and the accounts of his visits to the lead mines of Missouri and those at Galena, Illinois, and Dubuque, Iowa, are his chief tangible contributions to mining geology. The contagious enthusiasm of his expressions concerning future possibilities was incalculable in its effect. Some idea of the psychological importance of his writings can be gained by comparing Schoolcraft's statements with those of some of his most highly esteemed scientific contemporaries.

As early as 1822, Schoolcraft pointed out the relatively low cost of water carriage, and the unusual facilities for free and direct communication between the copper country and its market, New York City, via the Great Lakes and the Erie Canal—soon to be completed. At the same time he mentioned a canal at Sault Ste. Marie as a still further advantage that might soon be expected. Three years later than this, William H. Keating, professor of mineralogy and chemistry at the University of Pennsylvania, and geologist with the Long Expedition to the Upper Mississippi, wrote pessimistically: "The question which appears to us of far greater importance is not where the copper lies, but what shall we do with it if it should be found. We are very doubtful whether any other advantage would result from it, at least for a century to come, than the mere addition in books of science of a new locality of this metal."

The rightness of Schoolcraft is vividly witnessed by the fact that development of the Michigan copper country began in 1845. By 1846 Mackinac Island was crowded with people on their way to or from it. Up to 1889 the combined mines had produced over 1,000,000,000 pounds of the refined metal. The output for 1889 alone amounted to 87,455,675 pounds. As early as 1839 an abortive attempt was made by the State of

Michigan to build the St. Marys Canal at the Sault. When it was finally opened, June 18, 1855, copper was the cargo of the first vessel that locked down.

Schoolcraft's account of native copper on the shore of Lake Superior was one of the articles on the geology and mineralogy of North America that were eagerly seized upon by foreign scientists, as well as those interested from a spirit of gain only. His essay on the subject, published in advance of his report to the War Department, in the *American Journal of Science*, was one of those extracted for a pamphlet in German published in Hamburg in 1822.

Although the purpose of his trip to Missouri was mainly to study the lead deposits, his *A View of the Lead Mines of Missouri* offered some useful geological information about a region that then was practically unexplored. His cabinet collection, illustrating fully the mineralogy of the country, also, to some extent, reflected its structural characteristics. This investigation, unlike most of Schoolcraft's travels, was largely on foot and unrestricted by other objectives. He described the whole mineral country as "bottomed" on primitive limestone, though he found quartz rock and later sand rock very common in the southern section. Secondary limestone was also met with, but was far less common than in Ohio, Indiana, Connecticut, and Illinois, the ore itself being found in the decomposition products from the primitive limestone. He mentioned the occurrence of granite in Washington and Madison Counties, also greenstone porphyry and iron ore, and correctly described the granite as being the only mass of its kind known to exist between the primitive ranges of the Allegheny and Rocky mountains, being surrounded on all sides and to an almost immeasurable extent with secondary limestone. On Dormant Walls below Herculaneum he noted traces of an ancient ocean two hundred feet above the existing level of the Mississippi.

A descriptive catalogue of the minerals of the Western country was included. Among them mention was made of the flint from Girardeau County; several varieties of quartz, including the Arkansas novaculite; a red pipe-stone from the

Falls of St. Anthony, which is evidently the catlinite of later writers but which he called steatite; and other minerals, including baryte, fluorite, blende, antimony, native copper, etc. He described briefly the micaceous iron ore of Iron Mountain, Missouri; publicized reports of manganese and lead findings in Kentucky; recognized the importance of coal and iron near Pittsburgh, Pennsylvania, and foresaw that the coal measures might extend into New York State.

His narrative of the Cass expedition of 1820 abounds in mineralogical and geological notes. These are in large part of an economic nature. The occurrence of gypsum at St. Martins Island, Michigan, was mentioned, the island of Michilimackinac itself being of "transition and compact" limestone. A colored section was given showing the relative position of granite and overlying sandstone between Presque Isle and Garlic River. The sandstone he described as overlapping the granite and fitting into its irregularities in a manner that "shows it to have assumed that position subsequently to the upheaving of the granite." The age of this sand rock he was unable to satisfactorily determine, though its position seemed to him to indicate a near alliance to the "Old red sandstone." The correct position of this sandstone remained long a matter of doubt and dispute. It is now considered as of Potsdam age. He recognized Lake Superior as the theater of ancient extensive volcanic action, and noted old water lines high on Arched Rock on Mackinac Island and other places.

Writing on the prevailing theories as to the origin and distribution of metals and gems, he remarked, "There is no reason that can be drawn from philosophical investigations to prove that these substances may not be abundantly found in the climates of the north, even upon the banks of the frozen ocean," their distribution being apparently wholly independent of climatic conditions.

The Dubuque lead ore he described as occurring in detached masses in the ocherous alluvial soil resting upon a calcareous rock referable to the Transition class (in the revision of his work, published in 1832, he made this Carboniferous), and also in veins penetrating the rock. He did not seem to recognize that the ore was originally in the limestone, from which it was liberated by decomposition and left to accumulate in the residual clay, representing the insoluble constituents.

The presence of extensive beds of coal about forty miles southwest of Chicago, on the Fox River, was noted and the suggestion advanced that this formation might extend under the lake and be found in Michigan. The fact that bricks made from clay occurring near Milwaukee turned white was also mentioned. These are the bricks that later gave Milwaukee the name of the Cream City, because of the color of its buildings.

In his *Travels in the Central Portions of the Mississippi Valley*, Schoolcraft advanced the idea that there had been at some former period an obstruction in the channel of the Mississippi River at or near Grand Tower, in southern Illinois, whereby there was produced a stagnation of the current at an elevation of about 130 feet above the present ordinary water-mark. This was made sufficiently evident to him by the general elevation and direction of the hills, which for several hundred miles above are separated by a valley from twenty to twenty-five miles wide. Wherever these hills disclosed rocky and precipitous fronts a series of distinctly-marked old water lines were observed. The Grand Tower and the contiguous promontories were regarded as but the dilapidated remains of this barrier. On the breaking away of the obstructions the water gradually receded into existing channels, by which the inland sea was gradually drained.

While with this expedition of 1821, he noted signs of rich coal deposits at Terre Haute, Indiana, visited the fluor spar deposits in Pope County, Illinois, and revisited the lead mines in Missouri. "To satisfy the just requisitions of a temperate criticism" of his *A View of the Lead Mines of Missouri* and "in some measure to merit the commendations of a generous one," —also because no more formal and extended description had been offered in the interim—Schoolcraft devoted some thirty-six pages of his *Travels* to a more scientific description of the

SCHOOLCRAFT'S SECTION OF PRESQUE ISLE.

formations in the lead mining counties of Missouri. He did not recognize that the extensive deposits of galena in the red marl had their source in the breaking down of the superior stratum of galeniferous limestone; but he did refute the theory of Maclure who referred their origin to distant regions. The Appendix of this volume presents his letter concerning the resources of the western country, in 1819, as published by the New York Corresponding Association for the Promotion of Internal Improvement; also a colored geological sketch, both topographical and sectional, of the lead mine district of Missouri, embracing the granitical tract of St. Michael.

In calling attention to the glaciated area of Missouri, he correctly related the drift to the primitive formations of Lake Superior. He recorded drift findings over a wide section of the country, in New York State, around the southern shores of the Great Lakes, in the Maumee Valley, the Central and Upper Mississippi basin, and in Missouri. Though he did not hit upon the now accepted glacial theory for the agency of transportation, he made a valuable accumulation of data. Also he did not fail to notice the absence of drift boulders in parts of Illinois.

His geological work was of the greatest value in the then existing condition of knowledge regarding the regions visited, the lead districts of the Mississippi Valley and the copper regions of Lake Superior especially profiting by his activities.

Schoolcraft's labors in this field of science fall almost entirely within its earliest era in the United States. At the beginning of this period, the foreign literature extant was not large, and even then for the most part quite inaccessible to the average American student. There was a general lack of knowledge of the composition of rocks and of chemical methods. Rocks and minerals were bunched together indiscriminately. Some of his own palaeontological contributions are examples of the almost medieval notions of his day.

None of the sciences were taught in American colleges and other institutions of learning in this country. In fact the general trend of public opinion was decidedly against the study of geology, or the investigation of any question which might lead to the discovery of supposed inconsistencies in the Mosaic account of creation.

It was an event of great importance when, in 1802, Benjamin Silliman was appointed to a professorship of chemistry and natural science in Yale College. Interestingly enough, at that time Mr. Silliman was a young man of twenty-two, recently admitted to the bar and serving as a tutor in law, who had not even the most rudimentary knowledge of the science he was to teach. Professor Silliman tried to read up on chemistry in secret with no success, but eventually attended five months lectures on the subject in the Medical School of Philadelphia. His *American Journal of Science,* founded in 1818, became one of the oldest and perhaps the most important geological periodical extant in America. Schoolcraft was one of its earliest contributors and carried on a considerable and mutually helpful correspondence with Professor Silliman.

Douglass Houghton, M.D., Detroit, as physician, botanist and geologist to the Henry R. Schoolcraft expeditions in 1831 and 1832, gained experience under Schoolcraft that not only stimulated his natural love for adventurous exploration but also instructed him in those methods of travel and sustenance in the wilderness of which he made such effective use during the progress of the Geological Survey of Michigan.

When the first American society devoted mainly to geological and allied subjects was organized, in 1819, in the philosophy room of Yale College, as the American Geological Society, Henry Rowe Schoolcraft was among the more prominent members.

Yet with the publication of his *Travels in the Central Portions of the Mississippi Valley* in 1825, geology had ceased to be his major pursuit.

As long as he lived, it never ceased, however, to be one of his compelling interests and an enthusiasm to communicate to others. The mineralogical gleanings of his childhood were among the few treasures he kept when he converted his belongings into cash in order to go West. Interesting earth creations always enmeshed him.   At Mt. Vernon at the tomb of Washington for the first time, he was not too much overwhelmed by patriotic and historic emotions to overlook a bit of rock that merited a place in his cabinet.   On his way to Detroit in 1820, he carried his specimens in a banker's box for safer keeping—which so advertised the fact of preciousness that someone thought it heavy with money and stole it.   At Potosi, in Missouri, he inspired a multitude of miners to collect for him, all interested in carrying to him anything they found in their pits and leads which assumed a new or curious character.   He was a clearing house for all their questions as well as those from many other quarters.   His personal enthusiasm, and generous giving of his time to answering inquiries, stirred interest in those around him and many in far places, in fact across the oceans.

Even the northern Indians, suspicious of white men and fearful of their manitos, felt the contagion.   Schoolcraft's activities with his mineralogical hammer, on the Cass expedition in 1820, were

narrowly watched by the Indians, who wondered what such a scrutiny should mean. The French, said the chief to one of our interpreters, formerly held possession of this country; and, afterwards, came the British. They contented themselves with common things, and never disturbed these rocks, which have been lying here forever. But the moment the Americans get possession of the country, they must come and knock off pieces of the rock, and look at them. It is marvellous!

The Indians, he remarked,

are firmly impressed with a belief that any information communicated to the whites, disclosing the position of mines or metallic treasures situated upon their grounds, is displeasing to their manitos, and even to the Great Spirit himself, from whom they profess to derive every good and valuable gift: and that this offence never fails to be visited upon them in the loss of property, in the want of success in their customary pursuits or pastimes, in untimely death, or some other singular disaster or untoward event.

Nevertheless he made the Ojibways, as well as the traders, his collaborators at Sault Ste. Marie:

I had, the prior year, set up my mineralogical cabinet in my office, and stated to the Indians, who roved over large tracts, my solicitude to collect specimens of the mineral productions of the country of every description, and, indeed, of its zoology, always acknowledging their comity, in bringing me specimens in any department of natural history, by some small present; and I found this to be a means of extending my inquiries.

In 1938 there were two thousand five hundred museums in the United States—perhaps a quarter of all in the entire world—with an investment of one hundred and fifty million dollars and a combined annual operating income of eighteen million dollars. In Schoolcraft's day there were no institutionalized museums in the country.

It is an impressive remembrance that in his time, when Mackinac Island was the extreme end of the civilized earth, and Sault Ste. Marie the most northerly point in the United States to which the Indian title had been extinguished, the walls of the spacious main rooms of the Indian Agency on the St. Marys River were lined with cabinets and constituted a museum extraordinary in America.

Schoolcraft made a practice of sending unusual items and duplicates to Eastern organizations interested in natural history, thereby enlarging the nuclei from which numerous state, college, and university museums were later formed. From the Sault, back of the beyond in the North American wilderness, a continuing stream of correspondence went back and forth to men and publications that led the whole world in their fields. Science, for once marching abreast with commerce and the military, had a frontier outpost on Lake Superior.

In 1832 his eager excitement on the verge of reaching Lake Itasca did not down his desire to examine personally the formation at the Naiwa River Rapids, although his expedition had Douglass Houghton as official geologist.

The ardor that had been kindled in the gorges of the Tawasentha still burned consumingly when Schoolcraft later, as member of the first Board of Regents of the University of Michigan, played his important part in securing a mineralogical collection for that institution—regardless of whether they had proper facilities to house it! The price paid for the unusual Baron Lederer cabinet, and the proportion of this amount to the entire appropriation for the University that year, bear witness to unmistakable intensity of interest and exertion of influence. It gave the University and Michigan the nucleus of what has always since been an outstanding museum of its kind.

The trend of Schoolcraft's career, however, had changed in 1820. That was the year he had first seen Jane Johnston at Sault Ste. Marie, and had traveled the full length of the Mississippi—to within a few days' journey of its source.

Explorer-Geographer

1st voice: From as far West as Idaho,
Down from the glacier peaks of the Rockies—
From as far East as New York,
Down from the turkey ridges of the Alleghenies!
Down from Minnesota, 2500 miles,
The Mississippi River runs to the gulf!

2nd voice: Carrying every drop of water that flows down from two-thirds the continent—
Carrying every brook and rill,
Rivulet and creek—
Carrying all the rivers that run down two-thirds the continent
The Mississippi runs to the Gulf of Mexico!

3rd voice: For the water comes downhill,
Spring and fall, down from the cut-over mountains, down from the plowed-off slopes,
From as far West as Idaho and as far East as New York,
Down every brook and rill, rivulet and creek,
Carrying every drop of water that flows down two-thirds the continent,
The Mississippi River runs to the Gulf of Mexico!
—Pare Lorentz

THE lines quoted above convey inaccuracies. However, like many dramatic utterances, they have an impressive value that makes up, in a measure, for departure from actual fact. They are given merely to aid in the astounding realization that the Mississippi basin extends nearly to the Pacific Ocean westward, easterly almost to the Atlantic, and to a point north of Duluth on Lake Superior.   Counting as a part of it the longest branch of the drainage system, the Missouri, which far overtops the central stem, it is the longest river in the world—4200 miles.   The main north and south stem of the system, which rises in the highlands of Minnesota, has a length of 2555 miles. The total navigable length of the Mississippi and its tributaries is 9,000 miles, measured in straight lines, and over 14,000 following the river windings.   Twenty-one States are intersected by the navigable waters of this great system.   Its drainage basin covers an area of about 1,257,000 square miles, or over two-fifths of the total area of the United States.

As explorer of the source of the Mississippi River in the highlands of Minnesota, Schoolcraft won a place among those who have attached their names to that of the great Father of Waters into historical immortality.

The American Geographical Society of New York stands at the head of such organizations in the world.   Even the Royal Society of London, England, is not its superior.   The *Atlas of the Historical Geography of the United States,* published by this great American organization in conjunction with the Carnegie Institution of Washington, is the most comprehensive work of its kind that has ever been published for any country.   One map in this authoritative masterpiece shows American explorations west of the Mississippi River during the years 1803 to 1852.   The expeditions illustrated were selected from a long list, on the basis of the historical importance of the exploration, its priority in visiting new regions, and the value of the geographical or other scientific facts discovered.   Among these important few was chosen Henry Rowe Schoolcraft's exploration of 1832, because of his discovery and naming of Lake Itasca, source of the Mississippi.

The Itasca Lake basin was set aside as a State park by Minnesota, with the assistance of the Federal government, in 1891. With additions it now comprises some thirty-two thousand acres, in which there are three hundred sixty-five lakes.   The

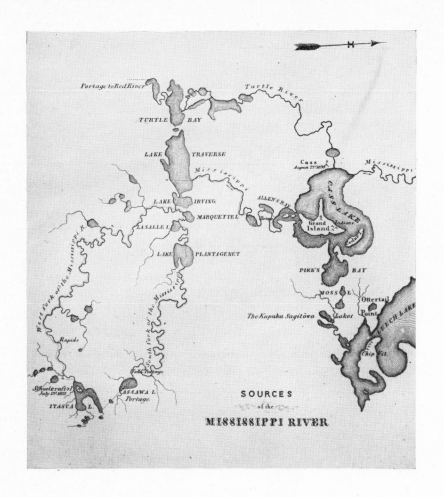

Portage to Red River

Turtle River

TURTLE BAY

LAKE TRAVERSE

Mississippi

Cass
August 27ᵗʰ 1820

Mississippi

LAKE IRVING

ALLEN'S BAY

CASS LAKE

LASALLE L.

MARQUETTE L.

Grand
Island

Indians

LAKE PLANTAGENET

PIKE'S BAY

MOSS L.

West Fork of the Mississippi R.

Ottertail
Point

The Kapuka Sagitôwa

Lakes

LEECH LAKE

South Fork of the Mississippi

Rapids

Chip Vel.

Falls Portage

Schoolcraft L.
July 13ᵗʰ 1832

CASSAWA L.
Portage

ITASCA L.

SOURCES
of the

MISSISSIPPI RIVER

"first bridge across the Mississippi" consists of four stepping-stones. A rustic sign near it bears the inscription of the altitude, 1467 feet, and the distance to the Gulf of Mexico, 2546 miles.

On October 13, 1940, the United States Office of Education at Washington produced, over the National Broadcasting Company networks, a radio dramatization entitled *Discovering the Source of the Mississippi*. This tribute to Schoolcraft's greatest explorational achievement was presented for, and in collaboration with the Smithsonian Institution.

Schoolcraft knew the story of the River as he knew the vast stream itself, with his mind and with his heart.

The Mississippi River was first seen by white men, at Chickasaw Bluff, near Memphis, Tennessee, by De Soto and his expedition of 1541. De Soto died and was buried in the stream to forestall outrages by the Indians. His men sailed down the River to its mouth, which the Spaniards, and La Salle later, tried in vain to find from the Gulf.

Jolliet, with Marquette, explored the Mississippi from the mouth of the Wisconsin River, near Prairie du Chien, Wisconsin, to within half a league of Arkansas, where threatening Indians and fear of the Spanish caused him to turn back, for fear the news of what already had been discovered should be lost. He had been told by Indians that the source of the great river lay in several lakes north of the point at which he first entered it; and that it went straight south from where he left it, so that he could be certain its mouth was not on the northeast coast or the west coast but in Florida or the Gulf of Mexico. He discovered it on June 17, 1673, and journeyed on it for a month, till July 17, when he entered the Illinois River on his return journey northward.

La Salle, it is now established beyond all reasonable doubt, first saw the Mississippi February 6, 1682, at the junction of the Illinois and traced its course to the delta, where he divided his party into three, each of which followed a debouching stream to the ocean and met to celebrate the discovery of the great river's mouth. His explorations determined the connection between the earlier findings of De Soto and Jolliet. Henri de Tonti, one of La Salle's companions, published an account of this. Father Louis Hennepin, another member of La Salle's party, in 1680 at his instance explored the Mississippi from the mouth of the Illinois southward a short distance, then northward one hundred and fifty leagues above that confluence, after which he and his associates were taken prisoner and carried nineteen days' journey toward its sources. It was Hennepin who named the Falls of St. Anthony and the River St. Francis.

Zebulon Montgomery Pike left Fort Bellefontaine, Missouri, at least four months too late in the season in 1805. Winter overtook him a hundred and twenty miles above the Falls of St. Anthony. On snow shoes, with light sledges, he pushed on determinedly to Upper Red Cedar Lake, the highest point to which he penetrated. Almost nine months were spent in this exploration. Lieutenant Pike was misled in placing the source of the river in Turtle Lake. His reports were limited in scope because of the season, as well as the fact that there was no scientific observer and no Indian interpreter on his staff.

Lewis Cass has a place among the explorers of the Upper Mississippi. He suggested such an expedition, in November, 1819, to Secretary of War John C. Calhoun. Information about the Indians and the British fur trade, the extinction of Indian title to land sufficient for a military post at Sault Ste. Marie, and the Ontonagon copper boulder were expressly mentioned as objectives. General reference was made to exploration of the southern shore of Lake Superior and the water communication between that Lake and the Mississippi, to obtain correct topographical delineation, collect botanical, zoological and geological information, and ascertain the existent and future value of the region. Michigan's population, although increasing fast in the previous two or three years, had only reached 8,765, and it was thought desirable to take all practicable measures to obtain and publish a knowledge of the country and its resources, to encourage settlements. "In addition to these objects," wrote General Cass, "I think it very important to carry the flag of the United States unto those remote regions, where it has never been borne by any person in public station." In the preliminary correspondence nothing appears to have been said about an exploration of the sources of the Mississippi, which is first mentioned after the council with the Chippewas at Sandy Lake, as a sub-expedition of two light canoes, provisioned for twelve days.

The Cass expedition left Detroit May 24, 1820. Governor Cass took the Indian tribes as the subject of his own personal observations. Captain D. B. Douglass, Professor of Engineering at West Point, was topographer and astronomer. The geology and mineralogy of the region were the concern of Henry Rowe Schoolcraft, also as much of its zoology and botany as water transit would permit. The plan of procedure in brief in Schoolcraft's words,

embraced the circumnavigation of the coasts of Lakes Huron, Michigan, and Superior. From the head of the latter, we ascended the rapid River of St. Louis to a summit which descends west to the Upper Mississippi, the waters of which we entered about five hundred miles above the Falls of St. Anthony, and some three hundred miles above the ulterior point reached with boats by Lieutenant Pike in December, 1805.

From this point we ascended the Mississippi, by its involutions, to its upper falls at Pakagama, where it dashes over a rock formation. A vast plateau of grass and aquatic plants succeeds, through which it winds as in a labyrinth. On this plateau we encountered and passed across the southern Lake Winnipek. Beyond this, the stream appears to be but little diminished, unless it be in its depth. It is eventually traced to a very large lake called Upper Lac Cedar Rouge, but to which we applied the name of Cass Lake. This is the apparent navigable source of the river, and was our terminal point.

By this time it was late in the summer. They were then, according to the Indians, six days' journey below a lake called LaBiche which gave the River rise. The water in the remote streams and rapids was at all times shallow but was particularly so that season, and it was not practicable to reach these remote sources of the river with boats or canoes of the size they had. These facts, in conjunction with the actual state of their provisions, made Cass decide to abandon the attempt. Another type of man might have accepted the challenge of conditions and overcome them. Forced marches, with lighter canoes and necessary portages, might have attained the goal. But Cass, with all his greatness, was more the military and civil leader than the explorer. On the Ontonagon River he had stopped short of the copper boulder and was lost returning to the canoes with his Indian guide.

We descended the river to the influx of the Wisconsin . . . thence we came through the Wisconsin and Fox valleys to Green Bay, on an arm of Lake Michigan, and having circumnavigated the latter, returned through Lakes Huron and St. Clair to Detroit. The line of travel is about four thousand two hundred miles.

As the sub-expedition at Cass Lake in 1820 turned back with its object unaccomplished, two men carried in their hearts the strong desire to return some day and finish what they had begun. One was Governor Cass, who was ardently an explorer in spirit if only to a certain point in practice. The other was Henry Rowe Schoolcraft, who had learned to fight on through tangled wilderness in spite of everything. When Cass became Secretary of War in 1831 he obtained the power to make the final exploration possible, and Schoolcraft had the mental perseverance and physical endurance to carry it through.

Schoolcraft had native physical strength and stamina. The weakness of ignorance he had overcome by sheer grit. The older brother who set out to drive him by sleigh to Olean in 1818, discouraged by hardships, dropped out before that minor journey was completed. Schoolcraft kept going. He learned to shoot a squirrel without blowing it to pieces, to light a camp fire, cook, to hobble a horse, to starve and keep on traveling. In Missouri he showed himself the complete tenderfoot by wearing unsuitable clothing, carrying inadequate equipment, killing a horse, ruining provisions and powder in fording a creek, and many similar performances. The expedition of 1820 to the Northwest, that through the central Mississippi valley in 1821, and ten years as Indian Agent at Sault Ste. Marie developed his knowledge and his hardihood. In 1825, 1826, and 1827, he attended convocations of the Indian tribes at far points, which imposed the necessity of passing through places where none but the robust, the fearless and the enterprising could go.

A mission to conciliate the Chippewas and Sioux in the Upper Mississippi Valley in 1830, which Schoolcraft instinctively associated with the exploration of the region, was received too late that year to permit of execution.

An expedition in 1831, for the same official purpose, did not require that the broad table-lands on which the Mississippi River originates should be visited. Fur traders represented that a visit to that section was necessary, because of Indian turmoil; but at the same time stated the waters were too low in the streams at the sources of the Mississippi to render explorations practicable. They said it was not even feasible that season to enter the Mississippi by way of the Brule or Misakoda River. This information, obtained by Schoolcraft en route on Lake Superior, was confirmed when he reached Chequamegon. So, says Schoolcraft,

I entered the Muskigo or Mauvais River, and ascended this stream by all its bad rafts, rapids, and portages, to the upper waters of the River St. Croix of the Mississippi. Crossing the intermediate table-lands, with their intricate system of lakes and portages to Lac Courtoreille, or Ottawa Lake, I entered one of the main sources of Chippewa River, and descended this prime tributary stream to its entrance into the Mississippi, at the foot of Lake Pepin. From the latter point I descended to Prairie du Chien, and to Galena in Illinois. Dispatching the men and canoes from this place back to ascend the Wisconsin River, and meet me at the portage of Fort Winnebago, I crossed the lead-mine country by land, by the way of the Pekatolica, Blue Mound, and Four Lakes, to the source of the Fox River, and rejoining my canoes here, descended this stream to Green Bay, and returned to my starting-point by the way of Michilimackinac and the Straits of St. Mary. Two months and twelve days were employed on the journey, during which a line of forests and Indian trails had been passed, of two thousand three hundred miles.

They had left Point Iroquois, near Sault Ste. Marie, June 27, and returned to the Sault September 4, 1831. February 13, 1832, Schoolcraft submitted in a letter to Washington the project of another voyage to the Northwest, to start early that year.

So, finally, May 3, 1832, instructions were issued by Secretary of War Cass for an expedition to the tribes on the sources of the Mississippi north and west of St. Anthony's Falls. Black Hawk had raised the standard of revolt on Rock River, and the tribes of the Upper Mississippi were believed to be extensively in accord with his views. Before Schoolcraft reached the headwaters of the Mississippi, the Indian agent St. Vrain had been murdered, and General Scott, with the whole disposable army of the United States had taken the field at Chicago.

The memorable Schoolcraft expedition left Sault Ste. Marie June 7, 1832. From the western end of Lake Superior on June 23, it began the ascent of the St. Louis River, and the Savannah Summit to Sandy Lake. Here he summoned a general council of the lower tribes, to assemble at the mouth of the River De Corbeau on July 20. A boat with presents and supplies was sent down the Mississippi to await the return of the party through that tributary.

Lightened of baggage, Schoolcraft led his associates up the main channel of the river to, and across, Pakagama Falls, through Little and Great Winnipeg Lakes, to Upper Red Cedar or Cass Lake. The latter point he reached July 10, exactly ten days earlier in the season than the Cass Expedition in 1820. In addition, he found that the state of the water on these summits was favorable to their ascent. Ozawindib, the Chippewa chief at Grand Isle in Cass Lake, said that his hunting-grounds embraced the source of the Mississippi. He advised smaller canoes, less laden. Schoolcraft encamped his extra men on the island, with the heavy canoes, provisions, and baggage, and procured five hunting canoes each capable of carrying one sitter and two paddlers. With his party of sixteen, including three Chippewas and eight engagees, he left Cass Lake early the next morning. Ozawindib, who was to be the guide, drew a rough map of the route. They traveled westward, to a lake he named Andrusia for Andrew Jackson; then through Lake

Pamitascodiac. Ten rapids, for their number named Metoswa by the Indians, were encountered.

In 1820, reaching the head of the Pakagama Falls, Schoolcraft had written:

We appear to have reached a vast geological plateau consisting of horizontal deposits of clay and drift on the nucleus of granitical and metamorphic rocks which underlie the sources of the Mississippi River. The vast and irregular bodies of water called Leech Lake, Winnipek, and Cass Lakes, together with a thousand lesser lakes of a mile or two in circumference, lie on this great diluvial summit. These lakes spread east and west over a surface of not less than two hundred miles. Most of them are connected with channels of communication forming a tortuous and intricate system of waters, only well known to the Indians; and there seems the less wonder that the absolute and most remote source of the Mississippi has so long remained a matter of doubt.

Now, in 1832, he found a further reason, in the lake beyond Metoswa Rapids called, like too many others, Lac Traverse, by the French. Schoolcraft renamed it Queen Anne's Lake. The meaningful Indian name, Pemidjegumaug, which he thought cacophonous, means Crosswater. This is now Lake Bemidji.

The peculiarity recognized by the graphic Indian appellation, consisted in the entrance of the Mississippi into its extreme south end, and the passage of that River through or across part of it to an exit at a short distance from the point of entrance. Here was a further explanation why the actual source of the Mississippi had so long eluded scrutiny. The utmost northing of the great river is in this lake. From its unexpected point of exit, the course is nearly due south, out of every old line of travel or commerce in the fur trade, into a remote elevated region never visited except by Indian hunters.

Southward he went now toward the long-sought source, with mounting, irrepressible excitement. The Mississippi River had become, and would be always, almost an obsession with him. Writing in the preface of his *Memoirs,* he said, twenty years later, "Ten years ago I returned from the area of the Mississippi Valley to New York, my native State, after many years' residence and exploratory travels of that quarter of the Union." Actually his residence at Sault Ste. Marie and Mackinac Island, Michigan, had been in the basin of the Great Lakes but a grand conception of the vast river had seized his imagination. He had envisioned it first, with great emotional enlargement, at the birthpoint of the Ohio, where the Allegheny and Monongahela join. His first sight of it at the mouth of the Ohio River inspired a paeon of exultation and prophecy. The junction of the Missouri with the southflowing stem of it set him to profound ponderings. Its nourishment by a thousand crystal Ozark springs was known to him with intimacy as well as its ancient relation to the noble northern Lakes. The imponderable things of past and future made manifest in its delta stirred him deeply. He knew the history of the men who had explored it from the Gulf of Mexico to Cass Lake. There was no one more fit, either practically or poetically, to complete its exploration.

A hundred yards or so south of "Queen Anne's Lake" the Mississippi extended into another sheet of water. "Washington Irving Lake!" said Schoolcraft. Straight south they continued through it, and beyond it half a mile, where the primary forks of the Mississippi were reached.

Ozawindib shot his canoe out of the stronger current of the larger branch, flowing from the west, into the smaller entering at an acute angle from the east. The latter led more directly to the base of the last summit.

There were frequent small lakes; an intricacy of meanderings; shores too marshy for footing; rain. Meals, wetness, did not matter. After the portage around the Naiwa rapids, there was another lake,—and in this the head of the Schoolcraft branch of the primary forks was reached. Then came the last portage to the source of the main fork—their final objective!

It was fourteen years since Schoolcraft, at Olean, New York, had hurled himself forward toward the mighty Mississippi on the wild spring flood of the Monongahela on the first ark of the season. Now he was approaching its ultimate and long elusive northern source with even greater eagerness. He

kept close to the guide's heels. When Ozawindib announced
they were now ascending the last elevation, Schoolcraft pushed
forward, outwent him on the trail, got the initial glimpse of the
lake they had been searching for and stood first on its shore.
He was the first white man to identify the source of this river
of world grandeur. He was the one man living, and perhaps
the only one so far in history, who had traversed the Father
of Waters from its delta to its beginning among this maze of
northern waters. Perhaps he had explored more of it and its
tributaries than any other man, not excepting even Meriwether Lewis and Clark. It was *his* river!—in a way. He loved
it, had faith in it, prophesied for it. It was part of him and he
was part of it. In that dramatic moment, among northern
woods and waters, Henry Rowe Schoolcraft personified the
spirit of that flood of humans who had "meant in their generation to plough the Mississippi from its head to its foot" and
had done it!

The expedition encamped on the island, now named
Schoolcraft, in Lac LaBiche, which he renamed Itasca.

While his tent was being pitched and supper cooked, he
scrutinized the shores of Schoolcraft Island for crustacea.
Lake Itasca was circumnavigated. A sketch of it was made,
showing the island and a southern arm fed by a little brook
with lakelet expansions. He composed two stanzas to free his
emotions. It was not quite three hundred years since the discovery of the lower portion of the Mississippi by De Soto.
Methodically he made the entry in his journal, under the date
July 13, 1832.

July 20 he was due to meet the Indian general council at
the mouth of the River De Corbeau. The time was short.
Before nightfall they were twenty-five miles down river, strain-
ing to make the rendezvous on the appointed day. The up-
stream journey from Cass Lake covered one hundred and
twenty-five miles; the return, on the main branch, was one
hundred and sixty-five.

Before leaving Schoolcraft Island a spruce tree was cut
and prepared as a flagstaff. As they departed, a United States

flag was hoisted, and left flying. Ozawindib and his companions understood and fired a salute.

This was Schoolcraft's crowning discovery. It added to geographical knowledge many details of the upper reaches of the Mississippi, and corrected errors. He published an account of it, with maps, in 1834. A map also accompanied the House Document recording it.

He had contributed to geographical knowledge of the country earlier, in the less dramatic but nevertheless important zone between the Missouri River and the White River of Arkansas, in 1818 and 1819. There he had recognized and mapped its granite peaks, gathered facts about mines and minerals, and crossed and recrossed its rocky ridges at the heads as well as mouths of the numerous spring-fed Ozark streams.

This is the fifth river I have passed since leaving Poke Bayou, in a short distance of ninety miles, all running parallel with each other from west to east, separated by similar ridges of calcareous rock, having analogous alluvions on their banks, and all discharging their waters into Black River, which, like an artificial drain, runs nearly from north to south, and, catching their waters, conveys them through White River into the Mississippi. That singular stream, which itself preserves an exact parallelism with the Mississippi during its whole course, is not less remarkable for the number of streams it receives from the west, than for receiving no tributary of any magnitude in its whole course from the east. This is owing to a singular configuration of the country, the examination of which would, perhaps, prove very interesting to the geologist as well as the geographer, and possibly throw some new light on the subject of alluvial deposits.

He traveled on foot considerable distances along Pine River and James River, two major forks of the White River, which enabled him to present an excellent view of the drainage system of the region. Because of his travels and observations, the northern part of the White River basin—a considerable stream previously unnoticed by geographers or only noticed to attest their want of information respecting it—was geographically clarified.

DISCOVERY OF LAKE ITASCA, SOURCE OF THE MISSISSIPPI, BY SCHOOLCRAFT IN 1832. FROM AN ENGRAVING BY EAST-
MAN FROM A SKETCH BY SCHOOLCRAFT.

Schoolcraft added to the maps of the United States in still another way.

It is to be noted that when Shakespeare wrote "What's in a name?" he left the matter as a question. Every Michiganian, like Henry Rowe Schoolcraft, should have a definite opinion on the subject.

There is a possibility, for instance, that if Schoolcraft's mother-in-law, the Pocahontas of Michigan, had had as short a name as the Virginia Indian girl, instead of Ozhaw-guscoday-wayquay, she might today occupy a prominently picturesque place in the general background of American history. Michigan was unfortunate in this slight respect.

In another phase of the question of names, however, the State is to be congratulated. It might have been called Cherronesus instead of Michigan! The cumbrous Greek word meaning peninsula was actually applied to the Lower Peninsula of the State by a committee of the Congress of the Confederation, of which Thomas Jefferson was chairman. That was in 1784, in the report of a plan for the government of the Northwest Territory, which proposed its ultimate division into ten states. One of the ten was to be called Michigania, but the territory therein extended westward from Lake Michigan to the Mississippi River, including a large part of the present State of Wisconsin.

It seems to be reasonably clear that the meaning of Michigan is the Great Lake. No name could be more appropriate for the region which the State of Michigan embraces. For Michigan is actually *the* Great Lake State, having 40,000 square miles of Great Lakes area within its boundaries. It has two-thirds of the American-owned waters of the Great Lakes— more than four times the area of Great Lakes waters possessed by any other Great Lakes State. More than half of the American shore line of the Great Lakes lies in Michigan—2389 miles out of 4343. Seven other states share the remainder. Michigan has more than two square miles of fresh water for every three square miles of land—that is, a greater proportion of fresh water to land than any other State or province or country in the world! Consequently, Michigan, *the* Great Lake State, is a most appropriate naming. Cherronesus, for peninsula, when Michigan now is *two* peninsulas, would be inaccurate as well as clumsy. There is much more involved in the naming of places than the light lines of the bard of Avon indicate.

Schoolcraft's relation to geographical terminology in the United States is faceted. He gave much more than ordinary thought to the subject, and wielded unusual influence. He not only recorded the meanings of names, but created and conferred them. And he himself has been memorialized in this department of geography.

Practically he was concerned with the idea of reducing the number of dead letters reported as received annually at Washington because of misdirection, much of which was supposed to result from great repetition of old township, city, county and village names. From the aesthetic angle he thought that Mud Creek, Jack's Corner, and Shingle Hollow left much to be desired. He says:

The sonorousness and appropriate character of the Indian names has often been admired. In so rapidly settling a country as the West, where the areas occupied so far outran the capacity to provide original names, the inconvenient repetition of old and time-honored names of Europe might be often avoided by appeal to the various Indian vocabularies.

In 1818, at Shawneetown, he encountered a minor unpleasantness because of his interest in the Indian appellation with one "high-feeling personage who did not like the manner in which I associated the modern town with reminiscences of the savages."

In 1821, he mentioned Damascus, Ohio, for the single reason of reprehending "the vile taste for foreign and outlandish names which prevails so extensively throughout our country, to the exclusion of pre-existing French or aboriginal names that are in many instances equally sonorous and pleasing to the ear and always more significant and appropriate." Originally Damascus had been Prairie du Masque. "When the inhabitants thought proper to apply for the appointment of a postmaster, it was deemed a suitable occasion to discard the current name, and from a little similarity of sound . . . the lonely, rural, little Prairie du Masque was changed into the high sounding, eastern title of Damascus."

"To facilitate geological reference and combine an allusion to the once powerful tribe that for so many years resided along its eastern base" he bestowed the name Shaunee or Oshawana Mountains on the prominent tract of highland in southwest Illinois.

Schoolcraft had marked literary leanings. The conflict between poetic imagination and scientific accuracy is evident in his contributions to geographical nomenclature. Desire for euphony, and reliance on connotations that are too subtle, sometimes triumphed. Dictionaries, grammars and other authorities on language have their function in recording the consensus of usage. They may also be gentle guides in desirable directions. Schoolcraft had a tendency to try to create beauty and consistency by simple fiat.

One of his ways of making names was to combine other languages with the Indian, sometimes adding syllables for euphony. He had more than one synthetic system, largely his own. The meanings of some of his inventions have since become vague or have altogether vanished.

A stream in Minnesota was designated Allenoga—"putting the Iroquois local terminal in *oga* to the name of the worthy officer who traced out the first true map of the actual sources of the Mississippi."

Algonac was derived from the first two syllables of *Algonkin* and the first syllable of *akee,* meaning earth or land.

He named a lake in Minnesota Illigan, because signs of a war party had been seen there, deriving the word from *in-in-eeg,* meaning men, and *sa-gi-e-gan,* lake, making "the usual transition of *n* to *l* of the old Algonquin."

His anagrammatic interest is excellently illustrated by the name Colcaspi which he gave to the largest island in Cass Lake, Minnesota. This was composed of the names of Schoolcraft, Cass and Pike, the geographical discoverers, in reversed order, of the region.   Colcaspi Island is the Gitchiminis of the Indians, translated as Grand Isle by the French.   In contrast with the confusing commonness of the French name, Colcaspi has uniqueness.

Schoolcraft wished to rename Lake Superior Lake Algoma, a compound of his own signifying Algonquin Sea.   He wrote:

The Algonquins, who, in the Chippewa tribe, were found in possession of it, on the arrival of the French . . . applied the same radical word to it which they bestow on the sea, namely, *gum-ee* (collected water), or, as it is sometimes pronounced, *gom-ee,* or *go-ma;* with this difference, that the adjective big (*gitche*) prefixed to this term for Lake Superior, is repeated when it is applied to the sea. . . . The word did not commend itself to French or English ears so much as to lead to its adoption.   By taking the syllable *Al* from *Algonquin,* as a prefix, instead of *gitche,* we have the more poetic combination of Algoma.

Schoolcraft's name for Lake Superior met the same fate as that of the Indians, but survived by attaching itself to a neighboring District in Ontario.

Most famous of all the names of "Schoolcraft manufacture" is that of Lake Itasca.   He had the name ready some weeks before the actual discovery.   While traveling westward on Lake Superior in 1832, he inquired of the Reverend William T. Boutwell, who had been designated by a Board of Missions to accompany the expedition, the Greek expression for "true source."   Mr. Boutwell's knowledge of that language was not equal to this, but he offered, as substitute, two Latin words, *veritas* for truth and *caput* for head.   Utilizing these, with regard to length and euphony, Schoolcraft created Itasca from the last syllable of one and the first syllable of the other.   Then he was glad to note it had a feminine ending in *a,* and immediately personified it in some verses.   It is an interesting example of his imaginative process, like that by which he transmuted the valley of the Normanskill, in New York State, to the Vale of Norma in a poem.

Excellent illustrations of changes for the sake of pleasantness of sound are Lake Andrusia, named for President Andrew Jackson, and Lake Cassina (now Cass Lake), in Minnesota.

Schoolcraft also enriched the geography of America by pure Indian names and fitting English ones. Kubba-Kunna, or the Rest in the Path, of the Chippewas, the site of crossing of one of their noted land-trails, he renamed Lake Plantagenet. He attached the memory of Washington Irving, Marquette, La Salle to various lakes; that of De Soto to a river; and the southern arm of Cass Lake was called Pike's Bay for the officer who crossed it on the ice in January, 1806.

In Michigan his contribution in this respect was especially outstanding, through permeating influence as well as his own acts.

As a member of the Legislative Council of the Territory of Michigan, he brought in a motion, in 1829, to appoint a committee to prepare a list of names proper for use in naming territorial subdivisions. This passed, and he was made chairman. The committee brought in a considerable list, at least ten of which were used by the Council. A number of these names were of Indian origin.

Schoolcraft also obtained from General Brady the names of the officers who had served reputably in the Indian campaigns of General Wayne to perpetuate their memory in the territory they had helped to win by naming townships for them.

Douglass Houghton, first state geologist of Michigan, committed to Schoolcraft the topic of Indian terminology and the bestowal of new names from the aboriginal vocabulary. Schoolcraft worked out quite a complete plan by which, taking the Indian roots and terminations, adding elements necessary for euphony and varying the combinations, he could produce a large number of words of pleasing sound, of descriptive character. This principle he used in several of the Michigan names. In January, 1838, he sent to Governor Mason a plan for a system of Indian names, which the Governor communicated to the Legislature.

In 1840, at the request of Douglass Houghton, the State Legislature provided for the completion of the subdivision of the Lower Peninsula of Michigan. Twenty-eight new counties were laid out and named at this time. All but one of the names were of Indian origin. It is probable that Henry Rowe Schoolcraft had much to do with their selection. Apparently, however, they did not all meet with popular approval. When the Legislature of 1843 met it renamed sixteen of the twenty-eight. Five of the new names were of Irish origin. Popular tradition has it that these were substituted at the instance of Charles O'Malley of Mackinac, who had quarreled with School-craft and took his revenge in this manner. Some of the other changes, however, were to names of distinctly Schoolcraft origin. On the whole the alterations were for the worse. For Indian names, generally those of chiefs connected with the early history of the State, names of no local significance were substituted. In connection with the Irish names of Michigan counties, the possible influence of the Johnston family on Schoolcraft might be considered. John Johnston, a member of the Historical Society of Michigan and a close friend of Schoolcraft as well as his father-in-law, was a native of Antrim County, Ireland. Schoolcraft's wife, Jane Johnston, lived awhile in Wexford County there.

An interesting paper by William L. Jenks, published in *Michigan Pioneer and Historical Collections,* volume 38, gives an idea of the general part played by Schoolcraft in the selection and interpretation of county names in Michigan. Some of his specific contributions follow.

Alcona is undoubtedly a word manufactured according to the Schoolcraft formula in which *al* is the Arabic for the; *co* is the root of a word meaning plain or prairie; and *na* is a termination denoting excellence. The name, therefore, has the meaning, the fine or excellent plain.

Allegan, suggested by Schoolcraft, is a derivative word, from the first syllable of Algonkin, and *e-gan,* the final two of the Chippewa *sa-gi-e-gan,* which means a lake.

Alpena was constructed by Schoolcraft from the Arabic *al* for the, and either *pinai* meaning partridge, or *penaysee* meaning bird.

Arenac was made by combining the Latin word *arena* meaning sand, with *ac* from *auk* or *akke,* an Indian word meaning land or earth or idea of locality.

When Chippewa County was created, in December, 1826, the name, in memory of one of the greatest of all Indian tribes, was chosen from a list of three that had been suggested by Schoolcraft, on request.

Iosco was a favorite name with Schoolcraft. Its meaning is uncertain. In one place in his writings he defines it as water of light; but in another he explains it as a synthesis of three words meaning to be, father, and plain, which is difficult to interpret. He used the word as a poetic name for the town in Albany County, New York, where he was born; in *Iosco, or the Vale of Norma* and in the tale, "The Rabid Wolf." The word appears also in "Iosco, or a Visit to the Sun and Moon," a tale from the Ottawa, said to have been related by Chusco, an Ottawa chief, as published by Schoolcraft in his *Algic Researches* in 1839. In this, Iosco is the name of the eldest of six Indian youths whose travels and adventures are related. In the version of this tale published in 1856 in *The Myth of Hiawatha,* the youngest of six, a boy, bears the name Ioscoda. It is possible that Iosco may have been the Indian name for the Hungerkill.

Isabella was proposed by Schoolcraft in memory of Queen Isabella of Spain.

Kalkaska, in the act of 1843, was spelled Calcasca. In its present form it looks like a genuine Indian word. If it is, its derivation may be from the Chippewa and mean burned over. Possibly it was manufactured by Schoolcraft, although that is not known. One might hazard the suggestion that it is a combination of Calcraft (for Schoolcraft) and Cass?

Leelanau County had its name suggested by Schoolcraft in 1829. In one of his books he gives the word as meaning delight of life. "Leelinau, an Ojibwa tale," the story of an Indian maiden living on the south shore of Lake Superior, appears in Schoolcraft's *Algic Researches* and again in *The Myth of Hiawatha.* In the latter version the heroine says,

"From her baby name of Neenizu, my dear life, she was called Leelinau."

Oscoda, meaning pebbly prairie, was formed by School-craft from *os* for *ossin,* stone or pebble, and *coda* from *muskoda,* prairie.

Tuscola is thought to be of Schoolcraft origin. In one place he gives its meaning as warrior prairie and in another as deriving from words or roots meaning level lands.

After Schoolcraft left Michigan, an act was approved by the Legislature, March 9, 1843, that greatly reduced the limits of the old counties of Chippewa and Michilimackinac, and divided the rest of the Upper Peninsula into four counties. Of these one was named in honor of Henry Rowe Schoolcraft. A town in Kalamazoo County, Michigan, also bears his name, through the friendship of Senator Lucius Lyon. Mackinac Island, Michigan, has a point known as Schoolcraft's Rest. In Minnesota there is Schoolcraft Island in Lake Itasca; and the smaller of the two streams of the ultimate fork of the Mississippi is called Schoolcraft River.

During April, 1839, he wrote,

In ascending the Hudson, with so good an interpreter at my side as Mrs. Schoolcraft, whom I have carried through a perfect course of philological training in the English, Latin, and Hebrew principles of formation, I analyzed many of the old Indian names, which, until we reached Albany, are all in a peculiar dialect of the Algonquin.

A considerable paper by him, on the valley of the Hudson, written for the New-York Historical Society as part one of a report on the aboriginal names and geographical terminology of the State of New York, was printed in the Proceedings of that Society for 1844. In the same year, on October 28, he wrote a "Letter on City Names" to the mayor of New York City. A two-column newspaper clipping of this communication is preserved in the Manuscript Division of the Library of Congress.

A proposed extensive contribution to the geographical terminology of the United States was never published. A series of extracts from this *Cyclopaedia Indianensis* appears in

Oneóta. Copies of a printed prospectus of this work are in existence.

Timeliness, vision, and enthusiasm added vastly to the importance of Schoolcraft's contributions to geography.

These factors, on his return from Missouri in 1819, expressed in the immediate publication of his *A View of the Lead Mines of Missouri,* had first brought his capabilities as a geographer before the public in America and Europe. His travels in the Ozarks were published in England in 1821.

The immediacy of the need for information about the Great Lakes and Upper Mississippi country was even clearer to him. It is significant that when the Cass expedition left Detroit in 1820 there was, in all the Territory of Michigan, only one short road—from Maumee Rapids to River Raisin and Detroit. Michigan highways then were lakes and rivers linked by portages.

The *New York Statesman* said of Schoolcraft's journal of the 1820 expedition before it was off the press: "We have always been surprised that, while we have had so many travelers through the valley of the Ohio and Lower Mississippi, no one should have thought of filling up the chasm in our northwestern geography."

The older members of the Cass expedition took no initiative toward publication of their observations. A joint work by all was agreed on, with Schoolcraft, but consistently delayed. This seems to have been unavoidable.

On the eve of disbanding the staff of the expedition of 1820, Governor Cass wrote a highly laudatory recommendation for Captain David B. Douglass, its topographer and astronomer, and Henry Rowe Schoolcraft, in which great praise was given both equally and the expectation expressed that both in future would assume distinguished stations. Captain Douglass went back to West Point to an eminent professional career. Henry Rowe Schoolcraft on his return worked night and day to get his journal of the exploration into print and available for general use. Some thirty years later, when Schoolcraft published his *Summary Narrative* of the Mississippi expeditions of 1820 and 1832, Professor Douglass's maps and figures had in large part been superseded.

While it brings out vividly one of the remarkable qualities of Schoolcraft, there is no detraction of David Douglass in this comparison. Professor Douglass had been given a chair in mathematics at West Point which required the teaching of a new phase of that subject. No textbook was available except in French and he could not read that language. The popular demand for the knowledge that he had gathered on the north-western expedition did not impress him as much as the unusual exactions of his new position. Schoolcraft, on the contrary, had no interest or urge except the all-devouring ones of enthusiasm for the brand new country and the conviction that facts about it were an actual public necessity. He reported them white hot, while of most value. His narrative journal was off the press early in the spring of 1821. Copies found their way to England, where it was praised by prominent geographers. In helping to make the country known, Schoolcraft created for himself an enduring place in national memory.

Another comparison serves to emphasize a characteristic value of his activities.

William Maclure, sometimes referred to as the father of American geology, in 1825 refused to invest money in real estate in the city of Philadelphia, with the comment that "Land in the cities can no longer rise in value. The communistic society must prevail, and in the course of a few years Philadelphia must be deserted. Those who live long enough may come back here and see the foxes looking out of the windows." Schoolcraft, out of the depths of a post-war depression in 1818, looked at the town of Pittsburgh, and at Cincinnati with its rows of abandoned half-built houses, and predicted for them glowing futures.

Maclure in 1809 saw insuperable mountain barriers, separating the continent north and south into three distinct nations, two of them narrowly confined on the coasts, open to aggression and necessarily warlike; one in the great central valley, isolated, a land of agriculture and peace. Schoolcraft saw not only the giant ranges, and the vastness of the region between them. He caught the significance of the grand system of rivers that was to bind to the nation this basin, "destined to be the first kingdom on the globe." He envisioned it tied even closer by innumerable possible canals, its distances contracted even by trans-continental railroads.

Of the Ohio he had said: "This splendid valley is one of the prominent creations of the universe. Its fertility and beauty are unequaled; and its capacities of sustaining a dense population cannot be overrated." It offered possibilities of hydraulic power that were amazing. "Yet all this is but an element in the vast system of western waters." Then when he reached the Mississippi he wrote, "I had lost all my standards of comparison . . . like a man suddenly ushered into a new world." He saw the Mississippi in its totality.

Then he descended to practicality and particulars. The superiority of inland navigation in that region to that of any country in the world to him meant possibilities of exchange and manufacture and agriculture. He appreciated the commanding position of St. Louis in the geography of the country, not only on bluffs above the river, but interpreted in relation to the whole Mississippi and the Missouri river system and the agricultural potentialities of the whole Mississippi valley, and saw that city as the leading primary fur market of the world and its future great development as the emporium of the western country.

In his travels in 1821, twelve years before Chicago began to be built, he foresaw that point as the great packing center of the future.

The want of a good market, constant in its demand, and convenient of access, appears, at present, to oppose the most serious obstacle to the prosperity of the farming and mercantile interest in this quarter. Should the contemplated canal at Chicago be constructed, we have little doubt but the trade of this part of the State of Illinois will pass through that channel. The produce of the country is of a description that ought to find its way to a northern market; and that, too, without passing through a tropical climate. Cattle and hogs may be driven to Chicago, at the present moment, with nearly the same expense that they can to St. Louis, and if slaughtered and packed at the former place, would remain in better preservation than if carried out at the mouths of the Mississippi. . . .

Although our journey has produced a conviction, that the difficulty and expense which will attend this work [canal between Lake Michigan and the Illinois] are greatly underrated; it has also impressed us with a more exalted opinion of this projected communication, and the ability of the country through which it must pass, eventually to complete and maintain it. If the present scanty population and feeble means of this part of Illinois, has convinced us that the commencement and completion of this important work, are more remote than we before supposed, its final execution is not the less certain, and we regard the plan as one entitled to every rational and proper aid. There are few portions of the western country, where the progress of settlement is more certain, or which will admit of a more dense population; and the first efforts of such a community if enlightened and enterprising, will be to place themselves on an equality with other states, by opening the way to a northern market.

He suggested that a safe and permanent harbor might be constructed at Chicago by making an artificial island off the mouth of Chicago Creek, with stone brought from Green Bay. That was in 1821. In 1855, he predicted it would be another Nineveh—great city of the plains—more than any other city of the West, because of its position. "Its growth cannot be limited, or can scarcely be estimated."

His narrative of the 1820 Cass expedition was an especially constructive force. Surveyor General Edward Tiffin's report, containing gross misrepresentations of the quality of Michigan land, after the War of 1812, resulted in Congress changing the location of the soldiers' bounty lands to Illinois and Missouri, which diverted the westward stream of emigrants from Michigan. The tenor of Schoolcraft's account, to the contrary, was: "Such a country—for its scenery, its magnificence, and resources, and the strong influence it is destined ultimately to have on the commerce, civilization, and progress of the country—the sun does not shine on!" His *Narrative*, which had wide circulation, did much to counteract the unfavorable impression of Michigan that the Tiffin report had spread. In any event, though in 1818 deemed inaccessible from swamps, by

1824 the state was known to possess qualities of so different a nature that it attracted crowds of emigrants from the fertile banks of the Genesee and diverted in a measure the current of migration from the Wabash and the Illinois.

When the Ohio-Michigan controversy was raging, Schoolcraft was one of the few who understood and maintained that the Upper Peninsula would be of far greater value and importance to the State than the seven-mile strip of Southern Michigan that was involved. More than mineral wealth based his conclusions. He was aware of the potential water power of the Fox River in Wisconsin; and turned from a discussion of the Tahquamenon Falls as a Chippewa favorite locality for fairies, to call attention to their hydraulic possibilities.

Geographic knowledge he applied at once to life. A longitudinal line, dropped south from the western extremity of Lake Superior would pass through Jefferson City, Missouri, he observed; and then proceeded:

When, therefore, a ship canal shall be made at St. Mary's Falls, vessels of large tonnage may sail from Oswego (by the Welland Canal) and Buffalo, through a line of inter-oceanic seas, nearer to the foot of the Rocky Mountains, by several hundred miles, than by any other possible route. A railroad line from Fond du Lac (Duluth) west to the Columbia valley, would also form the shortest and most direct transit route from the Pacific to New York. Such a road would have the advantage of passing through a region favorable to agriculture, which cannot but develop abundant resources.

He wisely judged that free range would endure in the Ozarks much longer than in adjoining prairie States, as indeed it has done for more than a hundred years in certain counties like Oregon. He was right in deeming the limestone hills ideal for sheep-raising, though he did not associate with this fact, as a deterrent, his observations on the unconscionable number of dogs that the natives kept. It was clear insight that made him predict a great future for cotton in Arkansas. Of Iowa, he said, "No Western State is believed to contain a less proportionate quantity of land unsuited to the plough."

In 1843 he was advocating the necessity of improving the

channel through the St. Clair Flats, in order to facilitate communication between Buffalo and Chicago; and, he continued,

when this line of commerce requires to be diverted north, through the straits of St. Mary's into Lake Superior, a period rapidly approaching, a short canal of three-fourths of a mile will be required at the Sault Ste-Marie, and some excavation made, so as to permit vessels of heavy tonnage to cross the bar in Lake George of those straits.

"These things," he says, after suggesting canal or even railroad connections between Green Bay and Galena, in 1831,

may seem too much like making arrangements for the next generation. But we cannot fix bounds to the efforts of our spreading population, and spirit of enterprise. Nor, after what we have seen in the way of internal improvement, in our own day and generation, should we deem anything too hard to be accomplished.

There is no branch of the science known as inspirational or prophetic geography. If there were, Schoolcraft would be inscribed as a master in that phase.

His contributions to geography were indeed many and in various branches. In fact, in all the period of his explorations, even when he had achieved national and international recognition as a geologist, his point of view was really that of a geographer. His concern was always that of the present and future more than with the past. Although interested in mounds, fossils, rocks, minerals and in formations that record the history of the making of the earth, he was acutely on the alert for all details concerning soil, climate, drainage, transportation, and all factors that influence the distribution of plant, animal, and human life. A good portion of his economic or engineering geology, with its comprehensive background of local conditions, could easily be classed as commercial geography. His reporting of plants and animals and birds and shells, as of given places, leans toward phytogeography and zoogeography rather than botany and zoology as now understood.

Though he had said to himself, when he reached the head of the Ohio,—"Now I am in the great geological basin of the West!"—actually he visioned it in even a larger way, as an area teeming with possibilities for a vast future population.   Henry Rowe Schoolcraft was a great constructive geographer.

In 1828 Schoolcraft was offered an unusual opportunity with the Department of the Navy to extend his explorations on a world scale.   He was tendered appointment as head of the scientific corps of a United States expedition to the South Seas—the first American expedition for foreign discovery. This was urged on him in several letters written to him at the Sault.   He refused it.   By that time the natural sciences, with all their luring facets, had been superseded in his mind by sentimental, practical, and scientific interest in the North American Indians, a practically unknown branch of the human race.

Three Decades with the United States Office of Indian Affairs

Although Henry Rowe Schoolcraft was practically thirty when he found his avenue of sustained endeavor in association with the North American Indian, he had been in contact with the race, psychologically, through three generations of his forebears.   He was destined to continue the attachment throughout his life, and then, in the intimacy of intermingled blood and bone, in his children.   As long as he lived the American Indian never ceased to be, for him, a national responsibility and a human problem, as well as a subject for scientific observation and research.

Schoolcraft's great-grandfather, James Calcraft, had known the Indians in the conflict between England and France; his grandfather, John, in the American Revolution.   Lawrence, his father, had come to close quarters with them in the Mohawk Valley during the Revolution, and knew all too well their activities in the War of 1812.   Their part in this last phase of the Revolution was scarred into the mind of Schoolcraft himself, intensifying all the family feeling he had inherited.

Above the town where he was born the Iroquois war and trading trail had wound for sixteen miles across the Pine Plains. Below was their ancient burying ground.   The name of Tawasentha was constant music in his ears long before it reached its crescendo in Longfellow's *Hiawatha*. This, on the first settlement of the country, had been the seat of an Indian population. The tale of the Indian Hormaun who haunted the region, seeking his hundredth victim, vividly impressed his mind in youth.

The records of the old Dowesburgh Glass Works in Albany County, New York, show that Indians were employed at times to weave basketry around demijohns. This was before young Schoolcraft was on the scene. He makes no mention of them.

My earliest impressions of the Indian race were drawn from the fireside rehearsals of incidents which had happened during the perilous times of the American revolution; in which my father was a zealous actor, and were all inseparably connected with the fearful ideas of the Indian yell, the tomahawk, the scalping knife, and the fire brand. In these recitals, the Indian was depicted as the very impersonation of evil—a sort of wild demon, who delighted in nothing so much as blood and murder. Whether he had mind, was governed by any reasons, or even had any soul, nobody inquired, and nobody cared. It was always represented as a meritorious act in old revolutionary reminiscences, to have killed one of them in the border wars, and thus aided in ridding the land of a cruel and unnatural race, in whom all feelings of pity, justice, and mercy, were supposed to be obliterated. These early ideas were sustained by printed narratives of captivity and hair-breadth escapes of men and women from their clutches, which, from time to time, fell into my hands, so that long before I was ten years old, I had a most definite and terrific idea impressed on my imagination of what was sometimes called in my native precincts, "the bow and arrow race."

To give a definite conception of the Indian man, there lived in my native valley, a family of Indians of the Iroquois stock, who often went off to their people in the west, and as often returned again, as if they were a troop of genii, or the ghosts of the departed, who came to haunt the nut wood forests, and sub-vallies of the sylvan Tawasenthaw, which their ancestors had formerly possessed, and to which they still claimed some right. In this family, which was of the Oneida tribe, and consisted of the husband and wife, with two grown up sons, I first saw those characteristic features of the race,— namely, a red skin, with bright black eyes, and black straight hair. They were mild and docile in their deportment, and were on friendly terms with the whole settlement, whom they furnished with neatly made baskets of the linden wood, split very thin, and coloured to impart variety, and with nice ash brooms. These fabrics made them welcome guests with every good housewife, who had forgotten the horrific stories of the revolution, and who was ever ready to give a chair and a plate, and a lodging place by the kitchen fire, to poor old Isaac and Anna, for so they had been named. What their original names were, nobody knew; they had lived so long in the valley that they spoke the Dutch language, and never made use of their own, except when talking together; and I recollect, we thought it a matter of wonder, when they discoursed in Indian, whether such a guttural jargon, could possibly be the medium of conveying any very definite ideas. It seemed to be one undistinguished tissue of hard sounds, blending all parts of speech together.

Had the boys of my own age, and I may say, the grown people, stopped to reflect, and been led to consider this family and their race in America, independently of their gross acts, under the strong excitements of war and revenge, goaded by wrongs, and led on by the class of revolutionary tories, more implacable than even themselves, we must have seen, in the peaceable lives, quiet manners, and benevolent dispositions of these four people, a contradiction to, at least, some part, of the sweeping conclusions above noticed. But no such thoughts occurred. The word "Indian," was synonymous then, as perhaps now, with half the opprobrious epithets in the dictionary. I recollect to have myself made a few lines, in early life, on the subject, which ran thus:—

> Indians they were, ere Colon crossed the sea,
> And ages hence, they shall but Indians be.

According to his own account, it was while at Vernon, in Oneida County, New York, for a few months in his seventeenth year, that he first began to take notice of the manners and customs of the Indian race. A remnant of the old Mohegans remained in that neighborhood. A few miles away was Oneida Castle, then the residence of the ancient Oneida tribe of the Iroquois. Throngs of both tribes were daily in the village.

On his way down the Ohio, eight years later, he saw the Seneca reservation on the Allegheny River and passed some of that tribe in their immensely long pine canoes. They were picturesque, unreal. At Smithfield, Ohio, he met some of General Jackson's volunteers, just back from his wars against the Creeks and Seminoles, who related some of the incidents of their campaign. That, too, seemed far off.

In Missouri, though the hills re-echoed with warnings about the Osage tribe, he saw nothing of them, during his invasion of their territory, except a deserted camp or two and an occasional abandoned hut. At worst they seemed petty thieves and temporary kidnapers. A settlement of Delawares aroused his wish to stay a while in order to observe them, but his companion on the expedition was unwilling. He noted in his diary that the decision to settle Cherokee Indians along the south bank of the White River was causing discontent among the whites who had improved small farms in that zone. The race seemed vaguely vanishing.

He had visited the great mound at Grave Creek Flats, the mound and elevated square at Marietta, the mounds and Indian burying ground near St. Louis, and the Indian, never a reality to him, had already receded to a place among antiquities.

The Indians in the canoe fleet of Governor Cass's expedition of 1820, when Schoolcraft joined it at Detroit, were still striking illustrations out of old romance to him. The scenery and history and geology of Mackinac Island inspired twelve pages of his journal; the lines of Indian wigwams and canoes along the beach elicited spare mention. It was at Sault Ste. Marie, stronghold of the Chippewas, that he plunged into the reality of actual contact with a shock.

There are occasional incidents in history that manifest so vividly an admirable human quality that they are told and retold to succeeding generations. They become little classics in themselves because of something they contribute to fortify the spirit of the human race. The individual courage of Lewis Cass at Sault Ste. Marie in 1820 is on its way to a place among these priceless memories. It was Schoolcraft's good fortune to be the first narrator of the story, which should be glowingly presented to each generation of Americans as part of their inheritance.

One object of the expedition of 1820 was to establish a fort at Sault Ste. Marie, where the Indians were unfriendly toward the United States. They had fought on the side of the British in the War of 1812 and assisted the latter in capturing Mackinac Island. The Americans had retaliated later. Resentments still festered. Meanwhile the British maintained a powerful hold on their imaginations. This was continually strengthened by presents given at Fort Malden on the Detroit River, and at Drummond Island. At the Sault no sign of possession had been maintained by the United States since the war. The Chippewas regarded the Americans as enemies.

Into this hotbed of hostility came General Cass, June 15, 1820, to secure the cession of sufficient Indian land to establish a garrison. A few years earlier General Macomb's party had been fired on by drunken Indians at Point aux Pins. It was only eight years since the Chicago massacre. Twelve years were to elapse before the murder of the Indian agent St. Vrain and the Black Hawk War.

To adjust the relations of the tribe with the United States, a council was convened with the chiefs on the day following our arrival. This council was assembled at the Governor's marquée, which was graced by the national ensign, and prepared for the interview with the usual presents. The chiefs, clothed in their best habiliments, and arrayed in feathers and British medals, seated themselves, with their usual dignity, in great order, and the business was opened with the usual ceremony of smoking the peace pipe. When this had been finished, and the interpreter taken his position, he was directed to explain the views of the Government, in visiting the country, to remind them that their ancestors had formerly conceded the occupancy of the place to the French, to whose national rights and prerogatives the Americans had succeeded, and, by a few direct and well-timed historical and practical remarks, to secure their assent to its reoccupancy. The utmost attention was bestowed while this address was being made, and it was evident, from the glances of the hearers, that it was received with unfriendly feelings, and several chiefs spoke in reply. They were averse to the proposition, and first endeavored to evade it by pretending to know nothing of such former grants. This point being restated by the American commissioner, and pressed home strongly, was eventually dropped by them. Still, they continued to speak in an evasive and desultory manner, which had the effect of a negative. It was evident that there was a want of agreement, and some animated discussion arose among themselves. Two classes of persons appeared among the chiefs. Some appeared in favor of settling a boundary to the ancient precinct of French occupancy, provided it was not intended to be occupied by a garrison, saying, in the symbolic language of Indians, that they were afraid, in that case, their young men might kill the cattle of the garrison. Governor Cass, understanding this, replied that, as to the establishment of a garrison, they need not give themselves any uneasiness—it was a settled point, and so sure as the sun that was then rising would set, so sure would there be an American garrison sent to that point, whether they renewed the grant or not. This decisive language had a sensible effect. High words followed between the chiefs. The head chief of the band, Shingabawossin, a tall, stately man, of prudent views, evidently sided with the moderates, and was evasive in his speech. A chief called Shingwauk, or the Little Pine, who had conducted the last war party from the village in 1814, was inclined to side with the hostiles. There was a chief present called Sassaba, a tall, martial-looking man, of the reigning family of chiefs of the Crane Totem, who had lost a brother in the battle of the Thames. He wore a scarlet uniform, with epaulets, and nourished a deep resentment against the United States. He stuck his war lance furiously in the ground before him, at the beginning of his harangue, and, assuming a savage wildness of air, appeared to produce a corresponding effect upon the other Indian speakers, and employed the strongest gesticulation. His address brought the deliberations to a close, after they had continued some hours, by a defiant tone; and, as he left the marquée, he kicked away the presents laid before the council. Great agitation ensued. The council was then summarily dissolved, the Indians went to their hill, and we to our tents.

It has been stated that the encampment of the Indians was situated on an eminence a few hundred yards west from our position on the shore, and separated from us by a small ravine. We had scarcely reached our tents, when it was announced that the Indians had raised the British flag in their camp. They felt their superiority in number, and did not disguise their insolence. Affairs had reached a crisis. A conflict seemed inevitable. Governor Cass instantly ordered the expedition under arms. He then called the interpreter, and proceeded with him, naked-handed and alone, to Sassaba's lodge at the hostile camp. Being armed with short rifles, we requested to be allowed to accompany him as a body-guard, but he decidedly refused this. On reaching the lodge of the hostile chief, before whose door the flag had been raised, he pulled it down with his own hands. He then entered the lodge, and addressing the chief calmly but firmly, told him that it was an indignity which they could not be permitted to offer; that the flag was the distinguishing symbol of nationality; that two flags of diverse kind could not wave in peace upon the same territory; that they were forbid the use of any but our own, and should they again attempt it, the United States would set a strong foot upon their rock and crush them. He then brought the captured flag with him to his tent.

In a few moments after his return from the Indian camp, that camp was cleared by the Indians of their women and children, who fled with precipitation in their canoes across the river. Thus prepared for battle, we momently expected to hear the war-whoop. I had myself examined and filled my shot-pouch, and stood ready, rifle in hand, with my companions, awaiting their attack. But we waited in vain. It was an hour of indecision among the Indians. They deliberated, doubtingly, and it soon became evident that the crisis had passed. Finding no hostile demonstration from the hill, Lieutenants Pierce and Mackay directed their respective commands to retire to their tents.

The intrepid act of Governor Cass had struck the Indians with amazement, while it betokened a knowledge of Indian character of which we never dreamed. This people possess a singular respect for bravery. The march of our force, on that occasion, would have been responded to, instantly, by eighty or a hundred Indian guns; but to behold an unarmed man walk boldly into their camp and seize the symbol of their power, betokened a cast of character which brought them to reflection. On one person in particular the act had a controlling effect. When it was told to the daughter of Wabojeeg (Mrs. Johnston), she told the chief that their meditated scheme of resistance to the Americans was madness; the day for such resistance was passed; and this man, Cass, had the air of a great man, and could carry his flag through the country. The party were also under the hospitality of her roof. She counselled peace. To these words Shingabawossin responded; he was seconded by Shingwakonce, or the Little Pine. Of this effort we knew nothing at the moment, but the facts were afterwards learned. It was evident, before the day had passed, that a better state of feeling existed among the Indians. The chief Shingabawossin, under the friendly influences referred to, renewed the negotiations. Towards evening a council of the chiefs was convened in one of the buildings of this Pocahontean counsellor, and the treaty of the 16th June, 1820, signed. In this treaty every leading man united, except Sassaba. The Little Pine signed it, under one of his synonymous names, Lavoine Bart. By this treaty the Chippewas cede four miles square, reserving the right of a place to fish at the rapids, perpetually. The consideration for this cession, or acknowledgment of title, was promptly paid in merchandise.

The same eventful thirty-six hours gave him also such a contact with the Indians as was later to change the current of his life.

It required but little observation to explore the village of St. Mary's. It consisted of some fifteen or twenty buildings of all sorts, occupied by descendants of the original French settlers, all of whom drew their living from the fur trade. . . . Most of the French habitations stood in the midst of picketed lots. There were about forty or fifty lodges, or two hundred Chippewas, fifty or sixty of whom were warriors. . . . The principal buildings and outhouses were those of Mr. John Johnston . . . the principal inhabitant . . . a native of the County of Antrim, Ireland, where his connections are persons of rank. He is a polite, intelligent, and well-bred man, from a manifestly refined circle; who, soon after the close of the American Revolution, settled here, and married the daughter of a distinguished Indian chief. Although now absent on a visit to Europe, his family received us with marked urbanity and hospitality, and invited the gentlemen composing the travelling family of Governor Cass to take all our meals with them. Everything at this mansion was done with ceremonious attention to the highest rules of English social life; Miss Jane, the eldest daughter, who had received her education in Ireland, presiding.

Swiftly, during the brief stop at the Sault, Schoolcraft had run the gamut of acquaintance with the Indians, from full-blood painted warrior, through the common run of the mixed breeds, to the Johnston household, with the exceptional Indian mother and unusual Indian-Scotch-Irish children, presided over by the extraordinary eldest sister Jane. Thereafter he was never to be free from knowing them.

Schoolcraft's duty in connection with the expedition was in the field of natural history, especially geology. Governor Cass took for his province the observation of the Indians. But, beginning at Sault Ste. Marie and continuing till the exploring party was safe back at its starting point, the aborigines commanded an expanding place in Schoolcraft's interest and in his notebook.

When the expedition of 1820 was disbanded, at Detroit, Governor Cass spoke to Schoolcraft about a situation as Secretary to the Commissioners appointed to confer with the

Indians at Chicago the following summer. The opportunity interested him. Meantime he returned to New York. His narrative of the 1820 exploration issued from the press May 20, 1821. May 22, Schoolcraft received a letter from Governor Cass confirming his previous offer. He accepted eagerly.

The purpose of the treaty at Chicago was to extinguish the Indian title to that portion of country included between the northern boundary line of the State of Indiana, and Grand River of Michigan, embracing in longitude all that part of the peninsula within these boundaries which still remained unpurchased. Governor Cass and Solomon Sibley were the commissioners. The usual route from Detroit to Chicago was either by way of an Indian trail from the sources of the river Raisin, about three hundred miles, or by ship through the Great Lakes, somewhat more than twice that distance. Since government business required the presence of Governor Cass on the Wabash, it was decided to proceed by means of the Maumee to the Wabash and afterward by way of the Ohio, Mississippi and Illinois Rivers.

The party left Detroit July 3, 1821, and reached Chicago on the 14th of August. The proceedings of the formal council, which started August 17, are given in Schoolcraft's *Travels in the Central Portions of the Mississippi Valley,* up to the point of an adjournment for consultation on the twenty-third. At this stage of the negotiations Schoolcraft was stricken with a sudden attack of bilious fever. No further notes, therefore, were taken. For this reason also Schoolcraft's name does not appear as a witness to the treaty, which was formally signed August 29, 1821. A copy of the ratified document appears in the appendix of Schoolcraft's *Travels* published in 1825. For a valuable consideration in annuities and goods, about five million acres of choice lands were ceded.

Governor Cass and his party returned to Michigan by the Indian trail. After several weeks of convalescence Schoolcraft left Chicago on the schooner *Decatur,* September 23, reached Detroit October 6, and proceeded east to Vernon, New York.

Soon thereafter Schoolcraft received news from a friend

in Washington regarding the probability of his appointment as Indian Agent at the proposed new post at Sault Ste. Marie, Michigan.   This letter, dated November 4, 1821, reads:

The proposition to remove from Sackett's Harbor to the Sault of St. Mary a battalion of the army, and to establish a military post at the latter place, has been submitted by Mr. Calhoun to the President.   The pressure of other subjects has required an investigation and decision since his return; so that he has not yet been able to examine this matter.   Mr. Calhoun is himself decidedly in favor of the measure, and I have no doubt but that such will be the result of the Presidential deliberation.   The question is too plain, and the considerations connected with it too obvious and important, to allow any prominent difficulties to intrude themselves between the conception and the execution of the measure.   If a post be established, it is almost certain that an Indian agency will be located there, and, in the event, it is quite certain that you will be appointed the agent.

At Albany, New York, January 5, 1822, he received another friendly reassurance from Washington: "The occupation of the Sault has been decided on, and I have but little doubt of your appointment to the agency.   Make your mind easy.   I am certain the government will not forget you, and I never can. I shall not lose sight of your interest a moment."

Secretary of War Calhoun had extended the time for the completion of his geological report of the expedition of 1820. Now it was ready.   He presented it in person, at Washington, in April, 1822.   There he learned that some question connected with the establishment of an agency in Florida complicated the matter of his appointment at the Sault.   Otherwise it appeared to be a mere question of time.   "The Secretary of War left me no room to doubt that his feelings were altogether friendly.   Mr. Monroe was also friendly."

At length Congress passed an act that left Secretary Calhoun free to carry out his intentions, by the creation of a separate Indian agency for Florida.   This enabled him to transfer one of the western agencies, namely, at Vincennes, Indiana, where the Indian business had ceased, to the foot of Lake Superior, at the ancient French village of Sault de Ste. Marie,

Michigan. If the act had not passed, it would have been necessary to transfer this agency to Florida.

Mr. Monroe immediately sent in my nomination for this old agency to the Senate, by whom it was favorably acted on the 8th of May. The gentleman (Mr. J. B. Thomas, Senator from Illinois) whose boat I had been instrumental in saving in my descent of the Ohio in the spring of 1818, I believe, moved its confirmation. It was from him, at any rate, that I the same day obtained the information of the Senate's action.

Governor Cass was Superintendent of Indian Affairs on the northwestern frontier. Schoolcraft obtained instructions from him at Detroit and embarked there July 2, 1822, for the Sault, on the new steamer *Superior* which had been chartered by the government to transport a battalion of the 2nd Regiment of Infantry under Colonel Brady from Sackett's Harbor, to the new post. On the 6th they anchored at the foot of the Neebish Rapids, fearing that the water was too low on the bar of Lake George, and the men ascended the remaining fifteen miles in small boats.

Schoolcraft was Indian Agent from May 8, 1822, until April 17, 1841. On first assuming this responsibility he wrote:

I had now attained a fixed position; not such as I desired in the outset, and had striven for, but one that offered an interesting class of duties, in the performance of which there was a wide field for honorable exertion, and, if it was embraced, also of historical inquiry and research. The taste for natural history might certainly be transferred to that point, where the opportunity for discovery was the greatest. At any rate, the trial of a residence on that remote frontier might readily be made, and I may say it was in fact made only as a temporary matter. It was an ancient agency in which General Harrison had long exercised his superior authority over the fierce and wild tribes of the West, which was an additional stimulus to exertion, after its removal to Lake Superior.

Years afterwards he summarized his work as Indian Agent at the Sault as follows. It was not . . . an ordinary task to induce this important tribe to acknowledge fealty to the American government. Firmness of purpose, combined with mildness of manner, were eminently necessary. The establishment of an agency, a smithy, and an armorer's shop, the supply of food to them in their necessity, and the bestowal of presents, were important means.   The display of so considerable a force on the frontier, as the garrison of Fort Brady, enabled the agent to act efficiently.   By acting in concurrence with the military, an effective controlling power was established.   Murderers of white men were demanded from the Indians; the country was cleared of freed men, or discharged boatmen, who had taken up a permanent residence among the Indians; and none but licensed traders, with their boatmen, were permitted to pass into the country.   Ardent spirits were excluded.   Sensing that the Indians were always gratified with the comity and ceremony of diplomatic attention, he accorded them dignified reception, and he encouraged their fondness for making trips from distant parts of the country.   He also rendered himself acceptable to the Indians by other means which were merely incidental.   His requests that they bring any specimens of animals, birds and organic forms that they thought new, and his inquiries regarding their language, customs, traditions and antiquities furnished material for conversation and led to common understanding.   The remote chiefs soon began to visit the agency.   The pacific results of this intercourse soon began to appear.

Henry Rowe Schoolcraft was the first and only Indian Agent to be located at Sault Ste. Marie, Michigan.   His arrival was on July 6, 1822, with the detachment of troops that established what has since been named Fort Brady.   When the Agency headquarters was transferred to Mackinac, he left the Sault (according to his letter to Governor Porter) May 27, 1833.

His first night as Indian Agent at Sault Ste. Marie was spent in the tent of Captain Alexander R. Thompson, as companion guest with Commandant Brady.   The settlement was taxed to accommodate the influx of its new military population.

Next day he and Captain Brant, the quartermaster, hired for a joint office a small log building which had been occupied by one of Mr. John Johnston's hands.   This was the first

Agency building at the Sault. It was about twelve by fourteen feet, with a small window in front and in rear, and "a very rural" fireplace in one corner.

July 9 he hired an interpreter for the government—in fact, as long as he was Indian Agent he never was without one. The same day he held his first public council with the Indians.

Four years later, after several changes, he secured permission from the authorities at Washington, and an allotment of two thousand dollars from Governor Cass, to build the Agency of mansional proportions that he called Elmwood. Of this he wrote: "A site was selected on a handsomely elevated bank of the river, covered with elms, about half a mile east of the fort, where the foundation of a spacious building and office were laid in the autumn of 1826, and the frame raised as early in the ensuing spring as the snow left the ground." He occupied it in October, 1827. Including the Agency offices, it had fifteen rooms—three stories and a basement—and such luxuries as double window-sashes. This is the monumental building that still stands in the Sault, near the canal, on the property of the Union Carbide Company. Subsequently, during the occupancy of the Scranton family, it was remodeled. Impressive now, it must have been much more so in its frontier day.

Letters to his subordinates throw interesting light upon the official Indian activities it housed:

It has been the design of the department to concentrate in the building the usual office for receiving their visits and transacting their business, both during the payment of the annuities and at other seasons, together with rooms for storing & issuing provisions & other articles, and apartments for temporary visitors. . . . Fuel will be provided to warm the apartments, which it is expected, will be used with economy. The expression, "Indians visiting the post," is construed to mean Indians visiting the Agency on business. To none others do the laws or instructions apply, at this time, and it is proper for you to discountenance the visits of the idle or intemperate. . . . Seven bbls. flour, one of pork, one of fish, and six of corn are assigned to be given out, occasionally, to destitute or sick Inds. only.

In April, 1832, while Stevens Thomson Mason was Secretary of Michigan Territory, Acting Governor, and Superintendent of Indian Affairs, the War Department directed the consolidation of the Indian Agencies at Michilimackinac and Sault Ste. Marie, under Schoolcraft, into what for a time was called the Northwestern Agency but later became more commonly known as the Mackinac Agency. Schoolcraft had the option of headquarters at either point. He chose to move to Mackinac Island, and left a subagent at Sault Ste. Marie.

The old Indian Agency that was Schoolcraft's Mackinac Island home was destroyed by fire many years ago.

Previous to July 2, 1836, the territorial governors served in ex officio capacity as Superintendents of Indian Affairs. After that date there were, of course, no territorial governors in Michigan to hold that office. Theoretically, state governors could not hold it since they were not Federal officials. Near the close of the session in 1836, Congress passed an act devolving the duties of this position on the agent at Michilimackinac. Instructions were issued July 10 carrying the Act into effect. Schoolcraft thus served in a dual capacity for five years, as Acting Superintendent of Indian Affairs as well as Indian Agent. Following this appointment Schoolcraft moved his headquarters to Detroit, though he spent his summers and one winter thereafter, at Mackinac.

In 1839, while in New York at the beginning of a leave of absence for a trip to Europe, he was obliged to return to Detroit in order to assume the duties of Chief Disbursing Agent.

He was spending the summer as usual at Mackinac Island in 1841 when he determined to resign and move to New York, in order to be close to printers and publishers, and also to make the long-desired European journey. His last letter as Acting Superintendent of Indian Affairs was dated April 17, 1841, which is the date of the appointment of Robert Stuart, his successor in both offices. His long connection with the Indian Office was temporarily severed, to be resumed in 1847 and continued for ten years thereafter in a different capacity.

Some of the difficulties of the Indian situation at the Sault

ELMWOOD, OLD INDIAN AGENCY AT SAULT STE. MARIE, MICHIGAN. BUILT
UNDER SCHOOLCRAFT'S DIRECTION IN 1827.

and in the Lake Superior region should be recalled in a review of Schoolcraft's labors on that frontier.

In 1822, the United States abolished its system of government trading houses. Although this enabled American fur traders to compete with the British, and from that time the influence of the British over the Indians was appreciably checked, the Indians were kept as far as possible under their control, and England still retained a foothold on American territory. Despite the fact that the commissioners under the Treaty of Ghent had determined, in 1822, that Drummond Island, at the mouth of the St. Marys River, belonged to the United States, the British maintained a post there until November 14, 1828. It was complained that American Indians to the number of four thousand received presents and annuities there in 1826 for their services to Great Britain.

In addition to this complication, there was continuous trouble among the Indians themselves. The Chippewas and Sioux were ancient enemies. The boundaries of their respective territories were ill-defined. They trespassed on each other's lands in hunting. Memories of old injuries and existing frictions resulted in sporadic war-parties, and constant fear and uncertainties.

Another cause of Indian restlessness was the introduction of a fast increasing population in the Mississippi valley and the Great Lakes basin. Tact and strength were required to maintain peace between the Indians and the white settlers. In 1831, especially, circumstances inclined the tribes on the Upper Mississippi to hostilities and extensive combinations. Schoolcraft, therefore, was directed by the government to conduct an expedition through the country lying south and west of Lake Superior, which from the earliest dates had been the fastnesses of numerous warlike tribes. This he accomplished satisfactorily, visiting the leading chiefs, and counseling them to the policy of peace.

In 1832, the Sauks and Foxes resolved to re-occupy lands which they had previously relinquished in the Rock River valley. This brought them into collision with the citizens and militia of Illinois and resulted in a general conflict, which, from its prominent Indian leader, has been called the Black Hawk War. From accounts of the previous year, its combinations embraced nine of the leading tribes. It was uncertain how far they extended. Mr. Schoolcraft accordingly was selected by the Indian and War Department, to conduct a second expedition to the headwaters of the Mississippi, in 1832.

The information obtained on this journey demonstrated that the Chippewas and Sioux, whatever sympathies they had with Black Hawk and his scheme, were not committed to his project by any overt participation in it. This was considered due, in large part, to Schoolcraft's presence and activities in the Mississippi country the preceding year. The Indians were vaccinated, as directed by an act of Congress, and their numbers definitely ascertained. Meantime, while the expedition was pursuing its explorations, the Sauk chief had commenced the war and been driven to the mouth of the Bad Axe River, between the Falls of St. Anthony and Prairie du Chien. Without being apprized of the impending danger, the Schoolcraft expedition unwittingly avoided it, after ascending the river to the influx of the St. Croix by passing up that river into the waters on Lake Superior.

In addition to his contributions toward peace on these two expeditions, he was associated officially with a number of treaty councils during a period of eighteen years.

At Chicago, he was secretary to the Commissioners who negotiated the treaty signed there August 29, 1821.

His name is affixed as a witness to the treaty with the Chippewas at Sault Ste. Marie, June 16, 1820; and to those of 1825, 1826, and 1827, at Prairie du Chien, Fond du Lac (Superior), and Butte des Morts.

He negotiated and signed the treaty with the Ottawas and Chippewas, March 28, 1836, at Washington, D. C.; treaty with Chippewas, Swan Creek and Black River Bands, at Washington, May 9, 1836; treaty with Chippewas, January 14, 1837, replacing treaty of May 20, 1836, that was rejected by the Government; treaty with Chippewas from Saginaw, at Flint,

December 20, 1837; and treaty with Chippewas, January 23, 1838.

The treaties of 1825, 1826 and 1827 embodied a new course. They proceeded toward settlement of internal disputes between the tribes by fixing the boundaries to their respective territories, thus laying the foundation of lasting peace on the frontiers. They contained no cession of territory.

Governor Cass and General William Clark from St. Louis were the Commissioners at the treaty of August 19, 1825, at Prairie du Chien, with the Sioux, Chippewas, Sauks and Foxes, Menominees, Iowas, Winnebagos, Ottawas, and Potawatamis, which began the work of establishing boundaries between the Sioux and Chippewas.

One year later, August 5, 1826, at Fond du Lac on Lake Superior, the Chippewas signed a treaty approving the boundary lines settled upon at Prairie du Chien; and ceding to the United States the right to search for and remove metals or minerals from any part of their country but not to gain title to the lands. Shingabawossin, of Sault Ste. Marie, one of the delegation accompanying Schoolcraft and doubtless influenced by him, was principal speaker and head chief, and helped in an important way to overcome the Indians' reluctance to part with their mineral rights. An attempt made by the expedition to move and ship the large copper boulder on the Ontonagon was unsuccessful. Nevertheless "the closed lake," as Superior was called in 1820, had yielded before the Anglo-Saxon power. Governor Cass and Thomas L. McKenney, Commissioner of Indian Affairs, negotiated this treaty.

At the signing of the treaty of Butte des Morts, on the Fox River, August 11, 1827, with Governor Cass and Commissioner McKenney as negotiators, Schoolcraft was present with a delegation of Chippewas from the midlands, on the sources of the Ontonagon, Wisconsin, Chippewa, and Menominee rivers, and again had the opportunity to witness and record Governor Cass's indomitable courage and sense, in overawing the hostile Winnebagos. This treaty completed the settlement of Indian boundaries begun in 1825.

On March 28, 1836—his forty-third birthday—he completed, as commissioner, the treaty he considered the zenith of his career. Through this the United States became possessed of vast territory worth many millions of dollars. His part in this was active, rather than instrumental, his attitude that of a diplomat rather than of an agent. With the approbation and aid of the Secretary of War, in the face of difficulties and embarrassments that no person of less superior qualifications could have overcome, he effected an agreement which was not only favorable in its terms to the Indians but distinctly so to the United States, and vastly important to the best interests and prosperity of Michigan.

He had reported, in February, 1834,

an official visit from Indians of the settlement of L'Arbre Croche, who wished to see the President on the subject of their lands. . . . Drummond Island had been abandoned. They thought themselves entitled to compensation for it. They were poor and indebted to traders. The settlements would soon intrude on their territories. Wood was now cut for the use of steamboats and not paid for. This was the first move of the Lake Indians, leading in the sequel to the important treaty of March 28, 1836.

The Department instructed him to ascertain whether the Indians north of Grand River would sell their lands, and on what terms, in September, 1835. The Indians were so eager that some of them set out at once for Washington. About the situation Schoolcraft wrote in his *Memoirs* October 31, that year:

Circumstances had now inclined the Chippewa and Ottawa tribes of Indians to cede to the United States a portion of their extensive territory. Game had failed in the greater part of it, and they had no other method of raising funds to pay their large outstanding credits to the class of traders, and to provide for an interval of transition, which must indeed happen, in view of their future improvement, between the hunter and agricultural state.

The Drummond Island band had, for a year or two, advocated a sale. The Ottawas of the peninsula determined to send a delegation to Washington on the subject. I could not hesitate as to the course which duty prescribed to me, under these important circumstances, and determined to proceed to Washington, although the

Secretary and acting Governor of the Territory, Mr. Horner, on being consulted by letter, refused his assent to this step. His want of proper information on the subject, being but recently come to the territory, did not appear to be such as to justify me in remaining on the island, while the question had been carried by the Indians themselves to, and was, probably, to be decided at Washington before another season. I determined, therefore, to proceed to Washington, taking one of the latest vessels for the season, on their return from the ports on Lake Michigan.

Later, at Washington, March 28, 1836, he continued:

My reception here has been most cordial, and such as to assure me in the propriety of the step I took, in resolving to proceed to the capital, without the approval of the secretary and acting governor (Horner), who was, indeed, from his recent arrival and little experience in this matter, quite in the dark respecting the true condition of Indian affairs in Michigan. The self-constituted Ottawa delegation of chiefs from the lower peninsula had preceded me a few days. After a conference between them and the Secretary of War, they were referred to me, under authority from the President, communicated by special appointment, as commissioner for treating with them. It was found that the deputation was quite too local for the transaction of any general business. The Ottawas, from the valley of Grand River, an important section, were unrepresented. The various bands of Chippewas living intercalated among them, on the lower peninsula, extending down the Huron shore to Thunder Bay, were unapprized of the movement. The Chippewas of the upper peninsula, north of Michilimackinack, were entirely unrepresented. I immediately wrote, authorizing deputations to be sent from each of the unrepresented districts, and transmitting funds for the purpose. This authority to collect delegates from the two nations, whose interests in the lands were held in common, was promptly and efficiently carried out; and, when the chiefs and delegates arrived, they were assembled in public council, at the Masonic Hall, corner of $4\frac{1}{2}$ street, and negotiations formally opened. These meetings were continued from day to day, and resulted in an important cession of territory, comprising all their lands lying in the lower peninsula of Michigan, north of Grand River and west of Thunder Bay; and on the upper peninsula, extending from Drummond Island and Detour, through the Straits of St. Mary, west to Chocolate River, on Lake Superior, and thence southerly to Green Bay. This cession was obtained on the principle of making limited reserves for the principal villages, and granting the mass of Indian population the right to live on and occupy any portion of the lands until it is actually required for settlement. The compensation, for all objects, was about two millions of dollars. It had been arranged to close and sign the treaty on the 26th of March, but some objections were made by the Ottawas to a matter of detail, which led to a renewed discussion, and it was not until the 28th that the treaty was signed. . . .

Liberal provisions were made for their education and instruction in agriculture and the arts. Their outstanding debts to the merchants were provided for, and such aid given them in the initial labor of subsisting themselves, as were required by a gradual change from the life of hunters to that of husbandmen. About twelve and a half cents per acre was given for the entire area, which includes some secondary lands and portions of muskeegs and waste grounds about the lakes—which it was, however, thought ought, in justice to the Indians, to be included in the cession. The whole area could not be certainly told, but was estimated at about sixteen millions of acres.

By this purchase of all Indian lands north of the Grand River and Thunder Bay in Lake Huron, comprising the northern one-third of the Lower Peninsula and the eastern half of the Upper Peninsula, Schoolcraft had performed an unusual service for the State. Ignoring the authority of the ex officio Superintendent of Indian Affairs, the unhappy Governor Horner of Michigan Territory, he had gone to Washington. Instead of bargaining with the representatives of a few bands who were there, he had sent for delegations from a wide section of the Territory and put through a cession on a large scale instead of making a minor treaty. He had treated the Indians generously. The first payment of their annuities was made in the fall of 1836. The Indians were happy; and Michigan entered upon statehood under vastly improved circumstances because of the completion of extinction of the Indian title to practically all of the Lower Peninsula, and an immense territory beyond the Straits of Mackinac. The State ought to be eternally grateful to Schoolcraft's memory.

The other treaties which he negotiated as Commissioner were important though less sweeping in their significance. His *Memoirs* state:

About the beginning of May a delegation of Saginaws [Chippewas from Saginaw] arrived, for the purpose of ceding to the government the reservations in Michigan, made under the treaty of 1819.

This delegation was referred to me, with instructions to form a treaty with them. The terms of it were agreed on in several interviews, and the treaty was signed on the 20th of May, 1836.

However, the terms, particularly the advance of money stipulated to be made, were deemed too liberal by the Senate and the treaty was rejected, to be replaced by that of January 14, 1837.

Another,

A third delegation of Chippewas, from Michigan, having separate interest in the regions of Swan Creek and Black River, presented themselves, with the view of ceding the reservations made to them by a treaty concluded by General Hull, November 17th, 1807. They were also referred to me to adjust the terms of a sale of these reservations. The treaty was signed by their chiefs on the 9th of May, 1836.

The treaty of January 14, 1837, signed at Schoolcraft's office in Detroit, after he was Acting Superintendent of Indian Affairs as well as Indian Agent, secured cession from the Chippewa chiefs at Saginaw of the reservations covered by the rejected treaty of May 20, 1836. More than 100,000 acres at Detroit were in the main relinquished here. The tribe was allowed the entire proceeds of the sale of their lands.

A supplementary treaty with the Chippewas of Saginaw was signed by him at Flint December 20, 1837; and another was negotiated by him January 23, 1838, according to the records of the Office of Indian Affairs.

In addition to his valuable activities as Agent in Michigan, Schoolcraft served the government by means of his international point of view and alert national interest. When the *London Times* had criticized the United States and Governor Cass for driving "another hard bargain" with the "miserable Indians," at Chicago, in 1821, Schoolcraft replied to it effectively with comments and severe counter-charges against the British in his *Travels in the Central Portions of the Mississippi Valley*. Thirty years later, one of his aims in his six-volume work was to show how gratuitous were such imputations against the character of the government of the United States in its dealings with the Indians—to make manifest the conviction that

no stock of the aborigines found by civilized nations on the globe, have received the same amount of considerate and benevolent and humane treatment, as denoted by its laws, its treaties, and general administration of Indian affairs, . . . and this in the face of the most hostile, wrongheaded, and capricious conduct on their part, that ever signalized the history of a barbarous people.

His correspondence with Major Delafield, boundary commissioner appointed by authority of the Treaty of Ghent, shows that he kept in intimate touch with difficulties along the Canadian border.   That his comprehension was not confined merely to the region of his own Agency appears in the following note made January 10, 1836:

I addressed a memoir to the Secretary of War on the state of Indian affairs in Oregon.   My position at St. Mary's being on the great line of communication between Montreal and the principal posts at Vancouver, &c., north of the Columbia, has afforded me opportunities of becoming familiar with the leading policy of the Hudson's Bay factors in relation to that region.   The means pursued are such as must influence all the Indian tribes in that quarter strongly in favor of the political power wielded by that company, and as strongly against the government of the United States, which has not a shadow of a power of any kind on the Pacific.   Silently, but surely, a vast influence is being built up on those coasts, adverse to our claims to the territory, and it cannot be long till those intrepid factors, sustained by the government at home, will assert it in a manner not easy to be resisted.   I embodied these ideas strongly in my paper.   The Secretary was arrested by the justice of my conclusions, and seemed disposed to do something, but the subject was, apparently, weighed down and forgotten in the press of other matters.

Such incidents as these, and the courage, vision, and executive ability manifested in connection with the Treaty of 1836, explain the standing that Henry Rowe Schoolcraft had at Washington under successive administrations.   It was the recognition given his tireless industry and character as well as his intelligence.   In time he became known as "Uncle Sam's Pet."   His success and his principles, especially with regard to the sale of liquor to the Indians, aroused jealousies and made him enemies. The appraisal of the lifelong friendship of Lewis Cass alone far outweighs the combined attacks of all his detractors.

At the same time that he was working for the welfare of the general public, he was earnestly devoted to the cause of the American Indian. As much as any white man could be under the hopeless circumstances, he was indeed the "Red Man's Friend." The blame for the invasion of the country of one people by another is not all, always, on the side of the invaders. The sins and weaknesses of those in original possession are factors in the case. The continuous warfare of the Indians amongst themselves, their lack of knowledge of how to use the land, their natural indolence and improvidence, fought against them, on the side of the whites. The fur trade not only hastened the exhaustion of the country from which they previously had as hunters found their food and clothing, but gave them whisky which lessened their ambition and ability to hunt and brought them many forms of disease and wretchedness. There was nothing much that any one man could do for them, or even that the United States could do, beyond helping them to help, and not to hurt, themselves.

Jane Johnston Schoolcraft, herself half Indian, could only pity them and say "My people are like children. They do not know what they need."

What could be done for such unfortunates as this?

The negotiations with the commissioners at Chicago had been protracted many days by the various propositions and modifications proposed on each side. When the terms had been finally settled, impatience on the part of the Indians became the ruling passion with those who had before evinced the greatest disposition to procrastinate and delay; and they could hardly wait for the necessary writings to be drawn. But it was the present of liquor which they had stipulated should accompany the goods, which caused the greatest impatience. "My Father," said the venerable Topinabee, the most aged and respected chief of this nation, addressing himself to Governor Cass, "we are very thirsty for some of that milk you have brought for us. We wish it to be given to us. We can no longer restrain our thirst." Being told that the goods were not yet ready to be issued—"Give us," he rejoined, "the whiskey! we care not for the rest."

Schoolcraft did his honest best for them, with hopeless sympathy, and sternness. His outward attitude toward the Indian is illustrated by the following, written in anticipation of the Black Hawk outbreak during his expedition of 1832:

I had caused my canoe, after it had been finished in most perfect style of art known to this kind of vessel, to be painted with Chinese vermilion, from stem to stern. Ten years' residence among the tribes, in an official capacity, had convinced me that fear is the controlling principle of the Indian mind, and that the persuasions to a life of peace, are most effectively made under the symbols of war. To beg, to solicit, to creep and cringe to this race, whether in public or private, is a delusive, if not a fatal course; and though I was told by one or two of my neighbors that it was not well, on this occasion, to put my canoe in the symbolic garb of war, I did not think so. I carried, indeed, emphatically, messages of peace from the executive head of the Government, and had the means of insuring respect for these messages, by displaying the symbol of authority at the stern of each vessel, by an escort of soldiery, and by presents, and the services of a physician to arrest one of the most fatal of diseases which have ever afflicted the Indian race.

The feeling in his heart toward them is expressed by what he wrote in 1853 of an experience in August 1820:

We passed, this day, several encampments and villages of Winnebagoes and Menomonies—tribes, who, with the erratic habits of the Tartars, or Bedouins, once spread their tents in the Fox and Wisconsin valleys, but have now relinquished them to the European race; and it does not, at this distance of time, seem important to denote the particular spots where they once boiled their kettles of corn, or thumped their magic drums. God have mercy on them in their wild wanderings!

His place and connections at Washington, as well as at the capital of Michigan, were strong influences in securing liquor legislation and other measures for the best interests of the Indian and the nation.

One means of appreciating his constructive activity for the welfare of the Indians is to compare the treatment accorded them in the Treaty of 1836 with what occurred in some of the later negotiations. Their scattered bands, without power to enforce any demands, were paid at the rate of 12½ cents an acre. For a just estimate of this transaction, it is illuminating to know that the United States paid approximately two cents an acre for Alaska, in 1867, to the powerful, established government of Russia, and about four cents an acre to France for Louisiana Territory. The accounts of the Indians with the traders were all settled, some of them debts of thirty years' standing, and there was money and gifts for every Indian besides. The treaty provided for a system of annuities; every man, woman and child received a specified individual share.

From 1836 he believed that the Chippewas and Ottawas could not permanently thrive as distinct tribes on their existing locations in Michigan. By 1844 there was a question in his mind whether even in Indian Territory the red race would be left long undisturbed. The western Indian lands lay across the path of white expansion. It seemed impossible that they could continue to live apart, unto themselves, even west of the Mississippi.

Even before this, however, without the definiteness of final conviction, he had proceeded by instinct and with sense to prepare for this eventuality. Estimating in the Northwest that every hunter, with those dependent on him, required fifty thousand acres, or a little more than two entire townships for his hunting needs, it early became conclusive in his mind that Indian education should stress agriculture. He was personally interested in and responsible for the location of the Indian center at the Old Mission on Grand Traverse Bay, where, according to treaty terms, a blacksmith, a carpenter, and an Indian farmer were stationed in 1839.

The Algic Society, founded in Detroit in the fall of 1832 in the main "to aid and encourage missionary schools and agricultural effort," seems to have been the result of his efforts and to have been carried on largely by him. His *Memoirs* under date of February 28, that year, record "initial steps . . . for forming an association of persons interested in the cause of the reclamation of the Indians." Even the name of the Society was his creation. He was its first president. It was intended, by furthering ethnologic inquiries and consolidating their results with philanthropic efforts, "to offer facilities to laborers on the frontiers, and answer inquiries made by agents authorized by the General Boards from the old States." At its first meeting it resolved, among other things, to have prepared "a succinct Temperance and Peace Circular, suited to the wants and situation of the Northwestern Tribes, to be addressed, through the intervention of the Hon. the Secretary of War, to the Agents of the Government and Officers commanding posts on the frontiers, and also to persons engaged in the fur trade; to travelers, and to gentlemen residing in the country, requesting their aid in spreading its influence;" to ascertain the number of missionaries then amongst them (the different bands of the Algonquin stock), and the extent of the field of labor which they present; and to "aid in sending a winter express to the missionaries who are now stationed near the western extremity of Lake Superior."

Advocating Christianization of the Indians as a first necessary step in their civilization, he worked tirelessly with individual missionaries, for mission schools, and mission boards. He was a loyal supporter of the mission at Mackinac Island. When a move against it was made in 1829, by an attempt to repeal the law exempting persons engaged in it from militia and jury service, and a formal attack on its mode of management and character was delivered in the Legislative Council, as a member of that body he brought in a report, which was adopted and printed, repelling the charges as entirely unjust. When Mr. Ferry resigned in 1834 and the Mission Board was unable to provide a successor, Schoolcraft himself occasionally conducted services in the Old Mission Church.

In his communication to the American Lyceum in 1834 on the best method of education for the Indians, there were valuable suggestions. He condemned free boarding schools at remote points from their settlements. The cost of feeding and clothing consumed funds needed for more widespread instruction. Students of such institutions, on returning to their homes, too often were objects of distrust, without influence and estranged, who lapsed into despondency or worse. "If the mass of a tribe be degraded, it is of little avail that a few be educated." Free boarding schools he considered

a positive injury instead of a benefit to both parents and children. . . . It is a position which forms the very basis of civilization, that each member of society must support himself by his own industry. And it seems important to teach this truth early to the Indians. If they are ever to exist as a happy, united and independent people, it must be through faithful individual exertions on their own part.

Local schools, in simple buildings, to which the Indians themselves contributed, would win their confidence and prove of immediate and constant helpfulness to all of them. Schoolcraft, in his grasp of the idea that the thing to do, as quickly as possible, was to make self-supporting, self-respecting citizens of the Indians, anticipated by exactly one hundred years the spirit of the reorganization of methods of the United States Office of Indian Affairs that took place in 1934.

Schoolcraft's *Thirty Years with the Indian Tribes*, together with his other published journals after 1820, are interesting further sources of information about the activities in Michigan of the Office of Indian Affairs. These writings supplement in a valuable way his official reports and communications, about which something may be found later in this book, under Bibliography.

In 1847, six years after he had ceased to be Indian Agent and Acting Superintendent of Indian Affairs in Michigan, he renewed official connection with the Department, at Washington, as Special Agent, in a new field recently set apart from other social sciences under the name of ethnology.

Pioneer in American Archaeology and Ethnology

Henry Rowe Schoolcraft's work in ethnology constitutes one of the most important contributions that have been made to the literature of this continent. Yet the field was not of his own choosing. It grew up about him and enmeshed him, in spite of his desire and definite plan to be a mineralogist and mining engineer.

Governor Cass, during his long public life, had a wide experience with the Indians and collected much material on their language, characteristics, and traditions. He published a number of articles about them; and the giving of Indian names to counties in Michigan was begun and furthered by him. Perhaps the beginning of Schoolcraft's actual concentration on American ethnology was the Cass questionnaire given to him as he hurried in 1822 to his new post as Indian Agent at Sault Ste. Marie, Michigan.

"Among the papers which were put in my hands at Detroit," he wrote, "I found a printed copy of Governor Cass's Indian queries, based on his promise to Douglass, by which I was gratified to perceive that his mind was earnestly engaged in the subject, which he sought a body of original materials to illustrate. I determined to be a laborer in this new field."

However, his interest in the subject had already been aroused to keenness, as his journal of the 1820 expedition records. After the hostile demonstration at the Sault, there were friendly parties of Indians in canoes, friendly villages at Ontonagon and LaPointe, and the council at Sandy Lake. An Indian dance, and the story of the lone survivor of a war-party, provided him with more than entertainment. He noted with alertness an instance of picture-writing by the Indian guides; the attitude of one of them toward a bear that had been killed; an Indian grave with a bear totem; burial on scaffolds; and peeled, clay-painted poles still standing in a clearing made by a jossakeed. Exploration of the lead mines at Dubuque, Iowa, resulted in an account of the Fox Indians who owned and worked them.

His experience with the aborigines widened, on his Central Mississippi journey in 1821. The Indian battles in the Raisin Valley, Michigan, of Fallen Timbers, Ohio, and Fort Wayne and Tippecanoe, Indiana, emerged out of the past for him. He visited the Indian School at Fort Wayne. In southern Illinois, he wished to name a height of land Shawano for the vanished tribe. At the treaty council of Chicago, though seized with illness, he was vividly impressed by Indian sincerity and eloquence and slavery to liquor.

Of the evolution of his attitude toward the race he wrote:

Fortunately I was still young when my sphere of observation was enlarged, by seeing masses of them, in their native forests; and I, after a few years, assumed a position as government agent to one of the leading tribes, at an age when opinions are not too firmly rooted to permit change. My opinions were still, very much however, what they had been in boyhood. I looked upon them as very cannibals and blood-thirsty fellows, who were only waiting a good opportunity to knock one in the head. But I regarded them as a curious subject of observation. The remembrance of poor old Isaac, had shown me that there was some feeling and humanity in their breasts. I had seen many of them in my travels in the west, and I felt inclined to inquire into the traits of a people, among whom my duties had placed me. I had, from early youth, felt pleased with the study of natural history, and I thought the Indian, at least in his languages, might be studied with something of the same mode of exactitude. I had a strong propensity, at this time of life, for analysis, and I believed that something like an analytical process might be applied to enquiries, at least in the department of philology. Whenever a fact occurred, in the progress of my official duties, which I deemed characteristic, I made note of it, and in this way preserved a sort of skeleton of dates and events, which, it was believed, would be a source of useful future reference.

This statement embodies Schoolcraft's general approach to ethnology—his urge to observe, record and collect, and his propensity for philosophic rather than scientific methods of interpretation.

At the end of his third day as Indian Agent at the Sault, he noted in his diary that, in order to cultivate the best understanding with the Ojibway tribe, as well as for his amusement, he "commenced a vocabulary, and resolved to study their language, manners, customs, &c."

Chapters XVIII and XIX of his *Travels in the Central Portions of the Mississippi Valley,* published in 1825, indicate the new focal point of interest. One chapter has to do with observations, interspersed with anecdotes, illustrative of Indian customs and character; the other with facts and translations attesting the existence of imaginative tales and oral poetry among the Chippewas.

In making the portage from the Maumee to the Wabash, on this journey, Schoolcraft experienced a night in an Indian wigwam, whose hospitality was as memorable as its drunken riot.   This, and an Indian village at the junction of the Little River with the Wabash, inspired a lengthy consideration of the Indian, including a portion of a memorandum addressed to the Secretary of War October 24, 1821, by Governor Cass.   Schoolcraft, on his own part, continued the subject by quoting from the *Quarterly Review* of December, 1824, that

our acquaintance with the peculiarities of Indian customs and character, has unfortunately, in general, been derived from the reports of traders—usually the most ignorant, and depraved, and dishonest part of the transatlantic white population: or of persons totally uneducated, who have lived in captivity, or from choice among them; or of well-meaning, but illiterate and simple missionaries.

Then he goes on to mention Heckewelder as having only opened the door of inquiry.

It remains for others to enlarge and compare, to continue and perfect what has been so well begun.   To accumulate materials is our first duty.   The labour of generalization must follow, but it is a labour for which the whole mass of our present information affords but feeble and doubtful aids.

Also in this volume, he made the statement:

The collection of the traditions existing among the Indians is of itself a labour that demands years.   The comparison of these traditions with the observations of the discoverers and early French, English, Spanish, and Scandinavian writers upon the aborigines, requires access to antique works, many of which are rarely to be found in America, and some of which are even difficult to be procured in Europe.   The rejection of all that is vague, contradictory, or irrelevant, in these two great means of information, and the selection and composition of anything like a clear, methodical, and authentic history of our Indians, is a work that must demand time, and means and powers of discrimination, neither of which we possess.

Schoolcraft, while he spent most of his leisure time studying the Indians, somehow had the sense to know that he could not, in his period, with the facilities at his command, do work of final interpretation and generalization such as is being done now by the efforts of enlightened scholarship and the cooperation of great libraries throughout the world. It would have been a waste of precious time, for no permanent good. Such a definitive production as *The Indians of the Western Great Lakes, 1615–1760,* by Dr. W. V. Kinietz, issued in 1940, by the University of Michigan Press, has only recently been possible. Schoolcraft's contribution was to garner for the students of tomorrow. This he did, with tireless energy.

It may have been the effect of the constant procession of deaths in his family, especially of those younger than himself, or premonitory symptoms of the paralysis that was to come. Whatever the reason, his disinclination to attempt to organize his material was deliberate. Referring to himself, as editor, in the third person, he wrote in the preface to *Oneóta,* in 1845:

These accumulations . . . assumed such a shape as to require much leisure for their consideration, and rendered it less and less probable, every year, that this amount of leisure could be had. Besides, he doubted in the end, and as years advanced, whether he should not be doing better to print the rough materials of this part of his collection, than to attempt to give a polish and elementary completeness to them, which, after all his best efforts, it might be found more appropriately the vocation of another to execute.

One of the Ojibway fables that Schoolcraft recorded runs as follows:

Manibozho, when he had killed a moose, was greatly troubled as to the manner in which he should eat the animal. "If I begin at the head," said he, "they will say I eat him head first. If I begin at the side, they will say I eat him sideways. If I begin at the tail, they will say I eat him tail first."

While he deliberated, the wind caused two limbs of a tree that touched to make a harsh creaking noise. "I cannot eat with this noise," said he, and immediately climbed the tree to prevent it, where he was caught by the arm and held fast between the two trees. Whilst thus held, a pack of hungry wolves came that way and devoured the carcass of the moose before his eyes.

Schoolcraft took the meaning of this to heart and quibbled away no valuable time on questions of manner or method in collecting Indian lore.

His writings, after almost a hundred years, are still a mass of unsorted, unsmelted ore of ethnology. As this book is being written, however, a great step is being taken toward recovery and refinement of its precious content. An index of his six-volume masterpiece has just been completed by the Bureau of Ethnology of the Smithsonian Institution, and will soon be available to scholars. Such an undertaking, at this day, is an eloquent tribute to the importance of his contribution.

The Ojibway language—its vocabulary and grammar—more than any other phase of Indian life inspired his concentrated study. Yet even in this, his contribution has been to the wealth of material rather than to final analysis. This was the first thing he undertook at the Sault for his amusement. He worked on it assiduously. When his dog chewed the manuscript, with all its complicated grammatical listings, into bits, he conquered his discouragement, gathered the wet shreds, and laboriously puzzled the record together again.

He was one of the earliest to perceive that classification of the various tribes must be made eventually on the basis of language. In his *Travels* published in 1825 he made the comment, "No successful effort has yet been made, to classify the numerous tribes of our Indians, by the only standard which can be depended on,—their languages." A long footnote in the same book gives the material on the vocabulary and grammar of the Potawatamis that Dr. Wolcott sent to Governor Cass.

In the summer of 1827 at Butte des Morts, he

embraced the opportunity of the delay created by the Winnebago outbreak, and the presence of the Stockbridges [Mohegans] on the treaty ground, to obtain from them some outlines of their history and language. Every day, the chiefs and old men came to my quarters, and spent some time with me. Metoxon gave me the words for a vocabulary of the language, and, together with Quinney, entered so far into its principles, and furnished such examples, as led me, at once, to perceive that it was of the Algonquin type, near akin, indeed, to the Chippewa, and the conclusion followed, that all the New England dialects, which were cognate with this, were of the same type. The history of this people clears up, with such disclosures, and the fact shows us how little we can know of their history without the languages.

In various places Schoolcraft gives divergent spellings and definitions of Chippewa words. It would be strange if he did not. Such differences existed. The name Cheboygan for instance, appears to be someone's interpretation of "jee-bah-bee-yah," as applied by Sugar Island Chippewas to "a way around," i.e., a channel connecting two bodies of water. A valuable vocabulary table in Schoolcraft's six-volume work illustrates the variations in usage and pronunciation among several bands of the same tribe. There are also discrepancies among members of the same Indian family on Sugar Island. Although the spelling and pronunciation of Baraga have come to be to Chippewa what Parisian is to the French language and Castilian to the Spanish, it is the standard merely by acceptance. The pronunciations and definitions given by Ozhaw-guscoday-wayquay, daughter of Waub-ojeeg, and her family, as School-craft tried to preserve them, are as authoritative a development of the language as any. In the old days, as Dr. Wolcott observed, Indian interpreters knew nothing. Modern phonographic recordings of the sound of Ojibway words are not beyond question. They are simply the habit and understanding of individuals, who, like many of Schoolcraft's or Baraga's informants, may be wrong. All together merely have contributed material for comparative study.

At the end of three weeks in the Sault, Schoolcraft wrote:

The study of the language, and the formation of a vocabulary and grammar have almost imperceptibly become an absorbing object. . . . The plan interests me so much, that I actually regret the time that is lost from it, in the ordinary visits of comity and ceremony, which are, however, necessary. My method is to interrogate all persons visiting the office, white and red, who promise to be useful subjects of information during the day, and to test my inquiries in the evening by reference to the Johnstons, who, being educated, and speaking at once both the English and Odjibwa correctly, offer a higher and more reliable standard than usual. . . .

Mrs. Johnston is a woman of excellent judgment and good sense; she is referred to on abstruse points of the Indian ceremonies and usages, so that I have in fact stumbled, as it were, on the only family in North West America who could, in Indian lore, have acted as my "guide, philosopher and friend."

Continuing arduously through the years the studies of the Indian language, thus begun the third day of his residence, he made a "complete lexicon," and "reduced its grammar to a philosophical system." "It is really surprising," wrote General Cass, in a letter in 1824, in view of these researches, "that so little valuable information has been given to the world on these subjects."

Mr. Duponceau, President of the American Philosophical Society, who translated into French, for the National Institute of France, from two of Schoolcraft's lectures on Ojibway grammar before the Algic Society, wrote with reference to them, in 1834: "His description of the composition of words in the Chippewa language is the most elegant I have yet seen. He is an able and most perspicuous writer, and treats his subject philosophically."

In 1855, writing about the dictionary he had compiled, Schoolcraft notes in the appendix of his *Summary Narrative:*

On referring to the manuscript of this vocabulary, it is found to fill a large folio volume, which puts it out of my power to insert it in this connection. It is hoped to bring it into the series of the ethnological volumes, now in the process of being published at Philadelphia, under the auspices of Congress.

That anticipation never was fulfilled. His work remains unpublished, but is preserved in the Schoolcraft papers of the Library of Congress as a large boxed sheaf of papers marked "Ojibwa vocabulary." Pages 203–210 of his *Narrative of an Expedition . . . in 1832* give a word list through A and B.

Schoolcraft explained some of his ethnological points of view as follows:

The author . . . has made observations which do not, in all

respects, coincide with the commonly received opinions, and drawn some conclusions which are directly adverse to them. He has been placed in scenes and circumstances of varied interest, and met with many characters, in the course of four and twenty years' residence and travel in the wilds of America, who would have struck any observer as original and interesting. With numbers of them, he has formed an intimate acquaintance, and with not a few, contracted lasting friendships. Connected with them by a long residence, by the exercise of official duties, and by still more delicate and sacred ties, he has been regarded by them as one identified with their history, and received many marks of their confidence.

His marriage, in 1823, to Miss Jane Johnston, granddaughter of the Ojibway chief Waub-ojeeg, gave him a much superior point of vantage, so far as understanding of the Indian was concerned, than that possessed by most of the thousands of white men who have entered into miscegenatory arrangements with Indian women. To begin with, as he himself stresses, his was not a questionable association but an honorable connection with the race, such as to denote respect and inspire trust in return. His half-Indian wife had a good English schooling. Although educated Indians at the time were not a rarity, it is noteworthy that educated Indians are not always gifted along the lines of language and literature, just as all educated white men—then and now—are not informed and able in these fields. Jane Johnston Schoolcraft was not only cultured but had literary talent. She wrote excellent verse. Her Scotch-Irish father had a genteel Irish education, had collected an unusual library in the wilderness, and showed some skill in both prose and lyric composition. Most significant, however, are the facts that Jane Johnston Schoolcraft's grandfather, the Ojibway chief Waub-ojeeg, was outstanding, actually famous, in his tribe as a story-teller and a creator of songs; and that Jane Schoolcraft's full-blood Ojibway mother inherited, in addition to her father's strength of mind and character, Waub-ojeeg's gifts of memory, imagination, and expression. Henry Rowe Schoolcraft, with his own marked literary inclinations, eager interest, and tremendous energy, married into the most highly-developed literary family of the Lake Superior Indians. He gained not only the psychological advantage of intimate understanding, by means of which to learn and evaluate subtle phases of Indian thought that custom and suspicion of the whites tended to bury in oblivion; he also secured a favored place at an artesian outlet of Indian imaginative lore.

As early as 1820 he had recorded, en route:

A brilliant mass of native copper, weighing ten or twelve pounds, was found by an Indian, some years ago, on the shores of this lake. The moment he espied it, his imagination was fired, and he fancied he beheld the form of a beautiful female, standing in the water. Glittering in radiancy, she held out in her hand a lump of gold. He paddled his canoe towards her, furtively and slow, but, as he advanced, a transformation gradually ensued. Her eyes lost their brilliancy, her face the glow of life and health, her arms disappeared; and when he reached the spot, the object had changed into a stone monument of the human form, with the tail of a fish. Amazed, he sat awhile in silence; then, lighting his pipe, he offered it the incense of tobacco, and addressed it, as the guardian angel of his country. Lifting the miraculous image gently into his canoe, he took his seat, with his face in an opposite direction, and paddled towards shore, on reaching which, and turning round to the object of his regard, he discovered, in its place, nothing but a lump of shining virgin copper.

Such are the imaginative efforts of this race, who look to the eyes of civilization as if they had themselves faces of stone, and hearts of adamant.

Less than a month after his establishment at Sault Ste. Marie he recorded, in July, 1822:

Nothing has surprised me more in the conversations which I have had with persons acquainted with the Indian customs and character, than to find that the Chippewas amuse themselves with oral tales of a mythological or allegorical character. Some of these tales, which I have heard, are quite fanciful, and the wildest of them are very characteristic of their notions and customs. They often take the form of allegory, and in this shape appear designed to teach some truth or illustrate some maxim. The fact, indeed, of such a fund of fictitious legendary matter is quite a discovery. . . . What have all the voyagers and remarkers . . . been about, not to have discovered this curious trait, which lifts up indeed a curtain, as it were, upon the Indian mind, and exhibits it in an entirely new character?

He gathered these tales eagerly, from the Johnstons, from old story-tellers at their fireside, from visitors at the Agency, through many winters.

Francis W. Shearman, who spent the frozen season of 1836 in the family of Mr. Schoolcraft at Mackinac Island, records continuance of Schoolcraft's custom: "As the Indians came to the Agency, they were requested to relate some one or more of their favorite legends."

A unique opportunity had come to Schoolcraft. He recognized and was equal to it. Beyond question the legends were oral when he discovered them. Through his quick appreciation of their value and his natural instinct to chronicle and make chroniclers of others, he was the direct means of fixing them in writing. In "Mash-kwa-sha-kwong," on pages 139–145 of *Oneóta,* he has preserved one of the tales exactly at the point of passing from tradition to the written word.

His feeling of scientific responsibility in regard to this folklore is evident in the following, written May 25, 1835, in his *Memoirs:*

I have long deliberated what I should do with my materials, denoting a kind of oral literature among the Chippewas and other tribes, in the shape of legends and wild tales of the imagination. The narrations themselves are often so incongruous, grotesque, and fragmentary, as to require some hand better than mine, to put them in shape. And yet, I feel that nearly all their value, as indices of Indian imagination, must depend on preserving their original form. Some little time since, I wrote to Washington Irving on the subject. In a response of this date, he observes:

"The little I have seen of our Indian tribes has awakened an earnest anxiety to know more concerning them, and, if possible, to embody some of their fast-fading characteristics and traditions in our popular literature. My own personal opportunities of observing them must, necessarily, be few and casual; but I would gladly avail myself of any information derived from others who have been enabled to mingle among them, and capacitated to perceive and appreciate their habits, customs, and moral qualities. I know of no one to whom I would look with more confidence, in these respects, than to yourself; and, I assure you, I should receive as high and unexpected favors any communication of the kind you suggest, that would aid me in furnishing biographies, tales or sketches, illustrative

of Indian life, Indian character, and Indian mythology and superstitions."

Schoolcraft was not satisfied by Irving's attitude.

I had never regarded these manuscripts, gleaned from the lodges
with no little pains-taking, as mere materials to be worked up by the
literary loom, although the work should be done by one of the most
popular and fascinating American pens. I feared that the roughness,
which gave them their characteristic originality and Doric truthful-
ness, would be smoothed and polished off to assume the shape of a
sort of Indo-American series of tales; a cross between the Anglo-
Saxon and the Algonquin.

On January 26, 1838, Schoolcraft noted in his *Memoirs:*

Completed the revision of a body of Indian oral legends, collected
during many years with labor. These oral tales show up the Indian
in a new light. Their chief value consists in their exhibition of
aboriginal opinions. But, if published, incredulity will start up
critics to call their authenticity in question. There are so many
Indian tales fancied, by writers, that it will hardly be admitted that
there exist any real legends. If there be any literary labor which has
cost me more than usual pains, it is this. I have weeded out many
vulgarisms. I have endeavored to restore the simplicity of the original style. In this I have not always fully succeeded, and it has been
sometimes found necessary, to avoid incongruity, to break a legend
in two, or cut it short off.

With folklore, as with all gifts, it is unprofitable to be
critical in the ways of gratefulness. Whatever may have
attached to the Schoolcraft versions of Ojibway tales, either
from the Celtic admixture in the Johnston family or from the
personality of Schoolcraft himself, we can only count ourselves
fortunate to have the material in as pure a form as it has been
given us. The artists commissioned by Pisistratus to preserve the Homeric legends undoubtedly added to, subtracted
from, and rearranged the material they found. Geoffrey of
Monmouth must have somewhat molded the Arthurian legends
that he collected. No matter. They perpetuated glimpses of
individualities and customs and ways of thinking that otherwise would have been lost. Schoolcraft snatched from oblivion
an important body of the tales of dark and dawn in North
America. He deserves whole-hearted gratitude.

Two slender volumes of Indian folklore were issued June 1, 1839. The press was uniformly generous and kind, if not always understanding. Schoolcraft wrote:

It is difficult for an editor to judge, from the mere face of the volumes, what an amount of auxiliary labor it has required to collect these legends from the Indian wigwams. They had to be gleaned and translated from time to time. Seventeen years have passed since I first began them—not that anything like this time, or the half of it, has been devoted to it. It was one of my amusements in the long winter evenings—the only time of the year when Indians will tell stories and legends. They required pruning and dressing, like wild vines in a garden. But they are, exclusively (with the exception of the allegory of the vine and oak), wild vines, and not pumpings up of my own fancy. The attempts to lop off excrescences are not, perhaps, always happy. There might, perhaps, have been a fuller adherence to the original language and expressions; but if so, what a world of verbiage must have been retained. The Indians are prolix, and attach value to many minutiae in the relation which not only does not help forward the denouement, but is tedious and witless to the last degree. The gems of the legends—the essential points—the invention and thought-work are all preserved.

Their chief value I have ever thought to consist in the insight they give into the dark cave of the Indian mind—its beliefs, dogmas, and opinions—its secret modes of turning over thought—its real philosophy; and it is for this trait that I believe posterity will sustain the book.

American ethnology was fortunate to have, in his position, in his period, a man of Schoolcraft's interest and energy, with so much of the scholar's viewpoint as is expressed in that last paragraph and in the indubitably scientific title, *Algic Researches*.

His genius in ethnology as elsewhere was to whip up facts where only a vacuum had been before, to create enthusiasm out of inertness, to organize idle interest into cooperative activity. He enlisted, in the work of garnering, many individuals who otherwise would never have contributed. With those already in the field he collaborated unstintedly. He fueled and fanned interest wherever a spark showed.

In a letter dated November 8, 1837, to one of the Johnstons, he urged:

Write to me by all the expresses, and do not forget my desire to bring forward my work on the intellectual character of the Indians, their traditions, tales, &c. It is in your power to contribute important aid, as you have heretofore done, and your name and labours shall be duly noticed.

His organizing efforts appeared as early as 1819, when in his *A View of the Lead Mines of Missouri*, he advocated a society for the study of the antiquities of America. The Historical Society of Michigan, and the Algic Society in Detroit, were in part manifestations of his devotion to the study of the American Indian and his organizing energy in that direction.

The Algic Society, of which he was principal founder and first president, was constituted in Detroit in October, 1832. The adjective in the name was derived by Schoolcraft himself from the words *Algonquin* and *akee,* earth or land, to denote a genus or family of tribes who take their characteristic from the use of the Algonquin language. It is interesting to observe, in this organization, a combination of practical philanthropy, literary activity, and scholarly reasearch.

One of its objects was to collect and disseminate practical information respecting their language, history, traditions, customs, and character; their numbers and condition; the geographical features of the country they inhabit; and its natural history and productions. . . . The place was deemed favorable . . . for the collection of original information.

"It was not intended to be exclusively a missionary or educational society, but also, to collect scientific and statistical information essential to both objects," for the use of laborers on the frontiers and to answer inquiries made by agents authorized by the General Boards from the old States. It resolved to "procure an exact statistical account of the names, numbers and location of the different bands of Indians, of the Algonquin stock, now living within the limits of the United States."

As President of the Algic Society, Schoolcraft was requested by resolution to deliver, at convenient times, a course of lectures on the grammatical construction of the Algonquin language, as spoken by the Northwestern Tribes, and to procure, from living and authentic sources, a full and complete lexicon of that language for the use of the organization. These lectures were delivered before the St. Marys committee, whose members, together with those resident at Michilimackinac, constituted a standing committee of the Society. Two of the lectures were published, as an appendix, under the title "Indian Language," in his *Narrative of an Expedition through the Upper Mississippi to Itasca Lake*, in 1834; and two in *Oneóta*. All four lectures may be found in Schoolcraft's *Summary Narrative . . .*, published in 1855. The first two have been credited with translation in full in French by Peter Stephen Duponceau for the prize-winning paper on the Algonquin language, before the National Institute of France; though the *Historical Magazine* of May, 1865, in a considered and considerate evaluation of Schoolcraft's work, after his death, says the statement about the award is not true.

The facts appear to be that M. Duponceau wrote voluntarily to Schoolcraft in October, 1834:

I have read with very great pleasure, your interesting narrative of the expedition to the sources of the Mississippi, and particularly your lectures on the Chippewa language, and the vocabulary which follows it. It is one of the most philosophical works on the Indian languages I have ever read; it gives a true view of their structure, without exaggeration or censure, and must satisfy the mind of every rational man.

The following year, on February 28, Mr. Schoolcraft quotes in his *Memoirs* another communication from the distinguished philologist:

The philosophy of our Indian languages has become very fashionable among the learned in Europe. The Institute of France has offered a premium of a gold medal, of the value of 1200 francs, for the best essay on the grammatical construction of the family of North American languages, of which the Chippewa, the Delaware and Mohegan are considered the principal branches, of course including the Iroquois, Wyandot, Naudowessie, &c. The premium is to be awarded on the first of May next. I would have informed you of it at the time, if it had not been made a sine qua non that the memoirs should be written in Latin or French. I have, therefore, ventured on sending one, in which I have availed myself of your excellent grammar, giving credit for it, as in duty bound. I have literally translated what you say at the beginning of your first and of your second lecture, which will be found the best part of my work, as it is impossible to describe the character of those languages with more clearness and elegance.

In Duponceau's *Systéme grammatical des langues,* published in Paris in 1838, Schoolcraft's lectures are quoted on pages 131 to 134; his conclusions are compared with those of Charlevoix on pages 134 to 136; and his lectures then analyzed, passim to page 147.

This essay, in May, 1835, won for M. Duponceau the Volney cash prize of *Linguistique* from the French Institute. According to no less an authority than the first and most learned philologist of America, Peter Duponceau himself, his literal translation from Schoolcraft was the best part of the work that gained the award.

That is high praise enough for Schoolcraft or any scholar. Also it affords an amazing picture of the place in the learned circles of the world that was attained, through Schoolcraft, by the little frontier settlement of Sault Ste. Marie where the lectures were delivered. In addition, this must be interpreted as distinguished recognition indeed for the achievements of the Algic Society of Michigan as an organization for the promotion of the study of ethnology.

At the first anniversary of the Algic Society, held in Detroit, October 12, 1833, Schoolcraft submitted a report of the proceedings of the St. Marys Committee, and delivered "a poetic address on the character of the race." There are one or two indications of meetings being held during the succeeding eight or ten years, but the information available concerning the operation of the Society is meager. The Detroit Public Library has the Constitution of the Society printed in Detroit in 1833, which gives, in addition, an abstract of proceedings of several meetings held in Detroit during the month of October, 1832; a long list of officers and members both honorary and active; an address delivered presumably by Mr. Schoolcraft at the time of its organization; and an abstract of proceedings of the St. Marys Committee for December, 1832, and January, 1833. The minutes of the monthly meetings of the St. Marys Committee showed that a valuable body of information had been collected respecting the population and statistics of the Chippewa nation, the grammatical structure of their language, etc.

The above statement of one phase of the objectives and activities of the Algic Society may give Sault Ste. Marie and Detroit and Michigan some shadow of a claim to the organization of the first ethnological society in America, or at least one of the first. Whatever its status, in many ways it promoted the study of ethnology at home and abroad.

Schoolcraft personally was, beyond question, importantly concerned in the founding of the first ethnological society in the United States. It was in New York, in 1819, that he had published his first book, the final page of which was devoted to a statement of the need of such an organization. In the same city, in 1842, soon after he had moved his residence there, "he was instrumental, with Mr. John R. Bartlett, Mr. H. C. Murphy, Mr. Folsom and other ethnologists, in forming the American Ethnological Society." Schoolcraft was a charter member and served as one of the early vice-presidents of this important body.

When the Board of Regents of the Smithsonian Institution held their first meeting, at Washington, D. C., in September, 1846, Schoolcraft submitted a plan for the investigation of American ethnology. This was reprinted in the Annual Report of that Institution for 1885, with the comment:

The following programme, though never officially adopted by the Smithsonian Institution, embodies the result of much study by the distinguished author; and even after the lapse of forty years possesses sufficient interest and suggestiveness to justify its publication.

He was an instigational influence in starting the first ethnological periodical in the world. As early as March 20, 1825, he wrote, in his *Memoirs*, "The plan of a magazine devoted to Indian subjects, which has been discussed between Mr.

Conant, Mr. Dwight, and myself, is now definitely arranged with Messrs. Wilder and Campbell, publishers." Nothing came of this projected New York City publication, apparently.

Publisher or no publisher he would not be turned from his purpose. He issued and circulated such a periodical, as a manuscript magazine, at Sault Ste. Marie, Michigan, late the same year.

It is debatable whether *Oneóta,* in its first published form of eight numbers, in paper covers, irregularly issued beginning in August, 1844, may properly be regarded as a periodical. Like magazines in general, it is a miscellany. Articles by others than Schoolcraft are included, and solicited. Some of its features continue serially from one number to another. It is definitely an ethnological publication, and its tone is that of a journal, encouraging and trying to coordinate interest in its special field.

He saw the fruition of his efforts after twenty years, when, as a charter member of the American Ethnological Society, its transactions were first published in 1845. They antedated those of the Ethnological Society of England by three years. Schoolcraft, thus, was a pioneer in the field of ethnological periodical publication, not only in the United States but in the world.

After he had ceased to be connected with the conduct of official Indian affairs in Michigan, and following a visit to Europe in 1842, Schoolcraft traveled through western Virginia, Ohio, Southern Michigan, and into Ontario as far as Dundas where his wife had died during his absence across the ocean. The chief subject of his printed account of this journey was American archaeology.

The mound at the mouth of the Normanskill, which gave it the Mohawk name of Tawasentha, "place of many dead," had seized his imagination early and held it throughout life. Of this ancient monument he said, in 1860, in an essay on Albany County, New York, in Munsell's *Annals of Albany:*

This curious natural mound, or hillock, is connected with the diluvial formation, by a narrow rock, or peninsula. It was a spot sacred to sepulture, from the earliest time; and furnished them a natural cognomen for the stream. There is no object of higher antiquarian interest in the vicinity, and it is worthy of municipal care.

In his twenty-fourth year, in a published notice concerning some archaeological discoveries made in Hamburg, Erie County, New York, he first noted the necessity of discriminating between the antique European and the aboriginal period, in American archaeology. This appears to be the same paper that is reprinted in his *A View of the Lead Mines of Missouri,* in 1819, in connection with glass beads found on Big River, Missouri. A number of other such items, including discussions of an antique silver cup found in a mound near Marietta, Ohio, and of supposed dwarf skeletons unearthed near St. Louis, Missouri, were printed in this work on the mines of Missouri.

He displayed an unusual amateur interest in archaeology on that first western expedition, by visiting and describing the mounds at Marietta and those in Illinois opposite St. Louis, and by studying Governor Clark's Indian museum at the latter city. At Bull Shoals, on the White River, in Arkansas, he noted what he described as the

seat of metallurgical operations prior to the deposition of alluvial soils on its banks. . . . Beneath this soil are imbedded the reliqua in question. Thus imbedded masses of a metallic alloy, manifestly the production of art, with bits of earthen pots, and arrow-heads chipped out of flint, horn-stone, and jasper, are found. The metallic alloy appears, from hardness and colour, to be lead united with silver or tin. It is not well refined, although it may be easily cut with a knife. The earthenware appears to have been submitted to the action of fire, and has suffered no decay.

He procured specimens for himself, and sent duplicates to Dr. Samuel L. Mitchill of New York.

In his narrative of the expedition to the Upper Mississippi in 1820, he incorporated Carver's description of the earthworks below Lake Pepin. This mound, and stories of others on the River St. Peter, helped to make exploration of that tributary one of his long-cherished, though ultimately disappointed, ambitions.

A deepening interest is shown in his *Travels in the Central Portions of the Mississippi Valley*. The supposed prints of human feet in rock found near St. Louis claimed considerable attention. He included a letter describing them in situ; gave his own account of the slab as he saw it at Harmony, Indiana; and included in the appendix an engraving by Inman from a tracing that he himself made. The *American Journal of Science* carried an account of his observations, with the figure drawn by Schoolcraft. Twenty miles below Harmony, on the Wabash River, he noted bones and antique pottery that had been revealed by the inroads of that stream upon a burial mound, with an appreciation of the necessity of discriminating between recent and more ancient monuments. At the salt mines of Illinois he observed at a depth of eighty feet vessels of eight or ten-gallon capacity; recalling that at an early iron age in Saxony and Lorraine brine-springs were evaporated by running the liquid over heated pottery of the coarsest description, and that a similar process was employed on the coasts of Belgium and Brittany. He described with interest the ancient works at Marietta, Ohio, and the truncated-cone mounds at Vincennes, Indiana; presented a picture of Mount Joliet, Illinois, in the appendix; and revisited the Belleville, Illinois, mounds near St. Louis.

So great was his interest in what he saw at Grave Creek Flats that he revisited the place twenty-two years later. Grave Creek Mound meantime, in 1838, had been excavated. In fact, archaeology was completely dominant as his study in the expedition of 1843, following his trip to Europe, which may possibly have sharpened his appreciation of that phase of study. In any event his record of that journey, as given in *Oneóta* is largely confined to descriptions and discussions of Grave Creek Flats; garden beds in Michigan; various objects found at Oakland, Thunder Bay, and Isle Ronde, Michigan, and on St. Joseph Island, Ontario; and to an examination of an extensive burying ground near Dundas, in the last-named Province.

The first year of the existence of the American Ethnological Society, he read at least two papers before it: one on the

Washington March 25th 1848

Dear Sir,

I have received your favour of the 7th Feb. by the hands of Mr Brockway enclosed to the Commissioner. The account of the old monument on the apex of a mountain near lake St. Croix, is very curious, & interesting. I should be happy to obtain a plan & drawing, & have written to Mr David Dale Owen, who is charged with the public surveys of the lands between the St. Croix & Chippewa rivers. I am in hopes that some of his people have been led to it. I am told that Bruce is a man of veracity, & am therefore in hopes that the discovery will not prove an illusion. Should it not, it must add an important element to our antiquarian knowledge. If you obtain any thing further, be sure to let me know it.

Ever truly Yours,

Henry R Schoolcraft

A LETTER FROM SCHOOLCRAFT TO GEORGE JOHNSTON (SEE PAGE 595).

The lake

in the inscription, that have a foreign look. Such are several figures like this Y. The square piece on the heads of men, thus 8, looks as if meant for a hat. Were there ancient frontlets like this? Point out these things, & to Wau-bo-jeeg & his mother.

With regard to the land claims, the Com. of the General Land office, thinks the law defective, & is embarrassed about writing instructions I think he may send out, Mr Wilson, the chief clerk, to see to them.

As to Eliza & look to Mr

inscribed stone known as the Dighton Rock in the town of Assonet, Massachusetts, comprising a full analysis of the characters found on it, with their explanation furnished by an Indian of the Chippewa tribe; and another on some curious evidences of an era of ancient semi-civilization in the West, noticed in the progress of settlements in the Mississippi valley and the lakes. An article by him on Grave Creek Mound is the third in the first volume of the *Transactions* of the Society.

In 1845, at the time of the taking of the State census, the Legislature of New York authorized Schoolcraft to enumerate and collect other statistics of the Iroquois or Six Nations. This valuable report to the Secretary of New York State was reissued in 1846 in a volume entitled *Notes on the Iroquois;* and a popular account, under the same title, in 1847.

The desirability of collecting and preserving similar facts about all the Indian tribes of the United States impressed him to the point where he was able to communicate this conviction to the powers in Washington. A memorial presented to Congress November 30, 1846, bearing the signatures of twenty-nine citizens including Schoolcraft, requested that the Indian Bureau be directed to collect and digest such statistics and materials as might illustrate the history, present condition, and prospects of the Indian tribes in the United States. This paper, in the promulgation of which Schoolcraft was leader, brought the subject of the American aborigines to the notice of the members of Congress in an important way. Schoolcraft expressed the opinion, enforcing it by facts drawn from many years' experience and residence on the frontiers, that the Indian question was misunderstood; the authentic published materials from which the Indians were to be judged were fragmentary and scanty; and that the public policy respecting them, and the mode of applying their funds and dealing with them, was in many respects unjust.

During the following session, on March 3, 1847, an Act of Congress, carrying an appropriation, was passed, authorizing the Secretary of War to have this work done; and Schoolcraft was appointed on the following March 18 "in the office of Indian affairs, to aid and assist in collecting and digesting a census and statistics of the various Indian tribes, & such material as will tend to illustrate their history, present conditions and future prospects," the appointment to become effective upon his entering upon his duties, and "to exist during the pleasure of the Secretary of War." His title, when given, seems to have been Special Agent. Schoolcraft immediately prepared and issued blank forms, calling on the officers of the department for the necessary statistical facts. At the same time a comprehensive system of questionnaires was distributed in an endeavor to elicit the true condition of the Indian tribes from men of experience in all parts of the Union.

Work on the resulting *Historical and Statistical Information Respecting the History, Condition and Prospects of the Indian Tribes of the United States* occupied his time for ten years, most of the remainder of his life, after March, 1847. His earlier tentative title, *Ethnological Researches,* as used on page 603 of his *Memoirs,* for some reason was abandoned. The first volume appeared in 1851; Volume V, the last issued at government expense, in the summer of 1855. J. B. Lippincott and Company published Volume VI in 1857. Schoolcraft was on the payroll of the Interior Department to the end of 1857, when his connection with that Office ended, apparently (except for a brief period, from November 26, 1858, to March 13, 1859, involving service as interpreter and a trip from Washington to Detroit and return).

The six elaborate quarto volumes issued from the press under Schoolcraft's supervision, in a period when the field of criticism was suffering from a sensationally acrid spell. Longfellow's *Hiawatha* was dismissed with a sneer, as perhaps a good dictionary of Indian names. The current offerings of Thackeray and Tennyson were subjected to supercilious and rough handling. The work of Schoolcraft was and has been hailed with everything from merciless revilings to utmost adulation.

The appended estimate from the *Historical Magazine* of May, 1865, following his death, appears to be fair and considerate.

These [volumes] in a manner resume his other labors and are his great historic work. . . . In the vast array of matter here presented [in an outline of the contents of the first five volumes], others contributed much, chiefly in the departments of physical geography, tribal organization, history and government, topical history, physical type and intellectual capacity, as well as the numerous vocabularies embraced in the work. Still an immense part is directly the work of Mr. Schoolcraft. This embraces almost every branch of knowledge concerning the Indian tribes, the relics of the past, tribal customs, religion, arts, government, trade, dress, language, intercourse with others in peace and war. The subjects are treated cursorily: few articles are exhaustive treatises on any given point, and the author, taking a few facts or statements, the result of his own observations or that of others, rises to general views and theories preferring philosophical systems to a marshalling of facts and authorities. His style, too, is peculiar; with all our tendency to innovation, few Americans have coined so many new words as Mr. Schoolcraft, some of which will remain as part and parcel of the language, while others, lacking analogy or an etymological basis, never met with favor. Some words may indeed be the coinage of the printer; few works having suffered more than these noble volumes at the hands of the compositors, and in the new edition announced Messrs. Lippincott owe it to themselves to have the plates thoroughly revised.

The sixth volume is of a different character, and bears as its title "History of the Indian Tribes of the United States, their present condition and prospects, and a sketch of their ancient status, by Henry Rowe Schoolcraft, LL.D., &c. In one volume, part vi. of the series." From what we have already said of the author's natural bent of mind and maturer mode of thought and views, we are not here to expect a history of the various tribes in our territory drawn up in a condensed form, by a careful collection and judicious comparison of all the fragmentary items of information afforded us by the earliest writers and their successors in later times. As the author remarks: "personal inquiries, however efficiently made, are alone inadequate to the compilation of Indian history. Books are required; and whoever endeavors to trace the subject will find many of these to be rare, and only extant in foreign libraries." "A hurried collection of the incidents of that history during the long period of three centuries and a half has necessarily rendered this view brief and summary."

The whole volume, with the exception of the chapters on the Andastes, is, we believe, exclusively the work of Mr. Schoolcraft. . . .

After . . . separate views of tribes, the author passes to general views, bringing the history down to the present time. It is not the annals of the tribes showing their wars, development, increase or decline, civilization or progress, but rather a history of the country, regarded in the light of the intercourse of the whites with the aborigines. This was, we presume, more especially the idea of government in commencing the work.

Mr. Schoolcraft's last labor aptly closes his contributions to American history, topography, archaeology and linguistics. It is an immense repository to which students will long resort for aid in their investigations, and the full index promised with the new edition will facilitate greatly its use and enhance its value. . . . Though material for two volumes more were prepared, government suspended the publication. . . .

The late Mr. Schoolcraft, from his earlier writings, and more especially from the position which for some years past he occupied under the American government, and the series of volumes on the Indians which under his supervision were issued in so magnificent a form by the national press, has long been regarded at home and abroad as the highest authority in all relating to the aborigines of the country.

A discussion of the first three volumes of the quarto edition, in the *North American Review* of July, 1853, was harsh in its criticism of the great number of illustrations, as compared with the brevity of text; its undigested presentation; errors; and especially of its cost to the government, which was represented, in detail, from the records of Congressional appropriations, as amounting to $80,856.50 for the first three volumes, and as likely to reach $130,000 for five volumes. Some writers on Schoolcraft have quoted the cost as high as $600,000!

No official summation of expenditures seems ever to have been made. The original report of Congress called for an appropriation of five thousand a year for two years. Volume IV, which may be regarded as representative, cost $12,400 for 1200 copies; $1,896 for paper; $1,900 for drawings and other illustrations. Schoolcraft's salary on the payroll of the Office of Indian Affairs was $1600 a year at the beginning, $2,000 at the end of the project. The cost to the government, therefore, for five volumes, may have been $81,000 plus $32,000, exclusive of Schoolcraft's salary for ten years. Volume VI was issued by J. B. Lippincott & Co., apparently at no cost to the nation except for Schoolcraft's time.

The volumes themselves were appraised as, on the whole, "the most sumptuous that have yet appeared in our country, and their publication may fairly be said to form an era in the art of American book making."

There is no doubt that through Schoolcraft's convictions and persuasive efforts, the infant science of ethnology achieved governmental recognition to an unprecedented degree and was accorded a dignity of publication that aroused jealousy on the part of workers in other fields. Henry Rowe Schoolcraft had the vision and intellectual fire to carry on research unremittingly, in his own self-acquired fashion, during the groping period of the science; and the physical stamina to persevere in recording what he found when his hands were knotted into uselessness by rheumatism and paralysis. Nobody else had the strength of purpose to do what he did, much less do it better.

One notable Schoolcraftian characteristic was that he endeavored to let nothing escape him. Chaff was stored with the grain, for the possible iota of good it might some day be discovered to contain. A nursery or cradle song, a principle of grammar, a psychological peculiarity, the meanings of a few geographical names, he set them down, organized them in a fashion, published them to preserve them. The field was new and vast. His time was uncertain. Even his major work he published, as he did *Oneóta,* in subdivisions that ran serially from tome to tome.

The absence of detail in regard to many tribes only magnifies the fact that, with all the opportunity of the period, while there were many Indians and numerous Indian agents, there was only one Schoolcraft. "Both the Indian and the local officials have been either adverse to the object, imprecise in their statements, or generally indifferent to the investigation." As to the nomad tribes, "Much of the country is a terra incognita, and some of the agents located at remote points have not been in a position to report at all. Most of the tribes, conscious of having but little to exhibit, have been unwilling to report their condition." The Superintendent of Indian Affairs for California wrote to him in 1855, in response to the official questionnaire: "The settlement of this section of the country by the whites . . . began about the year 1851. . . . I regret that at present I cannot give a more detailed account of the character, number and mode of living of the Indians, as much of the country has as yet been but little explored." Yet, notwithstanding every discouragement, the material submitted, which was the result of elaborate researches, was more accurate and comprehensive than any previously obtained. There were insuperable difficulties. He did his best and kept on publishing what could be secured. In a clearcut way he recognized his opportunity and responsibility: to collect and to preserve. The time for this was passing. For organization and generalization there would be the endless future. Modestly he appraised his life's achievement in Volume VI:

In forming an estimate of the man [the Indian], in ascertaining his faults and virtues, studying his physical and mental development, and inquiring into his history, the author has spent many years of active life on the American frontier. To this object the exploration of its geography and mineralogy became at length subordinate; and if assiduity merited success, he might claim it.

An article published in the *American Geologist* in 1890, a quarter of a century after his death, reads:

His six quarto volumes, *Archives of Aboriginal Knowledge*, comprising antiquities, languages, ethnology and general history of the Indian tribes of North America, attracted much attention at the time as a valuable addition to Indian archaeology and history, and Mr. Schoolcraft received numerous tokens of appreciation not only in this country, but from many scientific and historical associations in foreign lands. At the time of its publication a scholar writing to the *Philadelphia Bulletin* said: "*The ethnological researches respecting the red men of America* by Henry R. Schoolcraft, is a monument of genius, reflecting honor on the country, and placing its author among the very highest scholars of the age and of the world. In it we find accumulated with a research which defies appreciation, an industry which is incredible, and a quick piercing genius which reads the value of every fact at a glance, a mass of material which will in future ages reveal to the scholar facts which we are as yet far from being able to develop. We know that the work and the author have been praised ere now, but we have never yet heard the one or the other estimated as they deserve; for certain we are that Germany has no better reason to boast of Hammer, Purgstall, Kaiser or Grimm; France of Michelet or Lajard; or England of any of her long array of antiquarians from Leland to Palsgrave, than we have to boast of Schoolcraft, as shown in the great work in question."

Schoolcraft's memoirs, *Thirty Years with the Indian Tribes,* published in 1851, contain much material about the race. No man was more familiar with their habits or better understood their wishes, aspirations, or peculiar conditions; and no one more truly sympathized with them. His writings will forever be associated, as an invaluable source, with matters concerning the Indians of the United States. To estimate his contribution, it is only necessary to imagine the void if his work had not been done.

The science of American ethnology had its conception in his mind as much and as early as in that of any individual. He assisted in a major way at its birth; nourished its infancy; gave it a rich endowment in its youth; and, in its maturity, is still a substantial source for its advancement and enrichment. He began early its extension beyond the continent to the hemisphere, and in many ways promoted its interests abroad.

Science, as well as art, has its geniuses and its Andrea del Sartos. In the broad conception of things, Schoolcraft is the da Vinci of American ethnology.

HISTORIAN

THE establishment of the first Michigan Historical Society and the activity of that body for the initial thirteen-year span of its existence was due to Schoolcraft more than any other individual. He founded the organization. It suspended animation for many years soon after he left the State.

Schoolcraft was elected a member of the Legislative Council of the Territory of Michigan in 1828. To take part in its proceedings he went to Detroit from the Sault. His constituents were few. Their ideas were unformed and not vocal. He was free to follow his own trends. Among other things, he says, "I directed myself to the incorporation of a historical society." After consultation with some literary friends School-craft introduced a bill, during the first session of the Third Legislative Council. This contained the wise plan of "consti-tuting the members of the Legislative Council of the Territory as members ex officio, in order to give the society official countenance and to secure a convenient place for meetings." The list of original corporators that he drew up included the names of the influential men of the time in Michigan, and his own. The charter of "The Historical Society of Michigan" was approved June 23, 1828.

Schoolcraft's resourcefulness in such matters was prodigi-ous. He secured paying members for the Society from the circle of his family, friends, and associates. At the first meet-ing, July 3, 1828, in Detroit, his father-in-law, John Johnston of the Sault, and Robert Stuart of Mackinac Island, were two of the four members elected. Schoolcraft suggested honorary members whose names added much to the prestige of the Society. The distinction of a first anniversary address by Governor Cass was arranged. Schoolcraft gave the second annual address himself, June 4, 1830, at the Capitol. These papers, when published, were sent to older organizations of the kind in the East and to individuals eminent in government and in scholarly pursuits. This circularization not only advanced the standing of the Society but secured exchanges and gifts which forwarded the work of his committee for the collection of books and pamphlets on the history of the United States and Michigan in particular. His own contributions added to this nucleus of a library and to that of a historical museum.

One example of the carrying power of his personal interest is afforded by the effort to establish a periodical to promote the interests of the Society. In 1830, a committee was appointed to consider the expediency of this. Schoolcraft was a member. Nothing came of the gesture. Schoolcraft, however, did not give up the idea individually. July 1, 1840, he wrote in his *Memoirs* that he was trying to gather materials for the publica-tion of a volume of collections by the Society. He had enough of his own manuscripts for several volumes. Several gentlemen of national prominence whom he had addressed for contributions were interested but too busy.   From other sources several manuscript communications had been obtained.   By the spring of 1841 he had proceeded so far as to procure an estimate of the cost of a volume, "for which I am taking every means of preparing the materials.   I am satisfied that without publication the Historical Society cannot acquire a basis with the literary world to stand upon."   Unfortunately no funds were available, or procurable.

The most striking indication of his influence on the birth and life of the organization is the parallel between his presence and its activity.

Governor Cass, who as its first president gave the infant Historical Society the encouragement of his keen interest and the prestige of his position and personality, had been in Detroit the better part of two decades.   It was no coincidence that the Society sprang into being less than two months after Schoolcraft, with his genius for scholarly organization, arrived in the frontier capital as a member of the Legislative Council.

Schoolcraft's two terms in the Council ended in 1831. With this his protracted visits in the Territorial capital ceased. After the annual meeting of the Michigan Historical Society in September, 1832, it lapsed into inaction.   Significantly it revived, after an interregnum of five years, shortly after Schoolcraft moved to Detroit as Superintendent of Indian Affairs. Then it had its first gathering in his office, March 18, 1837, and elected him president.   Schoolcraft left Detroit and Michigan in 1841.   The last recorded reference to a meeting of the Society was an adjournment to January 30, 1841.   For sixteen years following there was apparently no activity.   Schoolcraft clearly was the Atlas of Michigan's earliest historical organization.   When it began its third phase of existence, in 1857, at the time he was in Washington, D. C., he was made an honorary member.

Historical and Scientific Sketches of Michigan, a publication of the Michigan Historical Society, appeared in 1834.   So wise an authority as Justice James V. Campbell wrote of it, in his *Outlines of the Political History of Michigan,* that "it remains among the best synopses of the State's history that have ever been prepared." This contains two addresses by Schoolcraft: one before the Historical Society and another for the Detroit Lyceum. It may easily prove, on investigation, that he had more to do with the editing and publishing of this volume than is now apparent. In this connection the following facts are worth consideration.

The enterprising George L. Whitney, although he had been in Detroit for several years, did not undertake to publish these addresses of 1830 and 1831 until the summer of 1834, as shown by a footnote on page 215. That summer Schoolcraft, then living at Mackinac Island, made at least two visits to Detroit, in spite of an outbreak of cholera in that city. George L. Whitney was at this time printing at least two other books for Schoolcraft: *The Man of Bronze,* and the *Narrative* of his expedition of 1832. Mr. Whitney had Schoolcraft to thank for the contract to print the *Narrative* for Harper and Brothers, New York publishers. Schoolcraft, driven by a deep-rooted conviction that the Historical Society of Michigan needed to publish in order to gain prestige, spent thought and time for more than a decade trying to provide for this. Each time he received a journal from one of the many Eastern societies of which he was a member, there was a troubled resurgence of his activity. It is only reasonable that he would attempt to persuade the printer Whitney, on the basis of two jobs already given him in 1834, to publish the *Sketches.* The popularity of Schoolcraft's preceding travel books and the even wider appeal of his forthcoming story of the discovery of the source of the Mississippi, with consequent arousal of general curiosity about the Territory of Michigan, would have been strong arguments that the *Sketches* might command an unusual market.

The disproportion of the reference in the preface of the *Sketches* in apology for the inclusion of a geological item might be construed as evidence of Schoolcraft's hand in editing the volume. That he had something to do with its preparation is clear from two footnotes added by him: one mentioning the

Algic Society in 1833; another describing an event in the spring of 1834.

In any event it is significant to note that, without consideration of the fact that more than a quarter of the space given to Schoolcraft is crowded with type of foot-note size, by actual page count Schoolcraft's writings constitute more than one-third of the volume.

From 1842 to 1847, after Schoolcraft returned from Europe and before he moved to Washington, D. C., he was active in the affairs of the New-York Historical Society. His name appeared at the head of a committee which issued a circular from the rooms of that organization in 1844, asking information regarding the Indian names for all geographical features in New York State, for use in making a map. Earlier the same year he had presented a report to the Society on the aboriginal names and geographical terminology of the State. In 1842 he read a paper before it on the subject of scientific associations abroad; and, in 1845, one on the siege and defense of Fort Schuyler. He delivered the anniversary address for the Society in 1846, and on another occasion gave a paper on antique earthen vessels found in tumuli in certain Southern States. The same year he spoke before an association of young men at Aurora, New York, who were interested in the investigation of Iroquois history.

The 1847 edition of his *Notes on the Iroquois* is in the form of a popular narrative history.

Schoolcraft chose historical subjects for some of his imaginative flights such as *Alhalla,* which is a tale of the Creek war; *Helderbergia,* based on the anti-rent disturbances in the vicinity of Albany, New York; and *A Curt History of the United States after the Hebraic Manner.*

An interest in the biographical facet of history is evidenced in numerous footnotes; an account of Moses Austin and his family in Missouri and Texas; sketches of various Indian individuals in *Oneóta* and elsewhere; and a short biography of Lewis Cass. Schoolcraft's correspondence with the Austins, as yet unpublished, is noteworthy. In the years immediately following Schoolcraft's first visit to Missouri, Moses Austin found himself facing bankruptcy. Under urgent need of selling his Missouri holdings, he commissioned Schoolcraft to auction them, if necessary, in New York. These letters illuminate not only the life of the Austin family but a colorful page of the story of the Southwest. Incidentally, the degree of confidence placed in one so young, especially on such short acquaintance, bears witness to the rare qualities of Schoolcraft.

His historical perception and enthusiasm caused the writing of memoirs which otherwise would never have been undertaken. Not only did he inspire the recording of much traditional and recent history of the Chippewa nation, from his first wife's Indian mother's memory; he encouraged her Irish father, John Johnston, to write a series of communications showing transition from Old World culture to American frontier life; and secured from her brothers intimate stories of the early fur trade and certain untoward incidents between the Chippewas and American forces. From John Baptiste Perrault, impoverished old French *coureur de bois* to whom he had offered the shelter of his basement at the Sault, he obtained written reminiscences. Without his advice, his second wife, Mary Howard Schoolcraft, would not have published her rare pre-Civil War account of life on a South Carolina plantation, with its intimate glimpses of Schoolcraft in his later years.

In his various writings, though enmeshed by contemporary incidents and enamored of future possibilities, he always gave intelligent regard to the historic past. His extremely practical *A View of the Lead Mines of Missouri* incorporated, for the first time in print, the oldest historical facts about mining in that State taken from legal documents dating from the French operations, beginning 1720, under Renault. *Travels in the Central Portions of the Mississippi Valley* shows particular regard for the historic background of the region traversed—Fort Maumee; Fort Meigs; Anglo-American relations after 1783; Indian Wars on the western frontiers—General Harmar's campaign, the expeditions of Generals Scott, Wilkinson, St. Clair, and William Henry Harrison, the importance of

General Wayne's victory, the treaty of Greenville; the capture of Vincennes. The appendix of that volume contains General Wayne's official account of the Battle of Presque Isle. The narratives of his explorations of the sources of the Mississippi are introduced by accounts of previous exploration of that River and the Northwest.

His travels and his *Memoirs* are particularly rich in material for the student of Schoolcraft's own time, not only for detailed and general description of wide stretches of new territory, but also because of his accounts of many major incidents, situations, and viewpoints: The taking down of the British flag at Sault Ste. Marie by General Cass, with other anecdotes about him, his writings and collections; a description of the site of Fort Mackinac south of the Straits, in 1820; the Toledo War in embryo; the Rappite colony and Indiana settlements on the Wabash in 1821; the growing preoccupation with the problem of slavery.

The correspondence of Schoolcraft with his father and other associates from 1809 to 1824 has preserved facts that provide a new view of the development of glass factories in the New England-New York State area. It records the vicissitudes of various plants, the source of their material, the migrations of labor, and the interchange of ideas consequent upon exchange of workmen.

Schoolcraft's contribution to the history of Missouri is considerable. Two of his books are devoted to this region. *A View of the Lead Mines of Missouri* tells in the main the story of the development of its mineral resources from the 1712 grant of Louis XIV to Anthony Crozat; through the importation of 500 slaves from San Domingo by Renault in 1720; the rediscovery of lead under Spanish rule in 1780; and the operation of the mines down to the creation of Arkansas Territory in 1819. But it contains also many valuable details about cities, counties, buildings, canals, roads, bridges, ferries, agriculture, manufactures, exports and imports, education, and religion in the region in 1818–1819. His *Journal of a Tour into the Interior of Missouri and Arkansaw* gives interesting pictures of the progenitors of the modern mountain people of Missouri, as do several articles in *Oneóta*. In *Travels in the Central Portions of the Mississippi Valley* there are three chapters given to consideration of the geology of Missouri, with something about the Missouri Question in 1821. The early pages of his *Memoirs* contain additional material on that State. His poem *Transallegania* is an imaginative treatment of the earthquake of New Madrid.

All of this general historical activity was incidental to his major work in relation to the American Indian. Schoolcraft seems to have first expressed realization of the need for an authentic history of that race when, as Secretary to General Cass, he wrote an account of the journey through the Central Mississippi Valley that led to the Chicago Treaty with the Indians in 1821. Before he died his position in the field of Indian history was so authoritative that Bancroft, eminent among American historians, sought information from him for the preparation of the aboriginal section of his masterpiece, and submitted that portion of his manuscript to Schoolcraft for criticism and suggestions. Schoolcraft's own writings, and the accounts of others that were collected by him, in regard to the Indians from their earliest contact with the white man, are to be found for the most part in his *Historical and Statistical Information Respecting the History, Condition and Prospects of the Indian Tribes of the United States,* as well as in many of his other books and pamphlets.

HIS GOLCONDIAN VERSATILITY

MRS. H., who lived in a half-finished log cabin at the junction of Beaver Creek and the White River in the Ozark Mountains, according to Schoolcraft's journal,

had a brass ring which she had worn for several years, and declared it to be an infallible remedy for the cramp, which she was much troubled with before putting on the ring, but had not had the slightest return of it since. She was now in much distress, on account of having lately broken it so that it could not be worn, and observing that I collected ores and minerals, thought I might possess some skill in working metals, and solicited me to mend it. It was in vain I represented it was not the case; that I had no blow-pipe, or other necessary apparatus for that purpose; she was convinced I could do it, and I did not wish to show a disobliging disposition by refusing to make the attempt. By cutting several small stems of cane of different thicknesses, and fitting one into the other until the aperture was drawn down to the required degree of fineness, I soon made a blow-pipe. A hollow cut in a billet of wood, and filled with live hickory coals, answered instead of a lamp; and with a small bit of silver, and a little borax applied to the ring, and submitted to the influence of my wooden blow-pipe, I soon soldered the ring, and afterwards filed off the redundant silver with a file that happened to be among the moveable property of our host. When I made Mrs. H. a table out of the butt of an enormous white ash-log, she declared I must be a carpenter; when I relieved her child from a bilious attack, she was inclined to consider me a physician; but she was now convinced I was a silversmith.

Instinctively Mrs. H. was right, in principle.

Schoolcraft at times exercised civil authority as a justice of the peace and legislator; or asserted the military power of his territorial commission as captain of an independent company of militia infantry; or, in the province of the clergy, by virtue of his zeal and knowledge, in emergencies officiated at church services and funerals. He was so constituted that he could combine with success the business objectives of a government department, the interests of many sciences, and the missionary efforts of religious organizations, as he so notably exemplified in his expedition of 1832.

In the sciences of mineralogy, geology, geography and ethnology he made his mark nationally and internationally. He also made distinct contributions in other subjects toward the information of his times and the extension of the boundaries of knowledge. He gathered, preserved, and communicated every detail that came to his attention that he thought might conceivably be of assistance to contemporary or future scholarship.

This wide diffusion of effort was due not only to the catholicity of his curiosity but to the unzoned condition of science in his day. The various subdivisions as we now know them were only beginning to be distinguished from each other.

The subject of the "natural history" of Michigan, on which he lectured before the Lyceum at Detroit in 1831, referred to studies in the branches now known as zoology, botany, mineralogy, chemistry, and so on. But Schoolcraft's eager interests were even wider than that elastic term.

Throughout his writings, although he was untrained as a zoologist or botanist, he made mentions and lists of the fauna and flora encountered in Missouri, the Mississippi Valley, and the Great Lakes region. His notes in the journals of his explorations range from comment on dyes made from vegetable sources by the Indians in the Ozarks, to recognition of *Acer negundo* along the waters of the St. Peters and sweet grass on the neighboring prairies. He observed that braids of *Holcus fragrans* were used by Indian women to decorate their deerskin clothing, and that the inner bark of the box elder, mixed with common nettle, was employed, in a strong decoction, as a cure for syphilis. When the New York Lyceum inquired of him about the wolverine, alluding to it as a species of the glutton, he replied that Indians said there was no animal in their country deserving such a name—the only creature they knew that might qualify was the horse, which was eating all the time. The Chippewas called the wolverine underground drummer, gwin-gwe-au-ga. In discussing the wild life of Michigan before the Detroit Lyceum, Schoolcraft bore witness to the existence of the *Gulo luscus* in the State in earlier days—which sometimes is erroneously questioned—and described its characteristics. One of his myths preserves a story of its strength and indomitability, which may more reasonably explain why natives of Michigan are nicknamed Wolverines.

He discovered a species of squirrel in the vicinity of the Falls of St. Anthony which had not before been described. The story of the existence of a specimen of pouched rat, which had hitherto been questioned, was supported by a second specimen found by Schoolcraft. A skeleton of a paddlefish of the Mississippi, though incomplete was better than that possessed by any other collection.

He reported two kinds of rattlesnakes in the valley of the

Wisconsin, displaying sufficient of the collector's zeal and courage to climb a cliff to a small cave and kill one of the larger
kind, barred crotalis, that was four feet long, unusually thick,
and had nine rattles.

The beginning of the zone of the parrakeet near the mouth
of the Ohio was noticed by him.   He mentions the magpie and
three-toed woodpecker as far north as Lac du Flambeau; the
mockingbird as seen once or twice as far north as the Island of
Mackinac, but never at the Sault or on the St. Marys; and a
flock of pigeons flying low over the mouth of the Montreal
River.   In the spring of 1823 a species of grosbeak visited
Sault Ste. Marie of which he transmitted a specimen to the
New York Lyceum of Natural History, where it received the
name of evening grosbeak.   The latter was his one addition to
ornithology.   The new species was named *Fringilia vespertina*
by William Cooper, from the supposition that it sings during
the evening.   The Chippewas call it paush-kun-da-mo because
of its thick and penetrating bill.   He observed a dead pelican
on a small Minnesota island in a lake above Pakagama Falls.

In 1828 Schoolcraft contributed a large box of stuffed
birds and quadrupeds to the Lyceum of Natural History of
New York.   Among the twenty-three specimens included were
a lynx of the northern species rarely seen even in public collections of the time in the East; a spruce partridge, of which there
was then no other example in New York City; a three-toed
woodpecker, up to that time unlisted in published works on
ornithology in America; and three species of lake tortoise that
the Lyceum had been trying for a year to obtain in order to
complete a paper on the subject.   The other items in his gift,
while better known, were valuable in advancing knowledge of
the geographical distribution of their kinds.

His mode of travel, following streams which were the only
thoroughfares, gave small opportunity of meeting the larger
animals in their natural haunts, but he examined the skins at
trading places and heard accounts of persons who had engaged
in their capture.   He wrote an article on the limits of the range
of the *Cervus sylvestris* in the northwestern parts of the United

States.   However, the streams, shrunk to their lowest summer level, afforded him unusual opportunity to enlarge the boundaries of species and varieties in conchology.   His interest in this study amounted almost to an obsession.   On the Fox River where the water was shallow and warm and the progress of the expedition slow, he often waded from bar to bar collecting fresh-water shells.

While awaiting preparations for ascending the Wisconsin, he found Prairie du Chien a remarkable locality for large unios and some other fresh-water species.   Some specimens of *Unio crassus,* found on a nearby island in the Mississippi, were three times the size of any noticed in America or Europe and put conchologists in doubt whether the species should not be named giganteus.   Previously in coming down the Mississippi he had procured some fine and large examples of *Unio purpureus.*

On the Fox he found almost innumerable species of unios, one of them the smallest and most beautiful of all the genus yet discovered in America.   One specimen with green-rayed beaks, on a yellow surface and iridescent nacre, having a peculiar structure, transmitted to Isaac Lea of Philadelphia, was by that investigator named *Unio Schoolcraftensis.*

On the expedition with General Cass to Chicago in 1821, up the Maumee and down the Wabash, he made a valuable shell collection which was lost.   This included items that he considered new or undescribed.   Even in the vast excitement of discovery of the source of the Mississippi and recording that event, he scrutinized the shores near his encampment and observed among innumerable other shells a hitherto unknown kind.

His collection of 1820 was referred to members of the New York Lyceum of Natural History and the Academy of Natural Sciences at Philadelphia, and the results of their examinations were published in two of the leading scientific journals of the country.   The number of species by which the science was enriched was more than ten, and a new impulse was given to the study of fresh-water conchology.

The *Summary Narrative* of his Mississippi explorations

contains, in its appendixes, a list of animal life observed by Henry R. Schoolcraft in 1820; a catalogue of shells collected by him in 1832 and those gathered in association with Captain David B. Douglass in 1820; a paper by John Torrey on the plants collected by Captain Douglass in 1820, and a list of those gathered by Dr. Douglass Houghton in 1831 and 1832, covering 246 specimens; together with bibliographical reference to discussions in various scientific publications.

In fact the 313 pages of Addenda to that *Narrative* are a witness to his unwearying attempt to be useful. All the scientific reports of the Mississippi expeditions of 1820 and 1832 appear to be given in some form or other, either as digests or as data indicating where the reports may be found.

When, in passing along the river Des Plaines he found a remarkably well characterized specimen of a fossil tree, completely converted to stone, he at once prepared a descriptive memoir, which was published in a scientific periodical in advance of inclusion in a book of his travels. Another contribution to palaeontology was his description of the rock, in possession of the Rappites at Harmony, Indiana, which bore, supposedly, the prints of human feet.

Schoolcraft's work on *Vitreology,* in so far as it was written, was in part an application of chemistry to the process of glass manufacture.

When canoe travel on Lake Superior separated him from land phenomena, he made and recorded the results of immersions of a thermometer several times each day, from which he drew the generalization that in a distance of five hundred miles and a time of fourteen days, the temperature did not vary more than two degrees below or above the average temperature of 55 in mere surface observations. Among other facts contributed to oceanography are similar data on other Great Lakes. He also noted the appearance of tides at the mouth of the Fox River in Wisconsin and the lake tide at the junction of Swan Creek with the Maumee. An article on the tide of Lake Superior was published by him in 1831.

In the appendixes to the *Summary Narrative* he preserved

for topographers J. N. Nicollet's 1836 table of geographical positions on the Mississippi River showing distances and altitudes at various points on the river from its mouth to its source; also the observations taken by Captain Douglass in 1820.

Even the province of the meteorologist attracted his attention. He recorded temperatures and weather conditions in 1820 at Geneva and Buffalo, New York; Detroit, Mackinac Island, and Sault Ste. Marie, Michigan; Lake Superior; and the headwaters of the Mississippi River. These he published together with supplementary accounts at several points along the route.

As a youth in Vermont, studying privately under a college professor, he had incidentally delved in the science of medicine.

Horticulture and landscape design were hobbies with him. When choosing the site of Elmwood at Sault Ste. Marie, he left standing many elms, maples, mountain ash and other native forest trees. Afterward he planted other trees to add to the natural attractions, and tried every flowering plant and fruit that would thrive in the climate. In making a lawn, he knew enough to sow the marshy land along the river shore with red-top, which thrives in moist soil and gives it firmness. The flower-beds and fruit trees and vegetable garden that he planted and the walks and arbors he constructed about the Old Agency at Mackinac, remained for many years the pride of the Island.

In the interest of agriculture and conservation he contributed an article to a Michigan periodical on the use of ornamental and shade trees on farms, to dissuade settlers from the common practice of denuding their lands. As early as 1819 he had written for the *Ploughboy,* first agricultural magazine in New York and second in the United States. He forwarded the knowledge of farming methods among the Indians by every means in his power.

To what we now know as the bibliographical branch of library science he contributed a list of books, translations of the Scriptures, and other publications in the Indian tongue.

He was Sault Ste. Marie's first librarian, serving Fort Brady in that capacity from its establishment till February 7, 1823.

His "early bias for the philosophy of language" keenly concentrated on that of the Chippewas, led him to extensive research in grammar and lexicography and even into phonetics and comparative linguistics. His interest in the remote origin of the Indian race caused him not only to study Hebrew but to have his wife, Jane Johnston Schoolcraft, learn it, in the hope that she might possibly discover some subtle relationship.

Schoolcraft bore a high reputation in learned circles, not only in Michigan and the Northwest, but in all America and the world. It was the day of oppression for science. That interest was an exceedingly small spark. Schoolcraft contributed memorably not only in providing tinder and fuel, but by fanning the flame, and inspiring others to keep up the fire.

Widely-traveled in new regions, his opportunity to see and hear and correlate was extraordinary. As an observer and collector he was alert, omnivorous, intelligent; and as a recorder honest, painstaking, tireless.

No man ever lived who took more delight in both the discovery and dissemination of knowledge—each in equal degree. He had a positive genius for the awakening of intellectual interest, for its organization and its nourishment.

By means of personal contact with leaders not only in science but in government he advanced the cause of many branches of research. Complete faith in his objectives enabled him to approach fearlessly both the great and the near-great.

Conscientious devotion to his voluminous correspondence, and enterprise in that direction, improved his opportunity not only for increasing his own knowledge but sharing what he found.

His constant collection of specimens enriched the cabinets of many individuals and fed embryo public museums.

In 1842 John J. Audubon wrote: "Having not only heard, but also read of your having rendered essential services to Charles Bonaparte, Mr. Cooper of this city, and other eminent naturalists, I think perhaps you would not look upon my endeavors to advance science as unworthy of the same species of assistance at your hands." What Audubon desired was the cooperation of Schoolcraft in his proposed work on American quadrupeds, corresponding in style of execution to his great work on ornithology.

As a lecturer Schoolcraft was fluent, interesting, convincing, and made a good appearance.

The boy who at fifteen organized a society of his elders at Hamilton, New York, for the discussion of subjects of popular and learned interest, at the age of twenty-five and thirty inspired Missouri miners and Lake Superior Indians to collaborate with him in mineralogy; at thirty-five established the Michigan Historical Society; in his fifties was co-founder of the American Ethnological Society; and in 1842 attended and addressed the Twelfth meeting of the British Association for the Advancement of Science at Manchester, England.

His contribution was first as a collector of facts and specimens; then in dignified publicity. General Cass in 1820 estimated Captain Douglass and Henry Schoolcraft as equally promising, but the talented mathematician and topographer never found time to assemble and publish his findings. Schoolcraft got things into print and before the public at once, when they could be used and useful. If he built no bridges, in terms of modern scholarship, it was because his was not the time for bridges to be built. There were rivers of ignorance barring the advance of knowledge in all directions. Some crossed these barriers and left little to help others—collected material but did nothing with it. Schoolcraft zealously set out stepping-stones on many trails to help the march of science on its way. For his own period he built temporary crossings; then heaped up everything he could find, in order that those who should come later might construct permanently. He had not time to arrange the rough material, neatly finished, in order, for the future's use. His opportunity as he saw it was to snatch tirelessly whatever he thought might be useful out of the course of the destructive flood of time.

He was a scientist of parts, in truth.

That was not all. In addition he was a trusted government employee, an industrialist, a mining engineer, an explorer, a historian, an educator, a legislator, social reformer, religious leader, editor and author, painter and poet.

Henry Rowe Schoolcraft was a member of the American Philosophical Society, Philadelphia; the American Antiquarian Society, Worcester; the American Geological Society, New Haven; of the Historical Society of Connecticut; the American Academy of Natural Sciences of Philadelphia; the Albany Institute, at the State Capitol, Albany, New York; membre ord. de la Société Ethnologique de Paris; resident member of the National Institute at Washington; corresponding member of the Royal Geographical Society of London, England, of the Royal Society of Northern Antiquaries, Copenhagen, of the Hartford Natural History Society, of the New York Lyceum of Natural History, of the Brooklyn Lyceum, of the Lyceums of Natural History of Troy and Hudson, New York; honorary member of the Natural History Society of Montreal, Canada East, of the New-York Historical Society, of the Rhode Island Historical Society, of the Historical Society of Georgia, of the Ohio Historical and Philosophical Society, of the Pennsylvania Historical Society, and of the Goethean and of the Philo L. Collegiate Societies of Pennsylvania; vice-president of the Society for Diffusing Useful Knowledge; a founder and first president of the Algic Society for Meliorating the Condition of the Native Race in the United States; a founder and president of the Michigan Historical Society; an organizer and vice-president of the Detroit Lyceum;* co-founder and vice-presi-

* Schoolcraft was elected a member of the first Detroit Lyceum in 1820. The second Detroit Lyceum, also known as the Lyceum of Michigan, was organized December 6, 1830. It had as president the Governor of the Territory, Lewis Cass; for vice-presidents, H. R. Schoolcraft and H. Whiting. William Ward was secretary; A. S. Porter, treasurer; J. L. Whiting, W. L. Newberry, and L. Lyon, executive committee. Its public meetings ended, apparently, with that of May 12, 1831, less than a month after Schoolcraft left Detroit at the close of his final term in the Legislative Council. The president of the Lyceum, who had been appointed Secretary of War, was in Detroit until the last week in July, and the other officers of

dent of the American Ethnological Society, New York. He collaborated with, and may have been a member of, the American Lyceum. The University of Geneva in 1846 conferred on him an honorary doctorate of laws.

An indication of the contemporary recognition accorded him is the fact that he was offered an appointment as head of the scientific corps of the first American foreign expedition of discovery, planned to visit the South Seas, in 1828. Under the conditions existing, Schoolcraft preferred to remain at Sault Ste. Marie, Michigan, to observe and write.

Journalist, Editor, Author

To Schoolcraft the ink of the printer was as natural a medium as that of the pen. He had no prejudices about the avenue of publication. His intent was first his own entertainment and improvement; then communication—by the publication first at hand.

Henry Wadsworth Longfellow was once offered a thousand dollars by a leading American newspaper for a poem of any length on any subject. He did not accept, because of some idea of the inferiority of the daily press. Schoolcraft's desire to express himself in the purest language and on the highest plane of thought was evidenced early and in marked degree; but his impulse to communicate and to be useful were even stronger.

It was as a contributor to a local newspaper that Schoolcraft began his literary and scientific career, as a boy, in 1808. Later he used the columns of such publications as the *Utica* (New York) *Patriot* (September, 1817), St. Louis *Missouri Gazette* (November 6, 1818), the *Ploughboy* (1819), and others in Vermont and in Kentucky.

Promptly following his return from the Northwest in 1820, he furnished Nathaniel H. Carter, publisher of a newspaper at Albany, New York, with a story on the zoology of the country he had just visited.

---

the organization remained there indefinitely. Suspension of the second Lyceum's activities appears to have coincided with Schoolcraft's departure.

Detroit newspapers published his poems. He was the outstanding author in the Territory. He wrote an article by request in 1841 for Michigan's first agricultural newspaper, the *Michigan Farmer,* published by Josiah Snow.

The story of his journey through western Virginia, Ohio, Michigan, and Canada, in 1843, was first published as a kind of feature story in the form of letters addressed to William L. Stone, editor of the *New York Commercial Advertiser.*

Schoolcraft had respect for the newspaper and a keen appreciation of its possibilities.

In a letter to Nathaniel Carter he made clear one phase of his attitude toward the daily press: "If it is the writer of books who truly increases information, every decade's experience more and more convinces me that it is the editor of a diurnal journal who diffuses it, by his brief critical notices, or by giving a favorable or unfavorable impetus to public opinion."

He saw the opportunity and responsibility of the newspaper not only to preserve the facts of today for future historians, but to garner facts and traditions of the fast-fading past. Properly used, he saw it as a potent scientific tool. More than once, in his serially-published *Oneóta,* he called on all who were interested in ethnology and other antiquities to send such facts to him, or to local newspapers, so that valuable material should not vanish from men's minds into oblivion.

He had what is known in the journalistic world as news sense, not only relating to items and articles, but also to books. This led him to send out new information with dispatch, while it was at the peak of its interest and usefulness. This strong news instinct completely dominated his artistic vanity.

Schoolcraft's swift printing of *A View of the Lead Mines of Missouri,* which was completely new material in 1819, exemplifies his ability to recognize timely matter and the success this gift brought him.

While other members of the expedition of 1820 dallied, desiring to expand their notes, Schoolcraft followed his urge to tell what he had found at once. His *Narrative Journal* brought him wide acclaim. It communicated to the world not only new and valuable facts but his own fire of enthusiasm for the Northwest and its unfolding possibilities. In fact, his observations and communication of them conspicuously affected the course of events in Michigan. What he wrote had a great deal to do in overcoming adverse reports which for a time had turned westward migration away from that Territory.

Schoolcraft comprehended that old material, forgotten, again becomes legitimate news when public attention assumes a fresh focus on the subject. This is particularly evidenced by his republication of his collection of Indian myths. First issued as a contribution to ethnology under the uninviting title of *Algic Researches* in 1839, they were in 1853 included in the comprehensive government volumes on the Indians for students of Indian history and ethnology. Then came the publication of Longfellow's *Song of Hiawatha* in 1855. The tremendous popularity of this poem based on Schoolcraft's collection made the latter a news item of immediate importance, especially in view of the hot controversy as to whether Longfellow had plagiarized the material from European sources. It was a matter of moment to American literature, and a contribution to the information of the general reading public, that Schoolcraft's collection should be publicized at once. He responded quickly, abandoning the first, scientific, title for the news-title, *The Myth of Hiawatha*. This was a service to the nation; and a successful venture for himself, as *Algic Researches* had not been.

The same journalistic adaptation to change in public interest is also shown in the alteration of the title of his proposed encyclopedia. The prospectus of this, issued in 1842, was simply geographical in scope, and the title was *Cyclopaedia Indianensis*. It was never published. An extract from the manuscript appears in Section I of *Oneóta* under the title, "Geographical Terminology of the United States." Subsequent excerpts used in the *Oneóta* series have the heading "Ethnology" with an explanation for his renaming the proposed work, *Schoolcraft's American Cyclopaedia, or Ethnological*

Gazetteer of the Indian Tribes of the American Continent, North and South. He had changed its subject from geography to ethnology, and extended its field from North America to the western hemisphere, to keep pace with the progressing world.

Newspaper items on scientific subjects that showed evidence of more than passing value he gave wider circulation and rescued from oblivion by inclusion in his books.

Schoolcraft was an editor and publisher by nature. From boyhood he seemed to realize the educational and inspirational value of publication, as well for the writer as for the reader. One year after his first appearance in print in the local paper, he had in circulation a medium of his own.

The first magazine he instigated, at the age of sixteen, as the organ of a literary society he had organized the year before in Hamilton, New York, was named *The Cricket or Whispers from a Voice in the Corner.* Numbers I and II, each containing four pages, were issued in 1809. With the third number, the same size, produced in the same village, the name was changed to *The Cricket or Parapetic* [sic] *Student.* The new alternate title seems to indicate that Schoolcraft knew at that time he was about to leave the little town.

The following prospectus, in the first number of this periodical, shows, by vivid contrast with the poverty of his equipment, the power of the urge that impelled him:

In this little sheet, we have neither history nor philosophy to offer. We have, in fact, scarcely anything else. A few persons finding themselves in an out-of-the-way place, with very few books, & very little means, have associated for literary convena without hardly knowing what literature is. One of our number thinks, it is a term relating to the acts of the human intellect, and we are nearly all agreed, that it may be promoted by putting our joint stock of poor wits together, small as they are, hoping, that they may be heard as the humble whispers of thought, if not entitled to the character of well formed thought itself. To submit occasional selections, from these literary confabulations, is the object of the editor. We have no printer, but send around our sheet in manuscript.

A bundle of twenty-three issues, or portions of issues, of such a magazine, is in the Division of Manuscripts of the Library of Congress. It shows that he continued this kind of periodical at various times and places in the East,—Vernon and Geneva, New York, and Lake Dunmore, Vermont,—from 1810 to 1813. One number, dated Potosi, 1818, may easily be the first magazine produced in Missouri. The name of the original publication was altered; then other titles were given, in succession. Schoolcraft always had difficulty finding titles.

The most sustained of these Schoolcraft manuscript periodicals was *The Muzziniegun or Literary Voyager* of Sault Ste. Marie, Michigan. Of this the Smithsonian collection has twelve issues or parts of issues, numbered from Two to Sixteen, dated from December, 1826, to April 28, 1827. The pagination is consecutive. The last page known to exist is 369.

A suggestion of a possible earlier venture at the Sault under another name, occurs in December, 1822, in his *Memoirs*. What came of that is not known. *The Literary Voyager* is first mentioned February 1, 1826: "As one of the little means of supporting existence in so remote a spot, and keeping alive, at the same time, the spark of literary excitement, I began, in December, a manuscript jeu d'esprit newspaper, to be put in covers and sent from house to house, with the perhaps too ambitious cognomen of 'The Literary Voyager.'" December 1, 1826, there is the note: "I have also resumed, as an alternate amusement, 'The Literary Voyager.'" This product of winter leisure may still have been alive in 1829.

The Literary Voyager is distinctly different from any of Schoolcraft's earlier manuscript magazines. The contributors still used pseudonyms. Instead of philosophy in verse and prose, the contents are largely Indian tales, legends, and bits of history. The size of the page was much larger, and the average number in an issue was 23 instead of 2 to 4. Although the chief purpose of the publication was the amusement of its contributors, it circulated not only in the Sault but among Schoolcraft's friends in the East. Later almost every article was published at least once. The Reverend Peter Dougherty mentions in his diary, in July, 1838, reading it at Mackinac Island. He gives the dates of its publication as 1826 and 1827.

The significant fact is, that, without printing press or type-writer, merely by force of his own interest and energy, Henry Rowe Schoolcraft produced and circulated in the frontier settlement of Sault Ste. Marie, the first magazine in Michigan. This was at a time when the earliest newspapers of the Territory, in Detroit, were having a struggle to exist.

Further, this Sault Ste. Marie manuscript periodical is, embryonically, the first ethnological magazine in America. If not scientifically ethnological that is because it antedated any such science as ethnology.

After Schoolcraft moved to Mackinac Island he began another magazine of the same kind. This was *The Bow and Arrow.* Only the first leaf of the first number has been preserved. The date is October 1, 1833.

These manuscript magazines, and especially *The Literary Voyager* of Sault Ste. Marie, were the precursors of a series of printed publications beginning in August, 1844, in New York, under the title of *Oneóta, or Characteristics of the Red Race* of *America.*

The word *Oneóta,* used as a symbol for the Red Race, refers to a huge boulder around which the Oneida Indians met in council and from which their name, the People of the Stone, derives. The *Oneóta* series present ten different departments,—some or all of them represented in each number,—incidents and observations in the Indian territories; Indian tales; manners, customs, and opinions; biographical sketches of Indians; their traditions as to their origin and history; their languages; ethnology; picture writing; their antiquities; their songs, music, poetry. Some of the articles were continued through successive numbers. Eight issues of this miscellany, as initially announced, were later bound together and issued as a single volume, but the editorial attitude became progressively that of a magazine. Contributors were sought. Material by various individuals other than the editor was included. It was promised that the series would be extended if sufficient interest was shown. Although most of the items were written by Schoolcraft, the compilation is first of all a product of his editorial interest and labor, exactly as the Sault Ste. Marie manuscript series, with continuous pagination, was. This first serial, *Oneóta,* therefore, appears to have been a phase of his early conviction and years of effort in the direction of an American ethnological periodical. The first bound volume was issued in 1845 under the same title as the parts. Numerous editions of the collection, under differing titles, were published afterwards.

Schoolcraft was interested in at least three other editorial ventures in Michigan, in addition to his literary-ethnological manuscript magazines at Sault Ste. Marie and Mackinac Island.

As soon as the Michigan Historical Society had been established under his instigation in 1828, Schoolcraft began his efforts to launch a publication for that organization. He collected enough material for several volumes and procured estimates of printing costs, but funds were not forthcoming for such an undertaking up to the time he left the State—or for many years thereafter.

Indubitably he was editor of *The Souvenir of the Lakes: An Annual for 1831,* published by George L. Whitney at Detroit in the year named. Through the kindness of Doctor William Kline Kelsey, profound Commentator of the *Detroit News,* a reprint of this rare item, with valuable information concerning it, has come into our hands.

About 1830 the Annuals began to displace Walter Scott's novels, Young's *Night Thoughts,* Milton, Thomson, and Zimmerman's *Solitude,* as Christmas and New Year's gifts. The letterpress of these highly ornamented, fancy leather publications consisted of poems, sketches and tales. Usually they were embellished with mezzotint engravings. The vogue came to America from England, where the issuance of literary annuals began in 1823. These gift-books filled a real place in American literary life. They provided an outlet for writing to timid and aspiring literary men, helped build up a national literature, gave impetus to the movement for local portraiture, and fostered local pride.

The first American example of importance was the *Atlantic Souvenir* for 1826, which attempted to show what America could offer as the product of American authors and American artists. Thirty-four of these annuals, under twenty-five different titles, appeared before 1830. By 1857, at which time such publications had practically ceased, 440 had been issued. Of these only two were published west of the Appalachian mountains: *The Western Souvenir* at Cincinnati in 1829, and *The Souvenir of the Lakes* at Detroit in 1831.

The Souvenir of the Lakes was advertised in the *Detroit Journal and Michigan Advertiser,* January 5, 1831, as a volume whose contents were all of home origin, and whose Indian tales were taken down from the mouths of the natives. It was far less pretentious even than the modest Cincinnati annual. It lacked binding ornamentation, had no engravings, and was small. Its literary pieces were merely creditable performances. No authors' names were given. Of the ten contributions, two are certainly by Schoolcraft: "Annamikees," and "To a Young Lady." The preface to "Ozhawongeezhick" is probably by him. The verse portion of the latter is unquestionably from his portfolio of Indian material. It was published prior to May, 1823, in one of his manuscript magazines at the Sault, and was written by the wife of Captain Thompson of Fort Brady. Mary, Mrs. Thompson's pseudonym in this instance, is also used under two other of the included poems. A fourth piece from Schoolcraft's collection of manuscripts is "A Wyandot Tradition." This he used again some years later in *Oneóta* with the name of J. H. Kinzie attached as author. "A Visit to the Cave in Put-in-Bay Island" has been traced to his close friend, Henry Whiting. Some of the unidentified poems may be by Schoolcraft or his father-in-law. Beyond doubt the bulk of the contents was either written or supplied by Schoolcraft, and the editorial urge and responsibility also may safely be imputed to him.

An Ohio historian has said:

That Cincinnati, the cultural and literary capital of the West, should imitate the East in compiling an annual comes as no surprise, but that a frontier community in Michigan Territory should produce such a volume is an event for which one is unprepared. Though it possesses no great merit, the *Souvenir of the Lakes* is clear evidence that the Detroit-Maumee area had literary pride as early as 1831, and that the Lakes Huron and Erie and the tribes that once roamed their shores afforded material for a Western gift-book which, though greatly out-rivaled by ornate Eastern volumes, was one of the early gestures toward literature culture in the Great Lakes region.

In 1838 Schoolcraft led in launching the Michigan *Journal of Education,* the first common school journal in the United States, and in 1841, on the eve of his removal to New York, he was trying to revive it or have another publication of the kind established.

His greatest work as an editor, of course, was that in connection with his *Historical and Statistical Information Respecting the History, Condition and Prospects of the Indian Tribes of the United States.*

An alphabetical list of the writings of Henry Rowe Schoolcraft is provided in the Bibliography of this volume. His major works are also given in the order of their appearance under Chronology.

The number of items in the Bibliography and the number of works actually written by Schoolcraft are in more than ordinary disproportion. The same production often appears in various forms, under altered or completely different titles, in reissues, or revised editions, or in other compilations. For this reason, a minutely detailed catalog of all of Schoolcraft's writings, published and unpublished, would be a contribution to scholarship.

A comprehensive index of his productions would be useful in research. Toward this an important step has been taken by the Bureau of American Ethnology of the Smithsonian Institution, with its index to his six quarto volumes.

Some day there may be a complete popular edition of his writings, omitting duplications. Certainly there is a place for new editions of some of his most readable productions, such as his *Memoirs* and books of travel. Most Schoolcraft items are now so rare that they are kept in library vaults for the use of students rather than the general public. They range in price from ten dollars for the *Memoirs,* and fifty for *Iosco,* to one hundred fifty for his six-volume magnum opus.

The reports and papers of Schoolcraft, as a geologist, and then as Indian Agent, covering his official activities in Michigan, New York, and Washington, constitute a library in themselves. He was not only an alert and conscientious government employee, but a careful record-keeper and a prolific correspondent. For the period during which his observations were made, they were highly valuable, creditable as well to himself as to the authority he fearlessly represented.

The collections of his personal manuscripts and papers, many of them unpublished, are almost discouragingly voluminous.

He contributed widely and constantly to newspapers and periodicals. His field was scientific, literary, and popular. Articles by him were sought by leading publications, and by new and uncertain ventures desiring the prestige of his name as a contributor. Eminent editors, such as Professor Benjamin Silliman of the *American Journal of Science,* kept up interesting correspondence with him.

It is impossible to draw a line between Schoolcraft's scientific and literary writings. Science was not at the time specialized. It sprouted and blossomed generally in the broad field of literature. His productions may be classified in such varied divisions as education, sociology, geology, mining engineering, ethnology, geography, history, linguistics, and literature.

Schoolcraft's major work, *Historical and Statistical Information Respecting the History, Condition and Prospects of the Indian Tribes of the United States,* in six volumes, of the sixth of which he was author as well as editor, has already been amply considered under his contribution to ethnology. The same is true of the miscellany, *Oneóta,* with its numerous reissues.

His earliest book ventures were in technical fields. The first has been something of a mystery.

As a youth Schoolcraft prepared material for a volume in

which he aimed to demonstrate the importance of an acquaintance with chemistry and mineralogy in the preparation and fusion of numerous substances in the mineral kingdom, which result in the different conditions of the various glasses, enamels, and so forth. Combining the knowledge gained from private instruction in chemistry with the opportunity of having under his charge extensive glassworks, he experimented with the arts under his direction and formulated principles which formed the basis of a treatise entitled "Vitreology." A copy of a printed prospectus for the work, with the names of some Zanesville subscribers affixed, is in the Smithsonian Collection of Schoolcraft's papers. *Antiques* for April, 1939, reprints it in full. Although there are several references to such a work, no copies of a book have been discovered.

"The portions published," wrote Schoolcraft, "and the entire plan and merits of it, were warmly approved" by a number of persons. The printed proposal outlines discussion of the practical problems of the manufacture of glass,—the selection of materials, and questions concerning fuel, labor and the construction of furnaces and pots,—from the standpoint of American rather than European needs in the way of practical skill and scientific knowledge. Other sections covered the origin of glassmaking; the ornamentation of glass,—cutting, etching, grinding, gilding; the art of painting on glass; the preparation of colors and description of furnace used for burning the colors; and other technical matters. Quite recently, among the Schoolcraft Papers in the Manuscript Division of the Library of Congress, a small bound manuscript volume entitled "Vitriology" has been discovered.

Schoolcraft's *A View of the Lead Mines of Missouri* has been discussed in detail in a preceding chapter. This first elaborate and detailed account of a mining district in the United States was regarded as particularly interesting and important, an acquisition to the means of information respecting the nation's mineral resources, and a regular volume of reference. Incidentally it contained considerable material of popular and scientific appeal. *The New York Literary Journal* reprinted five long sections from it by way of review.

The travel writings of Schoolcraft, which have been referred to often in connection with his contribution to the various sciences, also have a place in the general literature of the United States.

Henry Rowe Schoolcraft is one of the outstanding travelers in American history. He knew the Mississippi Basin from the Allegheny at Olean, New York, and from the extremities of the Wabash River; had explored its tributary system in Missouri, Arkansas, and what is now Wisconsin and Minnesota; and had traced the present and ancient water channels to Lake Michigan. He was the only man in his time who had traversed the length of the great river from its source in the Itasca basin, which he himself discovered, to its mouth. All the Great Lakes were familiar to him. The shores of the Lakes beyond the frontier town of Detroit he had investigated in minutiae.

Some idea of the pioneering quality of his explorations may be gained by knowing that when he visited Dubuque in 1820 there was no white resident and not a dwelling superior to an Indian wigwam in the present limits of the State of Iowa. He was in Wisconsin sixteen years before it had legal existence as a Territory. Accepting Dr. Johnson's characterization of a house as a residence having one story over another, there was not a house on the banks of the Illinois River, and few huts. Missouri Territory when he visited it in 1818 extended from Louisiana to the International Boundary Line on the north and to the Rocky Mountains on the West. Arkansas Territory was created while he was back in the hills away from civilization.

To read what Schoolcraft wrote about his journeys is a fascinating series of experiences by proxy. Alert and comprehensively observing, he was interested in and knew more about more things than other travel writers. In all his writings he is never happier or more readable than in these straight-forward, simple narratives.

The first of these was confined to a few pages in *A View of the Lead Mines of Missouri,* telling of a voyage from the mouth of the Ohio to St. Louis—one hundred seventy miles on the Mississippi River in twenty-three days. Parts of the diary of his penetration of the Ozarks were published in the *Belles-lettres Repository,* in 1820, from which they were taken by Sir Richard Phillips and included in his *Voyages and Travels,* published in London, England, in 1821. The title, in this collection, is *Journal of a Tour into the Interior of Missouri and Arkansaw, from Potosi, or Mine a Burton, in Missouri Territory, in a South-West Direction, toward the Rocky Mountains; Performed in the Years 1818 and 1819.*

This expedition for mineralogical investigation was his own idea and undertaking. Of the party he organized, all but one man failed him. He had bought a horse and constructed a packsaddle with his own hands, and resolved to proceed no matter what occurred. The journey, from November 5, 1818, to February 4, 1819, led more than nine hundred miles through barren, wild and mountainous scenes.

His Ozark narrative is the story of a complete tenderfoot, with small means, much ingenuity, and all the courage and determination in the world, who kept on his way despite a series of near-tragic mishaps, across rocky ridges that cut his shoes to pieces and along briary creekbeds that tore his unfit clothes to ribbons, to certain lead diggings two hundred miles beyond the last white man's habitation on the White River, through country where the occasional Caucasian hunter was almost as wild as the Indian and as treacherous. They almost lost their horse when it mired down; ruined their supplies at a deep ford; and lived on acorns. Schoolcraft did almost every possible thing he should not have done, and few that he should have, but he got there just the same! The diary of his ninety-day trip is short, but packed with interest.

Schoolcraft's *Narrative Journal of Travels Through the Northwestern Regions of the United States . . . in the year 1820,* which was published in 1821, is firsthand, first-class reporting of one of the most colorful expeditions in the history of the Northwest Territory. The party of about forty persons included eight or ten Indians, in a canoe, as hunters, in their picturesque costumes; ten Canadian voyageurs, guides, interpreters, a topographer, Schoolcraft as geologist, and a small detachment of infantry. The flotilla of birchbark canoes, with the colors flying from each stern, left Detroit to carry the American flag for the first time officially into the country beyond the Straits of Mackinac where the Indians were still wards of the British Indian Department and hostile to the United States. Among other objectives they planned to investigate the Lake Superior copper stories and to make a treaty with the Indians for land for a needed garrison at Sault Ste. Marie. It was a grand tour, by water and portages, of the American shores of the Great Lakes and the Upper Mississippi. The whole setting was novel. Some incidents were dramatic in the extreme. Schoolcraft's narrative shows accurate and logical powers of observation. His account is at once authoritative and enmeshing. The book was immediately and eminently successful. An edition of twelve hundred copies was sold out in a few weeks. It established his reputation as a scientific and judicious traveler. Those who read his narrative become in pleasurable memory a member of that epoch-making expedition.

There were three ways to go from Detroit to Chicago in 1821. One was on horseback along the Indian trail across the lower peninsula of Michigan. Another was by slow sailing vessels, through Lakes Huron and Michigan. The third, chosen by Governor Lewis Cass, on his way to negotiate a treaty with the Indians at Fort Dearborn, was up the Maumee River, then, after a portage, down the Wabash, across Illinois to St. Louis, up the Mississippi and the Illinois and along the Des Plaines Rivers, to the head of Lake Michigan. Schoolcraft, secretary to Commissioner Cass, chronicled the journey in his *Travels in the Central Portions of the Mississippi Valley* (1825). Their river trail ran through a wilderness marked by new settlements, signs of the already vanishing Indian, and memories of recent Indian wars. Fort Wayne consisted of eighteen log buildings, exclusive of the fort, and had a population of one hundred. The elder Rappe was at the head of his unique colony at Harmony, Indiana. Governor William Clark, companion of Meriwether Lewis on his expedition to the Pacific, was still living at St. Louis. On the banks of Chicago River three thousand Indians assembled under the guns of Fort Dearborn. Many of the younger generation, by reading this narrative, might relive with keen enjoyment the experiences of their pioneering forebears.

One of the incidental aims of the Cass expedition of 1820 had been to explore the ultimate northern source of the Mississippi River. Circumstances, it was decided, rendered this impracticable. Schoolcraft kept alive his desire toward that objective and achieved it twelve years afterwards. His *Narrative of an Expedition through the Upper Mississippi to Itasca Lake . . . in 1832,* published in 1834, is an account of the final discovery by white men of the Itasca basin as the source of the Mississippi River. This expedition is one of significance in its period.

In 1853 Schoolcraft issued his *Scenes and Adventures in the Semi-Alpine Region of the Ozark Mountains of Missouri and Arkansas.* Thirty-odd years had passed since parts of the diary of his Ozark expedition had been printed in an American periodical and reprinted in an English collection of travels. This first American edition in book form was drawn from the original manuscript journal, with the perspective of three decades and a special attempt to relate his knowledge of the country to a study of De Soto's explorations. A revision of most of *A View of the Lead Mines of Missouri* appears as an appendix.

Governor Cass had said in 1820 if Schoolcraft should "carry into effect the intention, which he now meditates, of publishing his journal of the tour, enriched with the history of the facts which have been collected, and with those scientific and practical reflections and observations, which few men are more competent to make, his work will rank among the most important accessions which have ever been made to our national literature." Because the exploration of the upper

MAP OF EXPEDITION OF 1821.

reaches of the Mississippi was accomplished in two voyages, 1820, and 1832, and his two books about these were simply narratives, Schoolcraft, in 1855, combined the two accounts, under the title *Summary Narrative of an Exploratory Expedition to the Sources of the Mississippi River, in 1820; Resumed and Completed, by the Discovery of Its Origin in Itasca Lake, in 1832*. This 1855 account is a concise summary, rather than a mere revision of the two prior narrations in journal form, with some additions from the original manuscript journals. The volume also incorporates, as addenda, the official correspondence and reports relating to both expeditions, together with extensive references to scientific material gathered.

Schoolcraft's memoirs are enjoyable, instructive reading. They were published in 1851, in a volume of 703 pages, under the title *Personal Memoirs of a Residence of Thirty Years with the Indian Tribes on the American Frontiers. With Brief Notices of Passing Events, Facts, and Opinions*. This is not an autobiography, nor a methodical record of his times, but rather a chronological presentation of illustrative memoranda for the ultimate historian. It covers an important part of the time of the settlement of the Mississippi Valley and the Great Lakes region. Anecdotes and incidents succeed each other without any attempt at method. They embrace social events, boat arrivals, visits with noted men and women, bits of correspondence, notes on climate, reflections on current events, wild life, Indian matters, and many others. The story these incidentally tell is that of the Anglo-Saxon race occupying the sites of the Indian wigwams. Plumed sachems, farmers, legislators, statesmen, speculators, professional and scientific men, and missionaries of the gospel, figure in their respective capacities. The charm of the *Memoirs* lies in Schoolcraft's wide interest in human affairs, and in his penetration.

Schoolcraft had ability above the ordinary as an essayist. Such papers as his address before the Chippewa County Temperance Society in 1832, and his paper on the education of the American Indian are examples of logical analysis, orderly development, and measured and impressive presentation.

"The Rabid Wolf," a tale of the Normanskill, that verges on the short story in its form, is excellently told. In this a slightly humorous attitude, sometimes not altogether happy in his writings, is a distinctly pleasing feature. Schoolcraft displays here a gift he used too seldom. In this direction he might have done much original and fine work.

His collection of Indian myths he at first presented as simply and accurately as possible for the purposes of scientific study. The information on Indian philosophy and their mode of reasoning on life, death, and immortality revealed in *Algic Researches,* establishes that work among the unique contributions to American literature. The reissue of this, with editorial changes, under the title of *The Myth of Hiawatha,* in 1856, emphasized the literary rather than the scientific value of the aboriginal stories. Of this Schoolcraft had been aware from the beginning. The success of *The Song of Hiawatha* had merely signalized it. Since then the individual tales, and the collection, have passed through many editings, at his hands and those of others. These primitive stories, preserved by Schoolcraft, have proved pure springs to feed a new continental river in the realm of the world's literature. "Iadilla; or The Origin of the Robin," in *Algic Researches,* may be cited as an example of Schoolcraft at his best.

Although he had never neglected more practical studies for its sake, first of all Schoolcraft had been moved in his youth by the spirit of poetry. "The whole valley of the Norman's Kill abounds in lovely and rural scenes, and quiet retreats and waterfalls, which are suited to nourish poetic tastes." These he indulged from his thirteenth year, periodically writing, and as judgment ripened, destroying volumes of manuscripts. His first published piece in 1808 was a lyric on the death of a young friend, which excited local notice and was attributed to a person of literary celebrity.

His verse, although often amateurish, at times reaches a high plane. It was a natural form of expression throughout his life. His occasional poems are numerous. They range widely in subject, and in time, from a translation from the German of

Gessner's "The Bird," in 1819; the whitefish of the St. Marys River; the discovery of the source of the Mississippi; and a rose plucked on Lake Itasca to carry to a loved one as a remembrance of the discovery day.

Some of his efforts were sufficiently sustained to justify separate printing in pamphlet form.

Transallegania, or the Groans of Missouri, contains 571 lines, in rhymed couplets of eleven syllables. It is the imaginative story of a congress of minerals in a cave in the Ozarks to protest upon the encroachment of men. The upheaval from their anvil chorus of complaint results in the earthquake of New Madrid. A mention of Lake Superior copper, which he had dreams of investigating some day, is interesting:

> Our home is a region all distant and drear,
> Where the tempest is howling one half of the year;
> Where the rock towers high, and the waters divide,
> And Superior lashes the shore at our side.
> Here, lone and neglected, my family groans
> Confined by the pressure of ponderous stones.

The poem has some good lines:

> And however the mortals on earth may deny it,
> There is more to be got without fighting, than by it;
> For though they gain treaties, they lose it in bones.

His *Helderbergia: Or the Apotheosis of the Heroes of the Antirent War,* published in 1855, is a mock-heroic account of the attempt of armed forces to suppress widespread resistance, in Albany County, New York, to the old patroon system of landholding which disturbed the population of that region for decades.

> Ah deeds like *theirs* and *ours* shall live,
>   when history is a blot,
> And heaven's apocalyptic hail, Napoleon, is forgot.

> On rushed the army—quick the bridge was crost
> Where nothing but a bleating flock assailed the host.

> To crown the victory it needs but now,
>   To roast "the mighty chine," and fill the bowl;

Let each proclaim the gastronomic vow,
  Nor fear in wine to bathe the noble soul;
Feasts are the tests of triumphs of the mind,
  And let anatomists write rules of art,
The gullet is that mass of muscles kind,
  That forms the highway to the human heart;
By eating, man expresses what he thinks,
And when he doubts of principles involved, he drinks.

Another of his longer poems, written at Sault Ste. Marie, is *The Rise of the West, or A Prospect of the Mississippi Valley.* This is a series of reminiscences of that noble stream and of the settlement of its banks by Anglo-Saxons.

His best work in poetry may be *Iosco, or the Vale of Norma,* of which a private edition of fifty copies was published anonymously in Detroit in 1838. In this, as in "The Rabid Wolf," Iosco is his imaginative name for Hamilton, New York, the place of his birth. This tribute to his early home and the friends of his boyhood has emotional and intellectual as well as artistic quality of a superior order.

As a young man he wrote in his diary and scratched on the wall of an Ozark cavern the following unformed philosophy of life:

O thou, who, clothed with magic spell,
Delight'st in lonely wilds to dwell,
Resting in rift, or wrapt in air,
Remote from mortal ken or care,
Spirit of Caverns, goddess blest!
Hear a suppliant's fond request
  .   .   .   .

Let me dream of friendship true,
And that human ills are few;
Let me dream that boyhood's schemes
Are not, what I've found them—dreams;
And his hopes, however gay,
Have not flitted fast away.
Let me dream life is no bubble,
That the world is free of trouble,
And my heart's a stranger still
To the cares that fain would kill.
Let me dream I e'er shall find
Honour fair, or fortune kind,

And that time shall sweetly fling
In my path perpetual spring.
Let me dream my bosom never
Felt the pang from friends to sever;
And that life is not replete,
Or with loss, pain, woe, deceit,
Let me dream misfortune's smart
Ne'er hath wrung my bleeding heart,
Nor from home its potent sway
Drove me far, oh far away.
Let me dream my journey here
Is not fraught with toil severe;
That the barren is not dreary,
Nor my daily marches weary;
And the cliff, the brake, the brier,
Never wound, and never tire;
Stony couch and chilly sky,
Trackless desart, mountain dry,
These afflict not, but beguile
Time away, like beauty's smile.
Let me dream it, for I know,
When I wake, it is not so.

Twenty years later, in the midst of a situation that was sheer and inescapable tragedy, he expressed his mature convictions in *Iosco:*

Frequent, in days remembrance loves to greet,
I bent my footsteps to a lone retreat,
High o'er the vale, yet crowned with solemn shade,
For inborn thought and contemplation made;
There, free from all that busy life assails,
I weighed the world in boyhood's golden scales;
And found it, to my much admiring sight,
All sun, all hope, all beauteous and all bright.
So is it still;—if viewed by wisdom's plan,
Shown in the peaceful, honest, happy man.

To the American Indian he gave the best of his mind and heart, in literature as in all phases of life.

He had a clear vision of the possibilities of their myths as material for American literature, both prose and poetry. The windswept freshness of their conceptions contrasted like Indian summer colorings with the sere mythologies of Europe.

There is poetry in their very names of places: Ticonderoga, the place of the separation of waters; Dionderoga, the place of the inflowing of waters; Saratoga, the place of the bursting out of waters; Ontario, a beautiful prospect of rocks, hills, and waters; Ohio, the beautiful river—these, and a thousand other names which are familiar to the ear, denote a capacity for, and love of harmony in the collocation of syllables expressive of poetic thought. But the great source of a future poetic fabric, to be erected on the frame-work of Indian words, when the Indian himself shall have passed away, exists in their mythology, which provides, by a skilful cultivation of personification, not only for every passion and affection of the human heart, but every phenomenon of the skies, the air, and the earth. The Indian has placed these imaginary gods wherever, in the geography of the land, reverence or awe is to be inspired. Every mountain, lake, and waterfall is placed under such guardianship. All nature, every class of the animal and vegetable creation, the very sounds of life, the murmuring of the breeze, the dashing of water, every phenomenon of light or electricity, is made intelligent of human events, and speaks the language of a god.

W. H. C. Hosmer, Whittier, and Lowell, as well as Longfellow, found inspirational subject matter in Schoolcraft's writings.

Charles Fenno Hoffmann's Indian poems won his helpful applause. Schoolcraft read and furnished notes for Captain Whiting's "Sanillac." He took constructive interest in all such efforts. "I regard every attempt of the kind as meritorious, although it may be the lot of but few to succeed," he said.

He found time himself, away from graver matters, to give Indian subjects literary form. Some of his lyrics were written in connection with Indian legends. A small volume of *Indian Melodies* was published by him in 1830. Short collections of verse on Indian topics were included at the end of *The Indian in His Wigwam,* as "Music and Cradle Songs," and at the end of *The Myth of Hiawatha* under the title of "Wild Notes of the Pibbigwun." "Geehale" and "The Iroquois" were published anonymously. A long poem entitled "Illula, the Pride of the Lakes" was still a manuscript draft when he died.

His longer published poems include *The Man of Bronze, or Portraitures of Indian Character,* and *The Appeal of Pontiac.*

Outstanding among his sustained works in verse is *Alhalla; or, The Lord of Talladega. A Tale of the Creek War.* This Indian narrative romance, written in 1821, published in 1843, tells of a traveler, a missionary and a trader who find their way to a lonely island in Lake Superior. There they find Alhalla, a former chief of Talladega, in voluntary exile, and listen to his long story of war on the Southern plains, the treachery of the whites, the supposed slaying of his daughter's fiancé, the death of his nation with the fall of Tuscaloosa. The Indian guide of the visiting party remarks that he has seen a strange Indian in the vicinity. This proves to be the beloved of the chief's daughter. Miraculously he had escaped death and without respite had been searching for her. The story has that much of a happy ending.

There are some minor anticipations of *Hiawatha* in *Alhalla.* In both the scene is laid in the Lake Superior country and a Creation tradition is introduced. Although as poetry *Alhalla* was a failure, historically it is of great importance. Most significant is the fact that it was written in trochaic tetrameter and that its preface contains a statement which unquestionably influenced Longfellow in his happy choice of meter for *Hiawatha.*

Schoolcraft, acutely aware of the possibilities of Indian mythology as material for imaginative literature, for years actively sought exactly what was given in *Hiawatha.* His attempt to enlist the interest of Washington Irving through correspondence was fruitless, but his published material enmeshed Longfellow. *Hiawatha* was the result of completely conscious collaboration, on both sides. Thus, although Schoolcraft fell short himself of being a poet of distinction, his intelligent and untiring interest in that form of art made him a major contributor to American poetry.

In Politics

For a decade Schoolcraft had performed each year, except 1823, a journey of more or less peril and adventure in the great American wilderness west of the Alleghenies. So he recorded, in his *Memoirs,* in October, 1828. Continuing, he noted, "I had now attained a point, ardently sought, for many years, where I was likely to be permitted to sit down quietly at home, and leave traveling to others." He had just moved into his new Elmwood—"a quiet home, a retired, convenient, tasteful, and even elegant seat, which filled every wish of retired intellectual enjoyment, where I was encompassed by books, studies, cabinets, and domestic affections."

Then, before a month passed, he was elected a member of the Third Legislative Council of the Territory of Michigan— "an office not solicited, and which is not declined." He had previously been justice of the peace for Michilimackinac County, and, after Chippewa County was created, was the first to serve the new county in that capacity.

Governor Cass wrote to him from Detroit soon afterward:

We have understood that you have been elected a member of the legislative council, and there is a prevalent wish that this report may prove true. I mention the subject now, to inform you that the council will probably be convened about the beginning of May, in order that you may make the necessary preparations for visiting this place at that time.

Schoolcraft was a member of the Michigan Legislative Council from 1828 to 1832.

Of the first session of the Third Legislative Council, which took him from the Sault from April 27 until the beginning of July, 1828, his *Memoirs* say:

There were just thirteen men, only one of whom was a demagogue, and had gained his election by going about from house to house asking votes. The worst trait in the majority was a total want of moral courage, and a disposition to favor a negligent and indebted population, by passing a species of stop laws, and divorce laws, and of running after local and temporary expedients, to the lowering of the tone of just legislation. I had no constituents at home to hold me up to promises on these heads. I was every way independent, in a political sense, and could square my course at all times, by pursuing the right, instead of being forced into the expedient, in cases where there was a conflict between the two. This made my position agreeable.

I was appointed chairman of the committee on expenditures,

and a member of the judiciary, &c. I directed my attention to the incorporation of a Historical Society; to the preparation of a system of township names derived from the aboriginal languages; and to some efforts for bettering the condition of the natives, by making it penal to sell or give them ardent spirits, and thus desired to render my position as a legislator useful, where there was but little chance of general action. As chairman of the committee on expenditures, I kept the public expenditures snug, and, in every respect, conformable to the laws of congress. The session was closed . . . early enough to permit me to return to St. Mary's, to attend to the summer visits of the interior traders and Indians.

The second session of the Third Legislative Council likewise gave its attention largely to local and specific acts. "Deeming it ever better to keep good old laws than to try ill-digested and doubtful new ones, I used my influence to repress the spirit of legislating for the sake of legislation, wherever I saw appearances of it." He extended his activities in the preceding session by securing something like protection for that part of the Indian population which had amalgamated with European blood, defeated an attack upon the Mackinac Mission, and added to his system of names for new townships a list of officers who served in the 1791–1793 Indian campaigns of General Wayne.

He was reelected to the Fourth Legislative Council in 1830. In April, 1831, having served four years, he declined reelection by a public notice to the electors of his district, on the understanding that the President had expressed an opinion that government officers should not engage in the business of legislation.

It is genuine sacrifice to give precious time, in uneventful years, to undramatic service of which the most that may be said is that it is conscientious and efficient. Schoolcraft, however, seems never to have been too busy to respond to a call when he could be of use. Like an enthusiastic individual Chamber of Commerce of America, it pleased him to answer promptly such inquiries as that of an unknown individual who asked something about the future of St. Louis, Missouri, which he perhaps best could answer. In or out of office, he was an alert public representative. As such in December, 1837, he wrote Lucius Lyon urging a Congressional appropriation for piers necessary to protect and make permanent the proposed State Canal at the Sault, at the same time raising the question of the building of that canal across a part of the Indian reservation made in 1820.

In addition to such everyday activities, it was also Schoolcraft's happiness to render Michigan signal public service more than once.

After the Territory had suffered so keenly from adverse early government reports that the tide of Western migration was for a time turned into other regions, Schoolcraft's journals of travel in the Great Lakes country beyond Detroit were an important factor in reversing this unfortunate trend. His factual yet glowing narratives achieved something of best-seller popularity and influence.

His personal contact also was pervasive. Commenting on a prospective missionary's nervous queries about the climate at Mackinac Island, he made the following statement:

> The air is a perfect restorative to invalids and never fails to provoke appetite and health. It is already a partial resort for persons out of health, and cannot fail to be appreciated as a watering place in the summer months as the country increases in population. To Chicago, St. Louis, Natchez, and New Orleans, as well as Detroit, Cleveland, Cincinnati, and Buffalo, I should suppose it to be a perfect Montpelier in the summer season.

This was indeed vision, in the year 1835. His eager championship was an immeasurable asset to Michigan in its infancy.

Schoolcraft's specimens of copper, and accounts of Indian traditions concerning this mineral, given to foreign ministers and others at Washington by Secretary of War Calhoun, added to Michigan's repute abroad. At home, his convictions concerning the mineral prospects of the country beyond the Straits of Mackinac were a factor in hastening the addition of much territory to the public domain.

A unique and memorable contribution to the progress of the embryo State of Michigan, as well as to the nation, is detailed in the following communication of Senator Lucius

Lyon to Morse and Bagg of *The Detroit Free Press,* under date of March 31, 1836:

Enclosed I send you a letter on a subject of much interest to the people of our State, which you can use as you think proper:—

On the 28th inst. a treaty was concluded here by Henry R. Schoolcraft, commissioner on the part of the United States, with the chiefs of the Ottawa and Chippewa nations of Indians, by which they cede to the United States the country lying within the following described boundaries, to-wit: Beginning at the mouth of the Grand river of Lake Michigan, on the north bank thereof and following up the same to the line called for in the first article of the treaty of Chicago of the 29th of August, 1821, thence in a direct line to the head of Thunder Bay river, thence with the line established by the treaty of Saginaw of the 24th September, 1819, to the mouth of said river, thence northeast to the boundary line in Lake Huron between the United States and British province of Upper Canada, thence north-westwardly, following the said line, as established by the Commissioners acting under the treaty of Ghent through the straits and River St. Mary's to a point in Lake Superior north of the mouth of Gitchy Seebing or Chocolate river, then south to the mouth of said river and up its channel to the source thereof, thence in a direct line to the head of the South Konawba river of Green Bay (near the Menominee river) thence down the south bank of said river to its mouth, thence in a direct line through the ship channel into Green Bay to the outer part thereof, thence south to a point in Lake Michigan west of the north cape entrance of Grand river, and thence east to the place of beginning, comprehending all the lands and islands not reserved. The principal reservations are the Beaver Island of Lake Michigan and five different tracts in the peninsula between Lakes Michigan and Huron, viz., one tract of 50,000 acres to be located on Little Traverse Bay, one tract of 20,000 acres to be located on the north shore of Grand Traverse Bay, one tract of 70,000 acres to be located by Chingassanoo or the Big Sail on the Cheboygan river and one tract of 1,000 acres to be located by Mageekeeis on Thunder Bay river. These are all the reservations made in the lower peninsula. The purchase is estimated to amount to 16,000,000 of acres, 10,000,000 on the lower peninsula and 6,000,000 on the upper peninsula and the government pays for it in the whole the sum of $1,601,600 as follows:—

Cash annuities $30,000, for 20 years $600,000
For education, teachers, schoolhouses, etc. 100,000
For missionary purposes, $3,000 per year for 20
    years 60,000

For agriculture	10,000
For vaccine matter, medicine, etc.	6,000
Annuities of provisions, salt, tobacco, etc.	14,000
Blacksmiths, farmers, mechanics, shops, etc. ..	93,600
Commutation of claims of individuals for lands	48,000
Goods and provisions to be delivered by the quartermaster some time next summer ...	150,000
Payments due to chiefs	30,000
Value of improvements on the lands bought and expenses of holding the treaty, about	40,000
Commutation of reservations of lands for half breeds	150,000
Payment of just debts of the two nations not exceeding	300,000
Whole cost of purchase	$1,601,600

This treaty, so just to the Indians, so favorable in its terms for the United States and so important to the best interests and prosperity of Michigan has been effected by Mr. Schoolcraft with the approbation and aid of the secretary of war and in the face of difficulties and embarrassments which no person of less superior qualifications could have overcome. Michigan ought to be grateful for their services. Of the country purchased about 4,000,000 acres extending from the Grand river north is known to be fine land for settlement and within a very few years we shall, no doubt, see towns springing up at the mouths of all the rivers flowing into Lake Michigan for a hundred miles north of Grand river, if not all around the lower peninsula. The upper peninsula is known to contain vast forests of the very best pine, which is even now much wanted in Ohio, Indiana, Illinois and the southern part of Michigan and Wisconsin, and must very shortly furnish the material of a highly valuable grade.

Following these two major performances, Schoolcraft again played a leading role in the birth drama of the State during the struggle that centered on the seven-mile strip on its southern boundary and on the Upper Peninsula of Michigan.

All the country west of Lake Michigan, north of Indiana and Illinois, and east of the Mississippi River had been added to the Territory of Michigan in 1818, temporarily, for administrative purposes. In 1824 Congress was petitioned by the inhabitants of the annexed region, and by those of Michilimackinac, for a separate organization to be known as Chippewa

Territory. The petition was repeated in 1826, and later the name was changed to Huron Territory. In 1829, a bill was presented in the Michigan Territorial Legislative Council to ask Congress to annex to the proposed new Territory of Wisconsin all that part of Michigan Territory lying north of the Straits of Mackinac. Such a memorial was actually accepted by the Council, the vote being seven to six. A few days later, however, wiser counsel prevailed. The question was reconsidered. The memorial was recommitted and not again reported. In 1833, when the Legislative Council proposed to memorialize Congress for permission to form a state within the limits fixed by the Act of 1805, Mr. Martin, then representing the Counties of Michilimackinac and Chippewa, objected to the boundaries on the ground that the citizens of the Island of Mackinac, and the country lying north of the Straits of that name, wished to be attached to the new Territory to be set off west of Lake Michigan. Mr. Martin launched several other unsuccessful plans to attach the northern country to Wisconsin. The continued disaffection of the northern counties was shown again in the Constitutional Convention of 1835.

At the time the Toledo War developed, the situation in Michigan in regard to the Upper Peninsula was apparently this: The Lower Peninsula did not exactly want to let it go, on the general principle of keeping what it could; but regarded the Lake Superior and Mississippi region as an expensive burden; while all the time the Upper Peninsula was clamoring for another seat of government of its own, more understanding, more reachable, and more representative, on the west side of Lake Michigan.

Schoolcraft had been Indian Agent at Sault Ste. Marie two years when the petition was made for organization of a new county on the St. Marys and in the basin of Lake Superior westward to the Mississippi. In response to a request, Schoolcraft submitted a choice of three names for the proposed county: Algonac, Allegan, and Chippewa. The organizing bill was passed December 26, 1826. The name of Chippewa was selected for the county.

In 1829, when the Legislative Council of the Territory voted to ask Congress to annex to the proposed new Territory of Wisconsin all that part of Michigan Territory lying north of the Straits of Mackinac, Schoolcraft was one of the seven members whose votes carried the short-lived memorial. In 1831, in "Notes on a Tour from Galena, in Illinois, to Fort Winnebago on the Source of the Fox River, in Wisconsin," he pointed out the need for a seat of territorial government at some point west of Lake Michigan.

The trouble with Ohio over its seizure of the seven-mile-wide strip that belonged to Michigan congealed the attitude of the nearly-born State. Public opinion in Michigan was united and volcanic. When offered the Upper Peninsula, as a compromise, in place of the disputed southern strip, it was determined in its refusal. It objected seriously to taking "that barren region." The seven-mile strip, or nothing, was its actual battle cry.

Yielding to the popular clamor, Senator Norvell and Delegate Crary, at Washington, rigidly opposed the Act of Congress that gave statehood to a Michigan with the compromised boundaries. Senator Lucius Lyon alone from Michigan stood for acceptance.

Senator Lyon knew for a certainty that the die was cast. Ohio was to have its way. Michigan's fight was unavailing. The powers that were had so decreed. He favored accepting the Upper Peninsula, not as a compromise, but as a compensation. To two men he owed the support that held him firm in his position.

General Cass, then Secretary of War, was troubled personally as well as officially by the crisis. He knew that the matter had been decided. He desired earnestly to have the conflict cease. Also he knew something of the value of the country beyond the Straits of Mackinac. Behind the scenes he encouraged Senator Lyon. They were old and close friends.

Senator Lyon had another powerful champion, not barred by circumstances from fighting in the open. This was Schoolcraft. The two had been intimate friends for years. Senator

Lyon not only knew Schoolcraft's evaluation of the country in his books, but personally.   He had lived with the Schoolcrafts in Detroit.

The Committee which considered the question in Congress had Schoolcraft's report regarding the value of the region. Schoolcraft also appeared in person before the Senate Committee to describe the Upper Lakes country.   He was at the time in Washington negotiating an Indian treaty.   Enlarging on its resources, he convincingly presented his opinion that it would be found of far greater value and importance to the State than the seven-mile strip surrendered.

Thus supported, Lucius Lyon, in flat opposition to the wishes of his angry constituents, advocated the Act that established Michigan's statehood with approximately its present boundaries.   At the following election they took their revenge. But he had gained a kingdom in acres and in mineral wealth for Michigan; and Schoolcraft had held up his hand through moments of weakening.   The true value of the region was known to few, if any.   In Schoolcraft's own individual self he had enough of the secret, and abundant strength, to sway the battle for Michigan, when the solid public opinion of the State unknowingly was inimical to its best interest.

After the fight in Congress was over; after the Upper Peninsula had been annexed to the Lower Peninsula by that body but before a Michigan convention had ratified the Act of Congress, in August 1836, Senator Norvell wrote to Mr. Schoolcraft "requesting information concerning the nature and extent of the territory thus attached . . . as may enable the people of Michigan duly to appreciate the importance of the acquisition."   The prestige of Schoolcraft as a national authority, and as a person free from suspicion of political motives, was thus sought by a chief opponent of the Act, in an effort to relieve the tense Michigan situation.   There was nothing perfunctory in Schoolcraft's response.   His *Letters of Albion* were designed to emphasize how much more the State had gained than it had lost.

From 1837 to 1841 Schoolcraft was a member of the first

Board of Regents of the reorganized University of Michigan. What he did for the State and the nation in ensuring successful continuance of that resurgence is another compelling story.

Vital Figure in Early American Education

The formal schooling of Henry Rowe Schoolcraft was curtailed, and in certain respects his self-education was inadequate. This only throws into more dramatic chiaroscuro his remarkable urge toward acquisition of knowledge for himself, and his extraordinary propulsion of the means of providing it for others.

His correspondence, lectures, published writings, collections, and organizational activity, all begun early and carried on continuously through many decades, make a massive contribution to education. His supreme desire, to be useful, although not at all confined to the discovery and diffusion of knowledge, was emphasized in that direction.

James Calcraft, his great-grandfather, had been a schoolteacher. A thirst for knowledge ran in the great-grandson's veins and some sound sense of pedagogic things was in his marrow.

As early as 1819 he saw and advocated the advantages of teaching mining engineering in the mineral district of the Ozarks.

What he saw of attempts to educate the Indians stripped certain problems of all education to their elemental simplicity.

Somewhat adapting the import of the Ordinance of 1787 to the Indian temperament, he placed the morality of temperance in advance of religion as well as before knowledge.

Notwithstanding all his zeal to spread the benefits of education, he held such common-sense views as many modern school administrators and social reformers would do well to study. Some of the characteristics of the Indian are also present in the Negro, the poor white, and the slum-dweller. Schoolcraft saw the vanity of great and sudden efforts to remodel the constitution of their peculiar society, to produce effects in a brief period which demand a long one—"to make, as it were, the red man, a white man, in a day."

"Knowledge, to be attractive to the Indian tribes, must possess a decidedly practical character." The first thing was to convince them of the superiority of agriculture over mere gardening, of grazing over hunting, of pacific over warlike achievements, of written over oral laws, of temperance over intemperance, of industry over inanity." Schoolcraft recognized the imperative need of simple, strong foundations.

The source of effective instruction lies not in the school building but in the instructor. How self-evident this sounds! And yet how far have we departed from its sane simplicity!

A circle of Indian children, gathered under a grove, might be as certainly taught the alphabet and digits, as if they were covered with a costly canopy. Buildings become necessary only to avoid the common changes of the atmosphere, and to ensure the observance of order. But such buildings require nothing beyond the simplest arrangements of a school house. . . . Large expenditures in the shape of buildings and fixtures, diminish the means applicable to instruction.

"The art and spirit of teaching," "perseverance and discrimination in the order in which facts are presented to the youthful mind," and "personal exertion and ingenuity on the part of the instructor,"—these he recognized as the essentials.

Schools, to be largely beneficial to the tribes, must be local. A school situated without the boundaries of the tribe, is also measurably without the boundary of a moral influence upon it. Experience has fully demonstrated the futility of attempts to change the moral condition of tribes by educating a select number of their youths at colleges and other remote points, while no simultaneous efforts were made with the body of the tribe itself. . . . Children who are drawn away to foreign boarding schools, become estranged from their tribes, and when they return, it is too often found that they have acquired a species of knowledge which places them so far above their people, that they become objects of distrust. . . . Neither can such isolated scholars themselves maintain the state of artificial elevation, in which adventitious circumstances have placed them. . . . Despondency or intemperance often ensue. . . . The whole failure, in these cases, has resulted from the want of local district schools, and other sources of instruction to raise the mass;—for if the mass of a tribe be degraded, it is of little avail that a few be educated.

In this statement lies the answer to the present condition of the Southern Negro and the mountain white.

Mission schools for Indians, however, were better than none; and when an attack was launched in the Michigan Legislative Council against the institution on Mackinac Island, Schoolcraft set himself successfully to defeat the unfriendly measure.

His essay on "Education of the Indian Race," originally written for the American Lyceum in 1834, reprinted in *Oneóta*, is worthy of wider note than its restricted title indicates.

He was a "natural" Regent for the University of Michigan and a giant in the educational history of that State.

The first phase of the development of the University of Michigan began August 26, 1817, with an act to establish the Catholepistemiad or University of Michigania. Its hold on life was tenuous. A reorganization to strengthen it was made April 30, 1821, by an act establishing in the City of Detroit an institution to be called the University of Michigan, transferring to it all possessions of the original body. A second, and successful reorganization, occurred March 21, 1837. The three are, in law as in spirit, one and the same institution.

For a third time the University experienced a life-and-death struggle. Professor Andrew Ten Brook in *American State Universities,* in his particular account of the University of Michigan, says:

State institutions, strictly such, had never prospered in this country. This fact was notorious, and was indeed regarded by almost all classes as decisive against the prosperity, and, of course, the life itself of this institution.

All the successful institutions of this country were under the control of bodies of religious men, strictly as such, or of close corporations. Their leaders had been chosen with an eye to their interest in the work, and their qualifications for it. . . . No class of men could thus fully identify themselves with this university, at least in its beginnings. The various religious denominations, and their members, as individuals, looked upon it as quite foreign to themselves; it would of course, they thought, be managed by the politicians, whose counsels would be divided by party and personal strifes, making the institution powerless for good; while it existed, it would rather impede than promote the true work of education, and only cause delay in the founding of colleges by the various Christian bodies of the State.

"The men officially bound to administer this trust . . . harbored all shades of doubt, especially the darker ones, in regard to the success of the enterprise." They were "moved more by a sense of present obligation, than by the hope of future and permanent results."

"There was nowhere any enthusiastic, or even hopeful feeling in regard to the university." "Petitions were sent to the legislature for transfer of the fund to common schools."

However true this may have been of public opinion in Michigan and of the Regents in general, it is antipodal to the temperament of Regent Schoolcraft, his previous performance, and his decisive, even over-optimistic action while a member of the Board. He brought to its meetings some things of incalculable value: faith in education, faith in America, faith in God; and his own indomitable way of forging ahead in spite of all obstacles. In his mind there was never a shadow of doubt about the future of America, either intellectually or economically.

Schoolcraft was appointed a member of the first Board of Regents of the University of Michigan March 21, 1837. At the first meeting of the Board, June 5, 1837, at Ann Arbor, his name was drawn for a full four-year term, which expired April 16, 1841. The brief summary of his life in the *Proceedings of the Board of Regents of the University of Michigan, 1837–1864,* states that he attended the meetings of the Board with regularity, took a prominent part in its deliberations, and had great influence in shaping its early policy. Even this contained statement is rich in commendation, considering the number of influential citizens of Michigan who refused appointment, resigned because they could not find time for the duties involved, or attended meetings so irregularly that the transaction of business was made extremely difficult because of inability to assemble a quorum. His friend, Senator Lucius Lyon, resigned after two years.

An example of Schoolcraftian action is provided in the purchase by the Regents of a fine collection of European minerals obtained from the Imperial Cabinet of Vienna. Unquestionably he was the one responsible. Schoolcraft had been interested in this collection for more than ten years. In fact he had at one time negotiated with Baron Lederer about exchanging his large mass of Lake Superior copper for specimens from the Austrian collection. It is significant also that Dr. John Torrey, of New York City, who was a party to the transaction, had been Schoolcraft's friend for almost twenty years.

At the second November meeting in 1837, Schoolcraft submitted a resolution directing the appropriate committee of the Regents to inquire into (1) the expediency of employing, at the earliest practicable period, a suitable agent to visit Europe for the purpose of procuring the necessary philosophical apparatus and standard books for the University; (2) the propriety of instituting such inquiries and taking such preliminary steps as might be proper, to lay the foundation of a suitable collection of specimens for the University cabinet, in the various departments of natural history; (3) to ask the State Geologist to secure the large mass of native copper from the Ontonagon for the University (it is now in the Smithsonian Institution), recommending that expense of transportation be paid out of University funds.

At the same meeting this committee reported correspondence with Dr. Torrey of New York relative to a cabinet of minerals owned by L. Lederer—2600 specimens of foreign minerals, many said to be rare and perhaps not elsewhere to be obtained, —priced at $4500. It was recommended that an agent be authorized to examine the collection and arrange for its purchase. Schoolcraft thereupon submitted a resolution that Dr. John Torrey be directed to examine Baron Lederer's cabinet, report on its value, and make necessary preliminary arrangements for its purchase. It was on motion of Mr. Schoolcraft,

January 6, 1838, that the President was directed to authorize Dr. Torrey to make the purchase, for $4000.

Such knowledge, forthright action, confidence to the point of rashness, and yet sense based on far vision are characteristic of Henry Rowe Schoolcraft and what his presence meant to apathetic Michigan and a half-hopeless Board. Professor Ten Brook says of the incident: This "seems a large amount to pay in anticipation of the existence of both an endowment and an institution, and yet as this was nearly all that was expended for such purpose, it can not well be deemed injudicious." President Tappan said: "By a wise purchase, early made, the Cabinet of Minerals had always been extensive."

The Regents might vote to purchase a mineralogical collection and a library, but the matter of financing arrangements was difficult. About a million dollars had been virtually promised to the University, but cash was necessary. Providentially Schoolcraft was appointed on the finance committee, November 14, 1837. He had the kind of determination that had carried him six thousand miles on sixty dollars; urged him on into unknown Ozark country when his companions failed him; led him to chop logs and help build a cabin as the price of a guide. Combined with this he had the enterprise that had built a mansion for an Indian Agency at the Sault, and was soon to secure more than a hundred thousand dollars from Congress for a publication on the American Indian. It was important also that Schoolcraft had served as chairman of the finance committee of the Legislative Council of the Territory of Michigan.

At the meeting of March 3, 1838, he presented a motion that "a standing committee of three be appointed on the organization and government of the University, who shall be charged with reporting to this Board as early as practicable the best plan for putting the University into operation at the earliest practicable period." This was adopted. Schoolcraft was made chairman. He was no novice in the launching of new enterprises. As a young man he had superintended and established a number of glass factories. In addition to driving executive ability he had practical knowledge.

A resolution submitted by him at the same meeting, and adopted, required:

That a committee on building be appointed, to consist of three members, who shall be charged with the following duties: (1) To fix upon and recommend to this Board a plan for the University buildings; (2) To prepare accurate estimates of the stone, lime, brick, timber, iron, and other materials required, with their probable cost, delivered on the ground, and the periods at which the delivery is required to be made; (3) To contract under the direction of the Board for such materials, on printed proposals, designating the articles, dates of delivery, and sureties required, and stipulating to make the respective payments at such periods as the University funds may justify; (4) The propriety of employing a suitable architect to superintend, under their directions, the erection of the buildings, and the arrangement of the grounds.

He immediately presented, at the same gathering of the Boad, two other resolutions of epochal importance: The first to inquire into the feasibility of obtaining a loan of $150,000 State bonds, for twenty years; the other, adopted, authorizing the President of the Board to ascertain whether a loan of State bonds to the amount of $150,000 could be obtained for twenty years. This was in anticipation of the approximately million dollar fund virtually promised.

Of this, Professor Ten Brook wrote after thirty-five years:

We may look upon this action from the distance, and find in it much to censure as premature and imprudent, as bringing into peril the university fund, as threatening to strangle at its birth the great enterprise which it proposed to hasten into life and into a full development of its beneficent career; even the closest scrutiny and most careful investigation of facts will rather increase than diminish the number and strength of the grounds of censure; and yet, after all, there will be found reason to believe that the very boldness of the act and the incentives to exertion generated in the straits into which it brought the board, really saved the institution, and contributed to make it what it is. . . . It checked, by its embarrassments, the reckless course which would have annihilated the fund, and proved a stimulus to exertion, an antidote to apathy.

Schoolcraft's report as chairman of the committee on organization and government was presented, without delay, March 24, 1838, and accepted.

A loan of one hundred thousand dollars was secured.

The plans for college buildings and professors' houses, drawn up by an architect from New Haven, as approved by the Regents and the Governor, would have cost half a million. Fortunately Superintendent of Public Instruction Pierce opposed them, the Regents receded, and the University campus plans were drastically reduced.

The first buildings, including four dwellings and one dormitory 110×40 feet, were either completed, or so nearly so, in the summer of 1841, as to allow the opening of instruction. Governor Barry, who came to the chief executive chair of Michigan on January 1, 1842, is said to have remarked that, as the State had the buildings and had no other use for them, it was probably best to continue the school—showing that the balance of the scale between suspending and going forward may have been turned in favor of the latter by the bare fact of having these architectural preparations.   However this may be, it is a fact that no enterprise ever stood in more absolute indecision between advancing and retreating than did the University of Michigan from 1839 to 1843.

Schoolcraft's activities on the Board were various.   He was a member of the committee on professorships, one of the auditors of the accounts of the treasurer of the Board, member of the committee on amendments to the organic laws of the University and of the committee on amendments to the laws for the government of the branches.   He presented the report for the library committee December 22, 1840, showing 3700 volumes, reporting the original purchase by Professor Asa Gray.   It is noteworthy that twelve years later the collection had increased by only 800 items.   Appointed to the committee on the Annual Report of the Board to the Superintendent of Public Instruction, December 22, 1840, he presented it January 5, 1841.   It was the third such report, but the first to be entered upon the records of the *Regents Proceedings*.

His work as chairman on the committee on branches, to which he was appointed at the first November meeting in 1837, was of profound influence.   The establishment of union schools, at various points throughout the State, by use of University funds and under University management, for the time being bridged the gap between the free common schools and the University. The original intention was to have a branch for every county. At first there were plans for eight, and at the end of the first year five had actually been established with 161 students. The branches were discontinued in 1846, but in the intervening time were of great service. They hastened preparation of the first classes for the University and kept up the succession. Even more, they did much to beget desire throughout the State for preparatory schools.

In a still more fundamental way, the work of the committee on branches affected the future of the University.

Dr. Ten Brook in his history of the institution makes the following illuminating comment:

In tracing the history of institutions, we often find the germ of the whole future wrapped up in the actuating principles of their founders. This may be true in regard to the University of Michigan, and a brief review of some of those principles may be of interest, as serving to account for results.

The annual report of the regents, made at the close of the year during which the work of instruction at Ann Arbor was begun, states some views which had operated in the management of the branches, and foreshadowed those which were to prevail in the establishment and prosecution of the work in the university proper. This report was doubtless written by Mr. Schoolcraft, and bears the names of Henry R. Schoolcraft, Zina Pitcher, and George Duffield. That part of it which is pertinent to our present purpose is as follows:

"In organizing a board of regents to carry out the views of the legislature in the establishment of a university, it is conceived to have been the primary object of this body to extend its benefits as widely, and at as early a period, throughout the state, as the wants of the community and the means at their disposal would admit.

"And their attention was therefore called at an early day to the location and establishment of branches of the university at suitable points, where the branches of a classical and English education, preparatory to the entrance of the students into the parent institution, should be taught. This object has been steadily pursued, not only from its being the appointed means for preparing classes for their final collegiate course, but from the additional consideration, that, in a new and hastily settled community, it would be one of the best and most practical means of arousing attention to the value and importance of the plan of education submitted to the people in the organic act, and of thus preparing the public mind to appreciate and foster it. To this end the most competent men were sought as principals of the branches, liberal salaries paid them, and every facility afforded in connection with the citizens of the respective sites of the branches, to render the means of instruction both efficient and reputable. The committee on the branches, charged with this duty, have encountered an arduous task in the management of the correspondence, the selection of principals and teachers, the examination of reports, and the pecuniary questions which required decision and adjustment, and the board owes to it much of the success which has attended the effort. It was conceived that the requirement of the act and the duty of the board in this respect would not have been fully performed by merely obtaining instructors of competent literary and natural abilities, disconnected from their moral influence, both in the branches and in the communities in which they are located. And it has ever constituted an object to find men, both as principals and subordinates, who united sound learning and apt judgment, and practical piety. And the confident hope is indulged that the importance attached to this principle in these selections for office, has produced a benign result.

"Of the seven branches established, five are under the direction of clergymen, and two of laymen, of various religious denominations. Two clergymen are also embraced among the assistants and tutors, the whole number of whom add to their literary qualifications those arising from religious considerations. The board can not, they believe, be mistaken in the importance they attach to the connection between learning and morals, science and religion; and at any rate, they would be unjust to themselves not to express the belief that success can not permanently crown the institution committed to their management, after this ligament is severed."

In this report, Mr. Schoolcraft has stated the claims of piety as a qualification for an instructor's position, and the preference of the board for clergymen, in stronger terms than he could have used had he belonged to that profession.

This policy disarmed the kind of opposition that pointed out that the first organization of the Board of Regents included no clerical members; that stigmatized the University then in futuro as an infidel affair, and urged an act for the incorporation of a sectarian college upon the Legislature.

The principles stated in Regent Schoolcraft's report, as governing the action of the Board in relation to the branches, were well supported in the following year in relation to the central institution. This trend "gradually conciliated the religious public, attached them more and more to the university, and inspired a degree of confidence which was wholesome in its influence . . ." It "held the religious element among the people at least from a decision adverse to the university."

The famous sentence from the Ordinance of 1787 carved on the façade of Angell Hall in Ann Arbor early in the succeeding century, as everybody knows reads: "Religion, morality, and knowledge being necessary to good government and the happiness of mankind, schools and the means of education shall forever be encouraged." For a long time, however, there was a tendency to slight the first three words.

In recent years, the administration, under the present President of the University, Dr. Alexander Grant Ruthven, has taken a number of positive steps to align its policy with the vision of Schoolcraft, set forth a hundred years ago in words which bear repeating: "The board can not, they believe, be mistaken in the importance they attach to the connection between learning and morals, science and religion; and at any rate, they would be unjust to themselves not to express the belief that success can not permanently crown the institution committed to their management, after this ligament is severed."

This attitude and action of Schoolcraft gave the University of Michigan its chance for life a hundred years ago. The same principle applied today is restoring its vitality.

It is a big statement, but justified in the light of the foregoing, that in all likelihood Michigan owes to Schoolcraft more than to any other individual the fact that its state university, in the organizational phase beginning in 1837, did not die quickly as previous birth-efforts had done. Certainly he was a great factor in that final, successful effort. The spirit of the other members of the first Board of Regents has not been made manifest. We do know his. Its strength and acts were of his kind. What he did not do himself, he typifies.

The question of Schoolcraft's own scholarship falls into the background. His mistakes in foreign languages and philology are trivia. His lack of all academic training except some extramural studies is entirely to his credit. On a poor background he wrote a shining record. Schoolcraft is not to be judged, finally, as a representative of American scholarship at its perfection, but as a great representative of the American spirit that made American scholarship eventually a reality. He was a true scholar. No man ever had more love of learning, or belief in it, or vision for it, or courage, or worked more tirelessly in its behalf.

America owes Schoolcraft profound recognition for his Herculean acts that enabled the University of Michigan to live and breathe and go on to become one of the leading educational institutions of the world.

His contribution to education in Michigan outside of the University was greatest in his work as chairman of the Regents' committee on university branches. There are evidences also of more general activities.

Having heard of a report by Professor Stowe of Cincinnati to the General Assembly of the state of Ohio on the mode of teaching and state of common school education in Europe, he was instrumental in procuring an authentic copy for the use of the Board of Regents of the University, in 1838.

A circular dated June 1839 at New York City, calling a national convention in Philadelphia to discuss elementary education, subscribed to by one representative from each of five States and addressed to the governor and members of the Legislature of Michigan, was signed by Henry R. Schoolcraft for Michigan. All five signatories were presumably members of the American Lyceum, by which the convention was proposed. This circular was printed in the *Journal of Education* of Michigan, at Schoolcraft's request, in August of that year. This item is interesting evidence of Schoolcraft's leadership in

education, not only in the State but in the nation.   His work
as chairman of the committee on branches of the University,
with its contribution to the establishment of secondary schools,
alone entitles him to recognition as one of the founders of the
public school system of the State of Michigan.

The importance of Schoolcraft's part in launching the
Journal of Education of Michigan also has yet to be realized,
as well as the claim of that publication to national prominence.

To begin with, as pointed out by Dr. Milo Milton Quaife
of the Burton Historical Collection, of Detroit, in a letter to
the authors, Michigan's *Journal of Education* has the distinction of being the first educational journal published in the
United States.   Beginning at Detroit in March, 1838, it clearly
antedated two other periodicals for which the same claim has
been made.   The initial number of the *Connecticut Common
School Journal* appeared August, 1838.   That of Horace
Mann's *Common School Journal,* issued in November of the
same year, was noted in Number 12 of Volume I of the Michigan *Journal of Education.*

The 1877 *History of Calhoun County,* Michigan, published in Philadelphia, says that F. W. Shearman actually
edited the *Journal of Education,* apparently under Mr. Pierce's
general authority and direction, and lists Schoolcraft as one of
the outstanding contributors.   No articles signed or initialed
by Schoolcraft are found in any of its numbers.   A book review
of his *Algic Researches,* and "A Shawnee Tale," from that collection, appear in Volume II, Number 5, July 1839; and a circular on elementary education, received from him, was printed
the month following.   Volume I, Number 5, contains an article
entitled "Typical Use of the Indian Pipe," by "Tzotiav," which
may have been a pseudonym of Schoolcraft.

Not much is known about the *Journal of Education.*   The
one original file known to exist is preserved in the library of
Michigan State Normal College at Ypsilanti, Michigan.   A
photostat copy of this is in the University Library at Ann
Arbor.

It was an eight-page paper, ten by twelve inches, with

three columns to the page, published monthly, from March, 1838, Volume I, Number 1, to December 1839, Volume II, Number 10. The first nine numbers were issued at Detroit, Michigan. At the start J. D. Pierce was listed as publisher. Communications were to be sent to the publishers at Marshall, Calhoun County, Michigan, but subscriptions could be paid to Alexander McFarren of Detroit where the paper was printed by J. S. & S. A. Bagg, Printers. Beginning with Volume II, Number 1, William S. Lee, Office of Indian Affairs, Detroit, was listed as one of the two subscription agents. With Number 10 of Volume I, the place of publication was changed from Detroit to Marshall, where the printing was done by Henry C. Bunce. J. D. Pierce is listed as publisher until November, 1838, Number 9 of Volume I, when Francis Willett Shearman became editor and co-publisher, which arrangement continued as long as the magazine lasted.

Intended as official organ of the state superintendent of public instruction, to be used by that officer as a means of communication between himself and subordinate school officials, it was not for teachers alone but to arouse interest in education and stimulate activity in the organization of schools. Although it lived only two years it circulated generally throughout the State in the interests of education, and was an able advocate of common and higher school systems. Dr. Charles O. Hoyt and Dr. Richard Clyde Ford, in their *John D. Pierce, Founder of the Michigan School System,* said: "As one reads it today, almost seventy years after its publication, there is the conviction that it would rank at par with any educational paper now published. . . . This initial movement of an educational publication in the Northwest may be regarded as one of Mr. Pierce's greatest achievements."

It would appear on examination that the distinction thus accorded John D. Pierce must be shared, if not entirely yielded, to Henry Rowe Schoolcraft.

In his memoirs, January 22, 1838, Schoolcraft recorded: "The friends of education in Michigan, having assembled in convention, issue a circular calling attention to that vital subject, and recommend a Journal of Public Instruction to the patronage of the people."

Among the Schoolcraft papers in the Smithsonian Collection is a printed circular, undated but issued January 22, 1838, at Detroit, that reads as follows:

To Parents, Teachers, and the Friends of Education generally, in the State of Michigan.

At the late convention in this city, of gentlemen from different sections of the state, interested in the promotion of common school education, the following, among other resolutions, was adopted:

"Resolved, That a committee of three be appointed, to take into consideration the importance of engaging an able and qualified editor, to conduct a monthly periodical, devoted exclusively to the subject of common school education; and if thought expedient, to employ such editor, and devise ways and means for the remuneration of his services."

Having been appointed said committee, the undersigned, after mature consideration of the subject referred to them, have come to the unanimous conclusion, that a publication of the character contemplated in the resolution, would be eminently serviceable to the cause of education, and entitled to the countenance and patronage of every enlightened and patriotic citizen. Its design is to awaken a deeper interest throughout the state, in the importance of primary education, to elevate the character of common schools, by communicating important principles and suggestions, connected with the management and instruction of youth, and to spread before the community such facts and information as will interest all who feel any concern in the subject of popular education.

The committee have great pleasure in announcing, that they have engaged as editor of the proposed journal the Superintendent of Public Instruction, Mr. John D. Pierce. To literary qualifications of a high order, Mr. P. unites the advantage of former experience as a practical teacher, and of minute and extensive acquaintance with the condition and wants of every portion of the state. Under such auspices, the committee cannot doubt, that the publication will be a most valuable auxiliary in the cause of education, and they appeal with equal earnestness and confidence to their fellow citizens, to encourage and sustain the enterprise.

The committee are desirous, if possible, to send it into every town, and every school district in the state; and they respectfully solicit the co-operation of gentlemen in every town, postmasters, and common school inspectors in particular, in procuring at least four subscribers for each school district, and remitting payment to Alexander McFarren, of this city, before the 1st of March.

Printers throughout the state are requested to insert this circular a few weeks gratis.

H. R. SCHOOLCRAFT,
GEORGE WILSON,
I. M. NEWCOMBE.

TERMS.

THE JOURNAL OF PUBLIC INSTRUCTION,

Will be published monthly in this city, under the editorial charge of John D. Pierce, and will be afforded to subscribers at 75 cents per annum. Payment in all cases required in advance.

It is clear that the idea of the periodical was introduced in a general meeting. A resolution was passed to appoint a committee for the purpose; Schoolcraft headed the committee; and it is common practice that the proponent of a resolution is made chairman. This committee announced that they had decided in favor of such a publication and had engaged Mr. John D. Pierce as editor. The name of the superintendent of public instruction would, of course, ex-officio, carry maximum prestige. The Committee asked for at least four subscribers for each school district; and the Smithsonian copy of the circular lists the unusual number of fifteen subscriptions from Michilimackinac. The fact that at a later time subscriptions could be paid to an individual at the Office of Indian Affairs in Detroit is another pointer toward Schoolcraft. After John D. Pierce had been engaged as editor and had issued eight numbers, another editor was secured. This was Francis Willett Shearman, the nephew of Henry Rowe Schoolcraft who had been instrumental in bringing him to Michigan in 1836 to aid in Indian affairs at Mackinac Island. The 1877 *History of Calhoun County* says that F. W. Shearman "actually edited the *Journal,* apparently under Mr. Pierce's general authority and direction."

Perhaps most significant of all the evidence of Schoolcraft's propulsion in the matter is the fact that, after this periodical ceased, we find him again, April 19, 1841, writing to the new, recently-appointed superintendent of public instruction, F. Sawyer, Esq., of Ann Arbor, suggesting the publication of an educational journal. Following his letter a circular was sent to inspectors in relation to the publication of a common school journal, in June, 1841. This was only a few months before Schoolcraft moved to New York from Michigan. Nothing came of this second attempt in the State to publish such a periodical.

This series of circumstances, added to the known almost-mania of Schoolcraft to get a publication out for every organization or interest with which he was ever connected, gives him a claim superior to that of Mr. Pierce to the credit for launching this periodical.

The distinction of having the first educational journal ever published in the United States is one which infant Michigan may well have taken pride in. Detroit shares in the honor. And it is one more amazing mark for Schoolcraft, that, with the Michigan *Journal of Education,* he was ahead of Horace Mann in that great pioneer's own field.

Uncompromising Antagonist of Alcohol

At the time of his election to the Territorial Council in 1828, Schoolcraft made the following comment:

Party spirit has not yet reached and distracted this Territory. So far as I know, political divisions of a general character, have not entered into society. The chief magistrate [General Cass] is an eminently conservative man, and by his moderation of tone and suavity of manners, has been instrumental in keeping political society in a state of tranquillity. All our parties have been founded on personal preference. If there has been any more general principle developed in the legislature it has been a *promptly debt paying,* and a *not promptly debt paying party*—a *non divorce,* and a *divorce party.* I have been ever of the former class of thinkers; and shall let my votes tell for the right and good old way—*i.e.,* pay your debts and keep your wife.

He did not refer here to his stand in the legislative chamber as everywhere, in the struggle of *man versus alcohol.* His fight against the liquor evil is a major characteristic of his constructive life.

Schoolcraft was personally a teetotaler. He did not smoke. It was part of his character to be temperate in all things, except industry.

His attitude toward the giving of liquor to Indians was not fixed at the beginning. In 1820, anticipating from reports that the Fox Indians at Dubuque would not be willing to let him, or any white man, view their lead diggings, he provided himself with presents of tobacco and whisky. These he made use of successfully when other means of persuasion had entirely failed. This is in complete contrast with his later policy.

The following year he had an unpleasantly intimate glimpse of the effects of whisky on the Indian, when obliged to seek accommodations overnight in an Indian village on the headwaters of the Wabash. The riot of an all-night carousal— the talking, singing, crying, at the same time; the quarreling that began when the liquor was exhausted; and the momentary expectation of murder—left a dark impression. A few days later the supply canoe of the Cass expedition was ambushed by Indians and robbed, for the sole purpose of securing the barrel of whisky carried.

But a truly unforgettable instance of the debasement of the Indian by his appetite for alcohol was soon to be presented. Schoolcraft, as secretary of the commission that effected the Treaty of 1821 at Chicago, records conversations between General Cass and two Indian chiefs as follows:

Metea, in giving reasons for the refusal of the Indians to conclude a treaty, said to General Cass, among other things,

"My Father,—You have denied us the smallest favours. When I came to ask you yesterday for only a gill of whiskey a-piece for my young men; you refused it. You must reflect that we have feelings as well as you."

"When you asked me for the whiskey," Governor Cass replied, "You ought not to have blushed because I refused it, but because you asked for it. I told you, some days ago, you should have no more whiskey—that I had stopped it all up tight, so that none could get out. Do your people suppose I would tell them a lie?

"If we wished to get your lands without paying a just equivalent for them, we have nothing to do but to get you all intoxicated, and we could purchase as much land as we pleased. You perfectly know that when in liquor you have not your proper senses, and are wholly unfit to transact any business, especially business of so weighty a nature. When intoxicated, you may be induced to sign any paper—you then fall asleep, and when you awake, find you have lost all your lands. But instead of pursuing this course, we keep the whiskey from you, that you may make the best bargain for yourselves, your women and children. I am surprised particularly, that your *old* men should come forward continually crying whiskey! whiskey! whiskey!

"The little liquor you asked for, would neither make me, nor my friend (Mr. Sibley), richer nor poorer. The worth of the whiskey is trifling—too trifling to merit a moment's consideration, but we denied it to you only to keep you sober, that you should be able to see justice done to yourselves.

"This passion for strong drink has injured your nation more than any other thing—more than all the other causes put together. It is not a long period since you were a powerful and independent tribe—now, you are reduced to a handful, and it is all owing to ardent spirits. . . . How should we look, should we hereafter meet you in council, and you should get up and say, We were drunk when we signed this treaty!

"We are daily giving you as much as you can eat: you are receiving a liberal allowance of provisions every morning, and cannot complain that there is anything wanting to render your situation comfortable. We neither spare nor value the expense of it. If you *will* drink and *must* drink, at least wait until a proper time."

Notwithstanding this stern admonition, at the close of the protracted negotiations, when they were told that the goods agreed on were not yet ready to be issued, Topinabee cried out, "Give us the whiskey! We care not for the rest."

Conditions at Sault Ste. Marie were beyond believing. A few weeks after his arrival there in 1822, a Chippewa Indian—the husband of Jane Johnston's full-blood Indian cousin—was murdered in a drunken brawl. Soon afterwards Sassaba, the chief who had led the demonstration against General Cass in 1820, and four other Chippewas, returning from a drinking party, were drowned and carried over the Falls. When the Reverend Mr. Bingham reached the Sault in 1828 he was astounded to learn that every male Indian in the town carried liquor in his medicine pouch, and that the stores and military canteens between them were planning to dispose of fifteen thousand gallons of whisky before spring. At least that was the quantity they had purchased to last until the opening of navigation. In 1829, Sutler Hulbert at Fort Brady, and other merchants, poured whisky in the street, as a public notice of their revolt against conditions, as well as evidence of the effect of Abel Bingham's preaching. The English author, Mrs. Jameson, recorded in 1837 that, when she decided to shoot the Rapids, she experienced considerable difficulty in finding an Indian in the village who was sufficiently sober to undertake the trip.

An early essay of Schoolcraft on Indian customs and character, published, in 1825, in *Travels in the Central Portions of the Mississippi Valley,* contains the statement:

The most prominent trait in the character of all the tribes at the present day; the trait which obtrudes itself first to our notice; which exercises, and which is calculated hereafter to exercise the most important influence upon their present and future condition, and upon their ultimate fate, is their strong, deep, and universal passion for ardent spirits. . . . It exists more extensively at the present day than at any former period; . . . its baneful current is spreading deeper and wider every hour, carrying want, disease, crime and depopulation in its course, and threatening to sweep before it the enfeebled remains of this once mighty people.

The Indians were not grateful for the efforts to save them from themselves. In 1825, at Prairie du Chien,

At the close of the treaty, an experiment was made on the moral sense of the Indians, with regard to intoxicating liquors, which was evidently of too refined a character for their just appreciation. It had been said by the tribes that the true reason for the Commissioners of the United States government speaking against the use of ardent spirits by the Indians, and refusing to give them, was not a sense of its bad effects, so much, as the fear of the expense. To show them that the government was above such a petty principle, the Commissioners had a long row of tin camp kettles, holding several gallons each, placed on the grass, from one end of the council house to the other, and then, after some suitable remarks, each kettle was spilled out in their presence. The thing was evidently ill relished by the Indians.

Laws of Congress forbade the sale of intoxicating liquors

to Indians only upon Indian territories. They could buy it in towns and villages and even from isolated white settlers, too many of whom were glad to manufacture home-made whisky for the revenue. In fact, the general situation was altogether bad. The westward movement of the white population began before the temperance reformation. Bad water, home-sickness, all shades of discouragement, and tedious and depressing fevers, drove many to seek relief in the common use of alcoholic drinks. Whisky made from fruits and grains which had no market was cheap and universally used, and even the religious conscience of the day did not forbid this practice, unless carried to the evident disturbance of reason.

On the boundary the competition between British and American traders made the situation particularly difficult. Schoolcraft's endeavors to save the Indians from their terrible enslavement made him bitter, even vicious enemies, in both races.

His stand began at home. Of course Schoolcraft himself is the agent mentioned in the following incident recorded by him:

One measure was found to be efficacious in establishing a systematic mode of doing business: this was to exclude from an interview, and to refuse to transact any business at all with drunken Indians, and not to allow any one in a state of intoxication to enter the office, or the dwelling of the agent. As whiskey was freely sold in the village, intoxication was a very prevalent vice; and, when excited, the Indian is noisy, and will endeavor to force his way into any part of the private dwelling in which he may chance to be.

The principal chief at Sault Ste. Marie was a tall and dignified man called Shingabawossin. . . . His armorial badge was the Crane totem, the distinguishing mark of the reigning clan. Shingabawossin had, in his youth, been on the warpath; but he was at this period principally respected for his prudence and wisdom in council. He was about six feet three inches in height, straight in form, having a Roman cast of countenance, and mild manners; he was a good speaker, but prone to repetition. He had three brothers, likewise chiefs, and a large retinue of cousins-german, and other relatives, who generally followed him. The attainment of his good will ensured the friendship of the tribe, through whom an extensive influence was established with the interior bands.

The agent told the Indians in a quiet way, that the President had not sent him to transact business with drunken Indians, and that such persons must never enter his office or house. He enforced this precept, soon after, by taking Shingabawossin by the shoulders, when he was in liquor, as well as very noisy, leading him to the door, and giving him a sudden push forward, which prostrated him on the ground at a little distance. If the king of the Chippewas could be so treated, it was naturally inferred that the subject might meet with harsher usage. The resulting effect was that no further trouble ever arose from this cause.

Boatmen, on his expeditions, were engaged with the express stipulation that they should drink no whisky, but should have instead a liberal food allowance. This was for example to the Indians, as well as general safety and efficiency and morals.

Courageously, and at cost of a dastardly attack later, Schoolcraft discharged his wife's scapegrace brother from the Indian service at Mackinac because of drunkenness.

Regardless of the practice of other Indian agents, he rigidly enforced what liquor laws there were and threw all his influence into the scale to pass even stricter regulations.

The following letter, written at St. Peters, July 25, 1832, to General Joseph M. Street, Indian Agent at Prairie du Chien, shows one phase of the difficulties he encountered:

I arrived at this place yesterday from the sources of the Mississippi, having visited the Chippewa bands and trading-posts in that quarter. Much complaint is made respecting the conduct of the persons licensed by you last year, who located themselves at the Granite Rocks, and on the St. Croix. No doubt can exist that each of them took in, and used in their trade, a considerable quantity of whiskey. And I am now enabled to say, that they each located themselves at points within the limits of my agency, where there are no trading-posts established. My lowest trading-post on the Mississippi, is the Pierced Prairie, eighteen miles below the mouth of the De Corbeau. It embraces one mile square, upon which traders are required to be located. On the St. Croix, the posts established and confirmed by the Department are Snake River and Yellow River, and embrace each, as the permanent place of location, one mile square. I report these facts for your information, and not to enable you to grant licenses for these posts, as the instructions of the Department give to each agent the exclusive control of the subject of granting licenses for the respective agencies.

Much solicitude is felt by me to exclude ardent spirits wholly from the Chippewas and Ottowas, the latter of whom have, by a recent order, been placed under my charge. I am fully satisfied that ardent spirits are not necessary to the successful prosecution of the trade, that they are deeply pernicious to the Indians, and that both their use and abuse is derogatory to the character of a wise and sober government. Their exclusion in every shape, and every quantity, is an object of primary moment; and it is an object which I feel it a duty to persevere in the attainment of, however traders may bluster. I feel a reasonable confidence in stating, that no whiskey has been used in my agency during the last two years, except the limited quantity taken by special permission of the Secretary of War, for the trade of the Hudson's Bay lines; and saving also the quantity clandestinely introduced from Prairie du Chien and St. Peters.

I know, sir, that an appeal to you on this subject cannot be lost, and that your feelings and judgment fully approve of temperance measures. But it requires active, persevering, unyielding efforts. And in all such efforts, judiciously urged, I am satisfied that the government will sustain the agents in a dignified discharge of their duties. Let us proceed in the accomplishment of this object with firmness, and with a determination never to relinquish it, until ardent spirits are entirely excluded from the Indian country.

P.S. Capt. Jouett, commanding at this post, has recently seized sixteen kegs of high-wines. . . .

The Indians in his territory resented the results of his efforts. At Leech Lake, in 1832, complaining against his traders, they cited the exclusion of liquor as one grievance. At the same time they admitted that formerly it was brought in to buy up wild rice, a practice that left them destitute at the beginning of cold weather. Schoolcraft made no attempt to dodge the issue:

So far as related to the traders withdrawing the article of whiskey from the trade, I felt it due to say that no hard feelings should be entertained towards them. That it was excluded by the office. That the Indians should, in justice blame me, or blame the government, and not the traders. I was satisfied that the use of whiskey was very hurtful to them in every situation, and felt determined to employ every means which the control of the Agency of the North-West gave to me, to exclude the article wholly and rigidly from the Chippewas, and to set the mark of disapprobation upon every trader who should make the attempt to introduce it.

The fur traders were harder to contend with than the Indians.

When the War Department laid down the principle that the quantity of whisky should be limited to two barrels for each post, the traders agitated for the establishment of three more posts, in order to get more liquor. They claimed that without more they could not compete with the British. Schoolcraft fearlessly opposed the American traders on this issue at every point, and kept an alert eye for liquor smuggling.

In 1828, an Indian requested permission to take inland, for his own use, two kegs of whisky which had been presented to him. This method of evading the intercourse act by presenting or selling liquor in a territory where laws of Congress did not operate, thus shifting on the Indian the risk and responsibility of taking it inland, was an example of the ingenuity of the Fur Company and their servants.

Guelle Plat, a chief, asked permission to take some whisky inland from the Sault. In reply to Schoolcraft's objections, he said, "Indians die whether they drink whisky or not."

Three days later, convinced that he could not change the ruling, he made ready to go home, observing that there was one thing in which he had observed a great difference between the practices of this, and St. Peters agency. There, whisky was given out in abundance—at the Sault he saw it was the practice to give none.

An illuminating glimpse of the friction between Henry Rowe Schoolcraft and Robert Stuart,—eminent citizen of Mackinac Island, who succeeded Schoolcraft as Indian Agent and Superintendent of Indian Affairs for Michigan in 1841,— is outlined in the following passage from the Schoolcraft *Memoirs* in 1829:

Mr. Robert Stuart, Agent to the American Fur Company, writes from Mackinac, that some of the American Fur Company's clerks are not inclined to take whisky, under the general government permit, *provided their opponents take none.* This tampering with the subject and with me, in the conduct of the agent of that company, whose duty it is rigidly to exclude the article by every means, would accord better, it should seem, with the spirit of one who had not recently taken obligations which are applicable to all times and all space. . . . The traders and citizens generally, on the frontiers, are leagued in their *supposed* interests to break down, or evade the laws, Congressional and territorial, which exclude it, or make it an offence to sell or give it. If an agent aims honestly to put the law in force, he must expect to encounter obloquy. If he appeals to the local courts, it is ten to one that nine-tenths of his jury are offenders in this very thing. So far as the American Fur Company is concerned, it is seen, I think, by the course of the managers, that it would conduce to better hunts if the Indians were kept sober, and liquor were rigidly excluded; but the argument is, that *on the lines*—that the Hudson's Bay Company use it, and that their trade would suffer if they had not *some*. And they thus override the agents, by appealing to higher powers, and so get permits annually, for a limited quantity, of which *they* and not the *agents* are the judges. In this way the independence of the agents is constantly kept down, and made to bend to a species of mock popular will.

In view of the counteracting influence of the American Fur Company on this frontier, it would be better for the credit of morals, properly so considered, if the chief agent of that concern at Michilimackinac were not a professor of religion, or otherwise, if he were in a position to act out its precepts boldly and frankly on this subject. For, as it now is, his position is perpetually mistaken. A temperance man, he is yet a member of a local temperance society, which only operates against the retailers, but leaves members free to sell by the barrel. Bound, by the principles of law, not to introduce whisky into the interior, he yet sells it to others, knowing their intention to be to run it over the lines, in spite of the agents. This is done by white and red men. And he obtains "permits" besides, as head of the company, at headquarters at Washington, to take in, openly, a certain quantity of high wines every year. Talk to that gentleman on the subject, and he is eloquent in defense of temperance.

A Washington official, after a trip on the Lakes to Green Bay, Wisconsin, wrote Schoolcraft, in the summer of 1830:

I conceive it my duty to inform you that I have obtained information from the contractor himself [one of the owners of the steamer on which he traveled] that, under the head of "provisions" he has contracted to deliver, and has actually delivered, two hundred barrels of whisky and two hundred barrels of high wines, at the place for the American Fur Company, which, no doubt, is designed to be sent into the Indian country the ensuing fall.

Schoolcraft saw that there could be no compromise. "Those who advocate the moderate use of distilled spirits, are, indeed, the real advocates of intemperance." For the Indians —as for others—freedom from the curse of alcoholic appetite was the undebatably first need. "Without temperance nothing can be accomplished," he wrote, in an address on Indian education. "There can be no Christianity; no well-attended schools; no well-cultivated farms; no comfortable buildings; no comely dress; no personal cleanliness; no adequate means of subsistence; no general health, or sound prosperity. Without temperance, the Bible and the school book may be carried to the Indians, but they will be carried as sealed books."

While a member of the Territorial Council of Michigan, among the laws in behalf of the Indians that Schoolcraft introduced and had passed, was one that made it a penal offence to sell or give ardent spirits to the Indians. Michigan, thus, was ahead of the nation in its attack on this problem. An Act of Congress, July 9, 1832, prohibited absolutely the introduction of liquor into the Indian country; but by 1836 in Michigan there was but little land in that category.

The Indian, however, Schoolcraft realized, could not be emancipated by a white man similarly enslaved. An Indian living at Porcupine Hills, near Little Traverse Bay, on Lake Michigan, when asked if he were sober, replied that he considered himself so, although he imitated the white men by taking a glass in the morning.

"This is wrong," said Schoolcraft, "you should not do so, but abandon the habit at once, lest it should imperceptibly overcome you."

"I will do so," replied the Red Man, after a moment's thought, "as soon as I see the white men abandon the use of it."

In addition to Schoolcraft's personal feeling, and his desire to relieve the sad situation of the Indian, he had other reasons for his activities in the growing temperance movement. His younger brother James, whom he had brought to the Sault and given a start in life, had succumbed to the sinister habit and Schoolcraft saw that young life already darkening toward its tragic end.

Schoolcraft's address, on the occasion of the first public meeting of the Chippewa County Temperance Society, at Sault Ste. Marie, Michigan, May 8, 1832, gives, among other effective data, an outline of the history of the introduction of liquor among the Indians, by the various European nations, and the conscienceless use of it during the period of economic and political rivalries as the price of furs and also the price of blood. This address, written in excellent essay form, shows as careful preparation as if intended for the most important scholarly organization in America.   Schoolcraft gave the cause his best.

The whisky-fighting phase of Schoolcraft's public activities emphasizes his integrity and his consistent, forthright courage both moral and physical.   The dangers encountered, because of his uncompromising stand and actions, approximated those of Indian warfare.

A Force for Religious Faith

In Michigan, from 1838 to 1840, John D. Pierce, first Superintendent of Public Instruction, was pleading for the teaching of natural science.   "In all our schools fate seems to have laid its heavy hand upon the study of the sciences."

If it was a time of repression for science, it was also a period of stress for religion.   Each feared the other.   Leaders on both sides fought for the actual life of the cause dearest to them.   It is a monument to Schoolcraft's magnitude that, in the thick of what seemed then a battle to the death, he was the protagonist of *both!*   He comprehended what is only in recent years being clearly envisioned, that there is no essential conflict—that faith underlies reason and carries on when it fails.

The ragged faces and hanging position of many parts of the sides and roof of this cave, added to its sombre colour, which has been heightened by soot smoke, its great extent, singular ramifications, and the death-like stillness which pervades such ample spaces situated so far below ground, inspire both wonder and awe, and we did not return from our examination, without feeling impressions in regard to our own origin, nature, and end, and the mysterious connection between the Creator of these stupendous works and ourselves, which many have before felt, but none have yet been satisfied about. In contemplating this connection, we feel humiliated; human reason has no clue by which the mystery may be solved, and we imperceptibly became silent, absorbed in our own reflections.

This was written in the Ozarks in 1819. About the outward and visible signs of religion in that region he was not so hopeful. In fact, the conditions that disturbed him have not, in the more remote corners of the hills, been much improved in a century.

The sabbath is not known by any cessation of the usual avocations of the hunter in this region. To him all days are equally unhallowed, and the first and the last day of the week find him alike sunk in unconcerned sloth, and stupid ignorance. He neither thinks for himself, nor reads the thoughts of others, and if he ever acknowledges his dependence upon the Supreme Being, it must be in that silent awe produced by the furious tempest, when the earth trembles with concussive thunders, and lightning shatters the oaks around his cottage, that cottage which certainly never echoed the voice of human prayer.

In his hard-driving, hour-packing and minute-snatching life of many interests, he yet found time to keep the Fourth Commandment. Of his expedition in 1832, he wrote:

At this place, I remained encamped, it being the Sabbath day, and rested on the 22d, which had a good effect on the whole party, engaged as it had been, night and day, in pushing its way to accomplish certain results, and it prepared them to spring to their paddles the more cheerfully on Monday morning. Indeed, it had been part of my plan of travel, from the outset, to give the men this rest and opportunity to recruit every seventh day, and I always found that they did more work in the long run, from it. . . . And, indeed, although I had frequently travelled with Canadian canoemen, I never knew a crew who worked so cheerfully, and travelled so far, per diem, on the mean of the week, as these six days' working canoemen.

Beginning with the summer of 1824 he had interdicted all

Sunday visits of Indians at the Sault Ste. Marie, Michigan, Indian agency.

Schoolcraft recognized the church as a fundamental necessity of sound national and community life.   At Merom, Indiana, he took occasion to note, in 1821, "the repetition of an amusing mistake of our canoemen, who are Canadian Frenchmen, and of course Roman Catholics, with respect to the public buildings erected for county purposes, at the numerous towns we have passed;—which they never fail to admire as being most commodious chapels."   On this he comments:

Does not this trifling incident prove more than the mere visual aberrance of unlettered peasants?   Does it not indicate one of those traits in the character of a people which may be seized upon to mark a predominance of national customs or manners—to distinguish an American from a striking French custom?   When the latter plant a colony, or found a settlement, one of the earliest and most important preliminaries regards the means of ensuring the speedy erection of a house of worship.   The chapel of the cross, like the tabernacle of Judah, is first set up.   Happy would it be if we were always equally attentive to this subject, in the foundation of our infant towns and settlements—we allude, more particularly, to those west of the Alleghanies.   Our first public edifice is a court-house, a jail, then a schoolhouse, perhaps an academy, where religious exercises may be occasionally held; but a house of public worship is the result of a more mature state of the settlement.   If we have sometimes been branded as litigious, it is not altogether without foundation; and, notwithstanding the very humble estimate which foreign reviewers have been pleased to make of our literary character and attainments, we are inclined to think there is still more likelihood of our obtaining the reputation of a learned, than of a pious people.

Later, on the same expedition, he elaborated this prophetic point.

While we are called on, at almost every stage of our journey, to notice the towns and villages, which are springing up throughout this naturally favoured [western] country and those varied improvements in its condition which have literally caused the wilderness to blossom as the rose, it may not be improper to cast a passing glance at a topic so vitally connected with its future march to opulence and power, that we think it cannot fail to recommend itself to every intelligent and reflecting mind.   We allude to that paucity of

HENRY ROWE SCHOOLCRAFT.

the external evidences of Christianity, evinced by the want of houses of public worship, which, it is believed, cannot prevail, in any country, in the degree that has been witnessed, without at the same time indicating a corresponding laxity and depraved moral tone in the public mind. In all our extensive route through this country, a considerable portion of which has been over districts more or less matured, as to the period of settlement, it has been our fortune to witness only two houses dedicated to the public worship of God; while we have seen but a solitary copy of the Scriptures, at any house where we have had occasion to stop. So singular a supineness on a subject so vitally important, has been deemed worthy of observation; and we embrace the occasion to subjoin a single inquiry. What rational hope of true greatness and lasting prosperity can a people promise themselves, who have not made the Christian faith the foundation of their civil and moral institutions? Let the history of fallen nations furnish the reply. . . .

Shall, then, the descendants of the pious pilgrims from Britain,— the hardy planters who followed the track of Cabot, of Hudson, and of Raleigh;—and the descendants of Penn, of Baltimore, and of Oglethorpe,—shall they, with the accumulated lights and experience of ages before them, purpose to lay the foundations of a great empire beyond the summits of the Alleghanies, without addressing themselves early, fervently, and continually to the inscrutable "Maker of heaven and earth?"

We are aware that it has not been customary for travellers to give so general a scope to their passing observations on the subject of religion as connected with the character and prosperity of a country. But with those men whose good opinion is "worth ambition," we shall find a full apology. We cannot persuade ourselves to forego an expression of our deep sense of the mighty consequences, which hinge upon a depraved and infidel rejection of the authority, and protecting providence of the Almighty, "who layeth the beams of his chambers in the waters, and maketh the clouds his chariot, and walketh upon the wings of the wind."

In all the writings of Schoolcraft there are few changes from the ruling mood of ringing optimism. In perceiving this shadow across the nation's shining future, Schoolcraft's vision was again manifest.

Guerilla warfare is ineffectual. The forces for good must organize against the forces for evil and disintegration. Schoolcraft was a leading member of the church, just as he was of many other societies for constructive activity.

What he wrote about the churchlessness of frontier towns was not idle comment. Three months after he arrived at Sault Ste. Marie, Michigan, as Indian Agent, he launched for that community its first self-initiated movement for a church. When the history of that town as a military outpost began, in the summer of 1822, with the establishment of Fort Brady, there was no clergyman in the settlement. In October of that year Schoolcraft drew up a paper authorizing Colonel Brady to procure a proper person to lead in public worship, and, incidentally, to give part-time instruction. Though the subscriptions of four individuals totaled seventy-five dollars, only ninety-seven dollars in all was guaranteed. For lack of funds the plan had to be abandoned.

Late in the autumn of 1823 the Reverend Robert McMurtrie Laird of Princess Anne, Maryland, arrived unheralded as a volunteer to minister to the soldiery and the settlers, but riotousness ruled out religion at the Sault still. Dr. Laird found so little to encourage him that he left as soon as the ice went out of the river in the spring, but Schoolcraft's warm friendship and personal interest in his labors evoked a lifelong gratefulness.

The work of the Reverend Abel Bingham, Baptist missionary among the Indians at the Sault beginning in 1828, had Schoolcraft's whole-hearted cooperation.

Finally the Reverend Jeremiah Porter came. Schoolcraft, at the time a non-resident member of the mission church at Mackinac Island, sent a bark canoe from the Sault to Mackinac expressly for Reverend Mr. Porter and aided in every practical as well as sympathetic way. So it was that in 1831, two years before he organized the first Presbyterian church in the village of Chicago, Illinois, Dr. Porter established the first Presbyterian church of Sault Ste. Marie, Michigan. January 31, 1832, Schoolcraft wrote in his diary: "I was now to spend a winter to aid a preacher. . . ." Mr. and Mrs. Henry Rowe Schoolcraft were among the first five members of the new church. Mrs. Johnston, the mother of Mrs. Schoolcraft, at once vacated one of her buildings in order that seats and a small platform and pulpit might transform it to a place of worship. In the autumn of the following year, she built a church for the small congregation—a wooden structure without a steeple—and she and her other daughters and her son George joined. Schoolcraft notes that this may be the first instance of a Christian church built by a full-blooded Indian. Undoubtedly the action of his wife's mother was due in some measure to his personal influence.

Schoolcraft's profession of faith was no perfunctory matter. He recorded it, in his *Memoirs* February 7, 1831:

This day is very memorable in my private history, for my having assumed, after long delay, the moral intrepidity to acknowledge, *publicly,* a truth which has never been lost sight of since my intercourse with the Reverend Mr. Laird, in the, to me, memorable winter of 1824—when it first flashed, as it were, on my mind. That truth was the divine atonement for human sin made by the long foretold, the rejected, the persecuted, the crucified Messiah.

His activity for religion as well as science is perfectly exemplified in the establishment by him of the Algic Society. This organization for both missionary and scholarly purposes is not peculiar because of this combination, but because the combination itself is extraordinary. Zealots are usually for either one of these two interests, whole-heartedly. Schoolcraft was with all his might for both.

In his essay on the *Education of the Indian Race* for the American Lyceum, he wrote:

It is an object of the highest moment with all who purpose to better the condition of the Indians, to begin their labours by the introduction of Christianity. This should be the corner stone. We are not willing to stop here. It should also cement the materials of the whole edifice. And it should constitute the capitals and ornaments of its final finish. Without it, there may indeed, be a pseudo civilization. Several of the states of antiquity are pronounced to have been eminently civilized before the Christian era. But we are inclined to think it was the civilization of the head, rather than the heart. Body and mind were brought to unite their aid in this effort. Sculpture, painting, and architecture, were carried to their highest pitch. All the arts, which require great physical skill were successfully cultivated. History and poetry were unexcelled. But they owed no part of their excellence to the virtues of society. Viewed in the era of its highest refinements, it was corrupt to the core. Profligacy, revenge, and refined error, in morals and philosophy were its striking characteristics. There was an utter destitution of moral loveliness. And we cannot select an era in ancient history which will bear the scrutinizing glare of Biblical truth. The very highest efforts of Greece and Rome were made in times of the greatest moral lassitude, affording proof that while the mind was disciplined for its most extraordinary achievements, and while the taste was cultivated, and the manners refined, the affections of the heart, like an uncaged lion, were left to rage in all their native fury. We merely allude to this species of civilization for the purpose of pointing out its enormities. And to illustrate the position, that mere civilization of manners, and changes of philosophical opinions, will not, as a necessary consequence, produce Christianity, although they may alike precede or follow it. While we may confidently appeal to history to show, that the introduction of the Gospel among the rudest nations, has without producing luxury, been attended by an almost immediate reformation of manners and a resort to the arts of civilization.

We are aware that we are trenching on disputed ground, and that many have entertained a different theory respecting the Indian race. By these, Christianity has been deemed the peculiar growth of a more advanced period of attainment. It has been deemed necessary first to learn to build and sow, and then to learn to pray. It has been regarded, so to say, as the fruit rather than the seed of civilization. We believe this opinion to be unsound, as a practicable maxim. We do not know that the church of Christ, has, at any period of its history, had doubts respecting the perfect applicability of the gospel to uncivilized nations. Paul had none. The Moravians had none, when they entered the missionary fields of India and Greenland. Elliot had none. Brainerd and Martyn had none. And whatever of doubt there may still rest on the minds of candid inquirers after truth, on this point, the history and progress of missions, in our day, and in our own land, furnishes a triumphant answer on the subject. The sublime experiment of Owyhee alone, settles the question. They found the true God first, and all else followed.

So far as my own observation has gone on the American frontiers, I feel impelled by the force of facts to affirm, that, as a general axiom, Christianity must be regarded as the precursor of civilization. That with the Red man, as with the White, it is a cause, and not an effect.

While he was at the Sault, Schoolcraft was the focal point

of missionary affairs in the Michigan Great Lakes region to the northern headwaters of the Mississippi. A specific case was that of the Reverend W. T. Boutwell. Schoolcraft helped the young missionary one winter at the Sault in his study of the Ojibway language. He made a place for Mr. Boutwell in his expedition to the Upper Mississippi in 1832, for the information it might afford him and the mission field in general. Having organized the Algic Society in Michigan to help, as President of that society and head of the Sault Ste. Marie group which formed its active committee, he sent practical aid in the form of supplies to Boutwell's mission at LaPointe. These activities, that centered easily in one so eager and resourceful, moved with him to Mackinac Island.

The Indian mission at Mackinac, established in 1823, was the first Protestant organization north of Detroit. Presbyterian in form and within the bounds of the Presbytery of Detroit, it was designed principally as a school. Its first administrator was the Reverend William M. Ferry, who was also the Protestant pastor of the village. In the records of the meeting of the Presbytery of Detroit held January 17, 1837, the name of Henry R. Schoolcraft appears as an elder from the Mackinac church. He was set apart as such January 25, 1834. The following glimpse of Schoolcraft in relation to "The Old Mission Church of Mackinac Island," is given by the Reverend Doctor Meade C. Williams:

> During his eight years' residence on the Island, this remarkable man, while enthusiastically engaged in antiquarian researches, noting every local phenomenon of science, studying Indian languages and customs, keeping abreast of the fresh literature of the day, writing articles for journals and reviews, corresponding with scholars and societies in Europe, and entertaining distinguished guests at his home in the Old Agency, was ever actively concerned in the details of the little church. He attended Session meetings, and social prayer meetings, giving counsel and fellowship, and in all ways seeking the peace and prosperity of the church.

The hymnbooks were printed in English on one page and on the opposite in Indian, following a plan arranged by Schoolcraft.

When the mission was the object of attack in the Legislative Council of Michigan, Schoolcraft, then a member of the Council, defended the institution effectively. He championed the Reverend Doctor Ferry when he was under fire, and when that able administrator resigned, corresponded unwearyingly with mission boards in the East in a vain attempt to find a successor. A visitor in 1835 recorded:

They have no protestant clergyman at Mackina. Mr. Schoolcraft read a very good sermon and conducted the service. . . .
A settled clergyman is very much wanted at Mackina. Mr. Schoolcraft does all that an individual who has many other duties can do; but they want some one who will devote his whole time and talents to the propagation of the truth. I was surprised to hear from Mr. Schoolcraft that they could not induce a Missionary to come here; the situation was objected to, I do not know why.

When the superintendent of the mission Sabbath school was absent for the greater part of one year, Schoolcraft substituted. During the period when there was no pastor on the Island, he conducted religious services at the funeral of a young New Hampshire emigrant who had died on board a steamer en route from Detroit to the West.

Schoolcraft's activities as a church member and able Christian leader were continued during his residence at Detroit. On March 7, 1838, he recorded that the friends of the Sunday School Union in Michigan "issued a circular this day making an appeal which deserves a hearty response." Knowing his propensity for getting up petitions, one wonders if this may not be another of Schoolcraft's initiatory enterprises for the general good. He contributed articles to the publication of the Home Missions Board.

Exercised earnestly, in his capacity as Regent of the University of Michigan, Schoolcraft's religious faith permeated the entire State in his time and into the future beyond today.

Someone, perhaps Mary Howard Schoolcraft, said of him: "The ennobling influences of Bible truth have mellowed and devoted to the most unselfish and exalted aims his natural determination and enthusiasm of character."

One of the chief manifestations of Schoolcraft's religious feeling was his conviction that it was his duty to sustain the Christian ministry. On the frontier he provided living quarters for them in his home. In Washington, after he was unable to go out, he often gathered a few members of the profession about him to spend an evening.

He realized the imperfection, mental and moral, of Christian ministers. He knew they could not excel in every science, and he thought it no diminution of their worth as religious teachers when, in interpreting some portion of God's word in the light of science, he differed from them. He knew, too, that they, like Elijah, the greatest of prophets, were men of "like passions" with other men, and though it grieved him when any one, as he thought, was turned away from his high mission to seek an applause less than that which comes from the Divine Master, he had no censoriousness to exercise toward them.

A few days before his death, in a conversation with his friend, the Reverend Doctor Samson,

he went over in a calm and delightful review his whole course as a Christian man. When allusion was made to the services he had rendered to science by his laborious and sacrificing life, he exclaimed with earnestness, "that is nothing, *nothing,* compared with my interest in Jesus Christ as my Redeemer." . . . He was of a deep religious spirit and a rich Christian experience. . . . Unlike many professional and controversial defenders of the truth, he had a profound conviction of the authenticity and inspiration of the Sacred Scriptures and spoke as one, every power of whose mind had been mastered and bowed in reverent subjection before a teacher manifestly divine.

Schoolcraft was interested eagerly in all knowledge. But he put first things first. The following is the finest single paragraph he ever wrote:

Christianity everywhere inculcates order, obedience, wisdom and virtue. Its order, educed from chaos, as depicted in Genesis, leads the mind through an infinite and connected series of beautiful creations of both animate and inanimate classes, from "nature up to nature's God." And its maxims of obedience, wisdom and virtue, are the most perfect and sublime to which the human intellect can refer. An Indian can be made to comprehend these truths, as displayed in the Bible. Considered merely as a code of morals, and were there no futurity to test their immutability, the maxims of Christianity, which he can be taught, will produce the greatest amount of happiness to families, and to communities. They are so interwoven in their practical application with the duties and relations of life, and evince so intimate a knowledge of human nature, that they are found to be adapted to all periods and states of human life. Cannot an Indian be made to understand them? They form a system which applies to man in the forest, as well as the field, in the wigwam as well as the palace, in his infancy and in his age; in his weakness and in his strength; in his joy and in his sorrow; in his life and in his death.

The funeral services of Henry Rowe Schoolcraft were conducted by the Reverend Doctor Gurley of the New York Avenue Presbyterian Church, Washington, D. C., of which he had been a member; by the Reverend Doctor Hall of the Epiphany Episcopal Church; and by the Reverend Doctor George W. Samson, President of Columbia College. The story of Schoolcraft's successful life and triumphant death, as given in Dr. Samson's memorial address, was published widely as an important contribution by the late eminent man of science to the rising generation.

Man may be great only in the proportion that he adds, by faith, some of God's stature to his own.

Schoolcraft knew radiantly that God was his immeasurably major discovery.

HOME, FAMILY, AND FRIENDS

THE personal story of Henry Rowe Schoolcraft falls naturally into three periods, centering successively in New York State, in Michigan, and at Washington, D. C.; or, in a more general way, about his unsettled youth, from 1793 to 1819; his association with Jane Johnston, the first Mrs. Schoolcraft, from 1820 to 1842; and his later years, from 1843 to 1864, the last seventeen of which were shared by his second wife, Mary Howard.

A concise chronology of the events of his life is included in this volume for ready reference.

An artistic portrayal of his years in the Lake Superior

country with Jane Johnston Schoolcraft is given in a strong, fine narrative, *The Invasion,* by Janet Lewis. The historical accuracy of this story is high and its details are imaginative and delicate.

A new point of view toward this best-known portion of his life, as well as a picture of his years after 1847, is afforded by pages 467 to 558 of a neglected book by Mary Howard Schoolcraft, published in 1860, somewhat misleadingly entitled *The Black Gauntlet: A Tale of Plantation Life in South Carolina.*

Schoolcraft's published memoirs, *Thirty Years with the Indian Tribes,* issued in 1851, give a general review of the years from 1809 through 1821, from his memory and correspondence; then entries in diary form beginning January 1, 1822, and ending August 10, 1841, with a brief reference to his European journey performed after that date. The book is prefaced by a twenty-one page biographical sketch, unsigned.

1793–1819

The place of his birth and the home of his boyhood never lost its special hold on Schoolcraft's heart. *Iosco,* his poetic tribute to Hamilton, New York, gives many happy glimpses of it.

His dearest brother was buried there:

> North, scattering tombs, upon the sandy moor,
> Marked the repose of all the village poor;
> For few were rich, or if a rich man died,
> He was interred by some proud river's side.
> One paling there, beyond each other part,
> Recalls the early sorrows of my heart,
> For there reclines the man I loved the best,
> By mind and manners prematurely blest,—
> An elder brother,—who was all to me,
> That brother, teacher, sage, or friend could be;
> Kind turned he oft, by books and winning art,
> To fit my mind for life's maturer part,
> And graced with pleasing tact of taste and tale,
> First led my steps in fancy's flowery vale:
> Well I remember, one cold winter's day,
> They bore him slowly to his rest away,
> By tap of muffled drum and solemn tread,

For he in life, a gallant corps had led,
And drew a throng from all the neighbouring plain,
That spoke affection, honor, love and pain.

The Albany County region and a troubled period of local history inspired his mock-heroic *Helderbergia* in 1855. The inescapable fragrance of the memories of childhood can give grace even to lines that limp.   He loved it—

. . . that prime valley—once the Indian's pride,
By Belgic voices christened Norman's kill,
But called by him in affluence of words
The Tawasentha.

Dear to him also to the end of his days was the gradually dwindling little town of Hamilton, now Guilderland,

. . . on the Hungerkill,
Where art had now its former cares forsook;
Place—once renowned for furnaces, that threw
Their rolling volumes to the amber skies,
Where reeking glassmen their bright fabrics blew
'Neath roofs that shamed the piny hills for size.

*   *   *

'Twas eke a plain, where mystic cross-roads meet,
And witches and hobgoblins, black and sour,
Had oft been seen to howl along the street,
In misty nights, and wreak their evil power,
For Guilderland—it was a haunted town
Where night was full surcharged with evil sprites,
And demons dark, who weighed the people down
With dead lights, spooks, and mystic candlelights
And daylight deviltries, which smarted like a whipping,
From learned doctors of the rap or table tipping.

*   *   *

Hard by the field arose the shapely manse
Of Ascan—chief, grown old in former wars,
When bold Montgomery poised th' invading lance,
Against Britannia. . . .
At his evening board
The modern heroes sat, and learned the tale of thralls
And tyranny, by vengeance, fire and sword. . . .

This cameo sketch of his father, Lawrence Schoolcraft, is supplemented by another in his tale of "The Rabid Wolf."

One of the parties in chase of the mad animal through the streets of Hamilton, at midnight

was led by old Colonel S., a revolutionary soldier, a field-officer of the county militia, and the superintendent of the extensive manufacturing establishment from which the village drew its prosperity. He was armed with a fusil of the olden time, well charged, and having been roused from his bed in a hurry, could not at the moment find his hat, and clapt on an old revolutionary cocked hat, which hung in the room. His appearance was most opportune; he halted on the brow of the hill, and as the wolf bounded on he levelled his piece at the passing fugitive, and fired.

The achievements of Lawrence Schoolcraft as a soldier and as a pioneer in American glass manufacturing are given at some length elsewhere in this book. The length of his life remains uncertain. He died June 7, 1840. More than once in the *Memoirs* he is said to have been in his eighty-fourth year. According to a genealogical record in possession of the Schoharie County Historical Society he was born February 8, 1757. The birth date in the copy of the epitaph printed in the *Memoirs* in February 3, 1757. Neither birth date agrees with the repeated statement that he had just entered his seventeenth year when the American Revolution broke out. The inscription on the actual monument, which Henry Rowe Schoolcraft himself had erected a few weeks after his father's death, records that he was born February 3, 1759, which is in accord with the statement that he had just passed sixteen on April 13, 1775. The figure for his age at death is not legible on the tombstone.

Of Schoolcraft's mother, Margaret Ann Barbara Rowe, little is known. Mary Howard Schoolcraft says that she was never reconciled to the intermarriage of two of her children with the Indian race. When James Schoolcraft was committed to jail on Mackinac Island, in expectation that the boy he had stabbed at the Sault would die, he still had grace enough to cry that it would break his mother's heart. Henry Rowe Schoolcraft recorded the news of her death, February 16, 1832:

She was seventy-five years of age, and a Christian—and died as she had lived, in a full hope. I had read the letters before breakfast, and while the family were assembling for prayers. I had announced the fact with great composure, and afterward proceeded to read in course the 42d Psalm, and went on well, until I came to the verse—"Why art thou cast down, O my soul? and why art thou disquieted within me? Hope thou in God: for I shall yet praise him, who is the health of my countenance, and my God." The emotions of this painful event, which I had striven to conceal, swelled up in all their reality, my utterance was suddenly choked, and I was obliged to close the book, and wait for calmness to go on.

According to her epitaph, she was seventy-two.

Although Schoolcraft says little about Vernon, Oneida County, New York, he returned a good many times to his father's later home there, from his intermittent western travels and after he established a home of his own at Sault Ste. Marie. Schoolcraft and his father were friends. Their correspondence through the years preserves valuable historical as well as personal details.

One of a large family, his attachment to his sisters and brothers was manifested practically. Just how many of them he took to Michigan for a start in life is not certain. In April, 1825, he stopped at his brother-in-law's a week or two in Vernon and "took along to the West, which had been favorable to me, my youngest brother James, and my sister Maria Eliza."

James Lawrence Schoolcraft, who married Anna Maria Johnston, a sister of Jane Johnston Schoolcraft, did not do so well. His drinking, gaming, keeping bad company and generally running wild made him a constant source of anxiety and grief to his older brother. He was a trader at the Sault. In 1838 he went as a delegate with a deputation of Indians to look over lands under consideration as a reservation for them in the West. His stormy career at Sault Ste. Marie ended abruptly July 6, 1846, when he was killed by an army musket ball fired from ambush.

For years it was believed this was the act of John Tanner, the unfortunate white man stolen and brought up by Indians, whose morose and embittered life faded out at the same time.

Tanner had served as interpreter for Henry Rowe Schoolcraft in 1828 and 1829, but had been discharged because of his manner both toward Schoolcraft and the Indians. Rapidly his state of mind grew worse. His mistreatment of his second wife and their child aroused the neighborhood. She left and divorced him. Schoolcraft put a bill through the Legislative Council to have the child taken from him. Tanner blamed all his troubles on Schoolcraft and the Baptist missionary, Abel Bingham. Threats and actual untoward actions caused both to fear and watch him. His warnings had included the families of both. Tanner disappeared under suspicious circumstances, at the time James Schoolcraft was murdered.

Though it has been said that Henry Rowe Schoolcraft held to the idea Tanner was the guilty man, it is now considered more probable that Second Lieutenant Bryant P. Tilden, Jr., was responsible for the death. He and James Schoolcraft had quarreled at a party on the preceding Fourth of July over a young French girl. Tilden had threatened publicly to kill James. His words were recalled, when the body was found, but there was no evidence except the threat and the kind of bullet. Tanner as well as Tilden had borrowed an army rifle. The case against Tanner appeared strong.

The Johnston women at the time preferred the idea of revenge rather than the woman motive. Later, however, local tradition at the Sault, particularly in the Johnston family, perpetuated the story that after the Mexican War Tilden was transferred to a post near Seattle, where, in a deathbed confession, he acknowledged it was he who had ambushed and slain James Schoolcraft, because of a quarrel over a woman.

Actual War Department records show that one Bryant P. Tilden, born in Massachusetts and appointed from that State, was admitted to the United States Military Academy at West Point as a cadet July 1, 1836; was graduated and commissioned a 2nd Lieutenant, 2nd Regiment United States Infantry, July 1, 1840; was promoted to 1st Lieutenant February 16, 1847; that he was tried, convicted and sentenced to be hung by a military commission in Mexico, for murder and burglary, but that this sentence was postponed by Major General Butler and the prisoner ordered to accompany his regiment to the United States; that he resigned June 6, 1848, intending to remain in Mexico. This ended his connection with the Army.

The authoritative Cullum's Biographical Register of the Graduates of the United States Military Academy gives Tilden's subsequent career as follows: He was principal of a scientific school at Boston, Massachusetts, from 1849 to 1850; for the next nine years was a civil and mining engineer, employed in making railroad surveys in New York and Massachusetts, and geological explorations of the coal lands of McKean County, Pennsylvania; and died December 27, 1859, at the age of 42, at Olean, New York.

Almost a hundred years have passed, and the Sault's most famous murder case has not been solved. Perhaps it is an example of the perfectly planned crime. In view of the Mexican murder and burglary phase of Tilden's career, it is strange that no one has ever suggested that he may have killed Tanner as well as James Schoolcraft. Tanner was a perfect object on which to concentrate suspicion. His house was burned. He was never heard of again. He was known to have converted all his belongings into cash the night of the Fourth.

The tragic death of his brother was not so great a grief to Henry Rowe Schoolcraft as his actual life had been. Some years earlier James had escaped the sadder fate of being murderer instead of the one murdered, in a similar stabbing affair, by the narrow margin of the unexpected recovery of his victim. This had happened at the Thanksgiving Day Ball at the Sault in 1831, when Schoolcraft was in Detroit. At the time, James, aged twenty-two, was the only local magistrate. Beyond doubt, the fate of this amiable, promising young brother was one reason for Schoolcraft's uncompromising attitude toward liquor.

Other members of his family, contrastingly, were sources of comfort and happiness. Maria Eliza Schoolcraft married John Hulbert, post sutler at Fort Brady. Her husband, like her older brother, was a member of the mission church at

Mackinac and one of the first five members of the first Presbyterian Church at Sault Ste. Marie. Maria Eliza joined the little congregation in its first year. Her grandson, Judge Henry Schoolcraft Hulbert, in 1942 is vice-president of the National Bank of Detroit and a distinguished citizen of Michigan. He is one of the three men concerned in carrying on scholarly investigations at Lake Angelus which have recently been sponsored by the University of Michigan and which for years have commanded the attention of astronomers throughout the world.

Peter, the older brother who had been associated with him in glassmaking, had moved to Geneva, New York. His sister, Margaret Helen, born June 18, 1806, died April 12, 1829, of tuberculosis. Catharine (or Catherine) married Willett H. Shearman (or Sherman) at Vernon. She died January 9, 1834. Her son, Francis Willett Shearman, lived afterwards at Marshall, Michigan. James Schoolcraft Sherman, the child of her son, Richard U. Sherman, was vice-president of the United States with Taft from 1908 to 1912 and held the renomination for vice-president at the time of his death.

W. H. Shearman, who changed his name to Sherman soon after 1825, remained in close touch with his brother-in-law in Michigan. After Mr. Shearman's son Francis was graduated from Hamilton College, Schoolcraft gave him a place in the Indian Agency at Mackinac Island during the winter of 1836 when there was much to do in fulfilment of the treaty of that year. Francis W. Shearman later became editor and co-publisher of the pioneer *Journal of Education* of Michigan, from November, 1838, till it ceased in December, 1839. From 1849 to 1855 he was Superintendent of Public Instruction for Michigan, and was the author of an important educational publication, *Public Instruction and School Law,* in 1852.

The Pettibone brothers of Vernon, New York, remained his friends as long as they lived. With Rufus, the lawyer, and his family, he had traveled westward in 1818 from Olean to Pittsburgh. Later he visited them at St. Louis, Missouri, where they settled. Levi was his sole companion on the Ozark expedition.

New York City was kind to him importantly on his return in 1819, when he most needed it, at the pivotal point of his life. His visit to the Conants there, in 1825, with Jane and little Penaysee, never ceased to be a vibrant memory.

His attachment to Albany County was enduring. Its expression took form, in one phase, in his anti-rent-war poem, *Helderbergia,* in 1855, and his contribution to the 1860 Albany Almanac. Much of his early printing was done at the State capital. In 1821 the great Governor De Witt Clinton welcomed him to work in his own library. Afterwards he was able to reciprocate in some small measure, as by sending Governor Clinton a supply of wild rice that he wished for foreign distribution. De Witt Clinton's example and advice and warmth of friendship were formative influences in his career.

No wonder he wrote, in his *Memoirs,* New Year's, 1822: "Albany is a dear place for the first of January; not only the houses of every one, but the hearts of every one seem open on this day." What he felt was the reflection of his own feeling toward the State and County of his birth.

Looking back across nearly fifty years and thousands of miles he wrote lovingly of his friends of the long ago in New York State:

> Peace to your shades! Your promises benign,
> And hope of years, were all as fair as mine;
> But vanished as the mist that once o'erhung
> The well known vistas, where we all were young;
> Nor will I bring your memory in review,
> By aught ye did, or aught ye failed to do,
> Nor whisper in my line, a single breath,
> To mar the ties of friendship and of death.
> And ye who still remain,—a scattered few,
> Where e'er ye dwell, and whatsoe'er pursue,
> Whether with honor crowned, or treasure blest,
> Or wandering hapless in the distant west,
> Oh call to mind an early written line,
> That virtue only stamps the man divine,

Nor boots it then, where'er ye meet the foe,
On Roxo's wave, or Athabasca's snow.

1820–1842

When Schoolcraft first saw the Sault in 1820, it consisted in the large of some fifteen or twenty buildings of all sorts, occupied by the descendants of the original French settlers, all of whom drew their living from the fur trade, and all of whom had married Indian women. This was in addition to the Indian village, at that time augmented by its summer visitors. Outstanding, however, was the home of John Johnston, the first English settler: a long, low well-built log house in a beautiful old-fashioned garden. Roses in perfection, hyacinths, lilacs, pinks, sweet william, violets, bachelor buttons, marigolds and other flowers of long ago grew luxuriantly in front of the portico toward the river. In a kitchen garden back of the house there were radishes, lettuce, carrots, and long rows of currant bushes.

In 1822 the Johnstons were expecting to raise twelve hundred bushels of potatoes and had some fine fields of peas and herdgrass.

As that comfortable home had seemed to him in the summer of 1820, it must have again impressed itself in July, 1822, with the added emphasis of vivid memories. On the great sideboard in the dining-room were many pieces of solid silver service brought from Ireland. Old portraits in gold frames hung on the walls. About the rooms were many foreign articles. The logs were rubbed with beeswax to a fine luster.

In contrast to the officers' mess at embryo Fort Brady, and the aloneness of a small log cabin, no wonder the privilege of eating at the Johnston table, and admission to its fireside circle, appealed to him. He began to take his meals with the Johnstons July 16, 1822, ten days after his arrival at the Sault. Before the month was out he had been tendered, and accepted, a room under their roof.

Mrs. Johnston—Ozhaw-guscoday-wayquay—was not only a strong character. She was motherly. Mrs. Thomas D. Gilbert, who was the Reverend Abel Bingham's daughter, described her:

Uneducated in books, reared among a savage people, she possessed that innate dignity, intelligence, self-respect and courage which rises to occasion, superior to circumstance. She adapted herself perfectly to her strange position. As the head of the household she was loved by her family and met on equal terms guests of the house from palace or wigwam.

A passage from Mrs. Jameson's book brings out this home-making phase of Mrs. Johnston's personality and Schoolcraft's attitude to her:

A woman whose habits and manners were those of a genuine Indian squaw, and whose talents and domestic virtues commanded the highest respect, was as you may suppose an object of the deepest interest to me. I observed that not only her own children, but her two sons-in-law, Mr. McMurray and Mr. Schoolcraft, both educated in good society, the one a clergyman, and the other a man of science and literature, looked up to this remarkable woman with sentiments of affection and veneration.

The old lady herself is rather large in person, with the strongest marked Indian features, a countenance open, benevolent and intelligent, and manner perfectly easy, simple, yet with something of motherly dignity becoming the mother of a large family. She received us most affectionately and we entered into conversation. Mrs. Schoolcraft, who looked all animation and happiness, acted as interpreter. Mrs. Johnston speaks no English, but can understand it a little, and the Canadian French still better, but in her own language she is eloquent, and her voice, like that of her people, low and musical. Many kind words were exchanged, and when I said anything that pleased her, she laughed softly like a child. I was not well and much fevered, and I remember she took me in her arms, laid me on a couch, and began to rub my feet, soothing and caressing me. She called me Nindannis, daughter, and I called her Neengai, mother. She set before us the best dressed and best served dinner I had seen since I left Toronto, and presided at her table, and did the honors of the house with unembarrassed and unaffected propriety.

John Johnston had been absent, on his second visit to England and Ireland, in 1820. Schoolcraft saw him for the first time in July, 1822, and liked him instantaneously. The cross-currents of war cause many kinds of devastation. The utterances of small jealousy and competitors' enmity may be repeated ad infinitum, for historical completeness and also in ignorance, but Schoolcraft's *Memoir of John Johnston* is an

SAULT STE. MARIE IN 1820. SHOWS NORTH-WEST COMPANY'S POST ON CANADIAN SHORE AND INDIANS FISHING AT FOOT OF THE FALLS. FROM A SKETCH BY SCHOOLCRAFT.

enduring monument to this man's integrity. There is nothing perfunctory about Schoolcraft's sketch. It is no subtle defense of Schoolcraft's marriage to John Johnston's daughter. Forth-right, earnest, warmly affectionate and even reverential, it is an eloquent tribute such as he might have expressed for his own loved father. In some ways John Johnston was closer than his father. Similarly Schoolcraft must have been to Johnston more sympathetically understanding than any of his sons. They were natural companions. Schoolcraft was the same age as Johnston's eldest child.

Governor Cass wrote of Mr. Johnston: "He was really no common man. To preserve the manners of a perfect gentle-man, and the intelligence of a well educated man, in the dreary wastes around him, and his seclusion from all society but that of his own family, required a vigour and elasticity of mind rarely to be found."

John Johnston came of a Scotch-Irish family of the landed gentry of Ulster. His grandfather, William Johnston, had planned and executed, at his own expense, the waterworks of Belfast. His three older uncles were schoolfellows at Armagh of Lord Macartney and of Lord Dorchester who was afterwards Governor General of Canada. Of the three brothers of his father who served in the British army, one became a lieutenant colonel in India, and another a chaplain. A fourth uncle was a lieutenant colonel of marines. His two aunts who married became the wives of clergymen. Among his cousins were a lieutenant general of engineers and an attorney general of Ireland. John Johnston's father, William, had chosen the navy as a career. Later he was appointed surveyor of Portrush in northern Ireland, and married the eldest daughter of John McNeil, Esquire, by whom he obtained the estate of Craige at Coulresheskan,—near Coleraine, where his grandfather in later years was Collector and one of his uncles was the Anglican rector. At Craige, in the extreme northeast of Ireland, not far from the Giant's Causeway, in Antrim County, John Johnston was born August 25, 1762. When he was seven his father died. His education consisted of English and Latin grammar and

ancient and modern history, gained chiefly under the direction
of his mother, his aunt Nancy Johnston, a neighbor clergyman,
and a tutor. Opportunities for the severer branches of study
were neglected by him because of his ardent preference for
hunting, belles lettres, and the gay atmosphere of drawing-
rooms. His youth, he has recorded, was wasted in light but
never low pursuits. He was instinctively a gentleman.

The Belfast waterworks had meantime been mismanaged.
Undertaking its superintendence in his seventeenth year, he
improved the situation, but the forty-one-year franchise given
his grandfather was on the eve of expiration, and uncertainties
regarding its renewal led him to realize what money he could
on it—four hundred pounds—and seek to repair his family's
fortunes in one of the colonies. Circumstances directed him
to Canada, which he entered, by way of New York, in 1790, at
the beginning of his twenty-ninth year. When expectations
centering in Lord Dorchester at Quebec were at least temporarily disappointed, he established himself at Montreal, where
he made friendly connections with Sir John Johnson, and
associated especially with Andrew Tod of the fur-baron family.
Through the latter he went on an expedition to Lake Superior,
which resulted in his entering the fur trade there. He spent
the winters of 1791 and 1792 at LaPointe, in territory not yet
reached by any actual extension of American authority; then,
still a loyal British subject in a region that was de facto wholly
British, settled at the Sault in 1793 with his Indian wife.
Almost at once he achieved recognized position. Soon he had
considerable means.

When John Johnston's mother, who had wished to adopt
and educate his eldest daughter, died in 1804, his sister, Mrs.
Moore, of Wexford, Ireland, having no child of her own, desired
to carry out the plan. Accordingly he took nine-year-old Jane
to Ireland in 1809. However, a rigorous ocean voyage late in
the autumn, the moisture of the climate, and the death of Mr.
Moore, combined so greatly to undermine her spirits and consistently affect her health that it was deemed best to take her
back to her North American home. Father and daughter left

Wexford in April, and London in June, the following year; were received by Governor Hull at Detroit on their return to Michigan; and reached the Sault happily in November, 1810.

Although influential members of his family in Ireland had offered to find a suitable position for him there, his strong attachment to his wife and children decided him against accepting. He relinquished all ideas of a permanent return, and planned instead to retire to the vicinity of Montreal, where his wife could be happy, he could farm to his heart's content, and his children could have the advantages of education. The handsome property he had acquired as an outfitter for the fur trade proved he had mercantile ability, but the details of business had always been distasteful.

The War of 1812 followed. Its consequences involved Mr. Johnston and his family deeply.

As an outfitter operating independently of the giant fur companies, he experienced conflicts of interest that were inevitable. Johnston's polished manners and refined pursuits, in what was then the rough, "farthest fixed settlement in British North America," gave rise to petty misunderstandings, which, in that Roman Catholic community, were no doubt emphasized because he had for his background in youth one of the most decidedly Protestant counties in Ireland. Unfriendly misinformation given about him led to a catastrophe.

In the summer of 1814 a detachment of American troops came up the St. Marys River in boats and, after they burned the buildings of the North-West Company, crossed to the west side of the river and completely sacked and pillaged his stores and dwelling house, under the misapprehension that he was an agent of that organization. The fruits of twenty-three years were swept away in a few days. Goods and property to the value of ten thousand pounds were destroyed or carried away, besides losses in his business of an irreparable character.

Restitution was denied by the British, on the ground that he lived south of the line fixed in 1783—although they had not recognized that line in toto prior to the Treaty of Ghent. The United States made no amends for the damage to private property. Mr. Johnston made a number of trips to Montreal and York in Canada, and to New York, and a second and last visit to Ireland in 1819–1820, to press payment of his claims. All were in vain. He sold his estate of Craige for 3,250 pounds sterling to finance further undertakings at the Sault, but infirmities, increased business difficulties, and interest on compounded debts slowly were dragging him down.

Harsh terms have been applied to Johnston for the part he played in aiding the British in the War of 1812. At worst, perhaps, he was an active Tory in that last convulsion of the Revolution. It would seem, however, that he had certainly forfeited all right to consideration of his claims against the American government; otherwise the standing of his wife and his son-in-law with Governor Cass, and the justness and influence of the latter, would have secured redress for him. However this may be, John Johnston was an American in spirit long before he died; and four of his grandsons gave their lives to preserve the Union.

In his *Memoirs* Schoolcraft speaks of their first meeting in 1822:

Prominent among the number of residents who came to greet us was Mr. John Johnston, a gentleman from the north of Ireland, of whose romantic settlement and adventures here we had heard at Detroit. He gave us a warm welcome. . . . Mr. J. is slightly lame, walking with a cane. He is of the medium stature, with blue eyes, fair complexion, hair which still bears traces of its original light brown, and possesses manners and conversation so entirely easy and polite as to impress us all very favorably. . . . At this remote point, so far from the outer verge of civilization, we found in Mr. Johnston a man of singular energy and independence of character, from one of the most refined circles of Europe; who had pushed his way here to the foot of Lake Superior about the year 1793; had engaged in the fur trade, to repair the shattered fortunes of his house; had married the daughter of the ruling Ogima or Forest King of the Chippewas; had raised and educated a large family, and was then living, in the only building in the place deserving the name of a comfortable residence, with the manners and conversation of a perfect gentleman, the sentiments of a man of honor, and the liberality of a lord. He had a library of the best English works; spent most of his time in reading and conducting the affairs of an extensive business; was a man of social qualities, a practical philanthropist, a well-read historian, something of a poet.

John Johnston had studied French in Canada the winter of 1790. At LaPointe in 1791 and 1792 he had concentrated on the language of the Ojibways and their lore, though he had afterwards destroyed his notes in the latter field and never taken others on discovering that someone had been hoaxing him. Schoolcraft was delighted to find, among the interesting equipment of this new friend, someone who "knew the difference, in reference to the Chippewa language, between the conjugation of a verb and the declension of a noun." In fact this was rare fortune.

Mr. Johnston's small but select library of history, divinity and classics furnished a pleasing resource during the long winter evenings that characterize the latitude of Sault Ste. Marie.

It was his custom on these occasions, to gather his family around the table, and while his daughters were employed at their needlework, he either read himself, or listened to one of his sons, adding his comments upon any passages that required it, or upon any improprieties or deficiencies in emphasis, punctuation, or personal manners. In this way information was diffused, and often rendered intelligible to the younger members of the group and he thus renewed, in his own family, the scenes in which he had been an actor at his mother's house, in his youth.

Schoolcraft, who knew him well, says that he had a general acquaintance with ancient and modern history, combined with an accurate and discriminating knowledge of English history, poetry and belles lettres up to the time of Johnson and Goldsmith; also that he had read with enjoyment and proper appraisal the works of Washington Irving and Cooper.

In his choice of reading, however, he never neglected his Bible, nor made it a book of secondary consequence. He devoted a portion of every morning and evening to its perusal. His family assembled in his sitting-room in the evening, and were dismissed with prayer. They were again assembled in the morning with prayer. One of his daughters usually placed a cushion for him to kneel upon.

"I remained to family worship in the evening," recorded Schoolcraft, December 29, 1822.

At Schoolcraft's urging, Johnston began, not long before he died, an autobiography in the form of letters, but finished only his first thirty years. Some of the odes and occasional poems that he wrote, from youth to a short time before his death, "give him claims beyond that of a mere amateur." "It is certainly some merit, in an age like this, when poetry and infidelity have shaken hands, to have written two thousand lines and upwards, without uttering one word offensive to virtue and piety, or a single sentiment tending to tolerate a sceptical philosophy." "We think . . . the 'War Song' unrivalled in its way, and as far as known without a prototype in English poetry." Schoolcraft ventured these criticisms with diffidence, hoping "if they should subject the writer to the charge of partiality, his respect and veneration for the memory of the Man, will plead some excuse for his admiration of the Author."

This was the unexpected comrade in arts and letters and father in religion and philosophy that Schoolcraft found beyond "the outer verge of civilization." And always with John Johnston there was his exotic, gentle daughter Jane, with her tremulous, liquid Ojibway quality of utterance, cultivated Irish accent, and lingering old-world memories, whose mind he had assiduously cultivated that she might be his intellectual associate in exile.

Strong attachment to his wife and children was one of Johnston's most admirable traits. In 1828 he wrote, in a letter from New York, "All that is rich, splendid and luxuriant is lost upon me. One smile of affection from those I love, is worth all the rest of the world." Henry Rowe Schoolcraft was nearly thirty. He had been a wanderer for fifteen years. Domestic by nature according to his own estimate, he must have been home-hungry. The reigning spirit of the Johnston household warmed his heart.

The seventh of thirteen children, Schoolcraft undoubtedly felt much at home among the numerous Johnstons.

There was a family picnic at Gros Cap, on the Canadian shore of Lake Superior. Schoolcraft never had found time for the frivolities, but he enjoyed this outing.

JANE JOHNSTON SCHOOLCRAFT—MRS. HENRY ROWE SCHOOLCRAFT.

> An even temper, mild, enduring, kind,
> A sound, discreet, and regulated mind,
> Improved by reading, by reflection formed,
> By reason guided, by religion warmed.
> This have I often prayed "heaven's last best gift" to be,
> This have I oft, with joy, remarked in thee.
>
> * * *
>
> In virtue principled, in love sincere,
> In manners guarded, in expression clear,
> Kind to all others in a just degree,
> But fixed, devoted, loving only me.
> This have I ever hoped "heaven's last best gift" would be,
> This have I sought, and heaven-blest, found in thee.
>
> —"The Choice" (1823)

Saut Ste Marie March 2
182[...]

My very dear Brother;

Altho' I have scarcely strength enough
to guide my pen, or to hold my aching head up, yet the
thought of its being a gratification to you to receive a few lines
from me, induces me to exert myself, tho' it will make my
poor wounded heart bleed afresh, & I know it will draw the
ready tear of sympathy from your eyes, as well as sincere
sorrow from your heart; When I tell you that it has [pleased]
the Almighty to take to himself, my beloved and ever
to be lamented Son William Henry, he died of the Croup, the
13th of this month, about 11 0clock at night — If ever a human
being went direct to the Mansions of everlasting bliss; he has,
it is a consoling thought to me that my Sweet Willy is rejoicing with exceeding joy before the throne of his Heavenly
Father, & there he will never know pain or sickness more.
O' my dear Brother if we, who still remain on earth would
strive with all our hearts to live, so as to become Partakers [of]
everlasting happiness, how gladly will the blessed Spirit of
[our] beautious Willy meet & welcome us to Heaven; when
[we] shall be obliged to leave our earthly tabernacle. — I can
say more. Papa Mamama & all the family are well & desire th[eir]
love to you — both Papa & Mr Schoolcraft are writing & [will]
no doubt give you all the news. Heaven [bless] you my dear Bro[ther]
believe me as ever your affectionate Sister
Jane Schoolc[raft]

LETTER FROM JANE JOHNSTON SCHOOLCRAFT TO GEORGE JOHNSTON (SEE PAGE 576).

A sugaring-off party on Sugar Island once would have seemed a waste of precious hours. It did not now.

On October 12, 1823, Henry R. Schoolcraft was married to Miss Jane Johnston at Sault Ste. Marie, Michigan, by the Reverend R. M. Laird.

Notwithstanding diminishing resources, John Johnston built an extension on his log house for the event. This portion of the building is still standing—where Schoolcraft wrote the *Travels in the Central Portions of the Mississippi Valley* and recorded embryonically *The Song of Hiawatha;* overcame the disappointment of his hopes that had centered in Missouri, experienced growing recognition as explorer, scientist, and author, and discovered his life work—his first home, associated with all his earliest happiness: first love, marriage, and his son, first-born.

Jane and Henry Schoolcraft began housekeeping in the so-called Allen house, on the eminence west of the Fort, in the spring of 1825 on their return from a visit to New York, with furniture purchased at Buffalo. It was "a pretty and attractive residence." But March 28, 1827, they closed it, leaving the furniture still standing, and took refuge at Mr. Johnston's. So insupportable were the memories of their dead child, they could not wait for the completion of Elmwood, then under construction. Thus the old log house added to its dear associations the birth of Jane Susan Anne.

"No part of my life had so completely all the elements of entire contentment, as my residence at the wild and picturesque homestead of Elmwood." He moved his family there in October of that year.

Few sites command a more varied or magnificent view. The broad and limpid St. Mary, nearly a mile wide, runs in front of the grounds. The Falls, whose murmuring sound falls pleasantly on the ear, are in plain view. The wide vista of waters is perpetually filled by canoes and boats passing across to the opposite settlement on the British shore. The picturesque Indian costume gives an oriental cast to the moving panorama. The azure mountains of Lake Superior rise in the distance. Sailing vessels and steamboats from Detroit, Cleaveland, and Buffalo, occasionally glide by, and to this wide and magnificent view, as seen by daylight, by sunset, and by moonlight, the frequent displays of aurora borealis give an attraction of no ordinary force.

In selecting this spot, I had left standing a large part of the fine elms, maples, mountain ash, and other native forest trees, and the building was, in fact, embowered by tall clumps of the richest foliage. I indulged an early taste in horticulture, and planting trees to add to the natural attractions of the spot, which, from the chief trees upon it was named "Elmwood," and every flowering plant and fruit that would thrive in the climate, was tried. Part of the grounds were laid down in grass. Portions of them on the water's edge that were low and quaggy, were sowed with the redtop, which will thrive in very moist soil, and gives it firmness. The building was ample, containing fifteen rooms, including the office, and was executed, in all respects, in the best modern style.

He planted elms on the circle of the drive leading to the door.

This was the peak of his happiness: convenience, even luxury, and a wild, new world awaiting investigation on every hand; high-ceilinged, spacious rooms lined with cabinets for his books and various collections; a garden; a beloved and loving wife; small, winsome Janee; and the coming of his doubly precious second son, John Johnston, who was born October 2, 1829. Here he was honored by election to the Legislative Council of the Territory; helped found the Michigan Historical Society, and the Algic Society of Detroit, Mackinac, and Sault Ste. Marie; aided in a great local temperance upheaval and in the establishment and building of a first Presbyterian Church; publicly acknowledged his faith in Christ and experienced new inner radiance; achieved, at last, the final exploration of the Mississippi River's source in the Itasca basin; prepared the manuscript of another book; had time for the pleasant diversion of writing verse.

The farther he moved away from Lake Superior by that much the noon-sun of his joy dropped imperceptibly from its meridian.

Schoolcraft's love of gardening blossomed at Mackinac Island. He took his family there in 1833, in May, having left

the Sault on the twenty-seventh of that month. The Old
Indian Agency in the East Fort garden, long since destroyed
by fire, possessed a charm that has given it a place in literature.

Mrs. Eliza Steele, in *A Summer Journey in the West,*
mentioning "the celebrated family of Schoolcraft," speaks of
the Agency house and gardens as among the most conspicuous
of the buildings of the town at the foot of the bluff.

Anna Brownell Jameson could write of it more intimately:

On a little platform, not quite half way up the wooded height
which overlooks the bay, embowered in foliage, and sheltered from
the tyrannous breathing of the north by the precipitous cliff, rising
almost perpendicularly behind, stands the house in which I find
myself at present a grateful and contented inmate. The ground in
front sloping down to the shore, is laid out in a garden, with an
avenue of fruit trees, the gate at the end opening on the very edge of
the lake. From the porch I look down upon the scene I have endeavoured—how inadequately!—to describe to you: the little
crescent bay; the village of Mackinac; the beach thickly studded
with Indian lodges; canoes fishing, or darting hither and thither,
light and buoyant as sea-birds: a tall, graceful schooner swinging at
anchor. Opposite rises the Island of Bois-blanc, with its tufted and
most luxuriant foliage. To the east we see the open lake, and in the
far western distance the promontory of Michilimackinac and the
strait of that name, the portal of Lake Michigan.

It is by Constance Fenimore Woolson, in "The Old
Agency," that the now vanished landmark has been painted
for the ages with vivid coloring and emotional perspective:

Stretching back from the white limestone road that bordered
the little port, its garden surrounded by an ancient stockade ten feet
in height, with a massive, slow-swinging gate in front, defended by
loopholes—a broad garden with a central avenue of cherry trees, on
each side arbors, paths, heart-shaped flower beds, and behind the
limestone cliffs crowned with cedars; a house large on the ground,
with wings and various additions built out as if at random; on each
side and behind, rough outside chimneys clamped to the wall. In
the roof over the central part, dormer windows showed a low second
story. Here and there at irregular intervals were outside doors.
Within were suites of rooms, large and small, showing traces of
workmanship elaborate for such a remote locality: the doors were
ornamented with scroll work, and the two large apartments on each

side of the entrance hall possessed chimney-pieces and central hooks for chandeliers. It had candelabra on its high mantels, brass and-irons on its many hearthstones. Beyond and behind stretched out the wings. Coming to what appeared to be the end of the house on the west, there unexpectedly began a new series of rooms turning toward the north, each with its outside door. You opened a door, expecting to step out into the garden and found yourself in a set of little rooms running off on a tangent, one after the other. . . . But the Agency gloried in its irregularities, and defied criticism. . . . The windows had wooden shutters fastened back with irons shaped like the letter S, and on the central door was a brass knocker, and a plate bearing the words, "United States Agency." . . . The officers of the little Fort on the height, the chief factors of the fur company, and the United States Indian agent, formed the feudal aristocracy of the Island; but the agent had the most imposing mansion, and often have I seen the old house shining with lights across its whole broadside of windows. . . . The garden . . . was the pride of the Island. Its prim arbors, its spring and springhouse, its flower-beds, where with infinite pains, a few hardy plants were induced to blossom; its cherry-tree avenue, whose early red fruit the short summer could scarcely ripen; its annual attempts at vegetables, which never came to maturity,—formed topics for conversation in court circles.

Schoolcraft's home at Mackinac was a social center, and many travelers of distinction found a generous hospitality under his roof. No one was more influential than he in the affairs of the Island during his residence there. He enjoyed an ever-widening and more distinguished correspondence. His accumulation of manuscript notes increased prodigiously. The *Narrative* of his crowning expedition of 1832 was published during this period. A viewpoint overlooking Haldimand Bay is still known as Schoolcraft's Rest.

The children were still at home, at Mackinac, most of the time, perhaps all but the summer there in 1839. Their portraits were painted in oil by a visiting artist. Schoolcraft carried on studies with them, and with Jane.

Although he moved to Detroit in 1836, after he became Superintendent of Indian Affairs as well as Agent, he continued until he left the State to be a summer resident of Mackinac—he and General Cass were first of the long line that followed; and Mackinac Island shares with Detroit in the associations of

Schoolcraft's last five years in Michigan: his satisfaction in helping to organize the University of Michigan and the secondary school system of the State; negotiation of his famous treaty of 1836 with the Indians, and especially the distribution of its immediate benefits to a multitude of happy aborigines; the publication, at last, of his collection of Indian legends; his mounting prestige; contact with the leading minds and most adventurous spirits of the United States and Europe. Perhaps it was at Mackinac that the darkest shadow began to move across his life, as Mary Howard Schoolcraft intimates, in the discovery of a chief cause of his wife's illness.

What time he spent in Detroit, between summering at Mackinac, making a census of improvements on Indian lands, dispensing Indian payments in the winter of 1836, absences in New York and Washington, was brightened with friendly and intellectual contacts.

He and Captain Henry Whiting had much in common. Dr. Zina Pitcher, then a fellow-Regent of the University, had been at Fort Brady at the Sault. Senator Lucius Lyon, with whom he worked closely in the matter of the Toledo War and the Upper Peninsula, who named a town and township for him, lived with them as a member of their family. Still fresh were the memories of invigorating days with Governor Cass, by this time gone to Washington. There was the particular fragrance of the spring of 1830, when the Schoolcrafts had been guests for a while at the executive mansion. Jane and the new baby had been taken for carriage drives by General Cass's daughter Elizabeth. Miss Elizabeth accompanied the Schoolcrafts on a trip to Niagara Falls, which Mr. Schoolcraft thought might be the first excursion made by anyone from Detroit to that point for no purpose other than to view the natural phenomenon. It was during that sojourn in Detroit that their two surviving children were baptized, July 4, 1830, by the Reverend Richard Bury, at St. Paul's Episcopal Church: Jane Susan Anne Schoolcraft, and John Johnston Schoolcraft.

At Mackinac Island Schoolcraft himself had taught his children, and sent them to the Mission School when convinced of its efficiency. For a while Johnston went to the Bacon School in Detroit. November 14, 1838, Schoolcraft recorded in his diary: "I embarked in a steamer, with my family, for New York, having the double object of placing my children at eligible boarding-schools, and seeking the renovation of Mrs. S.'s health." The richness of his home life was diminishing. As always he had the joy of arduous work for countless intellectual organizations and activities. But his wife's health was steadily failing. Jane's life was his; and it was waning.

There is no doubt but that he loved her. His mother's disapproval of miscegenation, on general principles, and his second wife's natural inclination to discount her husband's previous attachment, mean nothing at all. Schoolcraft's first marriage was infinitely more than a mere matter of propinquity and honor. Jane had beauty, intelligence, culture of an unusual kind, literary interests, and an exotic but gentle charm. Physically, mentally and spiritually she was out of the ordinary. A revelation of Schoolcraft's feeling for her is given in the record of his journey homeward to the Sault in 1825 by way of Green Bay and Mackinac.

"There is something in the air exhilarating," he wrote happily, when the wind rose in his favor.

I have been passing in retrospect, the various journeys I have made, but during none has my anxieties to return been so great as this. . . . No man was more unlikely to be a traveler than myself. I always thought myself to be domestic in my feelings, habits, and inclinations, and even in very early youth, proposed to live a life of domestic felicity. I thought such a life inseparable from the married state . . . Notwithstanding this way of thinking, my life has been a series of active employment and arduous journeyings. . . .

Two days later, at Mackinac Island, he found someone from the Sault "who reported friends all well. This was a great relief to my mind, as I had been for a number of days under the impression that some one near and dear to me was ill." Eagerly he had anticipated reaching home September 6, but was delayed three days by weather conditions between Mackinac Island and the Sault. Marooned at Outard Point he mourned:

I feel solitary. The loud dashing of the waves on shore, and the darkness and dreariness of all without my tent, conspire to give a saddened train to my reflections. I endeavored to divert myself, soon after landing, by a stroll along the shore. I sought in vain among the loose fragments of rock for some specimens worthy of preservation . . . I amused myself with the reflection that I should, perhaps, meet you coming from an opposite direction on the beach, and I half fancied that, perhaps, it would actually take place. Vain sport of the mind! It served to cheat away a tedious hour, and I returned to my tent fatigued and half sick.

His journal had no entry for the day of his homecoming. "The excitement of getting back and finding all well drove away almost all other thoughts."

His confession at the time of the death of their infant son that "idolatry such as ours for a child was fit to be rebuked" is a manifestation of complete sympathy and understanding.

Schoolcraft had no misgivings about the wisdom of his choice. Jane had acquitted herself memorably the first time he had seen her, in her exacting position as hostess, at her father's table, to the Governor of the Territory and his staff. Under similar conditions she continued to inspire commendation. He considered that two diverse sources of pride of ancestry met in her family:

That of the noble and free sons of the forest, and that of ancestral origin founded on the notice of British aristocracy. With me, the former was of the highest honor, when I beheld it, as it was in her case, united to manners and education in a marked degree gentle, polished, retiring, and refined.

Her father, naturally, became her earliest instructor, and directed her reading, and from him she derived that purity of language, correct pronunciation, and propriety of taste and manners which distinguished her. Under his direction she perused some of the best historians, the lives of Plutarch, the Spectator, and British essayists generally with the best dramatists and poets. And under his delicate and well timed commendations and criticisms, she not only acquired more than the ordinary proficiency in some of the branches of an English education but also a correct judgment and taste in literary merit.

From the aunt for whom she was named, with whom she had spent part of her tenth and eleventh years, in Wexford, Ireland, she had "profited in many lessons of female etiquette, of which she always retained the most perfect remembrance."

One of her father's letters to her from Montreal, a few years after her return from Ireland, is illuminating:

I received my dearest Jane's affectionate and sensible, and well written letter, with the most sincere pleasure. The improvement of your mind is dearer to me, than every other accomplishment. External manners are soon acquired, but if instruction is neglected in youth, it can never be regained. Your being sequestered from the world at present, is therefore, a blessing from providence as you have now the time and means of storing your mind with good and religious ideas, that in a future day will be of more use in directing your conduct and preserving you from the snares of a base and wicked world, than the greatest fortune could possibly do. I hope you will be able to keep your word respecting the improvement of your dear little sisters.

Many persons of intellect and refinement warmly approved of Schoolcraft's young half-Indian wife. She was the subject, first, of curiosity, then of surprise, complete capitulation, and eloquent appraisal.

During his visit to the East in 1825, he left Jane for some weeks, with her young son and a maid, with his New York friends, the Conants. Subsequently the latter wrote him that they "were not less surprised than recompensed to find such gentleness, urbanity, affection, and intelligence, under circumstances so illy calculated, as might be supposed, to produce such amiable virtues."

The Honorable Thomas L. McKenney, Commissioner of Indian Affairs, in a letter to his wife, described Mrs. Schoolcraft as follows:

She is a little taller and thinner, but in other respects, as to figure, resembles her sister, Mrs. McMurray, and has her face precisely. Her voice is feeble and tremulous; her utterance slow and distinct. There is something silvery in it. Mildness of expression, and softness, and delicacy of manners, as well as of voice, characterize her. She dresses with great taste, and in all respects in the costume of our fashionables, but wears leggins of black silk, drawn and ruffled around the ankles, resembling those worn by our little girls. I think them ornamental. You would never judge either from her complexion or language or from any other circumstance, that her mother was a Chippewa, except that her moderately high cheek-bones, her dark and fine eye, and breadth of jaw slightly indicate it; and you would never believe it, except on her own confession or upon some equally responsible testimony, were you to hear her converse, or see her beautiful and some of them highly-finished compositions, in both prose and poetry. You would not believe it, not because such attainments might not be universal, but because, from lack of the means necessary for their accomplishment, such cases are so rare. Mrs. Schoolcraft is indebted mainly to her father, who is doatingly fond of her, for her handsome and polished acquirements. She accompanied him some years ago, and before her marriage, to Europe; and has been the companion of his solitude, in all that related to mind, for he seems to have educated her for the sake of enjoying its exercise. Mrs. Schoolcraft is, I should judge, about twenty-two years of age. [She was twenty-six.] She would be an ornament to any society and with better health (for at present she enjoys this great blessing but partially) would take a first rank among the best improved, whether in acquirements, taste or graces.

Anna Brownell Murphy, Irish wife of Robert Jameson, Chancellor of the Province of Toronto, on a western literary tour in 1837, was the guest of the Schoolcrafts at Mackinac Island. Among her recorded impressions are the following:

About ten o'clock I ventured to call on Mr. Schoolcraft, and was received by him with grave and quiet politeness. They were prepared he said, for my arrival, and then he apologized for whatever might be deficient in my reception, and for the absence of his wife, by informing me that she was ill, and had not left her room for some days.

Much was I discomposed and shocked to find myself an intruder under such circumstances! I said no, and begged that they would not think of me—that I could easily provide for myself—and so I could and would. I would have laid myself down in one of the Indian lodges rather than have been de trop. But Mr. Schoolcraft said, with much kindness, that they knew already of my arrival by one of my fellow passengers—that a room was prepared for me, a servant already sent down for my goods and Mrs. Schoolcraft, who was a little better that morning, hoped to see me.

I am charmed with Mrs. Schoolcraft. When able to appear, she received me with true lady-like simplicity. The damp, tremulous hand, the soft, plaintive voice, the touching expression of her countenance, told too plainly of resigned and habitual suffering.

Mrs. Schoolcraft's features are more decidedly Indian than those of her sister, Mrs. McMurray. Her accent is slightly foreign—her choice of language pure and remarkably elegant. In the course of an hour's talk all my sympathies were enlisted in her behalf and I thought that she on her part was inclined to return those benignant feelings. Then she has two sweet children about eight and nine years old—no fear, you see, that we shall soon be the best friends in the world!

The most delightful as well as most profitable hours I spent here, are those passed in the society of Mrs. Schoolcraft. Her genuine refinement and simplicity, and native taste for literature, are charming; and the exceeding delicacy of her health, and the trials to which it is exposed, interest all my womanly sympathies. While in conversation with her, new ideas of the Indian character suggest themselves; new sources of information are opened to me, such as are granted to few, and such as I gratefully appreciate. She is proud of her Indian origin; she takes an enthusiastic and enlightened interest in the welfare of her people, and in their conversion to Christianity, being herself most unaffectedly pious.

Mrs. Steele, writing in *A Summer Journey in the West,* in 1840, says she would have taken Mrs. Schoolcraft for a Spanish lady, from her accent, the deep brunette of her smooth skin, and her dark hair and eyes; and that her grace and beauty made a keen impression.

She was considered one of the most beautiful women in the Northwest.

A manuscript diary of the Reverend Peter Dougherty, in possession of the University of Michigan Historical Collections, affords a glimpse of Mrs. Schoolcraft in 1838:

Mr. Schoolcraft had gone to Washington.

Saturday July 7th. After some preparation I called on Mrs. Schoolcraft and was happy to find her better than I had expected. When she learned my name and business she ventured out of her room which she had not done before for some time. She was very feeble but I found her a very pleasant and an unusually intelligent woman. After returning to my boarding house she sent the servant to invite me to tea in the evening. After returning from the excursion on the water, went up and found tea ready and Mrs. Schoolcraft informed me she had made preparation for my accommodation while remaining in the place. She appears to be a woman of a truly

Your affectionate Father

Henry R Schoolcraft

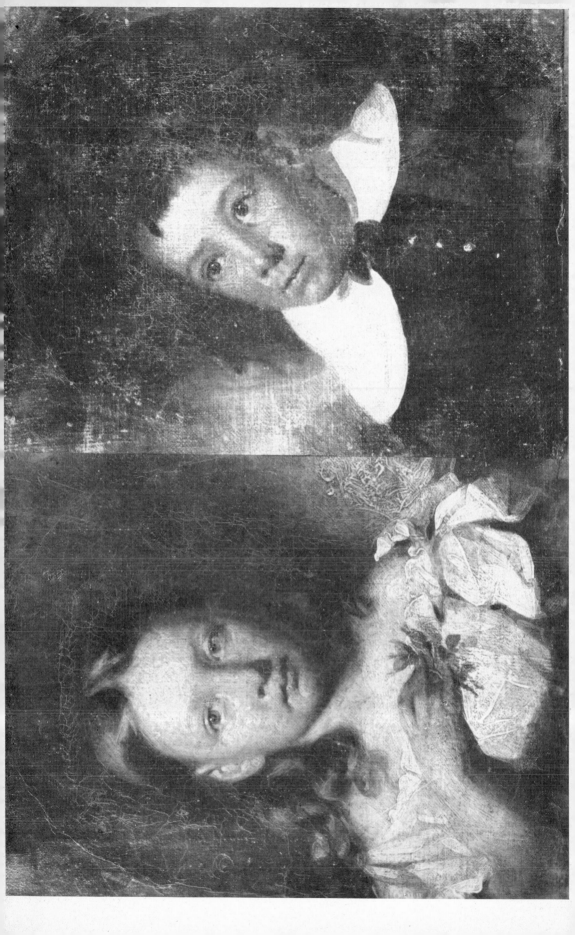

benevolent heart, all frankness and kindness. She is a woman of a highly cultivated mind.

Monday July 9th. Am delighted with Mrs. Schoolcraft who shows every attention to my comfort. She has two children—Jane about eleven and John about nine. Her little girl is a sweet little thing.

Thursday July 12th. Went to Round Island this morning and took Mr. Schoolcraft's children as my only companions.

Saturday July 14th. . . . Little Jane gave me three mococks full of sugar and worked outside with porcupine quills. Mrs. Schoolcraft about the same—very feeble.

Monday July 16th. Mrs. Schoolcraft showed me a manuscript newspaper published at St. Mary's by Mr. Schoolcraft in 1826 and 1827.

Tuesday July 17th. Read in Mr. Schoolcraft's journal and manuscript newspaper. Went in to see Mrs. Schoolcraft. She was thrown into quite an excitement which brought on a palpitation of the heart by a person coming to the door who she thought was Mr. Schoolcraft. Went again to her room in the afternoon and had some conversation respecting the natives.

The friendship that existed in Detroit and Washington between the Schoolcraft family and Governor Cass and his daughter is in itself eloquent attestation to Mrs. Schoolcraft's quality.

As she had been a devoted daughter to her father, and to her Indian mother whose presence seemed almost necessary to her complete happiness, Jane Schoolcraft was a loving mother to her own children. What discipline she exercised was, after the Ojibway manner, without cross words. Her daughter and son returned her affection with lifelong, utter idolatry. There is a pretty picture of the little family at Elmwood in one of her letters to her husband in 1831:

I wish it was in your power to bring along with you a good little girl who can speak English, for I do not see how I can manage during the summer (if my life is spared) without some assistance in the care of the children. I feel anxious, more particularly on Jane's account, for she is now at that age when children are apt to be biased by the habits of those they associate with, and as I cannot be with her all the time, the greater will be the necessity of the person to whom she is entrusted (let it be ever so short a time) to be one who has been brought up by pious, and, of course, conscientious parents, where no bad example can be apprehended.   I feel daily the importance of bringing up children, not merely to pass with advantage through the world, but with advantage to their souls to all eternity. . . .

Little Janee improves rapidly under her [Anna Maria's] tuition.   Janee [three and a half years of age] has commenced saying by heart two pieces out of the little book you sent her.   One is "My Mother," and the other is, "How doth the little busy Bee."   It is pleasant to see her smooth down her apron and hear her say, "So I shall stand by my father, and say my lessons, and he will call me his dear little Tee-gee, and say I am a good girl."   She will do this with so much gravity, and then skip about in an instant after and repeat, half singing, "My father will come home again in the spring, when the birds sing and the grass and flowers come out of the ground; he will call me his wild Irish girl."

Janee has just come into the room, and insists on my telling you that she can spell her name very prettily, "Schoolcraft and all." She seems anxious to gain your approbation for her acquirements, and I encourage the feeling in order to excite attention to her lessons, as she is so full of life and spirits that it is hard to get her to keep still long enough to recite them properly.   Johnston has improved more than you can imagine, and has such endearing ways that one cannot help loving the dear child.   Oh, that they would both grow up wise unto salvation, and I should be happy.

Mrs. Jameson remarked that Mrs. Schoolcraft always spoke to her children and domestics in the Chippewa tongue. The following lines in that language were written by her in 1839, after leaving Johnston at school in Princeton and Janee at Philadelphia.   The translation is by her husband.

> Nyau nin de nain dum
> May kow e yaun in
> Ain dah nuk ki yaun
> Waus sa wa kom eg
> Ain dah nuk ki yaun
>
> Ne dau nis ainse e
> Ne gwis is ainse e
> Ishe nau gun ug wau
> Waus sa wa kom eg
>
> She gwau go sha ween
> Ba sho waud e we

Nin zhe ka we yea
Ishe ez hau jau yaun
Ain dah nuk ke yaun

Ain dah nuk ke yaun
Nin zhe ke we yea
Ishe ke way aun e
Nyau ne gush kain dum

Lines of Mrs. Schoolcraft on Leaving Her Children at School in the East and Returning to Her Native Country

When memory turns to my country so dear,
My heart fills with pleasure and throbs with a fear.
My country, my country! my own native land!
So lovely in aspect, in features so grand;
Far, far in the west!   What are cities to me,
Oh, land of my mother! compared unto thee?

Fair land of the lakes!   Thou art blest to my sight,
With thy beaming bright waters and landscapes of light;
The breeze and the murmur, the dash and the roar,
That summer and autumn cast over the shore,
They spring to my thoughts like the lullaby tongue
That soothed me to slumber when cradled and young.

One feeling more strongly still binds me to thee
Here roved my forefathers, in liberty free;
Here shook they the war lance and sported the plume,
Ere Europe had cast o'er their country a gloom;
Nor thought they that kingdoms more happy could be,
While lords of a land so resplendent and free.

Yet it is not alone that my country is fair,
And my home and my friends are inviting me there.
While they beckon me onward, my heart is still here,
With my sweet, lovely daughter and bonny boy dear.
And oh! what's the joy that a home can impart,
Removed from the dear ones who cling to my heart.

It is learning that calls them, but, tell me, can schools
Repay for my love or give nature new rules?
They may teach them the lore of the wit and the sage,
To be grave in their youth and gay in old age;
But oh! my poor heart, what are schools to the view,
While severed from children thou lovest so true?

I return to my country—I haste on my way—
For duty commands me, and duty must sway.
Yet I leave the bright land where my little ones dwell
With a sober regret and a bitter farewell;
For there I must leave the dear jewels I love,
The dearest of gifts from my Master above.

At Mackinac Island, the Maternal Association, a praying band of mothers anxious for their children, met at her home. Some of those who attended were Indian mothers. To these the exercises were interpreted by Mrs. Schoolcraft.

A Christian by training from childhood, she had made a translation of the Lord's Prayer in Chippewa, and, occasionally, as delicate and declining health permitted, some other select pieces from the Sacred Writings, and hymns. The words of a psalm composed by her in Chippewa, with an English translation, are given in *Oneóta*.

Her cultivated and naturally superior intelligence was eagerly applied in efforts to forward the interests of her husband. She studied languages with him, especially the Ojibway, and even Latin and Hebrew. Her translation of the Chippewa tale, "Little Spirit," is included in *Oneóta*. A short poem written by her after the death of her first child appears in Mr. Schoolcraft's memoirs.

Obahbahm-wawa-geezhagoquay, her Indian name, signifies literally The Sound That the Stars Make Rushing Through the Sky. It has been translated, much less appropriately, The Music of the Spheres. Her English name, Jane, was in honor of her Scotch-Irish aunt in Wexford, Ireland.

Schoolcraft sailed for Europe, for a long-postponed brief visit, May 9, 1842. Their two children were at school in the East. Mrs. Schoolcraft was visiting her sister Charlotte, the wife of Archdeacon William McMurray, at Dundas in Upper Canada. There she was seized with an illness which proved fatal.

The stone that marks her grave in the churchyard of St. John's Anglican Church in the neighboring community of Ancaster, Ontario, was so badly weathered in 1940 that the last eight lines were not decipherable, but fortunately the entire inscription has been preserved, as follows, in the *Journal and Transactions of the Wentworth (Ontario) Historical Society:*

JANE,

Wife of

HENRY R. SCHOOLCRAFT, ESQ.,

Born at St. Mary's Falls, Jan. 31st, 1800.
She died at Dundas, May 22nd, 1842,
In the arms of her sister, during a visit at the home
of the Rector of this church, while her husband was absent
in England, and her children at a distant school.
She was the eldest daughter of
John Johnston, Esq., and Susan, daughter of Waubojeeg,
a celebrated War Chief and civil ruler of the Ojibewa Tribe.
Carefully educated and of polished manners and
conversation, she was early fitted to adorn society, yet
of retiring and modest deportment. Early im-
bued with the principles of true piety, she patiently
submitted to the illness which for several years marked her
decline, and was inspired through seasons of
bodily and mental depression with the lively hope of
a blessed immortality.

Henry Rowe Schoolcraft visited her grave on his return from Europe. He placed the monument there. Through all the years of her lingering illness, each of their many separations had left them fearful she would not live to see him again. The foreboding had at last come true.

There are tragedies more intolerable than the bereavement of death. For Schoolcraft this Valley of the Shadow had been his for half a decade.

Mary Howard Schoolcraft, who had a genius for pouring out the cruel truth, even about herself, to the last, bitterest drop, has intimated unmistakably that Jane Schoolcraft's illness was, at the last, drug addiction. In *The Black Gauntlet*, there is a glimpse of a Schoolcraft who has not hitherto been known:—silent and overwhelmed, drawing tight the strings of the purse that had previously smoothed his wife's pathway to destruction; his children, loving their mother blindly, innocently helping her to thwart him, turning against their father for his efforts to save her; his sending them away to school, depriving himself of the happiness of their presence, in order to guard Jane better and to save them from danger of a like misfortune.

He had need of all the courage that faith in God's goodness could give him.

Jane had done much to lead him to that refuge and security.

Jane Johnston Schoolcraft was a unique personality of gentleness and charm, who carried from the red race to the white a tenuous ray of imagination and spirituality. She received in return the light of Christianity that led her, as it can all mankind in spite of weakness, to the assurance of peace in Immortality.

Henry Rowe Schoolcraft and Jane Johnston had three children. With the death of these their line ceased.

Briefest and most touching is the life story of little William Henry, the darkness of whose loss became a light. Penaysee, Bird, they called him lovingly. His mother gave him a pet name of her own. Born in the old Johnston house at Sault Ste. Marie, Michigan, June 27, 1824, he died suddenly of croup before he was three years old. Three of his grandparents and his father were superior individuals of the white race. His mother's mother was a thoroughbred Indian. Like his sister and brother, he was a quarter-breed.

When the bright, promising baby died, his father was a stricken man, deeming it a warning from Heaven that his hopes had been too firmly set on earthly things. It is a deep glimpse into Schoolcraft's heart that he should take his first Bible, the one that he had carried from childhood, and place it in the coffin-pillow under his dead baby's head.

Little William Henry's Indian cousins were laid in the earth with bow and arrow playthings to comfort them across the Great Divide. Little William Henry took his father's cherished Bible, but gave him in return a strength that he had need of.

There were two cemeteries at Sault Ste. Marie in 1827: the old Indian burial ground and the new plot for Fort Brady. A place was granted this baby among the soldiers' graves. Years afterwards, when these were moved to Riverside Cemetery, the small one was permitted to remain in martial company. So it was lost and forgotten, until Lena and Paul and Ruth Chandler rediscovered it, after a long search, in 1941. The grave at Riverside is in the section for soldiers, north of their flagpole, the second grave in the first row from the pole. The stone is much darkened by weathering but the legend is clear:

> In Memory of
> William Henry
> the Dearly beloved Son
> of Henry R. and
> Jane Schoolcraft
> born June 27th 1824
> died March 13th 1827
> Ae 2 years, 8 mos, 14 das
> Sweet William

1843–1864

Schoolcraft had traveled almost continuously from early youth. Yet for the first time in his life he now found himself without a home.

His mother and father were buried at Vernon, New York. Their children—his numerous sisters and brothers—were dead or dispersed.

Whatever part of Jane Johnston's family had been his was also gone.

Her father, whom he had loved and admired and named his second son for, had contracted a malignant fever on a trip to New York and barely reached the Sault before he died of it, September 22, 1828. Susan Johnston had beaten an Irish sterling spoon into a coffin plate. Schoolcraft had engraved on it the name and dates and helped to lay him away beside little William Henry.

Mrs. Johnston, consistently admirable, carried on ably for the family despite the straitened circumstances in which she had been left. From the land reserved to her personally, by treaty, she manufactured maple sugar—thirty-five hundred pounds of it in 1837. Each fall she went with her people in canoes to the entrance of Lake Superior to fish in the bays and creeks for a fortnight and bring back a load of fish cured for the winter. Widowed and self-supporting, she gave the first building to the Sault Ste. Marie Presbyterian Church in 1832. Her remarkable life ended soon after that of her loved daughter Jane. She took her place for the long sleep beside her husband and first grandchild in November, 1843.

These had belonged to Schoolcraft, and he to them. They were no more. The rest of the Johnstons he had done much for when he had been able, and he kept on doing for them what he could from time to time, but they were not his family.

Returning from his tour through western Virginia, Ohio, and Michigan, to Ancaster and Dundas, Ontario, in 1843, he made New York his headquarters. Janee and Johnston and he had a hotel suite together. His daughter was already a lovely and accomplished young woman. Johnston was equally gifted, but to no apparent purpose. At their father's suggestion the two edited a small manuscript periodical, for home amusement, that ran from August 31, 1844, to March 1, 1846.

As always he was eagerly interested and occupied. With Charles Fenno Hoffman and others he collected information for a state map for the New-York Historical Society which was to show the aboriginal names of places. He lectured on historical and ethnological subjects. He issued an ethnological publication in eight parts, which he later bound together as *Oneóta*.

His distinguished friends included Albert Gallatin, with whom and others he helped to organize the American Ethnological Society.

In 1845, during the official census of New York State, he was engaged to enumerate the Iroquois. After submitting his report he issued a reprint of it; then published a popular historical interpretation of the figures and facts. A similar census, he and his ethnological associates agreed, ought to be made at once, before it was too late, for all the Indians in the United

States. They drew up a petition, and Schoolcraft carried it to Washington personally. This was in 1846.

In church at the capital one Sunday, as a guest in the pew of a friend—who might have been John Calhoun?—he was introduced to Miss Mary E. Howard, of Grahamville, South Carolina. Their interest in each other was instantaneous. They were married within a few months, and for seventeen years she was as great a help to him, in a different way, as Jane Johnston had been.

Perhaps no two women ever were more different. Mary Howard Schoolcraft was, by her own account, as unpopular as Jane Johnston Schoolcraft had been universally beloved. Not gentle nor gracious nor winsome nor delicate nor retiring, she was strong-minded, proud, quick, bitter—a fearlessly outspoken fighter for her cause, her people, or herself, with something from the tortured imaginings of her childhood that drove her to sadistic reiterance of what she thought the truth. She was a handsome woman, intellectual, self-educated, high-minded, and spiritual in a sometimes forbidding way. The Cinderella of her family—and not a patient but a rebellious one—she left her story hidden, for the world to find and ponder and to be rather sorry for her instead of really liking her. Her life reads like fiction, commanding keen interest and admiration, and often sympathy, but never love. The temperamental outbursts growing out of her unhappy childhood doubtless added much discomfort to Henry Rowe Schoolcraft's last years. This must have been especially true during the period of the War of the States. Her blazing, heavily-documented conviction regarding the justice of Negro slavery, and the opposed point of view of the three others in the family, probably caused many a taut hour in the Schoolcraft home. But she was tremendously interested in his work, an eager and an able amanuensis, and radiantly devoted to him throughout the long period of his physical affliction.

She was past thirty when she met and was married to Henry Rowe Schoolcraft. Those preceding thirty-odd years that became a part of his later life, are worth many pages here and an understanding volume of their own. The following paragraphs are based on investigations in the Howard-Hogg family records in Georgia and South Carolina; a visit to the beautiful country of her birth; and her own writings, especially *The Black Gauntlet: A Tale of Plantation Life in South Carolina,* published by J. B. Lippincott & Co., Philadelphia, 1860, four years before her husband's death. Some quotations from this narrative that throw light upon the life of Henry Schoolcraft are included in this book as an addendum.

Mary Howard was born in August, 1812, on the Orange Grove portion of Hogg's Neck Plantation, in Beaufort District, South Carolina, on the bank of the Broad River about eight miles from Grahamville. Her earliest memories were of affluence and pampering, in a world of which she was the special princess. A mansion, and many slaves who lived in a long line of neat white-and-green cabins along the river bank, were hers to command, until her mother died, when she was three. When she was some years older and could run away from a world that seemed all wrong, she turned from the broad rich acres that produced the famed Sea Island cotton that had made her family's wealth and explored the tangled forest and the farther reaches of the marshy river, with its fringe of live oaks hung with Spanish moss and its maze of islands which were no longer islands when the tide went out. The family graveyard, where generations upon generations of her father's forebears, and her own idolized mother, were buried, became her happiest retreat.

Her mother was the granddaughter of an Anglican bishop of Charleston, South Carolina; her father, the only son of a descendant of a first settler of the Broad River country. Of the ten children of her father's first marriage, four survived childhood. Mary was the youngest. One brother, John Howard, became a general in the Mexican War. Her sister, Jane Howard, married Captain Alexander Moultrie, a grand-nephew of the Revolutionary hero. Her eldest brother became a minister of note.

A beautiful, seventeen-year-old stepmother, brought home within a year after her mother's death, was one of the

Mrs H R Schoolcraft

Gen John Howard..   315. C. Street, S. East
    Grahamville   Capital Hill
        South Carolina.   Washington 1875
                                September

My dear Brother.
            For the first twenty years of our
existence we are taught fables, and traditions, as re-
= ligion, that it takes twenty more years to un-
= root. Thus are we cheated out of our lives, and
live in slavish bondage to error, when the
truth, makes every spirit as free as the
eagle that soars up to the skies. When
I study the history of man, and see what he
has believed in, with fervent faith, I begin
to doubt whether his intellect, is as respec-
= table as the instincts of beasts: It has not
been a hundred years, since our fellow sin-
= ners, allowed freedom of opinion; an attribute
of human dignity, that God has always left
free. We talk of Christianity, very flippantly,
as the moral catholicon; and yet one has studied
the history of the church, when its powen-
veiled kings, and kingdoms; when it
numbered two hundred millions of
converts, that does not hang his head

PART OF LETTER FROM MARY HOWARD SCHOOLCRAFT TO HER BROTHER. FROM ORIGINAL IN THE COLLECTION
MRS. GEORGIA H. DOVE, BALTIMORE, MARYLAND.

things that warped the life of Mary Howard. Another twisting influence was the backwash of the War of 1812. Prices of
cotton and Negroes fell precipitously. Her father had made
an agreement that proved disastrous. The needs of four
young children in his second family and the demands of the
three older than herself left Mary in between, forever wearing
others' clothes, her need of education always pushed aside by
other problems. When her father, crushed physically as well as
financially, died in 1825, Orange Grove passed into her
brothers' hands and Mary was sent to board at Grahamville
with her stepmother.

A thousand slights, big and little, past and present, compounded themselves in her imaginings. She adored her small
half-brothers and sisters, and was bitterly jealous of them.
Fierce pride and warm love for her family fought with an-
guished personal feelings. And she did not hide her thoughts.

She knew her life was warped. It seemed in memory all
deprivation and continuous criticism. Everybody knew she
was a hoyden, and said so, until being a hoyden was her idea of
being lost in sin. Despite circumstances she found a way of
her own to develop her native abilities. She studied the dic-
tion of ministers. But her chief inspiration was the society of,
and the books provided by, a brilliant Southern woman, their
nearest neighbor and her dead mother's closest friend, Mrs.
Thomas Heyward, widow of the South Carolina Signer. In
time Mary Howard became the local authority on matters of
learning and a leader in social reform. Although reduced to
what she considered penury at the time of her marriage, she
was then the owner of twenty-two Negro slaves as well as other
property, and numbered many notables among her friends,
among them the Governor of South Carolina.

She tells frankly of her one youthful love. The sensitive
suffering of years had been completely erased by a burst of pure
joy. Then the brilliant young minister with whom she had
plighted troth became suddenly insane and after some years
died in that condition. The shock deranged her own mind
temporarily.

These things she had lived through in her lonely, intellectual, and finally God-fearing way. Some of Schoolcraft's trials were complicated, without doubt, by her outbreaks of ungovernable emotional intensity; yet she contributed vastly to his achievements and comfort and content.

Mary Howard and Henry Rowe Schoolcraft were married January 13, 1847, at the home of her sister—Hickory Hill, the plantation of Captain Alexander Moultrie—in St. Luke's Parish, Beaufort District, South Carolina, near Walterboro.

There are no newspapers or court-house records of that date left in Beaufort District, due to the occupation of this town and county by Federal forces from 1862 to 1865. The court house was burned; the old library with its files and the Stoney Creek Presbyterian Church with its records also were destroyed during the War.

Before the ceremony, by prenuptial agreement, Mary Howard's Negroes were deeded in trust to her brother, John H. Howard, who was to turn over to her the income from the work of these people. This was to evade the unfair law of the time that gave the property of a woman to her husband.

The trip through the coastal waters of South Carolina to Savannah, Georgia, to get a steamboat to New York, was made in a small boat with slaves for oarsmen. Two giant Africans made a seat with their interlocked wrists and hands to carry the bride and groom together out through the shallow water to the waiting boat. That was as it had been done for her mother and father!

They were a few days at Savannah, waiting for the New York steamer. Mary and her brother John said their good-byes at leisure. Henry Schoolcraft examined the formation of Yamacraw Bluff. The three of them, and the oarsmen, stopped at the Pulaski House, which is still running in Savannah, under the same name, after a hundred years. The quarters where slaves were kept on such occasions, or while awaiting sale at the local market, may still be seen by flashlight under the old building.

The story of Henry Rowe Schoolcraft's first marriage as

recorded by his second wife is as Mary Howard Schoolcraft heard it on this voyage.

In New York City, she found the two children of Jane Johnston Schoolcraft quite naturally antagonistic. Eventually she won Janee. Johnston she accounted hopeless, in more ways than one. Schoolcraft suffered between them. But Mary Howard had the sense and strength to gain her husband's promise never to let such things come between them, and apparently he never did. As long as he lived he believed that she had been providentially sent to him to be his associate in the higher mission of giving a scientific form and literary finish to the results of his former explorations. When he entered the chill corridor of death, and she took him in her arms to try to warm him, he kept repeating her name as long as he could breathe, as if calling her to go with him. So recorded his friend, Dr. Samson.

With the sole exception of her dead mother, Henry Rowe Schoolcraft was the only human in whom Mary Howard did not see the flaw that marred perfection, or who escaped the barbed darts of her thoughts. "I have felt desolate from earliest childhood," she wrote, addressing him, in the dedication of her book; "ever lamenting the loss of an incomparable father and mother, and loving sisters, and brothers, and friends, all snatched from me by inevitable destiny; so that, in this wide world, I have found *you*, Ne na baim, my only unchanging earthly hope. You are, therefore, my all—for the heart needs a home in this world as well as the next." And again: "In the bodily afflictions that you have borne with the uncomplaining manliness, majesty, and serenity of Christianity, you have commanded the deepest moral appreciation and romance of a Southern woman's heart."

Within a few months after their marriage the Schoolcrafts moved from New York City to Washington, D. C. Schoolcraft's remaining years were spent at the national capital, chiefly in the task, as special Agent for the Indian Department, of compiling and issuing the six volumes that became his major work. This consumed ten years, from 1847 to 1857. In the same decade, however, he prepared and published his memoirs; issued a new edition of his Ozark travels; and summarized in one volume his two expeditions of discovery of the source of the Mississippi. The world-wide success of Longfellow's *Song of Hiawatha* in 1855 and re-echoed charges that the material had been stolen from the Finnish *Kalevala,* prompted Schoolcraft to republish, in 1856, his *Algic Researches,* with some changes, as *The Myth of Hiawatha.* Thanks to Mary Howard School-craft he was able to do all this in spite of handicaps that fell heavily on the last fifteen years of his life.

Not long after his settlement in Washington, according to the Reverend Doctor Gurley, the reaction from his former ex-posures began to show itself in his physical frame. He was crippled by rheumatic affections. For a while this merely pre-vented him from appearing much in society. After 1850 he moved his office to his home and seldom went to the War De-partment. In 1851 he was able to travel to Philadelphia about printing matters, though he could go about his house only on crutches. During the winter of 1858–59, he made a trip to De-troit for the Office of Indian Affairs. Later he could not be moved except in a wheel chair, and during the last three or four years he was confined to his bed with his limbs bent completely under him.

He had had a vigorous constitution. In Missouri in 1819 he had worked himself sick on the manuscript on the lead mines, but the jaundice that developed was soon cured. Two years later, at Chicago, he contracted an acute bilious fever of the worst type and narrowly escaped death. A foreshadowing of future trouble came as he hastened toward the Sault in 1822. An attack of fever and ague was quickly terminated by re-newed doses of mercury in rapid succession, but the treatment prostrated his strength and induced at first tic douloureux— and eventually a paralysis of the left cheek. In a letter of August 7, 1828, he mentions an "affection of the right arm and leg since July 1" that for a time nearly deprived him of the use of his pen.

According to Mary Howard Schoolcraft, he was stricken

with paralysis in 1849. He was confined to his home by it. His hands were rendered useless. The direct cause, she asserts, was the culmination of long anxiety and a shock arising from the conduct of his son John Johnston. There is the possibility that the derangement of his whole nervous system might have been aggravated by her own intense emotional reaction. While he was facing his intolerable situation she shut herself in her own room for three days and three nights.

Schoolcraft's letters indicate difficulties with his son. One of them, dated August 23, 1847, substantiates his wife's account of a visit to John Johnston in New York City soon after their marriage with the fact that they moved him to 96 Cliff Street, nearer to his business. He wrote George Johnston April 9, 1852: "John has been wandering about, and not only has no money to make such (land) entries, if I approved them, but is wholly incompetent to manage or keep any property."

Mary Howard says in so many words that Johnston found the unhappy trail that led his mother to an early grave; that he was a gambler and had embezzled Schoolcraft's friends in New York far beyond power to make restitution; and that he repaid their efforts to cure him, in their Washington home, by rifling his father's safe and vanishing. His private school education, his exceptional talents, his unmistakable Indian characteristics, and his father's name he had combined successfully in his unfortunate trend.

After Mary Howard Schoolcraft's reminiscences, thinly disguised with fictitious names of individuals and places, had been printed, in 1860, with her husband's approval, only two more references to Johnston have been found.

The War Department records show that John Johnston Schoolcraft, aged thirty-two years, born in St. Mary's, Michigan, was enrolled and mustered into service June 20, 1861, at Washington, D. C., as a private, Company H, 82nd New York Infantry. He was wounded in the battle of Gettysburg, July 2, 1863, and was honorably discharged April 29, 1864, at Harewood Hospital, Washington, D. C., on a surgeon's certificate of disability on account of hypertrophy of the heart.

His sister provided the statement, published some twenty-five years later, that Johnston had served under General McClellan and was in the seven days' battles around Richmond; that he succumbed to the hardships of a soldier's life and died in the hospital at Elmira, New York, in April, 1865, surviving his father one year.

John Johnston Schoolcraft is buried in the soldiers' plot at Woodlawn Cemetery, at Elmira, in Lot 31 of Section O. He is recorded there as a member of the National Reserve Corps. The date of his death was April 28, his age thirty-five.

Janee—Jane Susan Anne Schoolcraft—was, contrastively, a source of joy all the days of her life.

At Mackinac Island the Reverend Peter Dougherty, who saw a good deal of both the Schoolcraft children, wrote in his diary, perhaps significantly: "She (Mrs. Schoolcraft) has two children—Jane about eleven and John about nine. Her little girl is a sweet little thing."

That was the summer of 1838. In December following she was taken to the private school of the Misses Guild in Philadelphia, from which the report was sent to her father, in the summer of 1839, at Mackinac, that she had improved in music, had commenced drawing, and had a taste for both.

By 1840 Johnston had been changed from the Round Hill School at Princeton to another in Brooklyn. Janee still wrote from Philadelphia: "I am getting along in my studies very well. I love music as much as ever. I like my French studies much. I have got all p's for my lessons, but one g. G is for good, and p for perfect." Her letters comforted and cheered her father.

Mary Howard Schoolcraft, who says that Johnston looked entirely Indian, writes in detail of Janee's Nordic beauty: "The girl had a profusion of golden hair floating in ringlets over shoulders as white and transparent as wax-work. Her eyes were tender, intelligent, and blue as the sky; her limbs were moulded in faultless symmetry, although her stature was delicately unobtrusive." Also "she had real genius, highly cultivated by study of the most improving books, and a taste for music, of which she was very fond."

Like her mother, wherever she went she was beloved.

Though a poetic genius, there was no conceit, no arrogance, or didactic assumption of wisdom in her modestly-expressed opinions in company.

Janee, strange to say, though not half so beautiful as Sarah Rebecca, had a great many more beaux and lovers; for though mentally stoical as a philosopher, there was a sort of physical, impromptu nervousness of manner, that had all the pleasing effect of child-like frankness and artlessness.

Among her numerous admirers, Charles Fenno Hoffman, a celebrated poet of the day, was her choice. Her father had proposed him as an honorary member of the Michigan Historical Society many years before. The two had been co-workers in the New-York Historical Society. "A poet in his garret I had long heard of," wrote Schoolcraft after a first visit to Hoffman's lodgings,

but a liberal gentlemanly fellow, surrounded by all the elegances of life, I had not thought of as the domicile of the Muses. Mr. Hoffman impressed me as being very English in his appearance and manners. His forehead is quite Byronic in its craniological developments. His eye and countenance are of the most commanding character. Pity that such a handsome man, so active in everything that calls for the gun, the rod, the boat, the horse, the dog, should have been shorn of so essential a prerequisite as a leg. His conversational powers are quite extraordinary. I felt constantly as if I were in the presence of a lover of nature and natural things.

Educated at Columbia College, Hoffman had practiced law, edited a number of magazines, written two books on the West, a few novels. His fame rested chiefly upon his poems, first collected in *The Vigil of Faith*, in 1842, and especially his songs, which were once deservedly popular. Some of his verse appears in Schoolcraft's miscellany, *Oneóta*.

One week before the wedding day, in 1849, Hoffman became insane. He died in an asylum.

Mary Howard Schoolcraft, remembering a similar tragedy in her own life and fearful of the effect upon Janee, sent her away at once to South Carolina, in company with beautiful young Sarah Rebecca Howard, who at the time was visiting the Schoolcrafts in Washington.

Sarah Rebecca was the young half-sister of Mary Howard. Another member of Mary Howard's family at Grahamville was Benjamin Screven Howard, her youngest half-brother, born probably about 1823. Benjamin was Mary Howard's favorite. He was named for the Baptist minister in Charleston, South Carolina, who had taken her into his family for a while after her mother's death. Janee liked Benjamin sufficiently to shock her stepmother by consenting at once to marry him!

A glimpse of Janee at this important moment of her life is given in the Howard family records, as

a woman of very superior mind, and I may say, heart. She received, of course, a splendid education and was highly accomplished. It was on the occasion of her visit to Grahamville that I met her. She was not at all pretty, but the charm of her manners made you forget that. I remember as a child being afraid to meet her, but like all highly educated people she put you entirely at your ease.

Benjamin wished to go to California, in the gold rush, and return with a fortune for his bride. His sensible half-sister, soon to be his step-mother-in-law, decided otherwise. The Schoolcraft influence secured him a place at Washington, and the second Howard-Schoolcraft marriage was solemnized.

Happy as Henry Rowe Schoolcraft was then, notwithstanding his own physical plight, this union brought its element of sorrow. Benjamin Howard was of the South. When the War of the States came, in 1860, he left Washington to take office under the Confederate Government at Richmond, and, of course, Janee went with him. Her situation there, and Johnston's in the Union Army, together with Mary Howard's Southern background and fiery pro-slavery opinions, must have been a source of deep disturbance to him during his last years, through the long months of the War whose end he did not live to see.

"Jane Schoolcraft, wife of B. S. Howard, born October 14, 1829 [this should be 1827], died November 25, 1892," is the record on a tombstone in historic Hollywood Cemetery in Richmond, Virginia—where Jefferson Davis and his wife and his daughter Winnie and the rest of his family are buried; and President Tyler; and President Monroe; and many other famous Americans. "Light is sown for the righteous and gladness for the upright in heart," is inscribed below Jane Schoolcraft's name and dates.

The *Richmond Dispatch* of Saturday, November 26, 1892, reports the death of Mrs. Jane S. Howard, at 404 East Main Street, aged sixty-five, and informs:

Mrs. Howard was one of the best of women. She had long been an active worker in Dr. Hoge's church and was for a number of years in charge of the infant department of the Sunday School, where her true piety and sunny disposition made a lasting impression on the youthful minds under her charge.

Three days later, telling of her burial on November 27, the newspaper continues:

The death of this lady has cast a gloom over the entire congregation. The members of the Ladies Benevolent Society attended in a body, as did also the infant class of the Sunday School. Several Chinamen, of whom she was the teacher, were at the funeral.

The celebrated pastor of the Second Presbyterian Church of Richmond, the Reverend Dr. Moses D. Hoge, found it necessary to tell his congregation at her grave that he would not, even on this occasion, depart from his rule never to deliver a funeral eulogy. He disapproved of such addresses; and reiterated his request that none should be given when it came his time to be entrusted to the earth.

Dr. Hoge's attitude toward Jane Schoolcraft Howard was more than that of a pastor toward one of the most active members of his congregation. When Mrs. Hoge had died, young Mrs. Howard had mothered and practically raised his youngest child Hampden. Jane had no children of her own. She and her husband had lived with his family for many years and Jane had been more like a sister or a daughter. In fact, when she died, at her own request, she was buried in the family lot of one of Dr. Hoge's daughters, Mary Rochet Hoge Gilliam.

That was nearly fifty years ago. Yet today, lovely as old

Richmond is, its memories are richer and more fragrant because Janee Schoolcraft spent her life there. This is not because of the interest of her Indian ancestry, or the achievements of the man who was her father, but for herself. A half century after her death, there are distinguished Richmond citizens who still remember and revere her.

Benjamin Howard, after the Confederate Government ceased to exist, went into business in Richmond as a bookseller and stationer, first as a member of the firm of Sleight and Howard, then by himself. For a time he edited *The Central Presbyterian,* a religious weekly. Post-war times were difficult for everyone. Janee established a small private school for girls and boys, to help make their living.

Mr. Harry C. Beattie (whose mother's first husband was a John L. Schoolcraft of Albany, New York) attended Jane Schoolcraft Howard's school in the 1870's. "The Lord never made a better woman than she was," was still his vivid impression of her in 1941. Her Indian blood was apparent, he said, chiefly in her high cheek-bones.

The perfect tribute to Jane Schoolcraft Howard was that of Madam Coleman Wortham, a granddaughter of the Reverend Dr. Hoge. She had seen in *The Richmond Times Dispatch* a reference to our search for information and had overcome her keen reluctance to communicate with strangers because of love for Mrs. Howard, and a great desire to do anything that might worthily preserve the memory of one who had been her beloved teacher and her family's friend. It was thanks to the hospitality of Madam Wortham, and in her gracious company, that we paid our respects to Jane Susan Anne Schoolcraft Howard, beloved citizen of Richmond, in her Southern resting place.

After the two children of Henry Rowe Schoolcraft were grown and had left home, he and his wife Mary adopted a child. In the Census Report of 1860 she appears as Alice Schoolcraft, aged eleven, born in Washington, D. C.

Another member of their household at that time was fifteen-year-old Charles Lullay, whom they had taken to educate as their own. Charles was the son of Major Lullay, of the entourage of Kossuth, the Hungarian exile, for whose rescue the United States had sent a special expedition to Turkey in 1850. The Lullays, who were Jews as well as Hungarians, had sunk into dire poverty by 1856 when Schoolcraft found them and took one of their sons. The boy defeated their plans for a college education by joining the United States Navy at the outbreak of the War of the States. Then the Schoolcrafts took his eight-year-old brother Julius Caesar. Charles Lullay was honorably discharged from the Navy in 1863 for bodily disability; managed with difficulty and the assistance of Mrs. Schoolcraft to support his family through the depression following the war, and was killed with four others in the great fire of March 8, 1867, in Washington, at the age of twenty-two.

Alice Schoolcraft is mentioned, though not by name, as standing by her foster-father's bed a week before he died. She was then fifteen.

A happy life may be achieved by rising superior to endless sorrows. Like other kinds of success, it can be created by certain qualities of character, no matter what the obstacles. In essence it is a conquest of self, and a deliverance of the key of that stronghold—in radiance not in resignation—to the Great Will for Good that may most understandably be known as God. This is the crowning summit of the range of all the experience of the human race. Schoolcraft conquered this Gaurisankar.

His original world, unbounded by horizons or hemispheres, in which he had hastened about physically as well as intellectually and contacted personally the brightest minds of the period, had narrowed down to a circle about a wheel chair.

In 1846 he was described as

a very remarkable looking gentleman . . . perhaps fifty years of age, though his very long, waving, affluent, chestnut-colored hair was scarcely tinged with envious grey. His features were large, his complexion florid, his eyes a brilliant blue, and his forehead . . . white, broad, and high. . . . His height measured six feet; his hands were aristocratically small, and delicately white; while his dress indicated that he had no ambition to be a dandy. . . . So noble, so lordly, so commanding a head . . . reminded . . . of the god Jupiter.

Toward the end of his life there is a picture of him as he lay with his withered legs bent under him, holding to a friend with the only limb he could use—his left hand.

One who knew him well remarked, in admiration: He loved to gather his friends about him.   His society was much sought. So completely did his great spirit rise above his physical condition that no one in his company for an hour would hear even an allusion to his infirmities or would even think of them as he sat and filled up the moments with fascinating discourse.

The one who knew him best said that his "manly, dignified, edifying Christian philosophy, under such a tantalizing bereavement of locomotive energy," made her "venerate him as Eve did her husband, before he was stripped of his God-like attributes."   Schoolcraft

was a constant wonder to her, from the Christian philosophy with which he sat down, chained to his seat, every day for ten or twelve years, without a murmur, though his brain was clear as the sunlight, his body without a pain, and his high-mettled spirit as vaulting as ever in its interest in politics, patriotism, literature, and everything worthy of a genial philosopher's consideration.   No man would have revelled more wholesomely than he in his former extraordinary powers of locomotion.   And yet when that gift, so common to all men, was hopelessly withdrawn from him, he seemed to be so content as almost to demonstrate gratitude that God, who had given him so many blessings, should *only* have visited him with painless *bodily* disability.

Schoolcraft had come to his helpless condition in spite of the fact that he had been the embodiment of temperance in all things.   He had risen early, retired early, eaten moderately of simple food, had never used a drop of stimulants, or smoked.

Of course he had overworked.   The mere labor of writing the enormous number of words that he turned out, without the aid of a typewriter, in the years before paralysis attacked him, shows his extraordinary application of energy.   He had waded cold northern streams for hours in his bare feet; let himself down into damp, unexplored limestone apertures; kept his notebook, sketchbook and pencil in hand early and late, by flickering campfire-light and in wave-drenched canoe. When others thought themselves too busy to prepare a needed address or lecture, Schoolcraft would make the time for it by giving up sleep for a night or two. Incessant toil had been one of his main leverages in life. "I have scarcely lain down one night without a feeling that the next day's success must depend upon a fresh appeal to continued effort."

That daily address—and character—had carried him, a meagerly-schooled boy, to international eminence in science and letters, a position of trust and respect in the government of the nation, to the friendship of such men as Lewis Cass and John Calhoun, influence with several generations of cabinet officers, and closeness to the President of the United States under a succession of administrations.

But his chain of new days on the earth came at last to its final links, and ended. He died December 10, 1864, in his seventy-second year, of dry mortification of the parts rendered useless by rheumatism and paralysis.

FINALITIES

MAN, inescapably aware of the mortality of the flesh, sometimes finds comfort in choosing where his bones may rest for the little time they remain to memorialize the spirit they once accompanied. The hope is unimportant, yet its frustration adds a tinge of sadness even to death.

Jane Johnston Schoolcraft longed for the grandeurs of the Lake Superior country and the presence of her children. She is buried, alone, among the green little hills and buckwheat-flowered valleys of Ancaster, Ontario.

Janee, alone, lies near the historic James River, in storied Richmond, Virginia, among friends her mother never knew.

Johnston's grave, by itself, is in Elmira, New York.

Of all of them, only little William Henry sleeps by the noble St. Marys, below the singing rapids, at the Sault.

Mary Howard Schoolcraft gave her reminiscences a fictitious happy ending by having Schoolcraft's health restored and returning with him to the plantation country of her birth, there to end their lives and be buried in her family graveyard, among the live oaks and Spanish moss, where generations upon generations of her ancestors rested. She could not then imagine that all but two or three of her forebears were to be torn from their graves and, with their monuments, carried out to sea by a typhoonic storm in 1940. When her time came, March 10, 1878, she took her place quietly beside the husband she revered, in Washington.

Verse may fall short of being poetry and yet be eloquent. Schoolcraft had scribbled, in 1818, the following quatrains:

> I will go by western fountain,
>   I will wander far and wide;
> Till some sunny spot invite me,
>   Till some guardian bid me bide.
>
> Snow or tempest—plain the drearest
>   Shall oppose a feeble bar,
> Since I go from friends the dearest,
>   'Tis no matter then how far.

Twenty years later he wrote of this in a different way:

> Nor was it mine to fear, in some lone gloom
> To die, and tremble lest I lacked a tomb.

But he never ceased to love the little valley where he was born—

> My Norma! . . .
> So fly my thoughts from these sublime displays,
> To thy lone woods, and quiet winding ways.

Possibly he had thoughts of resting, beside his beloved elder brother, in the little graveyard in Albany County.

Henry Rowe Schoolcraft was interred in site 33 in range 68 of the Congressional Cemetery in Washington, D. C.

It is said that this cemetery may easily comprehend more history than any other burying ground in the world. It was begun about 1800 by The Vestry of Christ Episcopal Church, Washington parish, and has been owned by them since that time. Many years ago, however, there were donated to the

Government a thousand burial sites, which constituted the first National Cemetery in which were buried soldiers, sailors and marines, high ranking officers, cabinet officers, members of Congress and the Senate, foreign dignitaries, and many prominent men who helped to shape the United States of America.

There is one monument on the Schoolcraft plot, in the center. On its east side is the inscription:

WRIGHT
Alice Schoolcraft
1849–1876

On the west side appears:

SCHOOLCRAFT
Henry Rowe
1793–1864
and wife
Mary Howard
died 1877

Mary Howard Schoolcraft actually died March 10, 1878, according to the cemetery record and contemporary newspapers. The date of her death is wrong in the inscription.

There is a story here. Eight lots were purchased in Henry Rowe Schoolcraft's name at the time of his death. Five are still vacant. There are three graves—and four recorded burials.

Alice A. Schoolcraft—Mrs. William W. Wright—and her child, not named, died in June, 1876. The infant was not buried with its mother, but with Schoolcraft. Twelve years after his passing, affection had not disentwined itself from him. He was given the companionship of his one representative in the third generation, an adopted daughter's only child.

Henry Rowe Schoolcraft is not only one of the most versatile and brilliant but one of the most human characters in the history of America.

SCHOOLCRAFT AND THE FINE ARTS

SHORTLY after the publication of Longfellow's *Song of Hiawatha, Harper's Monthly* referred to it as "that poem which has made the English critics shout for joy that at length there is an American poem." Its success was immediate and tremendous. Four thousand copies were sold on the day of publication. Two months later it was still selling at the rate of three hundred a day in Boston and had been accepted as *the* poem of the American Indian. Since then the poem has become part of the cultural background of every English-speaking school-child on earth as well as many who do not know a word of the English language.

All of this constituted a moving and profound satisfaction for Henry Rowe Schoolcraft. He lived to see the gems he had discovered and preserved mounted as he knew they could be. He was collaborator in a world classic!

The essential part that Schoolcraft played in the creation of *The Song of Hiawatha* was no accident. It was a natural culmination of his years of love and labor, and of his own artistic sensibility and effort. He was an important contributor in many fields. This was true among the arts as in other phases of human activity. He had more than one facet of genius.

To the Indians Henry Rowe Schoolcraft was a sun god.

The last of the blackgown missionaries to the Ojibways, the Reverend Father William F. Gagnieur, S.J., who knew some but not all of Schoolcraft's achievements, evaluated him as "an extraordinary man and an indefatigable worker. . . . There is not to be found his equal, in many respects, in the history of the United States."

James H. Baker, writing of the sources of the Mississippi River, said: "No American scholar will forget Schoolcraft, no more than he will neglect Audubon or bury Agassiz, and more and more as the Indian perishes will Schoolcraft be recognized as an authority and a classic."

Among American pioneers and builders, Schoolcraft has a prominent, permanent place. Michigan honors his name among those of its illustrious citizens. As the nation becomes more conscious of the drama of its infancy, Schoolcraft shall gain an increasing hold on popular imagination.

THE ONTONAGON BOULDER.   FROM A SKETCH BY SCHOOLCRAFT.

A good man, an active citizen, and an ardent patriot, Schoolcraft's predominant urge was to be useful. On this he concentrated the curiosity and alertness of the scientist, the practicality of the industrialist, and the instincts of a newspaperman. His zealous devotion to the material progress of the new country was in constant conflict with his aesthetic trends. Yet his interest and activity in art were never submerged.

His beloved drawing materials, taken to Missouri, had permitted him to illustrate his practical treatise on the lead mines with three engravings, one of them a view of the town of Potosi. The narrative of his experiences in 1820 was embellished by drawings, among the earliest creditable efforts of the kind in the Northwest. He used his skill to depict the prints of human feet in rock for an American scientific periodical; and to portray the Ontonagon copper boulder, geological formations, and Indian articles, in his official reports and other publications. Also he presented, by this medium, views of rivers and lakes, of Sault Ste. Marie in 1820, and of the Pictured Rocks of Lake Superior, with a purely artistic purpose in view. The illustration of his six-volume work with steel engravings from paintings by Seth Eastman is another manifestation of Schoolcraft's penchant.

One of his severest critics said, of the first three volumes of the government-subsidized quartos, that they were "the most sumptuous that have yet appeared in our country, and their publication may fairly be said to form an era in the art of American bookmaking." For this achievement Schoolcraft, the artist, must be credited.

As a glass manufacturer in his youth, he produced pieces that rank him not only as an able industrialist but an artisan of distinction. He carried on chemical research with enamels for pottery because of the same urge to create beauty. The making of synthetic gems aroused his interest.

The only building of his period in Northern Michigan that has any architectural pretensions is Elmwood, the first frame building erected in Sault Ste. Marie, Michigan, which Schoolcraft planned and constructed in 1827. Later occupants have altered its outside appearance but the rooms and hallways retain an impressive dignity and spaciousness. The old Johnston house at the Sault is a type of the best log architecture of the period in that region. That part built for Schoolcraft and his bride still stands, although a more recent owner covered the log walls on the outside with clapboarding. Sault Ste. Marie is fortunate in its possession of these two structures, which in due time will be seen in proper focus by the public as architectural as well as historic monuments.

Of all the arts, literature was Schoolcraft's earliest and latest and constant pursuit. Expression in writing came as natural to him as speech. A pioneer in preserving aboriginal myths and lyrics, he appreciated their value not only as psychological specimens for the ethnologist but as precious literary material. James Russell Lowell and Thomas Bailey Aldrich based writings on his publications. Among other artistic activities, Schoolcraft produced the first literary magazine in Michigan, at the Sault, as he had edited one at Hamilton, New York, and in other Eastern towns, in his youth. *The Souvenir of the Lakes,* issued in Detroit in 1831, is another evidence of his irrepressible interest in literary activity. He loved poetry and wrote many lines, of which some have superior merit. He was the leading litterateur of his day on the frontier, where he helped and encouraged others.

While Governor Cass planned a work on the American Indians of such magnitude that it was never completed, Schoolcraft, whose spirit drove him to such feats as five-day trips in three days, communicated his findings about the aborigines at the first opportunity he could make. So it was that he supplied not only the birchbark kindling, and a fanning Northern breeze, but all the necessary firewood to the spark of interest in the Indian that had long been banked and dormant in Henry Wadsworth Longfellow's mind and heart.

Without Schoolcraft's poetical interest in the subject, The Song of Hiawatha would never have been written.

Schoolcraft's work is perpetuated in the music and the

drama. The Indian tales that first delighted him, and through him inspired Longfellow, as *Hiawatha* have been set to music and are presented as a pageant, in London, England, in a classic, annual performance.

Some day a sculptor of genius shall immortalize the epic triad—

SCHOOLCRAFT—LONGFELLOW—HIAWATHA.

CHRONOLOGY OF HENRY ROWE SCHOOLCRAFT

1793: March 28, born, in Watervliet township, later Hamilton, now Guilderland village, Albany County, N. Y.

1805: Was reputed a learned boy.

1808: Organized a literary society; was sent to Philadelphia to purchase shipload of clay for glass factory; had verse and articles published locally. In October his father moved to Vernon, N. Y.

1809: Established manuscript magazine at Hamilton, N. Y. In late autumn left for Vernon, N. Y.

1810: February 4, signed agreement to superintend Ontario Glass Works, Geneva, N. Y. Went to Geneva early that spring.

1812: War with England began.

1813: Last week of March left Geneva, N. Y., for Salisbury, Vt.

April 24, was considering a U. S. military commission.

August 30, signed an agreement (predated July 15) to superintend Vermont Glass Factory on Lake Dunmore, Salisbury, Vt.

Studied privately under a professor at Middlebury, Vt.

1814: July 7, was initiated in Masonic Lodge at Salisbury, Vt.

After December 30, left Salisbury, Vt.

1815: February 1 his salary began, as partner and operating manager, with T. Twitchell, in contract dated July 25, 1815, to erect a plant at Keene, N. H., to manufacture flint glass, etc.

February 17, ratification of Treaty of Ghent reopened American market to foreign glass.

1816: Began writing book, *Vitreology*.

March 20, signed agreement with new partner, N. Sprague, at Keene, N. H.

1817: March 20, was writing letters to various glassworks in attempt to find employment.

April 5, estimated his assets at $3856.50; September 27, at $683.64.

Early winter, left Keene, N. H.

In November published prospectus of *Vitreology;* the following month was at Vernon, N. Y., soliciting subscriptions for it.

That winter he started West, going to his brother's at Geneva, N. Y.

1818: Early—February?—traveled by sleigh from Geneva to Olean, N. Y.

Middle of March, started down Allegheny River.

March 23, arrived at Pittsburgh, Pa.

In April reached Cincinnati, O., where he stayed three weeks.

July 1–23, traveled on Mississippi from mouth of Ohio River to Herculaneum, Mo.; 26–27, on foot to St. Louis.

August 2, reached Potosi, Mo.

November 6, left Potosi, Mo., on expedition into Ozarks.

1819: February 4, returned to Potosi, Mo.

February–March, wrote *A View of the Lead Mines of Missouri,* at Potosi.

August 3, reached New York City, by steamer via New Orleans.

In November *A View of the Lead Mines of Missouri* came off the press, and he went at once to Washington, D. C., to see Secretary Calhoun and others about creation of, and his appointment to, government lead mine superintendency.

1820: February 5, left Washington, D. C., for New York City.

His Ozark diary was published in *Belles-Lettres Repository.*

February 25, Calhoun wrote letter appointing Schoolcraft to staff of Cass expedition to the Northwest.

March 5, left New York City.

Transallegania published.

April 10, left Vernon, N. Y., for Detroit, Mich.

May 1, visited Niagara Falls.

May 8, reached Detroit, on steamer "Walk-in-the-Water."

May 24, left Detroit with Cass expedition.

June 15, first reached Sault Ste. Marie, Mich.

June 16, was witness to treaty with Chippewas, at Sault.

June 27–29, investigated copper boulder on Ontonagon River.

July 21, expedition reached and named Cass Lake in Upper Mississippi.

August 7, he visited lead mines of Dubuque, Iowa.

August 20, the expedition reached Green Bay, Wisconsin.

August 29–31, at Chicago, Illinois.

September 1–9, he investigated east shore of Lake Michigan to Mackinac I.

September 23–October 13, he spent at Detroit, Mich.

October 21, reached Vernon, N. Y., where he wrote his report on copper mines of Lake Superior, dated November 6.

December 7, proceeded to Albany, N. Y.

1821: January 8, began transcription of his journal of Cass expedition, in Governor Clinton's library.

April, at 71 Courtland, New York City.

May 14, dated introduction to *Narrative Journal of Travels . . . in the year 1820,* at Albany, N. Y., where it came off the press May 20.

May 22, Governor Cass formally offered him position as secretary to Indian treaty commissioners.

June 16, left New York City for Detroit, Mich.

July 3, left Detroit with expedition to Chicago, via Detroit, Maumee, Wabash, Ohio, Illinois and Des Plaines Rivers.

August 29, at Chicago when treaty was signed, but too ill to be a witness.

September 23–October 6, enroute on Great Lakes from Chicago to Detroit, where he stayed a few days.

Late in December reached Albany, N. Y., after convalescing at Vernon, N. Y.

Journal of a Tour into the Interior of Missouri and Arkansaw published in England.

1822: Read paper on fossil tree before American Geological Society.

In March, at Albany, N. Y., wrote general report to War Department on geology and mineralogy of 1820 expedition; late that month took it personally to Washington, D. C.

April 22, visited Mount Vernon.

May 8, was appointed U. S. Indian Agent at Sault Ste. Marie, Mich.

July 6, began duties at Sault.

1823: April 9, abandoned hope of Missouri lead mines superintendency.

October 12, married Jane Johnston at Sault Ste. Marie, Mich.

1824: June 27, his son William Henry was born.

In September left Sault with his family to superintend printing of new book in New York City.

1825: January 10, went to Washington, D. C.

Early in February, returned to New York City.

March 20, concluded arrangements with publisher for a magazine devoted to Indian subjects.

April 14, *Travels in Central Portions of the Mississippi Valley* . . . off the press.

April 20, left New York City.

May 6, reached Detroit, Mich.

June 28, left Sault, via Mackinac I., to join Cass-Clark Mississippi expedition.

August 19, was witness to Indian treaty at Prairie du Chien.

In December began publication of manuscript magazine at Sault Ste. Marie, Mich.

1826: July 11, left Sault with Cass expedition.

August 5, was witness to Chippewa treaty at Fond du Lac, Lake Superior.

August 18, returned to Sault.

In the fall, foundations of Indian Agency at Sault Ste. Marie, Mich., were laid.

1827: March 13, his son William Henry died.

June 3, left Sault for Mackinac I. to join Cass-McKenney expedition.

August 11, was witness to treaty of Butte des Morts.

October 14, his daughter, Jane Susan Anne, was born.

Late in October moved into new Agency, Elmwood, at the Sault.

November 1, was elected to Legislative Council of Michigan Territory.

1828: April 27, left Sault for Detroit to attend 1st session of 3d Legislative Council.

May 21, reached Detroit.

June 23, his bill incorporating Michigan Historical Society was passed.

July 1, left Detroit, after close of Legislative session, for Sault Ste. Marie, Mich.

1829: February 5, was offered appointment as head of scientific corps of proposed U. S. expedition to South Seas.

Late in August left Sault to attend 2d session of 3d Legislative Council of Michigan Territory.

October 2, his son John Johnston Schoolcraft was born at Sault Ste. Marie, Mich.

Late in October, left Detroit for the Sault.

1830: *The Rise of the West* and *Indian Melodies* were published.

Middle of May, went to Detroit with his family, having been elected to 4th Legislative Council of Michigan Territory.

June, gave annual address of Michigan Historical Society; and visited Niagara Falls with his family and Miss Cass.

In July returned to Sault Ste. Marie, Mich.

November 16, left the Sault for winter session of the Legislative Council, at Detroit, which he reached in December.

1831: January 27, lectured before the Detroit Lyceum.

Edited—probably instigated—*The Souvenir of the Lakes*.

Finished second and last term as member of Legislative Council of Michigan Territory.

April 25, reached Sault Ste. Marie, Mich.

June 27–September 4, headed expedition to Upper Mississippi.

1832: February 28, took initial steps toward establishment of Algic Society.

March 28, the War Department directed consolidation of Indian Agencies of Sault Ste. Marie and Michilimackinac.

May 8, gave address before Chippewa County Temperance Society at Sault Ste. Marie, Mich.

June 7–August 14, headed expedition to Upper Mississippi.

July 13, discovered source of Mississippi River in Lake Itasca.

August 14, reached Sault.

Middle of September, left Sault for Detroit to meet Secretary of War Cass.

About middle of October returned to Sault Ste. Marie.

1833: May 20, finished manuscript of his expedition to Itasca Lake.

May 27, left Sault Ste. Marie and moved his headquarters to Mackinac I.

June 10–July 28 he was away from Mackinac I., as a member of the party attending President Jackson on a tour of New England.

Early in October went to Detroit.

The Man of Bronze read before Algic Society.

End of October, returned to Mackinac I.

1834: *The Man of Bronze* published.

During summer, made two visits to Detroit.

Narrative of an expedition . . . to Itasca Lake published.

1835: In August, attended first land sales at Green Bay.

November 9, left Mackinac I. for Detroit.

November 21, reached Washington, D. C.

1836: March 28, negotiated treaty with Ottawas and Chippewas at Washington, D. C.

May 9, concluded another Indian treaty, at Washington.

Late in May, left Washington.

June 15, reached Mackinac I.

July 10, instructions were issued to carry into effect Act that devolved duties of Superintendent of Indian Affairs for Michigan on Agent at Michilimackinac. Schoolcraft was both Indian Agent and Superintendent from 1836 to 1841.

End of September, ended several classes of payments to Indians made under treaty of March 28, 1836.

October 27, moved from Mackinac I. to Indian Superintendency headquarters at Detroit; but continued to summer at Mackinac I.

1837: January 14, concluded treaty with Chippewas at Detroit.

February 1, delivered lecture on temperance at Presbyterian Church, Detroit.

March 22, Michigan Historical Society elected him President.

March 23, received commission from Governor Mason appointing him a Regent of the University of Michigan (served until 1841).

Prepared manuscript of *Algic Researches*.

June 4, at Mackinac I.

November 11, left Mackinac I. for Detroit.

December 20, negotiated treaty with Chippewas at Flint Village, Mich.

1838: January 12, communicated to Governor a new system of Indian names for counties and towns of Michigan.

January 22, led in launching Michigan *Journal of Education*.

January 23, negotiated treaty with Chippewas.

January 26, completed manuscript of *Algic Researches*.

April 21, left Detroit for Mackinac I.

June 5, concluded modifying treaty with Ottawas at Grand Rapids, Mich.

Late June, left Mackinac I. for Washington, D. C.; returned to Mackinac I. middle of July.

July 31–August 25, trip in Lake Superior country to estimate Indian improvements to be paid for by government.

October 29, returned to Detroit for winter.

November 14, left Detroit for New York City, with family.

December 12, left New York City; placed his son in private school at Princeton, his daughter in one in Philadelphia.

December 21, reached Washington, D. C.; on the 26th obtained leave of absence to visit Europe.

Iosco published, at Detroit.

1839: January 11–16, en route to New York City from Washington, D. C.

March 27, his leave of absence was rescinded.

April 8–18, en route from New York City to Detroit, Mich., to take over duties of principal disbursing officer of the Superintendency.

June 1, *Algic Researches* was published.

June 7, reached Mackinac I., where he established summer headquarters.

June 11– , appraised Indian improvements on Lake Huron, and inspected mission at Grand Traverse Bay.

July 6–26, to Detroit and back to Mackinac I.

August 16–24 and September 14–27, visited his official headquarters at Detroit and returned to Mackinac I., where he spent the winter of 1839–40.

1840: June 7, at Detroit en route to Washington, D. C.

July 24, left Washington.

Early in August, returned to Detroit; reached Mackinac I. beginning of September; November 1, returned to Detroit for winter.

1841: April 16, his term expired as Regent of the University of Michigan.

April 17, he ceased to be Indian Agent and Acting Superintendent of Indian Affairs for Michigan.

May 22, he went to Mackinac I.

In New York City, helped to organize American Ethnological Society (1842).

1842: May 9, sailed for Europe.

May 22, his first wife, Jane Johnston Schoolcraft, died, at Dundas, Upper Canada.

Visited England, France, Germany, Prussia, Belgium, and Holland; attended and addressed twelfth meeting of the British Association for the Advancement of Science.

December 6, read a paper on "Scientific Associations Abroad" before the New-York Historical Society.

1843: August 19, arrived at Wheeling, Virginia, from Baltimore, en route to Grave Creek Flats.

August 27, reached Massillon, O., after crossing Ohio by stage.

September 15, arrived in Detroit, Michigan, by boat from Cleveland.

October 26, at Dundas, Canada West.

Alhalla . . . published.

1844: March, in New York City, on committee of New-York Historical Society.

August, first paper-covered number of *Oneóta* published; followed by numbers 2–4 that year.

1845: In New York with his children.

Numbers 5–8 of paper-bound series of *Oneóta* published; then *Oneóta* in one volume.

Acted as agent in making census of Iroquois for State of New York.

June 19, gave address before New-York Historical Society.

August 14, addressed New Confederacy of the Iroquois.

1846: Made report on Iroquois to Secretary of State of New York; issued reprint as *Notes on the Iroquois*.

Addressed Iroquois study association at Aurora, N. Y.

November 17, gave 42d annual address of New-York Historical Society.

Memorialized Congress, with others, to collect and publish available information about all Indian tribes of United States.

College of Geneva conferred honorary degree of LL.D. on him.

Met Miss Mary E. Howard, in Washington, D. C.

1847: January 13, married Miss Howard, in Beaufort District, South Carolina.

March 3, was authorized by Congress to gather, collate and edit information on all Indian tribes of the United States. Was engaged on this, as Special Agent, in Office of Indian Affairs, until end of 1857.

Late in March, moved from New York City to Washington, D. C.

Published revised edition of *Oneóta* as *The Red Race of America* (*The Indian in His Wigwam*); and a popular version of *Notes on the Iroquois*.

Visited his son Johnston in New York City.

1848: Published other versions of *Oneóta* as *The Indian in His Wigwam*, one in New York City, another at Buffalo, N. Y.; and a biographical sketch of General Cass.

1849: In Washington, D. C. Published bibliography of books in Indian languages. Was stricken with paralysis. His daughter Jane married B. S. Howard.

1850: Was living in Washington on north side of E Street N, between 10th and 11th Street, West. Published revised edition of *Oneóta*, as *The American Indians*, at Auburn, N. Y.

1851: May 24, Part I of *Historical and Statistical Information* . . . (6 v., 1851–57), issued from press.

September 17–November 6, at Butler House, Philadelphia, seeing Part II of *Historical and Statistical Information* through the press.

Personal Memoirs . . . published; also other revised editions of *Oneóta*, as *The American Indians*, at Rochester and at Buffalo, N. Y.

1852: Part II of *Historical and Statistical Information* off the press.

April 9, at Washington, D. C.

June 6. By this time had his office at home but was still able to go occasionally to War Department.

1853: Part III of *Historical and Statistical Information* came off the press; also second printing of Part I, omitting first three words of title. *Scenes and Adventures in the Ozark Mountains* was published; also another revision of *Oneóta*, as *Western Scenes and Reminiscences*.

1854: Part IV of *Historical and Statistical Information* came off the press.

1855: Part V of *Historical and Statistical Information* came off the press; also *Summary Narrative* . . . , and *Helderbergia*.

In the fall, Longfellow's *Hiawatha* was published.

1856: One revision of *Algic Researches* published as *The Myth of Hiawatha;* another as *The Indian Fairy Book.*

1857: Part VI of *Historical and Statistical Information* published; and another edition of the legends, in New York City, as *The Indian Fairy Book.*

December 31, his connection with the Office of Indian Affairs, as Special Agent, ended.

1858: A three-volume French adaptation of his *Information Respecting the History,* etc., appeared.

November 26, to March 13, 1859, he was on the payroll of the Indian Office for services as an interpreter that involved a trip from Washington to Detroit, and return.

1860: Living in Washington, D. C., 256 F Street North between 13th and 14th Streets. His six-volume work was reissued under title of *Archives of Aboriginal Knowledge.*

1864: December 10, he died, at the address given above.

December 12 he was buried in the Congressional Cemetery.

1865: April 28, his son John Johnston, unmarried, died at Elmira, N. Y.

1869: A New York edition of the legends was issued as *The Indian Fairy Book.*

1870: His widow lived at 1321 F Street N. W., Washington, D. C.

1876: In June his adopted daughter, Alice Schoolcraft Wright, and her child, died, in Washington, D. C.

1877: An edition of the legends appeared as *The Enchanted Moccasins.*

1878: March 10, the death of Mary Howard Schoolcraft occurred at 122 E. Capitol St., Washington, D. C. She was buried March 14 beside her husband.

1884: A two-volume abridgement of his *Information respecting the History,* etc., was published under title of *The Indian Tribes of the United States.*

1885: Annual report of Smithsonian Institution reprinted his *Plan for the Investigation of American Ethnology.*

1892: November 25, his daughter, Jane Schoolcraft Howard, died, childless, at Richmond, Va.

1916   (ca.): Another edition of his legends, as *The Indian Fairy Book,* appeared.

1941: Bureau of American Ethnology of the Smithsonian Institution completed Index to his *Historical and Statistical Information.*

1942: *Schoolcraft-Longfellow-Hiawatha,* first biography of Schoolcraft, was published.

ADDENDA

The Birthplace of Schoolcraft

To dispel the confusion resulting from many changes in the name of the locality in which Henry Rowe Schoolcraft was born, an outline of the history of the neighborhood is given below.   This is as presented in a letter dated May 5, 1942, from the brilliant and profound Dr. Arthur Pound, a former editor of *The Atlantic Monthly,* now State Historian of New York.

Replying to your letter of April 25, 1942, I am able to give you the following information after consulting with Mr. Arthur B. Gregg, local historian of that region.

1630   Manor of Rensselaerswyck established.

1683   Albany County established; included Manor of Rensselaerswyck.

The region under discussion was called the Hellebergh, and the Reformed Dutch Church at Apple's Corners, now Osborn's Corners, is still officially "the Reformed Church of the Hellebergh."

1772   District of Rensselaerswyck.

1779   District of Rensselaerswyck divided into East and West Districts of Rensselaerswyck.

1788   West District of Rensselaerswyck became the Town of Watervliet, equivalent to a township although then of more extent.

1803   The Town of Guilderland was taken off the Town of Watervliet.

The location of the glassworks in 1785 was known as Dowesburgh.   This became in succession Hamilton (1797), Hamiltonville (1820), Guilderland village (ca. 1860).

The village nearer the center of the Town of Guilderland was known as Guilderland Center from about 1803 on.   Apple's Corners, now Osborn's Corners, lies one-half mile west of Guilderland Center. This is the site of the old Dutch Church where Henry Rowe Schoolcraft was christened.   The Henry in his name is said to be in honor of Henry Apple.   It is definitely established that Schoolcraft was born (1793) in what is known as the Schoolcraft House, a two-story dwelling still standing on Willow Street in the village of Guilderland (not Guilderland Center).

Note that neither Guilderland nor Guilderland Center are incorporated as villages. Although generally called villages they are more properly hamlets.

A laugh—Guilderland Center was for long locally called "Bangall."

We will greatly appreciate a copy of your work on Schoolcraft, and if you could spare another copy I am sure that Mr. Gregg would be delighted to have one.

Most cordially yours,
(Signed) ARTHUR POUND,
State Historian

SCHOOLCRAFT MANUSCRIPT LETTERS
IN THE PUBLIC LIBRARY OF
SAULT STE. MARIE, MICHIGAN

The Public Library at Sault Ste. Marie, Michigan, possesses an unusual collection of Schoolcraft items. Many of these are the gift of the late Justice Joseph Hall Steere of the Supreme Court of Michigan. Others have been secured from various members of the Johnston family as gifts or deposits, or by purchase.

The Library has practically all of Schoolcraft's books; 48 manuscript letters; the silver plate from John Johnston's casket, made by melting family spoons and inscribed by Schoolcraft; and portraits in oil, $9\frac{3}{8} \times 11\frac{5}{8}$, of Schoolcraft's children, Jane and Johnston, probably done at Mackinac Island, possibly by an artist of distinction. Notable among the books is a presentation copy of *Algic Researches* with the inscription: "With the respectful compliments of the author. To Miss Eliza Johnston of St. Mary's." There is a copy of the first part of *Oneóta,* in paper covers, dated August, 1844.

Among the letters is a copy of one addressed to Schoolcraft by Lewis Cass (No. 3); and one to Schoolcraft from George Copway, half-breed interpreter and Ojibway author (No. 8); a copy of a letter to Schoolcraft from Adjutant General R. Jones of the United States Army (No. 31A); a circular issued for the New-York Historical Society (No. 22); and single letters from Schoolcraft to Mrs. George Johnston (No. 32) and to Major W. V. Cobbs, Commanding Officer at Fort Brady (No. 15).

Most of the communications are from Henry R. Schoolcraft to George Johnston, his Irish-Ojibway brother-in-law, who was for a while sub-agent at LaPointe and at times an interpreter in the Indian Department. In general they have to do with Indian affairs, claims, and researches, and family matters both personal and financial.

Schoolcraft's letters are written on large official sheets which were doubled and sealed with the Indian Agency seal. The outside of the sheet was then used for the address. A few of them were copied for him by scribes, with only the signature in his handwriting. Those written by him are in a strong, flowing hand up to No. 37, dated October 10, 1849, which shows that he has recently suffered some violent physical and mental disturbance.

Two letters to George Johnston were written and signed by Jane Johnston Schoolcraft. Of these, No. 2 is an example of delicately beautiful penmanship. The ravages of illness on her mind and body are apparent in No. 20.

In editing these manuscripts, the old-fashioned double "s" and the use of superior letters in abbreviated words have been disregarded.

Changes by the writers of the letters are indicated in footnotes. No special attention is called to uncorrected inadvertencies. The latter first become noticeable in Schoolcraft's compositions in 1847. After 1849 their number and character appear to indicate that his mental as well as physical coordination was affected by his stroke. This would mean that he persevered in and completed his chief work in spite of a major editorial handicap.

1. HENRY R. SCHOOLCRAFT TO GEORGE JOHNSTON.
Dear Sir,

I omitted to request you to get a new mess basket for the Exp. from Mr Sibley. And a *canoe* & also a *boat* oilcloth. I shall send Mr Chapman's new boat with stores to Fond du Lac. Bring a bill.

If there is *one two* or *three good* canoemen at Mackinac, who will work for $20 a month & *no whiskey* bring them along.

Leave the little canoe, & bring over William's, which was left by Chapman.

truly yours
H R Schoolcraft

29 May [1826?]

George Johnston Esqr
    Mackinac

2. JANE JOHNSTON SCHOOLCRAFT TO GEORGE JOHNSTON.
    A facsimile of the first page of this letter faces page 523.

Saut Ste Marie, March 26th 1827—

My very dear Brother,

Altho' I have scarcely strength enough to guide my pen, or to hold my aching head up, yet the thought of its being a gratification to you to receive a few lines from me,[1] induces me to exert myself, tho' it will make my poor wounded heart bleed afresh, & I know it will draw the ready tear of sympathy from your eyes, as well as sincere sorrow from your heart, when I tell you that it has pleas'd the Almighty to take to himself, my beloved and *ever to be lamented* Son William Henry, he died of the Croup the 13th of this Month, about 11 oclock at night—If ever a human being went direct to the Mansions of everlasting bliss, he has, & it is a consoling thought to me that my *Sweet Willy* is rejoicing with exceeding joy before the throne of his Heavenly Father, where he will never know pain or sickness more. O! my dear Brother, *if we,* who still remain on earth would strive with all our hearts to live, so as to become partakers of everlasting happiness, how gladly will the blessed Spirit of *our dear, beautious Willy* meet & welcome us to Heaven, when *we too* shall be obliged to leave our earthly tabernacle—I cannot say more. Papa, Mamma & all the family are well & desire their love to you—both Papa & Mr Schoolcraft are writing they will no doubt give you all the News.   Heaven bless you my dear Brother

& believe me as ever your affectionate Sister
Jane Schoolcraft

I send you a piece of B— Crape for your hat—

JS.

To George Johnston Esqr
    Sub Agt, Ind. Dept
        Lapointe, Lake Superior
Tr Express

    [1] "Me" was interlineated.

3. LEWIS CASS TO HENRY R. SCHOOLCRAFT.

Copy   Detroit May 9th 1827
Sir

I have received the copies of Mr. Johnstons letters to you, and
one from you to him, and shall transmit them to the War Department—They are honourable evidencies of his zeal & attention, and
evince in a clear manner the advantages, which will result from the
establishment of his Sub Agency.

Very Respectfully, Sir,
Yr Obt Servt.
(Signed) Lewis Cass

Henry R Schoolcraft, Esqr
Indn Agent
Sault Ste. Marie

4. HENRY R. SCHOOLCRAFT TO GEORGE JOHNSTON.

Sault Ste. Marie August 7th 1828
Dear Sir,

Mr Audrain will conduct the boat carrying your supplies. It
has been thought advisable not to wait for any formal letter of appropriation from government, the season being already so far advanced
as barely to leave time for making the trip in good weather.

My public letters will advise you[1] on the subjects most necessary
to be acted on. And Mr Audrain will give you many particulars
respecting our domestic circumstances which I have not time, in fact,
to write. We are blessed with a continuance of health, not always
uniform, nor so perfect as we could desire, but more than sufficient
to make us grateful & thankful. The affection of my right arm & leg,
under which I have laboured since July 1, is not believed to be of a
dangerous character, although it has, for a time, nearly deprived me
of the use of my pen. Our little daughter Jane is daily improving in
health, stature & beauty.

I must still solicit your further attention to the mineralogy &
geology of the interesting regions surrounding you. And shall be
grateful for any thing you can pick up, or procure from the Indians.
Small presents of goods, for any thing of this kind they may present,
would encourage them.

The articles you have sent for the Lyceum, shall be forwarded
this fall, in your name. And any thing, in the way of curiosities, you
may design for Gov. Cass, will be delivered, agreeably to your wishes.

I send by Mr Audrain some of my latest papers, from which you will, however, glean scarcely any thing of interest.

As ever
Sincerely your friend,
and kinsman
Henry R Schoolcraft

G Johnston Esqr
>For George Johnston Esqr
>>Lapointe,
>>>Lake Superior

Fd by
>Mr Audrain

[1] This word was interlineated.

5. HENRY R. SCHOOLCRAFT TO GEORGE JOHNSTON.

Sault Ste Marie Sept. 24. 1828

Dear Sir

By the enclosed you will perceive that we have lost the best of fathers. This afflictive stroke came suddenly upon us. During his recent trip to New York he had contracted a malignant fever. He reached[1] the vicinity of St. Mary's, in a small vessel on the 17th, and was brought up upon a bed, in a barge, in so low a state, that he could scarcely recognize any of the family. On the 18th & 19th he revived so much as to converse freely. On the 20 & 21st he grew worse, but retained the possession of his senses. On the 22nd a visible declension took place. He made but few replies to any thing addressed to him after 1 o-clock, and expired at 8 in the evening, surrounded by his family. It is a strong consolation to reflect that he died, as he had lived, in full reliance upon the merits of Jesus. Every circumstance connected with his disease tends to confirm our belief, that he is numbered with the blessed. And he has bequeathed to his family a name of unsullied purity & honor.

The most kind & incessant attention was given, to alleviate his malady, by Dr James but with only partial success, although I am inclined to believe, that we owe to this gentleman the prolongation of his life, for some days.

I enclose you a lock of his hair, cut by my dearly beloved Jane. His mortal remains were this day followed to the grave by the collected population of the place, and deposited by the side of our ever dear son Willy.

Your Mother, Jane, Eliza, Charlotte, William, Anne & John present you their love in affliction.

Ever, sincerely yours
Henry R Schoolcraft.

Silver Plate upon the Coffin

John Johnston Esqr
Born (Ireland) August 25th 1762
Died Sept. 22nd 1828
Aged 66 years 27 days

Pall Bearers

Col. Lawrence	Lieut. Bradley
Capt Beall	Mr. Agnew
Capt Ransom	Mr. Havring
Capt Hoffman	Mr. Audrain

Mr. Audrain will write you on public business
S

George Johnston Esq
    Lapointe,
        Lake Superior
Per L. Nolin

   ¹ This word was interlineated.

6. HENRY R. SCHOOLCRAFT TO GEORGE JOHNSTON.
              Sault Ste Marie January 14. 1829.
Dear Sir,
    Since my last, little has occurred, either melancholy or important, to diversify the daily routine of domestic incidents. Your mother and family are at present in health, though their late afflictive loss has weighed heavily upon all. Charlotte has been dangerously ill, but is now restored to her usual health, and is, I believe, about to write to you. Jane, and our interesting little daughter (Jane Susan) are also well, comparatively speaking.
    Considerable sickness, & several deaths have marked the past & present season, both among the Indian as well as white population. The old chief Shingaba W'ossin died on the 15 Decr.
    The detachment of the 2nd Regt. was relieved at this post, by two companies of the 5th under Capt. Wilcox, on the 1st November. Forts Gratiot & Dearborne are re-occupied, & the garrison at Michilimackinac doubled. Trusting you will receive, from other sources, more minute information,
              I am, dear Sir,
                  As Ever, Yours,
                 Henry R Schoolcraft

G. Johnston Esqr

        (over)

Tell Nolin his wife & children are well & have been supplied with food & clothing.   I send you my last papers.

H R S

George Johnston Esqr.
LaPointe, Lake Superior

7. HENRY R. SCHOOLCRAFT TO GEORGE JOHNSTON.

Office of Indian Agency
Sault Ste Marie
May 23d 1829.

George Johnston Esqr.
Sub Agt. Ind. Dept.
Sir

The annual instructions received at this office on the 14th instant, make no provision for the support of the LaPointe Sub-agency during the present year, in consequence of which, it becomes necessary to suspend its operations.   You will therefore lose no time in repairing [to][1] this Agency for the purpose of reporting your account of expenditures directly to government, and giving your aid in transacting the business of the office.   Your withdrawal from the lake will be for the present year, and until further orders.   It is proper however, to observe, that this step proceeds wholly from the pecuniary state of the affairs of the Department, and not from any disappointment in the result anticipated from your labours, & exertions, which have been fully approved.

I am anxious that you should make the least possible delay, in your arrangements for leaving Lapointe, and have forwarded the necessary supplies by Nolin.   He also takes a quantity of spikes, &c, for repairing your boat, but should it be thought that too much time & expence would attend the repair, it will be desirable you should come down in canoes, to be manned by Indians.

I wish you to inform the Indians of your vicinity, that no presents will be issued at this office this year, and it is desirable, on all accounts, that they should be encouraged to remain at their villages during the summer.   The advantages of visiting the lower country, are always overated by the Indians of your post, and the risks & inconveniencies, but little thought of, but the subject invites their candid attention the present season, when it is n[ow][1] known to them that no presents whatever will be issued here, & that the British

have retired several hundred miles down the lake to the remote &
unhealthy site of Penetanguishshine.

I am Sir

Very respectfully

Your Obt. Servant

Henry R Schoolcraft

George Johnston Esqr
      Sub-Agent
         La Pointe

[1] There is a hole in the letter paper at this point.

8. GEORGE COPWAY TO HENRY R. SCHOOLCRAFT.

Baltimore July 19 1829

Henry R Schoolcraft
Dear Sir,
    These indians will tell you that they have deposited five Hun-
dred and fifty dollars in the Land office at Sault Saint Marie, having
given it into the hands of Mr Watson the one who is with them

Kashe yah she gave from his Tribe—	$325.00
Out of which his expenses to get to Washington was to be deducted	1,25
Leaving a Balance in to the hands of the above named gentleman	200
Oosh kab bai wis gave from his Tribe	$225.00
Out of which his expenses $100	$1,25.00
The Balance in the hand of the above named gentleman	$125.00
Kiski tah way gave	$120

You better see if these are proper receipts for the following sums of
money if you can for them and satisfy them if possible

Yours &

G Copway

9. HENRY R. SCHOOLCRAFT TO GEORGE JOHNSTON.

Detroit[1] 19th Sept. 1829

Dear Sir
    I received your letter enclosing the affidavit of Holliday,[2]
which will enable us to complete the memorial to Congress. I
have enquired of Wells respecting the pamphlet & revision. The
letters are missing, but one volume of the Repository, & a volume of
my Travels are bound, & will be brought up by me.
    Your other commissions will be executed. Your accounts have

been handed in, & will be forwarded to Washington for settlement & payment.

Very truly yours

Henry R Schoolcraft

George Johnston Esqr.

[Sault Ste Marie]

     ¹ "Sault Ste Marie" was written then struck through.

     ² A trader among the Indians at the post of L'Anse, on the south shore of Lake Superior.

10. HENRY R. SCHOOLCRAFT TO GEORGE JOHNSTON.

Michilimackinac Nov. 20 1830

Dear Sir,

    I omitted in my letter to Mr Audrain to annex the forms of certificates. They are added. It will be seen, on a comparison of the invoices that some errors were committed, in consequence of which it became necessary to make them anew. I rely on you, if the weather will permit, to come over with Indians to put on board the Marshall Ney, the vouchers & such letters as may be ready to send down. The Ney will be the last vessel from here, & will probably be here in 8 or 10 days at farthest.

Sincerely yours.

Henry R Schoolcraft.

I certify that four pieces of strouds assorted, of the within mentioned goods, were delivered by me to Chippeway Indians at the subagency of Lapointe during the fall & winter of 1826 & 1827.

G.J.

(date)

 1830   Sub Agnt.

I certify that I am satisfied the within mentioned goods were delivered to Chippeway Indians.

F.A.

(date)

 1830

George Johnston Esqr.

Sault Ste Marie.

11. HENRY R. SCHOOLCRAFT TO GEORGE JOHNSTON.

Indian Agency

Michilimackinac

April 20th 1835

Sir,

    I communicate with this, a letter from the Commissioners of

Indian Affairs, appointing you an interpreter on the boundary survey. It is essential that no time be lost in proceeding to St. Peters. The route by Lake Superior, indicated in Mr Herring's letter, will be preferable, as it will enable you to give the necessary notice to the Chippewa Indians.

I will request Mr Hulbert at St Maries, to furnish you fifty dollars worth of presents for the Chiefs who accompany you, which you will use your judgment in the selection of, and which you will certify to the delivery of.

The survey will, for the present, be confined to the line between the Chippewa's and Sioux, and will probably begin south of the Chippewa river. I should be pleased to have the following chiefs attend. Neenaba of Rice Lake, Mozojeed & Diable Rouge of Lac Couteroielle, & Little Crow & the Big Martin of Lac de Flambeau. On reaching the Saint Croix this party may be joined by the Buffalo & Chacopee of Snake river, and and by Kabamappa and a companion from above. At the crossing of Rum river, the Chippewa river Chiefs, may return if they wish, and their places be supplied by Grosse Guelle *Tere Fort* & some third man, from Mille Lac. If the Loon's Foot of Fond du lac will join this party, he will be found a discreet man. On crossing the Mississippi to Spunk [?] river (being the *first* above Sac river, which the treaty calls for) *Guelle Plat* of Leech Lake, should attend in person, or send a deputation who would meet the surveying party at that point, & would necessarily continue with it, to the termination of the line. I think these chiefs would secure justice to the nation, and conduct in such a manner as to produce a harmonious result, in the cases in which they will probably be called to act. Change them or add to the number, however, if circumstances require it.

Let the Chippewa Chiefs understand that a great number of deputies are not required for the sake of security. There will be a detachment of United States Infantry or Dragoons, all the way. Major Bean will execute the[1] survey & will chain and mark the line, under general instructions from Genl Clark.

Trusting that your part of the duties will be performed in strict justice and faithfulness to all parties, and with satisfaction to yourself.

I am Sir
Very respectfully
Your Obt Servt

Mr. George Johnston   Henry R Schoolcraft[2]
    Sault Ste Maries.

[1] The two preceding words were added later, in the margins.
[2] Only the signature is in Schoolcraft's handwriting.

12. JAMES LAWRENCE SCHOOLCRAFT.

This may certify that Mr George Johnston commenced preparing for his voyage to St. Peters, for the purpose of entering upon his duties as United States Interpreter for the Survey of the line between the Sioux and Chippewa Indians, on the 27th of the present month.

Saut Ste Marie 30th May 1835

Ja La Schoolcraft

13. HENRY R. SCHOOLCRAFT TO GEORGE JOHNSTON.

Detroit December 8th 1836

Dear Sir,

I enclose you the Receiver's certificates and receipts for five lots of land purchased for you in the county of Oakland, at the government price of one dollar & a quarter per acre, amounting to $581.15. Patents will issue in your name at Washington for these lands. In the meantime your deed for them, should you wish to sell, will be perfectly valid, taking the description inserted in the receipt. The lands have been examined by an agent previous to the purchase, and are excellent farming lands.

The remainder of the sum received from you for investment, I am desirous to vest in improved real estate in this quarter, or some of the rising towns in the State, and I have no doubt of my being able to succeed in finding property which will yield you a handsome interest.

With regard,

Yours sincerely,

Henry R Schoolcraft

14. HENRY R. SCHOOLCRAFT TO GEORGE JOHNSTON.

Detroit Feb. 7th 1837

My dear Sir,

I have duly received yours of the 9th Jan. Since the date of my previous letter, I have vested two thousand dollars of your funds in the Forsyth farm, and loaned out two thousand dollars at legal interest. The investment in the Forsyth property is made with others who have placed funds in my hands, and the proper evidence will be furnished to you on my return to Mackinac in the spring. All your investments are, in my opinion good, and will justify you in anticipating a handsome advance.

Accept our thanks for the information contained in your letter. We reciprocate the friendly inquiries of your cousin in London. I beg to refer you to Charlotte for the hea[l]th of Jane & the children & remain

> Very sincerely Yours
> Henry R Schoolcraft

M G. Johnston.
[Sault Ste. Marie]

15. HENRY R. SCHOOLCRAFT TO W. V. COBBS.

> Superintendency of Indian Affairs
> Detroit May 8th 1837

Sir,
I have the honor to forward to you, Copies of the revised regulations of the Department.

> I am Sir
> Very respectfully
> Yr. Obt. Servant.
> Henry R Schoolcraft[1]

Major W. V. Cobbs
Commanding Officer
Fort Brady

[1] Only the signature is in Schoolcraft's handwriting.

16. HENRY R. SCHOOLCRAFT TO GEORGE JOHNSTON.

> Detroit May 22nd 1837

Dear Sir,
I have been favoured with your several letters of the month of March. Since I last wrote to you I have vested two thousand dollars of the sum you placed in my hands in the Cass Front, being a part of city property, which is deemed a desirable investment, and also the sum of $1000 at Saganaw. There still remains in my hands, after including the previous purchases, and crediting your dividend on Mr Kearney's draft, a balance of $182.18¾, as you will perceive by the enclosed statement.

There will be some charges during the year on your city and other property, to meet which it would be proper to leave a small amount uninvested. Still the balance is greater than will be required for these purposes. I have deemed it best to make no further investment of the balance, until seeing you personally, or receiving your further directions.

> I am [always?]
> Very sincerely
> Yrs
> Henry R Schoolcraft

Mr George Johnston
Sault Ste Marie

17. HENRY R. SCHOOLCRAFT TO GEORGE JOHNSTON.

Detroit May 23rd 1837

Dear Sir,

I herein enclose you the scrip for your investment at Lower Sagana, together with the printed deed of trust & articles of association. I observe, that no share of this stock has been sold short of $1000.

Very truly Yrs

Henry R Schoolcraft

G Johnston Esqr
    Sault Ste Marie

18. HENRY R. SCHOOLCRAFT TO GEORGE JOHNSTON.

Detroit February 14th 1838

Dear Sir,

I will thank you to inform John, Tom, and McMurray &[1] Waishkey, that I have recently paid the county and town taxes on their lands in Oakland for 1837, as I have likewise done upon yours. The township tax is rather severe, being $2.50 on each 80 acre lot. That of the county is $1.50 upon the same quan[t]ity. The several payments will be duly noticed in my accounts with each.

I believe William & John are doing very well at Mr Bacon's. They appear to be very steady, and avail themselves regularly, every Sabbath, of a permission given them in the fall, to occupy seats in my pew. Mr Bacon also speaks in high terms of them.

It has occured to me, that probably old Nabunway could relate to you some of the Chippewa traditionary tales. And as I am desirous of increasing my collection of this species of oral Indian literature, I shall esteem it a favour, if you will pen down, any thing of this kind, & transmit it to me, by mail.

I am dear Sir,

With much regard

Yours truly

Henry R. Schoolcraft.

Mr Geo. Johnston
    Sault Ste Marie.

    [1] "McMurray &" was inserted in the margins.

19. HENRY R. SCHOOLCRAFT TO GEORGE JOHNSTON.

Mackinac May 17th 1838

Dear Sir,

I have only time, by the return of the canoe, to thank you for the interesting tales you have collected. They are valuable, not only as glimpses of Indian tradition, but as shewing their opinions on various subjects. And I cannot but hope that you may obtain others in the course of the season.

We are happy to hear that your mother is out of immediate danger, & that there is every prospect of her restoration to complete health.

Very truly Yrs
Henry R Schoolcraft

Mr G. Johnston
Sault Ste Marie

20. JANE JOHNSTON SCHOOLCRAFT TO GEORGE JOHNSTON.

Mackinac June 15th 1839.

My dear Brother,

I received your kind letter, & am sorry to find your finger is still so sore, I hope Louisa will get well in time, I am glad the Doctor is kind to her & hope will do her good eventually,—Mr Turner has reapedly enquired about you & seems to feel a deep interest in you.—Mr Schoolcraft arrived here last week, & is now gone round Lake Michigan to appraise the cultivated lands & I expect him here in about 16 days.—I have got letters from Janee & Johnston & am glad to say they are well & send their love to you & family,—Janee has improved in music & has commenced[1] drawing, she has a taste for both.—I do not know of an opportunity for St Maries, but I write in advance.—Will you come over again?—I feel anxious to keep house, as I am getting to be a *burden* on James & Ann.—I am happy to learn our dear Mother is so much better, Give my love to your dear children & accept the same for[2] yourself from your

Affectionate Sister
Jane J. Schoolcraft

To

George Johnston Esqr
St Maries

[1] First written "comenced." The letter "m" was interlineated.
[2] "For" was written over the word "from."

21. HENRY R. SCHOOLCRAFT TO GEORGE JOHNSTON.

Acting Superintending Indian Affairs
Michilimackinac June 20th 1839

Sir

I have received your letter & its enclosure from the chief at Lapointe. I will thank you to state to Pezhickee's son, that the government do not wish to extend their purchases from the Indians north, at this time. There is already a superabundance of public lands in the market, & rapidly as our population advances, still it will require time to occupy the vast domain in the west already purchased.

Very Respectfully
Yr. Obt. Servt.
Henry R Schoolcraft[1]

Mr. George Johnston
    Sault Ste Marie

[1] Only the signature is in Schoolcraft's handwriting.

22. HENRY R. SCHOOLCRAFT TO GEORGE JOHNSTON.

New York May 10th 1844

Geo Johnston Esq
    Dear Sir:
        The Committee would feel under deep obligations to you, if you would undertake to furnish them some names, with their etymology, from the Lake country.
George Johnston Esqr.
Grand Traverse Bay
Michigan.
Fd by J. L. Schoolcraft Esqr.
[The above note is written on the bottom of the printed form below:]

Rooms of the New-York Historical Society,
University of New-York, March, 1844.

Sir:
    The undersigned, having been appointed a committee, to prepare a Map of the State, with all the original Indian names, solicit information on this head. It is believed that sectional maps, made by the early surveyors, exist among family papers, and would be communicated, as well as, in some instances, manuscript journals and letters. Another source of information, is to be found in the names of creeks, rivers, and other boundary marks, in early deeds. Tradition, in townships and neighborhoods, is a third, and still fruitful source of preserving these names, the meaning of which, may sometimes be yet obtained, from the natives, or from interpreters.

    Every year carries to the grave, some of those pioneers and early settlers, who are the best qualified to give the desired information, and thus narrows the circle of tradition, at its highest source. This Society furnishes a safe and eligible repository for all such documents, whether presented, or deposited. It is an object of deep interest, with its members, to collect and preserve, the sonorous and appropriate Indian terminology of the State. The committee will make due acknowledgments, in their final report, for all aid in this species of research.

Communications may be made to either of the undersigned, or under cover, to George Folsom, Esq., the Domestic Corresponding Secretary.

> Henry R. Schoolcraft,
> C. Fenno Hoffman,
> S. Verplank,
> William L. Stone,   Committee
> B. F. Butler,
> Edward Robinson,
> Wm. W. Campbell.

23. HENRY R. SCHOOLCRAFT TO GEORGE JOHNSTON.

New York August 31st 1844

Dear Sir,

I have duly received, and thank you, for your favour of the 2nd instant. You are favourably situated, for collecting traditions & traits of the Red Race, and their character & history; and possessing as you do, a full knowledge of their language with more than the ordinary share of English literature & letters, you would be, almost inexcusable, not to employ your leisure moments, in putting on record all you can find, among them, worthy of it. It is a debt you owe to them, & to the country, and such labours, if well directed & well executed, will form your own best claim to remembrance. Life is, at best, but short, & he only lives well, who does something to benefit others. So far as you may transmit to me, any thing you may collect, in names, or lodge-tales, or picture writing, or any other branch, I can assure you, that you shall have final & full literary credit.

I have commenced a popular work, under the name of "Oneota," of which, I send you the first number. This will afford a good medium for many such collections.

I have not received from the Bishop, the expected copy of yr translation of the Ep. service, but expect it.

Jane and Johnston beg to be remembered to Louisa & William & John, and all.

> Yours truly
> Henry R Schoolcraft

George Johnston Esqr
Grand Traverse Bay
via Michilimackinac
Michigan

24. HENRY R. SCHOOLCRAFT TO GEORGE JOHNSTON.

New York March 19th 1845.

Dear Sir,

Your several letters of Dec. 8 and of January 20th & 21st, with their enclosures, were received here, during my absence, and have just been perused. Accept my thanks for the Indian names of the rivers of the *east* & *south* shores of lake Michigan, from old Mackinac to Chicago. In some cases, I cannot identify them, with the present popular names. When this defect is supplied, the list will be perfect. Also, for the curious tradition of the "apron"—which appears to me, however, to be one of questionable authority. I would therefore like to have you speak further with Eshquagonaby on the subject.

On the subject of the lease, Randolph & Brothers are wholly misinformed, as to the illegality of the sales for assessments & taxes by the corporation. Those sales were made, under acts of the N. Y. legislature, and the decision, in the supreme court of this State & of the Court of Errors, last fall, in the noted case of *Lovatt vs. Stryker,* was in favour of the purchaser and the legality of the acts of the Corporation, & not against them, as they erroneously, and by reference to T. Romeyn, state in their letter to you.

The lease is for a *long* period—I do not recollect the time in yours, but they are, in others, for 500 to 900 years. When you recollect that North America has been settled but 225 years, you will comprehend, how improbable it is, that at the end of 900 years, there will be any claimant for the lots. As to the *value* of the lots, men may differ. My estimate I consider fair. In 20 years, these lots will be worth five times the sum. The city is rapidly going up, & will cover them. A third subject, is connected with these lots. You will recollect that they were conveyed to you for your share of the last debt claim,—I, taking the risque of the *allowance,* or *disallowance* of it. It has been disallowed by the govt & rejected by the judge of the court. I have therefore recd nothing for the lots, & I have no expectations of *now* receiving any thing.

In allusion to your letter in which you speak of the trouble Steuart has put in your way, I think you had better leave him to himself, as he will probably, have as much to do, to sustain himself, as he can get along with. I have found, in my experience of life, that diligence in right action, is sure to give a man the best rewards; and I trust you will be capable of sustaining yourself & children—I have since '36, believed that the Chippewas & Ottawas could not permanently thrive, *as distinct tribes,*[1] on their present locations; and that the sooner they embrace the offer to remove west, the better. This was my advice, as Agent, at the Council of Assent to the treaty at Mackinac, & I have seen nothing to alter my views, but much to confirm them.

Jane & Johnston reciprocate your kind remembrances, and remain, with me,

Sincerely Yours
Henry R Schoolcraft

P.S. Anne was here, in the fall, & tells me that James, has divided the homestead. I have heard nothing from him on the subject, but trust he has proceeded legally & justly. Send your enclosures by private hands, or under cover to Membr of Congress, or addressed to John Bigelow, Secy Hist. Society,[2] to save postage.
Mr George Johnston
    Grand Traverse Bay
       via Michilimackinac Michigan.

[1] First written "as a distinct tribe."
[2] The preceding eight words were interlineated.

25. HENRY R. SCHOOLCRAFT TO GEORGE JOHNSTON.

Washington June 30th 1847

Dear Sir,

I have received your favour of the 25th of May, and given the subject the best consideration I am able. The delays in the payment of the Irish money seem to me, to be interminable. Nor do I see much greater prospects of bringing matters to a close at St. Mary's. There seems to me no colourable[1] ground for the Judge of Probate of your county, excusing Mr Brockway from entering on the whole subject, but exonerating him[2] from responsibility for a part. The inventory of articles had by your mother from the estate foots over $1200. It was made, very low, by Hoffman & James, & is now in my possession. There is no law to give a preference, in the matter of indebetedness, to the estate of James. Each of the heirs is equally entitled to a share of the personal property, houses & other appurtenances, and I trust, that after so long a delay, in bringing the estate to a close, it may be done with a single eye to justice. I have always found Anne reasonable, & I think she would be readily made to see, that any arrangement of the kind you mention, would, by giving an undue preference to herself, be injurious to the other heirs, & consequently liable to revision. No reference from her or Mr Hulbert has been made to me on the subject, & but for your kind letter I should have remain'd in perfect ignorance of what was going on.[3] I should be pleased, if you would furnish me a sketch of the division of the real estate, buildings, &c.

I gave Mr Clinton of Buffalo, a letter to you, at the time he was appointed a Commissioner to treat with the Chippewas of lake Superior and the Upper Mississippi, but he has subsequently declined & the business has been put into the hands of Mr Verplank of Batavia, with the aid of Mr Mix of the Indian office.   The object is to purchase all the land as far as the Mississippi river, & throw the Chippewa population on its west bank, along[2] with the Pillagers. I know not how such a proposition will be received by the Fond du Lac & Sandy lake & Mille Lac bands.   To the Pillagers, it would present itself, in another & better light.

Remember me to Mrs Johnston, Louisa & the children to whom Jane desires to send her respects & believe me to be,

As ever, yours truly

Henry R Schoolcraft

[1] First written "colorable."
[2] This word was interlineated.
[3] First written "should remain in ignorance on the subject."

26. HENRY R. SCHOOLCRAFT TO GEORGE JOHNSTON.

Washington Augt 23rd 1847

Dear Sir,

I have been favoured with your letters of the 15th July & 3rd August; and thank you for the information, they communicate.   I am truly surprized that John & Anne should have taken up the idea that they are entitled to more than their proportionate share of the fence on the lots, and that they should have proceeded to remove it, from the lots of their *brothers & sisters* and placed it, exclusively around their *own*.   Your proposal to fence the lots now left in common, including mine, I see no objections to.   I have no intention, at present to sell them.   They cannot but increase in value, as the country settles, & the place increases.   I should *not* feel willing to bind myself *not* to part with the land in a given number of years, but have no intention of doing so, at present.   Should you feel willing to enclose the lots on this basis, I should be pleased, & would esteem it[1] an act of kindness.   I dare say the land would remain under your charge, where I *now place it*, a sufficient number of years to reward you for the expense of fencing, estimating the rent at a fair & moderate sum.

I have recently received a new release from Mr McMurray respecting the Irish property, & have signed it, & sent it back, duly acknowledged, to him.   The instrument has been prepared by Mr Maddock in Dublin, and conveys very *full* powers to Mr Kearney, both respecting this £800 of John McNiel Esqr, but also[1] respecting every other claim, of *every kind*, which the sagacious Mr Kearney *may have*, or may *hereafter* find.   I pray God's will be done, and shall think myself happy to get rid of the matter. I do not wish to lay a straw in the way of the final close of the business. It is, on this basis, that I have, unhesitatingly, signed & transmitted the instrument.

The notices you give of the mineral wealth of the region of lake Superior, coincide with my early & oft repeated opinions on this subject. These opinions were as confidently expressed seven & twenty years ago, as today; and I think that the veins of ore are not confined to the upper portions of the lake Superior basin, but will be found much nearer to you.

Johnston is at New York, where Mrs S. & myself recently paid him a visit, to inspect his wardrobe & see about his affairs, and I transferred his lodgings to 96 Cliff street, which is nearer to his business. Jane is with us here, and is well & in fine health, and unites with me in love and remembrance to the children, & to Mrs Johnston.

Yours sincerely

Henry R. Schoolcraft

P.S. What is the fate of John Tanner? Is he living? What do the Indians say? Has he fled to Red to Red River? When was he last seen? Are all efforts of the civil powers to bring him to justice, at an end? What is the general state of morals and religion & temperance in the village of St. Mary's?

[1] This word was interlineated.

27. HENRY R. SCHOOLCRAFT TO GEORGE JOHNSTON.

Washington Augt 30th 1847

My dear Sir,

I will thank you to affix the Indian equivalents, in the true Chippewa dialect, to the English words & phrases, in the enclosed forms, which have been prepared and forwarded to me, from England. Please transmit your return & reply, to me,[1] under cover, addressed to the Hon. Wm Medill, Commissioner Indian Affairs, War Department, Washington.

Very truly Yours

Henry R. Schoolcraft

Geo. Johnston Esqr
  Sault Ste. Marie.

[1] The words "to me," were interlineated.

28. HENRY R. SCHOOLCRAFT TO GEORGE JOHNSTON.

Washington Dec 6th 1847

My dear Sir,

I received this morning your letter of the 22nd November, covering one from certain Chippewa[1] chiefs of villages to the Commissioner of Indian Affairs. I have laid this promptly before him, & been referred to the public letter book, shewing that a letter was addressed to you, on the same subject, on the 24th November last, in which you were informed that the contemplated visit could not be sanctioned for the want of funds here to defray the expense of the delegation. I had received a similar request to yours, from William, some time ago. The fact is, the conduct of William & Hamlin & of the Mackinac traders generally, some years ago, in spreading false reports here, & striving to get a draft of the L'Arbre Croche chiefs to them paid, to the amount of some $4000, produced effects, which are yet, probably, felt in the War office here. I do not know the objects wished by the chiefs; but am satisfied that it will require some effort to bring up for favourable decision, questions of dissatisfaction, arising from the treaty of 1836. The most just claims have been, in several cases, rejected. James, in his life time, was among the number of those who exerted an adverse influence on certain of these claims. Indian affairs, in your quarter have, indeed, fallen into a poor condition, and it will require no little effort to revive them. My time is occupied with investigations & labours of another kind, and I have paid very little attention, for years, to a quarter of the country, in which I formerly took so much interest.

Perhaps, what the chiefs have to say, they might appropriately embody in a memoir addressed to the President through the regular channel of the Indian office. Mr Ord, though a poor & inefficient agent, could not refuse to transmit such a document.

I thank you for the Chippewa song, and for your reply to my list of words prepared for obtaining their equivalents in various Indian dialects. I trust you will do justice to your position & knowledge of the Chippewa history &c by answering the pamphlet of queries, or such of them as you may select. I shall digest my report from all the replies received, as well as my own researches, but preserve the original reports, & have them printed for reference. Mr Baraga recently sent replies to my "Inquiries" by numbers, through Bishop Lefevre of Detroit. It is simple, and has this merit, but evinces but little knowlege of the Chippewa traditions & history, and very little reach of thought.

Jane unites in remembrance to Mary & the children.

I am Sir, as ever
Very truly
Your friend & Brother
Henry R. Schoolcraft.

¹ This word was interlineated.

29. HENRY R. SCHOOLCRAFT TO GEORGE JOHNSTON.

Washington March 25th 1848

Dear Sir,

I have received your favour of the 7th Feb. by the hands of Mr Brockway enclosed to the Commissioner. The account of the old monument on the apex of a mountain near lake St. Croix, is very curious, & interesting. I should be happy to obtain a[1] plan & drawings, & have written to Mr David Dale Owen, who is charged with the public surveys of the lands between the St. Croix & Chippewa rivers. I am in hopes that some of his people have been led to it. I am told that Bruce is a man of veracity, & am therefore in hopes that the discovery will not prove an illusion. Should it not, it must add a important element to our antiquarian knowledge. If you obtain any thing further, be sure to let me know it.

Ever truly Yours
Henry R Schoolcraft

[1] This word was interlineated.

30. HENRY R. SCHOOLCRAFT TO GEORGE JOHNSTON.

Washington May 16th 1848

My dear Sir,

I am just in the receipt of your favour of the 5th instant, and have but a few moments at my command to reply. But I employ those moments in expressing my thanks for your attention to matters more exalted in their character, than many others in the lake country, to whom I have endeavoured to prove myself a friend. You are the only man in the Johnston family, who shews any interest in matters of literature & research.

Mr Owen writes to me that he will have the matter of the reported "mound" in the St. Croix country examined. That country is remarkable for its mound-like masses of lime stone & sandstone rock, which stand like monuments, as if all the surrounding rock, had been washed away. I suspect Mr Bruce refers to one of these, which if I remember well, the Chippewa chiefs at Prairie du Chien in 1825, wished to make a part of the boundary line between them & the Sioux, & which they called the *Moose's rump,* or *hump.* Still the top of this elevation[1] might be the site of an artificial monument of the kind you suggest.

I shall be greatly obliged to you to continue your observations on the proposed tour this summer. I must also beg you, to copy for me, if you find them, any heiroglyphics, or picture writing, from the faces of rocks, blazed trees, grave-posts, or bark scrolls, which you may encounter, in wandering among the sterile hills of lake Superior. I am still anxious also, to increase my knowledge of the original & striking *mythology* of the Chippewas, & their beautiful story-craft.

Give my love & remembrance to all the inmates of your family circle. With regard to the title to the lands, I shall do all in my power to secure the passage of a just law. Meantime, I think you, & the heirs, should file the claim, as originally awarded in 1823, in the office of the Register of the land office at St. Mary's.

Very truly Yrs
Henry R Schoolcraft.

George Johnston Esqr
    Sault Ste Marie Michigan.

¹ This word was interlineated.

31. HENRY R. SCHOOLCRAFT TO GEORGE JOHNSTON.

Washington Augt 10th 1848

Dear Sir,

Annexed I furnish you a copy of a letter, from the Adjutant General,¹ in reply to one which I addressed him on the subject of Tilden. Should any thing further come to light, respecting his being concerned, either as *principal* or *accessory,* in the murder of James, I will thank you to inform me.

Very sincerely Yours,
Henry R Schoolcraft.

¹ The phrase "from the Adjutant General," was interlineated.

31A. R. JONES TO HENRY R. SCHOOLCRAFT.   (Copy.)

Adjutant General's Office
July 13th 1848.

Sir:

In reply to your inquiry of the 11th inst. I have to inform you that 2d Lieutenant *B. P. Tilden* Jr. 2d Infantry, and others were tried, convicted, & sentenced to be hung by a Military Commission in Mexico, for Murder & Burglary, which sentence was afterwards postponed by Major General Butler, & the prisoners ordered to accompany their Regiments to the United States. Lieutenant Tilden has since tendered his resignation intending to remain in Mexico, but no definitive action has yet been taken upon it. It is understood he is a native of Boston, where it is believed his family resides.

Respectfully Your Obt. Servt.
(Signed) R. Jones
Adjt Genl

H. R. Schoolcraft. Esq.
    Washington.
        D. C.

32. HENRY R. SCHOOLCRAFT TO MRS. GEORGE JOHNSTON.

Washington Nov. 7th 1848

Dear Madam,

Your letter was received a day or two since, & I take my earliest leisure moment to reply to it. I do this, the more early from the fact that it is written under some misapprehension of transactions alluded to by you. If George has been unfortunate in his investments, with his treaty money, it must be recollected, so have we all. All the Saganaw investments came to nothing. So far as I was interested, my interest was turned over to the government & sacrificed with the rest of my real & personal property. It took about $40,000 worth of land, bank stock &c to satisfy a judgment of less than $10,000. In this matter, if the *Johnstons had stood faithfully by me,* I should have carried all my claims before *the court,* & thereby *each* of the heirs, would have secured a *share.* But they all, *saving George & Charlotte,* turned against me, & did not see, that *my* defeat, must be *their* defeat. Prior to the trial, I purchased the shares of *William, George* & *Eliza* for lots in New York, which were valued at their then estimated worth. But, whatever, the result was, it was *an even transaction.* They were not to make good to me, *their claim* if I *lost* the trial, & I was not to[1] make good to them the *value of the lots,* if I *gained* it. *It was an even & equal transaction, property for property; riquese against risque.* I lost the claim & had *to repay its amount* to the govement. They held on to the lots, till they fell to next to nothing in value. By this exchange, they gave me nothing, & you say, the lots are worth nothing. Who then has gained, or lost any thing? Nobody! We are, as we were, before the trial, *even.* For the claim, you know, has been decided against *here,* by the *Commissioner & Secretary of War.* The court, *with the late Robert Stuart to back it,* decided against it at Detroit. And nothing has since been done with it. The attempt of the heirs to send *Mr Brockway,* to advocate it, ended in nothing. Any other attempt they make make will, probably, end in nothing. So much respecting my "letting you have," or loaning you money. As I do not owe a cent on this claim, there could be no expectation of payment. In other respects, I am unable wholly to lend you, even a tithe of the sum you ask. I am poor & without funds, just living as you do, from hand to mouth. But I deeply sympathize with you, in your poverty & trials, & pray God, to give you all grace to sustain them, not doubting, that "by perseverance in well doing" there is still a reward for you, even on this earth.

I think George entitled to the subagency, as you suggest,[2] & annex a form for a petition to the Secretary of War for his appointment, which I think he would do well to have copied, & signed by the democrats, *or Cass & Butler men,* of your precincts; and transmitted, through one of the Michigan *Senators,* or *Representatives* in Congress.   My aid here shall be freely given.   Fret not, but trust.

Very sincerely Yours
Henry R Schoolcraft

Mrs Mary R Johnston
 St Mary's
Jane & Johnston reciprocate your remembrance.

 [1] The word "to" was interlineated.
 [2] The words "as you suggest," were interlineated.

33. HENRY R. SCHOOLCRAFT TO GEORGE JOHNSTON.

Washington March 12th 1849

My Dear Sir,
 Your letter of the 29th January was duly received.   Mr Bingham submitted your recommendation to the Commissioner of Indian Affairs, but I cannot learn that any definite action took place on that, or the remonstrance of the chiefs, prior to Mr Polk's leaving the Presidential chair.

 With respect to the strikership, I immediately submitted an extract of your letter to the Commissioner.   The result was, that Mr Ord's nomination of his third son was rejected, and he was directed to find a person of the Chippewa blood, or to furnish a certificate that no such person, of suitable qualifications, could be found.

 I have abstained from entering into any of[1] the mining speculations in your quarter, since sending Mr Bradford into that area. I do not doubt but some of the disclosures made to you by[2] the Chippewas are valuable, and would justify exploration; but my health is such that I could not, if I were disposed to do so, pass another winter in those severe latitudes.

 So many geological smatterers & rank empirics have been in that field since the copper mania first broke out—so much pure trash, lies & nonsense, has[3] been published in reports, & formed the grave basis of mining companies, that an honest & modest observer of the phenomena of nature, would like to keep as far as possible from the vortex.

Very truly Yours
Henry R Schoolcraft

Geo. Johnston Esqr
 Sault Ste Marie

 [1] This word was interlineated.
 [2] First written "by you to."
 [3] "Has" was written over "have."

34. HENRY R. SCHOOLCRAFT TO GEORGE JOHNSTON.

Washington March 30th 1849.

Dear Sir.

I have received your letter of the 27th ultimo containing a vocabulary of the Chippewa language from No. 86 to 367, as numbered by you, for which you will please accept my thanks.

When you say "Che-mah-wing" To Cry "Che-sah-gee-ting," to love &c do you mean to express the idea that he cries, is crying, He loves, or is loving? Is the action of crying or loving *complete* and *finished* or is it *still going on*. If it is not finished, but is still going on, then the particle "Che" marks the difference between the indicative and present participle of the verb. If the act *is* finished, then I apprehend, that the participle crying as in English, which you put "mah-wing," means "he cries," and is nothing but the indicative present, without the particle "Che."

The inflection *ing,* in the Chippewa, denotes generally the senses which we express in English by the prepositions *in, at,* and seems to imply both the *position* and the *action* of things.

It was early observed, that the Indian languages were without auxiliary verbs. I found on reaching St Mary's in 1822, that the mode of expression with them is, I sick—I well, &c and not I (am) sick, I (am) well. But I also observed, very soon, that they had a fundamental verb, to denote abstract existence. This verb I communicated in 1825 to the North American Review, in its full conjugation, under the orthography of "I-aw." It is variously written *Ah-au, I-ah,* and *Ah-ah.* The latter is Peter Jones' mode. You have given it, in the very same words, in the composite phrase "Che-ah-yah yong," in answer to No 347 (my numbers) with the addition of the letter y, to the third syllable.

Do you, in this phrase, employ "Che" to denote the *time* of existence, and is not "yong," a mere grammatical inflection of correspondence to the time "Che." Your alternate word, "Che-be-mah-tiz-ing," would merely convey the sense of *He lives,* or *is living* in English. Which?

I should be pleased to hear from you on this subject.

Very Truly Yours

Henry R Schoolcraft.[1]

[1] Only the signature is in Schoolcraft's handwriting.

35. HENRY R. SCHOOLCRAFT TO GEORGE JOHNSTON.

Washington April 4th 1849

Dear Sir,

Your letter of Feb. 23rd, with the *first* part of your vocabulary from No 1 to 85, has come to hand since the arrival of the second, acknowledged in my letter of March 30th.

Is not the word "emah" an affirmative particle? If, for instance, "O-doan," be *his mouth,* as it unquestionably is, then what addition to the meaning is made by *emah.* Is it not but a re-affirmation of what we already had, giving a sense something like this— His mouth-it. To me it seems that *Doan,* is clearly the root, or elementary form of the word. O is, in very many words, the pronominal sign of the third person.

I notice the word Muezzin, as being in use in the Punjaub on the banks of the Indus, for the voice of the priest, or native worshiper in prayer. This reminds me of Muzzi-tau-guzzi, the voice or cry of animated nature in the Chippewa. What is your opinion on this head?

Very truly Yours
Henry R Schoolcraft[1]

G. Johnston Esqr.

[1] Only the signature is in Schoolcraft's handwriting.

36. Henry R. Schoolcraft to George Johnston.

Washington May 30th 1849

Dear Sir,

I have received your letter of the 15th instant, with its several enclosures of the 13th & 14th, respecting principles of the Indian language, for which you have my thanks.

With regard to your claim, I remark, that it is, in itself just, & should be paid out of the debt fund created by the treaty of March 28th 1836 for the payment the just debts of the Indians. The course taken by Mr Crawford & Mr Harris on the subject has much prejudiced these claims, & yours is[1] among those unjustly reported against by Mr Edm[o?]nds. Wrong as the action was, it has been formally *sanctioned by the Secretary of War in 1842,* Mr Spencer. Mr Bingham is no lawyer & possesses none of the qualifications for advocating such a claim, whatever other good qualities he possesses, & I do not doubt them. If there is any man who can succeed in bringing up the claim, it must be some such man as Charles H[?] Stewart Esqr.* But even this, may be in vain, while the Indian office is under its present management. It is now confidently asserted that we shall have a new commissioner, within a fortnight.

I do not think the visit of the chiefs you name, could have the slightest influence here. I have heard nothing about the removal of Mr Ord but suppose it will take place as a matter of course. I wrote to you, that he was checked in the further appointment of his sons as strikers, while there were persons of Indian descent competent to fill that situation.

Sincerely Yours
Henry R Schoolcraft

* Platt, Stewart & Eldridge of N. Y. Mr S. is the partner here.

P.S. Your letter on or having any relation to the inquiries I have in hand, should be closed to me, & then put in an envelope addressed [to?] Commissioner Indian Affairs, Department of the Interior, Washington.

¹ This word was interlineated.

37. HENRY R. SCHOOLCRAFT TO GEORGE JOHNSTON.

Washington Oct. 10th 1849

My dear Sir,

The establishment of the Home Department, and the transfer of the Indian office to it, has created a favourable aspect to claimants, in various ways. From some recent decisions, which I have seen, I am of opinion, that your claim, for an allowance made to you by the Indians & their agent, for debt,¹ at Michilimackinac, in the fall of 1837, might be re-opened & brought up,² & also, the claim for the other allowances, sold to me. If you will execute a power of attorney to me, with full powers, I will try it, if some decisions now pending are carried. There must be a certificate, from the county clerk,³ that the magistrate before whom it is acknowledged, is duly an officer.

Very truly Yours
Henry R Schoolcraft

Geo. Johnston Esqr.

P.S. Enclose your letters to me, under cover to Orlando Brown Com. Ind. Affairs. By this course you will save me the rather heavy expense of postage I have hereforore paid on you[r] letters.

Has Brockway left the Sault? If so a new administrator should be appointed.

H. R. S.

¹ The phrase "for debt" was added, in the margin.
² The sentence originally ended here. What follows was interlineated.
³ "From the county clerk," was interlineated.

38. HENRY R. SCHOOLCRAFT TO GEORGE JOHNSTON.

Washington May 24th 1851

Dear Sir,

I have received your letter of the 16th instant, and thank you¹ for the interest you continue to manifest in my affairs. But, so far as it respects the action of the persons you name, both white & red, the circumstances are beneath my contempt, and if any thing has been prepared to transmit to this place, it[1] can only render the writers despicable—if indeed, the names you mention deserve a moment's consideration.

I understand, that in the recent allowances made for DEBT, under the brokerage of Messrs Ewing & Chute, no recognition whatever, of the previous allowances made in 1837 was made. I have read all the lists & papers respecting these *new allowances,* which far transcend, the whole amount due the Indians, on the debt fund. They provide for a reduction *pro rata.* They go, on the principle of giving a sop to everyone, "Gray, Blanche & Sweetheart." People who never sold a yard of strouds, are put down. Old Biddle is satisfied with $18,000. Some members of the legislature were *greased,* I think,[2] as the claims went along, as I see there is a resolution that these claims "ought be paid." It is a regular scrabble for the Indians money. I am told the brokers get *half.* This will be about $60,000—quite a job. So things go now-a-days. It is the reign of purity!!

As to the old claims, I suppose these will be[1] swallow up all, and the Johnston heirs may whistle.

Some time ago the department sent Aitkin, the sub agent, a copy of an old Indian inscription, with a request to get Chingwauk, to interpret it. Nothing has been heard from him. I, therfore enclose you an order for it, and will thank you to invite the Little Pine to call on you & try to explain it, and send me the result, under cover to Hon. L. Lea, Commissioner of Indian Affairs. Make some presents to Little Pine for it, say $10 or 15$ of such things as he most wants, & send bills to the office (under cover as above) and they will be paid. The inscription is on Cunningham's island, lake Erie. It may relate to the[1] old Eries, or Mundwa[?] Iroquois.

Give my respects to Mrs Johnston & Louisa & the boys. And allow me to advise you, that, however, *others* may do, & prosper in wickedness, to cast your lot wholly with the people of the Lord.

Truly & sincerely Yours
Henry R. Schoolcraft.

George Johnston Esq
    Sault Ste Marie
        Chippewa Co
            Michigan

P.S. I sent to you, some months ago, a copy of my *recent national work* on the Indians. You do not appear to have received it. It contains a paper from you. I think it was sent by Adams' Express to Detroit—of course, *free of charge,* but some time having elapsed,

I do not exactly recollect, but will inquire at the office.[3] It contains Little Pine's explanation of the Dighton Rock inscription.

[1] This word was interlineated.
[2] The phrase "I think," was interlineated.
[3] This final clause, beginning with "but," was interlineated.

39. HENRY R. SCHOOLCRAFT TO GEORGE JOHNSTON.

Washington June 2nd 1851.

Dear Sir,

Your letter of the 24th May, came duly to hand. I immediately filed strong recommendation in your favour, before the Commissioner, and have had an interview with him, this morning, in relation thereto. He says that he has made it a rule, throught the United States, to make no appointments of interpreter, except on the recommendation of the agent, or Supt and that it would afford him pleasure to confirm your nomination, if it comes up to him. He advises, that you write to the agent at Detroit.

Mr Sprague, the late Representative in Congress from Western Michigan, will be the Agent & Acting Supt *on the 30th of June*—being appointed to succeed Mr Babcock. He is a gentleman of moral character & intelligence, and, I think, a letter from you would be successful. In the meantime, as I am personally acquainted with him,[1] I will write to him recommending your appointment in the strongest terms.

Ever yours
Henry R Schoolcraft

Geo. Johnston Esq
    Sault Ste Marie

[1] This word was interlineated.

40. HENRY R. SCHOOLCRAFT TO GEORGE JOHNSTON.

Washington 10th July 1851

Dear Sir,

I have your letter of June 6th. A letter has been written to Mr Aiken to deliver you the copy of the old inscription, found on a rock, on Cunningham's island, lake Erie—which I trust, you get the Little Pine to interpret.

I have heard nothing on the subject of you[r] nomination of the interpretership, & proposed residence at Elmwood, to take care of the grounds. I have strongly recommended it, both here & to Mr Sprague—the new Superintendent. But, since the recent proceedings to defraud the Indians of their vested funds, by surreptitious claims, I cannot, say what you may expect.

With regard to the land claims, I have called attention here, to that subject, & expect that instructions will be soon sent to the Sault Ste Marie Land office. Edwin Hulbert has written to me, that he can sell my lot. I am not anxious about it. What is it worth? First from the ship channel to the *Road,* & then back to the hill?

The death of Dr Morton at Philadelphia, is the true cause, probably, of your receiving no answer to your letter. I will enquire about his papers on [hybrids?] when I go on in the autumn.

Your volume of my researches, I found had not been sent, from the Indian office. It will now be sent by Adams' Express to to J L Whiting & Adams Detroit—free of charge to you, to that point.

Reciprocating compliments to yourself, Mary & the children, from Mrs. S. Jane & myself, I am

Yours ever
Henry R. Schoolcraft

G. Johnston Esq

41. HENRY R. SCHOOLCRAFT TO GEORGE JOHNSTON.

Washington July 25th 1851

Dear Sir,

In reply to your last letter (July 10) I remark, that there was authority, originally given to Mr A. to make Little Pine, some presents. The inscription has some *peculiarities,* & with my knowledge of the ancient history of Indians of lake Erie, I should not feel much embarrassed, myself, in decyphering it—having studied the art of pictography, under Little Pine. The old man is very politic, & a great worshipper of *the powers that be.* It would not have a bad effect, to let him know that I have, for *many years,*[1] & *now am,* sitting, near the President, where my powers & pay, are far higher than they ever were, in Michigan, & that all these letters, originate from me. When you receive Part 1 of my work, shew him at page 108 et seq. (plates 36 & 37) the use I have made of his descriptions of the figures on the DIGHTON ROCK, and impress on him the full credit I have given him for it, & the great reputation he gets by these things, whereby his *name* will live, when he is *dead.* I think this will touch him.

There are some things in the lake[2] Erie inscription, that have a *foreign look.* Such are several figures like this [*]. The *square piece* on the heads of men, thus [*], looks as if meant for a *hat.* Were there ancient frontlets like this? Point out these things to him, & to Waubojeeg & his mother.

With regard to the land claims, the Com. of the General Land office, thinks the law defective, & is embarrassed about writing instructions. I think he may send out, Mr Wilson, the chief clerk, to see to them.

As to Eliza's sale to Mr Edwin Hulbert, it is very far below its value. Edwin wrote to me about my claim. I told him[3] I did not wish to sell it, but that I valued the front lot at $3,000 & the back at $1500.

I notice what you say about the stone hammer. I shall be pleased to receive any thing in this way. Any thing *authentic* & *valuable* which you have, in Indian history & antiquities, my publication, furnishes the best medium for bringing before the public. Your Menominee tradition,[3] is in Part I. Your *Vieux Desert* matters will be in Part II.

Very truly ever yrs,
Henry R Schoolcraft

Geo. Johnston Esq
    Sault Ste Marie

* See partial reproduction of this letter, facing page 417. The handwriting plainly shows the severity of his illness in 1849.
[1] "For many years," was interlineated.
[2] The words "the lake" were interlineated.
[3] This word was interlineated.

42. HENRY R. SCHOOLCRAFT TO GEORGE JOHNSTON.

Washington 25th Aug 1851

Dear Sir,

I will thank you to send me samples of the Indian[1] mode of weaving & making bark bags, & other manufactures, if they have any, of native hemp, or fabrics of cloth. Cut elongated pieces from the *mushkamoots* of the size of a large letter, & send them, under cover, to Mr Lea.

I have received your letter, of the 2d Aug[2] respecting the inscription, & hope, ere this, you have made something out of the latter.[3] I am aware, that there are some things, which are not, apparently, according to the Indian pictographic method, in it; but prefer, without pointing them out, to let the Little Pine, indicate them.

If you could also send me specimens of the native hemp, or flax, or nettles, used in rope making &c, I should be pleased.

I have received your fine specimen of the mining hammer, which was duly delivered by Adams' Express, for w[h]ich accept my thanks.

Sincerely
Henry R. Schoolcraft

Geo. Johnston Esq
    Sault Ste Marie

   ¹ Repetition of "the Indian" was struck through.
   ² The phrase "of the 2d Aug" was interlineated.
   ³ Originally written "out of it."

43. HENRY R. SCHOOLCRAFT TO GEORGE JOHNSTON.

Philadelphia Sept. 17th 1851

Dear Sir,

I have duly received, at this place, your several letters of Augt 23rd 25th, and Septr 5th. by which, you acknowledge the receipt of the 1st vol. of my work on the Indian tribes, & transmit specimens of Indian *heiroglyphics,* & of their manner of *weaving.* I will thank you for further specimens of the latter, in which Indian materiel is wholly used. Also, for the mode used by the Indian women, in preparing *the thread.* Is there any machenery in *twisting the fibre,* or in *weaving it?*

The pictographs are interesting, but cannot be employed in my present volume. They require to be numbered,¹ and explained, separating those designed for particular purposes, as hunting, &c, &c.

I am now engaged in putting to press the SECOND part of my work, & shall not, probably return to Washington, till the middle of December.

The land claims, will I trust, all be satisfactorily adjusted. I will thank you to point out the bounds & metes, & the division, made by the Executor, among the heirs.

The additional debt claims of 1837 were, you are probably informed,² defeated by the large *bonus,* paid to Ewing & Co. So, I lose my N.Y. lots, & the shares purchased.

Mrs. S. & Jane are with me, or rather Jane will be here in a few days,³ and all reciprocate your remembrances.

Very truly Yours,
Henry R. Schoolcraft.

Geo. Johnston Esqr
PS. I trust to hear from you when you make progress with the Little Pine, or any other MEDA who is wise in the Ke-kee-win.

   ¹ First written "required to numbered."
   ² This word was interlineated.
   ³ The clause "or rather Jane will be here in a few days," was interlineated.

44. HENRY R. SCHOOLCRAFT TO GEORGE JOHNSTON.

Philadelphia Nov 6th 1851
(Butler House 8th & Chestnut)

Dear Sir,

Your communication of Oct. 4th has been duly received & the explanations given by Shingwaak examined. They appear plausible, to one conversant with the Indian pictography, & who knows the importance which they place on *dreams* & *visions* & *fasts,* though, it will still be inquired, why such elaborate labour was bestowed by them in engraving, on hard rock, such records?

It will not be possible, in the advanced state of the *2nd Vol.* to offer an explanation of it. But I shall endeavour to make use of his principle interpretations in the next, combined with the actual ancient history of the *lake Erie Indians.*

I have sent you[r] account to Washington for payment & have not yet received an answer.

I am, as ever
Very truly Yours
Henry R. Schoolcraft

Geo Johnston Esq
Sault Ste Marie Michigan

45. HENRY R. SCHOOLCRAFT TO GEORGE JOHNSTON.

Washington April 9th 1852

Dear Sir,

I have just received a letter from Mr Brown, advising me that you have caused the entry for my lands to be made in the name of my children. By what authority have you done this thing? Neither by my *request,* nor by any *colour of law,* & I will thank you immediately to go to the office, with Mr Brown, & correct the entry. There is no will in the case & I am the *legal representative,* & the title[1] cannot pass to them, without *me.* I have ever designed this property for them, & still do so,* but I feel this act is a piece of high-handed injustice & indignity. Would *McMurray,* would *Anne,* would *you yourself* be satisfied at this course?

I requested you[1] to take care of the property, by fencing it in, but nothing besides. I filed my claim here, in the General Land Office, & will take care of it, instanter.

Very respectfully
Henry R Schoolcraft

Mr G. Johnston.

John has been wand[er]ing about, and not only has no money to make such entries, if I approved them but is wholly incompetent to manage, or keep *any* property.

* His will, dated March 28, 1850, scrupulously separated all of his possessions and claims that came through Jane Johnston, to be divided equally between her two children; and as exclusively gave everything of his own to Mary Howard Schoolcraft, who, in a codicil June 28, 1856, was made sole executor of his estate.

¹ This word was interlineated.

46. HENRY R. SCHOOLCRAFT TO GEORGE JOHNSTON.

Washington June 16th 1852

Dear Sir,

I am reminded by your note to Mrs Schoolcraft, that I have not replied to your last letter. It was inadvertent. My time is so much occupied in the great national work, on which I am engaged, that my friends must make some excuses for me.

I received the squirrel skin, which you sent me. It is a new species of squirrel, and is now under examination. I should be pleased to get the head bones, with the teeth.

Your account for payments to Little Pine,¹ was forwarded by me, to Mr Mix² the chief clerk of the Ind. Office for payment, while I was in Philadelphia, last fall. I called his attention to it last spring.³ It had been overlooked, with some others of that kind, & the receipt *mislaid*. He promised immediate attention to it, & I presume he has transmitted the amount long ere this.

I beg to be remembered to Mrs Johnston & Louisa, in which Mrs. S. unites.

Very truly Yrs

Henry R. Schoolcraft

G. Johnston Esq
    Sault Ste Marie

¹ The word "which" was written following this, and afterward struck through.
² "Mr Mix" was interlineated.
³ This sentence was interlineated.

47. HENRY R. SCHOOLCRAFT TO GEORGE JOHNSTON.

Washington Feb. 21st 1853

My dear Sir,

Your letters to me of the 14th & 15th June have been overlaid by other matters, pressing on my attention & not designedly neglected. The chief Buffalo & his companions, visited my house, but their object here, was, I believe, wholly fruitless. It is in vain, when the Indians have made a bad bargain, as they did in 1842, to get affairs rectified afterwards. They must look sharp at first, and exercise foresight. By putting their hands to paper, in a hurry, & without fully understanding the terms of a treaty, they do injustice to themselves. Thus they have signed away lake Superior; but it is, to them, gone forever.

Your little claim for Chingwauk is, probably, mislaid or misunderstood. I have had my writing room & office, in my own house, these two years, & being lame seldom go to the War Office. I am, in consequence, not aware of what is done there. It seems to me, there should not be a moment's hesitation in paying you.

Mr Lea will probably be removed, under the new rule; but we have no certainty, that any person will be appointed his successor, who is versed in Indian affairs.

It appears to me, the definite action which has been taken by Congress and by the Michigan legislature, ensures the building of the St. Mary's canal; and this must give a value to property there, which it had not before. With a view to the laying out of streets & laying off lots,[1] on the property owned by me &[2] the heirs &c I have authorized Mr Brown the Register to concur in such proper steps as may be agreed on. Mr Whitney tells me it will be a suitable place for residences.

Remember me to Mrs J. & the family & believe me, as ever
Yours truly
Henry R. Schoolcraft

George Johnston Esq
Sault Ste Marie.

[1] The phrase "& laying off lots," was interlineated.
[2] The phrase "me &" was interlineated.

48. HENRY R. SCHOOLCRAFT TO GEORGE JOHNSTON.

Washington Oct. 1./53
Sir,

Your letter of April 6th, informing me that you had "attended regu[l]arly to my proportion of the claim,"—your subsequent letter, informing me that I was not the owner of any part of your father's estate, at St Mary's, & your s[t]ill subsequent letter, denoting that the lot, which I permitted you to fence in, had been regularly taxed to me, & requiring me to reimburse this tax, & give the free use of the land, besides,—these are the positions, assumed by you, have been received.

Did I know what to say to you, under these extraordinary &
conflicting statements, I should have immediately answered them.

Very respectfully

Henry R. Schoolcraft

Geo. Johnston Esq

Henry Rowe Schoolcraft in The Black Gauntlet

The Black Gauntlet, by Mary Howard Schoolcraft, second
wife of Henry Rowe Schoolcraft, was published by J. B. Lippincott & Co., Philadelphia, in 1860. On cursory examination it
has been described as a book about the South and slavery, also
even as a book about the Indians. It is really an autobiographical narrative, in the thinnest possible disguise, but so
thickly encased in a mass of proslavery argument, quoted
verses, historical passages, and footnotes, that it has lain effectually hidden for three-quarters of a century. In its last hundred pages it gives an account of the later years of Henry Rowe
Schoolcraft's life, about which little has been known and practically nothing has been written.

If there could be any doubt of its autobiographical authenticity, her personal footnotes, cleverly inserted perhaps a hundred pages from the points where they would be most revela-
tory, furnish conclusive proof. The facts about her father and
her family are in accord with genealogical records and writings,
with which they have been checked, in South Carolina and
Georgia.

The book was published four years before the death of
Schoolcraft. Its preface would indicate his full knowledge and
approval.

In the following excerpts fictitious names have been replaced by actual names with no other indication, after the first
occurrence, except the use of italics.

Ne na baim,* you have so repeatedly urged me to write sketches
of character in Washington (the omnium gatherum of the world);
and sketches of plantation life, in my own native State of South
Carolina, where my ancestors have lived from its earliest settlement,
that I have, for two months past, snatched every moment I could

* Ne na baim, Indian word meaning my husband.

dutifully spare from my innumerable domestic cares, to comply with your wishes, by describing every-day life on the plantations.

*   *   *

In writing these sketches of South Carolina, Ne na baim, God knows that I have no ambition to be an author;—and nothing but my romantic veneration, that makes your wishes my law, could have induced me to take up my pen, other than as your amanuensis. For twelve years that you have been imprisoned at home by a stroke of paralysis, I have felt no earthly aspiration beyond the honor of helping you to complete your voluminous history of the Red race of this continent, by becoming your assiduous copyist and constant nurse; for, in the bodily afflictions that you have borne with the uncomplaining manliness, majesty, and serenity of Christianity, you have commanded the deepest moral appreciation and romance of a Southern woman's heart.

If, therefore, your criticism of my sketches induces you to think them at all worthy of publication, my ambition will be entirely satisfied; for every sentiment I have uttered I am willing to leave as a souvenir to my friends; for they are the mellowed convictions of my mind and heart.

You have made me read aloud to you so many books, that almost involuntarily I have acquired a habit of quoting from the best authors. Blot out, however, every line you disapprove; for your appreciation is all I crave. Indeed, I have felt desolate from earliest childhood; ever lamenting the loss of an incomparable father and mother, and loving sisters, and brothers, and friends, all snatched from me by inevitable destiny; so that, in this wide world, I have found you, Ne na baim, my only unchanging earthly hope. You are, therefore, my all—for the heart needs a home in this world as well as the next; and I could now be contented to live alone with you, surrounded with books, in a wigwam, in the Oke-fe-no-ke Swamp, among the birds, the flowers, and the wild beasts; for the rattlesnake and the tiger are not so malignantly insatiable as the poisoned tongue of suspicion, detraction, and envy—that neither you nor I have been shielded from, though living in the strictest retirement for half a score of years, and not intentionally standing in the sunlight of a human being; but humbly thanking God every day for that sublime blessing of patience under your severe afflictions, that has through you magnified the religious enthusiasm of Job, who from the depths of misery cried out, with his whole heart, "Though God slay me, I will still trust in Him."

*   *   *

One day she [Musidora Wyndham, i.e., *Mary E. Howard*] went

to church [in Washington, D. C.], where she had been invited to sit in the pew of a friend. A very remarkable-looking gentleman arose from his seat, opened the door as she entered, and then seated himself by her side. He was perhaps fifty years of age, though his very long, waving, affluent, chestnut-colored hair, was scarcely tinged with envious grey; his features were large, his complexion florid, his eyes a brilliant blue, and his forehead was so white, broad, and high, that *Mary* was on the tenter-hooks of curiosity to find out who the majestic stranger was. His height measured six feet; his hands were aristocratically small, and delicately white; while his dress indicated that he had no ambition to be a dandy, or worshipper of his own personal beauty. *Mary* thought that, with the exception of her proud lover, Mr. Fletcher, she had never seen so noble, so lordly, so commanding a head, and she was reminded of a fancy sketch she had once seen, and greatly admired, of the god Jupiter. Impulsively she whispered to the ladies in the pew, and ascertained that he was the world-renowned scholar of England [*New York*], Mr. Walsingham [*Schoolcraft*].

To her great surprise, this distinguished personage, who had merely been introduced, in passing out of the pew, to *Mary,* called on her the next morning, and then the next, and the next—conversing a whole hour during each visit, with almost embarrassing intensity of interest. Indeed, he declared that he had often heard gifted women converse, but never in all his life had he listened to moral subjects canvassed with such sparkling truth and enthusiasm; and that, too, by a South Carolina lady, who is always represented by calumny to be almost oriental in the impractical, luxurious tendencies of her education. Of course, this enraptured genius called every morning and every evening, and planned walks in the Capitol grounds, and all places where curiosities were to be seen; and, indeed, he was so natural in his abstraction from every other object, save herself, on the avenue, that the gossips found out his whole secret long before he revealed it, by word of mouth, to *Mary* herself.

*   *   *

Having been very unfortunate in his first matrimonial romance, Mr. *Schoolcraft* never expected to marry again, but to give himself up entirely to those researches that were so fascinating to his intellect. His meeting with *Mary Howard,* that has been already detailed, was purely accidental. He was pleased with her noble person, bearing, and manners. Her figure was majestic, her carriage graceful and commanding; her air queenly, and her features classic. Her eyes liquid, dark, intellectual, and full of soul; her hair, like that of the Greeks, grew very low on the forehead, but phrenologically there was great height, breadth, and volume of brain.

But it was her extraordinary power of conversation that fascinated him. He listened to her with the intensely absorbed interest of a devotee. She had a natural flow of eloquence; moral sentences dropped from her lips with the naïveté of a child. She had read theology extensively; she was a critic of men and manners, and particularly acquainted with the eccentricities of clergymen, having known many of them intimately. She abounded in aphorisms, wise and witty; she was an excellent reasoner, her logic was most clear. Mr. *Schoolcraft* was perfectly charmed with her society, and very naturally was betrayed into the exposé of his feelings nolens volens.

* * *

In visiting the country, he had made himself familiar with its situation, geographical extent, and resources, having passed over the Alleghany mountains, visited the great valley of the West, and penetrated the great chain of American lakes; and from these various observations he indulged the highest anticipations of the future prosperity and glory of the country, and its final power and influence in the family of nations.

* * *

Mary was now invited by some of the members of Congress and their wives, from South Carolina, to join their party in spending two months at Point Comfort, and she determined to go with them, as the weather was intensely hot. As soon as Mr. *Schoolcraft* heard this arrangement, he instantly offered his hand to *Mary* in marriage, which she accepted; for she had long since ascertained through his tell-tale eye, the intense devotion of his heart; and, moreover, she thoroughly admired the manly simplicity of his manners; the deep sincerity of his mellowed Christian philosophy, the brilliancy of his genius, and last, not least, the physical handsomeness of her lover; and, beside all these stimulants to affection, it must be borne in mind that her orphaned, nay widowed heart (for she had grieved as much for Mr. Fletcher as if she had been his wife) had long yearned for human sympathy.

Mr. *Schoolcraft* was prevented from accompanying his lady-love, as he enthusiastically desired to do, by an imperative call from *New York,* to attend to his children there, who had got into difficulties during his absence.

Mary spent a month of exquisite enjoyment at the before-mentioned "watering place," where she met the most charming society, and was treated with distinguished consideration and friendship, so that she heard her own praises at every corner she turned in the hotel.

But in the midst of this refreshment to her mind and heart, she was hurried back to Carolina by the alarming illness of her sister

Britannia [*Jane*],* where, for seven months, she watched over her with one disease succeeding another, so that, finally, she was almost reduced herself to the same wretched condition that nervous fever had brought *Jane* to—who now, however, began to convalesce, and Mr. *Schoolcraft* arrived from *New York* to be married.

Mr. Lauderdale found out, to his deep chagrin, that all his atrocious calumnies and persecutions had, in the providence of God driven *Mary* out of his parish only to return in conquering triumph; for now she was to be the honored wife of one of *New York's* most resplendent geniuses, whose aristocratic descent and large fortune, and commanding moral and intellectual influence, would place her in the front rank of that noble society she was so fitted to grace.

Mr. Lauderdale immediately called on Mr. *Schoolcraft,* and also sent his wife to request *Mary* to commune again in his church; for she had never been able to get the consent of her feelings to receive the sacrament from the hands of a person she regarded as an unmitigated villain. He also was very anxious to perform the marriage ceremony; but as no other Episcopal clergyman could be, with etiquette, invited without his consent into the parish, *Mary* had already engaged a devotedly pious, gifted minister from another denomination.†

*   *   *

Mary and her husband found themselves ensconced in a comfortable stateroom, on board ship, where they had provided themselves with interesting books; for of course two such gifted, congenial lovers, did not need the society of the passengers, and therefore made arrangements (now that the hurry and bustle of the marriage-feasts and farewells were over) to spend their time quietly together; for hundreds of miles had separated them during their whole engagement. *Mary* was on the tenter-hooks of curiosity to learn her husband's whole previous career in life, and therefore he commenced his narration by enumerating all the circumstances that determined his domestic history. A very rich talented nobleman [*John Johnston*], of England, he said, had, in a spirit of romantic adventure, extended his travels into the wild woods of America, in the year 1800. After canvassing almost this whole continent, in his antiquarian researches, he accidentally became acquainted with the far-famed Indian king, Skenandoah [*Waub-ojeeg*].

Our young nobleman (the Earl of Nottingham) . . . soon

* Jane Howard, wife of Captain Alexander Moultrie of Hickory Hill Plantation, St. Luke's Parish, Beaufort District, S. C. She died July 5, 1848, at the age of thirty-seven and is buried at Grahamville, S. C.

† The Rev. Edward Palmer of the Stoney Creek Presbyterian Church near Walterboro, S. C.

after his acquaintance with the renowned Indian chief, the above-described Skenandoah, fell madly in love with one of his idolized grand-daughters, and begged Skenandoah for her for a wife.

The proud old warrior, greatly flattered, replied—"Oh, yes! you can have Mud-wa-wa-ge-si-co-gua (my music of the heavens), provided you marry her as the pale-faces marry their wives."

The infatuated young man rashly consented to this dangerous amalgamation of races, so that the romance of one of England's proudest Anglo-Saxon sons—one of the descendants of Japheth whom divine prophecy had lifted far above his brothers, Shem and Ham, forever—we find this nobleman's aristocracy culminating in his marriage with a genuine North American Indian squaw, who was, of course, one of the immediate descendants of the oldest families in America.

*   *   *

This Earl of Nottingham had six children by this extraordinary marriage, to all of whom he gave every possible advantage that his high station, wealth, and rich intellectual judgment could procure for them. His first child was a daughter of rare genius and accomplishments; all the rest were sons. As soon as this eccentric young lady took her place in society as a fascinating belle, Mr. *Schoolcraft* made her acquaintance, and his imagination became so electrified with the idea of another edition of the far-famed Pocahontas, that he visited this refined and gifted descendant of a native American king every day; charmed to discover that she not only wrote the tenderest wild poetry, but that pride of her race had excited her to perfect herself in the study of the Indian language. She was the very personation of her mother in her physique and in the modest charm of her bearing, but her mind had received the highest European polish and education.

Roland Walsingham [*Henry Rowe Schoolcraft*], thrown into every-day propinquity with this unique young Hebe, of course fell desperately in love with her; and, obtaining her father's ready consent, he married her just as he had attained a world-wide reputation.

He had by this marriage two children, a son and daughter, that he named Leonora [*Janee*] and Jefferson [*John Johnston*]. No two children on the face of the earth were more unlike in looks and character, although they were both equally talented. The girl had a profusion of golden hair floating in ringlets over shoulders as white and transparent as wax-work. Her eyes were tender, intelligent, and blue as the sky; her limbs were moulded in faultless symmetry, although her stature was delicately unobtrusive.

The boy, on the contrary, was so entirely an Indian in the whole tout ensemble of face and form, and bearing, and character, that the most far-seeing ethnologist could not have discerned a single globule of Anglo-Saxon blood in his dark lowering physiognomy.

*   *   *

Mr. *Schoolcraft* idolized his Pocahontas wife with that patronage that a man feels for a woman who is a child in character and impulse, though he was, nevertheless, often obliged to leave her, month after month, in his scientific explorations of various countries, and even when at home, he lived in his library fascinated with antiquarian and ethnological research; so that he only associated with his family at meals, and on the Sabbath, for no Puritan had ever been more exact than he in the observance of the Lord's day; and he found, in travelling in the woods, that his men were so recruited by this pious rest, that on Monday morning they could undergo double labor.

Mr. *Schoolcraft's* strong-minded mother had protested against his marriage with a descendant of the Indian race; and, indeed, her grief was so inconsolable that she died of a broken heart, for *Henry* had been her pride, her favorite son. The sequel proved how true were her parental instincts, for this amalgamation brought Mr. *Schoolcraft's* "grey hairs in sorrow to the grave."

After he had been married ten or fifteen years, and had enjoyed all the sweets of domestic love and harmony, he noticed that his wife's health became alarmingly prostrated, and that she almost lived in bed. The best physicians were employed—the best nurses engaged—and her Indian mother never left her bedside. At last the horrible fact was elucidated that she had for years indulged excessively in the use of opium, until the habit had become the morbid passion of her every-day existence, and, to hide it from her trusting husband, she had educated her two children in every species of secrecy and cunning, to procure the drug for her without their father's knowledge. She had expended thousands upon thousands to gratify this insane craving for the fascinations of imagination that De Quincey, the opium-eater, has so glowingly described. So that this refined, gifted, plausible, gentle, interesting woman, was the hopeless victim of that accursedly-inebriating, poisonous weed, before her doting husband found it out. He tried every counter-stimulant to the nerves that the most scientific medical skill could culminate, but all in vain. For six years her brilliant mind continued to sink deeper and deeper into inanity; and then she died, leaving a daughter she had educated to regard her father a tyrant, because of his unending watchfulness in trying to prevent an access to his purse, that, in his previous generosity, had been the cause of the ruin of her mind, and the wreck of her body. She died, leaving a son to follow her example in the use of the soul-destroying stimulant of opium.   *   *   *

Mr. *Schoolcraft's* only son, under the unhappy influence of his infatuated mother during his most imitative age, finally brought his father to the grave from remorse, that he had made so suicidal an experiment as to amalgamate in marriage with a race . . . inferior to his own.   *   *   *

Children who have had a mother that never punished, always indulged, and took their part right or wrong, never believe she can have any moral faults or weaknesses; so that, although Mr. *Schoolcraft* had sent his son and daughter away from home to distant schools, expressly because his wife was incapable, during the last six years of her life, of rearing them usefully, they taxed their memories with no souvenirs of their unfortunate mother, except that she had been an angel of kindness to them. So that now we find them, at the respective ages of seventeen and twenty, with little confidence in the love of a father whose wife had made so many concealments from him, and taught them the same want of frankness towards him. Indeed, when these two children heard he had married again, every spark of identity with his interests seemed banished from their sympathies, and their narrow-minded prejudices against a step-mother made them almost detest *Mary* before they ever saw her face. And when, after all the horrors of a stormy voyage, she arrived in *New York,* they received her with saturnine, freezing inhospitality.

Mr. *Schoolcraft,* from the time he became a widower, had broken up housekeeping, and taken a suite of rooms in a hotel; and, the morning after his arrival with his bride being Saturday, he ordered a coach, and took *Mary* out on a shopping excursion to gratify his pride by purchasing innumerable costly presents for his majestic lady-love. He even selected a gem of a bridal bonnet, and all the belongings of a lady's tasteful toilet; and, on Sunday morning, observed to her that, as his new wife, she would be the observed of all observers, among his literary friends who frequented the church to which he belonged. "Now, then," continued he, "Ne-ne-mo-sha, you must look your very prettiest to-day, as an illustration of my taste, in going all the way to the far-off sunny South to choose a ladye-love."

After her husband had dressed himself with more care than he had ever done in his life before (for literary men are proverbially abstracted about the clothes they put on) Mr. *Schoolcraft* repaired to his private parlor, to read his Bible until *Mary* was ready to accompany him to church. Just as she had progressed a little in arranging her toilet, she heard a rap at her door, and it proved to be her step-daughter, who wanted, she said, to warm her feet previous to going to church (though she was all dressed in furs). *Mary* very naturally said: "I am dressing, dear; won't you go to the parlor, where your father is, to warm your feet, as there is a large fire there?" Little did *Mary* dream that this was an unpardonable offence; but so it proved, for *Janee* ran down stairs with the tears streaming from her eyes, and said she had been driven from her own father's chamber-door.   Mr. *Schoolcraft,* with his feelings deeply hurt, rushed up stairs to know if it was possible that a woman he had married expressly to be a true mother to his children, should immediately have manifested such savage unkindness.

Poor *Mary* almost fainted with astonishment, for her impulses were as guiltless as an angel's towards *Janee;* and her proud heart hated to explain the truth, though her good sense finally triumphed, and she did so; but she could not restrain her tears the whole day in church, and never closed her eyes that night; for now she plainly perceived that no purity of intention, no high moral resolves to remove all the errors that the want of a mother's education of these children had engendered, and to strive every day for their happiness and best welfare for time and eternity, that she had vowed to her own heart should be her future vocation; she plainly perceived that such moral elevation would never be appreciated by themselves or their friends in a talented, accomplished step-mother; that her best feelings would be distorted, and all her exertions thrown away through sheer prejudice.

She therefore resolved to do what was right, and leave the judgment of her actions to God; but as her heart could not feel resigned to a thought ever darkening her husband's mind against her, she made him enter into a covenant with her, never to suspect her motives again as long as he lived; and this vow he kept most faithfully; and, perhaps, no husband and wife on this earth ever respected and appreciated each other more than they did ever afterwards.

Janee was so angry at her father's marriage, that she refused to visit any of his friends, with his wife and himself.   Indeed, she made an entire new set of acquaintances, with whom her parents had no congeniality or friendship.   She went to a different church, she excluded herself from the society her father had always been the ornament of, and the prejudiced world at once said her step-mother forced her into the shades of retirement.   While the fact was, that *Mary* made her beautiful presents to betray her into adorning her person, and securing admiration for her talents and accomplishments in company; for she had real genius, highly cultivated by study of the most improving books, and a taste for music, of which she was very fond.

Mary was delighted to see her attract the beaux of *New York*, though, of course, she was very decided as to what circle of civilization they moved in. But nothing could reconcile *Janee* to a stepmother, though *Mary* pardoned her narrow-mindedness, knowing the natural instinct against such an anomalous relation to be almost ineradicable where the children of the first marriage are grown up before the father places over them a second mother.

* * *

Mr. *Schoolcraft's* unpromising son, though only eighteen years of age, proved so morally hopeless in his character and dissipated habits, that his father procured for him a commission in the army, hoping thus to discipline him into regularity of tastes; but he passionately and stubbornly refused to accept the situation; and then his despairing father yielded to his earnest entreaty to become a merchant, and placed him with a great mercantile house in *New York*.

In the meantime, Mr. *Schoolcraft*, like most literary men, had trusted all his money matters to agents, and he awoke one morning to learn that three hundred thousand dollars worth of property had been squandered by their breach of trust to him, so that he seemed inextricably ruined. A week or two, however, after this calamitous discovery, he received the most flattering offers of employment for his talents in *Washington*.*

We find him then, transferred to Washington, District of Columbia, and a perfect enthusiast in his literary labors.

* * *

Mr. *Schoolcraft* now received letters so appalling as to the career of his talented son, whom he had left in a mercantile house in *New York*, that he requested a friend who was returning to *Washington* after a long absence abroad, to bring *Johnston Schoolcraft* along with him. Oh! how the father's heart was wrung when the unfortunate young man arrived in Washington—for intemperance, debauchery, and gambling had left their usual stereotyped mark on his wrecked form and withered countenance. Soon letters arrived from *New York* that he had used his father's honored name to obtain fabulous sums of money from the most prominent persons of Mr.

* A reference to some such financial situation is made by Mary Howard Schoolcraft in a letter written at Washington, D. C., March 21, 1847, to Mr. Schoolcraft in New York, where he was superintending the transfer of their belongings: "Jane, & yourself, can both appreciate what we will need, in keeping house as primitively as we expect to do."

Schoolcraft's acquaintance. It was indeed wonderful how this irresponsible young spendthrift had been able to deceive the most practical business men, so as to realize the largest drafts on the strength of innumerable false pretences. But his Indian dignity and modesty of bearing, and his imperturbability of countenance, presented an effectual shield against suspecting so highly educated a gentleman.

Indeed, he often boasted of his extraordinary talents in this respect, and confessed that with many common people, he had obtained moneyed sympathy by abusing his step-mother—and then, again, praising her when conversing with the most refined and morally elevated whom he intended to take a toll from, on account of their great respect for his father.

Mary's pride was so tortured (for it was impossible to refund the enormous sums of money thus swindled out of her husband's most appreciating friends) that she shut herself up in her chamber three days and three nights, in an anguish of mind, too intolerable for any consolation—for this insane gambler was her husband's only son, and bore his father's venerated name. Fasting and praying to God for help in this dire calamity, she besieged heaven to sustain her poor hopeless husband, whose intensely absorbing grief brought on a derangement of the whole nervous system, and in one week he was struck down with paralysis that no medical skill could reach.

Johnston, who daily witnessed the misery he had brought upon the whole family, was still not in the least weaned from his darling vices. Indeed, he seemed as insensible as a marble statue to every interest save that of selfish indulgence. Conscience never appeared to speak loud enough to arrest his attention even for a moment.

*　　*　　*

Johnston, while his noble father lay helpless and prostrate on his bed, waiting for death, *Johnston Schoolcraft* still kept running around and inventing new schemes for obtaining money from the friends of *Mary* and her now imprisoned husband; while these said friends respected them too much to publicly prosecute this infatuated member of their family.

*　　*　　*

Mary thoroughly believed in the expulsive power of a new affection in the heart of man, so she not only prayed and fasted before God, night and day, for the regeneration of her miserable step-son; but she also determined to wean him from vice by expending every energy on making his home pleasant to him. Whenever she could leave her helpless husband, she would run out and purchase presents so as to secure a recherché wardrobe for *Johnston,* "for dress has a moral effect upon the conduct of mankind. . . ."

Mary furnished a delightful chamber, and innumerable books and writing materials, and encouraged this morally sick patient to write criticisms of new works, that at one time he was very gifted in analyzing. She invited young ladies to stay with her to amuse him in the evenings, and she bought games for them to play with him, and taught him chess as the most interesting of them all. She required from her servants the most scrupulous deference to his orders, even to the neglect of her own. She sent for the best physicians to consult together about the propriety of carrying this not only morally, but physically, diseased young man, through a course of mercury, as an alterative to his shattered constitution. But the end of all these godlike exertions to rescue this poor fellow from the bottomless pit of infamy in this world and the next, was, that *Johnston Schoolcraft* broke open the safe where all his father's gold was deposited, and then ran away with the accumulated treasure from the sale of his works of the patient industry of Mr. *Schoolcraft;* leaving him hopelessly paralyzed, with no means of recruiting his scattered fortune. *Mary* and her husband never heard of him afterwards.* Thus was Mr. *Schoolcraft's* wise mother's prescience of the danger of amalgamation with a different race from his own, brought home to him in his advancing years with the arbitrariness of prophecy. * * *

Mr. *Schoolcraft,* in spite of his mother's superior age and experience, warning him against amalgamation with other races in marriage, thought the union of the American aborigines with the noble Anglo-Saxon would produce the highest specimen of humanity; and, with ethnological enthusiasm, he had given *Janee* and *Johnston* every advantage that education, travel, and the best society could germinate.

Mary, being settled in Washington as her home, now carried out her affectionate desire of introducing her step-mother's only daughter, Gulielma (*Sarah Rebecca*),† into the court atmosphere of the grand metropolis of the United States. She therefore sent to Carolina for this beautiful half-sister to come and live with her, and Mr. *Schoolcraft* was delighted with the arrangement.

* * *

Her (*Mary's*) whole mind was set on one absorbing idea, and that was to employ every gift she possessed in contriving amuse-

* This is a fictitious detail.

† Sarah Rebecca Howard, born at Grahamville, South Carolina, 1825; died 1902, unmarried. "Aunt Sal was a great deal with them and it was at their home in Washington she met the most distinguished men of that day."—Manuscript autobiography of Mrs. Thomas Heyward Howard.

ments out of the library for her long-imprisoned husband, who was a constant wonder to her, from the Christian philosophy with which he sat down, chained to his seat, every day for ten or twelve years, without a murmur, though his brain was clear as the sunlight, his body without a pain, and his high-mettled spirit as vaulting as ever in its interest in politics, patriotism, literature, and everything worthy of a genial philosopher's consideration. No man would have revelled more wholesomely than he in his former extraordinary powers of locomotion. And yet when that gift, so common to all men, was hopelessly withdrawn from him, he seemed to be so content as almost to demonstrate gratitude that God, who had given him so many blessings, should only have visited him with painless bodily disability. Such a manly, dignified, edifying Christian philosophy, under such a tantalizing bereavement of locomotive energy, made the morally appreciating *Mary* venerate him as Eve did her husband, before he was stripped of his god-like attributes.

Janee was now engaged to be married to a man of renown in the literary world; but the very week before the bridal ceremony was to take place, he died;* and *Mary,* fearing the effect of this disappointment, induced *Sarah* to visit Carolina, and take *Janee* along with her for six months.

In an incredibly short time, *Janee* had captivated another beau; and through the infallible expulsive power of a new affection, she felt it very plausible to marry him.

*   *   *

And who do you think, dear reader, was *Janee's* affianced? Why actually the most idolized and youngest brother of *Mary* herself; so that she was now to be placed in the droll position of mother and sister to her step-daughter, and mother and sister to a handsome brother she had been devoted to from his birth. She did not like the contradictory consanguinity that Cupid had so suddenly culminated; but as her husband was delighted with the match, she sent to Carolina for her mercurial pet brother,† a month after *Janee* had returned home to Washington.

In order to frustrate this young lover in his arrangements for going off to California to make a fortune, and then to return in three years, bringing twenty hundred pounds of gold dust to lay on the

* A footnote on page 352 states that the author's stepdaughter was engaged to be married to the celebrated poet, Charles Fenno Hoffman, who, just one week before his bridal day, became a raving maniac.

† Benjamin Screven Howard, born at Orange Grove, Hogg's Neck Plantation, near Grahamville, S. C., in 1823 or 1824. He survived Jane Schoolcraft and may have remarried and be buried at Fredericksburg, Va.

altar of Hymen—or rather, then to get married, and go to house-keeping—Mary determined to get the magnificent, gigantic, Adonis lover a place under the Government . . . and . . . after six months of extraordinary exertions *Benjamin* received a plausible office.

Though she [*Mary*] thoroughly despised Mr. and Mrs. Jellabee, the hypocritical abolitionists, *Janee* insisted that he should be the officiating clergyman. In a week after the bride and groom had been united in marriage, Mrs. Jellabee influenced *Janee* and *Benjamin* to leave Mr. *Schoolcraft's* large, elegantly furnished house, and go to board with a private family who were the enemies of her father and *Mary*. . . . *Mary* and her husband . . . could not at all hold intercourse with *Janee* and her husband, while they lived voluntarily with the enemies of their parents.

*　　*　　*

Janee and *Benjamin,* having lost many children, now became true penitents for their folly in listening to Mrs. Jellabee's advice, and forsaking their renowned father, Mr. *Schoolcraft,* in his severe bodily helplessness; and now, profiting by all the elevated examples of *Mary,* and her unwearied efforts to instil proper sentiments into their hearts and minds, they became most excellent Christians, and a comfort ever afterwards to their pious parents.

In all *Mary's* trials, God had spared her one, that she shuddered even to think of; her husband's brain was not in the least affected by his paralysis of body; indeed he seemed brighter in his intellect than ever, and the physician told her that a man who had the gout, or any ailment of his extremities, would be clearer and stronger in his head. She therefore became his amanuensis, and thus enabled him to publish works that will immortalize him forever. Poor fellow, he was so proud of his South Carolina wife, and her romantic adhesiveness to him, for better, for worse, for richer, for poorer, in sickness, and in health, that he found at the bottom of that ancient Pandora's box of evils, that blessed gift of hope, that seemed to circumvent every dart aimed at his heart, even by the grim tyrant Death.

Note.—As this book goes to press, the fact is finally established that Mary E. Howard was born Mary E. Hogg, youngest child of Elizabeth Bowles and James Hogg, Jr. (1778–1825). Her father changed his name from Hogg to Howard about 1815. His eldest surviving child, James E. Hogg, retained that name. The next son, John H. Hogg, became a general in the United States Army; then, afterward, was known as General John H. Howard. The four children of James Hogg-Howard's second marriage went by the name of Howard, as did the youngest two children of his first wife, Jane H. Howard and Mary E. Howard.

A BIBLIOGRAPHY OF HENRY ROWE SCHOOLCRAFT

The following has been prepared with the definite purpose of assembling information for the use of scholars and others who may be interested in pursuing the subject. A special effort has been made to present as exhaustive a list as possible, at this time, of all material, published and unpublished, by or about or concerning Schoolcraft. His frequent resort to pseudonyms, and the distribution of his writings among a great number and variety of periodicals, including newspapers, combine with other factors to make this an interesting field for further research.

BIOGRAPHICAL AND CRITICAL MATERIAL

Biographical Dictionaries, Encyclopedias

American encyclopedia. New York, D. Appleton & co., 1879. v. 8, p. 10.

Appleton's cyclopaedia of American biography. New York, D. Appleton & co., 1888. v. 5, p. 425–26.

Dictionary of American biography. 1935. v. 16, p. 456–57.

Johnson's new universal cyclopedia. New York, 1879.

National cyclopaedia of American biography. 1894. v. 5, p. 145.

Notable Americans. Boston, 1904. v. 9, in alphabetical position.

Books, Pamphlets

Austin, George L. Henry Wadsworth Longfellow. Boston, Lee and Shepard, 1888. p. 320–31.

Blois, John. Gazetteer. Detroit, 1838. (Mentions general indebtedness to Schoolcraft, quotes him briefly, p. vi, 170, 172.)

Brower, J. V. The Mississippi river and its sources. Minneapolis, Minnesota historical society. Collections, v. 7, 1893. 352 p. (Contains section on H. R. Schoolcraft, with pencil sketch of Jane Johnston Schoolcraft, p. 142–50.)

Bryce, George. The remarkable history of the Hudson's Bay Company. London, England, Sampson Low Marston & co., 1902. p. 332–33.

Catalogue of the books, pamphlets, autograph letters, original manuscripts, documents, &c. belonging to the late Henry R. Schoolcraft, the Indian historian, and to Mrs. [Mary H.] Schoolcraft . . . to be sold at auction . . . November 15 and 16, 1880, by Bangs and co. [New York, 1880] 34 p.

Dole, Nathan H.   Introduction to "The song of Hiawatha." (In: Longfellow, H. W.   The song of Hiawatha.   New York, Thomas Y. Crowell & co., 1899.)   (Contains a discussion of relationship to the "Kalevala," p. iii–xiii.)

Duponceau, Peter S.   Mémoire sur le système grammatical des langues de quelques nations indiennes de l'Amérique du Nord.   Paris, France, 1838.   p. 131–47.

Eaton, Amos.   An index to the geology of the Northern States . . . wholly written over anew and published under the direction of the Troy lyceum.   Troy, N. Y., 1820.   (Contains extract from Schoolcraft's communication read before the Troy lyceum on the subject of sandstone, limestone and other geological evidence in Missouri, Mississippi, and Arkansas, in footnote on p. 226–28; also references on p. x, 50, 111, 186, 233, 262, 268.)

Farmer, Silas.   History of Detroit and Wayne county and early Michigan.   3rd ed.   Detroit, pub. by S. Farmer & co., for Munsell & co., New York, 1890.

Fowle, Otto.   Sault Ste. Marie and its great waterway.   New York & London, G. P. Putnam's sons, 1925.   458 p.

Gilbert, E. W.   The exploration of western America, 1800–1850: an historical geography.   Cambridge, England, University Press, 1933.   p. 194–96.

Gregg, Arthur B.   Old Hellebergh—historical sketches of the West Manor of Rensselaerswyck, including an account of the anti-rent wars, the glass house, and Henry R. Schoolcraft.   Altamont, N. Y., Altamont Enterprise, 1936.   192 p.   p. 176–88 *et al.*

Griswold, Rufus W.   Henry Rowe Schoolcraft.   (In: The prose writers of America.   Philadelphia, Carey & Hart, 1849.   p. 298–302.)

Hoyt, Charles O., and Ford, R. Clyde.   John D. Pierce, founder of the Michigan school system.   Ypsilanti, Mich., 1905.

Jameson, Anna B.   Winter studies and summer rambles.   New York, Wiley and Putnam, 1839.   2 v.   (Describes visit with School-crafts in 1837.   This section is reprinted in: Michigan history maga-zine, v. 8, p. 140–69, April, 1924.)

Kappler, Charles J.   Indian affairs, laws and treaties.   Washington, D. C., Government printing office.   4 v.   (v. 2 contains text of treaties witnessed and signed by Schoolcraft.)

Lewis, Janet.   The invasion: a narrative of events concerning the Johnston family of St. Mary's.   New York, Harcourt, Brace and co., 1932.   356 p.   (Gives an intimate presentation of Schoolcraft's family life at Sault Ste. Marie and Mackinac Island, with pictorial map of region.)

Longfellow, Henry W.   The complete poetical works of Henry

Wadsworth Longfellow. Cambridge edition. Boston and New York, Houghton Mifflin co., 1863. 689 p. p. 113–64, 664–67.

Longfellow, Henry W. The song of Hiawatha. Boston, Houghton Mifflin co., 1883. 193 p. (Contains an informative introductory note, and an essay by Alice M. Longfellow.)

Longfellow, Samuel. Life of Henry Wadsworth Longfellow, with extracts from his journals and correspondence. Boston, Ticknor and co., 1886. v. 2, p. 247ff.

McKenney, Thomas L. Sketches of a tour to the lakes, of the character and customs of the Chippewa Indians, and of incidents connected with the treaty of Fond du Lac. Baltimore, Md., Fielding Lucas, 1827. 493 p.

Merrill, George P. Contributions to the history of American geology. No. 135. From the report of the U. S. National Museum for 1904. Washington, D. C., Government printing office, 1906. p. 239–45, 260, 262–64.

Nichols, Frances. Index to H. R. Schoolcraft's "Historical and statistical information, respecting the history, condition and prospects of the Indian tribes of the United States." Washington, D. C., Bureau of American ethnology, Smithsonian institution, 1942.

Paullin, Charles O. Atlas of the historical geography of the United States. Published jointly by Carnegie institution of Washington and the American geographical society of New York, 1932. p. 20, plate 39B.

Sabin, Joseph. A dictionary of books relating to America . . . v. 19, p. 53–63. (Lists some fifty of Schoolcraft's publications and gives interesting bibliographical notes about them.)

Samson, George W. Henry R. Schoolcraft. Washington, D. C., Chronicle print, 1864(?). 8 p. (Dr. Samson's remarks at the funeral services of H. R. Schoolcraft.)

Schoolcraft, Mrs. Henry R. (Mary E. Howard). The black gauntlet: a tale of plantation life in South Carolina. Philadelphia, J. B. Lippincott & co., 1860. p. 467–559.

Schoolcraft, Mrs. Henry R. (Mary E. Howard). The fire at the Central Hotel. Washington, D. C., 1867(?). 6 p. (A tribute to Charles Lullay.)

Sketches of the life of Henry R. Schoolcraft. (In: Schoolcraft, H. R. Personal memoirs . . . . Philadelphia, 1851. p. xxvii–xlviii.)

Steele, Eliza R. A summer journey in the west. New York, John S. Taylor and co., 1841.

Struve, Heinrich von. Beitrage zur Mineralogie u. Geologie des Nordlichen America's nach Amerikanischen Zeitschriften. Hamburg, Germany, 1822. 124 p. (Contains abstract of Schoolcraft's account, in American journal of science and arts, of native copper on southern shore of Lake Superior.)

Ten Brook, Andrew.   American state universities . . . a particular account of the rise and development of the University of Michigan . . . .   Cincinnati, O., Robert Clarke & co., 1875.

Whiting, Henry.   Remarks, on the supposed tides . . . of the . . . lakes.   (In: Historical and scientific sketches of Michigan . . . Detroit, 1834.)   (This includes a letter from Schoolcraft to Whiting, written from Detroit, Jan. 19, 1831.)

Williamson, Scott G.   The American craftsman.   New York, Crown publishers, 1940.   p. 195.

Wood, Edwin O.   Historic Mackinac.   New York, Macmillan co., 1918.   2 v., 697 and 773 p.

Youmans, William J., ed.   Henry Rowe Schoolcraft.   (In his: Pioneers of science in America.   New York, D. Appleton and co., 1896.   p. 300–10.)   (Biographical sketch.)

Periodical Articles

American historians—Henry Rowe Schoolcraft.   (In: Historical magazine, v. 9, no. 5, p. 137–40, May, 1865.)

Baker, James H.   The sources of the Mississippi.   Their discoverers, real and pretended.   (In: Minnesota historical society. Collections, v. 6, p. 1–22, 1894.)   (Defends Schoolcraft's claim.)

Barnes, D. H.   Species of bivalves collected in the northwest, by Mr. Schoolcraft and Captain Douglass, on the expedition to the sources of the Mississippi, in 1820.   (In: American journal of science and arts, v. 6, p. 120, 259.)

Boutwell, William T.   Schoolcraft's exploring tour of 1832. (In: Minnesota historical society.   Collections, v. 1, p. 153–76, 1872.)   (Extracts from Boutwell's journal.)

Gagnieur, William F.   What the Indians knew about Manistique and Schoolcraft county.   (In: Michigan history magazine, v. 10, p. 350–52, 357, July, 1926.)   (Contains a sketch of Schoolcraft.)

Gilbert, Mrs. Thomas D.   Memories of the Soo.   (In: Michigan pioneer and historical society.   Collections, v. 30, p. 623–33, 1906.)

Henry R. Schoolcraft.   (In: Association of American geographers.   Annals, v. 20, p. 120; v. 22, p. 129, 136.)   (Brief mentions.)

Henry R. Schoolcraft.   (In: Burton historical collection.   Leaflet, v. 1, no. 1, p. 1–16, Jan., 1922.)

Henry Rowe Schoolcraft.   (In: International magazine, v. 3, p. 300–2, June, 1851.)   (With portrait.)

Henry Rowe Schoolcraft. (In: National magazine, v. 6, p. 1–6, Jan., 1855.) (With portrait.)

Holden, Mrs. J. Rose. Historical data re state and church in Wentworth county. (In: Wentworth historical society. Journal and transactions, Hamilton, Canada, v. 3, p. 58–60, 1902.)

Holmes, J. C. The Michigan state historical society. (In: Michigan pioneer and historical society. Collections, v. 12, p. 316–50, 1888.)

Jameson, Anna B. (The description, in her "Winter studies and summer rambles," of a visit with the Schoolcrafts in 1837, is reprinted in: Michigan history magazine, v. 8, p. 140–69, April, 1924.)

Jenks, William L. History and meaning of the county names of Michigan. (In: Michigan pioneer and historical society. Collections, v. 38, p. 439–78, 1912.)

Kinietz, Vernon. Schoolcraft's manuscript magazines. (In: Bibliographical society of America. Papers, v. 35, p. 151–54, 1941.)

Lea, Isaac. Freshwater shells collected in the valleys of the Fox and Wisconsin, in 1820, by Mr. Schoolcraft. Read before the American philosophical society Mar. 16, 1832. (In: American philosophical society. Transactions, v. 5, article 2, sec. K, p. 37, plate III, fig. 9 &c, 1837.)

Michigan, University of. Board of regents. Proceedings, 1837–1864. Ann Arbor, Mich., 1915.

Mitchill, Samuel L. Description of two mammiferous animals of North America. (In: Medical repository, New York, v. 21—new series, v. 6, p. 248–49, 1821.)

Mitchill, Samuel L. The proteus of the North-American lakes. (In: American journal of science and arts, v. 4, no. 1, p. 181–83, 1822.)

Orians, G. H. The souvenir of the lakes. (In: Historical society of northwestern Ohio. Quarterly bulletin, v. 11, nos. 2 and 3, Apr. and July, 1939.) (Reprint, with foreword, of gift book probably compiled by Schoolcraft.) (Also issued as a separate.)

Ormsbee, Thomas H., and Allen, Florence C. Glassmaking at Lake Dunmore, Vermont. (In: American collector, New York City, v. 6, p. 6–7, Aug., 1937; p. 6, 7, 19, Sept., 1937.)

Osborn, Chase S. Longfellow-Schoolcraft-Ojibway special edition, Evening News, Sault Ste. Marie, Mich. Feb. 27, 1940.

Osborn, Chase S. and Stella B. A vital figure in early American education (with sketch from portrait). (In: Quarterly review of the Michigan alumnus, Ann Arbor, Mich., v. 48, no. 15, p. 129–38, Feb. 21, 1942.) (A chapter from their "Schoolcraft-Longfellow-Hiawatha.") (Also issued as a reprint, 12 p.)

Pettibone, Levi. With Schoolcraft in southwest Missouri in 1818. (In: Missouri historical society. Collections, v. 2, p. 46–51, Jan., 1900.)

Schramm, Wilbur L. Hiawatha and its predecessors. (In: Philological quarterly, Iowa City, Ia., v. 11, no. 4, p. 321–43, Oct., 1932.) (The "Kalevala" and Schoolcraft and other American sources for material and meter of "Hiawatha.")

Sketch of Henry Rowe Schoolcraft. (In: Annals of Iowa, v. 3, p. 495–503, July, 1865.)

Sketch of Henry R. Schoolcraft (with portrait). (In: Popular science monthly magazine, v. 37, p. 113–21, May, 1890.)

Soule, Anna M. The southern and western boundaries of Michigan. (In: Michigan pioneer and historical society. Collections, v. 27, p. 378–84, 1896.)

Streeter, Floyd B. Henry Rowe Schoolcraft. (In: American collector, Metuchen, N. J., v. 5, p. 2–8, Oct., 1927.) (Brief bibliography with biographical introduction.)

Torrey, John. Notice of the plants collected by Professor D. B. Douglass . . . in the expedition . . . during the summer of 1820, around the Great Lakes and the upper waters of the Mississippi. . . . (In: American journal of science and arts, v. 4, no. 1, p. 56, 1822.)

White, Harry H. Henry Rowe Schoolcraft, glassmaker. (In: Antiques, v. 34, no. 6, p. 301–3, Dec., 1938; v. 35, no. 2, p. 81–83, Feb., 1939, no. 4, p. 186–88, Apr., 1939.)

Williams, Meade C. The old mission church of Mackinac Island. (In: Michigan pioneer and historical society. Collections, v. 28, p. 191, 1900.)

Winchell, N. H. (and Howard, Jane Schoolcraft). Henry Rowe Schoolcraft. (In: American geologist, v. 5, p. 1–9, Jan., 1890.) (Sketch of Schoolcraft, with autographed portrait and 2-page bibliography.)

Woolsey, M. Letters on Lake Superior. (In: Southern literary messenger, v. 2, no. 3, p. 166–71, Feb., 1836.) (Mr. Woolsey accompanied Schoolcraft in 1831, as a volunteer, seeking health.)

Woolson, Constance Fenimore. The old agency. (In: The galaxy, New York, v. 18, p. 804–15, Dec., 1874.)

Printed Documents

United States. Statutes. (Contain the texts of the treaties listed below.) (The texts of these are also printed in v. 2 of Charles J. Kappler's "Indian affairs, laws and treaties." The original treaties are in the State Department files of the National Archives.) Treaties that Henry R. Schoolcraft was witness to:

With Chippewas, June 16, 1820 (7 Stat. 206)

With Sioux, Chippewas, Sacs and Foxes, Menominees, Iowas, Winnebagos, Ottawas, and Potawatamis, August 19, 1825 (7 Stat. 272)

With Chippewas, August 5, 1826 (7 Stat. 290)

With Chippewas, Menominees, and Winnebagos, August 11, 1827 (7 Stat. 303)

Treaties that Henry R. Schoolcraft was signer of:

With Ottawas and Chippewas, March 28, 1836 (7 Stat. 491)

With Chippewas, Swan Creek and Black River bands, May 9, 1836 (7 Stat. 503)

With Chippewas, January 14, 1837 (7 Stat. 528)

With Chippewas, December 20, 1837 (7 Stat. 547)

With Chippewas, January 23, 1838 (7 Stat. 565)

United States. Statutes. An act of Congress, requiring the Secretary of War to collect and digest such statistics and materials as may illustrate the history, the present condition, and future prospects of the Indian tribes of the United States, March 3, 1847 (9 Stat. 203–4). (Printed in: Acts of the 29th Congress. Washington, D. C., C. Alexander.   p. 137.)

Papers

Canada, Dominion of.   References to Schoolcraft, and an occasional letter by him, are to be found in the records of the British Indian agencies at Malden and Drummond Island, among the papers of the Department of Indian Affairs in the public archives at Ottawa; in various other collections in the public archives there, and at Montreal and Toronto; in the papers of the Redpath Library of McGill University, Montreal; and in the archiepiscopal archives of Canada in the archbishop's palace in Quebec.

Dougherty, Rev. Peter.   Manuscript diary written at Mackinac Island, 1838.   v. 1.   (In files of Michigan historical collections, Ann Arbor, Mich.)

Ferry, Rev. William M. and Amanda W.   Papers.   Typed copies of personal letters, many from Mackinac Island, with notes by members of the family.   v. 1, 1823–1831.   (In files of Michigan historical collections, Ann Arbor, Mich.)

Howard, Mrs. Thomas Heyward.   Manuscript autobiography. (In possession of her son, John W. Howard, Savannah, Georgia.)

Schoolcraft, Mary Howard.   Letters to her brother, General John Howard.   (In possession of Mrs. Georgia H. Dove, Garden Apts., Baltimore, Md.)

Shearman, Francis W.   Address (presumably given in Mar-

shall, Mich., prior to the Civil War).   (In files of Michigan historical collections, Ann Arbor, Mich.)

Taliaferro, Lawrence.   Papers.   (In files of Minnesota historical society, Saint Paul, Minn.)

Tunick, Irve.   Discovering the source of the Mississippi river.
(Manuscript of radio dramatization presented by the United States
Office of education, Federal security agency, for the Smithsonian in-
stitution, in "The world is yours" series, Oct. 13, 1940, over N. B. C.)

Works Written by Schoolcraft

Books, Pamphlets

An address at Aurora, Cayuga county, New York, before an
association of young men for investigating the Iroquois history.
Auburn, N. Y., 1846.   35 p.

An address delivered before the Chippewa county temperance
society, on the influence of ardent spirits, on the condition of the
North American Indians . . . May 8th, 1832.   Detroit, printed by
Geo. L. Whitney, 1832.   13 p.   (Noticed in: American journal of
science and arts, v. 24, p. 190.)   (Reprinted in: Oneóta, p. 413–25.)

An address delivered before the Was-ah Ho-de-no-son-ne or
New Confederacy of the Iroquois . . . at its third annual council,
August 14, 1845 . . . .   Rochester, N. Y., printed by Jerome &
brother, 1846.   48 p.   (The volume contains also: Genundewah, a
poem, by W. H. C. Hosmer . . . pronounced on the same occasion.
Sabin gives the date of delivery of the address as August 14, 1846.)

Algic researches, comprising inquiries respecting the mental
characteristics of the North American Indians.   First series.   Indian
tales and legends . . . .   New-York, Harper & brothers, 1839.   2 v.,
248 and 244 p.   No more published.   Later edition with some additions and omissions (Phila., 1856) pub. as: The myth of Hiawatha.
(Reviewed in North American review, v. 49, p. 354–72, 1839; also in
Journal of education, Marshall, Mich., v. 2, p. 40, July, 1839.)

Alhalla; or, the lord of Talladega.   A tale of the Creek war.
With some selected miscellanies, chiefly of early date.   By Henry
Rowe Colcraft.   New York & London, Wiley and Putnam, 1843.
116 p.   In verse.   (*Note*—Colcraft, or Calcraft, was the old family
name of the Schoolcrafts.)   (Contains fifteen poems.)

The American Indians.   Their history, condition and prospects,
from original notes and manuscripts . . . .   Together with an appendix, containing thrilling narratives, daring exploits, etc. etc.   New
revised edition.   Auburn, N. Y., 1850.   495 p.   Also: Rochester,
N. Y., Wanzer, Foot and co., 1851.   495 p.   Also: Buffalo, N. Y.,
George H. Derby and co., 1851.   495 p.   (Originally issued, 1844–
45, in eight paper-covered nos. with title: Oneóta . . . .   After-

wards issued under various titles. The present work was a new edition, with some additions, of the material published under the title: The Indian in his wigwam. In 1853 it was reissued under the title: Western scenes and reminiscences.)

Annual report of the acting superintendent of Indian affairs for Michigan, made to the Bureau of Indian affairs at Washington at the close of the fiscal year, 30th Sept., 1840. Detroit, Asahel S. Bagg, printer, 1840. 28 p. (Also in: Annual report of the commissioner of Indian affairs, 1840.)

Archives of aboriginal knowledge. Containing all the original papers laid before Congress respecting the history, antiquities, language, ethnology, pictography, rites, superstitions, and mythology, of the Indian tribes of the United States. Philadelphia, J. B. Lippincott & co., 1860. 6 v., paged as follows: xxviii, 13–575; xxiv, 17–614; 642; xxvi, 19–674; 718; xxviii, 25–756. A reissue of his: Historical and statistical information . . . 1851–57, with new titles and some additional pages.

A bibliographical catalogue of books, translations of the Scriptures, and other publications in the Indian tongues of the United States, with brief critical notices. (Anon.) Washington, D. C., C. Alexander, 1849. 27 p. Half title: Literature of the Indian language. (Lists 139 books and tracts owned by Schoolcraft. A reprint, expanded to 150 titles, is in v. 4, p. 523–51 of: Information respecting the history, condition and prospects of the Indian tribes of the United States . . . 1854.)

Constitution of the Algic society, instituted March 28, 1832, for encouraging missionary effort in evangelizing the north western tribes . . . to which is annexed an abstract of its proceedings, together with an introductory address by Henry R. Schoolcraft, Esq., president . . . . Detroit, Cleland & Sawyer, 1833. 23 p.

A curt history of the United States after the Hebraic manner. (In: The knickerbocker gallery, New York, 1855, p. 421–31.)

Cyclopedia Indianensis: or, A general description of the Indian tribes of North and South America . . . . By Henry R. Schoolcraft, assisted by a number of literary and scientific gentlemen in America and Europe. In 8 nos., to make 2 vols. royal 8 vo., 700 pages each. New-York, Platt and Peters, 1842. University press, John F. Trow, printer. 16 p. (A prospectus of a work never published.)

A discourse delivered on the anniversary of the historical society of Michigan, June 4, 1830 . . . . Detroit, printed by Geo. L. Whitney, 1830. 44 p. (Noticed in American journal of science and arts, v. 20, p. 166, 1831.) (Also in: Historical and scientific sketches of Michigan . . . . Detroit, 1834. p. 51–109.)

[A discourse before the Michigan historical society in 1831 . . . . Detroit, printed by Geo. L. Whitney, 1831. 59 p. (This item, listed by Sabin, apparently was an error. The Library of Congress in August, 1938, circularized all of its 63 cooperating libraries for information regarding it, but received no reply. Leading booksellers find no trace of such an item. Only four addresses were given before the Michigan historical society before its first activities lapsed. Of these Schoolcraft gave the one in 1830. In 1831, Schoolcraft gave an address before the Detroit lyceum. This Sabin lists as a third item, but it is likely the address erroneously recorded as a discourse before the Michigan historical society in 1831.)]

The enchanted moccasins, and other legends of the Americans (sic) Indians. Comp. from original sources by Cornelius Mathews . . . (Ed. 3) New York, Pulvanis, 1877. 338 p. (Original ed. pub. in 1869 as: The Indian fairy book.)

Expedition to the north-west Indians. Letter from the Secretary of War transmitting a map and report of Lieut. Allen and H. R. Schoolcraft's visit to the north-west Indians in 1832. (Washington, D. C., 1834.) 68 p. (Also pub. as government document.)

Extracts from a lecture delivered before the Detroit lyceum . . . relative to the natural history of Michigan. (In: Historical and scientific sketches of Michigan . . . . Detroit, 1834. p. 177–91.) (Delivered Jan. 27, 1831. Extracts originally printed in Detroit journal and Michigan advertiser, Feb. 16, 1831; corrections, Feb. 23, 1831, p. 2, col. 3; lecture in full, May 4, 1831.)

Helderbergia: or, The apotheosis of the heroes of the antirent war. Albany, N. Y., J. Munsell, 1855. 54 p. A poem.

Historical and statistical information respecting the history, condition and prospects of the Indian tribes of the United States. Collected and prepared under the direction of the Bureau of Indian affairs, per act of Congress of March 3d, 1847 . . . Illustrated by S. Eastman, Capt. U.S.A. Philadelphia, Lippincott, Grambo & co., 1851–57. 6 parts, as follows: Part I, 1851. Half title, "Ethnological researches . . ." iii–xviii, 13–568 p. Part II, 1852. Half title, "Ethnological researches . . ." (2), vii–xxiv, 17–608 p. Part III, 1853. Half title, "Ethnological researches . . ." v–635 p. Part IV, 1854. Half title, "Ethnological researches . . ." v–xxvi, 19–668 p. Part V, 1855. Half title, "Ethnological researches . . ." vii–712 p. Part VI, 1857. Half title, "General history of the North American Indians." (2), vii–xxviii, 25–756 p. (Reviewed adversely in North American review, v. 77, p. 245–62, July, 1853.) Later ed. has title: Information respecting the history . . . .*

* "The bibliographer's task is complicated by a change in printers during the course of the publication of the first edition and particularly by

Incentives to the study of the ancient period of American history. An address, delivered before the New-York historical society, at its forty-second anniversary, 17th November, 1846 . . . . New York, Press of the historical society, 1847. 38 p. (Also in: New-York historical society. Proceedings, 1846, bound in at end.)

The Indian fairy book. From the original legends. With illustrations by (John) McLenan. Engraved by (A. V. S.) Anthony. New York, Mason brothers, 1856. 338 p. (Legends originally collected and published in "Algic researches," 1839, and "The myth of Hiawatha," 1856, with many verbal changes by the editor, as well as changes of title.) Also, another edition. New York, Mason brothers, 1857. Also, another edition (published under the name of the editor, Cornelius Mathews). New York, Allen brothers, 1869. Also: The Indian fairy book, from the original legends; with eight illustrations in color by Florence Choate and Elizabeth Curtis. New York, Frederick A. Stokes co. (ca. 1916). 303 p.

The Indian in his wigwam, or, Characteristics of the red race of America . . . . New York, W. H. Graham, 1847. 416 p. Also, another edition. New York, W. H. Graham, 1848. 416 p. Also, another edition. Buffalo: Derby & Hewson, 1848. 416 p. (Frontispiece title: The red race of America . . . . Originally issued as:

---

the use of engraved and printed title pages in each volume which do not agree with each other or with the bastard title.

"The first volume of the first edition bore the title *Historical and statistical information respecting the history, condition and prospects of the Indian tribes of the United States.* The first three words of the title were dropped in the second and through the fifth volumes. The government stopped its subsidy of this work when the fifth volume came out but subsequently the sixth volume was brought out by the J. B. Lippincott and Co., successors to Lippincott, Grambo and Co. The first volume was also reprinted with the same title as the following volumes. Years of publication were I (1851) [2d printing 1853], II (1852), III (1853), IV (1854), V (1855), VI (1857).

"Then in 1860 the J. B. Lippincott and Co. brought out a reissue of the work with the title *Archives of Aboriginal Knowledge.* The engraved title page of this issue, however, was the same as the revised one of the previous edition. The text otherwise was the same page for page, but there was an index added to each volume.

"I should have added above that the publishing house brought out the first edition in two forms, one on thinner and slightly smaller paper than the other. In this smaller form, however, only the first five volumes were published."—Vernon Kinietz.

Oneóta . . . 1844–45.   Later reissued under various titles, such as:
The American Indians . . . .)

Indian melodies . . . .   New York, Elam Bliss, 1830.   52 p.

The Indian tribes of the United States: their history, antiquities, customs, religion, arts, language, traditions, oral legends and
myths.   Edited by Francis S. Drake . . . .   Philadelphia: J. B.
Lippincott & co.   London: 16 Southampton Street, Covent Garden.
1884.   2 v., 458 and 455 p.   (An abridgement of: Information respecting the history . . . ; with additions by the editor.)

Information respecting the history, condition and prospects of
the Indian tribes of the United States: collected and prepared under
the direction of the Bureau of Indian affairs . . . .   Illustrated by
S. Eastman, Capt. U. S. A. . . . .   Philadelphia, Lippincott, Grambo
and co., 1853–57.   (Same as "Historical and statistical information
. . . ." with titles of Part I changed to conform with other parts.   A
cheaper edition, comprising only the first five volumes, was published with the same title and imprint.)   Adapted in French as:
Mondot, Armand.   Histoire des Indiens des États-Unis . . . .   Paris,
1858.   352 p.   (3 v. in-fº.)

Inquiries, respecting the history, present condition and future
prospects of the Indian tribes of the United States.   (Washington,
D. C., 1847.)   55 p.   (Also issued as appendix to Part I of: Historical and statistical information . . . .   The same was extracted
and published as a separate.   Philadelphia: Lippincott, Grambo &
co.   Pages numbered 523–568.)

Iosco, or the vale of Norma.   A poem.   Detroit, Geo. L. Whitney, printer, 1838.   14 p.

Journal of a tour into the interior of Missouri and Arkansaw,
from Potosi, or Mine à Burton in Missouri territory, in a southwest
direction, toward the Rocky Mountains; performed in the years 1818
and 1819.   London, printed for Sir R. Phillips and co., 1821.   102 p.
(Forms no. 5 of v. 4 of: Phillips, Sir R., ed. and pub.   A collection
of modern and contemporary voyages & travels . . . .   Was also
issued separately, however.   Pages 92–102 contain a reprint of:
Transallegania, or The groans of Missouri . . . .   According to
Sabin, some copies have additional pages, numbered 103–28, which
are part of another work.   There is also another edition of the
Phillips collection in which Schoolcraft's "Journal" appears as no. 4
of v. 4.)   (This "Journal" was first printed in the New York literary journal and belles-lettres repository as a serial: v. 2, p. 256–65
Feb. 1, p. 330–44 Mar. 1, p. 393–408 Apr. 1; v. 3, p. 100–11 June 1,
p. 169–83 July 1; 1820.   From this the English edition was made in
1821.)   (An American, amplified edition was published as "Scenes

and adventures in the Semi-Alpine region of the Ozark mountains . . . ," Philadelphia, 1853.)

A journey up the Illinois river in 1821. (In: Quaife, M. M., ed. Pictures of Illinois one hundred years ago. Chicago, R. R. Donnelley & sons co., 1918. Lakeside Classics, v. 16.) (An abstract from: Travels in the central portions of the Mississippi valley.)

The man of bronze, or portraitures of Indian character, delivered before the Algic society at its annual meeting in 1834 [1833]. Detroit, 1834. 8vo.

A memoir on the geological position of a fossil tree, discovered in the secondary rocks of the river Des Plaines. Read before the American geological society . . . . Albany, N. Y., printed by E. and E. Hosford, 1822. 18 p. (Reviewed in North American review, v. 15, p. 249–50, July, 1822.) (Also, in: American journal of science and arts, v. 4, p. 285–91, Feb., 1822.) (Also published in: Summary narrative of an exploratory expedition . . . . Phila., 1855. p. 396–404.)

The myth of Hiawatha, and other oral legends, mythologic and allegoric, of the North American Indians. Philadelphia: J. B. Lippincott & co. London: Trübner & co. 1856. 343 p. (Material in this was published also in "Algic researches," 1839, and "The Indian fairy book," 1856.)

Narrative journal of travels through the northwestern regions of the United States; extending from Detroit through the great chain of American lakes, to the sources of the Mississippi river. Performed as a member of the expedition under Governor Cass. In the year 1820 . . . . Albany, N. Y., E. and E. Hosford, 1821. 419 p. (Reviewed in North American review, v. 15, p. 224–50, July, 1822. The material was partly reprinted in: Summary narrative of an exploratory expedition . . . 1855.)

Narrative of an expedition through the upper Mississippi to Itasca lake, the actual source of this river; embracing an exploratory trip through the St. Croix and Burntwood (or Broule) rivers; in 1832. . . . New York, Harper & brothers, 1834. 307 p. (Besides the narrative this work embraces the following by Schoolcraft: Localities of minerals observed in 1831 and 1832 in the northwest; Indian languages, part of a course of lectures delivered before the St. Mary's committee of the Algic society.) (Reviewed in Foreign quarterly review, v. 15, p. 325–36, July, 1835.) (The material was partly reprinted in: Summary narrative of an exploratory expedition . . . 1855.)

Natural history. The following extracts relative to the natural history of Michigan are taken from a lecture delivered before the

Detroit lyceum. (In: Historical and scientific sketches of Michigan. Detroit, Wells and Whitney, 1834. p. 177–91.)

Notes on the Iroquois; or Contributions to American history, antiquities, and general ethnology. Albany, N. Y., E. H. Pease & co., 1847. 498 p. (A popular account, in the form of a narrative history, based upon: Report of Mr. Schoolcraft, to the Secretary of State . . . 1846.)

Notes on the Iroquois: or, Contributions to the statistics, aboriginal history, antiquities and general ethnology of western New York . . . . New-York, Bartlett & Welford, 1846. 285 p. (A reissue, with special title and list of contents, of: Report of Mr. Schoolcraft, to the Secretary of State . . . 1846.)

Notices of some antique earthen vessels, found in the low tumuli of Florida, and in the caves and burial places of the Indian tribes north of those latitudes. Read at the monthly meeting of the New-York historical society, June, 1846 . . . . New York, W. Van Norden, 1847. 15 p. (Also, in: New-York historical society. Proceedings, 1846, p. 124–36.)

On reaching the source of the Mississippi river in 1832. A poem. (In: Literary world, no. 337, p. 559–60, July 16, 1853.) (Also in his: Summary narrative of an exploratory expedition, p. 243–44.)

Oneóta, or, The red race of America: their history, traditions, customs, poetry, picture-writing, etc. . . . New York, Burgess, Stringer, & co., 1844–45. 512 p. (Issued in 8 paper-covered numbers. The first 4 were published in 1844, beginning with Number I, in August; the last four appeared in 1845. The University of Illinois has an imperfect copy of this first edition.) Also, an edition of the same in 1 v. New York and London, Wiley & Putnam, 1845. 512 p. (The University of Michigan has this edition.) The work was afterwards reissued under various titles: The red race of America, 1847; The Indian in his wigwam, 1848; The American Indians, 1850; Western scenes and reminiscences, 1853.

Outlines of the life and character of Gen. Lewis Cass. Albany, N. Y., J. Munsell, 1848. 64 p.

Personal memoirs of a residence of thirty years with the Indian tribes on the American frontiers: with brief notices of passing events, facts, and opinions, A.D. 1812 to A.D. 1842. . . . Philadelphia, Lippincott, Grambo and co., 1851. 703 p.

Petition to Congress of Henry R. Schoolcraft, acting superintendent Indian affairs, Michigan, &c. (Washington, D. C., Gideon, printer, 1858.) 7 p. (A copy is in the E. E. Ayer Collection, Newberry Library, Chicago. Incomplete: includes only abstracts A and

B of the abstracts A, B, C, D, E, F, G, H, I, K listed in the author's introductory statement as found in his subjoined schedule of claim.)

Plan for the investigation of American ethnology . . . . Submitted to the board of regents of the Smithsonian institution, at their first meeting, at Washington, in September, 1846. New York, printed by E. O. Jenkins, 1846. 13 p. (Reprinted in: Smithsonian institution. Annual report, 1885. p. 907–14.)

The red race of America. New York, W. H. Graham, 1847. 416 p. (A new edition of: Oneóta, 1844–45. Contains the cover title: The Indian in his wigwam. Reissued under various titles.) Another edition. New York, W. H. Graham, 1848. 416 p.

Report of Mr. Schoolcraft, to the Secretary of State (New York) transmitting the census returns in relation to the Indians. (Albany, N. Y., 1846.) 285 p. (The census fills p. 3–20; a supplementary report on antiquities, history, and ethnology occupies p. 21–285. Reissued as: Notes on the Iroquois, 1846. A popular account was published under a title similar to the one just cited, in 1847.)

The rise of the west, or A prospect of the Mississippi valley. By H. R. S. . . . Detroit, printed by Geo. L. Whitney, 1830. 31 p. A poem. (Contains also: A retrospect; or the ages of Michigan. By H. W. A copy is in the Michigan State Library. "H. W." is supposed to have been Henry Whiting.) Also, another, "private edition." New-York, W. Applegate, printer, 1841. 20 p. (Duyckinck, in his "Cyclopaedia of American Literature," 1875, mentions an edition, Detroit: G. L. Whitney, 1827. 20 p.)

Scenes and adventures in the semi-Alpine region of the Ozark mountains of Missouri and Arkansas. . . . Philadelphia, Lippincott, Grambo & co., 1853. 256 p. (An American edition, amplified, of: Journal of a tour into the interior of Missouri . . . 1818 and 1819.) (Also contains, as an appendix, a new edition of: A view of the lead mines of Missouri.)

Sketch of the life and public services of Gen. Lewis Cass. Washington, D. C., printed at the Congressional Globe office, Jackson Hall, March, 1848. 8 p.

The souvenir of the lakes. Detroit, published by Geo. L. Whitney, 1831. 25 p. (An annual for 1831, edited by H. R. Schoolcraft, which contains verse and articles by him, both initialed and under pen names, as well as contributions by others.) (Contents reprinted, with photostat of original title page, in: Historical society of northwestern Ohio. Quarterly bulletin, v. 11, nos. 2 and 3, April and July, 1939; also issued as a separate.)

Suggestions for travelers visiting the ancient sites of Indian occupancy in America. (n.p., 184–?) 6 p.

Summary narrative of an exploratory expedition to the sources of the Mississippi river, in 1820: resumed and completed, by the discovery of its origin in Itasca lake, in 1832. . . . With appendixes, comprising the original report on the copper mines of Lake Superior, and observations on the geology of the lake basins, and the summit of the Mississippi; together with all the official reports and scientific papers of both expeditions.   Philadelphia, Lippincott, Grambo, and co., 1855. 596 p. (The first part is a revised edition of: Narrative journal of travels . . . , 1821. It occupies p. 37–220. The second part is an abridgement of: Narrative of an expedition . . . , 1834. It occupies p. 221–274.)

Transallegania, or The groans of Missouri. A poem. New York, printed for the author by J. Seymour, 1820. 24 p. (Also in: Belles-lettres repository, v. 2, p. 458–63, Apr. 1, 1820. From this it was reprinted in: Journal of a tour . . . , 1821.)

Travels in the central portions of the Mississippi valley: comprising observations on its mineral geography, internal resources, and aboriginal population . . . in the year 1821. New-York, Collins and Hannay, 1825. 459 p.

A view of the lead mines of Missouri; including some observations on the mineralogy, geology, geography, antiquities, soil, climate, population, and productions of Missouri and Arkansaw, and other sections of the western country. New York, Charles Wiley & co., 1819. 299 p. (Five extracts printed in: Belles-lettres repository, and monthly magazine, New York, v. 2, no. 3, p. 211–220, Jan. 1, 1820; reviewed in American journal of science and arts, v. 3, no. 1, p. 59–72, Feb., 1821.) (A revised edition was published as an appendix in: Scenes and adventures . . . , in 1853.)

Vitreology: or The art of making glass   embracing the manufacture of flint, window, mirror and bottle glass   the art of making colored glasses, or pastes, and smalt   remarks on the constitution of optical and burning glasses   some information on potters glazing and miscellaneous processes, receipts and remarks on subjects connected with the manufacture of glass   With an appendix: exhibiting an historical sketch of the manufacture, progress and present state of the glass manufacture, in the northern department of the United States. Prospectus. Utica, N. Y., Williams and Williams, November, 1817. (Prospectus of a work never published. A small bound manuscript volume entitled "Vitriology" is in the Manuscript division of the Library of Congress.)

Western scenes and reminiscences: together with thrilling legends and traditions of the red men of the forest. To which is added several narratives of adventures among the Indians. Auburn, N. Y.,

Derby and Miller.   Buffalo, N. Y., Derby Orton & Mulligan.   1853. 495 p.   (A reissue, with additions, of: Oneóta, 1844–45.)

Periodical Articles

Account of the mound at Grave Creek flats in Virginia.   (In: Geographical society.   Journal, v. 12, p. 259–60, 1842.)

Account of the native copper on the southern shore of Lake Superior, with historical citations and miscellaneous remarks, in a report to the Department of War.   (In: American journal of science and arts, v. 3, p. 201–16, June, 1821.)

The Alleghanic hand-book.   (In: the Alleghanian, v. 1, no. 6, p. 93, June 28, 1845.)   (A gazetteer of the nomenclature and re-membrancer of the red race of North America: comprising notices of their history, philology, biography, geography, mythology, ethnography, and antiquities.)

Anglo-Indian words.   No. I.   (In: the Alleghanian, v. 1, no. 2, p. 27, May 31, 1845.)

The ante-Columbian history of America.   (In: the American Biblical repository, 2d ser., v. 1, no. 2, p. 430–49, April, 1839.)   (A review of the Antiquitates Americanae, sive Scriptores septentrionales rerum ante-Columbianarum in America—Hafniae, 1837.   Discusses, in passing, Dighton Rock, of which an illustration is given.)

Bericht über das gediegene kupfer das sich an der Südküste des Ober-Sees in Nord-Amerika in Grossen Massen findet.   (In: Annalen der physik und chemie, v. 70, p. 337–48, 1822.)

Brief notices of a Runic inscription found in North America. Copenhagen, 1844.   (In: Société royale des antiquaires du Nord. Mémoires, II, 1840–44, p. 119–27.)

Discovery of a coal basin on the western border of the Lake of the Woods.   (In: American journal of science and arts, v. 69, p. 232–34, Mar., 1855.)

Dubuque in 1820, August 7th.   (In: Iowa historical record, v. 16, p. 100–06, 1902.)   (Abridged from chapter 15 of: Narrative journal of travels . . . , 1821.)

Fate of the red race in America.   (In: Democratic review, 1844.)   (Reprinted in: Oneóta, p. 487–510.)

Geological character of the limestone of the Missouri lead region. (In: American journal of science and arts, v. 3, p. 248–49, May, 1821.)

Geology of Albany county.   (In: Munsell's annals of Albany, 1860.)   (Also, in: Webster's calendar or the Albany almanac, no. 101.   Albany, N. Y., Joel Munsell's sons, 1884.)

A glossary of Anglo-Indian words and phrases.   No. II.   (In:

the Alleghanian, v. 1, no. 3, p. 44–45, June 7, 1845.)

A glossary of Anglo-Indian words and phrases. No. III. (In: the Alleghanian, v. 1, no. 4, p. 60–61, June 14, 1845.)

A glossary of Anglo-Indian words and phrases. No. IV. (In: the Alleghanian, v. 1, no. 5, p. 74–75, June 21, 1845.)

Historical considerations on the siege and defence of Fort Stanwix in 1776 [1777]. Read before the New-York historical society June 19th, 1845 . . . (In: New-York historical society. Proceedings, v. 3, p. 132–58, 1845. Also pub. as a separate by the society, 1846. 29 p.)

Incentives to the study of the ancient period of American history. An address, delivered before the New-York historical society, at its forty-second anniversary, 17th November, 1846 . . . (In: New-York historical society. Proceedings, 1846, bound in at end.) (Also published as a separate, New York, Press of the historical society, 1847. 38 p.)

*Indian serenade. (In: Littell's living age, v. 25, p. 45, April, 1850.)

Letter. (In: Literary and philosophical repertory, Middlebury, Vt. Feb., 1816.)

Letter containing observations of himself . . . and others during the exploring expedition to the N. west . . . . (In: American journal of science and arts, v. 6, no. 2, p. 362, May, 1823.)

Letters on the antiquities of the western country. By Henry R. Colcraft. (In: Commercial advertiser, New York, 1843. Aug. 25, p. 2, col. 3; Aug. 29, p. 2, col. 2; Aug. 30, p. 2, cols. 1 & 2; Sept.

* Part of this unsigned contribution is printed on pages 192–93. It is claimed for Schoolcraft by the authors for the following reasons: A considerable number of Schoolcraft's writings were published anonymously and have not yet been identified. It was easily possible for him to have been at Newark, where it was dated. George Johnston, Schoolcraft's brother-in-law and one of his most prolific sources for the oral literature of the Ojibways, was "for a few brief years" at LaPointe, as Schoolcraft's sub-agent, following 1826. Schoolcraft's correspondence with George Johnston extended over many years. During 1850, when the "Indian Serenade" was published, there was a hiatus in their exchange of letters (see page 601). The peculiar placing of commas preceding both parentheses of a pair, in the prefatory matter, is a characteristic of Schoolcraft's style. The "Serenade" was not included in "Wild Notes of the Pibbigwun" at the back of The Myth of Hiawatha for the same reason that Schoolcraft's "Odjibwa Song," which seems to be a companion piece, was omitted. That collection is of Schoolcraft's formal Indian verse. These two items are literal translations.

2, p. 2, col. 2; Sept. 19, p. 2, col. 1; Oct. 18, p. 2, col. 2.)   (Reprinted, with additional communications, in: Oneóta, p. 385–403.)

Memoir of John Johnston.   (Printed, from the Schoolcraft papers in the Library of Congress, in: Michigan pioneer and historical society.   Collections, v. 36, p. 53–94, 1908.)

A memoir on the history and physical geography of Minnesota. (In: Minnesota historical society.   Annals, no. 2, p. 144–57, 1851.) (Also in: Minnesota historical society.   Collections, v. 1, p. 108–32, 1872.)

Moowis, or the Indian coquette.   (In: The Columbian lady's and gentleman's magazine, v. 1, p. 90–91, Feb., 1844.)   (Reprinted in: Oneóta, p. 381–84.)

Mythology, superstitions, and languages of the North American Indians.   (In: Literary and theological review, New York, v. 2, p. 96–121, March, 1835.)   (Partially reprinted in Oneóta.)

Notes for memoir of Mrs. Henry Rowe Schoolcraft [Jane Johnston].   (Printed, from the Schoolcraft papers in the Library of Congress, in: Michigan pioneer and historical society.   Collections, v. 36, p. 95–100, 1908.)

Notice of a military journal of the French and Indian war.   (In: New-York historical society.   Proceedings, p. 58–64, 1843.)

Notice of a recently discovered copper mine on Lake Superior, with several other localities of minerals.   (In: American journal of science and arts, v. 7, p. 43–9, 1823.)

Notices of some antique earthen vessels, found in the low tumuli of Florida, and in the caves and burial places of the group of Indian tribes, north of those latitudes.   Read at the monthly meeting of the New-York historical society, June, 1846.   (In: New-York historical society.   Proceedings, p. 124–36, 1846.)   (Also published as a separate, New York, W. Van Norden, 1847.   15 p.)

Observations on the geology of Missouri, Arkansas and Illinois. (In: Ploughboy, v. 1, p. 353, April, 1820.)

Observations respecting the Grave Creek mound in west Virginia.   (In: American ethnological society.   Transactions, v. 1, p. 367–420, 1845.)

On the action of the North American lakes.   (In: Geologist, p. 287–88, 1842.)   (Noticed in: American journal of science and arts, v. 44, p. 368–70, 1843.)

On the production of sand storms and lacustrine beds by causes associated with the North American lakes.   (In: British association for the advancement of science.   Report, pt. 2, p. 42–44, 1842.) (Also in: American journal of science and arts, v. 44, p. 368–70, 1843.)

On the tide of Lake Superior.   (In: American journal of science and arts, v. 20, p. 213–14, 1831.)

Plan for American ethnological investigation.   By the late Henry R. Schoolcraft.   (In: Smithsonian institution.   Annual report, p. 907–14, 1885.)   (A reprint of: Plan for the investigation of American ethnology . . . , 1846.)

Remarkable fossil tree, found about fifty miles south west of Lake Michigan, by Gov. Cass and H. R. Schoolcraft in August, 1821 . . . .   (In: American journal of science and arts, v. 4, p. 285–91, Feb., 1822.)   (Also issued as a separate, Albany, N. Y., E. and E. Hosford, 1822, 18 p.)   (Also, included in: Summary narrative of an exploratory expedition . . . , 1855, p. 396–404.)   (Reviewed in: North American review, v. 15, p. 249–50, July, 1822.)

Remarks on native silver from Michigan.   (In: Lyceum of natural history of New York.   Annals, v. 1, pt. 2, p. 247–48, 1825.) (Also in: Schoolcraft's Summary narrative . . . , p. 532–33.)

Remarks on the prints of human feet, observed in the secondary limestone of the Mississippi valley.   (In: American journal of science and arts, v. 5, p. 223–31, Sept., 1822.)

Report of the aboriginal names and geographical terminology of the state of New York.   Pt. 1.   Valley of the Hudson.   Made to the New-York historical society and read at the meeting of the society, February, 1844.   (In: New-York historical society.   Proceedings, p. 77–115, 1844.)   (Also published as a separate, by the society, 1845.   43 p.)

Review of Beltrami's "Decouverts des sources du Mississippi et de la Riviere Sanglante . . . ."   (In: North American review, v. 27, p. 89–114, July, 1828.)

Review of Gallatin's "Synopsis of the Indian tribes within the United States . . ." in Archaeologia Americana.   (In: North American review, v. 45, p. 34–59, July, 1837.)

A Shawnee tale: the celestial sisters.   (In: Journal of education, Marshall, Mich., v. 2, p. 39, July, 1839.)   (An excerpt from: Algic researches.)

Territorial papers.   (In: Michigan pioneer and historical society.   Collections, v. 36 and 37.)   (Contain extracts from Schoolcraft papers in the Library of Congress, in v. 36, p. 383–620; and from Schoolcraft papers in the Smithsonian institution, in v. 37, p. 207–421.)

Utterances of Alalcol.   (In: The knickerbocker, or New-York monthly magazine, v. 57, no. 5, p. 539–42, May, 1861.)

Utterances of Alalcol.   An Indian poet.   (In: The knickerbocker, or New-York monthly magazine, v. 58, no. 2, p. 109–12, August, 1861.)

Printed Documents

Michigan. Legislature. House. Communication from Henry R. Schoolcraft, Esq., to His Excellency Governor Mason, relative to geographical names, &c. (House doc., no. 59, p. 559–62. Detroit, John S. Bagg, state printer, 1838.)

New York. Legislature. Senate. Communication from the Secretary of State, transmitting the report of Mr. Schoolcraft, one of the agents appointed to take the census . . . of the Indians . . . . In Senate, Jan. 22, 1846.

United States. Congress. Henry R. Schoolcraft—expedition into the Indian country . . . report . . . . (House ex. doc., no. 152, 22d Cong., 1st sess., v. 4, Mar. 7, 1832. Serial no. 219.)

United States. Congress. Letter on private land claims at Sault Ste. Marie, Mich., from H. R. Schoolcraft. (Senate doc., no. 425, 29th Cong., 1st sess., 1846. Serial no. 477.)

United States. Congress. Message from the President of the United States, transmitting a report of the Secretary of War, on the number, value & position, of the copper mines on the southern shore of Lake Superior. (Senate doc., no. 5, 17th Cong., 2d sess., v. 1, Dec. 11, 1822. Serial no. 730.)

United States. Congress. Narrative of expedition to the northwest Indians. (House doc., no. 323, 23d Cong., 1st sess., v. 4, 1833–1834.) (A map of the region explored accompanies this document.)

United States. Congress. Report . . . on the state of Indian statistics. (Senate ex. doc., no. 13, 33d Cong., 2d sess., v. 6, Dec. 27, 1854. Serial no. 751.)

United States. Department of Indian Affairs. Annual report 1838. (Contains an extract of Schoolcraft's report on the condition of the Indian tribes. No. 16.) p. 451–59.

United States. Department of Indian Affairs. Annual report 1839. (Contains a report from Schoolcraft from Michilimackinac. No. 44.) p. 476–82.

United States. Department of Indian Affairs. Annual report 1840. (Contains annual report of Schoolcraft as agent and acting superintendent of Indian affairs, Michigan. No. 29.) p. 340–50. (A reprint of this was issued, Detroit, Asahel S. Bagg, printer, 1840, 28 p.)

United States. Department of Indian Affairs. Annual report 1841. (Contains letter from Schoolcraft, written from Detroit as acting superintendent of Indian affairs, No. 5; and reply, No. 7.) p. 277–79.

United States. Department of Indian Affairs. Annual report 1856. (Contains letter, No. 107, dated May 26, 1855, from George W. Manypenny, commissioner of Indian affairs at Washington, to

Schoolcraft; and Schoolcraft's reply, dated May 28, 1855, No. 108.) p. 260–62.

Papers

LIBRARY OF CONGRESS

The papers of Henry Rowe Schoolcraft in the Division of Manuscripts of the Library of Congress are a basic collection of source-material regarding him. They were acquired partly by gift from Mrs. Henry R. Schoolcraft (2d), partly by transfer from the Smithsonian Institution.

PHYSICAL DESCRIPTION

The material consists of:

(a) 47 volumes, bound by the Library. Volumes 1–33 chiefly contain Schoolcraft's correspondence, dated between August 21, 1809, and December 26, 1864, and undated, with a few items which he had gathered of an earlier period. In addition, there are: two bound volumes of "Miscellaneous and printed matter"; two volumes of "Poems, notes on aborigines"; two volumes containing his "History of Indian Tribes"; two volumes of "Indian tales"; two volumes of "Travel notes, scientific memoranda"; two volumes of "Scientific, Indian material, Indian poetry"; and two volumes of miscellaneous "Literary" material. [Titles taken from those applied to the volumes by the Library.]

(b) 1 box of "Miscellany, clippings and duplicates."

(c) 1 volume of Accounts, 1814–1819. [Kept by John Johnston of St. Mary's Falls.]

(d) 1 large boxed sheaf of papers containing the "Ojibwa vocabulary."

(e) 2 large boxed sheaves of papers containing "Eoneguiski or the Cherokee chief."

(f) 1 package containing Schoolcraft's "Private Journal of Indian affairs, 1837–1839."

(g) 8 boxes of papers of Mrs. Henry R. Schoolcraft (Mary Howard), dated chiefly between 1865–1878, and undated. [Papers of hers prior to the first-mentioned date may be found in the bound volumes listed under "(a)".]

(h) 1 box containing assorted lists and inventories of the collection. [Garrison's *List of Manuscript Collections*, of 1932, speaks of the papers as inventoried, and there is mention in the files of the Division of Manuscripts of a 500-page typewritten list or inventory, but this volume cannot now be found. There are several typewritten notes, of various extent and dates, describing the collection, or parts of it. Among these is a five-page bibliography by J. S. Fox, 1906. There is also a large group of handwritten cards. All of these seem to antedate the binding of the papers.]

(i) There are also three small bound manuscript volumes: one entitled "Vitriology"; another, "Indian Maxims, Traits, and Apothegms"; and the third an "Essay on Indian Character in Four Parts."

CHIEF CONTENTS OF THE COLLECTION

The description of the Schoolcraft collection as a whole, found in the *Handbook of Manuscripts in the Library of Congress* (Washington, D. C., 1918; p. 357 *et seq.*), is well done, and quite adequately reveals the nature of the body of papers. An important modification is required, however, in view of the fact that in 1925 the papers, or the chief part of them, were bound. Thus bound, these papers make 40 "volumes," but the last seven volumes are each in two parts, which makes really 47 in all, as described above. From the numbering of the individual pieces, which does not seem to be entirely in order, there are probably something over 7,000 pages in these volumes.

Only a survey to discover the most important items in the collection has been made. As a preliminary, the following may be extracted from the *Handbook:*

". . . A journal of Indian affairs kept at the agency of Sault Ste. Marie, from July 6 to September 30, 1822; a small journal of Indian affairs kept at the agency of Sault Ste. Marie, from July 6 to September 30, 1822; a small journal of Indian affairs, 1824; a 'Memoir of the Life of John Johnston, Esq., late of Sault Ste. Marie,' by H. R. Schoolcraft . . . abstracts of accounts of the Indian Department, 1839; scrapbook, 1847–1849, mainly Indian affairs; scrapbook for the year 1854; a small book of original poetry, undated; a number of bank books of the Bank of Michigan, Riggs & Co., etc., in account with Schoolcraft, converted by a later hand into commonplace books.

". . . travel notes, personal business miscellany, papers relating to Lewis Cass, papers relating to Michigan, claims against Schoolcraft as Indian agent, and Schoolcraft's claim against the United States . . . 'Reminiscences of the Tawasentha Valley,' 1862 . . . a few genealogical notes; papers of Schoolcraft's father, Lawrence Schoolcraft; some early papers of the Territory of Michigan; letters and papers regarding the manufacture of glass; many letters of Lewis Cass to the various Departments regarding the military post at Detroit, 1818–1819; letters and verses of William H. Sankey; 'Rambles in the Ozark Mountains, 1818–1819'; and a report to the Secretary of the Treasury about the lead mines in Missouri.

"Single items are a portion of an undated letter of William Shirley, regarding an expedition into Canada, and Schoolcraft's commission as agent for the Ottawas and Chippewas, March 4, 1839.

"The correspondence includes letters from Lewis Cass, Daniel Livingston, G. M. Dallas, Reuben Haines, Charles C. Trowbridge, Benjamin Silliman, James D. Doty, Lucius Bull, De Witt Clinton, Nathaniel H. Carter, Edward Everett, Henry Whiting, Samuel S. Conant, John Johnston, B. F. Stickney, John Torrey, Theodore Dwight, Jr., Lyman M. Warren, Peter S. DuPonceau, Henry Newcombe, John Bigelow, E. Croswell, W. Gilmore Simms, Elisha Whittlesey, Buckingham Smith, Brantz Meyer, Benjamin B. French, D. D. Mitchell, John M. McCalla, William Duane, George Gibbs, Henry T. Tuckerman, J. Logan Chipman, S. Eastman, Peter Force and Lyman C. Draper.

"A letter of George Watterston, dated June 21, 1852, contains interesting information about John Howard Payne's observations among the Cherokees. A single letter from Washington Irving is also included.

"The correspondence and papers of Mrs. Schoolcraft . . . have to do, for the most part, with real estate transactions in the City of Washington."

In volumes 36 and 37 of *Michigan Pioneer and Historical Collections* a large group of Territorial Papers of Michigan are reprinted. Of the part of this material contained in Volume 36, the later pages, 383–620, are noted as being extracts from the Schoolcraft papers in the Library of Congress. A great body of typed transcripts of other of these papers is in the Burton Historical Collection of the Detroit Public Library.

NOTABLE ITEMS FOUND BY THE INVESTIGATOR, IN ADDITION TO THOSE CITED ABOVE

A sampling of the volumes of the Schoolcraft Papers has uncovered the following, in addition to those items already cited. It should be understood that this is not an exhaustive list, but merely an attempt to locate material not necessarily covered in the prepared

Bibliography. [Some of them, however, will be found to be manuscripts of part or whole of the published books.]

(1) Report of the Indian Department, 1840, printed by
    Asahel S. Bagg.

(2) Manuscript issues of *The Garland,* an informal peri-
    odical apparently made for family divertissement,
    "edited" by Jane S. A. Colcraft and John J. Colcraft,
    New York, beginning with Vol. 1, No. 1, for August
    31, 1844.   Each issue contains four carefully-written
    pages.   They are dated: Aug. 31, 1844; Sept. 7, 1844;
    Sept. 14, 1843 [*i.e.,* 1844]; Sept. 21, 1844; Sept. 28,
    1844; Oct. 5, 1844; Oct. 12, 1844; Oct. 19, 1844; Oct.
    26, 1844; Nov. 2, 1844; Nov. —, 1844; Feb. 15, 1845
    [Vol. 1, No. 12]; Nov. 23, 1844 [Vol. 2, No. 1]; Nov.
    30, 1844 [Vol. 2, No. 2]; Dec. 7, 1844; Dec. 14, 1844;
    Dec. 21, 1844; Dec. 28, 1844; Jan. 5, 1845; Jan. 11,
    1845; Jan. 18, 1845; Jan. 25, 1845; Feb. 1, 1845; Feb.
    8, 1845 [Vol. 2, No. 12]; June 21, 1845 [Vol. 3, No.
    1]; July 5, 1845; July 19, 1845; Feb. 22, 1846; and
    Mar. 1, 1846 [Vol. 3, No. 5].   It is possible that these
    contain material written by Henry Rowe Schoolcraft.

(3) Newsclipping containing "A Letter on City Names,"
    written by Henry Rowe Schoolcraft to Hon. James
    Harper, Mayor of the City of New York, Oct. 28,
    1844, 2 columns, without indication of name of news-
    paper in which it was published.

(4) Manuscript journal, from March 2 [1831?] to Apr.
    15, 1831; journal [of Indian journey?], Jan. 1, 1834–
    Sept. 6, 1834 [Vol. 34, Nos. 6866–91 and 6950–6996,
    respectively].

(5) Broadside: "Rooms of the New-York Historical Soci-
    ety, / UNIVERSITY OF NEW-YORK, March,
    1844. / SIR: The undersigned, having been appointed
    a committee, to prepare a Map of the State, with all
    the original Indian names, solicit information on this
    head . . . / . . ."   Subscription contains the names
    of Henry R. Schoolcraft and six others.   1 p.

(6) Broadside, undated, requesting support for the main-
    tenance of "THE HISTORICAL MAGAZINE,
    undertaken by Mr. RICHARDSON last year . . ."
    Subscription contains the names of Henry R. School-
    craft and five others.   1 p.

(7) Mutilated printed piece, containing "LEELINAU, /

OR / THE LOST DAUGHTER. / AN ODJIBWA TALE. / . . ." Pages [77]–84, which ends it.

(8) "SKETCH / OF / THE LIFE AND PUBLIC SER-VICES / OF / GEN. LEWIS CASS. / " Printed at the Congressional Globe Office, Jackson Hall, Washington, D. C.   8 p.   Dated March, 1848.

(9) Broadside prospectus of "Archives of Aboriginal Knowledge . . ."

(10) Broadside prospectus of "The history, condition, and prospects of the Indian tribes of the United States."

(11) Manuscript draft of work on the explorations of the Mississippi. Dated at end Jan. 11, 1848 [Vol. 39, Nos. 9034–9067].

(12) Lengthy manuscript draft of "Illula, The Pride of the Lakes." (Poem) [Vol. 39, Nos. 9068 and following].

(13) A brief autobiographical sketch, which contains this bibliographical information: ". . . In 1830, Mr. Schoolcraft published lectures on the Chippewa substantive, which were translated into French by Mr. Duponceau, and published by the Royal Academy in Paris . . ." Also, ". . . Mr. Schoolcraft has published 31 diverent [sic] works, a partial list of which, can be found in Duyckinck's Cyclopaedia of American Literature . . ." This sketch is embodied in a manuscript draft of a letter from [Mary Howard Schoolcraft] to Henry Morgan, June 1, 1864.

TRANSFER FROM SMITHSONIAN INSTITUTION, 1942

Until recently the library of the Smithsonian Institution at Washington had a considerable body of Schoolcraft papers that had not been turned over to the Library of Congress. These seem to have been bundled up indiscriminately by J. S. Fox, editor of the Schoolcraft Papers. They were found there comparatively recently. In January, 1942, all of this material, with the exception of correspondence between Schoolcraft and the Institution itself, was transferred to the Library of Congress. The preceding description of the Schoolcraft papers in the Manuscript Division of the Congressional Library must, therefore, be extended to include the former Smithsonian collection.

This consists of a more or less mixed aggregation of manuscripts, notes, sketches, correspondence, and newspaper clippings that has never been arranged or indexed. Roughly speaking there are about 32 file cases of miscellaneous clippings, notes, etc., 16 bound volumes of letters, and 3 bundles of mixed notes, etc. A cursory examination revealed the Bible of Henry Rowe Schoolcraft, with family records; twenty-three issues, or portions of issues, of manuscript magazines issued by Schoolcraft, under six different titles, from 1809 to 1833; manuscripts of Schoolcraft's books; sketches relating to the Upper Peninsula of Michigan, to Oregon, to Minnesota, and to the names of American lakes; criticisms; maps; correspondence with members of his family, with Lewis Cass and other public men; a volume of letters relating to the Indian agency; diaries, note-books, etc.; and newspaper articles relating to the Indians. These papers, while mostly of literary and ethnological value, also have historical and biographical interest. Extracts from the papers in this collection have been printed in Volume 37 of the *Michigan Pioneer and Historical Collections*, under the title "Territorial Papers," on pages 207–421. Typed transcripts of many other of these items that were formerly in the Smithsonian archives may be consulted in the Burton Historical Collection of the Public Library of Detroit, Michigan.

NATIONAL ARCHIVES

An appreciable quantity of Schoolcraft material is in this depository.

Among the records sent to the Office of Indian Affairs from Mackinac Island in 1889, and now in the National Archives, Washington, D. C., are the following letter books of Henry Rowe Schoolcraft which cover his outgoing correspondence for the entire period of his connection with the Indian administration in Michigan:

a. Letter book as Agent at Sault Ste. Marie, July 12, 1822, to May 2, 1833.   424 p.

b. Letter book as Agent at Mackinac Island, May 31, 1833, to July 1, 1836.   179 p.

c. Letter book as Agent at Mackinac and Acting Superintendent of Indian Affairs for Michigan, July 18, 1836, to June 26, 1839.   719 p.

d. Letter book as Agent at Mackinac and Acting Superintendent of Indian Affairs for Michigan, July 1, 1839, to April 30, 1841.   p. 1–500.   (Pages 501–699 contain letters of Robert Stuart, Schoolcraft's successor.)

Since their files of incoming letters of the Michigan Superintendency of Indian Affairs are fairly complete, the National Archives have the originals of many letters sent to his superior by Schoolcraft while Agent at Sault Ste. Marie and Mackinac (of which copies were made in the first two books listed above). And since their files of incoming letters of the Office of Indian Affairs in Washington are generally complete, they have the originals of most of the letters sent to Washington by Schoolcraft in the period covered by all four books listed above.

They also have in the Michigan Superintendency records or in the Washington Office records, copies or originals of the replies sent to Schoolcraft.

For the period subsequent to May 1, 1841, including the years when Schoolcraft worked under the supervision of the Office of Indian Affairs in compiling his six-volume work on the *History, Condition and Prospects of the Indian Tribes of the United States* (1851–57), the National Archives have, among the files of the Office of Indian Affairs, a great number of original letters and reports prepared by him.

Schoolcraft's original letters for this entire period (1822–1864) have not been segregated from the files nor has a list or calendar of such items been compiled.

The National Archives also have numerous Schoolcraft items for the years 1849–1864 in the Indian Division and Appointment Division files of the Secretary's Office, Department of the Interior, but these have not been segregated or listed.

The State Department files of the National Archives contain the original treaties that Schoolcraft was witness to or signer of.

OTHER COLLECTIONS

The Burton Historical Collection in the Public Library, Detroit, Michigan, has eleven wallets of Henry Rowe Schoolcraft Papers dating from 1809 to 1869. These consist of typed transcripts from the original manuscripts in the Smithsonian Institution and the Library of Congress. The documents published in Volumes 36 and 37 of the *Michigan Pioneer and Historical Collections* are not included among the present collection of transcripts. These papers amply reflect his wide range of activities: his relations with his father and family in New York State; the early glass industry; mineralogy and geology; Missouri affairs, lead mines, friendship with Moses and Stephen F. Austin; his appointments under and explorations with Governor Cass; numerous aspects of life in Michigan from 1822 to 1841, more especially Indian relations and scientific and literary studies and contacts; his subsequent life at New York and Washington. He was a friend of many prominent characters of his time, and although never greatly active in politics, considerable material of this character is included among his papers. After 1850 the volume of the correspondence becomes much diminished. Much of it concerns the various relatives of Schoolcraft and his wife. There are also interesting letters from his daughter, who married a Southern man and thereby became a resident and an adherent of the South in the great sectional struggle; and communications from his soldier son, who served in the 2d New York Volunteers.

In the Burton Historical Collection there are also many letters written by Schoolcraft,—to Trowbridge, Woodbridge, and other Detroit figures,—which are not filed as Schoolcraft Papers. They are in several other series, not calendared, arranged chronologically, and have to be hunted out. The Austin Wing collection contains some.

In the recently established Michigan Historical Collections of the University of Michigan, Ann Arbor, Michigan, is a letter from Schoolcraft to John Winder, July 30, 1829, A.L.S., 1 page, filed in the John Winder Papers. There are also the following, which have minor references to Schoolcraft and relate in general to his period at Mackinac Island: manuscript diary of the Reverend Peter Dougherty; papers of Francis W. Shearman; and the William M. Ferry papers.

The William L. Clements Library of the University of Michigan has a few of Schoolcraft's letters.

The unusual Schoolcraft collection of the Sault Ste. Marie, Michigan, Public Library includes 48 manuscript letters, most of them addressed to George Johnston by Schoolcraft. These letters are printed as an addendum to this volume.

The New-York Historical Society has a manuscript of Schoolcraft's relating to different tribes of Indians; a paper read by him before the Society, December 6, 1842, on "Scientific Associations Abroad"; and four of his letters, including one to Washington Irving, dated August 29, 1835, at Michilimackinac.

The Public Library of New York City in its manuscript division has five letters and a fragment, and a copy of the family record of Schoolcraft's marriage and children; also two original letters, and a photostat negative of a third, by Mary Howard Schoolcraft.

The Office of the Register of Wills of the District of Columbia, Washington, D. C., has the last will and testament of Henry R. Schoolcraft, with codicil thereto, filed January 28, 1865, as Admn. No. 5025, Old Series.

The late Mrs. E. D. Hayward of Keene, New Hampshire, had some Schoolcraft papers. Since her death in 1940, these letters, mostly personal, are in possession of her son, Ralph E. Hayward, of that city.

In 1880, Bangs and Co., a New York dealer, printed a catalogue offering for sale, after the death of the second Mrs. Schoolcraft, several thousand Schoolcraft letters and other papers. This gives the names and dates of many fine letters.   The purchaser of this collection is not known.

Judge Henry Schoolcraft Hulbert of Detroit, Michigan, a grandson of Maria Eliza Schoolcraft Hulbert, contributes the following interesting account of the loss of other Schoolcraft papers, in a letter dated December 9, 1940: "Some forty-five years ago, when the State of Minnesota established a historical society they were extremely anxious to include in it facsimiles of Schoolcraft papers and details concerning his early life, marriages, children, etc.   At that time, I was a very young man and tried enthusiastically to help them obtain what they needed, on the basis that they would obtain facsimiles and return the original papers to the owners.   Jane Schoolcraft very gladly contributed some of the most valuable material which she had and my own grandmother, who was living with me at that time, and who was Henry Schoolcraft's younger sister, also sent very valuable material and data which was in her possession. These were turned over by the State Commissioner to a curator, whose name has escaped me.   After a long correspondence, we discovered this material had never been used by the Commission and had disappeared.   I had little means at my disposal at that time to take steps for its recovery, so much of the material you require and which should be in our family, is probably in the archives of some historical museum."

INDEX

531, 536, 615; estate of, 608; illness, 528, 531, 532–533, 575; in Ireland, 362, 518, 529–530, 531; letters, 523, 533, 575, 576, 587; literary ability, 99, 405, 529, 531, 532, 534–536, 615; marriage, 58, 100, 506–507, 517, 523, 528, 564; as a mother, 533–536, 537–538, 616–617; her names, 98, 536; in New York City, 514; notes for memoir of, 642; penmanship, 523, 575; personal charm, 541, 549; portraits, 522, 624; quoted, 75, 393; religious faith, 500, 530, 532, 534, 536, 538, 576; Schoolcraft's attitude toward her, 364, 522, 528–530, 537–538, 578, 616

Schoolcraft, Jane Susan Anne. See Howard, Jane Schoolcraft

Schoolcraft, John, 296–297, 371

Schoolcraft, John Johnston: attitude toward his parents, 545, 616–617; birth, 524, 547, 565; burial, 548, 555; childhood, 527–528, 533–534, 536, 537–538, 587; christened, 527; Civil War record, 547–548, 550, 652; death, 548, 571; described, 547, 548, 615–616, 620; drug addiction, 617; education, 526, 527–528, 534, 536, 538, 547, 548, 568, 586, 621; irresponsible maturity, 545, 547–548, 608, 613, 615–616, 617, 619–621; letters, 652; literary activities, 540, 648; named for his grandfather, 539; in New York, 540, 547, 570, 589, 591, 593, 619; portrait, 526, 533, 574; in Washington, 547, 598, 619–621

Schoolcraft, John L., of Albany, 552

Schoolcraft, Lawrence, of Albany Co., N. Y., 296–299, 301, 302, 303, 307, 319, 371, 372, 517; correspondence, 429, 651; death, 509, 539; described, 508–509; glassmaker, 308–309, 313–315, 509; moved to Vernon, N. Y., 299, 562; papers, 646; parentage, 296

Schoolcraft, Lawrence, of Schoharie Co., N. Y., 296

Schoolcraft, Margaret A. B. Rowe, 298, 301, 302; averse to Indian marriage of her son, 509, 528, 616, 621; death of, 509–510, 539

Schoolcraft, Margaret Helen, 513

Schoolcraft, Maria Eliza. See Hulbert, Maria E. Schoolcraft

Schoolcraft, Mary Howard, 528, 541–544, 593, 604, 606; amanuensis for her husband, 541, 545, 546, 611, 623; attitude toward Schoolcraft, 541, 545, 554, 611, 622; birth, family, childhood, 541–543, 545, 550, 611, 623; in *The Black Gauntlet*, 509, 537, 541–550, 553–554, 555–556, 610–623; in Burton Historical Collection, 651; death and burial, 555–557, 571; described, 541, 612; donor of Schoolcraft papers, 645; enemies, 611, 614, 623; handwriting, 543; marriage, 506, 507, 541, 544–547, 569, 612–614; papers, 543, 619, 624, 630, 645, 647, 649, 652; photograph, 542; pro-slavery opinions, 550, 610; in Schoolcraft's will, 608; writings, 294, 428, 504, 507, 509, 527, 537, 542, 543, 546, 547, 548, 553–554, 610–623, 626

Schoolcraft, Peter, 315, 321, 350, 513, 563

Schoolcraft, William Henry: birth, 523, 538, 539, 564; death and burial, 523, 529, 538–539, 555, 565; grandparents buried beside him, 540, 578; letter about death of, 523, 576; in New York, 514, 530; verses on, 536

Schoolcraft, Mich., 364

Schoolcraft Co., Mich., 364, 627

Schoolcraft House, 302, 573

Schoolcraft I., 355, 356, 364

Schoolcraft River, 354, 364

Schramm, Wilbur L., 39–40, 629

Science: and religion, 341–342, 437, 479, 496–497, 505; as yet unzoned, 431–432

Scotch, 305, 307

Scott, Walter, 446

Scott, Winfield, 352, 428